reflective teaching
in primary schools

6th edition

Available titles in the *Reflective Teaching* series

Series Editors: Andrew Pollard and Amy Pollard

Reflective Teaching in Early Education, 2nd Edition, Jennifer Colwell and
   Amanda Ince et al.

Readings for Reflective Teaching in Early Education, edited by Jennifer Colwell and
   Andrew Pollard

Reflective Teaching in Secondary Schools, 6th Edition, Andrew Pollard and Caroline Daly et al.

Readings for Reflective Teaching in Schools, edited by Andrew Pollard

Reflective Teaching in Further, Adult and Vocational Education, 5th Edition,
   Sam Duncan and Margaret Gregson et al.

Readings for Reflective Teaching in Further, Adult and Vocational Education, edited by Margaret
   Gregson, Andrew Pollard, Lawrence Nixon and Trish Spedding

Reflective Teaching in Higher Education, 2nd Edition, Paul Ashwin et al.

reflective teaching

in primary schools

6th edition

Andrew Pollard and Dominic Wyse
with Ayshea Craig, Caroline Daly, Sinéad Harmey, Louise Hayward,
Steve Higgins, Amanda McCrory, Sarah Seleznyov and Ernest Spencer

BLOOMSBURY ACADEMIC
LONDON · NEW YORK · OXFORD · NEW DELHI · SYDNEY

BLOOMSBURY ACADEMIC
Bloomsbury Publishing Plc
50 Bedford Square, London, WC1B 3DP, UK
1385 Broadway, New York, NY 10018, USA
29 Earlsfort Terrace, Dublin 2, Ireland

BLOOMSBURY, BLOOMSBURY ACADEMIC and the Diana logo are trademarks of
Bloomsbury Publishing Plc

First published in Great Britain 2023

Copyright © Andrew Pollard, Dominic Wyse and Contributors, 2023

Andrew Pollard, Dominic Wyse and Contributors have asserted their right under the
Copyright, Designs and Patents Act, 1988, to be identified as Authors of this work.

For legal purposes the Acknowledgements on p. 575 constitute an extension of this
copyright page.

Cover design: Grace Ridge
Cover image © iStock (SolStock, monkeybusinessimages, DGL Images, Highwaystarz-
Photography and sturti / Getty Images

All rights reserved. No part of this publication may be reproduced or transmitted
in any form or by any means, electronic or mechanical, including photocopying,
recording, or any information storage or retrieval system, without prior
permission in writing from the publishers.

Bloomsbury Publishing Plc does not have any control over, or responsibility for,
any third-party websites referred to or in this book. All internet addresses given in this
book were correct at the time of going to press. The author and publisher regret
any inconvenience caused if addresses have changed or sites have ceased to exist,
but can accept no responsibility for any such changes.

A catalogue record for this book is available from the British Library.

A catalog record for this book is available from the Library of Congress.

ISBN: HB: 978-1-3502-6364-2
       PB: 978-1-3502-6363-5
       ePDF: 978-1-3502-6365-9
       eBook: 978-1-3502-6366-6

Series: Reflective Teaching

Typeset by RefineCatch Limited, Bungay, Suffolk
Printed and bound in Great Britain

To find out more about our authors and books visit www.bloomsbury.com
and sign up for our newsletters.

Contents

Introduction   vii
Using this book   x
A summary of the book   xii

Part one Becoming a reflective professional

1 **Identity** Who are we, and what do we stand for?   3
2 **Learning** How can we understand learners' development?   37
3 **Reflection** How can we develop the quality of our teaching?   79
4 **Principles** What are the foundations of effective teaching and learning?   105

Supplementary chapters at **reflectiveteaching.co.uk**
- **Observing** Children and young people as learners
- **Mentoring** Learning through mentoring in initial teacher education
- **Enquiry** Developing evidence-informed practice
- **Techniques of enquiry** Gathering and analysing evidence

Part two Creating conditions for learning

5 **Contexts** What is, and what might be?   139
6 **Relationships** How are we getting on together?   163
7 **Engagement** How are we managing behaviour?   195
8 **Spaces** How are we creating environments for learning?   229

Part three Teaching for learning

9 **Curriculum** What is to be taught and learned?   267
10 **Planning** How are we implementing the curriculum?   305
11 **Pedagogy** How can we develop effective strategies?   345
12 **Communication** How does use of language support learning?   371
13 **Assessment** How can assessment enhance learning?   403

Part four Reflecting on consequences

14 **Outcomes** How do we monitor pupil learning achievements?   441
15 **Social justice** Can we enable all children to succeed?   481

Supplementary chapter at **reflectiveteaching.co.uk**
- **Judgement** Assessment without levels

Part five Deepening understanding

16 **Teacher expertise** A holistic view   513
17 **Professional learning** How can we nurture career-long
    reflective teaching?   537
18 **Professionalism** How does reflective teaching contribute to society?   553

Supplementary chapters at **reflectiveteaching.co.uk**
- **Starting out** Learning as a newly qualified teacher
- **Improvement** Continuing professional development

Acknowledgements   575
Bibliography   577
Index   621

reflectiveteaching.co.uk

Introduction

This book offers *two* levels of support for teachers in initial teacher education or as part of teachers' continuing professional development.

- Comprehensive guidance on key issues in classroom practice – including relationships, behaviour, curriculum planning, learning and teaching strategies, assessment processes and evaluation.
- Uniquely, the book also introduces evidence-informed 'principles' and 'concepts' to support a deeper understanding of teacher expertise.

Reflective Teaching in Primary Schools 6th Edition thus supports both initial school-based training and extended career-long professionalism for primary school teachers.

Developed over three decades, the book, companion reader and website represent the accumulated understanding of generations of teachers and educationalists. This new sixth edition includes extensive revisions throughout, for example new case studies in many chapters, and a new structure for the final part of the book. In general this new edition also has more specialist material focused on work in primary schools.

Readings for Reflective Teaching in Schools provides a compact library which complements and extends the chapters in this book. It has been designed to provide convenient access to key texts and will be of particular help when library access may be difficult.

The associated website, reflectiveteaching.co.uk, offers an enormous range of supplementary resources including reflective activities, research briefings, advice on further reading and additional chapters. It also features a compendium of educational terms, a conceptual framework showcasing some of the UK's best educational research and extensive links to useful websites.

Underlying these materials, there are three key messages. The first is that it *is* now possible to identify teaching strategies which are more effective than others in most circumstances. Teachers therefore now have to be able to develop, improve, promote and defend their expertise by marshalling such evidence and by embedding enquiry and evaluation within routine practices. Second, all evidence has to be interpreted. To do this we need to understand the underlying principles of learning and teaching to which specific findings relate. Finally, we need to remember that education has moral purposes and social consequences. The provision we make impacts on the life-chances of the children and young people with whom we work and on our future as societies.

Whether you are a trainee, early career teacher, mentor or other experienced professional, we hope that you will find these materials helpful as you seek personal fulfilment through your work.

Suggestions on how to use the book, and a description of its content, follow.

Andrew Pollard and Dominic Wyse
June 2022

Using this book

This book contains a number of features to support both students and professionals, from their initial teacher training, right through their development into expert teachers. In developing skills and understanding, it helps to 'stand back' as well as engaging in the detail of educational issues – the structure of the book will help in this.

Headers on every page confirm the part and chapter you are in. Footers direct you to the location of additional chapter resources which are freely available at **reflectiveteaching.co.uk**.

The book contains many illustrations, activities and so on, and these are numbered in relation to the chapter in which they appear; for example, Reflective Activity 5.2 is in Chapter 5 and is the second activity there.

Within each chapter

Each chapter introduces and explores key issues using a combination of practitioner experience and contemporary research. The text is your guide. Additionally, you will find:

Reflective Activities Key points in each practical chapter are highlighted by suggested enquiries to be conducted in school. Each Reflective Activity comes with a full explanation of its aims, methods and follow-up required, and can be carried out individually or with colleagues.

Lesson Study These illustrate teacher enquiries, sometimes using the three-part structure of Lesson Study, to investigate practical issues. They also demonstrate what is possible when colleagues collaborate to improve their practice in ways which are more systematic than usual.

Expert Questions

What is an expert question?
These questions are intended to promote thinking and suggest the potential of conceptual analysis. In addition, they feed forward to the conceptual framework of Chapter 16, with its holistic representation of teacher expertise.

TLRP Principles

Experienced teachers become used to policies and practices which come and go – however, there are enduring features of effective teaching and learning on which most practitioners and researchers can agree. At the start of each chapter, these boxed features invite consideration of some of these 'principles' of teaching, as identified by a large UK research programme, TLRP (Teaching & Learning Research Programme).

Using this book   xi

At the end of each chapter

All chapters provide a review of available resources for follow up study, covering the free material on the chapter webpage at reflectiveteaching.co.uk, and providing additional resources such as:

Toolkit Evidence These research summaries focus on the costs and benefits of different approaches to improving pupil attainment. They review research and evaluate the evidence to inform classroom decision-making, particularly in relation to improving outcomes for disadvantaged pupils.

Research Briefings For a selection of influential research studies, we offer compact synopses to convey their intentions, key findings and practical implications – vital for modern teachers who have to evaluate research evidence over the course of their careers.

Readings for Reflective Teaching in Schools Students and teachers don't always have access to large educational libraries. Throughout this book, we provide links to the companion volume, *Readings for Reflective Teaching in Schools*: this offers excerpts from over 100 exceptional educational texts, and is organised to directly support this volume.

Online

This icon shows where related material can be found online, including on the book's dedicated website reflectiveteaching.co.uk/rtps6, which offers many free resources to support this book:

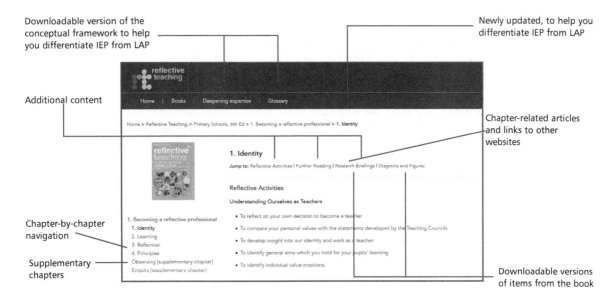

reflectiveteaching.co.uk

A summary of the book

PART 1: BECOMING A REFLECTIVE PROFESSIONAL introduces and structures the activity of becoming a teacher. We start in Chapter 1 with a focus on the decision to teach and on the significance of the contribution we can make as professionals. Then comes an introduction to ways of understanding 'learning' (Chapter 2) – which is the foundation of expert teacher judgement. Despite much complexity, *learning* is what it is all about! The chapter on reflective practice (Chapter 3) discusses how such processes can improve the quality of our teaching. And then it gets really interesting, with a review of ten principles of effective teaching and learning (Chapter 4). These come from a major UK research and development programme and also draw on accumulated evidence from around the world. Measured effects of particular strategies are related to underlying principles.

Four supplementary chapters are available on reflectiveteaching.co.uk – 'Observing', on studying learners; 'Mentoring', on support for initial training; 'Enquiry', on how to design small-scale classroom investigations; and 'Techniques of Enquiry', on how to gather and analyse evidence.

PART 2: CREATING CONDITIONS FOR LEARNING concerns the creation of classroom environments to support high-quality teaching and learning. We begin by considering the circumstances which impinge on families and schools (Chapter 5) – and we note the ways in which people contribute to and challenge such circumstances through their actions. We then move to the heart of classroom life with a focus on teacher–pupil relationships and inclusion (Chapter 6). Because such relationships are so crucial for classroom success, this is an extremely important chapter. Chapter 7 builds further and illustrates how positive cycles of behaviour can be created through firmness, fairness and engaging pupils in the curriculum. Finally, we consider a range of learning spaces in school and beyond (Chapter 8) and the affordances they offer for formal and informal learning. As well as the basic dimensions of classroom organisation, this chapter also addresses the use of technology, pupil organisation and team-working with teacher assistants.

PART 3: TEACHING FOR LEARNING supports the development of practice across the three classic dimensions of teaching – curriculum, pedagogy and assessment. Chapter 9 starts us off with a review of curricular aims and design principles, before progressing to a review of national curricula in the UK and the role of subject knowledge. 'Planning' (Chapter 10) puts these ideas into action and supports the development and evaluation of programmes of study, schemes of work and lesson plans. Chapter 11 offers ways of understanding pedagogy – and the development of a pedagogic repertoire. 'Communication' (Chapter 12) extends this with an introduction to the vital role of talking, listening, reading and writing across the curriculum. Perhaps the core instructional expertise of the teacher lies in the skill of dialogic teaching? Finally, this part concludes by demonstrating how assessment can be tied into teaching and learning processes in very constructive ways (Chapter 13). In short, through principled strategies for sharing goals, pupil engagement, authentic feedback, self-assessment and responsive teaching, excellent progress in learning can be made.

PART 4: REFLECTING ON CONSEQUENCES draws attention to what is achieved, and by whom, in our classrooms – what are the consequences of what we do? Chapter 14 reviews big issues in assessment, with particular attention on how schools measure pupil achievement and manage accountability. Whilst some problems are raised, positive uses of summative assessment data are also promoted. 'Social Justice' (Chapter 15) asks us to consider various dimensions of difference and also the ways in which routine processes differentiate between people. However, the emphasis is on accepting difference as part of the human condition and on how to build more inclusive classroom communities. On reflectiveteaching.co.uk there is a supplementary chapter on 'Judgement', focused on assessment without levels.

PART 5: DEEPENING UNDERSTANDING is the final, synoptic part of the book. It integrates major themes through discussion of teacher expertise and professionalism. 'Teacher Expertise' (Chapter 16) harvests and integrates powerful ideas from previous chapters into a holistic conceptual framework of enduring issues in teaching and learning. The chapter constructs a framework describing dimensions of expert thinking. In Chapter 17, 'Professional Learning', we consider the ways in which teachers continue to learn as part of their professional role. Finally, in Chapter 18, 'Professionalism', we look at the bigger picture once more to consider the role of the teaching profession in our societies and suggest how reflective teachers can contribute to democratic processes.

Supplementary chapters are available on the website, reflectiveteaching.co.uk, on succeeding as a newly qualified teacher ('Starting out') and on career and school development ('Improvement').

Part one

Becoming a reflective professional

1 **Identity** Who are we, and what do we stand for?   3

2 **Learning** How can we understand learner development?   37

3 **Reflection** How can we develop the quality of our
teaching?   79

4 **Principles** What are the foundations of effective
teaching and learning?   105

Supplementary chapters at reflectiveteaching.co.uk
- **Observing** Children and young people as learners
- **Mentoring** Learning through mentoring in initial
  teacher education
- **Enquiry** Developing evidence-informed practice
- **Techniques of enquiry** Gathering and analysing evidence

This part introduces and structures the activity of becoming a teacher.

We start with a chapter focused on ourselves and on the significance of the
contribution we can make as professional teachers. Then comes an

introduction to ways of understanding 'learning' (Chapter 2) – which is the foundation of teacher judgement. After all, despite much complexity, learning is what it is all about! The chapter on reflective practice (Chapter 3) discusses how such processes can improve the quality of our teaching. And then it gets really interesting, with a review of ten 'principles of effective teaching and learning' (Chapter 4). These come from a major UK research and development programme and also draw on accumulated evidence from around the world.

Chapter 1
Identity
Who are we, and what do we stand for?

| Introduction | 4 |

Understanding ourselves as teachers	5
Becoming a primary teacher	5
Values informing practice	6
Teacher identities	11
Primary teachers' work	13

Knowing children and young people as pupils	15
Pupil views of themselves in school	16
Pupil perspectives of teachers and school	17
Pupil cultures	19
Understanding pupil needs	20
Examining our perceptions of pupils	22

Learning and teaching through life	26
Pupil development and career	26
Teacher development and career	29

| Conclusion | 30 |

reflectiveteaching.co.uk/rtps6/part1_ch1

INTRODUCTION

This chapter is concerned with primary teachers and children in primary education, as well as with the feelings and perceptions we hold in relation to ourselves and others. A key issue is that of our 'identities' as unique individuals and how these identities relate to the cultures and opportunities within classrooms and schools. However, to understand identities we must recognise both social influences beyond the school and also learning and development throughout each stage of life. A school is after all a microcosm of the society in which we live.

The first part of the chapter focuses on the professional vocation and work of teachers. We consider why people choose to become primary teachers and the values that might inform and sustain our practice. We introduce what is known about primary teachers' work, including how primary teachers respond to complexity and uncertainty. This part also reflects the belief that there are always things that we can do to improve the quality of educational provision for all learners. To this end, whilst celebrating vocational commitment, this chapter also acknowledges the professional resilience needed to ensure a positive work life balance.

The second part of the chapter focuses on thinking about primary-aged children. We consider what we know about the particular identities and cultures of the children with whom we are privileged to work – in, and beyond, our schools. We challenge ourselves to consider how our values, biases and pre-existing understandings may influence how we think about pupils and their learning.

The third part considers the ways in which primary-aged children develop and learn through their schooling. Social, physical and psychological factors are addressed. The important role of the agency of children is highlighted and celebrated. Finally, our own biographies, and our commitment to teaching, are acknowledged. We again affirm the need to balance our personal and professional lives to achieve success in the classroom; embracing a healthy work–life balance to safeguard our own mental health and wellbeing whilst impacting positively on *all* children and the wider school community.

See Chapter 4

TLRP Principles

Two principles are of particular relevance to this chapter on identity and values in education:

Effective teaching and learning equips learners for life in its broadest sense. Learning should aim to help people to develop the intellectual, personal and social resources that will enable them to participate as active citizens, contribute to economic development and flourish as individuals in a diverse and changing society. This implies adopting a broad view of learning outcomes and ensuring that equity and social justice are taken seriously. (*Principle 1*)

Effective teaching and learning depends on teacher learning. The need for teachers to learn continuously in order to develop their knowledge and skills, and adapt and develop their roles, especially through classroom inquiry, should be recognised and supported. (*Principle 9*)

reflectiveteaching.co.uk/rtps6/part1_ch1

UNDERSTANDING OURSELVES AS TEACHERS

Becoming a teacher

Research has shown that initial motivation for, and commitment to, teaching are important factors that influence teachers' job satisfaction and retention (Fokkens-Bruinsma and Canrinus, 2012). Motives for choosing the teaching profession tend to fall into two broad categories: (1) intrinsic motivations such as liking and wanting to care for children and to impact positively on their lives, and (2) extrinsic motivations for example salary, pensions and holidays (Moses et al., 2017; Heinz, 2015).

A scoping review of seventy empirical studies between 2007 and 2016 by Fray and Gore (2018) examined why people choose both primary and secondary teaching. In relation to primary and early years teaching it was found that intrinsic motivations such as a commitment to the service to others, a desire to work with children as well as enjoying the company of children (Weiss and Kiel, 2013) were main motivations. This was sensitively described by Nias, whose classic study *Primary Teachers Talking* (1989) showed how identification with the role eventually became so strong for some that they saw themselves as 'persons-in-teaching' rather than just as people who happened to be employed as teachers with significant contributions.

There is also a well-established theme of idealism in the commitment of many aspiring teachers. The profession attracts those with a sense of moral purpose who decide that they want, through their work with children, to make a contribution to the future of our societies. The 'passion for teaching' of a large number of primary teachers has been recorded many times in the past, and remains evident today (Day and Gu, 2010; Gu, 2007, Reading 1.1).

Whilst the contemporary role of the teacher is challenging, the opportunity to support the development of young children holds considerable fascination and importance. There is also for many a strong commitment to social justice in providing opportunities for children from disadvantaged backgrounds to fulfil their potential and to provide life chances as expressed in Richardson's book, *Changing Life Chances* (2011).

The vocational commitment of student teachers is not, however, associated with complacency about the challenges of becoming a 'good teacher'. Most people when beginning to become a teacher are aware of the challenges which relate to a range of factors, from conceptual understanding to practical skills and opportunity (see Florian and Linklater, 2010 for a study of student teachers negotiating how to become inclusive practitioners). Fortunately, with apposite support, commitment can be nurtured until professional capabilities and self-efficacy are secure. However, a slightly uneven journey, characterised by ups and downs and a lot of hard work, is not unusual – though guides, such as 'Your Teaching Training Companion' (McGrath and Coles, 2016) and 'A Guide to Early Years and Primary Teaching' (Wyse and Rogers, 2016) help considerably.

The early years of classroom life for newly qualified teachers is crucial for career decisions. In a study of such experiences McNally and Blake (2010) found that establishing good relationships with pupils and with teacher colleagues often assumes huge importance – and feelings about teaching and personal self-confidence ebb and flow (see also **Research Briefing 1.1** on p. 35). They found that the struggle to establish competence and acceptance could be overwhelming and feelings sometimes veered from anxiety and despair to fulfilment and delight. The significance of this research is that it highlights aspects of the journey that we all share as teachers. The feelings associated with our first few weeks in the profession may stay with us in some form – a keen sense of moral purpose; excitement because of the responsibility and opportunities; and awe, wonder and uncertainty about how to fulfil our ambitions for both ourselves as teachers and for the children with whom we work. Gradually though, these commitments are tempered by experience (Quigley, 2016), but it is to be hoped that they never fade completely.

Like the student teachers in the research projects above, much of our motivation and resilience will be associated with our personal qualities. Moreover, these qualities will develop and sustain us throughout our careers – and contribute to 'reflective practice'. The process of reflection acknowledges dilemmas and the need for expert judgement in teaching. It is entirely understandable to feel such challenges – see Richardson's classic *Daring to Be a Teacher* (1990). *Reflective Teaching in Primary Schools* offers evidence-informed and constructive ways of managing challenges in the short term whilst also building principled, career-long expertise.

Reflective Activity 1.1

Aim: To reflect on your own decision to become a primary school teacher.

Evidence and reflection: Earlier we explored the importance of initial feelings in relation to motivation, aspiration and determination. Write a short piece for yourself, recollecting why you decided to train to become a teacher (you may wish to consider intrinsic and extrinsic motivations). If appropriate, also record your feelings at the point of qualifying.

Extension: Read what you have written and highlight where you have made reference to specific value commitments. List these, and try to identify personal experiences that informed why they were so important.

Share your thinking with colleagues and discuss the range of motivations which inform 'becoming a teacher'.

Values informing practice

The values we hold about the importance of education are critical to the decision to become primary teachers in the first place, and to sustaining our motivation and resilience throughout our career. The values that inform our practice are of varying degrees explicit, but it is important to try to identify them for at least three reasons. First, being clear about values can help us to assess whether we are consistent, both in what we as individuals

reflectiveteaching.co.uk/rtps6/part1_ch1

believe, and in reconciling differences which may exist in a school between colleagues working together. Second, it can help us to evaluate and respond to external pressures and requirements – as 'creative mediators' of policy (see Chapter 3, p. 96). Third, it can help us to assess whether what we believe is consistent with what we actually do: that is, whether our value system or philosophy is compatible with our actual classroom practice. This is important to reflect on because of the way our values inform our *agency* (our sense of, and exercising, what can be changed) as well as *purpose* (what we might want to change).

As well as an awareness of the values we held when we entered the profession (see **Reflective Activity 1.1**), we are also required to work with values shared within our profession. In addition to the values expressed by successive governments through the Departments for Education there are also professional bodies that promote key values. In the British Isles, the Department for Education (England) and the Chartered College of Teaching (CCT) (England), the General Teaching Councils (GTCs) (Scotland, Northern Ireland), Education Workforce Council (EWC) (Wales) and The Teaching Council (Ireland) articulate clear expectations regarding the shared values that should underpin teachers' work. In England, from 2017, professional values were enriched by the activities of the Chartered College of Teaching. The values and standards of such national bodies reflect a commitment and determination to improve educational provision. They challenge us to address the ways in which structures and systems of schooling currently contribute to inequalities and to professionalism.

Teachers' Standards, Department for Education, England

Part 1: Section 8: Fulfil wider professional responsibilities

- make a positive contribution to the wider life and ethos of the school
- develop effective professional relationships with colleagues, knowing how and when to draw on advice and specialist support
- deploy support staff effectively
- take responsibility for improving teaching through appropriate professional development, responding to advice and feedback from colleagues
- communicate effectively with parents with regard to pupils' achievements and well-being.

Part 2: Personal and professional conduct

A teacher is expected to demonstrate consistently high standards of personal and professional conduct.

The following statements define the behaviour and attitudes which set the required standard for conduct throughout a teacher's career.

Teachers uphold public trust in the profession and maintain high standards of ethics and behaviour, within and outside school, by:

- treating pupils with dignity, building relationships rooted in mutual respect, and at all times observing proper boundaries appropriate to a teacher's professional position having regard for the need to safeguard pupils' well-being, in accordance with statutory provisions

- showing tolerance of and respect for the rights of others
- not undermining fundamental British values, including democracy, the rule of law, individual liberty and mutual respect, and tolerance of those with different faiths and beliefs
- ensuring that personal beliefs are not expressed in ways which exploit pupils' vulnerability or might lead them to break the law.
- Teachers must have proper and professional regard for the ethos, policies and practices of the school in which they teach, and maintain high standards in their own attendance and punctuality.
- Teachers must have an understanding of, and always act within, the statutory frameworks which set out their professional duties and responsibilities.

GTC Scotland

Professional values and personal commitment

- The professional values of social justice, integrity, trust and respect and a professional commitment are at the core of Professional Standards.
- The values are reflected across the Professional Standards and are relevant to all registered teachers regardless of post. Values are complex and work to shape who teachers are as professionals.
- The educational experiences of all learners are shaped by the values and dispositions of those who work to educate them. In recognition of the importance of professional values, they have been placed at the *heart* of the Professional Standards.
- A commitment to the values underpin the range of relationships, the thinking and professional practice of teachers across Scotland.

EWC Wales

Code of Professional Conduct and Practice

This Code sets out the key principles of good conduct and professional practice EWC registrants uphold, and is intended to inform, support and guide all in their day to day conduct and practice. It is also information for parents, the public and stakeholders involved in the education of learners in Wales, and learners themselves, as to the standards they can expect from registrants.

Registrants commit to upholding Personal and Professional Responsibility

Registrants:

- recognise their personal responsibility as a role model and public figure, to uphold public trust and confidence in the education professions, both in and out of the workplace

reflectiveteaching.co.uk/rtps6/part1_ch1

Chapter 1 Identity   9

- conduct relationships with learners professionally by:
  - communicating with learners respectfully, in a way which is appropriate for them;
  - using all forms of communication appropriately and responsibly, particularly social media;
  - ensuring any physical contact is necessary, reasonable and proportionate;
  - contributing to the creation of a fair and inclusive learning environment by addressing discrimination, stereotyping and bullying;
  - maintaining professional boundaries.
- engage with learners to encourage confidence, empowerment, educational and personal development
- have a duty of care for learners' safety, physical, social, moral and educational well-being:
  - acting on anything which might put a learner's safety or welfare at risk;
  - reporting any safeguarding issue, or any other issue which may potentially harm a learner's safety or welfare.
- are mindful of their professional responsibility for the health, safety and well-being of colleagues, and themselves
- demonstrate a commitment to equality and diversity.

GTC Northern Ireland

Code of Values and Professional Practice

The Code seeks to:

- set out clearly the core values underpinning professional practice
- encourage attitudes and conduct commensurate with the core values of the profession
- provide a framework for evaluating both policies and practice; and
- affirm the diverse professional heritage of teachers and enhance the status of the profession in the eyes of the public.

Core values: trust, honesty, commitment, excellence, respect, fairness, equality, dignity, integrity, tolerance and service:

A commitment to serve lies at the heart of professional behaviour. In addition, members of the profession will exemplify the values listed above in their working and in their relationships with others; recognising in particular the unique and privileged relationship that exists between teachers and their pupils. In keeping with the spirit of professional service and commitment, teachers will at all times be conscious of their responsibilities to others: learners, colleagues and indeed the profession itself.

Teaching Council Ireland

The Code for Professional Conduct for Teachers

The Code is designed to guide teachers' professional judgement and practice and is underpinned by four core values: respect, care, integrity and trust.

reflectiveteaching.co.uk/rtps6/part1_ch1

Part 1 Becoming a reflective professional

Professional values and relationships

Teachers should:

- be caring, fair and committed to the best interests of the pupils/students entrusted to their care, and seek to motivate, inspire and celebrate effort and success
- acknowledge and respect the uniqueness, individuality and specific needs of pupils/students and promote their holistic development
- be committed to equality and inclusion and to respecting and accommodating diversity including those differences arising from gender, civil status, family status, sexual orientation, religion, age, disability, race, ethnicity, membership of the Traveller community and socio-economic status, and any further grounds as may be referenced in equality legislation in the future
- seek to develop positive relationships with pupils/students, colleagues, parents, school management and others in the school community, that are characterised by professional integrity and judgement
- work to establish and maintain a culture of mutual trust and respect in their schools.

Reflective Activity 1.2

Aim: To compare your personal values (see **Reflective Activity 1.1**) with the statements developed by the Teaching Councils and/or by government education departments.

Evidence and reflection: Were there values in your initial reflection that are not included in any of the national codes or standards? If so, why do you think this might be?

Are there ways in which the official codes and standards extend your value expectations?

How? Which aspects of your practice do they relate to? For example, in your initial reflections, did you, like GTC Northern Ireland, highlight the value of 'service'?

Extension: Isolate and compare each element of the statements of professional values. How would you explain the similarities and differences?

One of the arguments for developing codes or standards for professional practice is that they frame our practice and development in certain ways. They are intended to encourage us to be reflective and responsible, to remind us of professional values, aims and commitments *and* to consider indicators of their implementation and effect. Only then will we be able to judge whether what we *really* do matches what we say we value. Gaps between aspirations, values and outcomes are common in many walks of life but for teachers it is particularly important to examine why these may occur. After all, failure to adapt and change may have significant effects on the lives of others.

Of course, self-improvement is often based on the collection and analysis of evidence. So, the contemporary professional has to be willing to test their value positions and beliefs.

reflectiveteaching.co.uk/rtps6/part1_ch1

Indeed, the reflective practitioner, as we will later see, is able to justify their practices and provide a justification for them.

An important step in developing as reflective practitioners is to understand how our own personal values, beliefs and practices are influenced by our previous experiences, circumstances and understanding. We need to become 'reflexive' and thus able to question ourselves. Such reflexivity is an important aspect of reflective practice. Whilst the latter addresses a wide range of social, organisational, pedagogic and other factors, reflexivity focuses directly on our self-awareness and ability to reflect on ourselves (Feucht, Lunn Brownlee and Schraw, 2017).

For a supplementary approach to articulating values, aims and commitments see reflectiveteaching.co.uk.

Beliefs, of course, can be particularly difficult to change since they may rest on significant cultural and material foundations. Indeed, we may even feel that our beliefs are representations of 'objective truths' and that nothing more needs to be considered. Reflective practice requires an interesting combination of moral commitment and open-mindedness. Whilst being fully value committed, we must still aspire to learn and improve. We will explore this more fully in Chapter 3.

Teacher identities

What sort of a person do we think we are, and what sort of a teacher do we wish to become? In primary education, teachers often associate themselves with a pupil year or key phase of schooling such as the Early Years Foundation Stage (EYFS) Key Stage 1 (KS1) or Key Stage 2 (KS2). In earlier times these were known as infants and juniors. You will find that there are pedagogies specific to EYFS such as 'continuous provision', which you are unlikely to find in KS2. However, in spite of these phase designations, and some differences in pedagogies, it is important to remember that education should be continuous for learners.

The concept of 'identity' summarises the ways in which we think about ourselves. Our sense of personal identity forms through life and is particularly influenced by identification with 'significant others' such as parents, friends and, in due course, colleagues. It is argued that we often separate our thinking in terms of our 'personal' and 'professional' self and, in this section, we focus on the formation and development of professional identities as teachers (Quigley, 2016; Bennett, 2012). However, this is not to say how we self-identify does not underpin our professional identity. Social constructs such as class, gender, language and race influence teachers' construction of self and their social milieu. Perceptions and manifestations of these social constructs can therefore inform the way in which teachers and children perceive and measure the potential for success in the classroom (Nguyen, 2012).

As we have seen, most people enter the profession of teaching with a strong sense of personal commitment, and such values are seen by many people as professional characteristics. However, the progression from early idealism to long-term professionalism is often not straightforward. At each stage, we must wrestle with the tension between vocational commitment and practical challenges.

Initial teacher education brings the first round of such challenges. Maynard and Furlong (1993) identified five typical stages of initial school experience – 'early idealism', 'personal survival', 'recognising difficulties', 'hitting the plateau' and, finally, 'moving on'. For example, it may well be rather dispiriting if you come into school to help children with their learning only to find that you cannot get them to pay attention and take you seriously! But it is also reassuring to know that most people do, with the support of others, work their way through these initial challenges – and as they do so, a more professional teacher identity begins to develop.

In their few first years of teaching, teachers may experience a similar cycle. For example, Ewing and Manuel (2005) identified five stages from initial experiences to a more confident professionalism:

- early expectations and a sense of vocation;
- early days of the first teaching appointment;
- finding a place – the establishment phase;
- consolidating pedagogical content knowledge;
- building a professional identity and voice.

For a full account of this and helpful support, see the supplementary **Mentoring** chapter on reflectiveteaching.co.uk.

This process is also similar to that described by McNally and Blake (2010) and must succeed if a long-term teaching career is to be established. The issue of achieving personal fulfilment from teaching is obviously of great significance in this. It is most likely when there is congruence between each teacher's personal commitments and the roles which they fulfil in school. If personal and professional identities align, then a long-term career is much more likely.

The classic study of teacher careers as a whole is Huberman's *The Lives of Teachers* (1993). Huberman suggested that teacher careers typically develop through five stages. He saw initial training and early career learning as 'career entry' which, after five years or so, leads on to 'stabilisation' and then 'experimentation' for a long period, which may last for twenty years or more. After that, he suggested, there is typically a period of wind-down into 'serenity and conservatism' followed by 'disengagement' and eventual retirement.

Day and Gu (2010, see also Reading 1.1) bring this analysis up to date for UK circumstances, as informed by a large-scale study on teachers' work and lives (see TLRP **Research Briefing 1.1** on p. 35). They showed that the key contemporary factor in achieving satisfaction, commitment, wellbeing and effectiveness for teachers is the relative success with which various personal, work and external policy challenges are managed. In other words, given the challenges of teaching today, successful career teachers require strong personal and professional identities which derive coherence from underlying values and beliefs. Day et al. (2007) suggest that teachers who offer this combination of professional understanding and personal qualities are often particularly effective in terms of supporting pupil learning and are also better able to achieve a sustainable work–life balance. They are committed, but they also keep things in perspective.

Exploring a particular dimension of this, Hargreaves (1998) has written on the place of emotion in teaching. He argues that:

> As an emotional practice, teaching activates, colours and expresses teachers' own feelings and actions as well as the feelings and actions of others with whom teachers interact. All teaching is inextricably emotional either by design, or by default. (p. 5)

Hargreaves reminds us that it is not only the values we go into teaching with that matter, but how we feel able to put these into practice. Affective responses to classroom situations invariably do influence our actions and the ways in which we express what we value. Moreover, in such interactions with pupils and others, our professional success often depends significantly on how we make others feel. Becoming an effective teacher thus has a great deal to do with learning how to support, manage and develop oneself. This is reflected in the professional expectations and standards discussed on p. 7. The nature of personal and professional identities, and the ways in which we understand these to be 'in action' over our careers is therefore of great significance for teachers. We each reflect the uniqueness of our past experiences and circumstances – and these influences, of course, have very significant effects on our self-perceptions. In school settings, the influence of other colleagues on the school staff is often considerable. They represent 'significant others' providing feedback to us in relation to our self-presentation (Warwick, Hennessy and Mercer, 2011).

Our teacher colleagues, and others with roles in school and beyond, are likely to influence the development of our identities and self-confidence as teachers. If we don't relate well to them that may inhibit our personal and professional development. On the other hand, collaboration with colleagues when underpinned by open, trusting relationships enables authentic development of professional identities. This has been demonstrated for many years by research on school effectiveness which identifies the benefits of schools supporting teachers in taking risks, exploring new practices and creating 'learning communities' (Lave and Wenger, 1991) in which teachers are also learners (Burn, Hagger and Mutton, 2015; MacGilchrist, Myers and Read, 2004).

In summary, for teachers, the personal and the professional interrelate to a considerable extent. The nature, resilience and development of our identity over time will make a significant contribution to our professional success.

Primary teachers' work

In terms of responsibilities, primary teachers' work can be described with some precision, and indeed, employment contracts do exactly this. Teachers have a right to receive particulars of employment setting out expectations for their role and, if full-time in a

reflectiveteaching.co.uk/rtps6/part1_ch1

'maintained' school in England and Wales for example, they must be available for work for a maximum of 195 days or 1,265 hours of 'directed time' each year. A minimum of 10 per cent of timetabled teaching time should be designated (without pupil contact) for planning, preparation and assessment for fully qualified teachers. In the Newly Qualified Teaching (NQT) years, this is typically 20 per cent to give NQTs the time needed to engage with England's Early Careers Framework, which claims to outline the best available evidence of what teachers should know and be able to do. The Early Careers Framework was introduced in England in 2021 to provide a compulsory two-year induction package for NQTs, supported and fully funded by the Department for Education. It is claimed that benefits for NQTs include flexible online and face to face training modules, access to expert resources, as well as a one–one mentor. NQTs undertake two formal assessments at the end of each induction year, in addition to progress reviews in each term where there is not a formal assessment.

Whilst contractual conditions are extremely important, the most significant question concerns how we interpret both them and the role more generally. This question needs to be posed because, as we have already seen, teaching is a complex activity and contractual terms, whilst necessary, are not sufficient to fully account for the nature of being a teacher. Below, we offer a different but complementary approach.

Metaphor can enable us to understand complexity more clearly, and this certainly applies to interpretations of the nature of teaching. The most common metaphors used are the *art* of teaching (Egan, 2010), the *science* of teaching (e.g. Simon, 1985, Reading 11.3; Hattie, 2012, Reading 4.6) and the *craft* of teaching (e.g. Grimmett and Mackinnon, 1992; Brown and McIntyre, 1993; Day and Gu, 2010; see also Reading 11.1).

Expert Question

Effectiveness: are there improvements in standards, in both basic skills and other areas of curricular attainment, to satisfy society's educational goals?

This question contributes to a conceptual framework representing enduring issues and teacher expertise (see Chapter 16).

The metaphor of 'art' mphasizes the affective and creative aspects of teaching and learning as well as use of intuition in forming judgements. The 'science of teaching' conjures an image of the application of tested knowledge, whilst emphasis on the teacher's 'craft' affirms the particular significance of practical experience. There are many other common metaphors too, such as the 'teacher as gardener', which perhaps mphasizes the personal development of learners, or the image of 'conductor', which foregrounds the teacher role in orchestrating multiple, simultaneous classroom activities.

The choice of metaphor thus foregrounds particular aspects of teachers' expertise, knowledge and decision-making – creating, instructing, directing, coordinating, facilitating, nurturing etc.

Chapter 1 Identity

Reflective Activity 1.3

Aim: To develop insight into our identity and work as a primary teacher.

Evidence and reflection: The most established metaphors to describe teachers' work foreground the art, science and craft of teaching. Listed below are some additional metaphors that people have used to describe the work of teachers.

- architect
- conductor
- facilitator
- gardener.

Choose a couple of the metaphors discussed above and explore their strengths and limitations. For example, a conductor determines the tempi and dynamics of the playing of the different groups of musical instruments in an orchestra, reflecting the conductor's interpretation of a composer's music set out in a musical score. A gardener plans, nurtures and tends, but weeds . . .

Look over your lists. What do they reveal about how you understand the nature of teachers' work?

Extension: The issues raised could be discussed and analysed with colleagues. It might be helpful to try to identify aspects which are core to the role of teachers, and those which are more supplementary.

So far in this chapter, we have explored personal and professional values and demonstrated how teachers' own sense of identity is drawn on, and develops, during initial training and beyond. In a sense, the whole of this book is dedicated to helping us to analyse our own behaviour and its consequences. As we bring evidence to bear on our classroom practice, we can reflect on our value commitments and aspirations and on progress in the development of expertise (see Chapter 16).

We now move our focus onto children and young people, who remain central to the purpose of all our work.

KNOWING CHILDREN AND YOUNG PEOPLE AS PUPILS

Developing an understanding of primary-aged pupils requires a reflective teacher to empathise with their school experience as well as develop personal knowledge of and rapport with individual children. This is a foundation for establishing positive behaviour and a positive learning atmosphere in the classroom – and is key to school practices.

reflectiveteaching.co.uk/rtps6/part1_ch1

Pupil views of themselves in school

The way that primary-aged children think of themselves in school will directly influence their approach to learning, sometimes known as their 'learning disposition' (Flückiger, Dunn, and Stinson, 2018, Reading 2.6; Claxton, 2013, Reading 2.9). Some may be highly anxious and continually undervalue themselves. Others may seem overconfident and extremely resilient. Some may be very well aware of their own strengths and weaknesses whilst others may seem to have relatively naive views of themselves. Children may be gregarious, or loners, or they may in fact be lonely. For instance, Pollard and Filer traced the home, playground and classroom experiences of small groups of children through their primary and secondary school careers (1996, 1999, 2007, Reading 1.2; see also Warin, 2010).

Such studies show how pupils adopt particular strategies and identities as they manage relationships with peers and with teachers, and thus negotiate their way through schooling. These experiences contribute to each pupil's sense of identity and thence to confidence and achievement in learning. Qualitative research of this sort highlights the complexity of pupils' lives, and suggests that there are no simple explanations for how and why pupils respond to schooling as they do. Moreover, as the demographics of the population change, teachers may feel that the diversity of cultures, affecting expectations for childhood and education, amongst pupils and their families are increasingly varied. Having an understanding of a child's community cultural wealth (Yosso, 2005) is also important. Yosso (2005) proposes six forms of cultural capital: aspirational (children's hopes and dreams for the future); navigational (manoeuvring through social institutions); social (networks of people); linguistic (multiple languages, to which we would add dialects including different kinds of English language), familial (family and community knowledge) and resistant (challenging inequality). Understanding these forms can help teachers to avoid deficit models of some groups of pupils so that they can empower children and their learning.

A central strategy in the development of positive self-concepts among children in school lies in encouraging individuals to identify qualities within themselves which they can value (Lawrence, 1987, Reading 6.6). It is important to provide opportunities where a wide range of qualities can be appreciated. In classrooms where competitive achievement can be emphasised some pupils may quickly come to regard themselves unfavourably, or else learn to resent and oppose the values of the teacher. It is, however, possible to create a climate where many different qualities are valued and where pupils are encouraged to challenge themselves to improve their own individual performance. In this way pupil dignity can be protected and individual effort and engagement rewarded (see Chapters 6 and 15 on inclusive practices). One of the ways of contributing to such a climate is to encourage pupils to evaluate their own work and to set their own personal goals – as in 'assessment for learning' (see Chapter 13), often referred to as a 'success criteria' or 'steps to success' in primary schools. As we will see, it is important that such procedures are meaningful for children, reflect their agency, and are worthy of their respect.

Chapter 1 Identity

> ## Reflective Activity 1.4
>
> *Aim:* To explore one of the features of children's development: the multiple and sometimes contradictory expectations that different people have of children.
>
> *Evidence and reflection:* These issues can be explored through 'picture maps' about themselves. Pupils can draw or write about each perspective.
>
>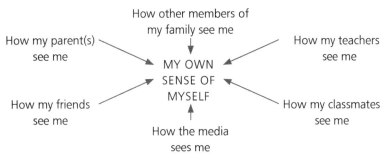
>
> *Follow-up:* The activity, as well as giving you insights into your pupils, may provide opportunities for discussion of how they could handle differing expectations of different people, and how it feels to feel uncertain of 'who we are'. You may also be able to discuss who they wish to become . . . and are becoming.

Pupil perspectives of teachers and school

Children's views of teachers have been studied for many years (Blishen, 1969; Meighan, 1978; Kyriacou, 2009; Pollard and Triggs, 2000). Their perceptions of trainee teachers have also been considered (Cooper and Hyland, 2000). Much of the evidence suggests that children like teachers who 'help them learn'. They expect teachers to teach, by which they seem to mean to take initiatives, to explain things clearly and to provide interesting activities. On the other hand, they also like teachers who are prepared to be flexible, to respond to the different interests of the individuals in the class and to provide some scope for pupil choice. Pupils dislike teachers who have favourites or who are unpredictable in their moods. Recent research carried out by Children in Scotland (2018), which in part informed the GTC Scotland's review of their Professional Standards for teaching (GTC S, 2018), found that 'kindness and fairness' are key to excellent teaching in the eyes of primary-aged children. The key findings of the report also stated that meeting the needs of all pupils as individuals using a relationship-based and rights-based approach was important. Overall, it seems that primary-aged children like teachers who are kind, firm, flexible, fair and who help them succeed as learners. You could check these findings with some of the pupils you teach.

> **Reflective Activity 1.5**
>
> *Aim:* To find out young people's criteria for a 'good teacher'.
>
> *Evidence and reflection:* Hold a discussion (with the whole class, or in small groups which can then report back to the whole class) on what makes a 'good teacher'. Perhaps the discussion could be couched in terms of suggestions for a student on how to become a good teacher.
>
> Discussions with pupils on such a topic must obviously be handled very carefully and only with the agreement of any teachers who are involved.
>
> *Follow-up:* Such information can be interesting in two ways:
>
> 1 It reveals something of the young people's expectations of what it is to be a good 'teacher'.
>
> 2 It can contribute to reflection on our own effectiveness as teachers and in implementing our values, aims and commitments. It could also lead to a reconsideration of those values, aims and commitments.

The personal development of pupils implies that they take increasing responsibility and exercise more autonomy as learners. Indeed, extensive classroom research (Rudduck and Flutter, 2004, Reading 1.3; Rudduck and McIntyre, 2007, **Research Briefing 1.2** on p. 36) has shown that authentic consultation with pupils about teaching and learning is extremely worthwhile. It facilitates the development of relationships (see Chapter 6) and improves learning because of the higher quality feedback loops which are created (see Chapter 13). Such processes call for a degree of managed power-sharing between teachers and pupils. The most significant manifestation of pupil recognition lies in 'making visible' the learning objectives and success criteria which are in play. Hattie (2009, 2012, Reading 4.6), summarising one of the largest-ever international syntheses of research, put this in terms of two high-level 'big ideas' which teachers should certainly adopt if they want to maximise effectiveness:

- I see learning through the eyes of my students.
- I help students to become their own teachers.

Authentic consultation, engagement and transparency with pupils may seem risky for some teachers since it involves opening up spaces and issues which might be contested. Ultimately, however, understanding *has* to be constructed by learners so that, sooner or later, they simply have to take control of their learning. A reflective teacher embraces and constructively manages this process.

Pupil cultures

So far, the focus has been on the teacher, the pupil and their mutual perceptions. However, it is most important to remember that, although the teacher is a central figure, classrooms are a meeting place for many children – indeed, Jackson (1968, Reading 6.1) referred to 'the crowd' as being a salient feature of classroom life. How children learn to cope with being one of a crowd, and how they relate to each other, is of consequence. This can affect how well the children settle in the class socially and, in turn, may affect their learning. There is, thus, a social dimension to classroom life.

Pupil culture has been described by Davies (1982, p. 33) as the result of children 'constructing their own reality with each other' and 'making sense of and developing strategies to cope with the adult world'. It thus reflects the children's collective perspectives and actions, many of which can be interpreted as defensive responses to adults.

Children's place in classrooms and schools is therefore an important means by which they can identify with each other, establish themselves as members of a group, try out different roles and begin to develop independence and responsibility. Young children often make friends with those who are immediately accessible and with whom they share common experiences (Rubin, 1980). Typically, their friends are children who live close by, who are in their class or who are the children of their parents' friends. When peer groups begin to form, each individual is likely to have to establish their membership of the group in a number of ways. For example, each member may be expected to contribute and conform to the norms which are shared by the group: for example, liking similar games, toys, television programmes; supporting the same football team or pop group; liking the same fashions. Group members will also be expected to be loyal to each other, 'stand up for their mates', play together and share things. Status is important in peer culture. As children establish their individual identities among their peers, each will be valued in particular ways. For young children this value may be based on prowess in the playground in activities such as skipping, dancing, chasing or football, as well having access to fashionable toys, clothes or activities.

The identities which children develop have serious implications for us as teachers because they often lead to significant differentiation as schools try to meet the needs of the children they serve. Processes of differentiation start during the early years at school, perhaps with the practical organisation of group work, and have been found to increase during students' school lives (Breakwell, 1986; Pollard and Filer, 1996; Ireson and Hallam, 2001, Reading 15.4). Pupil responses may eventually lead to a polarisation of pro-school and anti-school cultures (Lacey, 1970) and this has been cited as of particular significance in the underachievement of boys, when to 'be good' in school is considered 'uncool' (Raphael-Read, 1995; Evans, 2007). More recent research suggests that boys in primary schools believe that teachers view them as academically inferior to girls, impacting on children's motivation and confidence and subsequent performance (Hartley and Sutton, 2013). Self-image and status within a peer group thus have significant consequences for development during the school years – and these often last into adult lives. This is further discussed in Chapter 15.

One particular issue which should be watched for, in relation to pupils' relationships with each other, is that of bullying (Slee, 2017; Smith, 2014; Robinson Sleigh and Maines, 1995), both in and out of school and online. This is an unacceptable aspect of young people's culture and often reflects both its tendency to emphasise conformity and its concern with status – as well as, frequently, the relative insecurity of the perpetrators. Thus, children who are different in some way – new to school, overweight or possibly have an unusual accent or simply a different culture – are picked on physically and verbally and are excluded by other pupils as their unacceptability for cultural membership is asserted or as a pecking order is maintained. In its worst forms, this can degenerate into overt racism (Richardson and Miles, 2008), homophobia (DePalma and Atkinson, 2008) or sexual harassment (Lees, 1993).

Adult intervention must be firm, but also needs to be sensitive to the realities of the social situation and should take into account school policies for bullying and harassment as well as guidance given by the Department for Education (DfE), for example *Preventing and Tackling Bullying* (2017b) and *Cyber Bullying – Advice for Headteachers and Staff* (2014). Everyone needs friends and to feel accepted by others. Very often then, the teacher's task is to stop the bullying whilst facilitating the entry of the 'victim' into an appropriate niche within the pupil cultures of the school (Cowie and Wallace, 2000). Complex issues are raised on which new teachers should seek advice from more experienced colleagues and advocacy groups such as Scope (**scope.org.uk**) who have developed wide ranges of resources and guidance for teachers in primary schools.

Understanding pupil needs

Just as we need to consider our personal identities and circumstances as teachers, so a similar kind of 'biographical' knowledge about each child is valuable in understanding them as individual people and as learners. We are likely to find that many characteristics are shared in common, but others will be more unique and individual.

Many schools collect basic information about each child's medical history and educational progress, but such records, although sometimes helpful, rarely convey an impression of the 'whole child'. As a move in this direction, profiles, portfolios or 'records of achievement' used to be commonplace in schools. Increasingly, however, records tend to focus more narrowly on each child's progress and targets achieved in different subject areas, supplemented perhaps with examples of their work at different ages. However, they may be enhanced by including information about hobbies and interests, abilities and tastes, and materials which reflect each pupil's social attitudes, behaviour, out of school achievements and family context. Children are also encouraged to participate in decisions about what to include. Accessing such information can be achieved via a 'knowledge exchange' between home and school, as is modelled in the 'Home–school Knowledge Exchange' project (Feiler et al., 2007; Winter et al., 2009, see **Research Briefing 4.1** on p. 136). Home visits for early years children, although not a statutory requirement, are an opportunity for teachers to build trust with parents and have a better understanding of the home life of the children they teach. Such visits and records, coupled with building relationships with children and parents over time, provide context for understanding children in school through careful encouragement for parents to share their views and to ask questions.

> **Reflective Activity 1.6**
>
> *Aim:* To begin to construct a biographical understanding of a pupil.
>
> *Evidence and reflection:*
> - Take an interest in a pupil's general behaviour inside and outside the classroom. Consider how they interact with other pupils and how they tackle learning tasks.
> - Present open-ended opportunities where the child can write, draw, talk or otherwise communicate about themself. Discussions about friends, experiences, family or about favourite books or TV characters can be revealing. Make notes.
> - If possible, discuss the pupil with parents and other teachers.
> - Discuss the pupil's own perception of their individual needs with them.
> - Summarise what you have learned. Try not to take a deficit approach to a child's needs but rather one that starts with their strengths.
>
> *Follow-up:* Consider what implications your new understanding has for shaping the educational provision that is appropriate for the child concerned.

It is often argued that the 'needs' of the learner should be seen as the starting point for teaching and learning policies. However, the notion of appropriate needs is not straightforward, since it begs questions about prior aims, and judgements about what is worthwhile (Barrow, 1984). Nevertheless, it may be valuable for us as reflective teachers to articulate what we see as the basic 'needs' of the learners to whom we commit ourselves.

The classic work of Maslow (1954) is interesting here, since he linked the drive to have needs met with motivation in learning. Maslow proposed a hierarchy of basic needs, and proposed that the lower level order of needs must be met before people could fulfil higher level needs. This argument is represented as a pyramid (see Figure 1.1).

5 Self-actualisation needs
4 Esteem needs
3 Belongingness and love needs
2 Safety needs
1 Physiological needs

The lowest level (1) expresses our primary biological need for food, shelter, oxygen, water etc. The second level (2) encompasses the need for security and freedom from anxiety. The third level (3) includes the need to feel that one belongs, and to be loved and be able to love in return. The fourth level (4) addresses the need for prestige and status, to be successful and to feel good about oneself. The final level (5) might be seen as the ultimate goal of education – the need of people to fulfil their potential.

Teachers and pupils are no different in their humanity, and they therefore share the needs which each of these elements represent. To learn, and to work at teaching, physiological needs are basic – and we will explore one dimension of this in Chapter 8 when considering the physical qualities of classroom learning environments. More significantly, if a pupil is hungry or distressed, teaching and learning will be limited in how it can enhance learning capacity. Successful schools and classrooms enable both teachers and pupils to feel safe, respected and valued. The experience of being in school thus supports developing towards mutual self-actualisation. We can all take pleasure from success.

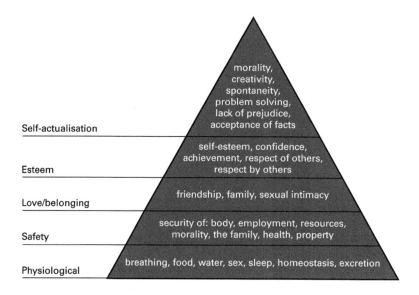

Figure 1.1 Maslow's hierarchy of needs (adapted from Maslow, 1954)

Examining our perceptions of pupils

So far, we have considered pupils' views of themselves, of teachers and of school. We have reviewed peer cultures and begun to understand the hierarchy of learner needs. How then, does this influence the expectations which we ourselves have about 'pupils' (Jones, 2009, Reading 1.5)?

We probably all have views about how we would like children to be as pupils – polite, attentive, cooperative, hard-working, engaged? And we also have ideas about the characteristics which may be less favoured. These conceptions tend to relate to the practical challenges of doing the job in the classroom. However, it has been found that teacher judgements are affected by the gender, ethnicity or social class of the pupils and even by their names (Meighan and Siraj-Blatchford, 1981). If, as teachers, we hold such preconceptions without reflecting on them, it can result in treating particular individuals or groups of pupils in ways which may not be fair or just. When the pupils then respond, original preconceptions may be reinforced. Labelling, or stereotyping, can thus lead to a phenomenon known as the 'self-fulfilling prophecy', resulting in considerable social injustices (Brophy and Good, 1974; Nash, 1976; Mortimore et al., 1988; Hart et al., 2004, Reading 1.4). This is particularly the case if patterns emerge in official assessment outcomes (Stobart, 2008, Reading 13.6; Filer, 2000).

As reflective teachers, we must focus on supporting and enhancing the achievement of *all* pupils in our care. We therefore need to occasionally step back from our initial or routine reactions to pupils, and interrogate our conscious or unconscious processes of categorisation and bias (see also Chapter 15, p. 491). For instance:

1. How does the school or classroom organisation differentiate between pupils, and what are the implications of this for teachers and pupils?

2. How do we personally acknowledge, categorise and label the pupils we work with?

3. How can we think about and work with pupils, moving beyond the labels?

Expert Question

Empowerment: *is our pedagogic repertoire successful in enhancing wellbeing, learning disposition, capabilities and agency?*

This question contributes to a conceptual framework representing enduring issues and teacher expertise (see Chapter 16).

Of course, teachers do have to develop ways of understanding and organising pupils in order to respond effectively to their educational needs. Within the classroom, however, this should be done with regard for the purposes of each particular situation or learning activity (see Chapter 15 for extensive discussion of inclusive practice). An inflexible form of classroom organisation is almost bound to disadvantage some students unnecessarily, if nothing else, by failing to recognise the individuality of everybody (Linklater, 2013).

Reflective Activity 1.7

Aim: To understand our perceptions of 'pupils'.

Evidence and reflection: First, without referring to the register or any lists, write down the names of the pupils in your class or tutor group. Note which order you have listed them in and which names you found hard to remember. What does the order tell you about which students are more memorable than others, and for what reasons?

Second, use your complete class list to generate the 'personal constructs' which you employ. To do this, look at each adjacent pair of names and write down the word that you think indicates how those two pupils are most alike. Then write down another word which shows how they are most different.

When you have done this with each pair, review the characteristics that you have identified.

Part 1 Becoming a reflective professional

What does this suggest to you about the concepts through which you distinguish children?

What additional qualities do the children have which these constructs do not seem to reflect and which perhaps you do not use?

Extension: Consider, perhaps with a colleague, the results of this activity and note any patterns that might exist: for example, whether some of your ideas relate more to boys than girls, or to children from different class, ethnicity or religious backgrounds. There may be some constructs that relate to such things as academic ability, physical attributes or behaviour towards teachers or other children. How might this be problematic for the identities of those pupils within your class, or for your expectations of them as learners?

Reflecting on our own thinking and practices helps us to understand the complexity of the classroom choices and decisions that are faced routinely every day. It helps us to ensure that future actions can be justified; that we continue to be professionally accountable.

There are various 'tools' available to support reflective practice. One helpful one is Hart's *Framework for Innovative Thinking* (2000). The essence of this framework is that it invites us to break down, or interrupt, our routine thinking and to try new ideas. The latter are framed in constructive, enabling and inclusive ways. Figure 1.2 summarises Hart's 'five moves', and Reflective Activity 1.8 invites us to try this out.

Figure 1.2
A framework for innovative thinking (adapted from Hart, 2000)

Five moves for innovative thinking	
Making connections	This move involves exploring how the specific characteristics of the child's response might be connected to features of the immediate and wider learning environment.
Contradicting	This move involves questioning the assumptions underlying a given interpretation by searching out a plausible alternative interpretation which casts the meaning of the situation in a new light. This helps to tease out the norms and expectations underlying the original interpretation so that it can be re-examined.
Taking a child's eye view	This move involves trying to enter the child's frame of reference and to see the meaning and logic of the child's response from the child's perspective.
Noting the impact of feelings	This move involves examining the part that our own feelings play in the meaning that we bestow on the situation and in leading us to a particular interpretation.
Postponing judgement in order to find out more	This move involves recognising that we may lack information or expertise needed to have confidence in our judgements. It involves holding back from further analysis and the attempt to arrive at judgements about the child's needs while we take steps to acquire further information.

reflectiveteaching.co.uk/rtps6/part1_ch1

Reflective Activity 1.8

Aim: To review the learning of a pupil in the light of Susan Hart's 'Framework for Innovative Thinking'.

Evidence and reflection: Think of a child or young person who is puzzling you, and review an example of their learning activities which surprised you or which you thought they might have done better.

Write a brief account of what happened.

Now use Hart's framework to reflect on what happened. Does it help in illuminating possible interpretations? What more would it be helpful to know? How might you find this out?

Extension: Share what you have written with a colleague who also knows the child or young person. How does their understanding match or contrast with yours? Why do you think this is? What teaching strategies seem most appropriate for the future?

Another contemporary lens for reflecting on our expectations of pupils is that of character education (Taylor, 2017). As a term, 'character education' is described as embracing 'all educational activities which help young people develop positive personal strengths and virtues'. The Association for Character Education elaborates this on their website:

> Character education is more than just a subject. It has a place in the culture and functions of families, classrooms, schools and other institutions. Character education is about helping students grasp what is ethically important in situations and how to act for the right reasons, so that they become more autonomous and reflective. Students need to decide the kind of person they wish to become and to learn to choose between alternatives. In this process, the ultimate aim of character education is the development of good sense or practical wisdom: the capacity to choose intelligently between alternatives. (character-education.org.uk)

One interesting way in which some primary schools incorporate character education is by taking an approach to teaching and learning called 'Philosophy for Children' (P4C, sapere.org.uk). See also the "Open Futures" site which shows an example of how P4C underpinned a new approach to the curriculum: https://www.openfutures.com. Philosophical questions centred around a stimulus, such as a story, video-clip or image, are open to examination, further questioning and enquiry. These questions are usually important to the lives of children but also contestable, central and common with multiple valid viewpoints. This approach, though modern in its form and impetus, has resonances with the classic commitment to holistic education of the 'whole child' in personal, social, moral and ethical dimensions – as well as simply the cognitive. In any event, it is a helpful frame of reference when considering aspirations for children.

LEARNING AND TEACHING THROUGH LIFE

Children and adults, pupils and teachers, occupy particular stages and roles through the life course. We all pass through infancy, childhood and adolescence before establishing ourselves as young adults. We then, often imperceptibly, progress into 'middle age' (with its rather elastic definition) and on towards retirement. 'Old age' then beckons – with even more learning challenges. In one sense then, although relevant historic periods generate particular circumstances, we already know something of our pupils, for we once inhabited that role too. And although we may look upon children and young people as 'in need of a good education', it is upon them that we will one day come to depend.

This section draws on our common experience to acknowledge and empathise with processes of development, becoming and contributing over time.

Pupil development and career

There are many different theories and perspectives on what the years from birth to age 18 mean in our society.

We can start by acknowledging that 'childhood' and 'adolescence' are social constructions. For example, during particular periods of history and in different parts of the world, young people are considered to have 'grown up' sufficiently to assume responsibilities at widely varying ages (Aries, 1962; Boas, 1966; James and Prout, 2003; James and James, 2004). Indeed, for some, contemporary western childhood is seen as reflecting adult priorities and ambitions (Moss and Petrie, 2005) or adult sentiment and nostalgia (Gillis, 1997).

Thus, whilst 'childhood' appears as a cultural feature of many societies, particularly in the western world, it is also possible to characterise young people simply as 'young people', rather than as 'children'. This suggestion is intended to disrupt the idea of children as *becoming* – with a focus on what the child is 'not yet'. On this argument, children and young people should thus be fully recognised as active and interactive agents (Jones, 2009, Reading 1.5; see also Mayall, 2002; Dahlberg, Moss and Pence, 1999) and as participants in society *during* childhood. Early phases of life have intrinsic value in themselves, not simply as preparations for future stages. This sort of approach can be illustrated by longitudinal studies of pupil learning and careers through primary and secondary school (Warin, 2010; Pollard and Filer, 1996, 1999, 2007, Reading 1.2). These sources provide detailed case studies of individual pupils as they develop through schooling, and document the ways in which relationships with family, friends and successive teachers influence the learning outcomes and the emergent identities of each child (see Figure 1.3).

Of course, there are extremely significant physiological changes too during infancy, childhood and adolescence. As we will see in Chapter 2, normal biological development is sequential. It follows that particular forms of educational provision are appropriate for children of different ages (a point which ambitious policymakers sometimes neglect). For example, it is implausible to require children to write, in a conventional sense, until their fine motor control has begun to develop (however, low expectations of children's writing need to be guarded against, see Bradford and Wyse, 2020). It is then possible to go with the flow of development to extend and refine that capability. This way of thinking is the source of the concept of 'readiness to learn' and has been applied in many domains. The problem of course, is that you might wait so long that teaching is neglected and children thus become disadvantaged. As with so many things in education we need balanced judgement in the light of important ideas which pull in slightly different directions. Moreover, the widening gap between the skills of children even at the earliest stages of schooling suggests the impact of environmental factors, and increasingly school is cast as the place where the gaps can be narrowed or closed. (For a discussion of how education policy has responded to poverty, see Burn and Childs, 2016.)

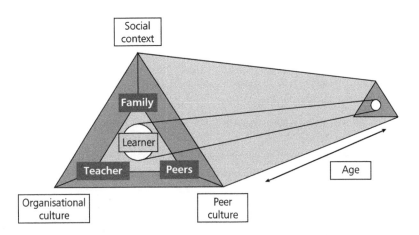

Figure 1.3 Social influences on learners through a school career

The physiological changes associated with puberty are many, and happen at different rates and stages, the average age of puberty for girls being 11 and boys 12, respectively. However, it is completely normal for puberty to begin at any point from the ages of 8 to 14. For primary teachers and schools, sex and relationships education has been highly controversial. Relationships education is currently statutory in England whereas sex education is not (McCrory and Worthington, 2018). However, the statutory National Curriculum for science in the Year 5 programme of study states that pupils should be taught to describe the changes of humans as they develop to old age. Non-statutory guidance states that pupils *should learn* about the changes experienced in puberty. Primary schools are therefore required to publish a clear statement of the Relationships and Sex Education (RSE) policy – including what will be taught so that parents can make an informed decision regarding withdrawing their children from sex education lessons.

Neuroscientists are contributing more and more to our understanding of how the brain develops and functions, and this is explored in Chapter 2. For the moment, we can simply note that whilst infancy appears to be particularly significant, later development through childhood and adolescence is also extremely important. Cognitive capacity is enhanced through use, and schooling is a primary source of structured experience for most young people.

reflectiveteaching.co.uk/rtps6/part1_ch1

Other psychological features of childhood and adolescence relate to changes in cognition. Whilst the thinking of children tends to be relatively bounded by direct experience, older children and young people gradually become more sophisticated in their manipulation of abstract concepts and complex thought (Inhelder and Piaget, 1958). They develop the ability to 'de-centre' by empathising with others, and can evaluate moral and ethical dilemmas (Kohlberg, 1976). Emotions and emotional states also play an important role in personal development – whether of children (Hyland, 2011) or even in teacher education (Shoffner, 2009).

All teachers thus have to consider and juggle with the developmental needs of learners in relation to curricular requirements and expectations. It is now possible to see the consequences of these social and developmental factors within our education systems over time. The National Child Development Study (NCDS) has been following the lives of around 17,000 people born in Britain in one week in 1958 (Elliott and Vaitilingam, 2008). Such longitudinal data has enabled analysis of the long-term consequences of early childhood and school experiences, and analysis has begun to identify factors that reinforce positive and negative developments in people's lives (Schoon, 2016; Elliott, 2013). Other cohort studies have been established which extend these analyses.

Feinstein, Vorhaus and Sabates (2008b, Reading 1.6) draw on such studies in a Government Foresight Study on 'learning through life'. They note that there are significant 'economic returns' to investment in education but also that 'intrinsic motivations are also important in individual decision-making' (p. 23). In an important analysis of the 'wider benefits of learning' they demonstrate how education fosters skills, confidence and qualifications which lead to many other benefits in later life and across society (see Figure 1.4).

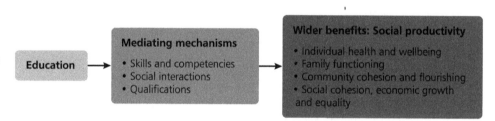

Figure 1.4
Mediating mechanisms for achievement of the wider benefits of learning (Feinstein et al., 2008b)

Feinstein et al. (2008b, p. 35) cite TLRP's 'evidence-informed principles' (see Chapter 3) as a contribution to the improvement of teaching and learning practices and argue that:

> Educational systems have a crucial role in equipping children and adults to withstand the economic, cultural and technological challenges they face in an increasingly globalised world. The fast pace of new technological developments and the intensification of economic pressures mean that the technical and academic skills of the working population are crucial for the UK economy. However, so are features of personal development such as resilience, self-regulation, a positive sense of self, and personal and social identity. The capability of individuals to function as civic agents with notions of personal responsibility, tolerance and respect depends on these wider features of identity which are strongly influenced by interactions with others in schools, workplaces, communities, neighbourhoods and through the media and other channels.

It is only in recent years that the career aspirations of primary and early years children have received any serious considerations from policymakers. The outcomes of the Drawing the Future project (Education and Employers et al., 2018) which surveyed 20,000 national and international primary-aged (7- to 11-year-old) children by asking them to draw what they wanted to be when they were older has interesting considerations for primary education. This research found that gender stereotyping continues to exist from the age of 7, that aspirations are still influenced by social background, and that there seems to have been a shift in the aspirations of children built largely upon new communication methods and the growth of online and console-based gaming; YouTube gaming 'vloggers' have now replaced TV and movie stars in the aspirations for 7- to 11-year-olds. Having said that, the outlook looked positive for STEM-related professions, although the most popular aspiration was being a 'sportsperson', followed closely by 'teacher'.

The implication of such research and of our brief consideration of pupil development and career in schools is to draw attention to the responsibility on us as teachers. Quite simply, our work contributes in significant ways to our national economy and cultures and, not least, to the future wellbeing of the country's citizens and the career aspirations of the children we teach. Although daunting, this task echoes with the ambitions voiced by the trainee teachers discussed at the beginning of this chapter. Moreover, their commitment serves to remind us not just of the economic reasons for this endeavour, but also the moral. To participate in the process of education is to participate in civil society. As we engage children in new learning, so we challenge ourselves, as reflective practitioners, to create new possibilities for all our futures.

Teacher development and career

Membership of the teaching profession represents a stage in the personal trajectory through life of each of us. For some, teaching will offer a long-term career. For others, our time as a teacher may be relatively brief, or even transitory. However, for all qualified teachers, official certification in that role affirms good knowledge of pedagogy and appropriate subject matter, understanding of learners and learning in school settings, and an important array of personal qualities. New teachers, in other words, are selected because of the competence they demonstrate and for the potential contributions which are anticipated.

The issues discussed above in relation to pupils also all apply again, albeit at different stages of life. Thus, social relations, experiences, identity and self-confidence complement physical, psychological and neurological maturity to offer social, affective and cognitive capability. We are simply the children of yesteryear, who have now grown up.

As we saw above (p. 12), Huberman (1993) proposed five stages of teacher development – career entry, stabilisation, experimentation, conservatism and disengagement. Day and Gu (2010) took this further in *The New Lives of Teachers* by linking the challenges of professional development with particular life and work scenarios. They argue that:

reflectiveteaching.co.uk/rtps6/part1_ch1

The relative success with which teachers manage various personal, work and external policy challenges is a key factor in the satisfaction, commitment, well-being and effectiveness of teachers. The influences of school leadership, culture, colleagues and conditions are also profound, and relate directly to teacher retention and the work–life balance agenda. (Day and Gu, 2010, prelim, see also **Reading 1.1**)

The social influences on teachers through a professional career are thus not dissimilar to those which affect pupils as they progress through schooling. We all have basic needs which must be satisfied to create conditions for success (Eyre, 2017). It is noticeable that, just as positive learning dispositions and resilience to new challenges are crucial to pupil success (see Claxton, 1999, **Reading 2.9**), so teacher commitment and resilience are essential to effectiveness over the whole of a career (Bennett, 2012).

The finding in Day et al.'s (2006) study that 'teachers do not necessarily become more effective over time' is challenging for us to think about. It draws attention to our own professional vulnerabilities and suggests that aspiration, good intentions or values are not enough. We also need to reflect on our practices, using evidence of various sorts to challenge ourselves in continuous cycles of improvement (see Chapter 3).

The notion 'warranted practice' has been used to emphasise the importance of progressive development in the work of teachers (Richardson, 1998). Ruthven (2005) used the term to describe the process teachers engage in to ensure continual improvement of provision, as well as meeting the demands of professional accountability. He suggests that educational reform depends on deeper understandings and flexible thinking about practice. For Ruthven, the term 'warranted' is used in two important senses. First, it provides reasoned grounds for the practice as intended; and second, it suggests that the practice as implemented in a particular setting is indeed likely to succeed in its aims. This perspective does not offer a 'cook book' prescription of 'what works', because teacher decision-making is seen as being contextual, dynamic and responsive to the needs of learners in each particular setting.

Our commitment to professionalism through a teaching career is expressed through our values, identities, and work as teachers. However, professionalism also needs to be underpinned by processes which enable us to routinely review and improve our own practices (see Chapter 3).

CONCLUSION

This chapter celebrates the idealism and moral purpose of primary teachers, but also recognises the personal and professional challenges. It reviews the significant array of factors shaping pupils' lives, and suggests how such knowledge may be used to support effective teaching and learning. Finally, it describes the trajectories through life of pupils and teachers, and acknowledges our common humanity.

We saw that the process of reflecting on our aims and values as teachers can help us in developing a realistic personal *and* professional identity. Further, it was suggested that, by

Chapter 1 Identity   31

understanding the many influences on our teaching more explicitly, we can identify where we are being most successful and perhaps where values and intention, evidence and practice do not match as well as they might.

It was suggested that, by maintaining awareness of the cultures of children and young people, their views of us as teachers and their perspectives on themselves and each other, we are better able to take account of their needs when developing opportunities for learning. We do, however, need to keep under scrutiny the concepts which we ourselves use to understand pupils.

Finally, we considered the significance of teaching and learning in the life course of children, and for ourselves.

> **Expert Question**
>
> **Warrant:** *are our teaching strategies evidence-informed, convincing and justifiable to stakeholders?*
>
> This question contributes to a conceptual framework underpinning professional expertise (see Chapter 16).

reflectiveteaching.co.uk/rtps6/part1_ch1

CHAPTER WEBPAGE

 reflectiveteaching.co.uk offers additional professional resources for this chapter. Go to: reflectiveteaching.co.uk/rtps6/part1_ch1

For instance, there are over twenty *Reflective Activities* which could be tried, including some focused on personal values and commitment to teaching, and others on knowing children and young people as 'pupils'.

There is an interesting *Research Briefing* on 'learning and identity across the life course', which really conveys why education is so important in enhancing, or constraining, life chances. Whilst that looks at the 'big picture', Alison Peacock has shown how opportunities and/or constraints can be embedded in routine classroom practices. Please take a look at her YouTube TED talk on 'Learning without Limits'. Such talks can be inspiring, and the associated research affirms the importance of such commitment.

For those who would like to follow up on the issues raised in the chapter, three sources of guidance and support are provided.

1. Suggestions for *Further Reading* are available by clicking a tab on the relevant chapter webpage. It provides a broad review of what is known about teacher identities, understanding pupils and the progress of teaching and learning though life. It is an excellent resource to inform a visit to a library, or for work on a project or essay.

2. Simplifying somewhat, a selection of suggestions has been picked out in the list of *Key Readings* below.

3. Making things really easy, and by-passing the library, it is possible to read short, edited versions of some of the best material in the companion volume, *Readings for Reflective Teaching in Schools*. Several of these readings are indicated below, and there is a synopsis for each one on the chapter webpage.

KEY READINGS

A classic introduction to the delights and challenges of teaching is:

Richardson, R. (1990) *Daring to Be a Teacher*. Stoke-on-Trent: Trentham Books.

Quigley offered advice drawing on extensive teaching experience. In both cases, there is a focus on personal development in the context of professional work.

Quigley, A. (2016) *The Confident Teacher. Developing Successful Habits of Mind, Body and Pedagogy*. London: Routledge.

Chapter 1 Identity

On teacher development and commitment through careers and lives, the classic account is Huberman's. We also have more contemporary work from Day and Gu as well as Eaude who focuses on the continuing professional development of teachers.

Huberman, M. (1993) *The Lives of Teachers.* London: Cassell.

Day, C. and Gu, Q. (2010) *The New Lives of Teachers.* London: Routledge. (see also **Reading 1.1**)

Eaude, T. (2018) *Developing the Expertise of Primary and Elementary Classroom Teachers. Professional Learning for a Changing World.* London: Bloomsbury.

For a thorough exploration of how student teachers learn from the expertise of practising teachers, see:

Hagger, H. and McIntyre, D. (2006) *Learning Teaching from Teachers – Realizing the Potential of School-Based Teacher Education.* Maidenhead: Open University Press.

Burn, K., Hagger, H. and Mutton, T. (2015) *Beginning Teachers' Learning: Making Experience Count.* St Albans: Critical Publishing.

There are many interesting books on children's culture, friendships and perspectives in school.

Devine, D. (2003) *Children, Power and Schooling. The Social Structuring of Childhood in the Primary School.* Stoke-on-Trent: Trentham. (**Reading 1.3**)

Carter, C. and Nutbrown, C. (2016). 'A pedagogy of friendship: young children's friendships and how schools can support them'. *International Journal of Early Years Education*, 24(4), 395–413.

For detailed case studies of children's developing identities and careers through schooling, see:

Pollard, A. and Filer, A. (1999) *The Social World of Pupil Career: Strategic Biographies through Primary School.* London: Cassell. (see also **Reading 1.2**)

Two important books which challenge all determinist ideas about 'ability' and 'grouping' are:

Hart, S., Dixon, A., Drummond, M-J. and McIntyre, D. (2004) *Learning Without Limits.* Maidenhead: Open University Press. (see also **Reading 1.4**)

Marks, R. (2016). *Ability-grouping in Primary Schools: Case Studies and Critical Debates.* St Albans: Critical Publishing.

A paper discussing how student teachers used this work to support and develop their own professional practice is:

Florian, L. and Linklater, H. (2010) 'Preparing teachers for inclusive education: using inclusive pedagogy to enhance teaching and learning for all'. *Cambridge Journal of Education* 40 (4), 369–86.

The long-term consequences of schooling are quantified in:

Feinstein, L., Vorhaus, J. and Sabates, R. (2008b) *Learning Through Life: Future Challenges*. Foresight Mental Capital and Wellbeing Project. London: The Government Office for Science. **(Reading 1.6)**

But note that although lifecourse outcomes are patterned, changes in fortunes can occur at any point as people react to their circumstances:

Schoon, I. (2016) *Human Development in Context* : The Study of Risk and Resilience. London: UCL IOE Press.

To explore the implication of the arguments in this chapter, try the readings in Chapter 17 of *Readings for Reflective Teaching in Schools* – such as:

Power, S. (2008) 'The imaginative professional'. In Cunningham, B. (ed.) *Exploring Professionalism*. London: UCL IOE Press. **(Reading 17.5)**

RESEARCH BRIEFING 1.1
Teacher careers and effectiveness

A large-scale and comprehensive TLRP project on teachers' work, lives and effectiveness, VITAE, researched teachers' professional identities through career phases. Teachers' sense of professional identity is affected by tensions between: their personal values and life experiences; the situated leadership and cultures of their schools; and the impact of external policies on their professional work. Outcomes, in terms of wellbeing, commitment and resilience, and hence effectiveness, depend on teachers' capacity to manage interactions between personal, work and professional factors.

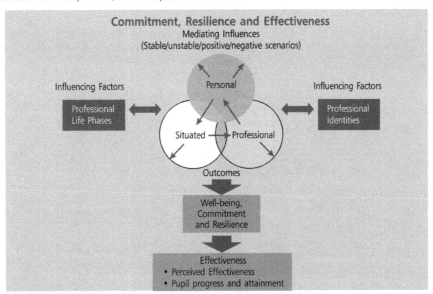

Key findings:	Implications:
Pupil attainment: Pupils of teachers who are committed and resilient are likely to attain more than pupils whose teachers are not.	Policy makers, national associations and head teachers concerned with raising standards in schools need to consider the connections between teachers' commitment, resilience and effectiveness.
Professional identity: Teachers' sense of positive professional identity is associated with well-being and job satisfaction and is a key factor in their effectiveness.	Strategies for sustaining commitment in initial and continuing professional development programmes should distinguish between the needs of teachers in different phases of their professional lives.
Challenge: The commitment and resilience of teachers in schools serving more disadvantaged communities are more persistently challenged than others.	Schools, especially those which serve disadvantaged communities, need to ensure that their continuing professional development (CPD) provision is relevant to the commitment, resilience and health needs of teachers.
Experience: Teachers do not necessarily become more effective over time. Teachers in later years are likely to be less effective.	National organisations and schools need strategies for professional learning and development to support teachers in the later stages of their careers.
Sustainability: Sustaining and enhancing teachers' commitment and resilience is a key quality and retention issue.	Efforts to support and enhance teacher quality should focus upon building, sustaining and retaining their commitment and resilience.

Further information
Day, C., Stobart, G., Sammons, P., Kington, A., Gu, Q., Smees, R., Mujtaba, T. and Woods, D. (2006) *Factors that make teachers more effective across their careers.* TLRP Research Briefing No 20 (available on the chapter page for this book at reflectiveteaching.co.uk).
Day, C., Stobart, G., Sammons, P. and Kington, A. (2007) *Teachers Matter.* Maidenhead: Open University Press. The TLRP Associate Project was funded by DfES and directed from the University of Nottingham.

RESEARCH BRIEFING 1.2
Consulting pupils about teaching and learning

TLRP's researcher/practitioner network on consulting pupils, led by Jean Rudduck, was influential in respect of policy on personalised learning. For example, 'pupil voice' was identified as enabling children to 'take ownership of their learning' and thus develop citizenship and a positive learning disposition. As the *2020 Vision* team put it in recommending effective pedagogies:

> Pupils are more likely to be engaged with the curriculum they are offered if they believe it is relevant and if they are given opportunities to take ownership of their learning. (DfES 2006, p. 26)

Many hundreds of teachers worked in Jean Rudduck's networks. They developed strategies for consulting pupils about teaching and learning in the classroom and for building pupil consultation into the organisation of the school. They found that pupil consultation on everyday, practical issues enhanced pupil self-esteem and also gradually changed the ways teaching and learning was thought about across the whole school. The figure below represents this impact.

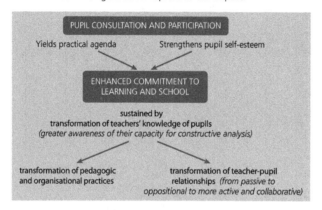

Key findings:	Implications:
For pupils: Being consulted produces a stronger sense of engagement with learning, an enhanced sense of agency and of self as learner.	If pupils feel that they are respected in school, then they are more likely to commit themselves to learning.
For teachers: Consulting pupils leads to deeper insights into children's abilities and learning preferences, leading to more responsive teaching and giving greater responsibility to pupils individually and as a group.	Pupils' accounts of what helps and what hinders them in learning can provide a practical agenda for improving teaching and learning.
For schools: Consulting pupils strengthens school policy and priority development by including pupils in substantive rather than marginal or tokenistic ways.	Pupil testimony can feed powerfully into whole school policy and planning – where this is enabled to happen.
For national policy: Pupil engagement suggests new insights and practical tools for school self-evaluation, strategic planning and improvement.	Classroom and school practice engaging pupils can provide the basis for further systematic inquiry and policy development.

The U.N. Convention on the Rights of the Child (1989) included children's right to be heard as one of its four basic principles. It is seen as integral to the Citizenship curriculum and lifelong learning. How to listen and learn, as well as to teach and lead, is the challenge for teachers, schools and their communities.

Further information

Rudduck, J., Arnot, M., Demetriou, H., Flutter, J., MacBeath, J., McIntyre, D., Myers, K., Pedder, D., Wang, B., Fielding, M., Bragg, S. and Reay, D. (2005) *Consulting Pupils about Teaching and Learning*. TLRP Research Briefing, No 5. (Available on the chapter page for this book at reflectiveteaching.co.uk).
Rudduck, J. and McIntyre, D. (2007) *Improving Learning through Consulting Pupils*. TLRP Improving Learning series. London: Routledge.
This TLRP network was directed from the University of Cambridge.

Chapter 2
Learning
How can we understand learners' development?

| Introduction | 38 |

Learning processes	**39**
Behaviourism	39
Constructivism	42
Social cognition	44

***Nature*, nurture and agency**	**49**
Personal development, health and wellbeing	49
Body and brain, mind and behaviour	51
'Intelligence' and expectations	53

***Nurture*, nature and agency**	**57**
Cognitive science and teaching	58
Culture, language and disposition	60
Personality, motivation and identity	63
Metacognition and thinking skills	66

Taking stock of learning	**69**
Key factors in learning	69
Metaphors of learning	70
Applying learning beyond school	72

| Conclusion | 73 |

Supplementary chapter at reflectiveteaching.co.uk
- **Observing** Children and young people as learners

reflectiveteaching.co.uk/rtps6/part1_ch2

INTRODUCTION

Learning can be thought of as the process by which people acquire, understand, apply and extend knowledge, concepts, skills and attitudes. Children and young people also discover their feelings towards themselves, towards each other and towards learning itself. These feelings influence learners' motivation about their learning and their engagement in learning activities. Learning is thus a combination of cognitive, social, affective and conative (motivational) elements. The teacher's recognition of what learners bring as individuals to their education is crucial.

See Chapter 4

TLRP Principles

Three principles are of particular relevance to this chapter on learning:

Effective teaching and learning recognises the importance of prior experience and learning. Teaching and learning should take account of what the learner knows already in order to plan their next steps. This includes building on prior learning but also taking account of the personal and cultural experiences of different groups of learners. (*Principle 3*)

Effective teaching and learning promotes the active engagement of the learner. A chief goal of teaching and learning should be the promotion of learners' independence and autonomy. This involves acquiring a repertoire of learning strategies and practices, developing positive attitudes towards learning, and confidence in oneself as a good learner. (*Principle 6*)

Effective teaching and learning recognises the significance of informal learning. Informal learning, such as learning out of school, should be recognised as at least as significant as formal learning and should therefore be valued and used appropriately in formal processes. (*Principle 8*)

How we understand children and their learning affects the choices that teachers make, day by day, encounter by encounter in the classroom. It influences how we interpret what children do and how we decide, as their teacher, what to do next. There is a tendency, in our culture, to attribute differences between children's learning and attainments to deficits in the young people themselves. However, a new mindset is turning this deficit approach around, enabling teachers to take a 'credit approach', seeing all children as rich, strong, powerful learners, as long as conducive classroom conditions and compelling opportunities for learning are provided (see Hart et al., 2004; Swann et al., 2012, Reading 1.4). Reflective teachers taking this credit approach focus on what pupils can do, not on what they cannot do. They are more interested in young people's desire to understand than in gaps in their knowledge. If we see all learners as powerful then we are inescapably committed to the educability of every child, and to building and using our professional expertise to seek, understand and remove barriers to learning.

In this chapter we focus first on processes of learning, and introduce three perspectives which have particularly influenced education – behaviourism, constructivism and socio-cultural perspectives. We then consider the classic debate about the relative roles of 'nature' and 'nurture' in education through a brief review of some biological, social and cultural factors – whilst emphasising the agency of learners and teachers.

LEARNING PROCESSES

Learning is a fascinating, but highly complex, aspect of human activity. In psychology, a distinction is often made between cognitive and affective development – contrasts being drawn between thought and feeling; rationality and emotion; and even some forms of knowledge and understanding. There are interesting interconnections of course – with one neuroscientific analysis entitled 'We feel, therefore we learn' (Immordino-Yang and Damasio, 2007, Reading 6.2). Indeed, attention, memory, decision-making and other cognitive capabilities are strongly influenced by affective dispositions and feelings. The latter respond in particular to characteristics of learning environments – such as homes, classrooms and even examination halls, as many of us will recognise from our own experience.

Of course, humans learned for many thousands of years before anyone thought that a 'curriculum' and 'schooling' were necessary. Indeed, at its simplest, learning can be seen as the product of a continuous interaction between *development* and *experience* through life, where schooling and the intentional curriculum can be seen as a formal part of those experiences. The learner understands their experiences in school in relation to their development and their wider experiences. The professional teacher's job is to understand the process as well as possible and to offer children the benefit of that understanding in designing teaching and learning activities.

For centuries, philosophers, psychologists and educationalists have analysed learning. The result is that there are many perspectives and theories which attempt to describe the process. We have simplified this complex field by identifying just three theories of learning which have been particularly influential on teaching and learning in schools. Each has merit in highlighting specific dimensions of learning which can help teachers understand the challenge that they face.

Behaviourism

This theory suggests that living creatures, animal or human, learn by building up associations or 'bonds' between their experience, their thinking and their behaviour. Thus, as long ago as 1911, Thorndike formulated two principles. First, the 'law of effect':

- The greater the satisfaction or discomfort, the greater the strengthening or weakening of the bond.

Second, the 'law of exercise': the relationship between the frequency of the response and learning:

- The probability of a response occurring in a given situation increases with the number of times that response has occurred in that situation in the past.

Thorndike confidently claimed that these 'laws' emerged clearly from 'every series of experiments on animal learning and in the entire history of the management of human affairs' (Thorndike, 1911, p. 244).

A variety of versions of behaviourism were developed and provided the dominant perspective on formal learning in English speaking countries until the 1960s. Perhaps the most significant of these psychologists was Skinner (e.g. 1968, see Reading 2.1) who, through his work with animals, developed a sophisticated theory of the role in learning of stimulus, response, reinforcement and consequence.

The influence of behaviourist theory in education has been immense because, in the early part of the twentieth century, it provided the foundations of work on a 'science of teaching' based on whole-class, didactic approaches through which knowledge and skills were to be taught. The 'law of effect' was reflected in elaborate systems and rituals for the reinforcement of correct pupil responses. The 'law of exercise' was reflected in an emphasis on practice and drill.

Behaviourist learning theory casts the learner in a relatively passive role, leaving the selection, pacing and evaluation of learning activity to the teacher. Subject expertise can thus be transmitted in a coherent, ordered and logical way, and control of the class tends to be tight – because pupils are often required to listen and respond. There is a problem though, in whether such teaching actually connects with the learner's existing understanding.

Teaching which has been influenced by behaviourism can be seen in all schools, and has been particularly influential on provision for children with special educational needs. The importance of recognising and reinforcing children's work and effort is well established, and reflects the work of Skinner (e.g. 1953) in demonstrating the limited value of 'punishment' (or other forms of negative reinforcement) as a means of supporting learning. The use of practice tasks is also well established, particularly for teaching aspects of the core curriculum such as numerical computation or spelling, and this type of work reflects the influence of the 'law of exercise'. The use of teacher-controlled explanation and question-and-answer routines is an important part of any teacher's pedagogic repertoire. These methods will be used, for instance, when new topics are being introduced and when taking stock of achievements. The idea of building progressive steps in learning (e.g. Gagné, 1965) is, of course, often reflected in the organisation of the curriculum. Behaviourism has also been influential in work with children who experience Special Educational Needs and Disabilities (SEND). It has also been influential in the design of approaches to learning which use digital technologies, particularly where technology has a teaching or tutorial role (Watters, 2021).

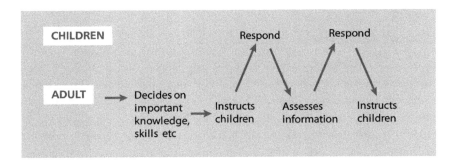

Figure 2.1 A behaviourist model of roles in the teaching–learning process

Figure 2.1 represents the roles of children and adult in behaviourist-influenced teaching and learning processes.

It is important to note some additional points about behaviourist approaches. First, there is a high degree of adult control in the process; deciding on the subject matter, providing explicit instruction, pacing the lesson, modelling, correcting, assessing and reinforcing pupil responses. In principle, this makes it relatively easy for teacher expositions and explanations to be logical, coherent, linear and progressive as particular subject matter and knowledge or skills are introduced to the pupils. However, there are also some difficulties with teaching in this way. The most important is the question of connecting with the existing understanding of the learner. In this respect, the strength of subject exposition can also be a weakness if a pupil does not recognise subject divisions as being relevant to daily experiences (see Chapter 9, p. 269). Such a mismatch, between existing knowledge and experience, and new learning, can reduce motivation and achievement as the child may not be able to use the knowledge which is offered to build a meaningful understanding. In such circumstances, learning tends to be superficial and fragmented. This problem may be made acute when large groups are taught because it is very hard for a teacher to 'pitch' the lesson appropriately for all learners.

The influence of behaviourism has been greatest on what are commonly termed 'traditional' teaching methods, and particularly those associated with whole-class, subject-based teaching such as mastery learning (Guskey, 2007). Careful programmes of explicit instruction and practice or reinforcement can meet particular needs – for example, digital technologies can be successfully designed to exploit these strengths through tutoring and feedback programs. Behaviourism is also evident in some models of formative assessment where the aim is to ensure pupils achieve a pre-determined goal (Pryor and Torrance, 1996). However, behaviourism is often oversimplified as a 'training' model and some in the media even seem to expect behaviourist assumptions to be applied to almost all teaching. Perhaps it is popular because of its association with teacher control, strict discipline and strong subject teaching focused on knowledge acquisition. However, the responsibility of teachers is to interact with pupils so that they learn successfully over time, not simply to expose them to subject matter which can be rehearsed and reproduced for a specific assessment or short-term goal. Teaching methods based on behaviourism must, therefore, be fit for their purpose (Kirschner and Hendrick, 2020).

Constructivism

This approach to understand learning suggests that people learn through an interaction between their own thinking and experience, and through the sequential development of more complex cognitive structures which help them understand the world around them. The most influential constructivist theorist was the Swiss psychologist Jean Piaget (e.g. 1926, 1950, 1961; see Reading 2.2). His ultimate goal was to create a 'genetic epistemology' – an understanding of the origin of knowledge in individuals derived from research into the interaction between people and their environment.

In Piaget's account, learning and the development of the mind involves three basic processes: assimilation, accommodation and equilibration. When children encounter new events and experiences, they 'assimilate' them into their current cognitive structures, or they make sense of them in terms of their current understanding. Sometimes, however, these understandings need to change to 'accommodate' the new information. This process of adjustment and change is 'equilibration'. This is finding a balance between existing understanding and making sense of new experiences which need new understandings. A child actively tries to make sense of their world as they experience it, so constructs and reconstructs these understandings or 'schema' in response to new events and experiences as they develop. Gradually then, children come to construct more detailed, complex and accurate understandings of the phenomena they experience.

Piaget proposed that there are characteristic stages in the successive development of these mental structures, stages that are distinctive because of the type of 'cognitive operation' with which children and young people process their experience. These stages are:

- sensorimotor (approximately birth–2 years);
- preoperational (approximately 2–7 years);
- concrete operations (approximately 7–12 years);
- formal operations (approximately 12 years onwards).

In each of the first three stages, the role of the child's direct experience is deemed to be crucial. It is only in the formal operations stage that abstract thinking is believed possible. In the sensorimotor and preoperational stages children are thought to be relatively individualistic and unable to work with others for long. Children are believed to behave rather like 'active scientists', enquiring, exploring and discovering as their curiosity and interests lead them to successive experiences. They actively make sense of these experiences and develop idiosyncratic theories of how the world works. Play and practical experimentation have a crucial role in the assimilation process at each stage (Piaget, 1951): a point that is particularly well understood by early childhood educators (Moyles, 2005; Parker-Rees and Leeson, 2015).

A student of Piaget's, Seymour Papert (1980), developed his ideas though activities in which children used computer environments to 'construct' programs and develop their understanding through this exploration, which he referred to as 'constructionism'.

reflectiveteaching.co.uk/rtps6/part1_ch2

(Somewhat confusingly, there is also a theory called 'social constructionism', used in sociology and communication theory, which draws on concepts such as narratives and identity (Berger and Luckmann, 1966), and considers how aspects of reality are socially constructed.)

The influence of constructivist theory in primary education in England was considerable in the UK following the report of the Plowden Committee (Central Advisory Council for Education (CACE), 1967, see also Reading 9.4), in which it was suggested that:

> Piaget's explanation appears to fit the observed facts of children's learning more satisfactorily than any other. It is in accord with what is generally regarded as the most effective primary school practice, as it has been worked out empirically. (CACE, 1967, para. 522)

The image of the active child as the agent of their own learning runs through Plowden. 'Child-centred' teaching approaches, based on interpretations of Piaget's work, were adopted with commitment by some teachers in the late 1960s and 1970s. Great imagination and care were put into providing varied and stimulating classroom environments from which children could derive challenging experiences (e.g. Marsh, 1970). Sophisticated forms of classroom organisation, such as the 'integrated day' (Brown and Precious, 1968; Walton, 1971) were introduced and developed to manage the problem of providing individual children with appropriate direct learning experiences. Despite these efforts, observational research showed that constructivist methods were not greatly reflected in the actual practice of teachers of older primary children (Galton, Simon and Croll, 1980). Constructivism has always been particularly influential in work with younger pupils with whom the benefits of working from children's interests, from play and from practical experience, are relatively clear-cut (Parker-Rees and Leeson, 2015; Lindon and Trodd, 2016; Doddington and Hilton, 2007). However, Piaget's work has also influenced important research on the development of thinking skills and 'cognitive acceleration' in science and maths across the age range (Shayer and Adey, 2002).

There have been a number of criticisms of Piaget's work, particularly because of the way in which seeing the development of young people in sequential structured stages can lead to underestimation of their capacities. Psychologists, such as Donaldson (1978) and Tizard and Hughes (1984), demonstrated that children's intellectual abilities are often greater than those reported by Piaget. Their findings emerged when children were observed in situations that were *meaningful* to them. In such circumstances, children also show considerably more social competence at younger ages than Piaget's theory suggests (Dunn, 1988; Siegler, 1997). From a different perspective, sociologists such as Walkerdine (1983, 1988) have argued that Piaget's stages became part of a child-centred ideology and a means through which teachers classify, compare and, thus, control children. Critics have also suggested that this form of constructivism over-emphasises self-discovery by the individual and ignores the social context in which learning takes place. In so doing, the potential of teachers, other adults and other children to support each child's learning may be under-estimated.

Constructivist learning theory, as adapted by educationalists, casts the learner in an active and independent role, leaving much of the selection, pacing and evaluation of the activity to be negotiated with the child. There is some emphasis on each pupil's interests and some compromise on the specific content of curriculum coverage with a focus on the development of children's understanding.

Figure 2.2 represents the roles of child and adult in constructivist-influenced teaching and learning processes.

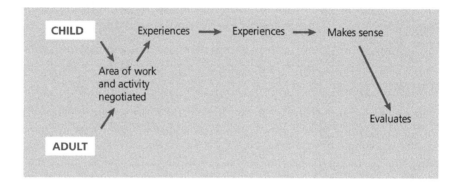

Figure 2.2 A constructivist model of roles in the teaching–learning process

Note here the *negotiation* of pupil activity and the emphasis placed on direct experience in learning. Together, these have the aim of creating high levels of pupil motivation and engagement. In the right circumstances, creativity and other forms of pupil achievement can reach exceptional levels of excellence. However, coverage of a particular curriculum is hard to monitor and the diversity of individual pupil interests tends to produce relatively complex forms of classroom organisation as a range of activities needs to be provided. Research shows that teachers then tend to be drawn into managing this complex environment rather than teaching itself (e.g. Galton, 1989; Alexander, Rose and Woodhead, 1992).

As with behaviourist approaches, professional judgements about 'fitness for purpose' should always guide decisions about the use of teaching methods based on constructivism.

Social cognition

This perspective on learning takes two main forms. On the one hand, it draws attention to the language and forms of understanding that are embedded in particular contexts and social practices – and sees these as important 'cultural resources' that are available to a learner from that setting. Studies with this emphasis are often referred to as *socio-cultural*. On the other hand, it draws attention to the key role of experienced participants in inducting less competent learners, and in 'mediating', 'scaffolding' and extending their understanding. Studies with this emphasis are sometimes known as *social constructivist or social constructionist*, because they retain the concern with learner activity, but also recognise the significance of social processes and interaction with others.

Socio-cultural theories of learning affirm the importance of recognising and building on pupils' family and community knowledge and the interaction with their peers, whilst also emphasising the role of teaching and instruction in extending such knowledge. The seminal writer on this approach was Vygotsky (1962, 1978, Reading 2.3), whose publications in Russian date from the 1930s. The increasing availability of Vygotsky's work in English coincided with reappraisals of the strengths and weaknesses of Piagetian theory. Psychologists such as Bruner (1986), Wood (1997) and Wertsch (1985) were able to demonstrate the considerable relevance of Vygotsky's work to modern education. This complemented empirical work by other child psychologists, and curriculum-development initiatives by subject specialists.

As we have seen, a key insight concerns the role of the culture and the social context of the learner in influencing understanding (Wells, 1999, Reading 2.5; Bruner, 1990, 2006, Reading 11.4; Pollard and Filer, 1996, Reading 1.2). This influence starts in informal ways from birth. Thus, infants and young children interact with their parents and family and, through experiencing the language and forms of behaviour of their culture, also assimilate particular cognitive skills, strategies, knowledge and understanding (Richards and Light, 1986; Dunn, 1988; González, Moll and Amanti, 2005). Cognition, language and forms of thought thus depend on the culture and social history of the learner as well as on any particular instruction which may be offered at any point in time. This influence of culture on learning continues throughout life; indeed, it is what makes learning meaningful. Ideas, language and concepts derived from interaction with others thus structure, challenge, enhance or constrain thinking.

An extremely practical conclusion from this is that teachers may therefore need to engage with children's existing cultural and conceptual understandings (and misunderstandings) before attempting further instruction. A review from the United States indicates that: 'if initial understanding is not engaged, pupils may fail to grasp new information and concepts, or may learn for the purposes of the test, but fail to transfer the learning to new situations' (Bransford, Brown and Cocking, 1999, p. 25, Reading 4.1). As we will see later in this chapter, this argument for 'deep' and 'connected' learning is also linked to learner identity. Does the learner feel comfortable with new, school knowledge? Can they incorporate it and feel supported by the significant others in their lives (such as parents or their peers), or do they experience apathy or even disapproval?

The second major aspect of socio-cultural perspectives on which we will focus concerns the mediation of understanding by more knowledgeable others. This is best illustrated through Vygotsky's concept of the 'zone of proximal development' (ZPD) (1978, Reading 2.3). This is:

> the distance between the actual developmental level (of the child) as determined through problem solving and the level of potential development as determined through problem solving under adult guidance or in collaboration with more capable peers. (Vygotsky, 1978, p. 86)

The ZPD concerns each person's potential to 'make sense'. Given a learner's present state of understanding, what developments can occur if they are given appropriate assistance by more capable others? If support is appropriate and meaningful, then, it is argued, the understanding of children can be extended far beyond that which they could reach alone.

Such assistance in learning can come in many ways. It may take the form of an explanation by or discussion with a knowledgeable teacher; it may reflect debate among a group of children as they strive to solve a problem or complete a task; it might come from discussion with a parent or from watching a particular television programme. In each case, the intervention functions to extend and to 'scaffold' the child's understanding across their ZPD for that particular issue. An appropriate analogy, suggested by Bruner, is that of building a house. Scaffolding is needed to provide access to the process as the house is gradually constructed from its foundations – but when it has been assembled and all the parts have been finished, the scaffolding can be removed. The building – the learner's understanding – will be complete.

The influence of socio-cultural theories of learning has grown steadily since the early 1980s. Perhaps this is because the approach seems to recognise both the needs of learners to develop their own, meaningful understandings and the role of interaction and communication in the learning process. Indeed, a key to the approach lies in specifying relationships between these factors. As Tharp and Gallimore (1988, Reading 11.4) suggest, learning can be seen as 'assisted performance'.

Figure 2.3, elaborated from Rowland (1987), represents the roles of children and adults in a social constructivist teaching and learning processes. Negotiation, focused perhaps on a National Curriculum topic, is followed by activity and discussion by children. However, the teacher then makes an intervention to provide support and instruction – a role which Rowland named as that of the 'reflective agent'. This draws attention to the fact that any intervention must be appropriate. It must connect with the understandings and purposes of the learners so that their thinking is extended. If this is to happen, teachers need to draw on both their subject knowledge and their understanding of children and young people in general, and of their class in particular. They must make an accurate judgement themselves about the most appropriate form of input. In this, various techniques of formative assessment (see Chapter 13) are likely to be helpful. If such judgements are astute then the input could take the children's thinking forward, across the ZPD and beyond the level of understanding which they would have reached alone. Clearly there could be successive cycles of this process.

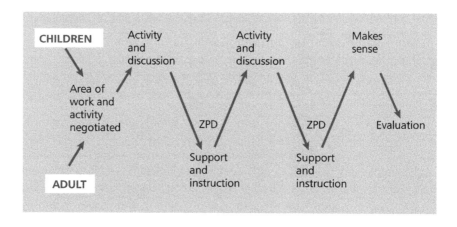

Figure 2.3 A social constructivist model of roles in the teaching–learning process

Reflective Activity 2.1

Aim: To observe learning and consider the insights of behaviourist, constructivist and socio-cultural perspectives on learning.

Evidence and reflection: Using the questions below, observe a short episode (up to twenty minutes) of one child's learning with an adult.

1. What was the child actually doing? 2. What was he/she learning? 3. How worthwhile was it? 4. What did you (the adult) do? 5. What did you learn? 6. What will you do next?	

Now consider the psychological rationale for the approach offered to the child and note down the key elements:

Behaviourist	Constructivist	Socio-cultural

Consider if the activity has implications for the repertoire of teaching strategies that you use.

Extension: Drawing on features of the three approaches, summarised in Figure 2.4, suggest ways in which the teaching strategies used could have strengthened the child's opportunity to learn.

SUMMARY

Figure 2.4 provides a very simple summary of some key points in the previous discussions of teacher–learner interaction. The table aims to contrast the different perspectives on learning. We return to some further socio-cultural factors later in this chapter.

So far we have considered three major theoretical influences on learning and teaching processes in schools. We now move on to focus more specifically on children and young people as learners, and on factors which influence individual differences in learning.

reflectiveteaching.co.uk/rtps6/part1_ch2

Part 1 Becoming a reflective professional

Figure 2.4 Some features of behaviourist, constructivist and social constructivist models of learning in school classrooms

	Behaviourism in classrooms	Constructivism in classrooms	Social cognition in classrooms
Image of learner	Passive/responsive Individual/collective Extrinsically motivated	Active Individual Intrinsically motivated	Active/interactive Social Socially motivated
Images of teaching and learning	Teacher transmits knowledge and skills Learning depends on teaching and systematic reinforcement of correct behaviours	Teacher gives child opportunity to construct Knowledge and skills gradually through experience Learning can be independent of teaching	Knowledge and skills are developed gradually through experience, interaction and adult support Learning comes through the interdependence of teacher and children
Typical child activities	Class listening to an adult Class working on an exercise Teacher providing feedback and evaluation	Individuals making, experimenting, playing or otherwise doing something	Class, group or individual discussion with an adult or other child/ren Group problem-solving Collaborative activities
Some characteristics	Draws directly on existing subject knowledge in a logical, linear manner When matched to existing understanding, can be a fast and effective way to learn	Uses direct experience and allows child to explore in their own way at their own pace Can build confidence and practical, insightful understanding	Encourages interaction and language development By structuring challenges can clarify thinking and extend meaningful understanding
Some issues	May not connect with existing understanding and may thus lead to superficiality Difficult to motivate all children in class equally Difficult to adapt structure of subject matter to varied pupil needs	Has significant resource and organisational implications Management of classroom often dominates actual teaching Anticipates motivation and responsible autonomy from children	Requires an appropriate, learning-oriented classroom climate Requires a high level of professional educational judgement, knowledge and skill Anticipates language, reasoning and social capability from children

reflectiveteaching.co.uk/rtps6/part1_ch2

NATURE, NURTURE AND AGENCY

The next two sections provide an interconnected introduction to some of the factors which influence learning. Debate about the relative importance of inheritance (genetic factors) and environmental factors influencing an individual's development and learning has continued for centuries, albeit in different forms. Most famously, this is the argument about the relative importance of 'nature' versus 'nurture'. Whilst the debate is unlikely to be settled any time soon, the interaction of genetics and environment is a complex and cumulative process. As teachers, we need to have some understanding of them both.

These sections also consider 'agency'. This refers to the capacity of humans to act on the basis of their sense of agency. Although we are very significantly influenced by our biology and individual circumstances, we are not determined by them. Indeed, in all circumstances, actions and choices always make a difference of some sort. It is the responsibility of teachers to understand learners and then to ensure that they are supported and challenged to exercise their agency, and strengthen and extend their learning capacity. This is the power of positive expectations, constructive thinking and professional commitment.

Personal development, health and wellbeing

Children's health and their physical and social development are crucial to their wellbeing and capacity to learn (Hugdahl, 1995; Cowie, 2012). The pioneering work of Tanner at the London Institute for Child Health (see Tanner, 1978) was influential in demonstrating patterns of normal development in children, and it was on the basis of such work that mass-screening procedures were introduced into the United Kingdom. There is much more awareness now of diversity, but measures such as height and weight are still used as indicators of child health, for instance, through the NHS '0 to 19 Healthy Child Programme' in England, thus enabling problems to be identified and help offered if necessary. School nurses provide services for pupils at any age, including advice to young people during adolescence.

Health has always been strongly associated with social conditions (Rutter and Madge, 1976; Wilkinson and Pickett, 2009; Phelan, Link and Tehranifar, 2010) and a general rise in average standards of living since the 1970s reduced the prominence of the issue for a time. However, since the banking crash of 2008, economic austerity has affected UK poverty levels and the circumstances of children have been badly affected (see the index of poverty and social exclusion provided annually by the Joseph Rowntree Foundation; see also Ball, 2003, Reading 5.3; Department for Children, Schools and Families (DCSF), 2009, Reading 5.4). The impact of the COVID-19 global pandemic is likely to exacerbate this. There have also been concerns about the mental health of children and young people – particularly in relation to anxiety caused by the growth of social media and frequency of assessment at school (Mental Health Foundation, 2017). Health across the

UK as a whole remains an issue of considerable concern, with the Children's Commissioner reporting 800,000 children and young people in England suffering from mental health difficulties in 2017 (Longfield, 2017).

Young people develop physically at very different rates and such differences can affect both children's capacity for new learning and their self-confidence. Differential rates of development should therefore be carefully considered by teachers, particularly if National Curriculum and assessment procedures make little explicit allowance for such variations. In this context, there is concern that young children may sometimes be required to do things, such as controlling a pencil, before they are sufficiently physically developed. Similarly, adolescence sees variable spurts of hormonal and physical change, with significant implications for emotional and other forms of development. At all ages, levels of attainment reflect present development rather than long-term learning capabilities, and this is a vital distinction. In particular, it is important to consider the relative age of children in a class, as those born early in the school year (September to December) tend to do better than those who are youngest in their year group (sometimes called 'summer born' children (Cobley et al., 2009).

Modern family lifestyles have also produced concerns about child health – arising particularly from the sleeping patterns, diet and lack of physical exercise of many children (Walker, 2017, National Audit Commission, 2001; Sustain, 2006). The general view, articulated for instance by Jamie Oliver, is that too many children consume too much fat, sugar and salt and that the exercise which they get is not sufficiently frequent or sustained to ensure healthy development of muscles and heart. Several cross-governmental schemes have existed to tackle the problem: Healthy Schools Programme, Food in Schools Programme, School Fruit and Vegetable Schemes, Physical Education, School Sport and Club Links are a few. Environmental issues such as toxicity in cities and the rapid development of child allergies are obviously additional concerns. More culturally related health problems of great seriousness include those associated with tobacco, alcohol, drugs and other substances which can be abused.

What do children and young people think of their own health and health care at home and school? Typically, when they are asked, they have strong views (Donnelly and Kilkelly, 2011). Mayall (1994) researched this question in London and found that they were both aware of many important health issues and capable of taking more responsibility than they were normally offered by adults. Those bodies had minds of their own, and wanted to be consulted! This extends to their involvement in education more broadly (Smith, 2007).

Reflective Activity 2.2

Aim: To evaluate the exercise taken by pupils in your class/es.

Evidence and reflection: We suggest that a simple daily record sheet is developed such as the one below. The task for an appropriate group of pupils could be to record their physical activity:

If you had any exercise at these times, please write in what you did:
- after getting up
- getting to school
- first lesson
- playtime
- second lesson
- dinner time
- third lesson
- getting home
- after school
- in the evening.

This could be completed retrospectively for one week.

Extension: Analyse your results. You will probably be able to see patterns in the type, amount and timing of activities. Perhaps there will be differences between boys and girls, or between children with gardens at home and those without. Do you judge that the amount of exercise is sufficient for healthy physical growth at the age of your sample of pupils?

Body and brain, mind and behaviour

The work of biologists and neuroscientists has attracted much attention in recent years and new knowledge is beginning to affect our understanding of human development and its implications for teaching and learning (Dowling, 1999; Goswami, 2008; The Royal Society, 2011a, b, Howard-Jones, 2014, **Reading 2.5**).

On the one hand, we have the extraordinary mapping of human DNA and some 30,000 genes from which each of our species is formed. Scientists can now document the proteins within the body, which are arguably even more significant (see Morange, 2001; Bear, Connors and Paradiso, 2020). On the other hand, there is often an assumption that biology is deterministic with the concept of the 'selfish gene' (Dawkins, 1978) which has developed into more wide-ranging socio-biological analyses and which demonstrate the interaction of *genes* and *culture* (for an influential early text, see Wilson and Lumsden, 1981). From the educational point of view, we must therefore accept the contribution of genetic variation (Asbury and Plomin, 2014; Knopik et al., 2016), whilst also affirming our responsibility with parents and others for helping each child to develop their learning capacity in the context of specific social, cultural and economic opportunities.

Trillions of networks of neural cells are interconnected within the brain by 'synapses', and it is the number and complexity of these that affect the brain's capacity. There are two ways in which synapses are added to the brain – in part determined by biology, and in part by each child's experiences. First, in the early stages of development, the brain over-produces synapses but then selectively prunes out those which are not used. As Bransford et al. put it (1999, p. 104, see also **Reading 4.1**):

the nervous system sets up a large number of connections. Experience then plays on these networks, selecting appropriate connections and removing inappropriate ones. What remains is a refined form that constitutes the sensory and cognitive bases for later phases of development.

The second way in which synapses are added is actually *driven* by experience, when additions occur as a biological consolidation of new learning. This process of adaption and development is known as 'plasticity', and operates throughout life. Such processes have enormous implications for teaching.

There is no doubt at all then, that children's mental capacities (or our own) are the product of the interaction of biological and environmental factors. In this context, it is helpful to distinguish between 'brain' (as a biological organ), 'mind' (the personal meanings which become embodied within a brain) and 'behaviour' (actions taken on the basis of thoughts and feelings). Of course, the mind strongly reflects the influence of culture. As leading neuroscientist Colin Blakemore (2000) wrote:

> if our behaviour were determined by our genes, we should be stuck in the world of the very first of our species who appeared some 100,000 years ago. But the extraordinary capacity of the brain to modify itself on the basis of its own experiences has fuelled a different form of evolution, the evolution of mind and culture.

There is a danger, however, in oversimplification of what is actually a complex, interacting cognitive system (Hellige, 1993). An excellent summary of contemporary knowledge can be found at: developingchild.harvard.edu/resources/inbrief-science-of-ecd/.

So how do we help children to enhance their learning capacity? One answer to this has been provided by those promoting forms of 'brain-based learning', 'neuro-linguistic programming, and 'brain-compatible classrooms'. These initiatives aim to enable teachers to consider the implications of research so that it can be drawn into classroom practice.

However, considerable caution is necessary because, as TLRP demonstrated (see **Research Briefing 2.1** on p. 78) much scientific knowledge on the brain is not yet sufficiently robust to underpin the conclusions that are sometimes drawn for educational practice – particularly if this occurs in a politicised context. One example of this is the work on 'working' and 'long-term' memory by the US neuroscientist, Daniel Willingham (2010). His work is worth serious consideration, but when drawn into debates on the new curriculum in England, it became reduced to the notion that memory has 'limited space' with the consequence that 'important' knowledge must be prioritised – thus risking a narrow curriculum. Indeed, there are rather too many neuro-myths in circulation at present and 'brain-based' schemes should be approached with caution (Darling-Hammond et al, 2020). The Royal Society has published summaries of existing knowledge with explicit warnings on these matters (2011a, b, Reading 2.5). As they put it: 'much of neuroscience is still "upstream" of application' (2011b, p. 76). 'Neuromyths' or misconceptions about the brain and what neuroscience means for teachers are widespread and it is important to be aware of what the science says, and what it does not say (Grospietsch and Mayer, 2019).

'Intelligence' and expectations

Teachers meet the specific needs of children by knowing them well. In particular, teachers must build on, and extend, the prior cognitive capability, knowledge and skills of pupils. Indeed, studies such as Hattie's (2009, Reading 4.6) have identified a high impact for prior attainment in subsequent learning. It is thus right and proper that concepts to describe the attributes of pupils should exist. However, such concepts should be accurate, discriminating and capable of impartial application. Notions of 'intelligence' have a long history but, given what we now know about the capability of people to develop themselves and the way people change over time, there are also dangers of stereotyping and inappropriate generalisation.

Although the validity and measurement of the concept of intelligence have been in dispute among psychologists for many years, the idea was once taken for granted and has passed into our culture to denote a generalised form of potential, labelled as 'ability'. It is part of our language and it influences our ways of thinking about people. For instance, parents often talk about their children in terms of 'brightness' or 'cleverness', and teachers routinely describe pupils and classroom groupings in terms of 'ability'. The concept of intelligence is important too because it is often used in the rhetoric of politicians and the media when they communicate with the public. It is thus routinely assumed that there *is* both a generalised trait of intelligence and that it is possible to measure it objectively and use it to predict future achievement. Psychologists such as Kline (1991) argue, on the basis of statistical factor analysis, that general ability remains a valid concept to describe an amalgam of inherited attributes. On the other hand, Howe (1990) used experimental and biographical evidence from different cultures to argue that there are many dimensions to ability and that generalised measures, such as IQ scores, are misleading.

One of the most important issues is that the concept of intelligence risks giving the impression that learning capabilities are fixed (see Figure 2.5 for some 'labels' denoting abilities which are in everyday use). However, as we have seen, neuroscientists suggest that the brain is 'plastic' and is moulded and developed by new experiences and opportunities. Indeed, many of the anecdotal stories of 'the teacher who changed my life' concern professionals who believed in a child's capability, and helped them to succeed in a new field of learning.

> **Expert Questions**
>
> **Validity:** *in terms of learning, do the forms of assessment used really measure what they are intended to measure?*
>
> **Dependability:** *are assessment processes understood and accepted as being robust and reliable?*
>
> These questions contribute to a conceptual framework underpinning professional expertise (see Chapter 16).

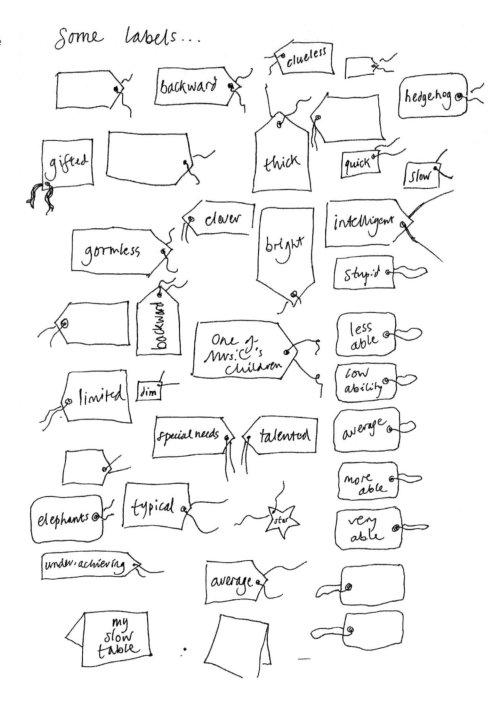

Figure 2.5
Everyday language embodying labelling (adapted from Hart et al., 2004)

Ability-based labelling can certainly restrict learner progress (Francis et al., 2020). For this reason, Hart et al. (2004, see Reading 1.4) investigated alternatives to ability-based pedagogy drawn from closely observed accounts of primary and secondary teachers' classroom practice. They found that the nine teachers in their study did not differentiate their teaching by accepting apparent differences in ability; they did not see children's achievements as predictable or inevitable. Instead, they demonstrated that there is always potential for change as a result of what both teachers and learners do in the present – transformability. However, the terminology of ability grouping is deeply entrenched in the language of schools (Francis et al., 2017).

A second phase of research (Swann et al., 2012) explored what becomes possible when a whole school's staff act together to create a learning environment free from ability labelling. The research described how a school community became committed to transformability, and how the children became more powerful learners. Together, the staff worked to shape curriculum and pedagogy, and to build inclusion and social justice through their unshakeable commitment to the educability of *every* child.

Research by Dweck over many years (e.g. 1986, 2000, Reading 2.6) demonstrates why such challenges to fixed-ability thinking are so important. Dweck studied, in particular, how children think about, explain and 'attribute' their own capability. Those who adopt an 'entity theory' of intelligence tend to believe that their personal capability is fixed, and that they either 'can' or 'cannot' succeed at the new challenges they meet in school. For this reason, they tend to adopt a form of 'learned helplessness' and dependency to accomplish school, and this disposition is likely to roll forwards into adult life (Yeager and Dweck, 2020). However, those who adopt an 'incremental theory' of their capability believe that they are able to learn and improve. They are thus likely to be more highly motivated, have greater engagement and take risks, exhibit 'resilience' (Claxton, 1999, Reading 2.9) and act independently. They exhibit 'mastery' rather than 'helplessness'. For instance, Figure 2.6 shows the drawings of two children who were asked to 'draw pictures of how they felt about school learning'. The work of Dweck has led to the development of approaches for schools such as 'Growth mindset' where children are encouraged to believe that they can succeed through effort to improve their own performance.

Differences between young people certainly exist and prior opportunities and experiences also vary widely. The key question for teachers is *how to account for such differences*. Indeed, teacher expectations have been demonstrated to be very significantly related to pupil outcomes (Gipps and MacGilchrist, 1999, Reading 6.5).

- If teachers account for differences between learners by believing in unalterable variation in 'ability' (in other words, that some children simply *are* more clever than others – and that is that), then they may place limits on learning, albeit unintentionally.

- If they believe that each person's capacity to learn can be continually developed and shaped by working together, then a whole new, exciting and unpredictable world of opportunity is made possible as the teacher commits to supporting future learning.

reflectiveteaching.co.uk/rtps6/part1_ch2

Figure 2.6 Sally and Andrew illustrate 'mastery' and 'helplessness' in learning

Sally communicates confidence, an understanding of progression and the need to practise to improve. Her pictures suggest that she has an 'incremental' view of her learning. Sally is on the way to becoming a 'lifelong learner' and a sound teaching goal would be to support her in finding new challenges.

Andrew's drawings seem to represent bewilderment, annoyance and anxiety, particularly about maths – and a retreat to sleep! Other pictures indicate how friends and the playground offer release. He appears to have an 'entity' model of his capacity in maths. It would be wonderful to be able to gradually help Andrew to develop a more positive view of himself as a learner of maths – but don't forget that he might be a splendid learner in other domains, including those out of school.

The beliefs and values about learners and learning that teachers bring to learning encounters thus have profound effects, for better or for worse, on all children's opportunities to learn in school. Put crudely, are some pupils 'written off', or do we really try to do our job as professional educators?

It is important to recognise this connection between a teacher's expectations and a pupil's beliefs.

In summary, it is worth remembering some simple points about 'intelligence', 'ability' and learning:

- the use of generalised terms such as intelligence or ability is imprecise, insecure and unreliable – but, unfortunately, commonly happens in everyday interactions;

- there are many differences between children and young people, and one challenge for teachers is to identify, develop and celebrate such diverse attributes;
- whatever a learner's present attainments, a teacher *can* influence the quality of pupil learning experiences and *can* thus influence future disposition and achievements.

> **Expert Question**
>
> **Expectation:** *does our school support high staff and pupil expectations and aspire for excellence?*
>
> This question contributes to a conceptual framework underpinning professional expertise (see Chapter 16).

> **Reflective Activity 2.3**
>
> *Aim:* To monitor the use and misuse of concepts of 'intelligence'.
>
> *Evidence and reflection:* A simple method is proposed based on noticing, recording and studying any use of language which denotes generalised ability. This could be done in a school, in discussion with governors, teachers, parents, non-teaching staff or pupils, from printed articles in newspapers and the educational press, from school or government documents, from the speeches of politicians. It will require active listening – becoming attuned to things which are said which are relevant – and the period of awareness may need to extend over a week or so.
>
> Whatever sources are chosen, the statements and the context in which these occur should be recorded in notes as accurately as possible.
>
> When you have a collection of statements, study them.
>
> Think about them in their context. For instance: Do they recognise the richness and diversity of pupils' present capabilities? What particular expectations about future attainment are implied?
>
> *Extension:* Try to monitor your own use of language. Be explicitly aware of the words and concepts which you use. Distinguish between *abilities* and *attainments*. Try to satisfy the criteria of accuracy, discrimination and impartiality in your thinking about children's capacities and potential.

As we have seen, whilst the influence of 'nature' is real, and intrinsic differences in capabilities do exist, these are profoundly mitigated by cultural factors and teacher/pupil actions. These impact on pupils' interpretation of performance and on their views of themselves as learners – and they therefore merit our specific attention.

In this section, we consider formal and informal 'nurturing', beginning with a particular form of teaching deriving from cognitive psychology and recently promoted by government agencies in England. We then move the focus to a broader range of social and cultural factors which contribute to 'nurture' and the learning environment. At the same time, we remain aware of biological factors and draw particular attention to the opportunities for teachers and pupils to take action to enhance learning.

Cognitive science and teaching

Much has been made of the notion of a science of learning and of developments in both cognitive science and the 'learning sciences' more broadly (Willingham, 2021). It is certainly true that our knowledge of learning and memory has developed extensively in the last twenty years. These ideas have extended our models of how the learning takes place and have stimulated ideas (and some prescriptions) concerning the effective forms of teaching. However, it is important to remember that findings from laboratory studies do not always transfer easily to the classroom, where the busy world of teaching and learning creates a hectic and messier context than studies where variables are controlled and measured.

The Education Endowment Foundation (EEF) published a review of cognitive science approaches in 2021 (Perry et al., 2021). The review acknowledges that cognitive science is increasingly being used to inform aspects of teaching practice. A number of areas of research have attracted interest, particularly topics like motivation and reward, working memory, long-term memory and cognitive load. Findings from two areas of cognitive science have been especially influential: cognitive psychology, which is underpinned by interpretive, behavioural and observational methods; and cognitive neuroscience, which is underpinned by brain-imaging technologies. A number of theoretical principles for effective learning have been derived from these research areas, including:

- spaced learning – distributing learning and retrieval opportunities over a longer period of time rather than concentrating them in 'massed' practice;
- interleaving – switching between different types of problem or different ideas within the same lesson or study session;
- retrieval practice – using a variety of strategies to recall information from memory, for example flash cards, practice tests or quizzing, or mind-mapping;
- strategies to manage cognitive load – focusing pupils on key information without overloading them, for example, by breaking down or 'chunking' subject content or using worked examples, exemplars, or 'scaffolds'; and
- dual coding – using both verbal and non-verbal information (such as words and pictures) to teach concepts; dual coding forms one part of a wider theory known as the cognitive theory of multimedia learning (CTML) (Sorden, 2012).

The EEF review concludes that while cognitive science approaches can have a meaningful impact on pupils' learning, the evidence about how they can be applied successfully in classrooms is still limited. In particular, research into how they can be effectively used in different year groups and subject areas is lacking. More information is needed to support teachers in bridging the gap between the theory that underpins cognitive science approaches and implementing these techniques well in their daily practice. This is particularly relevant for primary schools as much of the evidence is from studies of older children or adults with specific knowledge content as the learning outcome. Whilst this can be informative, it is unlikely to provide precise recommendations for practice. In England,

Chapter 2 Learning 59

a number of policy documents relating to initial teacher education and teacher development (e.g. the *ITT Core Content Framework*, DfE, 2021a) refer to research which takes a cognitive science perspective on learning, so it is important to understand the terminology and rationale (see the Glossary below). In considering implications for classroom practice, it is also important to bear in mind the nature of the learners, their capabilities and the desired learning.

Glossary of some cognitive science terms

Cognitive load This idea views the mind from an information-processing perspective, with a limit to each learner's 'working' memory. Three types of cognitive load are distinguished: intrinsic cognitive load, which is the effort needed for a specific activity, or perhaps how hard the task is; extraneous cognitive load, which involves how the information or tasks are presented to a learner; and germane cognitive load, which refers to the effort required for this content to be learned. The central idea is to ensure that the way tasks and information is presented (extraneous load) does not get in the way of the effort needed to learn (germane load). This could be, for example, by presenting information in sequential steps or by simplifying how it is presented. The challenge is to work out how to design learning tasks and activities so that they focus efficiently and effectively on the learning outcomes required without the explanation or the detail of the task getting in the way. Cognitive load can also be affected by how the learner is feeling and is reduced by stress and anxiety.

Interleaving This refers to the sequencing of learning activities so that similar items are interspersed with different but related types of items, rather than the items being presented consecutively. When learning tasks are interleaved, they are inevitably also spaced. This can make **spaced practice** (see below) and interleaving hard to distinguish. In spaced learning, spaces are usually filled with unrelated activities or the learning of unrelated topics. The challenge is to understand the relationship of the items so that the differences between items provide a helpful contrast.

Multimedia learning theory This is based on the idea from 'dual coding theory' that there are two main ways or channels by which we receive information, by seeing pictures or images by hearing or reading verbal information, and that we form mental representations using these two channels. Each channel has its own limits in terms of cognitive load. Providing information in both channels, pictures and words, can help learners form stronger mental representations, particularly if connections are made between the two channels. The challenge is to understand how to combine particular verbal and visual information so that it improves learning, rather than overloading a learner's working memory (see **cognitive load**).

Retrieval practice This refers to developing the speed and fluency of recall of information and is based on the idea that such recall is improved with practice and immediate feedback. A typical way of achieving this in a classroom would be through low-stakes quizzes, questions and tests. One of the challenges is in ensuring that learners can apply the knowledge learned rather than just recall it when prompted.

---

reflectiveteaching.co.uk/rtps6/part1_ch2

> **Spaced learning** This is based on the idea that material is more easily learned when it is separated by an 'inter-study interval'. This may be very brief (seconds or minutes) or very long (weeks or months). Spaced learning is also sometimes referred to as 'spaced practice', 'distributed practice', 'distributed learning' and 'the spacing effect'. Spaced learning is often contrasted with massed (or clustered) practice when content is practised or rehearsed in a single session or in close succession. The challenge is to work out how frequently the content needs to be repeated and how long to leave between activities.

Limitations in 'cognitive load' and 'working memory' clearly can have implications for how children should be taught. So this is a worthwhile contribution to this particular form of 'nurture'. However, the learning environment as a whole is much broader, and is influenced by a wide range of other factors too. We begin with a discussion of culture, language and learning disposition.

Culture, language and disposition

It has always been understood that home background, peer relationships, the cultures of different schools and, increasingly, the media influence how children learn. However, the development of constructivist and socio-cultural approaches has led to improved understanding of the processes which are at work (Wells, 1999, **Reading 2.4**; Bruner, 1990; Mercer, 1992, 1995; see also p. 42)

We can identify three particularly significant cultural influences on learning:

1 *Cultural resources and experiences:* Learning is a process of 'making sense' and whatever is taken as being meaningful ('makes sense') will be strongly influenced by the culture, knowledge, values and ideas of social groups which the learner has previously experienced. In our complex world of migration and change, diversity of language and experience is considerable – particularly in city schools. In any event, family and community cultures provide an initial framework for children's understanding. Thus, each child's early learning will tend to elaborate and extend the knowledge which is embedded in their experienced social system. Sometimes this is talked about as 'situated learning' (Lave and Wenger, 1991).

2 *The mediation of language:* Language is the medium of thinking and learning and is created, transmitted and sustained through interaction with other people within the cultures of different social settings. These settings influence the range of 'languages' we use – the register, styles, dialects etc. Language also embodies the 'cultural tools' through which new experiences are 'mediated' and interpreted as learners become inducted into the knowledge of their communities (Wertsch 1985,

1991). Sometimes this is known as 'cognitive apprenticeship' (Rogoff, 1990). See also Chapter 13.

3 *Learning disposition:* The term 'learning disposition' summarises the ways in which learners engage with any opportunity to learn. These may also be thought of as the habits that learners develop over time. As defined by Carr (2001, p. 10), they are 'participation repertoires from which a learner recognises, selects, edits, responds to, resists, searches for and constructs learning opportunities'. When children start school, patterns in how they approach learning will probably already be discernible, and the role of the teacher is to encourage, and invite, positive dispositions to form (Carr, 2008). In particular, opportunities (through tasks and activities) should be provided for positive engagement and learning dispositions and habits to be strengthened. Features of the classroom environment may invite or inhibit engagement, so the choices that teachers make are important.

The approach to learning adopted by each child is crucial to educational outcomes. Will a learner be open or closed to experience and support, will they be confident or fearful, willing to take risks or defensive? What is their self-belief, their 'identity' as a learner? Can they overcome setbacks, and will they become a 'lifelong learner'? The origins of disposition and learner identity reflect the learning cultures which each child has experienced (Pollard and Filer, 1996, see Reading 1.2), yet schools continue the process as the first formal institution which is experienced in a sustained way.

The major sources of such cultural influence are commonly seen as family and community, peers, the school and the media. We will consider each in turn.

Family and community. Family background has been recognised as being of crucial significance in educational achievement for many years. This occurs not just in material ways, depending on the wealth and income of families, nor simply because of ownership or otherwise of overt forms of 'cultural capital' (Bourdieu and Passeron, 1977). The most significant issues for school learning concern what the culture of the family and community provides in terms of frameworks of existing understanding, language for further development and the child's disposition regarding learning. The National Academies of Sciences, Engineering, and Medicine (2018) in the United States, in their review of how people learn, noted that school failure may at least partly be explained by the mismatch between what children and young people have learned in their home cultures and what is required of them in school. They also concluded that since learning is influenced in fundamental ways by the context in which it takes place, schools and classrooms should therefore be both learner and community centred.

> **Expert Question**
>
> **Connection:** *does the curriculum engage with the cultural resources and funds-of-knowledge of families and the community?*
>
> This question contributes to a conceptual framework underpinning professional expertise (see Chapter 16).

Peers at school. Peer group culture is important to children as a way of both enjoying and adapting to school life (Davies, 1982). Some peer cultures favour school attainment and are likely to reinforce teacher efforts to engender a positive approach to learning. Other peer cultures derive meaning from alternative values, and young people who are influenced by such cultures may approach school with minimal or even oppositional expectations. Such children will still be constructing understanding, but it may not be the type of understanding for which teachers would have aimed.

> **Expert Question**
>
> **Culture:** does the school support expansive learning by affirming learners' contributions, engaging partners and providing attractive opportunities?
>
> This question contributes to a conceptual framework underpinning professional expertise (see Chapter 16).

The school. Schools have their own unique cultures, created by those who work there and those who are associated with them. A school culture must be seen as a learning context which is at least as important as the bricks and mortar, books and equipment which make up the material environment of a school (see, for instance, Nias, Southworth and Campbell, 1992). Again, we have to ask how this culture influences the framework for understanding which is offered to pupils, the language in which teaching and learning is transacted and the stance which pupils adopt (Rudduck and McIntyre, 2007,

Reading 1.3). For instance, are children and young people encouraged to take risks in their learning?

The media and new technologies. The influence of the media is very considerable and has been extensively researched (Marsh, 2005; Buckingham, 2008, see also Kress, 2010, Reading 8.6). Some people have been concerned about the effects of such experience. With reading from paper in relative decline, some children and young people may watch many hours of television each week and use screens and mobile technologies in toys as well as in phones and tablets. Play and lifestyles are influenced by advertising and popular media, including the internet and social networking. Such experiences can be extremely educational in new ways. Key issues for learning include whether the stance adopted is passive or active, and how new cultural experiences are interpreted and used. Engagement with new media creates powerful opportunities for many, but there are access problems for others where technologies and support are not available.

Clearly, the nature of these influences on pupils will affect the way in which they approach learning at school. Reflective Activity 2.4 focuses on this issue.

> **Reflective Activity 2.4**
>
> *Aim:* To map the influence of culture on the learning disposition of a pupil.
>
> *Evidence and reflection:* This activity is directly based on the text on pp. 60–62. It provides an opportunity to review the range of influences on a child and their capacity as a learner. Drawing up a table, as illustrated below, is a helpful way of organising thoughts.

	Cultural resources and experiences	The mediation of language	Learning disposition
The influence of family and community			
The influence of peers and friends at school			
The influence of the school			
The influence of the media and of digital technologies			

Think of a child or young person whom you know well. Consider the way culture and experiences influence the child's understanding, the language they use and the learning disposition they adopt. Complete each cell of the table, as far as you can, to map what you know about the sources of influence on that child.

If you have time, it would be valuable to talk to the pupil and others – parents, peers and teachers – to improve the quality of your evidence.

Extension: Repeat this exercise with different pupils, or compare the results of similar activities by colleagues. What insights are produced by comparisons of children of different sex, ethnicity, religion, social class, attainment? You can see some examples of this sort of analysis in the final chapters of Pollard and Filer (1996, 1999).

In summary, children and young people are both reproduced by their culture, and produce new forms of it. However, culture and language always mediate thought, interpretation and learning. Thus, success or failure through curriculum tasks and short-term performance is given particular significance by the cultural interpretations that are made of it (Filer and Pollard, 2000, Reading 14.7). In these ways, culture both structures learning attainment and shapes the self-belief of the learner. What then, are the consequences for the personality, identity and motivation of the child?

Personality, motivation and identity

Psychologists' understanding of personality has, according to Hampson (1988), derived from three contributory strands of analysis. The first is the *lay perspective* – the understandings which are implicit in common-sense thinking of most of us about other people. This is evident in literature and in everyday action. It is a means by which people are able to anticipate the actions of others – ideas about the character and likely actions of others are used for both the prediction and explanation of behaviour.

Such understandings have influenced the second strand of analysis – that of *trait theorists*. Their work reflects a concerted attempt to identify personality dimensions and to objectively measure the resulting cognitive and *learning styles*. Among the most frequently identified dimensions of cognitive style are impulsivity/reflexivity (Kagan, 1964) and extroversion/introversion (Eysenck and Cookson, 1969). Such early work has been synthesised by Riding and Rayner (1998) into two orthogonal families – wholist/analytic and verbal/imager. Other accounts identify more general learning styles such as the concrete/abstract/sequential/random offered by Butler (1988) and the visual/auditory/tactile of Sarasin (1999). However, whilst a learning style approach draws attention to patterns of individual difference, it is not straightforward to translate it into specific classroom provision. Indeed, a systematic review of such research concluded that the scientific basis of 'learning styles' is very weak (Coffield et al., 2004, see also Pashler et al., 2008, and **Research Briefing 2.1** on neuroscience on p. 78). Further, this is another occasion when we need to be wary of inappropriately limiting the expectations that we make of children by assuming they learn in a particular way. Perhaps, in other circumstances, they might sometimes surprise us.

A third strand of personality analysis has been prominent, which Hampson (1988) calls the *self-perspective*. This approach sees the development of personality in close association with that of self-image and identity. Crucially, it draws attention to the capacity of humans to reflect on themselves, to take account of the views of others and to develop. The social context in which children grow up, their culture, interaction and experiences with significant people in their lives, is thus seen as being very important in influencing their views of self and consequent patterns of action.

A key aspect of this concerns the meaning which learning has for a child. In one sense, such motivation issues can be seen as being technical and related to specific tasks. Certainly, when children fail to see any purpose or meaning in an activity it is unlikely to be productive, however well intended and carefully planned. Sadly, as we saw in Chapter 1, a very common perception of children regarding schools is that lessons are 'boring' and, for this reason, engendering enthusiasm often requires sensitivity, flexibility, spontaneity and imagination from the teacher. The nature of this challenge is represented in Figure 2.7, which plots the relationship between new learning challenges and existing skills, knowledge and understanding. If too great a challenge is set for a child, then the situation of risk may produce withdrawal. Conversely, if the challenge is too little, then boredom and inappropriate behaviour may ensue. Targeting the effective learning in which the child will be highly motivated requires considerable skill and knowledge of both the subject matter and the child. Of course, motivation can stem from a wider range of factors too, from 'intrinsic' and 'extrinsic' interest to a fear of receiving negative sanctions.

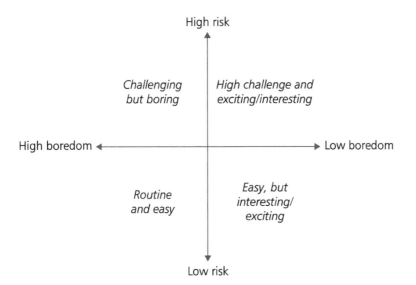

Figure 2.7 Risk, boredom and challenge

However, the most enduring form of motivation is connected to the evolving identity of each person and to their 'framework of meaningfulness' (National Research Council, 1999). For example, Pollard and Filer (1999, Reading 1.2) tracked two cohorts of English children from starting school at age 5 to GCSEs at age 16. They documented 'strategic biographies' of each child as they adapted to successive teachers and classrooms. In some settings, particular children felt affirmed as they developed new skills, appropriated new knowledge and fulfilled their learning identities *through* the school curriculum. Other settings were less conducive to such processes and the children felt little personal connection to the curriculum. It became something that was done to them, that they had to endure, rather than an activity through which they could experience personal development and understanding. For us all, deep and enduring learning only occurs when new knowledge has relevance and connects meaningfully with the personal narratives through which we make sense of life.

Similar ideas were explicitly endorsed by some UK governments in the early part of this century. For example, 'personalised learning' was suggested as a new concept for educational provision (Teaching and Learning Review Group, 2006, Reading 10.7) after many years of single-minded pressure for 'performance'. In England since 2012, revisions to the National Curriculum have introduced a far tighter focus on subject knowledge *per se* and we have seen increasing prescription in England in terms of the curriculum and approaches to teaching (see Chapter 9).

We also need to remember that learning can be emotionally challenging, and is certainly not simply cognitive and rational. Frijda (2001) suggests that emotions are subjective responses to events that are important to individuals. Positive or negative emotions

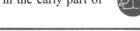

Expert Questions

Personalisation: *does the curriculum resonate with the social and cultural needs of diverse learners and provide appropriate elements of choice?*

Relevance: *is the curriculum presented in ways which are meaningful to learners and so that it can excite their imagination?*

These questions contribute to a conceptual framework underpinning professional expertise (see Chapter 16).

reflect the affirmation or threat to previous understandings and 'meaning structures' – or indeed, implications for a learner's personal identity, self-esteem or social status. Whilst it can be 'embarrassing' for a child to succeed, it is often humiliating to fail. Learning can thus be stressful at several levels (Lazarus, 1991, 1999).

One way of succeeding at school, and life, is to become very effective at 'learning how to learn', and it is to this powerful set of ideas that we now turn.

Metacognition and thinking capability

Humans have the unique capacity to reflect on their own thinking processes and to develop new strategies. This capacity for self-awareness regarding one's own mental powers is called 'metacognition' (Flavell, 1970, 1979). It has received strong endorsement and extension through the refinement of practical ways of developing 'thinking skills' (e.g. Fisher, 2008, **Reading 2.7**; McGuinness, 1999; McGregor, 2007). The synthesis of high-quality international research evidence on metacognition and self-regulation by the Education Endowment Foundation Toolkit demonstrates high effectiveness, with significant gains in learning outcomes (for more detail, see **Toolkit Evidence 2.1** on p. 77).

Metacognition is a particularly important capacity once children start to attend schools. Prior to this, at home, learning is largely self-directed and thinking tends to be embedded in immediate personal experience (Donaldson, 1978); at school, the agenda for learning increasingly becomes directed by teachers. Thinking is challenged to become more disciplined and deliberate; tasks are set, problems posed and instructions given; criteria for success and failure become more overt. The result of all this is that a new degree of self-control is required and, in order to achieve this self-control, new forms of reflective self-awareness become essential.

Vygotsky (1978; see Chapter 2, pp. 46–47) believed that learners, in working to understand and cross their 'zones of proximal development', could be supported by their own disciplined and reflective thinking. Tharp and Gallimore (1988, **Reading 11.4**) provide a particularly good illustration of this, with their four-stage theory of 'assisted performance'. The concept of 'Building Learning Power' (Claxton, 2002, 2004, 2011, **Reading 2.9**; Deakin Crick, 2006) is another version of these ideas. Indeed, experience has shown that guidance to children on how to review their learning needs to be direct.

> There is a need to be explicit about what we mean by better forms of thinking. If pupils are to become better thinkers – to learn meaningfully, to think flexibly and to make reasoned judgements – then they must be taught explicitly how to do it. (McGuinness, 1999, p. 3)

Indeed, successive studies and meta-analyses that have repeatedly confirmed the power of promoting metacognition and self-regulation clearly demonstrate the limited value of direct instruction alone (e.g. Hattie, 2009; see the EEF guidance report (2018a) and **Toolkit Evidence 2.1**). It is not enough for teachers to model the strategies that can be used to accomplish particular tasks; they also need to talk explicitly about those strategies, explaining why and how they are appropriate to use. Nor is it enough simply to coach pupils through successive steps, assuming that the learners will naturally come to internalise them and be able to reproduce them on subsequent occasions. If children are to develop as autonomous learners – increasingly able to work independently, and to apply methods learned in one context to analogous problems encountered in another – then they need to be encouraged to identify and articulate the approaches that they are using and to evaluate their usefulness in relation to specific problems.

TLRP's project on 'learning how to learn' (James et al., 2006, 2007, Reading 2.8) has been influential in England and took an expansive approach to the issues. The project explored the conditions in classrooms, schools and networks which enable pupils and teachers to engage in new practices that are conducive to learning how to learn. These extend the principle of using assessment and feedback to support learning, as we will see in Chapter 13.

Lesson Study 2.1 illustrates how a group of teachers researched on their own practice to support the critical thinking of young children – teaching for the development of metacognition.

LESSON STUDY 2.1

Shared, critical thinking for learning in the early years

The schools: The members of the Lesson Study Research group were practitioners from nurseries and Children's Centres serving diverse areas across the London Borough of Camden. Common to all settings was a high proportion of children with English as an additional language. The Lesson Study was carried out in 3 nursery classes with children aged from 3 to 4.

What we wanted the pupils to learn: We wanted to develop characteristics of effective learning through encouraging children to: develop their own ideas; use what they already know to learn new things; and choose ways to do things and find new ways of doing them.

What research is available: Building on research about metacognition (Chapter 2, p. 71), the EPPE project (Sylva et al., 2010), a unique, large-scale, longitudinal study of effective early years provision, found that the development of shared thinking and dialogue between children and skilled adults was particularly effective. We wanted to try this out.

What we discovered in our research lessons:
RL1: We wanted children to show perseverance and independence in solving a problem. We planned a very challenging activity which asked the children to fix a light on a spaceship in response to the story 'The Way Back Home'. The children were given wires, crocodile clips and bulbs, and through careful questioning were encouraged to use a trial-and-error approach. Through this activity, they learned how to make a circuit. We noticed that some children (mainly girls) were unwilling to get involved with the activity; they showed an unwillingness to take risks and a preference for adult direction. For this reason, we adjusted the focus of the second research lesson to make sure that the task was open ended.

RL2: The second research lesson focused on children choosing different ways of approaching an activity. Children worked in a group with the challenge of finding places on a plan where they could hide 'Moshi Monsters'. They were asked to share with the group the reasons for their choices. Although the aim was for the children to work together, there was very little collaborative interaction despite adult questions aimed at encouraging articulation of thinking. Two children copied the solution of another member of the group without being able to verbalise the reasons for this. We discovered that it was important for the children to have shared resources to encourage them to think together. As a result of this research lesson, it was agreed that the third lesson should encourage children to work together as a team whilst being prepared to try something different.

RL3: In the third research lesson, a group of boys worked together on a cooking activity whilst a girls only group co-operated on a construction task. These were activities which would not have been their first choice. Individuals in each group were asked to take on 'expert' roles (mixer, measurer, roller, writer, reader and photographer). Adults were able to walk away from the groups and allow the children to assign roles. All the children showed sustained interest and pride in their roles and were aware of those of each member of the group. The importance of children taking responsibility for their own learning was emphasised by the group.

What pupils learned: In terms of direct pupil outcomes, teachers commented: 'Children are more self-directed, confident in making their own choices and asking for adults' help and support where needed.'

> 'Children in the group were [initially] not confident in contributing to discussions. . . . [now] they feel confident to try out new vocabulary and language in a safe and supported environment.'

What we learned: We concluded that: open ended tasks are more likely to lead to risk taking and sustained shared thinking; flexibility and optionality are important to keep the interest of children and involve them in decision-making; it is important for groups of children to share resources and thus creating opportunities for shared thinking and problem solving.

Children were able to assign roles within a group without adult involvement. This ensured that they were enthusiastic about their roles and understood the responsibilities of their peers, thus encouraging shared thinking.

We were surprised by the high level of children's perseverance, particularly when there were very high expectations of learning, e.g. wiring a circuit.

We have changed our practice by offering a weekly 'challenge' linked to a story text; adapting the classroom environment to encourage shared and critical thinking; and planning new group work opportunities.

How we shared: This case study was shared with other practitioners who were part of a Camden-wide Early Years project. The project brought together practitioners working across the Early Years to consider ways of developing shared and sustained thinking. This was a very good way of building understanding of child development across the phase and there was a commitment from practitioners to continue this work. Members of the project, whether they had qualifications at degree or GCSE level, worked together very effectively as equals, respecting each other's contributions to the research.

reflectiveteaching.co.uk/rtps6/part1_ch2

TAKING STOCK OF LEARNING

Key factors in learning

This section offers a simple summary of the key factors that affect learning and motivation (see Figure 2.8). The interaction of nature and nurture, and the potential for agency, is readily apparent in the figure. Teachers, and pupils, can make a difference.

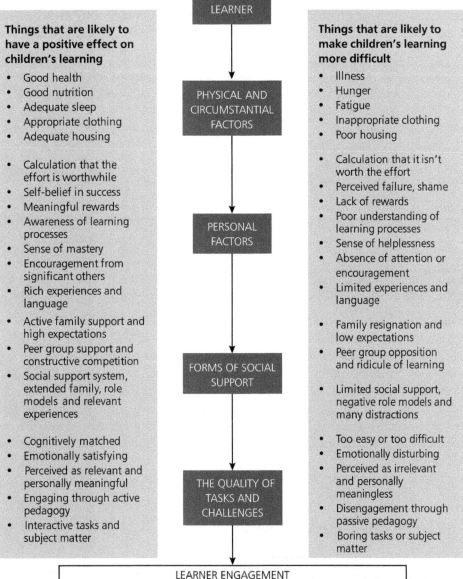

Figure 2.8 Factors affecting learning engagement (adapted from Bransford et al., 1999)

Things that are likely to have a positive effect on children's learning

- Good health
- Good nutrition
- Adequate sleep
- Appropriate clothing
- Adequate housing

- Calculation that the effort is worthwhile
- Self-belief in success
- Meaningful rewards
- Awareness of learning processes
- Sense of mastery
- Encouragement from significant others
- Rich experiences and language

- Active family support and high expectations
- Peer group support and constructive competition
- Social support system, extended family, role models and relevant experiences

- Cognitively matched
- Emotionally satisfying
- Perceived as relevant and personally meaningful
- Engaging through active pedagogy
- Interactive tasks and subject matter

LEARNER

↓

PHYSICAL AND CIRCUMSTANTIAL FACTORS

↓

PERSONAL FACTORS

↓

FORMS OF SOCIAL SUPPORT

↓

THE QUALITY OF TASKS AND CHALLENGES

↓

Things that are likely to make children's learning more difficult

- Illness
- Hunger
- Fatigue
- Inappropriate clothing
- Poor housing

- Calculation that it isn't worth the effort
- Perceived failure, shame
- Lack of rewards
- Poor understanding of learning processes
- Sense of helplessness
- Absence of attention or encouragement
- Limited experiences and language

- Family resignation and low expectations
- Peer group opposition and ridicule of learning
- Limited social support, negative role models and many distractions

- Too easy or too difficult
- Emotionally disturbing
- Perceived as irrelevant and personally meaningless
- Disengagement through passive pedagogy
- Boring tasks or subject matter

LEARNER ENGAGEMENT
Paying attention, concentrating, practising, reflecting, persevering: building and extending a meaningful conceptual framework.

reflectiveteaching.co.uk/rtps6/part1_ch2

Our understanding has moved a long way beyond simple theoretical models. We now know that the most effective, deep, long-term learning is meaningful and conceptual. This is hugely important for teaching, and Reflective Activity 2.5 encourages you to apply these insights to children in your class.

> ### Reflective Activity 2.5
>
>
> *Aim:* To review and apply knowledge about factors affecting learning.
>
> *Evidence and reflection:* Try to take stock of the issues that have been raised in this chapter. Although they are complex, they directly affect individuals such as the children in your class.
>
> Consider a boy and a girl with contrasting motivation towards learning. Using the structure provided by Figure 2.8, make notes on the factors which, in your opinion, affect their engagement with learning. Record physical and circumstantial factors, personal factors, forms of social support, and the quality of tasks and challenges which they typically meet in school.
>
> Does such a review help in understanding and making better provision for such children?
>
> *Extension:* To what extent have such factors affected your own engagement as a learner through your educational career? Over time, could you use this understanding to develop your personal learning effectiveness?

Metaphors of learning

Within our cultural history, theories about learning have come and gone. And although, as we have seen, contemporary sciences are gradually accumulating more stable knowledge, the field remains complex. It is helpful therefore to consider the resonance of two metaphors which attempt to make sense of this cultural variability and scientific complexity. We draw here on the work of Sfard (1998), whose paper was entitled: 'On the two metaphors for learning and the dangers of choosing just one'. Sfard suggests that metaphors provide a deceptively simple way of representing our tacit frameworks of understanding. In particular, they reach between culturally embedded intuition and more formal knowledge. As she put it: 'they enable conceptual osmosis between everyday and scientific discourses' (p. 4).

Learning as 'acquisition'

'Since the dawn of civilisation', human learning has been 'conceived as the acquisition of something' writes Sfard (1998, p. 5), whether this be knowledge *per se* or conceptual development. In either case, the image is of the 'human mind as a container to be filled with certain materials and of the learner becoming an owner of these materials' (p. 5). These entities may include knowledge, concepts, skills, facts, understanding, meaning, attitudes etc. They are to be acquired through remembering, internalisation, construction, appropriation, development etc., and with the help of teachers who guide, support, deliver, explain, mediate, test etc. Once acquired, the capabilities can be applied, transferred, shared with others etc. We discuss all of these aspects extensively in this book, for the metaphor is a fine representation of an established view of 'education' and is closely aligned with behaviourist theories of learning. National education systems rest on the foundation of this metaphor, and are designed in systematic ways to provide the conditions, support and instruction which will maximise learner attainment at each stage of development.

Learning as 'participation'

This alternative metaphor has rapidly grown in significance in the contemporary world, partly as a consequence of socio-cultural perspectives on learning. The emphasis is on the learner as 'a person interested in participation in certain kinds of activities' (Sfard, 1998, p. 6). So this is learning through activity; through direct, authentic engagement in an applied situation – learning through practice as a participant. With the support of parents, family and friends, a child might learn to 'play games', 'go shopping', identify with a football team – or to become a bit more independent by 'sleeping over' etc. Another obvious example is the priority given in contemporary teacher education to direct, participatory school experience. And there are many others. The metaphor thus affirms direct experience with participants or practitioners in real situations. Instead of prioritising formal knowledge, one becomes a participating member of a practice community (see Lave and Wenger, 1991). The metaphor has particular resonance in respect of informal and tacit learning (Thomas and Pattison, 2007, **Reading 2.9**) – including through use of new technologies (Buckingham, 2013; Kress, 2010, **Reading 8.6**). Indeed, in addition to the unbounded flow of information which is now available, social networking opens up a vast range of opportunities for participation. The potential for learning in entirely new participatory ways, building on global diversity, appears to be exponential. Figure 2.9 summarises these descriptions.

	Acquisition metaphor	Participation metaphor
Learning process	Acquisition of something	Becoming a participant
Pupil role	Recipient, constructor	Participant, apprentice
Teacher role	Provider, facilitator	Expert practitioner
Form of knowledge	Possession, commodity	Activity, practice
Form of knowing	Having, possessing	Belonging, communicating

Figure 2.9 Two metaphors for learning (adapted from Sfard, 1998)

We may wish to debate the relative advantages and disadvantages of these two metaphors for learning – and, when you look for it, such debate is a constant theme in popular culture. However, a reflective teacher should carefully note Sfard's argument that the metaphors represent two very important ways through which learning occurs. Put another way, the acquisition of capabilities through formal education is necessary but not sufficient, and the same can be said for participation in communities of practice. Acquisition alone risks bookish knowledge which can't easily be applied. Participation alone risks contextually bounded thinking. For analytic power and personal effectiveness which can be applied in and through practice, we need to understand both forms of learning. As we see below, this is not always easy to provide.

Applying learning beyond school

We move towards a conclusion in this chapter by drawing attention to a major problem of school learning. In the 'real world' outside, it is hard to actually *apply* the knowledge that has been learned in classrooms. This seems to be because of the very different frames of reference that structure thinking in the different settings – and echoes of our discussion about the metaphors of 'acquisition' and 'participation' will be readily apparent.

Routine activities at home, parks, shops or street are accomplished using a quite different set of procedures and forms of knowledge from the procedurally constrained requirements of school (for an indication of the potential, see Thomas and Pattison, 2007, Reading 2.10). Whilst the former tend to be pragmatic and informal, the latter are very carefully structured and formally assessed. The result, sadly, is that children often find it hard to make connections between their learning in these two worlds. For instance, Hughes et al. (2000) documented the gap between the abstract, formal knowledge of school mathematics and the authentic contexts in which it might have been applied (but often remained unused). Similar findings exist across the curriculum, from doing geography tasks in school, to getting lost when travelling; and from doing well in spelling tests, to being unable to write a real letter about something important.

Learning, in this sense, is about *making connections* between different forms of knowledge and across the two metaphors (see also **Research Briefing 4.1** on home–school knowledge exchange, p. 136). However, this is particularly difficult when understanding and skills are being developed and have not yet been confidently appropriated into identity and self-belief.

From a teacher perspective, we need to acknowledge that children probably know a lot more than we think they know. If only we could tap into the funds of knowledge that are sustained in the social practices of families, communities and networks, then pupils' learning might become much more authentic, flexible and sustained.

Expert Question

Connection: *does the curriculum engage with the cultural resources and funds-of-knowledge of families and the community?*

This question contributes to a conceptual framework underpinning professional expertise (see Chapter 16).

reflectiveteaching.co.uk/rtps6/part1_ch2

We thus have yet another topic on which a reflective and aware teacher can be really effective – this time in encouraging children to think about what they know, how they know it, how it fits into their lives and how they can apply such knowledge in the future.

CONCLUSION

Learning is an immensely complex topic and this chapter has simply touched the surface of some of the many issues which are involved. In one sense, perhaps the provisional nature of our understanding is no bad thing, because, if we knew it all, then one of the greatest sources of fascination and fulfilment in teaching would be diminished. The vocation of teaching will certainly always include this element of intellectual challenge as teachers seek to understand what children understand, and then to provide personalised support in relation to a set of curriculum goals.

In this chapter we reviewed three influential theories on children's learning and related these to school practices. We then considered how physical and biological factors in the body and brain interact with the social and cultural factors of family, community and the broader society elements of a long-established 'nature–nurture' debate. Whilst acknowledging differences between learners, we emphasised the agency of both teachers and pupils and their power to act in the present. Commitment to the learning capacity of all children is seen as a professional responsibility and a precondition for enhancing children's lives and system-wide improvement. Whatever pupil circumstances may be, teachers have the precious opportunity to influence their learning and their lives for the better.

reflectiveteaching.co.uk/rtps6/part1_ch2

CHAPTER WEBPAGE

reflectiveteaching.co.uk offers additional professional resources for this chapter. For the chapter webpage, go to: **reflectiveteaching.co.uk/rtps6/part1_ch2**

From the chapter webpage, you can download or print the *Reflective Activities* mentioned in the chapter above, and supplementary activities too. These dovetail into the structure of the chapter, and actively trying them out is an interesting and practical way of getting to grips with the issues covered. To take things further still, you could collaborate with others and compare results. The *Diagrams and Figures* from the chapter can also be accessed directly from the chapter webpage.

To reinforce key messages from the chapter, some particularly influential educationalists are worth following up online. For example, check out the Wikipedia entry for Jerome Bruner – particularly on developmental and educational psychology, language development and the influence of culture on learning. Or listen to one of Carol Dweck's YouTube talks, such as 'The Power of Believing That You Can Improve'. It's powerful stuff, and this focus on learning *per se* is revolutionising contemporary approaches to teaching.

Support in accessing relevant educational research is offered at three levels.

- First, the *Further Reading* section of the chapter webpage provides a wide-ranging review of different approaches to learning, and begins to tease out the implications of those of particular relevance to school education.
- Second, from the sources reviewed, some have been selected as *Key Readings* below.
- Finally, several of these also feature in condensed form within the portable mini-library of *Readings for Reflective Teaching in Schools*. A selection of the latter is indicated below.

KEY READINGS

On psychological approaches to learning, there are many introductory, overview texts – a very good example of which is that of Gallard and Cartmell:

> Gallard, D. and Cartmell, K.M. (2015) *Psychology and Education*. London: Routledge.

Wood offers a more detailed account, including reference to behaviourism, constructivism and, in particular, social constructivism. He discusses the implications for learning in school.

> Wood, D. (1997) *How Children Think and Learn: The Social Contexts of Cognitive Development.* London: Wiley-Blackwell. (see also Readings 2.1, 2.2 and 2.3 on Skinner, Piaget and Vygotsky)

Chapter 2 Learning 75

Research and debate on the implications of the neurobiology of the brain is growing, though caution is appropriate in such a new field of research. For an expert introduction, see:

Goswami, U. (2008) *Cognitive Development: The Learning Brain.* Hove: Psychology Press. (see also **Reading 2.5**)

Bruner's work extended for over fifty years, and powerfully promoted a 'cultural psychology' focused on the creation of understanding. See, for example:

Bruner, J. (1990) *Acts of Meaning.* Cambridge, MA: Harvard University Press. (**Reading 11.1**)

Across the world, there are significant attempts to take stock and review everything that is known about learning and schooling. Bransford, Brown and Cocking's book is one influential outcome.

Bransford, J.D., Brown, A.I. and Cocking, R.R. (eds) (1999) *How People Learn: Brain, Mind, Experience and School.* Washington, DC: National Academy Press. (**Reading 4.1**)

Cognitive science draws on models of information processing to analyse working memory and cognitive load – and has recently been influential. For an interesting introduction, see:

Willingham, D. (2021) *Why Don't Pupils Like School*, 2nd edn. Hoboken, NJ: Jossey Bass.

Whist 'intelligence' remains a powerful concept, the ways in which capability is interpreted, towards 'mastery' or 'helplessness', is now receiving particular attention. For an accessible account, see:

Dweck, C.S. (2006) *Mindset: The New Psychology of Success.* New York: Ballantine. (**Reading 2.6**)

The idea of 'building learning power' through developing resilience, resourcefulness, reflectiveness and reciprocity is worth considering. See:

Claxton, G. (2011) *Building Learning Power: Helping Young People Become Better Learners.* Bristol: The Learning Organization (TLO). (**Reading 2.9**)

For an approach to developing habits of mind which has been developed in the United States, see:

Kallick, B. and Zmuda, A. (2017) *Pupils at the Center: Personalized Learning with Habits of Mind.* Alexandria, VA: ASCD.

reflectiveteaching.co.uk/rtps6/part1_ch2

Among many interesting books on the development of metacognitive and thinking skills, see:

Fisher, R. (2008) *Teaching Thinking: Philosophical Enquiry in the Classroom.* London: Continuum. (Reading 2.7)

For some influential British studies of learning in schools, see:

James, M., Black, P., Carmichael, P., Conner, C., Dudley, P., Fox, A., Frost, D., Honour, L., MacBeath, J., McCormick, R., Marshall, B., Pedder, D., Procter, R., Swaffield, S. and Wiliam, D. (2006) *Learning How to Learn: Tools for Schools.* London: Routledge. (Reading 2.8)

James, M., McCormick, R., Black, P., Carmichael, P., Drummond, M-J., Fox, A., MacBeath, J., Marshall, B., Pedder, D., Procter, R., Swaffield, S., Swann, J. and Wiliam, D. (2007) *Improving Learning How to Learn: Classrooms, Schools and Networks.* London: Routledge.

An interesting book on informal learning out of school is:

Thomas, A. and Pattison, H. (2007) *How Children Learn at Home.* London: Continuum. (Reading 2.10)

Fascinating accounts of how children engage in activities in school:

Nuthall, G. (2007) *The Hidden Lives of Learners.* Wellington: NZCER Press.

Kallick, B. and Zmuda, A. (2017) *Pupils at the Center: Personalized Learning with Habits of Mind.* ASCD.

reflectiveteaching.co.uk/rtps6/part1_ch2

TOOLKIT EVIDENCE 2.1
Metacognition and self-regulated learning: transferring responsibility for learning

What is it?
Metacognition and self-regulated learning is when teaching includes an explicit focus on helping learners to think about their own learning and their engagement. This is by supporting them in taking responsibility for aspects of the learning process such as planning, monitoring and evaluating their own progress (metacognition), or managing their feelings and motivation towards their learning (self-regulation). This is usually by teaching specific strategies to set goals, and to monitor and evaluate their own progress in curriculum tasks. The intention is often to give pupils a repertoire of strategies to choose from during learning activities which are appropriate for the content being learned.

What does the evidence say?
Metacognition and self-regulation approaches have consistently high levels of impact, with pupils making an average of seven months' additional progress when compared with approaches which do not feature these aspects of learning. The evidence indicates that teaching these strategies can be particularly effective for low achieving and older pupils.

These strategies are often more effective when taught in collaborative groups so learners can support each other and make their thinking explicit through discussion.

The potential impact of these approaches is very high, but can be difficult to achieve as it requires pupils to take greater responsibility for their learning and develop their understanding of what is required to succeed. There is no simple method or trick for this. It is possible to support pupils' work too much, so that they do not learn to monitor and manage their own learning but come to rely on the prompts and support from the teacher.

How sound is the evidence?
A number of systematic reviews and meta-analyses have consistently found similar levels of impact for strategies related to metacognition and self-regulation. Most studies have looked at the impact on English or mathematics, though there is some evidence from other subject areas such as science, suggesting that the approach is likely to be widely applicable.

What do I need to think about?
- How much do you emphasise the *process* of learning, and what your pupils should think about, or pay attention to, as they undertake a task?
- We often model cognitive aspects of learning, but what about the affective and motivational? Where might learning be difficult and need resilience?
- What strategies do you teach your pupils for planning, for monitoring their own progress in activities and for evaluating these strategies?

Links and further reading
Schunk, D.H. and Zimmerman, B.J. (eds) (2012) *Motivation and Self-Regulated Learning: Theory, Research, and Applications*. London: Routledge.

The EEF Teaching and Learning Toolkit entry on metacognition and self-regulation: educationendowmentfoundation.org.uk/education-evidence/teaching-learning-toolkit/metacognition-and-self-regulation
See also the technical appendix for references to individual studies. They have also published a guidance report (EEF, 2018a) and a review of the underpinning evidence (Muijs and Bokhove, 2020).

See also
Metacognition and self-regulation (Toolkit Evidence 2.1)
Collaborative learning (Toolkit Evidence 11.3)
Feedback (Toolkit Evidence 13.1)

RESEARCH BRIEFING 2.1
Education and neuroscience

TLRP assembled leading practitioners, neuroscientists, psychologists and educationalists to review the impact of neuroscience on education. There was agreement about its enormous potential significance. There was also agreement that many applications were inappropriate and that some 'neuro-myths' in schools needed to be challenged.

Essentially, aspirations to apply 'brain science' too directly to 'practice' are misplaced. The model below represents the relationship between brain, mind and behaviour, and indicates the wide range of mediating environmental and intra-individual factors.

Figure 2.10 A model of brain, mind and behaviour (after Morton and Frith, 1995)

Examples of environmental factors	Examples of intra-individual factors	Factor affected
Oxygen Nutrition Toxins	Synaptogenesis Synaptic pruning Neuronal connections	BRAIN
Teaching Cultural institutions Social factors	Learning Memory Emotion	MIND
Temporary restrictions e.g. teaching tools	Performance Errors Improvement	BEHAVIOUR

Key findings:	Implications:
Nature/nurture: Biology is not destiny. Biology provides no simple limit to our learning, not least because our learning can influence our biology.	Teaching should aim to enable children's potential and to enrich their experience.
Neuro-myths: Education has invested an immense amount in 'brain-based' ideas that are not underpinned by recognisable scientific understanding of the brain. Many of these ideas remain untested and others are being revealed as ineffective, such as:	Professional judgement should be applied in respect of commercial 'brain-based' programmes
The belief that learning can be improved by presenting material to suit an individual's preferred 'learning style' is not supported by high quality evidence (Coffield et al., 2004).	Focusing on learning styles too narrowly could actually inhibit learner development more broadly.
Encouraging teachers to determine whether a child is left or right brained is misplaced. Performance at most everyday tasks, including learning activities, requires both hemispheres to work together in a sophisticated parallel fashion.	Right brain/left brain beliefs, particularly if linked to gendered assumptions, categorises children inappropriately.
Neuroscience: Some particular insights from neuroscientists and psychologists have broad implications for teaching and learning strategies which merit further exploration. For example:	There are grounds for 'cautious optimism'.
When we learn new information, the semantic links that form between this new information and our existing knowledge serve to make it meaningful. (Binder et al., 2003).	The construction of meaning is a key to understanding and remembering information.
Mental visualisation of an object engages most of the brain circuitry which is activated by actually seeing it (Kosslyn, 2005).	'Visualisation' has considerable power and usefulness as a learning tool.
Cautious optimism: We are still at an early stage in our understanding of the brain. There are methodological limitations and the transfer of concepts between neuroscience and education requires caution. Nevertheless, the potential is great.	There is a growing need for research collaborations between neuroscience, psychology and education that embrace insights and understanding from each perspective.

Chapter 3
Reflection
How can we develop the quality of our teaching?

| Introduction | 80 |

| Dilemmas, reflection and effectiveness | 81 |

Dilemmas and challenges in classroom life	81
Reflection and evidence-informed practice	83
Standards for effectiveness and career development	86

| The meaning of reflective teaching | 87 |

Aims and consequences	89
A cyclical process	91
Gathering and evaluating evidence	92
Attitudes towards teaching	94
Teacher judgement	95
Learning with colleagues	97
Reflective teaching as creative mediation	100

| Conclusion | 100 |

Supplementary chapters at reflectiveteaching.co.uk
- **Mentoring** Learning through mentoring in initial teacher education
- **Enquiry** Developing evidence-informed practice
- **Techniques of enquiry** Gathering and analysing evidence

INTRODUCTION

This book is based on the belief that teaching is a complex and highly skilled activity which, above all, requires classroom teachers to exercise judgement in deciding how to act. High-quality teaching, and thus pupil learning, is dependent on the existence of such professional expertise.

The process of reflective teaching supports the development, maintenance and extension of professional expertise. We can conceptualise successive levels of expertise in teaching – those that student teachers may attain at different stages in their courses; those of the new teacher after their induction to full-time school life; and those of the experienced, expert teacher. And as teaching is a dynamic and responsive process, it is a profession in which development and learning are continuous.

The process of reflection thus feeds a career-long spiral of professional development and capability (see Figure 3.1).

Figure 3.1 The spiral of professional development

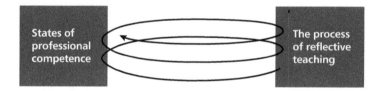

Reflective teaching should not only be personally fulfilling for teachers but should also lead to a steady increase in the quality of the education provided for children – teaching requires a sense of moral purpose. Indeed, we would argue that because it is evidence based, reflective practice supports initial training students, newly qualified teachers, teaching assistants and experienced professionals in satisfying both external performance requirements and the intrinsic commitments to education to which most teachers subscribe.

See Chapter 4

TLRP Principles

Two principles are of particular relevance to this chapter on reflective practice for the improvement of teaching:

Effective teaching and learning fosters both individual and social processes and outcomes. Learning is a social activity. Learners should be encouraged and helped to work with others, to share ideas and to build knowledge together. Consulting learners about their learning and giving them a voice is both an expectation and a right. (*Principle 7*)

Effective teaching and learning depends on teacher learning. The need for teachers to learn continuously in order to develop their knowledge and skills, and adapt and develop their roles, especially through classroom inquiry, should be recognised and supported. (*Principle 9*)

This chapter has three main parts. The first introduces some of *the dilemmas* and challenges which teachers and teaching assistants face; these are linked briefly to the idea of professional standards. In the second part, the meaning of reflective teaching is explored; seven major characteristics of reflective teaching are then identified and discussed. In exploring these characteristics, particular emphasis is placed on teaching as an evidence-informed profession and on the ways in which teachers might support one another's reflective practice. In the final part, we draw some conclusions that might inform the future actions of teachers and teaching assistants.

DILEMMAS, REFLECTION AND EFFECTIVENESS

Dilemmas and challenges in classroom life

The complicated nature of educational issues and the practical demands of classroom teaching ensure that a teacher's work is never finished. One need only review the foci of the various chapters in this book to gain a sense of the breadth of professional concerns that are within the purview of every teacher. Thus, when practicalities, performance standards, personal ideals and wider educational concerns are considered together, the job of reconciling the numerous requirements and possible conflicts may seem to be overwhelming. As a primary teacher explained to us:

> I love my work but it's a constant struggle to keep it all going. If I focus on one thing, I have to neglect another. For instance, if I talk to a group or to a particular child then I have to keep an eye on what the others are doing; if I hear someone read then I can't be in position to extend other children's language when opportunities arise; if I put out clay then I haven't got room for painting; if I go to evening courses then I can't prepare as well for the next day; if I spend time with my family then I worry about my class but if I rush around collecting materials or something then I feel guilty for neglecting the family. It's not easy . . . but I wouldn't do anything else.

This quote illustrates that the 'job' of becoming a teacher involves, amongst other things, learning a complex set of technical skills and understandings; positioning yourself within a larger community of practice; managing emotional dimensions of 'personal development'; and connecting, integrating and reconciling various sources of theory and experiences of practice. For beginning teachers it is first necessary to reconcile the realities of school experience with prior personal beliefs about children, subjects, teaching and learning (Luehmann, 2007).

Such dilemmas and tensions are endemic in the teaching role and it is not surprising that they are frequently expressed (Kimbrough, 2015). A classic analysis of the dilemmas which teachers face was provided by Berlak and Berlak (1981). The framework that they developed is simple but powerful. Its strength derives from the fact that, although they studied only three schools in detail, they took great care to relate their analysis of the

reflectiveteaching.co.uk/rtps6/part1_ch3

dilemmas which arose in the 'micro' world of the classroom to the major factors, beliefs and influences in society as a whole. Such factors, they argued, influence, structure and constrain the actions of teachers, children and parents. However, they do not do so in ways which are consistent, because of existing complexities and contradictions within school and education systems – hence the dilemmas which have to be faced. The resolution of such dilemmas calls for teachers to use professional judgement to assess the most appropriate course of action in any particular situation.

But what are the major dilemmas that have to be faced?

Figure 3.2 presents some of the dilemmas and challenges faced by teachers. You may like to consider what is particularly important to you, or what would you add?

Figure 3.2
Common dilemmas faced by teachers

Treating each child as a 'whole person'	Treating each child as a 'pupil'
Organising the children on an individual or group basis	Organising pupils as a class
Giving pupils a degree of control over their time, their activities and their work standards	Maintaining purposeful control over children's use of time, their activities and their work standards
Seeking to motivate the children through intrinsic engagement and enjoyment of activities	Offering reasons and rewards so that children are extrinsically motivated to tackle tasks
Providing a curriculum structure that enables children to feel in control of their learning	Providing a curriculum structure that reflects what the children need for them to understand and take a place in society
Showing connections in teaching and learning across subject boundaries	Maintaining the integrity of subject content in teaching and learning
Aiming for quality in school work	Aiming for quantity in school work
Focusing on the development of basic skills across the curriculum	Focusing on expressive and creative elements of subject and topic learning
Trying to build up cooperative and social skills	Developing self-reliance and self-confidence in individuals
Inducting the children into a 'common culture'	Affirming the variety of cultures in a diverse, multi-ethnic society
Allocating teacher time, attention and resources equally among all the children	Paying attention to the special needs of particular children
Maintaining consistent rules and understanding about behaviour and schoolwork	Being flexible and responsive to particular situations and individuals
Presenting oneself formally to the children	Being more open with the children
Working with 'professional levels' of application and care for the children	Considering one's personal needs as well as one's professional responsibilities

reflectiveteaching.co.uk/rtps6/part1_ch3

> **Reflective Activity 3.1**
>
> *Aim:* To review experienced dilemmas.
>
> *Evidence and reflection:* Think about your own situation and classroom experiences. Look carefully at Figure 3.2 and see whether any of the identified dilemmas provide a realistic reflection of those you are experiencing. Are there other dilemmas that relate to your specific context?
>
> Having carried out this exercise, try to identify the three most pressing dilemmas that you are facing. Think carefully about each of these and consider whether there are any measures that you might take to help mitigate them (for example, discussions with relevant colleagues about developing approaches to behaviour management; changing classroom assessment practices in line with recent CPD events; researching the classroom behaviour of individuals/groups in order to have the evidence for curriculum developments etc.).
>
> The important point here is to start with one dilemma and consider what evidence you need to be able to address it effectively, and where that evidence might come from. Progress will often be slow and incremental, but such professional development has powerful potential for change.
>
> *Extension:* Note that this Reflective Activity may well lead to a more formalised piece of classroom-based research; this is considered in **Reflective Activity 3.2** below.

This book provides a practical guide to ways of reflecting on such issues. Indeed, it offers strategies and advice for developing the necessary classroom expertise to resolve them. Resolution of such dilemmas will always be based on teacher judgement. However, in contemporary education, performance data and other evidence are now routinely used to augment (and sometimes challenge or refine) such judgements.

Reflection and evidence-informed practice

Three main sources of evidence are available to teachers. School performance or benchmark evidence, generated from assessment, inspection or intake data, is often made available to schools to support improvement strategies. Such data may also be provided to parents to inform school choice. It is also now very significant to school managers who must respond if trends appear, and for inspection teams and others who make judgements about school *and* teacher effectiveness. There are now sophisticated management information systems which enable, for instance, tracking of pupil progress and school self-evaluation in preparation for inspection (see Chapter 14, p. 450, also Readings 14.3 and 14.4). There are various systems for data collation, target setting and national comparison – such as, in England, Analyse School Performance (ASP) – a 2017 replacement for RAISEonline. In secondary education, most exam boards also provide feedback systems. Measures of pupil outcomes may be used in annual reviews of teacher performance. The government's emphasis on schools' statutory assessment data can also be seen in the 'School Inspection Data Summary (IDSR) Report Guide' (gov.uk/guidance/school-inspection-data-summary-report-idsr-guide#full-publication-update-history). At the other end of the scale, international, system-wide comparisons are also made with countries in Europe, the Americas and parts of Asia and Australasia through surveys such as the Programme for International Student Assessment (PISA) and Trends in International Mathematics and Science Study (TIMSS).

A second source of evidence comes from educational research and, in particular, from research reviews and summaries which interpret such research. In some aspects of primary education there are systematic reviews and meta-analyses which review robust research studies and compare evidence from multiple studies in a rigorous way. The research centre for Evidence-Policy and Practice in Education (eppi.ioe.ac.uk) pioneered systematic reviews of available evidence, and many university research teams now seek to maximise the impact of their work by directly engaging with practitioners. The British Educational Research Association (BERA) is the largest UK body for specialist researchers in the field (bera.ac.uk), and its Presidential Round Table reports are one example of the way that BERA reviews research evidence related to policy and practice. The National Foundation for Educational Research (nfer.ac.uk) continues to provide a range of independent evidence to support teaching and learning. However, establishment of a trustworthy UK aggregating service to enable access to the range of valuable work has proved difficult. Most recently, the British Academy (BA) and the Royal Society (RS) have advocated an Office for Educational Research (RS & BA, 2018). An 'evidence centre' and other collaborative initiatives have been debated and trialled, and there is a particularly influential DfE-funded contemporary resource in the 'toolkit' at educationendowmentfoundation.org.uk. This resource for schools is notable for the way in which it compares the measured impact and likely cost of various teaching strategies. The evidence on ten of the most effective teaching strategies is summarised in the relevant chapters of this book.

In addition to the report by the Royal Society and British Academy (RS & BA, 2018) for an analysis of an extensive range of sources, systems and processes affecting research on education, see the report of the UK Strategic Forum for Research in Education (Pollard and Oancea, 2010).

Further guidance is provided in Chapter 16, and up-to-date advice and relevant links are maintained on reflectiveteaching.co.uk.

The third source of evidence is, arguably, the most important for reflective practitioners for it suggests that teachers themselves collect their own classroom and school evidence. It suggests, in other words, that teachers take control of their own research and development. This builds on the long tradition of action research which was established by Lawrence Stenhouse (Reading 3.3). The Chartered College of Teaching; the General Teaching Councils in Northern Ireland and Scotland; the Education Workforce Council in Wales and the Teaching Council of Ireland (see Reading 17.3) are particular advocates of this sort of work. Indeed, the GTC for Northern Ireland actively promotes 'The Reflective Teacher' and encourages the professional community to 'take ownership'. The GTC for Scotland has been supporting professional development since 1966. In Wales, The National Strategy for Educational Research and Enquiry was initiated in 2021. More widely, teacher unions and organisations such as Educational International (ei-ie.org) support research activities that inform teaching and learning in various countries across the globe.

The model at Figure 3.3 summarises the relationship between classroom practice and enquiry. It suggests that a practical *problem* in the classroom can helpfully be considered in terms of the *issues* which might underlie it. Some careful thinking might help! As we saw above, this foregrounds an appreciation of classroom *dilemmas* – the challenge of deciding what to do when there are a number of competing possibilities (see p. 86). The essence of professional expertise in teaching is being able to make high-quality practical *judgements* (Heilbronn, 2010, Reading 3.6) to resolve such dilemmas. Figure 3.3 shows how evidence from classroom enquiry and other research sources can enhance such judgements.

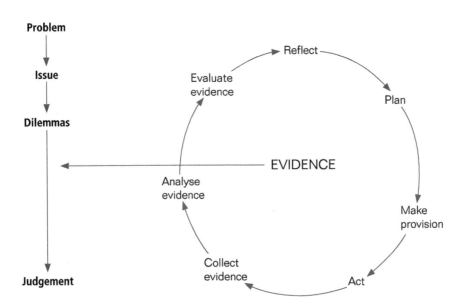

Figure 3.3
Evidence-informed practice

For example, pupils' inappropriate classroom behaviour may result in an immediate response from a teacher to assert control. However, later reflection might promote consideration of a number of possible longer-term issues. Are teacher–pupil relationships beginning to go awry for some reason? Do the children respect the authority of teachers and accept their actions as fair? Is the curriculum engaging the students, or causing them to become bored? Are the lessons well planned, offering focus, interest, progression and successful learning experiences? Each of these topics, and others, could merit further investigation through classroom enquiry.

Of course, the sources of evidence we have reviewed – using performance or benchmark data, interpreting educational research and professional enquiry by teachers themselves – actually complement each other. Reflective professionals should thus be able to draw on, or contribute to, many sources of evidence, and use them to inform their teaching practices. However, evidence in education must always be critically evaluated, as in other fields of social science or professional practice, because absolute 'truth' is not available, given the difficulties of research on people and teaching/learning processes. Further, because education is imbued with values, this raises some educational questions for which it is very difficult to determine educational decisions on evidence. This is the reason why the term 'evidence-informed' is preferred over 'evidence-based'. It shares an assertion of the importance of evidence in decision-making, but does not make inappropriate claims for precedence. Judgement remains essential for practitioners in classrooms and schools, just as it is necessary for administrators and politicians in relation to policy.

Practical guidance on 'Enquiry' for classroom research is available at reflectiveteaching.co.uk.

Standards for effectiveness and career development

In recent years, competency criteria and 'standards' have been set by governments in many countries to provide a framework for teacher training and further professional development. The evolution of such standards can take a considerable time and is often predicated on the political perspectives of particular governments. In most cases, such standards provide a statutory framework for continuing professional development and performance management, as well as for initial teacher education.

Broad standards and competences can be helpful in defining goals for students, mentors, headteachers, tutors and others who are engaged in teacher education and professional development. They can:

- set out clear expectations;
- help teachers to plan and monitor development, training and performance;
- maintain a focus on improving the achievement of pupils and educational quality;
- provide a basis for the professional recognition of teacher expertise.

However, we need to be clear about the status of such models and criteria. Those required where a centralised national curriculum and legally defined assessment procedures exist may well differ from those which are called for where teachers and schools are more engaged with a greater degree of partnership; for example, there is a substantial difference in the character of the standards in the different countries of the UK, in different states in North America and in various countries of the European Union. Those called for where class sizes are large and resources scarce (as in many parts of the world) may vary from those needed when much smaller classes or groups are taught with good access to suitable equipment. Further, it is worth considering that the standards required at any particular period in history are unlikely to remain constant. To illustrate this point, it is interesting to consider the requirements made of apprenticed 'pupil teachers' in England more than 175 years ago (see Figure 3.4).

> *Regulations respecting the education of pupil teachers.*
> *Minutes of the Committee of Council on Education, 1846.*
>
> Qualifications of candidates:
>
> To be at least 13 years of age.
>
> To not be subject to any bodily infirmity likely to impair their usefulness.
>
> To have a certificate of moral character.
>
> To read with fluency, ease and expression.
>
> To write in a neat hand with correct spelling and punctuation, a simple prose narrative read to them.
>
> To write from dictation sums in the first four rules of arithmetic, simple and compound: to work them correctly, and to know the table of weights and measures.
>
> To point out the parts of speech in a simple sentence.
>
> To have an elementary knowledge of geography.
>
> To repeat the Catechism and to show that they understand its meaning and are acquainted with the outline of Scripture history. (Where working in schools connected with the Church of England only.)
>
> To teach a junior class to the satisfaction of the Inspector.
>
> Girls should also be able to sew neatly and to knit.

Figure 3.4
Regulations for the education of pupil teachers, 1846

We have to remember then that officially endorsed standards are historically and contextually specific. Despite the moderating influence of available research, they are likely to be strongly influenced by the cultures, values and the priorities of decision-makers who happen to be in power at the time of their construction. During a forty-year career, a teacher is likely to experience many such systems, and historical or comparative reflection will help keep them in perspective. Indeed, Hay McBer's influential report on teacher effectiveness cautioned against over-conformity when they emphasised that 'teachers are not clones' and asserted that professionals always have to use their judgement about circumstances, pupils, contexts and teaching approaches (2000, para 1.1.4). The central point to be made here, then, is that whilst standards provide a framework for teacher actions and responsibilities, they are not a substitute for the practical judgements that are the central element of reflective and evidence-informed teaching (see Calderhead, 1994, Reading 3.5 for an elaboration of the complexities of teaching).

THE MEANING OF REFLECTIVE TEACHING

The concept of reflective teaching stems from Dewey (1933, Reading 3.1 who contrasted 'routine action' with 'reflective action'). According to Dewey, routine action is guided by

reflectiveteaching.co.uk/rtps6/part1_ch3

factors such as tradition, habit and authority, and by institutional definitions and expectations. By implication, it is relatively static and is thus unresponsive to changing priorities and circumstances. Reflective action, on the other hand, involves a willingness to engage in constant self-appraisal and development. Among other things, it implies flexibility, rigorous analysis and social awareness.

Reflective action, in Dewey's view, involves the 'active, persistent and careful consideration of any belief or supposed form of knowledge in the light of the grounds that support it' (1933, p. 9). Teachers who are unreflective about their teaching tend to accept the *status quo* in their schools and simply 'concentrate on finding the most efficient means to solve problems that have largely been defined for them' by others (Zeichner and Liston, 1996, p. 9). Of course, routine action based on ongoing assumptions is necessary, but Dewey argued that it is insufficient on its own. In Dewey's view, reflection 'enables us to direct our actions with foresight' (1933, p. 17).

Donald Schön (1983, Reading 3.2; 1987) extended these ideas in analysing the actions of many different professional occupations – medicine, law, engineering, management etc. Schön emphasised that most professionals face unique situations that require the use of knowledge and experience to inform action. This is an active, experimental and transactional process which Schön called 'professional artistry'. It is the 'kind of professional competence which practitioners display in unique, uncertain and conflicted situations of practice' (1987, p. 22) – a form of 'knowing-in-action'. Schön thus came to distinguish between 'reflection-on-action', which looks back to evaluate, and 'reflection-in-action', which enables immediate action. Both contribute to the capabilities of a reflective teacher.

Others, such as Solomon (1987), have made a powerful case for reflection as a social practice, in which the articulation of ideas *to others* is central to the development of an open, critical perspective. The support of colleagues and mentors is thus extremely helpful in building understanding – ideas which have been extended further with the concepts such as 'culture of collaboration', 'community of enquiry' and 'network learning' (see Reading 3.7).

Such ideas about what it is to be a reflective professional, when developed and applied to teaching, are both challenging and exciting. In this section, we review their implications by identifying and discussing seven key characteristics of reflective practice. These are that it:

1 implies an active concern with aims and consequences, as well as means and technical efficiency;

2 is applied in a cyclical or spiralling process, in which teachers monitor, evaluate and revise their own practice continuously;

3 requires competence in methods of evidence-informed classroom enquiry, to support the progressive development of higher standards of teaching;

4 requires attitudes of open-mindedness, responsibility and wholeheartedness;

5 is based on teacher judgement, informed by evidence and insights from other research;

6 along with professional learning and personal fulfilment, they are enhanced through collaboration and dialogue with colleagues;

reflectiveteaching.co.uk/rtps6/part1_ch3

7 enables teachers to creatively mediate externally developed frameworks for teaching and learning.

Each of these characteristics will now be considered more fully.

Aims and consequences

Reflective teaching implies an active concern with aims and consequences as well as means and technical competence.

This issue relates first to the immediate aims and consequences of classroom practice for these are any teacher's prime responsibility. However, classroom work cannot be isolated from the influence of the wider society and a reflective teacher must therefore consider both spheres.

An example from the history of educational policy making in England will illustrate the way in which changes outside schools influence actions within them. Following the initiation of a 'Great Debate' by Prime Minister Callaghan (1976) many of the 'taken-for-granteds' in education were challenged during the 1980s and 1990s. Successive Conservative governments introduced far-reaching and cumulative changes in all spheres of education. Many of these reforms were opposed by professional organisations (see for example, Haviland,

> **Expert Question**
>
> **Reflection:** *is our classroom practice based on incremental, evidence-informed and collaborative improvement strategies?*
>
> This question contributes to a conceptual framework underpinning professional expertise (see Chapter 16).

1988; Arnot and Barton, 1992) but with no noticeable effect on political decision-making. Indeed, the allegation was made that educational policy was being influenced by a closed system of beliefs – an 'ideology' deriving from a small number of right-wing politicians and pressure groups. Meanwhile, teachers and pupils worked to implement the new forms of curriculum, assessment, accountability, management and control which had been introduced, despite the fact that the profession at the time was largely opposed to the principles on which the reforms were based (see Osborn et al., 2000; Pollard et al., 1994).

The development of England's national curriculum of 2014 has also caused controversy in relation to some of the same issues that emerged previously in the development of the first national curriculum of the twentieth century in England as a result of the Education Reform Act 1988. All bar one of the experts on the group convened to advise Secretary of State for Education Michael Gove resigned in protest because the proposals for the national curriculum did not sufficiently reflect their review of the evidence (see the account by Mary James who was one of the expert group (BERA, 2012)).

Such stark examples of the contestation of aims, values and evidence in education raise questions concerning the relationship between professionals, parents and policymakers, and mirrors current developments in many countries around the world. It is possible to start from the seemingly uncontroversial argument that, in democratic societies, decisions about the aims of education should be 'democratically' determined. However, it has also

reflectiveteaching.co.uk/rtps6/part1_ch3

been suggested (for instance, by *Education International* representing 400 education organisations across the world) that teachers should adopt a role as active 'interpreters' of political policy. Indeed, that most teachers accept this argument is shown by the ways in which they have implemented legislation about which they had reservations. For example, where prescribed national curricula are to be implemented, the 'official' rationale may not match up to the day-to-day experience of classroom teachers. Reflective teachers are likely to use their initiative to adapt the curriculum so that it is more suitable for the pupils in their care (Ball, Maguire and Braun, 2011).

This stance accepts the authority of governments regarding educational goals, but asserts the need for practical judgement regarding implementation. It is thus very different from the idea of the wholly autonomous professional with which many teachers once identified. It can be argued that the existence of unconstrained autonomy is only reasonable and practical if ends, aims and values are completely uncontroversial. However, as soon as questions about educational aims and social values are seriously raised, then the position changes. In a democratic society, the debate appropriately extends to the political domain and this, of course, is what has happened in recent years in many countries.

This does not mean though, that teachers, even as interpreters of policy, should simply 'stand by' in the procedure. Indeed, there are two important roles that they can play. In the case of the first, an appropriate metaphor for the teacher's role is, as both White (1978) and Sachs (2003) have suggested, that of 'activist'. This recognises that school teachers are individual members of society who, within normal political processes, have rights to pursue their values and beliefs as guided by their own individual moral and ethical concerns. They should thus be as active as they wish to be in contributing to the formation of public policy. Second, whilst accepting a responsibility for translating politically determined aims into practice, teachers should speak out, as they have done many times in the past, if they view particular aims and policies as being professionally impracticable, educationally unsound or morally questionable. In such circumstances the professional experience, knowledge and judgements of teachers should be brought to bear on policymakers directly – whether or not the policymakers wish for or act on the advice which is offered (for interesting developments of this argument, see Thompson, 1997). Indeed, it is important that, within a modern democratic society, teachers should be entitled to not only a hearing, but also some influence, on educational policy. Sectoral and subject associations in the UK, such as the Association for the Study of Primary Education and the Geographical Association, together with the General Teaching Councils of most parts of the UK and teacher unions (whose influence may be particularly significant), provide collective forms of organisation for such voices.

The reflective teacher should thus be aware of the political process and of its legitimate oversight of public educational services. They should also be willing to contribute to it both as a citizen and as a professional (see also Chapter 17 and Readings 17.2, 17.5 and 17.7).

A cyclical process

Reflective teaching is applied in a cyclical or spiralling process, in which teachers monitor, evaluate and revise their own practice continuously.

This characteristic refers to the process of reflective teaching and provides the dynamic basis for teacher action. It is clearly evident in the thinking of Dewey, Schön and others, though the specific conception of a classroom-based, reflexive process stems from the teacher-based, action-research movement of which Lawrence Stenhouse was a key figure. He argued (1975, Reading 3.3) that teachers should act as 'researchers' of their own practice and should develop the curriculum through practical enquiry. Various alternative models have since become available (Carr and Kemmis, 1986; Elliott, 1991; McNiff, 1988) and, although there are some significant differences in these models, they all preserve a central concern with self-monitoring and reflection (see also Pring, 2010, Reading 3.4).

Teachers are principally expected to plan, make provision and act. Reflective teachers also need to monitor, observe and collect data on their own, and the children's, intentions, actions and feelings. This evidence then needs to be critically analysed and evaluated so that it can be shared, judgements made, and decisions taken. Finally, this may lead the teacher to revise their classroom policies, plans and provision before beginning the process again. It is a dynamic process which is intended to lead through successive cycles, or through a spiralling process, towards higher quality standards of teaching. This model is simple, comprehensive and certainly could be an extremely powerful influence on practice. It is consistent with the notion of reflective teaching, as described by both Dewey and Schön, and provides an essential clarification of the procedures for reflective teaching.

Figure 3.5 represents the key stages of the reflective process.

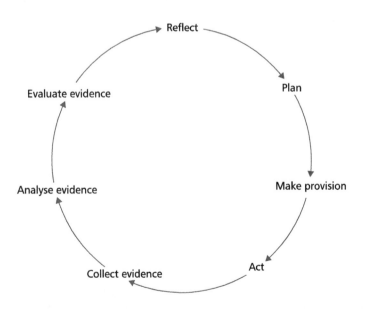

Figure 3.5 The process of reflective teaching

> **Reflective Activity 3.2**
>
> *Aim:* To explore how improvement can come from collecting evidence of our teaching.
>
> *Evidence and reflection:* The key to this process is to create a focus and to consider what evidence is required in order to make judgements about how to proceed. For example, you may be considering the progress of a particular child in a specific curriculum area or analysing the effectiveness of a method for encouraging group dialogue. Whatever your focus, the stages you'll consider are:
>
> 1 Which facet of classroom life should be investigated and why?
> 2 What evidence to collect, and how?
> 3 How can we analyse, interpret and apply the findings?
>
> This may seem rather formal, but these are all things you'll be thinking about in any situation where you are evaluating your classroom.
>
> To start with, pick a small issue or dilemma (see p. 87 and **Reflective Activity 3.1**) and see if you can construct a plan for evidence gathering, on which you can base subsequent action.
>
> *Extension:* Generally, teachers focus their first classroom-based research and development activity on an individual child or group of children. Is there a whole-class intervention that you would like to trial? How will the evidence base change for such work?

For detailed support on these three processes of classroom enquiry, see the supplementary chapter on *Enquiry* at **reflectiveteaching.co.uk**.

The cyclical model we have considered above is relatively open and can be interpreted in many ways. 'Lesson Study' is a rather more systematic version, in which colleagues cooperate as a sequence of 'research lessons' is taught. To provide indicative evidence of effectiveness, a small number of pupils may be focused on from lesson to lesson.

The process of Lesson Study is elaborated in Chapter 10, p. 341 in relation to curriculum evaluation and development. Many of the practical chapters in Parts 3 and 4 of this book feature illustrative Lesson Study cases. In these, practitioners from UK schools describe the process and outcomes of their reflective, research lesson sequences. Additional information about Lesson Study is available at **lessonstudy.co.uk**.

Further practical advice on how to carry out classroom enquiries is offered in supplementary material on **reflectiveteaching.co.uk**. This includes guidance on publicly available sources of research evidence and, being web-based, is updated regularly.

Gathering and evaluating evidence

Reflective teaching requires competence in methods of evidence-informed classroom enquiry, to support the progressive development of higher standards of teaching.

We can identify four key skills here: reviewing relevant, existing research; gathering new evidence; analysis; and evaluation. Each of these contribute to the cyclical process of reflection (see p. 95).

1 *Reviewing relevant, existing research.* The issue here is to learn as much as possible from others. Published research on the issue of concern may be reviewed. Internet-based search techniques make this an increasingly straightforward task as do other resources – including the Key Readings which conclude all chapters of this book and its associated book of linked Readings. Going into yet more depth, *Notes for Further Reading*, chapter-by-chapter, are offered on reflectiveteaching.co.uk. Many universities and publishers are now providing open access to more of their publications and careful internet searches are often rewarding.

2 *Gathering new evidence.* This relates to the essential issue of knowing what is going on in a classroom or school as a means of forming one's own opinion. It is concerned with collecting data, describing situations, processes, causes and effects with care and accuracy. Two sorts of data are particularly relevant. 'Objective' data are important, such as descriptions of what people actually do. Pupil performance data comes into this category of course (Ofsted, 2008, Reading 14.4), but is only part of the picture. Additionally, it is also vital to collect more subjective data which describe how people feel and think – their perceptions. The collection of both types of data calls for considerable skill on the part of any classroom investigator, particularly when they may be enquiring into their own practice.

3 *Analytical skills.* These skills are needed to address the issue of how to interpret descriptive data. Such 'facts' are not meaningful until they are placed in a framework that enables a reflective teacher to relate them one with the other and to begin to theorise about them.

4 *Evaluative skills.* Evaluative skills are involved in making judgements about the educational consequences of the results of the practical enquiry. Evaluation, in the light of aims, values and the experience of others enables the results of an enquiry to be applied to future policy and practice.

Increasingly the teaching community is engaged, at a classroom or school level, in enquiries into teaching and learning, in order to inform subsequent practice and the developmental priorities of a school. Many of such enquiries exhibit characteristics of case study and action research (Pring, 2010, Reading 3.4; Carr and Kemmis, 1986; Hamilton and Corbett-Whittier, 2013). The 'case' is often a class, a year group or the school cohort in which spiral of action research develops. A range of data collection methods may be used, focusing on pupil perspectives, direct observations, interpretations of attainment data etc.

Such work can both develop and legitimate school and classroom policies – and thus provide sound answers to challenges where a teacher or school is required to justify their practice.

> **Expert Question**
>
> **Warrant:** *are our teaching strategies evidence-informed, convincing and justifiable to stakeholders?*
>
> This question contributes to a conceptual framework underpinning professional expertise (see Chapter 16).

However, such competence is not sufficient in itself for a teacher who wishes to engage in reflective teaching. Certain attitudes are also necessary and need to be integrated and applied with enquiry skills.

Attitudes towards teaching

Reflective teaching requires attitudes of open-mindedness, responsibility and whole-heartedness.

In this section we draw directly on the thinking of Dewey.

Open-mindedness. As Dewey put it, open-mindedness is:

> An active desire to listen to more sides than one, to give heed to facts from whatever source they come, to give full attention to alternative possibilities, to recognise the possibility of error even in the beliefs which are dearest to us. (1933, p. 29)

Open-mindedness is an essential attribute for rigorous reflection because any sort of enquiry that is consciously based on partial evidence, only weakens itself. We thus use the concept in the sense of being willing to reflect upon ourselves and to challenge our own assumptions, prejudices and ideologies, as well as those of others – no easy task. However, to be open-minded regarding evidence and its interpretation is not the same thing as declining to take up a value position on important social and educational issues. This point brings us to the second attribute which Dewey saw as a prerequisite to reflective action – 'responsibility'.

Responsibility. Intellectual responsibility, according to Dewey, means:

> To consider the consequences of a projected step; it means to be willing to adopt these consequences when they follow reasonably. . . . Intellectual responsibility secures integrity. (1933, p. 30)

The position implied here is clearly related to the question of aims that we discussed on p. 92 above. However, in Dewey's writing the issue is relatively clearly bounded and he seems to be referring to classroom teaching and to school practices only. Tabachnick and Zeichner (1991) take this considerably further. Moral, ethical and political issues will be raised and must, they argue, be considered so that professional and personal judgements can be made about what is worthwhile. It clearly follows that a simple instrumental approach to teaching is not consistent with a reflective social awareness.

Wholeheartedness. 'Wholeheartedness', the third of Dewey's necessary attitudes, refers essentially to the way in which such consideration takes place. Dewey's suggestion was that reflective teachers should be dedicated, single-minded, energetic and enthusiastic. As he put it:

> There is no greater enemy of effective thinking than divided interest. . . . A genuine enthusiasm is an attitude that operates as an intellectual force. When a person is absorbed, the subject carries him on. (1933, p. 30)

Together, these three attitudes are vital ingredients of the professional commitment that needs to be demonstrated by all those who aim to be reflective teachers. Echoes with the issues discussed in Chapter 1 will be readily apparent.

In modern circumstances, these attitudes of open-mindedness, responsibility and wholeheartedness and are often challenged, as a result of continual change from the political centre in many countries. Halpin (2001) argues that maintaining 'intelligent hope' and imagining future possibilities are essential for committed educationalists. Beyond simple optimism, this requires 'a way of thinking about the present and the future that is permeated by critique, particularly of the kind that holds up to external scrutiny taken-for-granted current circumstances' (p. 117). Maintaining a constructive engagement, a willingness to imagine new futures, and a self-critical spirit are thus all connected to reflective practice.

Teacher judgement

Reflective teaching is based on teacher judgement, informed by evidence and insights from other research.

Teachers' knowledge has often been criticised. For instance, Bolster (1983) carried out an analysis of teachers as classroom decision-makers and suggested that, since teacher knowledge is specific and pragmatic, it is resistant to development. Bolster argued that teacher knowledge is based on individual experiences and is simply believed to be of value if it 'works' in practical situations. However, this gives little incentive to change, even in the light of evidence supporting alternative ideas or practices. On this analysis there is little need for teacher judgement, since teachers will stick to routinised practices.

For an alternative view we can again draw on Donald Schön's work (Schön, 1983, Reading 3.2) on the characteristics of 'reflective practitioners'. Schön contrasted 'scientific' professional work such as laboratory research, with 'caring' professional work such as education. He called the former 'high hard ground' and saw it as supported by quantitative and 'objective' evidence. On the other hand, the 'swampy lowlands' of the caring professions involve more interpersonal areas and qualitative issues. These complex 'lowlands', according to Schön, tend to become 'confusing messes' of intuitive action. He thus suggested that, although such 'messes' tend to be highly relevant in practical terms, they are not easily amenable to rigorous analysis because they draw, as we have seen, on a type of knowledge-in-action. It is spontaneous, intuitive, tacit and intangible but, it 'works' in practice.

Schön's ideas have received powerful empirical support, with the sophistication of teachers' classroom thinking and 'craft knowledge' being increasingly recognised and understood by both researchers (Calderhead, 1994, Reading 3.5; Brown and McIntyre, 1993; Warwick, Hennessy and Mercer, 2011) and some organisations with an influence on policymakers (OECD, 2005; Barber and Mourshed, 2007). It is clear that effective teachers make use of judgements all the time, as they adapt their teaching to the ever-changing learning challenges which their circumstances and pupils present to them.

There has also been much greater recognition of the role of intuition in the work of experienced teachers (Atkinson and Claxton, 2000; Tomlinson, 1999a and 1999b) and decision-making. Of course, reflective teachers need to recognise potential bias in their judgements as a result of their diverse experiences, and this again emphasises the need for open-mindedness.

Educational researchers' knowledge may be based on comparative, historical or philosophical research, on empirical study with large samples of classrooms, teachers, pupils or schools, on innovative methodologies, or on developing theoretical analyses. Many researchers certainly regard it as their duty to probe, analyse and evaluate – particularly with regard to the impact of policy – even though this is not always popular with governments. Whatever its character, such educational research has the potential to complement, contextualise and enhance the detailed and practical understandings of practising teachers.

In recent years, considerable effort has been made to improve the relevance, significance and impact of educational research, and to engage with practitioners and policymakers. Indeed, the best work is of very high quality and is an important source of ideas and evidence on teaching, learning, policy and practice. The BERA Close to Practice Research Project engaged with issues to do with educational research quality and the ways in which this work was relevant to practice and policy (e.g. see Wyse et al., 2020)

Over 100 selections of such work are provided in **Readings** and further advice (with regular updates) is offered through reflectiveteaching.co.uk.

Politicians' knowledge of education has often been criticised. However, governments have a democratic mandate and are appropriately concerned to ensure that educational services meet national needs. Teachers would thus be unjustified if they ignored the views of politicians, though independence, experience, judgement and expertise remain the defining characteristics of professionalism. Indeed, where politicians' views appear to be influenced by fashionable whims, media panics or party considerations rather than established educational needs, a certain amount of 'professional mediation' may be entirely justified (see p. 100).

Taken as a whole, we strongly advocate attempts to maximise the potential for collaboration between teachers, researchers and politicians. For such collaboration to be successful it must be based on a frank appreciation of each other's strengths and weaknesses. While recognising the danger of unjustified generalisation, we therefore identify these strengths and weaknesses (see Figure 3.6).

We arrive then, at a position that calls for attempts to draw on the strengths of the knowledge of teachers, researchers and politicians or policymakers. By doing this, we may overcome the weaknesses which exist in each position. This is what we mean by the statement that reflective teaching should be based on 'informed teacher judgement'. The implied collaborative endeavour underpins this whole book.

	Strengths	Weaknesses
Teachers' knowledge	• Often practically relevant and directly useful • Often communicated effectively to practitioners • Often concerned with the wholeness of classroom processes and experiences	• Often impressionistic and therefore lacking rigour • Usually based in particular situations which limits generalisation • Analysis is sometimes over-influenced by existing assumptions
Researchers' knowledge	• May be based on careful research with large samples and reliable methods • Often provides a clear and incisive analysis when studied • May offer novel views of situations and issues	• Tends to use jargon that may not communicate to practitioners in a straightforward way • Often seems obscure and difficult to relate to practical issues • Often fragments educational processes and experiences
Politicians' knowledge	• Often responsive to issues of public concern • May have a democratic mandate • May be backed by institutional, financial and legal resources	• Often over-influenced by short-term political considerations • Often reflects party political positions rather than educational needs • Is often imposed and may thus lack legitimacy

Figure 3.6 A comparison of teachers', researchers' and politicians' knowledge

Learning with colleagues

Reflective teaching, professional learning and personal fulfilment are enhanced through collaboration and dialogue with colleagues.

The value of engaging in reflective activity is almost always enhanced if it can be carried out in association with other colleagues, be they trainees, teaching assistants, teachers, mentors or tutors (Cordingley et al., 2003). The circumstances in schools, with very high proportions of contact-time with children, have constrained a great deal of such educational discussion between teachers in the past – though this is gradually changing as whole-school or even inter-school professional development assumes a greater priority. On teacher-education courses, despite the pressure of curricular requirements, reflection together in seminars, tutor groups and workshops, at college or in school, should bring valuable opportunities to share and compare, support and advise in reciprocal ways. Indeed, school settings are a particular example of the development of 'communities of practice', which Wenger analysed (1999, see also Reading 3.7). This concept of workplace communities of practice has also been powerfully developed beyond schools through the use of teacher networks.

Whether professional conversations occur between experienced teachers, as in lesson study in the UK (see Chapter 10), or between novice and experienced teachers as in school-based initial teacher education, consideration of professional ethics and structuring will ensure that the participants derive the maximum benefit from activity. For example:

- agreement about roles and relationships within such arrangements must be clear;
- the central focus of discussions should be on the benefits for children's learning that derive from the joint reflection;
- in cases where the focus is on developing the teaching of one person involved in the discussion, clear parameters for any teaching observations and subsequent conversations need to be agreed;
- decisions on future targets should be agreed together before discussion concludes.

It is important, of course, that trust between teachers and others is really secure – for without this, the sharing of ideas, concerns and challenges can seem threatening. Interestingly, Kettle and Sellars (1996), when studying developing reflective practice with trainee teachers, found that work with peers encouraged challenge to existing theories and preconceived views of teaching whilst modelling a collaborative style of professional development.

This sort of work can be extremely engaging. For instance, a group of teachers investigated 'talk in science' in their school . . . and the implications spread through the school. A sense of excitement is palpable in the lead teacher's report of the project:

> After a year of classroom analysis we, as the research group, have a wealth of data and we are now in a position to talk with enthusiasm and authority to other professionals about what we have learned about establishing a classroom climate which values this approach and encourages talk which is exploratory, responsive and relevant to individual needs. We are also able to extend our knowledge and understanding to influence future developments. (Flitton, 2010; see also Flitton and Warwick, 2012)

Wherever and whenever it occurs, collaborative, reflective discussion capitalises on the social nature of learning (Vygotsky, 1978, Reading 2.3). This is as significant for adults as it is for children, and it works through many of the same basic processes. Aims are thus clarified, experiences are shared, language and concepts for analysing practice are refined, the personal insecurities of innovation are reduced, evaluation becomes reciprocal and commitments are affirmed (see also Pring, 2010, Reading 3.4). Moreover, openness, activity and discussion gradually weave the values and self of individuals into the culture and mission of the school or course. This can be both personally fulfilling and educationally effective.

Given the enormous importance of coherence and progression in school provision, collaborative work is also a necessity. Work on school leadership suggests the imperative of senior management working actively and positively with staff to find institutional solutions to teaching dilemmas and challenges. Yet more detailed work on the nature of school cultures and the development of the 'intelligent school', whilst affirming the enormous value of whole-school staff teams working and learning together, has also shown the complexity and fragility of the process (MacGilchrist et al., 2004). Beyond schools, the development of 'networked learning communities' and other forms of web-supported activity are very exciting, though are not always sustained. Professional, subject and phase-based associations, together with professional teaching councils and unions, often provide important opportunities for collaborative work.

Whatever their circumstances, reflective teachers are likely to benefit from working, experimenting, talking and reflecting with others (for a proven systematic approach, see Reflective Activity 3.3). Apart from the benefits for learning and professional development, it is usually both more interesting and more fun.

Expert Question

Culture: *does the school support expansive learning by affirming learner contributions, engaging partners and providing attractive opportunities?*

This question contributes to a conceptual framework underpinning professional expertise (see Chapter 16).

More practical advice on mentoring is offered on reflectiveteaching.co.uk, where there is a supplementary chapter focused on this topic.

Reflective Activity 3.3

Aim: To deepen collaboration with colleagues.

Evidence and reflection: One way of doing this is through implementing regular Lesson Study lessons. Lesson Study is a highly specified form of classroom action research focusing on the development of teacher practice knowledge. Stemming from practice over many decades in Japan, lesson study offers a well-developed set of principles and procedures for supporting the professional development of teachers, focusing on the collective planning and analysis of 'research lessons'. It has several components:

- identifying themes and groups;
- formulating hypotheses and goals;
- joint research lesson planning;
- post research lesson discussion;
- passing on the knowledge gained.

Lesson Study involves groups of teachers collaboratively planning, teaching, observing and analysing learning and teaching in specified lessons. Essentially, Lesson Study provides a way of looking in detail at something teachers want to try out in a lesson series – this can be a big thing (e.g. developing dialogic group work) or a smaller thing (e.g. an approach to lesson introductions). There is a specific and agreed Lesson Study focus and observations relate to the children's experience of the intervention; this is different from many 'normal' lesson observations (which usually have a range of different foci and in which the focus of observation is usually the teacher). A Lesson Study consists of a series of 'research lessons' that are *jointly* planned, taught/observed and analysed by a Lesson Study group. A series is usually three lessons, though it can be longer; a minimum of two is absolutely essential to ensure that the teacher learning from the first lesson can be used in the second.

Extension: You may wish to develop this approach across your cluster of schools in order to share innovations and developments more widely.

This approach to collaborative professional development is applied to curriculum planning in Chapter 10, p. 341. See also Pete Dudley's website: **lessonstudy.co.uk**

Reflective teaching as creative mediation

Reflective teaching enables teachers to creatively mediate external requirements.

'Creative mediation' involves the interpretation of external requirements in the light of a teacher's knowledge of his or her pupils, values and educational principles. A study of change in education (Osborn et al., 2000) identified four different kinds of 'creative mediation' deployed by teachers to interpret such situations.

- *Protective mediation* calls for strategies to defend existing practices which are greatly valued (such as the desire to maintain an element of spontaneity in teaching in the face of assessment pressure).

- *Innovative mediation* is concerned with teachers finding strategies to work *within* the spaces and boundaries provided by new requirements – finding opportunities to be creative.

- *Collaborative mediation* refers to teachers working closely together to provide mutual support in satisfying and adapting new requirements.

- *Conspirational mediation* involves schools adopting more subversive strategies where teachers resist implementing those aspects of external requirements that they believe to be particularly inappropriate.

Such forms of mediation exemplify major strategies in the exercise of professional judgement (see also Chapter 17 and Readings 17.2, 17.3 and 17.5). Clearly, they need to be carefully justified – but the irony is that creative mediation is often the source of essential forms of innovation for future development. Indeed, innovative schools and teachers are often sought out by charities, think-tanks, teacher associations and even government agencies in the constant quest for improvement in the quality of educational services.

All education systems need to be able to guarantee consistency in entitlements to provide opportunities for all – but they also require some capacity for innovation and change. In applying principles and evidence through their practice, and making this public when appropriate, reflective teachers have a significant role in providing such leadership.

CONCLUSION

In this chapter we have considered the spiral of professional development and the potential to raise standards of teaching through evidence-informed judgement. We have outlined the seven key characteristics of reflective teaching.

Some readers may well be wondering if this rather a lot to expect. How is the time to be found? Isn't it all 'common sense' anyway? Two broad responses may be made. First, it is certainly the case that constantly engaging in classroom enquiry and reflective activities of the sort described in this book would be impossible. The point, however, is to use them as *learning experiences* which are undertaken from time to time in a 'mindful' and purposive way. Such experiences should lead to conclusions which can be applied in more routine circumstances. This is how professional expertise is actively developed. Second, there is certainly a good deal of 'common sense' in the process of reflective teaching. However, when reflective teaching is used as a means of professional development it is extended far beyond this underpinning. The whole activity is much more rigorous – carefully gathered evidence replaces subjective impressions, open-mindedness replaces prior expectations, insights from reading or constructive and structured critique from colleagues challenge what might previously have been taken for granted. 'Common sense' may well endorse the value of the basic, reflective idea but, ironically, one outcome of reflection is often to produce critique and movement beyond the limitations of common-sense thinking. That, in a sense, is the whole point, the reason why reflection is a necessary part of professional activity. The aim of reflective practice is thus to support a shift from routine actions rooted in common-sense thinking to reflective action stemming from professional understanding and expertise.

> **Expert Questions**
>
> **Effectiveness:** *are there improvements in standards, in both basic skills and other areas of curricular attainment, to satisfy society's educational goals?*
>
> **Empowerment:** *is our pedagogic repertoire successful in enhancing wellbeing, learning disposition, capabilities and agency?*
>
> These questions contribute to a conceptual framework underpinning professional expertise (see Chapter 16).

In summary, evidence-informed reflection makes an important contribution throughout professional life. Novice teachers, such as those in initial teacher education, may use it to improve on specific and immediate practical teaching skills. Competent teachers, such as those who are newly qualified, may use reflection as a means of self-consciously increasing understanding and capability, thus moving towards a more complete level of professionalism. Expert teachers will work at a higher level, understanding the various issues concerning children, curriculum, classroom and school so well that many decisions become almost intuitive (see Chapter 16 and Eaude, 2012, Reading 16.3). However, greater depth of reflection is always possible, for example through further study at master's and doctoral level and beyond. Reflective activity thus can be seen as making a central contribution throughout a professional career.

> **Expert Question**
>
> **Reflection:** *is our classroom practice based on incremental, evidence-informed and collaborative improvement strategies?*
>
> This question contributes to a conceptual framework underpinning professional expertise (see Chapter 16).

reflectiveteaching.co.uk/rtps6/part1_ch3

CHAPTER WEBPAGE

reflectiveteaching.co.uk offers additional professional resources for this chapter. For the chapter webpage, go to: reflectiveteaching.co.uk/rtps6/part1_ch3

This chapter is all about 'classroom reflection' and it is a salutary experience to do a web search on that, or related, terms. You can immediately see just how far Dewey's basic proposition, of challenging routine thinking, has spread. And of course, the contemporary emphasis in education is that such reflection should be informed by evidence.

Chapter 3's chapter webpage offers a set of *Research Briefings* which are particularly strong on the use of evidence. They cover issues such as collaboration between teachers and researchers, evidence-based policy, how to assess the 'warrant' of research findings, and the characteristics of different types of research review or synthesis. These all derive from the *Teaching and Learning Research Programme*, which drew together researchers and practitioners in a decade-long programme of research.

As with other chapters, there are three levels of advice and information for follow up reading.

1 *Further Reading* is a general overview of sources, following the structure of this chapter. It is available on the chapter webpage.

2 *Key Readings*, below, picks out a shorter list for those with a bit less time but still with access to a library.

3 *Readings for Reflective Teaching in Schools*, the companion volume, provides short, edited extracts of particularly helpful texts, all within tidy covers and structured to match this book. Many of these, of relevance to this particular chapter, are indicated below.

KEY READINGS

The dilemmas in educational decision-making, which suggest that reflection is a continually necessary element of teaching, are analysed in:

> Kimbrough, K. (2015) *Classroom Dilemmas: Solutions for Everyday Problems*. Lanham, Maryland: Rowman and Littlefield.
> Berlak, A. and Berlak, H. (1981) *Dilemmas of Schooling*. London: Methuen.

On the potential gains from self-evaluation, classroom research and enquiry, see:

> Stenhouse, L. (1975) *An Introduction to Curriculum Research and Development*. London: Heinemann. (Reading 3.3)

A classic work by Dewey which has strongly influenced the development of reflective practice is:

Dewey, J. (1933) *How We Think: A Restatement of the Relation of Reflective Thinking to the Educative Process.* Chicago: Henry Regnery. (Reading 3.1)

For analyses on the nature of professional knowledge and its potential to enhance learning, see:

Schön, D.A. (1983) *The Reflective Practitioner: How Professionals Think in Action.* London: Temple Smith. (Reading 3.2)

Heilbronn, R. and Yandell, J. (2011) *Critical Practice in Teacher Education: A Study of Professional Learning.* London: UCL IOE Press. (Reading 3.6)

Timperley, H. (2011) *Realising the Power of Professional Learning.* Maidenhead: Open University Press. (Reading 16.6)

For an overview of different forms of research in education, including the contribution of school-based action research, see:

Pring, R. (2010) *Philosophy of Educational Research.* London: Continuum. (Reading 3.4)

For an in-depth overview of research methodology in education linked with researchers' projects, see:

Wyse, D., Selwyn, N., Smith, E. and Suter, L. (eds) (2017). The BERA/SAGE Handbook of Educational Research. London: SAGE.

More specific guidance on conducting classroom and school research is on **reflectiveteaching.co.uk** and includes:

Gilchrist, G. (2018) *Practitioner Enquiry. Professional Development with Impact for Teachers, Schools and Systems.* London: Routledge.

Wilson, E. (ed.) (2017) *School-based Research. A Guide for Education Students.* London: Sage.

Menter, I., Elliot, D., Hall, J., Hulme, M., Lewin, J. and Lowden, K. (2010) *A Guide to Practitioner Research in Education.* Maidenhead: Open University Press.

Mitchell, N. and Pearson, J. (2012) *Inquiring in the Classroom. Asking the Questions that Matter about Teaching and Learning.* London: Continuum.

The significance of learning and developing practice with colleagues is elaborated in:

Wenger, E. (1999) *Communities of Practice: Learning, Meaning and Identity.* Cambridge: Cambridge University Press. (see also Reading 3.7)

McLaughlin, C., Black-Hawkins, K., Brindley, S., McIntyre, D. and Taber, K. (2006) *Researching Schools: Stories from a Schools-University Partnership.* Maidenhead: Open University Press.

Sachs provides arguments for morally informed and socially aware teachers:

Sachs, J. (2003) *The Activist Teaching Profession.* Buckingham: Open University Press. (see also Readings 17.5 and 17.7)

Chapter 4
Principles
What are the foundations of effective teaching and learning?

Introduction	106
Evidence-informed principles	106

TLRP's principles	109
Education for life	109
Valued knowledge	111
Prior experience	113
Scaffolding understanding	114
Assessment for learning	115
Active engagement	118
Social relationships	119
Informal learning	120
Teacher learning	123
Policy frameworks	124
At school level	125
In the locality of the school	125

International knowledge accumulation	127

Conclusion	130

reflectiveteaching.co.uk/rtps6/part1_ch4

INTRODUCTION

This chapter is focused on ten 'evidence-informed educational principles' which have been specifically identified to support the development of teachers' professional judgement – and, indeed, as a contribution to education policy making. Whilst the previous chapter focused on the *process* of reflective teaching, this one highlights some of the *enduring issues* with which teaching and learning are concerned.

The ten principles were conceptualised by the UK's Teaching and Learning Research Programme (2000–2012) by reviewing the outcomes of its many research projects, consulting with UK practitioners in each major educational sector, and comparing these findings with other research from around the world (see James and Pollard, 2012b).

The TLRP funded educational research for over a decade and involved over 100 projects and other initiatives. It represented a new style of social science which insists on engagement of potential users throughout the research process (Pollard, 2007). TLRP project teams thus worked closely with teacher practitioners and, in some cases, with policymakers. TLRP identified major themes, such as learning, teaching, assessment etc., to analyse across its projects – and this process finally enabled the distillation of ten evidence-informed principles. They represent a holistic summary, prepared for application, of 'what we think we know' about effective teaching, learning and education.

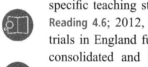

The same period has seen the development of meta-analyses of measured effects of specific teaching strategies. John Hattie's work has been groundbreaking (Hattie, 2009, Reading 4.6; 2012, Reading 16.5), and is complemented by a programme of randomised trials in England funded by the Education Endowment Foundation (EEF). This work is consolidated and presented to schools in the EEF Teaching and Learning Toolkit (educationendowmentfoundation.org.uk/toolkit). The Toolkit is particularly focused on disadvantaged pupils and the improvement of attainment through the use of specific teaching strategies.

When comparing TLRP's holistic principles with other studies that include effect sizes, they complement each other. It is vital to know which teaching strategies are likely to be most effective, and it is also essential to be able to interpret and understand teaching and learning processes, and to set them in the context of more wide-ranging educational purposes. We are thus developing, step by step, the means of really improving educational standards and life-chances for pupils. In the final part of the chapter we return to the theme of international knowledge accumulation.

Evidence-informed principles

Each of the ten principles which are described in this chapter has an extensive research base – they are 'evidence-informed'. They do not, however, seek to tell teachers what to do. Indeed, each principle is expressed at a level of generality which calls for contextual interpretation by a teacher in the light of their knowledge of the educational needs of pupils and the circumstances of the school in which they work. The principles are thus intended as a guide and support for teachers in making the professional judgements which they are uniquely positioned, and required, to make.

TLRP's approach promotes contextualised, evidence-informed teacher judgement. Other experts take similar positions:

> Bureaucratic solutions to problems of practice will always fail because effective teaching is not routine, students are not passive, and questions of practice are not simple, predictable, or standardised. Consequently, instructional decisions cannot be formulated on high then packaged and handed down to teachers. (Darling-Hammond, USA, 2007)

> TLRP 'insists that the articulation of evidence-informed pedagogic principles, which can inform teacher and policy-maker judgements rather than detailed instructional prescriptions that tell teachers what to do, is the most useful way to improve classroom practice at scale'. This is surely right: teaching and learning are deeply contextual and highly contingent. Certainly our experience in Singapore strongly supports this claim, particularly if backed up by contextually appropriate, iterative, authentic and extended professional learning experiences. (Hogan, Singapore, 2012, p. 97)

> The Teaching and Learning Toolkit will be most useful when in the hands of professionals. The aim of the Toolkit is to support teachers to make their own informed choices and adopt a more 'evidence-based' approach. The evidence it contains is a supplement to rather than a substitute for professional judgement; it provides no guaranteed solutions or quick fixes. (Higgins et al., 2013)

TLRP's ten principles are an attempt to pick out prominent patterns from the complexity of teaching and learning, and to shed light on them. They are statements of what we think we understand, at this point in time. The evidence-informed principles offer reference points, thus making it easier to take stock and review progress in educationally sound ways. But when particular classroom dilemmas arise, the principles will not actually determine a specific decision, for that is the job of the reflective teacher.

Our overarching guide is Principle 1, which is concerned with the most enduring objectives and moral purposes of education. A cluster of principles on curriculum, pedagogy and assessment then takes us to the heart of teacher expertise, whilst a further group highlights the personal and social processes which underpin learning. Finally, two principles draw attention to enabling conditions for success in practice and policy.

In the following section, we introduce and illustrate the ten principles as a whole. Issues associated with each principle are also discussed and elaborated in relevant chapters of the book (as indicated in Figure 4.1), and we return synoptically to them in new ways in Chapter 16 when reviewing the various dimensions of teacher expertise.

Figure 4.1 represents the ten principles holistically.

> ## Expert Question
>
> ***Principle:*** *is our pedagogy consistent with established principles for effective teaching and learning?*
>
> This question contributes to a conceptual framework underpinning professional expertise (see Chapter 16).

reflectiveteaching.co.uk/rtps6/part1_ch4

Effective teaching and learning

Figure 4.1 Ten evidence-informed educational principles for effective teaching and learning

TLRP'S PRINCIPLES

Education for life

Commitment to broad educational objectives has existed for a very long time in the UK and Republic of Ireland. For example, the general requirements of Section 78 of the Education Act 2002 state that a maintained school in England or Wales must offer:

A balanced and broadly based curriculum which promotes the spiritual, moral, cultural, mental and physical development of pupils at the school and of society, and prepares pupils at the school for the opportunities, responsibilities and experiences of later life.

Similar statements apply in Scotland and Northern Ireland. However, despite such affirmation, goals of this type have been historically vulnerable to erosion by the narrowing effects of high-stakes assessment and accountability.

TLRP also embraced a wide definition of educational values and purposes. The importance of attainments as measured by national tests and qualifications was recognised, but there was also interest in other outcomes. These included learner engagement, participation, skills, dispositions and the development of learning identities and autonomy. Such outcomes have the potential to contribute to a wide range of educational aims including those linked to economic productivity, social cohesion, cultural development, personal fulfilment and environmental sustainability. These are all important in a contemporary developed society.

The UK's long-standing commitment to broad, rich and inclusive forms of education thus gave rise to the first of TLRP's ten principles.

Principle 1: Effective teaching equips learners for life in its broadest sense.

Learning should aim to help individuals and groups to develop the intellectual, personal and social resources that will enable them to participate as active citizens, contribute to economic development and flourish as individuals in a diverse and changing society. This means adopting a broad conception of worthwhile learning outcomes and taking seriously issues of equity and social justice for all.

TLRP worked with the Philosophy of Education Society of Great Britain to examine the way in which this principle might inform policy and, by extension, practice. The philosophers argued that empirical evidence is not sufficient for decision-making in policy or practice, for it is always complemented by values. For example, Bridges suggested:

We should be more explicit about the educational and wider political values which frame policy and practice, and be more ready to subject these to careful scholarly, as well as democratic, scrutiny and criticism. (2009, p. 3)

There are many examples of the influence of values in policy making at the highest level. For example, consider the speech made by England's Secretary of State for Education, Michael Gove, when moving the second reading of the 2011 Education Bill in the Westminster Parliament:

reflectiveteaching.co.uk/rtps6/part1_ch4

> This Bill provides an historic opportunity for this country. It will help to guarantee every child a high quality education, which will equip them for the technological, economic, social and cultural challenges of the next century. Throughout history, the opportunities we give to our young people have far too often been a matter of time and chance. Accidents of birth or geography have determined children's fate, but education can change all that. Education allows each of us to become the author of our own life story. Instead of going down a path determined for us by external constraints, it allows each of us to shape our lives and the communities around us for the better.
> (Hansard, 8 February 2011)

A strong commitment to opportunity is espoused, but such rhetoric has to be reconciled with the realities of the academies programme in England, which the bill was designed to promote.

reflectiveteaching.co.uk features a video on this principle: Teaching should equip learners for life.

Research conducted by the Education Policy Institute (EPI) and London School of Economics (LSE) (Andrews et al., 2017) looked at the impacts of academies on educational outcomes in secondary schools, across the phases of 'academisation' and variety of forms it has taken. The findings identified considerable variety of impact on attainment, concluding that academies have not provided 'a panacea' (p. 7) for school improvement and that close attention is needed to the actual quality of provision within schools, rather than looking only at schooling structures as influencing students' life chances. As in all walks of life, the relationship between espoused goals and actual consequences has to take account of relevant evidence.

Vision and values are arguably even more important at other levels of the education system. When they engage with pupils, teachers can, without doubt, change lives – as we discussed in Chapter 1 of this book (see Gu, 2007, Reading 1.1). Qualitative sociologists have demonstrated how learners perceive and make sense of their school experiences. For example, one series of projects tracked two cohorts of children from age 4 to age 16 (Pollard and Filer, 1999, Reading 1.2). That work recorded how pupils progressively develop strategies to cope with the challenges of schooling over time, and how secure forms of learning become embedded in personal narratives and identities. It suggested that where school curricula fail to make meaningful connections with the learner, pupil performance and capability are likely to be shallow and transitory. Similar ideas were reflected in other TLRP projects. A developed example was provided by a study of further education experiences – *Transforming Learning Cultures* (James and Biesta, 2007) – which recognised the way in which institutional conditions enable or constrain opportunities for independent learning. Another was that of Crozier, Reay and Clayton (2010), who analysed disjunctions in the experiences of working-class students entering higher education. However, the analysis was developed most thoroughly by the *Learning Lives* project (Biesta et al., 2010), which studied learners across the lifecourse using a combination of evidence from a large-scale cohort study and case study interviews reviewing learning careers over time. This study was important for its lifelong reach and demonstration of the durability of attitudes deriving from early school experiences. In particular, it reported how narratives about learning and educational experiences are used as frameworks of interpretation in the development of identity, self-confidence and agency in later life. Other quantitative studies reinforce this analysis to demonstrate the 'wider benefits' of learning (Feinstein et al., 2008b, Reading 1.6).

Education, in other words, makes an enormous difference to the people we become. Teachers, have a unique privilege and responsibility to shape the next generation. That is why this principle of 'education for life' is so important. Teaching has moral purpose.

Reflective Activity 4.1

Aim: To reflect on the moral purposes of education in relation to learner development.

Evidence and reflection: Typically, this issue has particular resonance when applied to people who we know well – parents, partners or even ourselves. Think deeply about a person whose early upbringing and school education you know something about. How did those experiences influence the person they became? Can you see traces of adult qualities in those earlier experiences, or even identify patterns of development? Were there any particular critical incidents which made a difference in the life you are considering? Were there relationships of particular significance? Thinking of teachers, what specific memories arise? How would you summarise this review, in relation to the first TLRP Principle?

Extension: The next step is clearly to imagine the trajectories through life of some of the children and young people whom you teach. Consider the potential lifelong consequences of day-by-day experiences at school.

Valued knowledge

Principle 2: Effective teaching and learning engages with valued forms of knowledge. Teaching and learning should engage with the big ideas, facts, processes, language and narratives of subjects so that learners understand what constitutes quality and standards in particular disciplines.

There has always been debate about what a curriculum should consist of, how it should be organised, what constitutes valued knowledge in a subject or field, how such knowledge can be represented and communicated to learners, and how learners' knowledge, understanding and skills can be identified and evaluated (see Chapter 9). Such debates reflect the priorities in our culture and the capacity of particular stakeholders to promote their views. Analysts of such processes characterise the curriculum as a contested, social construction, with any particular settlement being influenced by the balance of power of the time. The early work of Young (1971) and Bernstein (1971) established this approach, and the history of UK curriculum 'reform' demonstrates the significance of the perspective.

However, from a different direction, the development of curricula has also involved philosophers, cognitive psychologists, subject specialists, curriculum developers and assessment experts – many of whom bring a far greater awareness of the distinctive character of particular bodies of knowledge. England's National Curriculum Review recognised that such experts bring: 'a view of disciplinary knowledge as a distinct way of investigating, knowing and making sense with particular foci, procedures and theories, reflecting both cumulative understanding and powerful ways of engaging with the future' (DfE, 2011a, p. 24). In this sense, disciplinary knowledge offers core foundations for education, from which the subjects of the curriculum are derived' (DfE, 2011a, footnote 58, p. 24). This perspective is also reflected in the *Early Career Framework* for teachers in England (DfE, 2019a). Interestingly, the later work of Young (2008, Reading 9.2) has contributed significantly to the commitment to 'bring knowledge back in', and a considerable amount of other work has developed in relation to Young's ideas and others' (e.g. the special issue of the curriculum journal that was also published in book form: Wyse, Hayward, Higgins and Livingston, 2014).

But the level at which the curriculum is applied is the domain of practising teachers, for it is they who put the 'curriculum into action' (Stenhouse, 1975, Reading 3.3). In the UK, it is common to think of curriculum 'elements' such as knowledge, concepts, skills and attitudes (Her Majesty's Inspectors, 1985), and a commitment to learning skills as well as content is firmly established. Skills depend on content. Indeed, some curricular innovations promote a particular emphasis on skills or competencies (e.g. the Royal Society of Arts (RSA)'s *Opening Minds*, 2013 or Claxton's *Building Learning Power*, 2011). In balancing these elements, Ryle's classic distinction between 'knowing that' and 'knowing how' (1945) has been particularly influential. Teachers know that both knowledge and skills are vital.

Building on the work of Polanyi (1962), Eraut's contribution to TLRP (2007) also argued for the significance of 'personal knowledge'. This type of knowledge foregrounds understanding and skills acquired during acculturation, social interaction and reflection on experience. Eraut argued that: 'A person's performance nearly always uses these kinds of knowledge in some integrated form, and is influenced by both context and feelings.' Such informal ways of 'making sense' have considerable significance for understanding and misunderstanding in schools. We will consider informal learning again in discussion of Principle 8.

TLRP's emphasis on 'valued forms of knowledge' has been described as 'an immensely important principle' by a leading educationalist in the Asia–Pacific region – David Hogan. However, work in Singapore has:

> focused a lot more analytical attention on the intellectual quality of the instructional and assessment tasks that students are asked to work on, and the extent to which the knowledge practices they engage in are informed by, and are consistent with, domain specific forms of disciplinary knowledge and epistemic norms. (Hogan, 2012, p. 103)

Hogan argues that the most important single factor in determining the quality of teaching, learning and outcomes lies in the nature of instructional tasks (see also Reading 4.2). Hattie's meta-analysis of global research makes the same point: 'what teachers *get students to do* in the class is the strongest component of the accomplished teacher's repertoire, rather than what the teacher specifically does' (2009, p. 35, Reading 4.6; also 2012, Reading 16.5).

Subject knowledge is undoubtedly of enormous significance in teacher effectiveness (see Chapter 9). This is one reason why 'lesson study' has become so well established in the Far East and why similarly focused approaches are developing rapidly around the world (see Chapter 10, Section 5.2).

Prior experience

Principle 3: Effective pedagogy recognises the importance of prior experience and learning. Pedagogy should take account of what the learner knows already in order for them, and those who support their learning, to plan their next steps. This includes building on prior learning but also taking account of the personal and cultural experiences of different groups of learners.

Whilst the nature of knowledge to be learned is important, few people now think that children arrive at school as 'empty vessels' to be filled. The principle of starting where children are and helping them to move on is widely recognised. The scientific foundation of this principle lies in the practical philosophy of Dewey, the constructivist psychology of Piaget and the socio-cultural perspectives of Vygotsky (see Chapter 2 and Readings 2.2 and 2.3). International evidence is also very extensive, including from synoptic reviews by the American Psychological Association (1997) and by European researchers (Dochy, Segers and Buehl, 1999). A famous quote by Ausubel put this clearly:

reflectiveteaching.co.uk features a video on this principle: Teaching should build on prior experience.

> If I had to reduce all of educational psychology to just one principle, I would say this: 'The most important single factor affecting learning is what the learner already knows. Ascertain this, and teach him accordingly.' (1968, p. vi)

One reason for affirming the importance of prior learning is cognitive, and has been demonstrated in subjects such as science where early misconceptions create barriers to later learning. Such misunderstandings need to be identified and addressed. One TLRP project developed and evaluated sequences for teaching science concepts and complemented this with banks of diagnostic questions to identify misconceptions (Millar et al., 2006). The researchers found that carefully designed probes can illuminate pupils' understanding of key concepts, and can thus inform judgements about 'next steps' in teaching. They also found that the level of pupils' understanding of many fundamental science ideas increases only slowly with age, so that pitching an appropriate level of challenge is essential. Of course, work of this sort influences the sequencing of content knowledge within national curricula.

A second rationale for focusing on prior learning is concerned with motivation and providing appropriate opportunities to learn. Here, it is essential to take account of the knowledge, understandings, skills and attitudes derived from the other worlds that pupils inhabit: from their homes, communities and peer groups. For example, a number of TLRP projects, ranging between those working with young children to others concerned with further and higher education, found benefits in teachers making more deliberate and positive use of the informal knowledge and understanding that children and young people acquire.

However, because of the extent of social inequality and difference within the UK (see Chapter 5), children and young people have extremely variable experience before and during their schooling. For some, there are continuities between home and school, whilst for others there are disjunctions. This has great significance for teaching and learning, and in building identities. This aspect of effective pedagogy will be revisited in discussion of Principles 7 and 8 on personal and social processes and relationships.

Whatever the merits of the case, with large classes it can be difficult to determine each pupil's prior knowledge, although school policies can help to encourage teachers' understanding of children's backgrounds including their interests and prior learning. Some barriers to learning undoubtedly stem from teachers' misplaced assumptions about pupils. However difficult, expert teachers are committed to seeking to understand learners so that appropriate starting points are identified. In summary, understanding pupils' prior experience from previous teaching and learning, from home and from their communities is difficult, but can significantly improve teacher judgements and thereby enhance pupils' confidence in learning.

Scaffolding understanding

Principle 4: Effective pedagogy requires learning to be scaffolded. Teachers, trainers and all those, including peers, who support the learning of others, should provide activities and structures of intellectual, social and emotional support to help learners to move forward in their learning. When these supports are removed the learning needs to be secure.

Scaffolding in teaching can be compared to building work; scaffolding creates a structure to support the construction activities as the house (or the learner's understanding) is being built. A scaffold does not bear any of the weight of the building, but it enables the builders to get the right resources to the level that the building is at. The idea was implicit in Vygotsky's work but was taken further in a classic paper by Wood, Bruner and Ross (1976; see also Tharp and Gallimore, 1988, Reading 11.4). An aspect of the work by Wood et al. that sometimes gets neglected is the idea that scaffolding should be removed as soon as the child is ready to learn independently. This can perhaps be linked with Vygotsky's idea of the Zone of Proximal Development (ZPD). Vygotsky's conception of learning also emphasises the importance of active choice and use of cultural tools, especially language, in learning. The role of the 'more expert other' in helping the novice to make progress beyond the level of their present understanding is equally crucial (see discussion of the zone of proximal development in Chapter 2). When these two elements are brought together, the pertinence of the concept of scaffolding becomes evident.

A major contribution to such scaffolding derives from teachers' understanding of both curricular knowledge and of how children and young people learn. They thus recognise when they should intervene to help the pupil move on to a higher level of understanding.

It is also worth drawing attention to the fact that TLRP's principle picks out provision of 'intellectual, social *and* emotional support'. It does this because discussion of these issues tends to focus on cognitive forms of scaffolding alone. However, the TLRP proposition is that social and emotional factors are also important, such as those associated with social expectations and feelings of personal security for example (see Immordino-Yang and Damasio, 2007, Reading 6.2). Because learning is intrinsically personal, intellectual progress is enabled or constrained by such factors and reflective teachers will consider how to provide for each of the three dimensions (see rows 3.1, 3.2 and 3.3 of the conceptual framework in Chapter 16, and discussion of Maslow in Chapter 1).

A crucial contribution to scaffolded learning derives from dialogue between teacher and learners, and through the feedback loops that this makes possible. To be effective, teacher support must be carefully matched to the current understanding or capabilities of the learner and must thus be informed by feedback from the student. As Hattie puts it, there should be explicit 'visibility' in the teaching–learning process.

reflectiveteaching.co.uk features a video on this principle: Teachers should scaffold learning with appropriate tools.

> The teacher must know when learning is correct or incorrect; learn when to experiment and learn from the experience; learn to monitor, seek and give feedback; and know to try alternative learning strategies when others do not work. . . . It is most important that teaching is visible to the student, and that learning is visible to the teacher. The more the student becomes the teacher and the more the teacher becomes the student, then the more successful are the outcomes. (Hattie, 2009, p. 25)

Dialogue is the most practical way of creating such visibility. The dialogic approach proposed by Alexander (2006, Reading 12.3) comprises a three-part repertoire informed by dialogic principles (see also Chapters 11 and 12). The repertoire consists of 'learning talk' (narrating, explaining, questioning, answering, analysing, speculating, imagining, exploring, evaluating, discussing, arguing, justifying and negotiating), 'teaching talk' (rote, recitation, exposition, discussion, dialogue) and 'interactive strategies' (whole-class teaching, teacher-led group work, pupil-led group work, one-to-one pupil discussion, one-to-one discussion between pupil and teacher). The principles that inform this repertoire are that genuine dialogue is collective, reciprocal, supportive, cumulative and purposeful. According to Alexander, the most vital of these is cumulation: that teachers and pupils build on their own and each other's ideas and chain them into coherent lines of thinking and enquiry.

The expert teacher facilitates, focuses, listens, analyses, contributes *and* teaches. This brings us to the role which assessment can play in learning.

Assessment for learning

Principle 5: Effective pedagogy needs assessment to be congruent with learning. Assessment should be designed and implemented with the goal of achieving maximum validity both in terms of learning outcomes and learning processes. It should help to advance learning as well as determine whether learning has occurred.

TLRPs *Learning How to Learn* project (James et al., 2007, Reading 2.8, **Research Briefing 13.1** on p. 436) elaborated the highly influential proposition that assessment should be used to 'advance learning' as well as measure it. The project built on work by the UK Assessment Reform Group which demonstrated that 'assessment for learning' practices can lead to improved learning and achievement (Black and Wiliam, 1998b; Black et al., 2003). The project found that four clusters of practices were necessary to support such learning, all of which are based on dialogue. They are: developing classroom talk and questioning to elicit understanding; giving appropriate feedback; sharing criteria of quality; and peer- and self-assessment (which incorporate elements of the three previous clusters). These assessment practices helped teachers to promote 'learning how to learn', which in turn enabled pupils to become more autonomous learners. The project found that classroom practice thus becomes better aligned with the educational values expressed by teachers, and less driven by a culture of performativity. Chapter 13 picks up on this analysis, when guiding principles and practical implications are discussed at length.

reflectiveteaching.co.uk
features a video on this principle: Assessment should support learning.

However, changes in practice are not easy to establish and the project demonstrated that, although advice on specific techniques is useful in the short term, longer-term development and sustainability depends on re-evaluating beliefs about learning, reviewing the way learning activities are structured, and rethinking classroom roles and relationships.

A related element of Principle 5 – 'Assessment should be designed and implemented with the goal of achieving maximum validity both in terms of learning outcomes and learning processes' – was addressed by other projects and thematic initiatives. Traditionally, the quality of assessments is judged by their reliability and their validity, which together indicate whether the inferences drawn from assessment results are dependable (see Chapter 14, Broadfoot, 2007, Reading 14.1). Often more attention is paid to reliability for two reasons. First, there are clear technical procedures for enhancing reliability. Second, the publication of unreliable results can have immediate and far-reaching political and personal consequences where data is used for accountability purposes. However, there is a sense in which even reliable assessment results have no worth if they are not valid – if they do not represent authentic learning.

One of TLRP's associated projects (Filer and Pollard, 2000, Reading 14.7) focused on assessment encounters from a sociological point of view. Children and young people develop their identities through successive experiences as they move through schooling, and experiences of assessment are shown to be among the most powerful of these. Assessment can thus be seen as a social process with significant consequences. Indeed, pupil performance is strongly influenced by the contexts and circumstances in which assessments take place, and results take meaning from social and cultural interpretation. If learners' sense of agency and identity is to be nurtured, the case for maintaining the validity of both assessment events and the inferences drawn from them is therefore overwhelming. But this is not easy to do when assessment data are also used as an indicator of school performance.

These problems occur wherever high-stakes assessment exists. For example, Singapore has testing at the end of primary school (Year 6), the end of secondary school (Year 10) and the end of Year 12. As Hogan explains:

By virtue of the tight nexus between social mobility patterns and national high stakes assessments, and the commitment of the government to 'meritocratic' sorting and allocation through national high stakes assessments, reliability remains the over-riding issue for parents and the government. This constrains the ability of the system to develop assessments that have greater authenticity and validity. At the same time, the character and logic of classroom instruction is directly shaped by national high stakes assessment – in Singapore, as they do elsewhere, teachers teach to the test. . . . In effect, although it places a floor on student learning, the national high stakes assessment system in Singapore places a ceiling on it as well. (2012, p. 105, **Reading 4.2**)

At the heart of the matter are concerns about fitness for purpose, and TLRP contested the common view that a single set of assessments could serve several purposes without distorting one purpose or another (Mansell and James, 2009, **Reading 14.5**). Above all, it was argued that assessment systems must be congruent with the overarching purpose of education systems to advance learning.

'Assessment should help advance learning as well as determine whether learning has taken place,' says TLRP's principle. This may sound obvious, but many teachers know that assessment requirements can militate against good learning. When staff end up 'teaching to the test' rather than teaching to the principles to which they are professionally committed, something is not right. An example of this can be seen in the Phonics Screening Check in England. This was designed as a diagnostic check of a child's knowledge of letters and sounds and consists of a series of real and pseudo words (these are phonetically plausible, but not real words with meaning). The check can inform a teacher, to some degree, of which letters and sounds a child is familiar with, and which letters or combinations of letters they have yet to learn. When it is used to evaluate how successful a class or school is at teaching reading it can lead to children being taught to read non-words and practising this skill, which may detract from developing fluent comprehension of what is being read and has an opportunity cost in terms of other learning activities.

Reflective Activity 4.2

Aim: To review TLRP's principles on knowledge, prior learning, pedagogy and assessment (see pp. 109–17).

Evidence and reflection: This cluster of four principles represents enduring issues in teaching – the interaction of knowledge and development, and the crucial instructional and feedback roles of the teacher. Tracing the linkages between these elements and applying them in and through practice is enough to fascinate and challenge most of us throughout our careers in teaching. One way of formalising that is to review each of the four sections above and pick out from each one or two key points which are most meaningful to you. How do your key points relate together? What might they mean for your practice?

Extension: If possible, compare your selection with the judgements of a colleague and discuss inter-relationships across the principles. Does such comparison enable you to better understand your own teaching? Are there skills or processes on which you and our colleague could work together in developing your expertise?

---

reflectiveteaching.co.uk/rtps6/part1_ch4

Active engagement

Principle 6: Effective pedagogy promotes the active engagement of the learner.
A chief goal of teaching and learning should be the promotion of learners' independence and autonomy. This involves acquiring a repertoire of learning strategies and practices, developing positive learning dispositions, and having the will and confidence to become agents in their own learning.

Almost all TLRP research projects affirmed the importance of developing active engagement, positive learning dispositions, self-confidence and learning awareness (see also Chapter 2, p. 65). Indeed, the programme developed in an era characterised within much of the UK by central control over curriculum, pedagogy and assessment, so that the motivation and engagement of under-performing learners had become an increasingly pressing contemporary issue. It remains a difficult judgement to ensure that national requirements provide enough guidance to ensure entitlements whilst also providing sufficient scope and support for teachers to respond to needs of the particular pupils for whom they are responsible (see Chapter 9). Concern for the quality of learning experiences is a further driver of this concern with active engagement.

reflectiveteaching.co.uk features a video on this principle: Learning should involve and engage the learner.

However, the most pragmatic reason for emphasising active engagement is simply that it is essential for learning. As we saw earlier, and in Chapter 3, Piaget's constructivist psychology emphasised processes of accommodation and assimilation through which learning takes place, and the example of Armstrong's work (1980) highlights the 'appropriation' of knowledge. Socio-cultural analysts envisage a learner whose capability and confidence are greatly influenced by others, and who develops independent agency and meaning within networks of social relationships. This capacity to sustain active engagement in purposive ways is encapsulated in Guy Claxton's conception of 'building learning power' through resilience, resourcefulness, reflection and reciprocity (2011, see also Reading 2.9 and the discussion in Chapter 9, p. 288).

More traditionally, psychological questions concerning the active engagement of learners have been framed in terms of motivation, with emphasis being placed on ways of involving individual learners in particular tasks. The work of Carol Dweck for instance, on 'mastery' and 'learned helplessness' as orientations to new learning challenges, has been very influential (1986, Chapter 3, p. 57, Reading 2.6). Her work has included approaches such as the development of a 'growth mindset', which has been both influential and controversial (Yeager and Dweck, 2020). The promotion of learner independence and autonomy has thus been seen as essential to the effectiveness of learning. For example, the EEF **Toolkit Evidence 2.1** on metacognition and self-regulated learning synthesises international studies and clearly demonstrates their importance.

In a commentary on TLRP's ten principles, Allal (2012) highlighted the ways in which this principle of active engagement links back to the scaffolding of understanding. In particular, she argued that this requires what she termed 'co-regulation':

> Scaffolding is a process that is elaborated on the basis of what the learner does and says (given his or her current developmental level), rather than a pre-existing support structure

that an expert prepares, introduces and later withdraws. The elaboration of scaffolding cannot take place without the active engagement of the learner. (2012, p. 65)

There is a resonance here with Hattie's call for 'visible' teaching and learning (2009, Reading 4.6) and with Alexander's emphasis on dialogue (2008b, Reading 12.3). They each make the point that the guidance provided by teacher scaffolding can only be accurately deployed and taken up except through the active engagement of the learner. In this way, and many more, TLRP Principles are interconnected.

Nor indeed, should we forget that when pupils are positively engaged in learning activities, behavioural problems tend to be very minor. We explore this more fully in Chapter 7.

Social relationships

Principle 7: Effective pedagogy fosters both individual and social processes and outcomes. Learners should be encouraged and helped to build relationships and communication with others for learning purposes, in order to assist the mutual construction of knowledge and enhance the achievements of individuals and groups. Consulting learners about their learning and giving them a voice is both an expectation and a right.

Learning is a social as well as an individual activity. It flourishes through interaction with other minds, when the conditions are right. Good teacher–pupil classroom relationships underpin such conditions. Or, to put it another way, teacher–pupil respect is the foundation of discipline, order *and* learning (see Chapters 6 and 7). More broadly, some TLRP projects used the concept of social capital (Putnam, 1995) to analyse available opportunities, whilst noting the formative role that school and classroom processes and peer relations can play in such accumulation. Social processes, at many levels, create conditions for individual learning.

TLRP's studies on group work (Baines, Blatchford and Kutnick, 2017), teacher learning (James et al., 2007) and inclusion (Ainscow, Booth and Dyson 2006), among others, show that when schools function as genuine learning communities, students and teachers thrive both collectively and as individuals. For example, pupils who worked effectively in groups also did measurably better on individual exams than those who had other forms of teaching and learning. The SPRinG (Social Pedagogic Research into Group-work) and Scottish SPRinG projects found that, in Key Stages 2 and 3, children who worked effectively together made gains in their inferential thinking and their higher cognitive understanding (see **Research Briefing 11.1** on p. 370). Group work also improved social relationships among pupils and between pupils and teachers.

reflectiveteaching.co.uk features a video on this principle: Social relationships are vital to learning.

Going further, Principle 7 suggests that 'consulting learners is both an expectation and a right'. In parallel with psychological research on pupil agency and learning, this reflects the humanistic tradition in British education drawing on the practitioner enquiry movement initiated by Stenhouse (1975, Reading 3.3). TLRP's network on *Consulting Pupils about*

Teaching and Learning was a manifestation of this commitment to practical theorising and improvement. The network directly engaged teachers, children and young people in reflection on their classroom practices and school experiences (Rudduck and McIntyre, 2007, Reading 1.3, see **Research Briefing 1.2**, p. 36). Indirectly, it connected with thousands more pupils in building from the UN Convention on the Rights of the Child (United Nations, 1989, see also Reading 17.6) to affirming the quality and constructive nature of feedback about teaching and learning that pupils were able to offer. Outcomes included enhanced commitment to learning and improved teacher–pupil relationships. Pupils were more likely to be engaged with schooling when they were consulted and their views treated with respect.

Here, then, we see the social awareness of a significant cluster of TLRP projects, and their attention to the construction of pupil meaning in relation to circumstances. It also concerns the realisation of rights, formation as a person, manifestation of citizenship and, ultimately, the contribution of individuals to history.

At its core though, consulting pupils strengthens their engagement with learning, gives teachers deeper insights into pupils' abilities and learning preferences and strengthens school policy and planning. Giving pupils a 'good listening to' challenges old habits.

Informal learning

Principle 8: Effective pedagogy recognises the significance of informal learning.
Informal learning, such as learning out of school or away from the workplace, should be recognised as at least as significant as formal learning and should therefore be valued and appropriately utilised in formal processes.

This principle can be stated simply, but has profound implications and challenges. Recognition of the social and cultural dimensions of learning in many TLRP projects produced a heightened awareness of learners, relationships and contexts (see also Chapter 2, p. 63). Over several years, researchers struggled with how to study, analyse and represent the learning that took place beyond formal educational settings.

UK Governments have recognised the significance of social context in relation to children and young people. For example, in England from 2003, the *Every Child Matters* agenda and integration of national health, social and educational provision into Children's Services across the whole country were evidence of holistic analysis and of attempts to promote inclusion through the coordination of services.

TLRP's own work in these areas was at rather different levels, whether in workplace, university or school education. Regarding school education, two areas of research stand out – home–school relationships and the influence of new technologies.

The *Home–School Knowledge Exchange* project (see Hughes and Pollard, 2000, **Research Briefing 4.1**, p. 136) investigated how the home and school environments for learning might complement each other. Focusing upon literacy and numeracy in these two worlds, the team helped teachers, parents and children to find new ways of exchanging knowledge between home and primary school, using videos, photographs, shoeboxes of artefacts etc. For example, primary pupils took photos to show the maths and literacy activities they were doing at home. Maths activities included cooking, shopping, playing board games, setting timers and consulting timetables. Children were also asked to collect a 'shoebox' of artefacts from home, *All About Me*, which offered teachers and other pupils insights into their interests and opportunities. The project team then investigated how this process of knowledge exchange could enhance learning and ease the transition to secondary school.

Explicit home–school knowledge exchange activities improved outcomes in the project schools, but this was mediated by social class, gender and attainment – factors that underline the importance of considering the character of informal learning with sensitivity in order to avoid negative consequences for particular groups of pupils (Thomas and Pattison, 2007, Reading 2.10).

The TLRP project on how to *enhance* home–school knowledge exchange complements international evidence (e.g. Jeynes, 2018, and see **Toolkit Evidence 4.1** from the Education Endowment Foundation on p. 135). As is explained there: 'Although parental involvement is consistently associated with pupils' success at school, the evidence about how to *increase* involvement to *improve* attainment is much less conclusive, particularly for disadvantaged families.'

TLRP's work on technology began with a project on the integration of ICT into everyday classroom practices. The *InterActive Education* project (Sutherland, Robertson and John, 2009) worked with primary and secondary school teachers to study how subject-knowledge could be used in teaching through the use of new technologies (see **Research Briefing 8.1** on p. 263). The use of mobile and other forms of technology is now so pervasive and so embedded within the cultures of children and young people that it provides a very strong illustration of the knowledge and experiential resources that exist beyond formal educational settings (Burnett and Merchant, 2020; Kress, 2010, Reading, 8.6). Access and knowledge are uneven, however, making the affordances of mobile devices difficult to harness in schools. The project found that technology could be particularly effective at enhancing subject knowledge when teachers were able to bridge between the idiosyncratic and the intended curricular learning using tailored software. The software was seen, in socio-cultural terms, as a mediating tool in support of the teaching–learning process (see also Mercer, Hennessy and Warwick, 2019).

Reflecting back on the project, Robertson and Dale (2009) write that there is a

> tendency to view schools as islands, loosely connected to society. . . . What young people learn in other places and spaces has little currency in the classroom . . . and . . . schools are represented as enduring features of the landscape, immune to change'.
> (p. 155)

They suggest that schools reflect an 'assemblage' of social relations, assumptions and organisational arrangements with significant effects on pupils, teachers, parents and others. Change, they suggest, is inevitable, as the impact of new technology and of learning beyond school accumulates. Their book concludes:

Maybe it is time to consider young people's out-of-school knowledge and cultures not as 'distractions' from the main business of schooling, but as rich, complex, diverse and powerful sources for learning and as an important place to start in designing education for the twenty-first century. (p. 176)

There is a significant resonance here with our earlier discussion of the metaphor of 'learning as participation' (see Chapter 2, p. 63).

The challenge with digital technologies is that new forms of technology are emerging all the time and influencing the way we work, learn, interact and socialise with each other across the whole of society. The global pandemic has forced change on education through distance learning technologies in ways which could not have been predicted. It has also highlighted the challenge of access to technology and equity in access to learning. As this chapter is being written it is hard to predict which changes will become embedded in schools and where practices in schools will return to previous norms. What we can learn from the history of digital technologies (Higgins, Xiao and Katsipataki, 2012) is that it is important to look beyond the technology and the activity surround it to the learning that is being supported (or not).

Reflective Activity 4.3

Aim: To review TLRP's principles on engagement, relationships and informal learning (see pp. 123–27).

Evidence and reflection: This group of principles concerns how teaching makes *connections* with the learner. Emphasising the construction of meaning, they acknowledge personal and social influences on children and young people in schools and beyond – as realised through both formal and informal learning processes. Once again, these are enduring issues – they are forever with us.

However, such principles imply wide-ranging awareness on the part of teachers, and speak to recognition of the 'participation metaphor' of learning as well as that of 'acquisition' (see Chapter 2, p. 62). How far do you feel that the role of the teacher can, or should, embrace such issues? Traditionally, the formal teacher role has been defined narrowly – though many teachers have stepped beyond this, sometimes routinely. How though, do you see the role today, and in the future?

Discuss the issues with colleagues. How can teaching and learning in school contribute to and draw on the learning which takes place beyond school? How can we, as teachers, make better connections with the frameworks of meaning and relationship which are of particular importance to the children and young people in our classrooms?

Extension: An excellent development of this activity would be to explore the issues directly through discussion with selected pupils or even with parents or other stakeholders in the community. How do learners' lives, as a whole, relate to experiences in and benefits from schooling?

Teacher learning

Principle 9: Effective pedagogy depends on the learning of all those who support the learning of others. The need for lecturers, teachers, trainers and co-workers to learn continuously in order to develop their knowledge and skill, and to adapt and develop their roles, especially through practice-based inquiry, should be recognised and supported.

This principle provides the rationale for this book as a whole – we need to be reflective, and thus commit to our own learning, because this enhances our effectiveness in supporting pupils.

Teacher learning is concerned with both what we do *and* how we think (see Wiliam, 2009, Reading 16.4). Put another way, the most effective forms of teaching depend not only on behavioural change and the acquisition of new knowledge about pedagogy, but also on the development of values and understanding. With the right school leadership and support, such learning is particularly effective in the workplace and through participation in collaborative activities with other teachers (see Chapters 3 and 16, in particular).

These conclusions began to emerge early in the life of TLRP. A summary of common themes by Mary James suggested:

1 Learning involves the acquisition of knowledge and skills *and* participation in social processes. Thus the development of supportive professional cultures is vitally important. Within schools, especially secondary schools, the focus is often the department or team. However, the very cohesion of these groups can create insularity and inhibit change. Rich and dynamic learning environments need to provide opportunities for boundary crossings, and to encourage learning from others in different communities of practice (see Chapter 3, p. 100).

2 Teachers are most ready to accept ideas for change if they resonate with their existing or previous beliefs and experience. However, this does not necessarily make them 'right' or appropriate. Teachers need to develop knowledge and skills to evaluate evidence and the confidence to challenge taken-for-granted assumptions, including their own. This is difficult (see Hargreaves, 2007, Reading 16.2) and it is often helpful to involve outsiders, perhaps researchers from universities or visiting teachers from other schools. Teachers need to be assured that it is acceptable and often fruitful to take risks – so a culture of trust and openness is crucial.

3 Evidence from research about effective practice is not always sufficiently accessible for teachers to use as a basis for action. Findings often need to be transformed into practical and concrete strategies that can be tried out. This may involve the production of concise and user-friendly materials, although ideas are often mediated best by talk and personal contacts with other teachers who have had some success in using them. (James, 2005, pp. 107–8)

Later TLRP studies emphasised the interaction of teacher characteristics (e.g. knowledge, attitudes and behaviour), cultural factors (e.g. school communities or professional networks) and structural factors (e.g. policy contexts). Where these were seen to be aligned as, for example, they have been in Finland, then teacher learning was likely to be most effective (see Sahlberg, 2012, Reading 4.3).

The character of teachers' professional lives was the particular focus of a TLRP associate project, *Variations in Teachers' Work, Lives, and their Effects on Pupils* (VITAE) (Day et al., 2007, Chapter 1, p. 5, Reading 1.1 and **Research Briefing 1.1** on p. 35). This longitudinal study of 300 teachers provided a new perspective on teachers' quality, retention and effectiveness over the whole of their careers.

The project found that:

1 Pupils of teachers who are committed and resilient are likely to attain more highly than pupils whose teachers are not.
2 Teachers' sense of positive professional identity is associated with wellbeing and job satisfaction, and this is a key factor in effectiveness.
3 The commitment and resilience of teachers in schools serving more disadvantaged communities tend to be persistently challenged.
4 Teachers do not necessarily become more effective over time – a minority risk becoming less effective in later years.
5 Sustaining and enhancing commitment and resilience is key to teachers' career decisions to continue or leave the profession.

The project thus concluded that strategies are needed for meeting the needs of teachers in each phase of their professional lives, and in particular communities. Learning with colleagues in school is particularly influential in creating commitment, resilience and wellbeing. These factors are also correlated with pupil outcomes – thus affirming the significance of teacher learning in effective education systems.

Policy frameworks

Principle 10: Effective pedagogy demands consistent policy frameworks with support for learning as their primary focus. Organisational and system level policies need to recognise the fundamental importance of continual learning – for individual, team, organisational and system success – and be designed to create effective learning environments for all learners.

There is growing international awareness of the significance of the coherence, or otherwise, of national systems. Curriculum requirements must articulate with assessment processes and qualifications; these must be supported by teacher education, recruitment, promotion and retention policies; which in turn must be linked to school priorities, leadership, organisation and pedagogic culture; and provision for funding and accountability to parents, community and other stakeholders must contribute appropriately too. Above all, all of these forms of provision must be focused on the contribution they can make to effective learning (Schmidt and Prawat, 2006). The system must be an educationally principled system – simply being tightly controlled is insufficient.

The coherence of national systems is manifested at several levels, and we will here identify three – school, locality and nation.

At school level

There has been an enormous amount of work on school effectiveness and improvement. MacGilchrist et al. (2004) argued that the four most important characteristics of an effective school are: high-quality leadership and management, a concentration on teaching and learning, a focus on pupils' rights and responsibilities, and the development of the school as a learning organisation. TLRP projects certainly found similar patterns. For example, within the *Learning How to Learn* project, Swaffield and MacBeath (2005) found that school leaders who prioritised developing a sense of purpose, supporting professional development, auditing expertise and supporting networking were significantly more effective in fostering learning how to learn in classrooms. Similarly, the *Pupil Consultation* project found that support and commitment of school leaders was vital to ensure that consultation led to changes in actual classroom practices (Rudduck and McIntyre, 2007).

In the locality of the school

The work which teachers and schools do is in service of the children, young people, families and employers within their community – though, of course, this can be a very complex set of relationships. Indeed, most schools, particularly in urban areas, serve several communities and provide for social groups in widely different circumstances.

Ideally, connections between schools and their communities are close, because of the significance of informal learning at home and in other out-of-school settings. Indeed, teachers are often well known in their communities. The school curriculum may even be explicitly tailored to local expectations about important knowledge, and those with significant roles in the community may contribute to the life of the school – for instance, as helpers, fund-raisers or governors. The RSA advocatied just such an 'area based curriculum' (Thomas, 2010, Reading 10.4).

Teachers and schools also have to demonstrate professional accountability and to be willing to justify pedagogic judgements and decisions. The established way of doing this is through the governing body of the school and the accountability structures of the local education authority. However, in England, local authorities now have very limited powers and most secondary schools, and a significant number of primaries, have assumed a new status as independent 'academies' or 'free schools'. Many schools are now directly funded by the DfE. It is not yet clear how this will affect the overall coherence and quality of national provision.

Nationally

The case for coherent, principled education policy is strong and there are some excellent examples of countries which seem to achieve this. Finland is the most often quoted (Sahlberg, 2012, Reading 4.3) but pp. 130–31, below, illustrate work from New Zealand, Singapore, Australia and the United States too, amongst many others. However, history suggests that this is not easy to achieve in large, complex societies.

For example, in 2003 the Labour Government in England published its *Every Child Matters* agenda which highlighted the importance of five wide-ranging outcomes for the education system: being healthy; staying safe; enjoying and achieving; making a positive contribution; and achieving economic wellbeing. And yet there was a tension between meeting these broad objectives, with which few disagreed, and focusing on narrow performance targets which that particular government also prioritised. Indeed, educationalists sometimes felt that progress was being made despite government policy rather than because of it. However, there have been exceptions and one might pick out policy for early years education which has been strongly influenced by research, including that of TLRP's associate project, EPPE (Sylva et al., 2010; 2013).

There is thus still much work to do to make policy better informed by research evidence, as the work of the UK *Strategic Forum for Research in Education* (Pollard and Oancea, 2010) has demonstrated. This is an area which is ripe for development, and new initiatives can be anticipated. For example, the British Academy and Royal Society produced their report *Harnessing Educational Research* (RS & BA, 2018) which included the recommendation for an Office for Educational Research. The British Educational Research Association's (BERA) *Close-to-Practice Research* and *State of the Discipline* projects also have a strong focus on the importance of the intersections between research, policy and practice and how these effect perceptions of education as an academic discipline and as a field of practice.

But values are always contested in a democracy, particularly in very unequal societies such as those in the UK (see Chapter 5, Green and Janmaat, 2011, Reading 5.2). Further, our education systems are also complex and only partially integrated across sectors. There are thus several structural reasons why coherence is difficult to achieve.

We need to be both realistic and optimistic about this goal. Although achieving *principled* educational coherence is difficult, incremental progress can be made if governments realise its significance. It remains important that all those with an interest in effective teaching and learning – pupils, parents, teachers, researchers, policymakers and the public at large – continue to strive together to establish socially just policies that truly support learning for the diverse needs of all learners in our communities.

Reflective Activity 4.4

Aim: To consider the roles of teacher learning and public policy development in educational improvement.

Evidence and reflection: People in particular roles or structural positions tend to develop shared perspectives, and these perspectives tend to reflect their material interests. So, politicians must struggle for power and then demonstrate that they can rule decisively. And teachers must achieve professional status and defend their autonomy and working conditions. But in fact, of course, both policymakers and teachers would claim that they 'act in the public interest'.

The truth is that the public interest cannot be fulfilled without the complementary efforts of all stakeholders working together. TLRP's principles were designed to offer a simple framework of educationally sound ideas on which to base such cooperation.

What scope do you see, on whatever scale, for developing your own learning as a teacher, and for constructively engaging with school, local or government decision-makers? (See Chapter 17 for further ideas on this.)

Extension: Working with some colleagues, consider some recent government policies on education which you know about. Are they coherent with other contemporary national policies? How do they relate to the evidence-informed principles proposed by TLRP? The *Early Career Framework* (DfE, 2019a) for teachers in England can be mapped to these ten principles. Which areas receive greater or less emphasis? What kinds of research are there cited in the framework, and what kinds are not cited?

INTERNATIONAL KNOWLEDGE ACCUMULATION

In this chapter so far, we have reviewed TLRP's ten evidence-informed principles for effective teaching and learning. These were developed in and for the UK. However, the extent of international collaboration in understanding education is now enormous – and indeed, is part of the role of academic researchers. Teams form, propositions are tested, papers are exchanged, findings debated, books written etc. From such processes, new frameworks of understanding are created.

In North America, there is an extensive and very well-established body of work. There are many contributions from the United States in particular. The work of, for example, Linda Darling-Hammond has added to the cumulative understanding over many years, and her review of *Teacher Education Around the World* (2017) is a recent contribution. See also, in particular, Darling-Hammond (1996; Darling-Hammond et al., 2008). An influential synthesis of US work is *How People Learn: Brain, Mind, Experience and School* (Bransford et al., 1999, Reading 4.1). This was produced by the Committee on Developments in the Science of Learning for the US National Academy of Sciences.

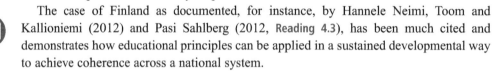

Research in Australia, New Zealand and parts of the Far East has also made significant contributions. For example, Bob Lingard and colleagues' longitudinal work on school reform and 'productive pedagogies' in Queensland, Australia, which has generated a lot of interest (see Lingard et al., 2003). *Best Practice Syntheses* from New Zealand have made a great contribution (e.g. Alton-Lee, 2003; Timperley et al., 2007, Reading 16.6) and from Singapore, work by David Hogan and colleagues (2013, Reading 4.2) has codified and measured instructional systems for improvement of teaching in core subjects. Hong Kong has harvested work from around the world and introduced its school curriculum through a consultative process over a ten-year period.

The case of Finland as documented, for instance, by Hannele Neimi, Toom and Kallioniemi (2012) and Pasi Sahlberg (2012, Reading 4.3), has been much cited and demonstrates how educational principles can be applied in a sustained developmental way to achieve coherence across a national system.

Comparative study remains a much-debated subject with significant concern in relation to 'policy borrowing'. Robin Alexander's tour de force, *Culture and Pedagogy* (2000) provided an exceptionally rich analysis of the interaction of culture, power, schools, curriculum and pedagogy in five countries – thus analysing both unique and common features. Reviews by international agencies, such as *The Nature of Learning* (Dumont, Istance and Benavides for the OECD, 2010, Reading 4.4), draw together research from a wide range of disciplines, and PISA survey analyses provide hugely influential feedback on national performance. However, they also inevitably mask many inter-cultural subtleties (Sturman, 2012, Reading 14.6). PISA ranks the performance of countries, subject to significant methodological qualifications, and analysis of these data has suggested a formula for success requiring high expectations combined with significant school autonomy to enable improvement practices to become embedded. The results have had a major impact on the development of education policy internationally and are an example of how assessment shapes educational policy and practice in unexpected ways (see Choi and Jerrim, 2016 for an account of the impact in Spain).

The National Foundation for Educational Research (NFER) provided a useful 'mapping of seminal reports on good teaching' from 2007–12 (Rowe, Wilkin and Wilson, 2012, Reading 4.5). The review collates overlapping conclusions in respect of the 'teaching environment', 'teaching approaches' and 'teacher characteristics' – see Figure 4.2. The authors draw attention to the need to 'understand the principles that underpin practice' and note that, whilst awareness of strategies and techniques is valuable, 'they are not enough, in themselves, to change practice' (p. 26). Indeed, it is interesting to see how the 'teaching approaches' resonate closely with TLRP's ten principles.

The most comprehensive and systematic synthesis of recent years has been the work of John Hattie (2009, Reading 4.6). He has developed techniques to measure 'effect sizes' across multiple research studies, thus ranking findings for their relative importance in teaching and learning.

This work is now cogently expressed in *Visible Learning for Teachers* (Hattie, 2012, Reading 16.5). Hattie summarises by proposing eight 'mind frames' for teachers. If, he suggests, they were established as 'theories of practice', then significant impacts on learning should follow (see Reading 10.7). These 'mind frames' again overlap with TLRP's principles in interesting ways.

Three cover dimensions of knowledge, learning, pedagogy and assessment:

- Teachers/leaders want to talk more about the learning than the teaching.
- Teachers/leaders engage in dialogue not monologue.
- Teachers/leaders see assessment as feedback about their impact.

Two others address engagement and relationships, whilst also reaching into informal settings to draw significant others into the learning process:

- Teachers/leaders believe that it is their role to develop positive relationships in classrooms/staffrooms.
- Teachers/leaders inform all about the language of learning.

The final three of Hattie's 'mind frames' relate to teacher learning and commitment.

- Teachers/leaders believe that their fundamental task is to evaluate the effect of their teaching on students' learning and achievement.
- Teachers/leaders believe that success and failure in student learning is about what they, as teachers or leaders, did or did not do.
- Teachers/leaders enjoy the challenge and never retreat from 'doing their best'.

The overlaps between synoptic studies of different sorts give confidence to the process of international knowledge accumulation. It remains very unlikely that we will ever be able to state exactly 'what works' in all specific educational contexts. However, as evidence accumulates, informed teachers and others can refine their understanding and improve their judgement. We are progressively able to say 'what is *likely* to work' (see, for example the EEF Teaching and Learning Toolkit (educationendowmentfoundation.org.uk/education-evidence/teaching-learning-toolkit) – which is drawn on throughout this book. This growing confidence reflects the development of knowledge and expertise.

It is thus becoming entirely reasonable that we should, as teachers, be able to justify (or 'warrant') our practices to others through the use of evidence of various sorts. It is also, of course, increasingly reasonable to expect governments to take note, so that policy is well aligned with knowledge about learning and teaching.

Figure 4.2 Key features in a repertoire of effective teaching (Rowe, Wilkin and Wilson, 2012)

Teaching environment	Teaching approaches	Teacher characteristics
• Calm, well-disciplined, orderly • Safe and secure • An ethos of aspiration and achievement for all • Positive emotional climate • Purposeful, stimulating • Bright, attractive and informative displays • Clean, tidy and well organised • New or redesigned buildings and spaces • Lower class sizes	• Interactive (e.g. working and learning together – social constructivism) • Use of teacher–pupil dialogue, questioning • Monitoring pupil progress (including the use of feedback) • Pupil assessment (including assessment for learning) • Pupil agency and voice (active engagement in their learning) • Enquiry-based • Effective planning and organisation • Scaffolding learning • Building on the prior experience and learning of pupils • Personalisation, responding to individual needs • Home–school learning, knowledge exchange • Use of new technology and ICT • Collaborative practice • Good use of teaching assistants • Creative use of visits and visiting experts	• Good subject knowledge • Self-efficacy and belief • High expectations • Motivational • Provides challenge • Innovative and proactive • Calm • Caring • Sensitive • Gives praise • Uses humour as a tool • Engenders trust and mutual respect • Flexible (where appropriate) • Builds positive relationships with pupils • Self-reflecting

CONCLUSION

In this chapter we have reviewed TLRP's ten evidence-informed principles which were developed to support the judgements of teachers and others in working towards high-quality teaching and learning.

Each principle focuses attention onto particular dimensions of teaching and learning. However, the principles should be seen as being interconnected. TLRP represented them 'in the round' to assert holism and to facilitate consideration of inter-relationships (see Figure 4.1). The salience of particular principles may change in relation to the specific circumstances or issues which a teacher faces, but none of them is likely to recede entirely.

reflectiveteaching.co.uk/rtps6/part1_ch4

The ten principles are used to structure reflection within this book because they tap into the enduring issues which teachers must face. At various points within the book, the text thus draws attention to particular principles in relation to the issues under consideration. The principles offer a framework for our understanding. They are also complemented through the book by the introduction of powerful concepts and Expert Questions for analysing teacher expertise. We will take stock of these elements as a whole in Chapter 16.

> **Expert Question**
>
> **Warrant:** *are our teaching strategies evidence-informed, convincing and justifiable to stakeholders?*
>
> This question contributes to a conceptual framework underpinning professional expertise (see Chapter 16).

The principles have a particular cutting edge when used to evaluate or review actual policy or practice. When that is done, there is often a gap between aspiration and achievement. This gives pause for thought, and can lead to new insights and developments. Why not apply the principles to interrogate a government policy document or, at the other end of the scale, to review some aspect of school provision, or a dimension of your classroom practice that has been concerning you?

As we have seen, TLRP's work is part of a continuing international effort to harvest, evaluate and synthesise global knowledge about teaching and learning. TLRP's principles represent a holistic understanding of teaching, learning and education. They complement more specific analyses of the measured effects of particular teaching strategies.

We conclude this chapter with an aim of of the Chartered College of Teaching, which once again indicates the role of evidence-informed, principled judgement at the heart of the teaching profession:

We are working to celebrate, support and connect teachers to take pride in their profession and provide the best possible education for children and young people. We are dedicated to bridging the gap between practice and research and equipping teachers from the second they enter the classroom with the knowledge and confidence to make the best decisions for their pupils. (Downloaded from chartered.college/aboutus/)

This book is designed to support the development of such decision-making, and TLRP's ten principles are offered as contributions to that goal.

reflectiveteaching.co.uk/rtps6/part1_ch4

CHAPTER WEBPAGE

reflectiveteaching.co.uk offers additional professional resources for this chapter. For the chapter webpage, go to: reflectiveteaching.co.uk/rtps6/part1_ch4

Chapter 4 addresses 'educational principles' – a concept which is fundamental to the approach to professional practice being advocated in the book. In this instance, the form of the highlighted principles derives from the *Teaching and Learning Research Programme*, and the chapter webpage gives access to an archive of synoptic TLRP material. To review this, look at the right-hand column, starting with 'TLRP's ten principles: a poster'.

The TLRP materials include direct links to six videos on YouTube. Led by teachers and illustrated in classroom settings, these are focused on principles with direct educational application – prior experience, scaffolding learning, assessment strategies, engagement, relationships.

Information on the many books published from the research programme is also listed, and such books are likely to be available in education libraries.

Key Readings, below, provides a shortlist of material directly related to the chapter for those with access to a library. It is focused on the issue of knowledge accumulation and is intended to demonstrate how, across the world, our educational understanding is building. TLRP's principles are just one attempt to synthesise this – other versions have existed and will be developed in the future in a sequence of extension, adaption and refinement.

Readings for Reflective Teaching in Schools is available for those who may not be able to access a library or who just want a very convenient source. Again, it aims to illustrate the way in which knowledge is accumulating globally. This is a continually developing field, both in terms of what we know about how children and young people learn, but also the way that teachers develop and improve. It will always be a challenge as a professional to keep up to date with contemporary research and scholarship in these areas.

KEY READINGS

Simple summaries of TLRP's findings are available in the form of a teacher guide, poster, DVD and commentary at this book's Chapter 4 webpage at **reflectiveteaching.co.uk**. The commentary is:

> James, M. and Pollard, A. (2006) *Improving Teaching and Learning in Schools*. London: TLRP.

For an extended academic review of the principles and international commentaries see:

> James, M. and Pollard, A. (2012a) *Principles for Effective Pedagogy: International Responses to Evidence from the UK Teaching and Learning Research Programme*. London: Routledge.

Synoptic reviews of cumulative evidence on teaching and learning include:

> Bransford, J. (ed.) (1999) *How People Learn: Brain, Mind, Experience and School.* Washington, DC: National Academy Press. (Reading 4.1)
> Muijs, D. and Reynolds, D. (2017) *Effective Teaching. Evidence and Practice.* London: SAGE. (Reading 8.7)
> Good, T. and Brophy, J. (2008) *Looking in Classrooms.* Boston: Pearson.
> Darling-Hammond, L. (1996) *The Right to Learn: A Blueprint for Creating Schools that Work.* San Francisco: Jossey-Bass.

Globally influential work drawing on development in Austalia, Canada, Singapore and Finland is:

> Hayes, D., Mills, M., Christie, P. and Linguard, R. (2006) *Teachers and Schooling Making a Difference.* Sydney: Allen and Unwin.
> Levin, B. (2008) *How to Change 5000 Schools.* Cambridge, MA: Harvard Eduction Press.
> Hogan, D., Chan, M., Rahim, R., Kwek, D., Aye, K. M., Loo, S. C., Sheng, Y. and Luo, W. (2013) 'Assessment and the logic of instructional practice in Secondary 3 English and Mathematics classes in Singapore'. *Review of Education*, 1 (1), 57–106. (see Reading 4.2)
> Sahlberg, P. (2012) *Finnish Lessons: What Can the World Learn from Educational Change in Finland?* Boston: Teachers' College Press. (Reading 4.3)

A special issue of the Teachers College Record in 2015 has a helpful critique of PISA. The editorial by Perry and Ercikan provides an overview of the articles:

> Perry, N. and Ercikan, K. (2015). Moving beyond country rankings in international assessments: The case of PISA. *Teachers College Record*, *117*(1), 1–10.

An OECD attempt to summarise the implications deriving from what is known about learning from across the world is:

> Dumont, H., Istance, D. and Benavides, F. (2010) *The Nature of Learning. Using Research to Inspire Practice.* Paris: OECD. (Reading 4.4)

UK synopses of contemporary studies on effective teaching are:

> Rowe, N., Wilkin, A. and Wilson, R. (2012) *Mapping of Seminal Reports on Good Teaching.* Slough: NFER. (Reading 4.5)
> Cassen, R., McNally, S. and Vignoles, A. (2015) *Making a Difference in Education. What the Evidence Says.* London: Routledge.
> Coe, R., Aloisi, C., Higgins, S. and Major, L.E. (2014) *What Makes Great Teaching? Review of the Underpinning Research.* London: Sutton Trust.

Two synopses of quantitative research, encouragingly consonant in general with the results of qualitative research and teacher experience, are:

Hattie, J. (2009) *Visible Learning: A Synthesis of Meta-Analyses Relating to Achievement*. London: Routledge. (Reading 4.6)

Marzano, R.J. (2009) *Designing and Teaching Learning Goals and Objectives*. Bloomington: Solution Tree.

For a UK website harvesting international evidence on particular teaching strategies and summarising knowledge from a programme of randomised trials in England, see: **educationendowmentfoundation.org.uk/education-evidence/teaching-learning-toolkit**

For more specialist insights, the handbook below indicates the range of scientific disciplines engaging with contemporary understanding of teaching and learning, and the nature of their contributions.

Sawyer, R.K. (2006) *The Cambridge Handbook of the Learning Sciences*. Cambridge: Cambridge University Press.

The insights from international research are also played out in particular ways in relation to learners of different ages, and thus for each sector of education. Among the most significant sectoral reviews are:

Early Childhood: The Effective Pre-School and Primary Education Project: Sylva, K., Melhuish, E., Sammons, P., Siraj-Blatchford, I. and Taggart, B. (2010) *Early Childhood Matters*. London: Routledge.

This book summarises the first large scale multi-level longitudinal study of young children's development and underpinned a significant expansion in early years provision in the UK. See **ucl.ac.uk/ioe/research/featured-research/effective-pre-school-primary-secondary-education-project**

Cambridge Primary Review (CPR): Alexander, R. (ed.) (2010) *Children, Their World, Their Education*, Final Report and Recommendations. London: Routledge.

The CPR was funded in 2006 by Esmee Fairbairn Foundation to evaluate the state of primary education by combining 'retrospective evidence with prospective vision'. The final report, based on extensive research, drew together over thirty interim reports. It subsequently developed into a regional organisation which lasted a decade. The riches of its residual website can be found at **cprtrust.org.uk**

Mental Capital and Well Being Report: Feinstein, L., Vorhaus, J. and Sabates, R. (2008b) *Learning through Life: Future Challenges*. London: Government Office for Science. (Reading 1.6)

The Office for Science's Foresight Programme advises the Government on how to achieve the best possible intellectual development for everyone. This Report considered factors which could affect 'learning through life' in future decades. The report is available from the book chapter page at **reflectiveteaching.co.uk**

TOOLKIT EVIDENCE 4.1
Parental engagement: working with parents for their children's learning

What is it?
Parental engagement is a broad term and covers the active involvement of parents in supporting their children's learning at school. This includes programmes focused on parents and their skills (such as improving literacy or digital skills), general approaches to encourage parents to support their children to read or do mathematics, and more intensive, targeted programmes for families in crisis.

What does the evidence say?
Although parental engagement is consistently associated with pupils' success at school, the evidence about how to *increase* involvement to *improve* attainment is much less conclusive. This is particularly the case for disadvantaged families. There is some evidence that supporting parents with their first child will have benefits for younger siblings. However, there are also examples where combining parental engagement with other approaches, such as extending early years provision, does not have any additional educational benefit. This suggests that developing effective parental involvement to improve their children's attainment is challenging and will need careful monitoring and evaluation. Two meta-analyses from the United States suggested that increasing parental involvement in primary and secondary schools had on average two to three months' benefit on learners' attainment.

How sound is the evidence?
Although there is a long history of research into parental involvement in schools, there is surprisingly little robust evidence of the impact of programmes that have tried to increase involvement to improve learning. The evidence is predominantly from primary level and the early years, though there are studies which have looked at secondary schools. Impact studies tend to focus on reading and mathematics attainment. Studies often report wider benefits from parental involvement in terms of attendance and behaviour.

What do I need to think about?
- Informal contact with parents is often easier to develop with younger children.
- How can you provide opportunities for the parents of older children? This will need to be flexible.
- Some parents will have had negative experiences in their own education; how can you make sure contact with school will be positive?
- Have you provided straightforward suggestions which all parents can use at home to help their children?

Links and further reading
Higgins, S. and Katsipataki, M. (2015) 'Evidence from meta-analysis about parental involvement in education which supports their children's learning'. *Journal of Children's* Services, 10(3), 1–11. doi:10.1108/JCS-02-2015-0009
Campbell, C. (2011) *How to Involve Hard-to-reach Parents: Encouraging Meaningful Parental Involvement with Schools*. Nottingham: NCSL. dera.ioe.ac.uk/12136/1/download%3Fid%3D156367%26filename%3Dhow-to-involve-hard-to-reach-parents-full-report.pdf
The EEF Teaching and Learning Toolkit entry on 'Parental engagement': educationendowmentfoundation.org.uk/education-evidence/teaching-learning-toolkit/parental-engagement. See also the technical appendix for references to the individual studies.

See also
Behaviour interventions (Toolkit Evidence 7.1)

Education Endowment Foundation

RESEARCH BRIEFING 4.1
Enhancing home–school knowledge exchange

Children learn in two different worlds, home and school. Yet the knowledge which exists in each of these worlds is often not fully recognised or understood in the other. Martin Hughes and his TLRP colleagues worked with teachers, parents and children to find new ways of exchanging knowledge between home and primary school. They looked in particular at how this process of knowledge exchange could enhance children's learning in literacy and mathematics and through the transition from primary to secondary school. The social and emotional aspects of learning, and of pupil identity, cannot be separated from academic performance. The child's home and school experiences are thus intimately connected in relation to learning.

Key findings:	Implications:
Exchange activities: Home–school knowledge exchange activities can have a positive impact on teachers, parents and children, and on attainment in literacy and mathematics. At primary–secondary school transfer, they can help to avoid the common post-transfer dip in pupil performance.	Greater priority should be given to exchanging knowledge between home and school, as a means of improving home–school relationships, raising attainment in literacy and mathematics and facilitating learning during primary–secondary school transfer.
Funds of knowledge: There are substantial 'funds of knowledge' in homes and communities which can be used to support children's learning. They are often embedded in national and ethnic cultures, and in the experience of family members. Popular culture is an important influence on children's funds of knowledge.	Schools need to recognise these funds of knowledge and find ways of making them more visible in the classroom and in the school. Exchange of videos, photographs and 'shoe-boxes' of significant items can be used to make this knowledge more tangible.
School transfer: Teachers, parents and children all have significant 'funds of knowledge' which can be drawn on to support transfer. Parents know about children's out-of-school lives while primary teachers have extensive knowledge of the children they have taught. This knowledge is often ignored by secondary teachers who want children to have a 'fresh start'.	Parents, teachers and children need to find ways of sharing and exchanging their different funds of knowledge. Transfer 'passports', photographs of out-of-school life and videos of secondary school can all be used. Drama activities can help children and parents share their hopes and fears about transfer.
At risk children: Some groups of children are particularly likely to be 'at risk' when transferring from primary to secondary school. These include children who are considered to be 'gifted and talented' as well as children whose families are considered to be 'hard to reach'.	Schools need to consider how they will provide support for these 'at risk' groups. More clearly targeted strategies at the start of secondary school can help to prevent later disengagement and under-performance.

Schools which take on the challenges of home–school knowledge exchange are likely to see a range of benefits for teachers, children and parents. Teachers can appreciate the additional knowledge they acquire about children's out-of-school lives and can use it to enrich their curricula. Parents can acquire a greater understanding of what is happening to their children in school, gain a greater appreciation of teachers' professional skills, and realise how they can complement the work of the school at home. Children can appreciate when aspects of their out-of-school lives are valued and respected in school, and when their work at school is better understood at home. As one parent commented about her child: 'I think she likes to show people things about herself and I think she really enjoys that . . . yeah I think she really liked to do that.'

Further information

Hughes, M. et al. (2007) *Enhancing Primary Literacy and Mathematics through Home–School Knowledge Exchange*. TLRP Research Briefing 22. London: TLRP.
Hughes, M. et al. (2008) *Supporting Primary–Secondary Transfer through Home–School Knowledge Exchange*. TLRP Research Briefing. London: TLRP. (Available on the chapter page for this book at reflectiveteaching.co.uk)
Feiler, A. et al. (2007) *Improving Primary Literacy: Linking Home and School*. London: Routledge.
Winter, J. et al. (2009) *Improving Primary Mathematics: Linking Home and School*. London: Routledge.
This project was directed from the University of Bristol.

Part two

Creating conditions for learning

5	**Contexts** What is, and what might be?	139
6	**Relationships** How are we getting on together?	163
7	**Engagement** How are we managing behaviour?	195
8	**Spaces** How are we creating environments for learning?	229

This part concerns the creation of classroom environments to support high-quality teaching and learning.

We begin by considering the circumstances which impinge on families and schools (Chapter 5) – and we note the ways in which people contribute to and challenge such circumstances through their actions.

We then move to the heart of classroom life with a focus on teacher–pupil relationships and classroom climate (Chapter 6). Because 'good relationships' are so enabling, this is an extremely important chapter.

Chapter 7 builds further and illustrates how positive cycles of behaviour can be created through firmness, fairness and engaging pupils in the curriculum.

Finally, we consider a range of learning spaces (Chapter 8) in school and beyond and we consider affordances they offer for formal and informal learning. As well as the basic dimensions of classroom organisation, this chapter also addresses the use of technology, pupil organisation and team-working with teacher assistants.

Chapter 5
Contexts
What is, and what might be?

Introduction	140

Social context	141
Ideology	142
Culture	145
Opportunity	147
Accountability	150

People and agency	153
Teachers	153
Pupils	155

Conclusion	158

Part 2 Creating conditions for learning

INTRODUCTION

The questions 'What Is, and What Might Be?' are inspired by Edmond Holmes' (1911) text of the same name. Holmes worked as Her Majesty's Chief Inspector of Schools. After he retired in 1911, he published *What Is and What Might Be* in 1911, offering a strongly critical view of the system within which he had worked and a glimpse of what an alternative system might look like.

In line with Holmes' (1911) thinking, this chapter provides a brief review of some of the contextual factors which are important in education, and of how teachers, children and families might respond. The influence of social context pervades everything that happens in schools and classrooms, and awareness of such issues is therefore an important contributing element of reflective teaching. This influence is felt at many levels – from the 'big picture' of government policies in Scotland, Wales, England, Northern Ireland, the Republic of Ireland or elsewhere, to the detail of community, school and family cultures and particular individual circumstances.

A second purpose of the chapter is to establish some principles concerning the relationships of individuals and society. Indeed, the chapter is very deliberately in two parts. The first, 'Social context', emphasises the ideas, social structures and distribution of resources which *structure* action in various ways. The second part, 'People and agency', is concerned with the factors which, in various senses, *enable* action by individual teachers and children.

A particular theoretical position thus underpins this chapter and, indeed, the book as a whole. At its core is the conception of a dialectical relationship between society and individuals. This suggests the existence of a constant interplay of social forces and individual actions (see, for example, Giddens, 1984). On the one hand, the decisions and actions which people make and take in their lives are constrained by social structures and by the historical processes which bring about such structures. On the other, each individual has a unique sense of self, derived from their personal history or biography. Individuals have a degree of free will in acting and in developing understandings with others. Sets of these understandings, which endure over time, form the basis of cultures. Such understandings can also lead to challenges to established social structures and thus to future changes.

The ways in which these processes play out are significantly influenced by the circumstances of various social groups in terms of power, wealth, status and opportunities (Reid 1998, Halsey, 1986). Individuals, each with their own background and sense of self, will react to such factors in a variety of ways. Some in powerful positions might wish to close ranks and defend themselves by suggesting that their position is inherited by right or earned by merit. Some among those who are less fortunate may accept the social order or even aspire to success in its terms. Others may try to contest it – for of course, to be able to question existing social arrangements is a fundamental right in our democratic societies.

The particular historical era in which we happen to live also makes a significant difference. Following the Second World War, the UK economy was still the third largest in the world (after the United States and the Soviet Union). Since then, our living standards have trebled and life expectancy has steadily risen. However, relative to some other countries such as Germany and the United States, our growth has been relatively faltering

reflectiveteaching.co.uk/rtps6/part2_ch5

and unbalanced. In the future, growth and competition from countries such as China and India will continue to force structural changes in our economy. In recent decades, these global forces have resulted in increasingly interventionist education policies from governments of both left and right. The form of intervention differs, but intervene they do. Educational provision, in other words, cannot escape its circumstances.

There is thus an enduring ebb and flow in social change – a process of tension and struggle. It is the product of a constant interaction between agency and circumstance, voluntarism and determinism, biography and history (Mills, 1959, Reading 5.1).

New priorities may emerge in future (see Collarbone, 2009, Reading 16.1). For instance, given the environmental challenges facing the world, it would not be surprising if schools were one day required to play a major role in introducing more sustainable ways of life to new generations. At the moment, governments sometimes appear to merely pay lip service to this issue, but events could make it a much higher priority. We cannot predict the future and the roles which education may be called upon to fulfil.

A reflective teacher has responsibilities within this process which should not be avoided.

The interaction of structure and agency can be seen in education, as in other fields of life. Amongst the many ways in which they may be realised, they can be seen to influence both national policy frameworks and everyday informal learning.

See Chapter 4

TLRP Principles

Two principles are of particular relevance to this chapter on the broader contexts in which teaching and learning take place:

Effective teaching and learning recognises the significance of informal learning. Informal learning, such as learning out of school, should be recognised as at least as significant as formal learning and should therefore be valued and used appropriately in formal processes. (*Principle 8*)

Effective teaching and learning demands consistent policy frameworks with support for teaching and learning as their primary focus. Policies at national, local and institutional levels need to recognise the fundamental importance of teaching and learning. They should be designed to create effective learning environments in which all learners can thrive. (*Principle 10*)

SOCIAL CONTEXT

We now consider four aspects of the social context which are particularly significant for practice in schools: ideology, culture, opportunity and accountability. The influence of each can be traced at national, regional, local and school levels so that, although such issues sometimes seem distant, they shape classroom activity in very real ways.

Part 2 Creating conditions for learning

Ideology

A dictionary definition of ideology states that it means a 'way of thinking'. However, particular sets of ideas are often used, consciously or unconsciously, to promote and legitimise the interests of specific groups of people. Indeed, if a particular way of thinking about a society is dominant at any point in time, it is likely to be an important influence on education and on teachers' actions. It may determine the types of schools which are created, produce a particular curriculum emphasis and even begin to frame the ways in which teachers think about their work and relate with children and young people.

For instance, in the United States of the 1950s and the Cold War, anti-communist feeling was so great that it not only led to the now discredited inquisitions of the McCarthy Committee but also to a range of nationalistic practices in schools, re-interpretations of history and pressures to compete with the 'enemy', particularly after the 1957 launch of the Russian *Sputnik* satellite. Similarly, in the USSR and Eastern Bloc countries, before the revolutionary changes which swept Eastern Europe in 1989, pupils were taught highly selective views of history, of the values and achievements of their societies. They too were encouraged to compete, particularly to sustain exceptional international achievements in areas such as science and sport. In both cases, despite widely differing circumstances, it can be seen that the ideologies of key political elites interacted with the 'common sense thinking' of the wider population to create particular ideological climates (see the work of Gramsci, 1978, for an analysis of such hegemonic phenomena). Although the influence of these ideological periods was enormous, they passed.

International comparison also enables us to place the 'taken for granted' into perspective and consider alternatives. A study by the LLAKEs research centre in London (Green and Janmaat, 2011, Reading 5.2) analysed the values and assumptions underpinning education policies in the western world. They identify three main positions:

- **Liberal** – with core beliefs in individual opportunities and rewards based on merit (English-speaking countries, particularly the United Kingdom and the United States).

- **Social market** – with solidarity depending more on the state and less on civil society (north west continental Europe, including Belgium, France, Germany, Netherlands).

- **Social democratic** – with egalitarian and solidaristic values and higher levels of social and political trust (Nordic countries, such as Denmark, Finland, Norway, Sweden).

Particular beliefs and values permeate perception and decision-making in these societies, and throw up a wide range of issues. For instance, a common question in some parts of the UK is: Why do we widely admire the achievements of the Nordic countries but in reality do so little to emulate them?

The ideologies which influence education in the UK also come and go. For example, there have been very different beliefs over the years about what kinds of schools should be provided and who should go to them. After the Second World War, it was thought that

reflectiveteaching.co.uk/rtps6/part2_ch5

the most appropriate way of organising secondary education was to have different types of school – grammar schools, technical schools and secondary moderns. Pupils would be selected for each of these schools on merit, based on how they performed in '11-plus' tests. However, it was not long before this 'tripartite' system came to be criticised for favouring well-off families rather than widening educational opportunities. This led to proposals for the introduction of a system of secondary schools, which would be 'comprehensive' in that there was to be no selection of students. By the 1960s, this view had become the new orthodoxy and, with support from all major political parties, comprehensive schools supported by local education authorities became the norm in most of England, Scotland and Wales. The commitment to the meritocratic ideal of 'opportunities for all' was distinctive, but comprehensives were criticised in the 1990s for being too complacent or, as an English Minister once put it, 'bog standard'. The Coalition Government in England from 2010 urged that schools should become responsive to their clientele by breaking free from local authorities and establishing themselves as independent 'academies', a policy that was not adopted by any other of the four nations. A mix of competition and collaboration between such schools has been expected to improve the performance of the system overall. More recently, in 2018, a new debate over grammar schools began, with the Conservative government allocating significant funds to support grammar schools to expend their intake, a policy that led to bitter debate in the education world.

Some historians have argued (for example, Simon, 1992) that forms of school organisation can best be understood in terms of the reproduction of social class structures and patterns of advantage and disadvantage. Indeed, authors such as Althusser (1971) saw education systems within capitalist societies as forms of an 'ideological state apparatus' designed to achieve broader social control in the interests of powerful elites. On the other hand, sociologists such as Collins (1977), Kogan (1978) and Archer (1979, Reading 17.1) have argued that educational policies and provision are the product of competing interest groups and that control and power is more diffuse.

Unfortunately, ideologies flourish in education about the curriculum, teaching methods, assessment requirements and many other issues. In the post-war years, civil servants had tended to moderate political manifestations of popular ideas – though this was, in itself, a reflection of their own 'assumptive world' (McPherson and Raab, 1988). However, in more recent decades there has been a considerable struggle for control between politicians, civil servants and professionals over education policy (Ball, 1990; Bowe, Ball and Gold, 1992, Reading 17.7). As they should, within reason in democracies, politicians gradually prevailed – but the tension can still be seen in animated media debates and moral panics about education issues, uneasy relationships between researchers and policymakers, and regular 'shake ups' of government education departments. One such notable instance was the incoming Secretary of State for Education Michael Gove's reference to academics and educationalists opposing his education reform agenda as the 'Blob' and 'Enemies of Promise' (Gove, 2014), responsible for damaging young people's education.

In recent years politicians have taken to claiming that their policies are 'evidence based' – though the academic community and journalists are sometimes rather sceptical of this assertion (see Benn and Downs, 2016). However, the commitment in principle to the use of evidence to inform policy and practice is a very important development. In 2011, the government invested £125 million in the Education Endowment Foundation (EEF), to help it develop a 'what works' centre for UK education. Whilst its focus on Randomised Control Trials as the 'gold standard' for research has been criticised, the EEF has become a widely used source of information for school leaders in recent years. Significant work has also been done on enabling wider access to research evidence through organisations such as the Economic and Social Research Council, the British Academy, Royal Society and, in education, the UK Strategic Forum for Research in Education (SFRE), Campaign for Evidence-Based Education (CEBE) and the British Educational Research Association (BERA). Most recently the Royal Society and the British Academy published 'Harnessing Educational Research' (RS & BA, 2018), which advocated setting up an Office for Educational Research with the purpose of addressing mismatches between the supply of research and the demand for research.

Even at national levels, ideologies interact with culture and identity as well as with material interests. For example, in England, as we will see in the discussion of accountability later in this chapter, the big story of the last thirty years has been the growth of centralised control over the education system. But this is not quite the same in Scotland, Northern Ireland or Wales, particularly since the 2016 Brexit vote catalysed moves towards further devolution, a process which has enabled the particular priorities of each country to be addressed. Consequently, the four education systems within the UK have become increasingly unique. Therefore, the Scottish Parliament now ensures that education policy responds to Scottish, rather than English, priorities. The Welsh Parliament does the same for Wales, and the Northern Ireland Assembly, with more limited powers, develops its own new policy initiatives. Such measures are influenced by *different* sets of beliefs and power relations. In Wales, for instance, the Curriculum for Wales Framework is distinctive (hwb.gov.wales/curriculum-for-wales/introduction/). Debate over the future of Northern Ireland's grammar schools continues, as it has for decades, though the last official 11-plus transfer test took place in 2008. Although integrated education has been expanding, over 90 per cent of Northern Ireland's pupils still attend either Catholic or Protestant schools. Meanwhile, as we will see in more detail later in this chapter, Scotland has taken distinctive positions, for instance the *Curriculum for Excellence* and professional development matters. The Republic of Ireland has been fully independent since 1922, and its education system of course reflects its history, culture and priorities (Coolahan et al., 2017). In 2020, Ireland began a first major review of its primary national curriculum for more than two decades. This was notable for the involvement of researchers from the beginning. For example, Manyukhina and Wyse's (2019) paper drew on work on knowledge and the curriculum commissioned by the National Council for Curriculum and Assessment (NCCA) who also commissioned a range of other research and appointed academic advisors to work with the NCCA on the consultative processes of developing the new curriculum (ncca.ie/en/primary/primary-developments/primary-curriculum-review-and-redevelopment/research-and-publications/).

> **Expert Question**
>
> **Effectiveness:** are there improvements in standards, in both basic skills and other areas of curricular attainment, to satisfy society's educational goals?
>
> This question contributes to a conceptual framework underpinning professional expertise (see Chapter 16).

The relationships between the four major parts of the UK have always been complex and, of course, they will continue to evolve. Whilst such complexity has increased since devolution and then Brexit, the basic educational issues to be tackled remain much the same. Education is inevitably concerned with the future, with opportunities and life chances, with productivity, wealth, community, identity and fulfilment. It is not surprising that it is contested. If possible, reflective teachers should develop their understanding at this enduring level.

In summary, the ideas, perspectives or beliefs which prevail at a particular point of time are likely to be reflected in public debate and education policy. Whilst the basic issues being contested are likely to remain much the same, the settlements reached will change and change again over a teaching career. At some point in time, critique and experience lead to evaluation, counter proposal, development and change (Bowe et al., 1992, Reading 17.7). Societies and dominant ideologies are never static, but awareness of the concept of ideology makes it more likely that reflective teachers will be able to evaluate the values or interests that may lie behind new ideas, policies or practices.

It is important to remember that no one, including ourselves, is immune to the influences of ideologies. For instance, professional ideologies are always likely to remain strong among teachers – they represent commitments, ideals *and* interests. Reflective teachers should be open-minded enough to constructively critique their own beliefs, as well as those of others.

Culture

Cultures can be seen as sets of shared perspectives. They often develop from collective activity and from the creative responses of groups to situations. Furthermore, cultures endure over time and thus represent sets of perspectives, values and practices into which individuals are likely to be socialised. The playground cultures of young children provide an example here. In one sense, children in friendship groups develop unique and particular ways of perceiving school life. Indeed, they use these as a means of understanding school and coping with it (Clarricoates, 1987; Davies, 1982; Pollard, 1987b). Yet at the same time, continuities in children's culture, from generation to generation, provide a context which young children absorb (Opie and Opie, 1959; Sluckin, 1981). For older students, pupil cultures are strongly influenced by social media, films, television, gaming, popular music, mobile phones and other styles and technologies – but they are played out through students' collective agency.

The community within the school provides another cultural context. This will influence and be influenced by the perspectives of parents, children and teachers. However, few communities can be characterised as single, united entities. Among the many divisions which may exist are those relating to ethnicity, language, religion, social class, gender, sexuality and to political or personal values. The existence of such cultural diversity is particularly important in many inner-city schools and reflective teachers are likely to explore the relationship between cultures in young people's homes, communities and school very carefully indeed (Vincent, 2000). A recent policy focus in England on the importance of 'cultural capital' and its associated definition within the 2019 Ofsted school inspection framework of 'the best that has been thought and said' provoked significant debate in recent years, its opponents citing a body of research which has shown problems arising when home cultures are not considered or attended to by teachers or school curricula. This debate includes the importance of not seeing working class culture as deficient (see Lareau, 1989; Ball, 1981a; Reay, 2018). Culture has also been highlighted through the recent Black Lives Matters movement with its subsequent focus on institutionalised forms of racism leading to underachievement for black and minority ethnic pupils (Maylor et al., 2009; Alexander and Shankley, 2020; Joseph-Salisbury, 2020; Doharty, 2019; Tikly, 2022), leading to calls to recruit a more diverse teaching staff and to diversify, and decolonise, the school curriculum. Stereotypical perceptions of teachers may also have gender or sexuality dimensions that could impinge in a number of ways on the educational opportunities of both girls and boys (for example, Younger and Warrington, 2007; Kehily, 2003; Skelton, 2001, Mac an Ghaill, 1994), as well as LGBTQ+ pupils (Bradlow et al., 2017).

There are also likely to be cultures among the adults within each school. Primary school staffrooms provide a backstage area where tensions are released, feelings are shared and understandings about school life are developed. This is the territory of the classroom teacher, and the resulting relationships usually provide a source of solidarity and sympathy when facing the daily pressures of classrooms (Nias, Southworth and Yeomans, 1989). While colleagues may be stimulating and supportive of experimentation, they can also become protective of existing practices and inhibit innovation (Pollard, 1987a; Sedgwick, 1988).

Cultures have an impact on learning and behaviour, as is being progressively demonstrated by the field of 'cultural psychology' (Heine, 2011; Wells, 1999, Reading 2.4; Bruner, 1986, 1990, Reading 11.1; see also Chapter 2). For instance, Wertsch (1991) argues that the thinking of any learner is dependent on the 'cultural tools' that they deploy. These concepts and artefacts frame and mediate understanding and thus shape development. They will thus certainly have a direct impact on school performance. Similarly, new learning may affect, or even change, the sense of identity of individuals, and such changes may or may not feel viable to them within their home culture. For instance, a classic study (Jackson and Marsden, 1962) showed the unease of working-class boys on being sent out of their communities to a grammar school, and similar problems may affect the performance of children from minority ethnic groups today. It has been argued that organisations like schools can helpfully be seen as 'communities of practice' (Wenger, 1999) which evolve and maintain strong norms of behaviour and thought. New members must learn how to conduct themselves and there may be a process of 'cognitive apprenticeship' (Rogoff, 1990) as new understanding is acquired. However, depending on the social, cultural and economic background of a new pupil or teacher, such induction may or may not be comfortable. Cultures can thus be exclusive as well as inclusive, particularly when organisations feel the need to assert a narrow range of goals. Sadly, exclusion from school has become a significant issue in recent years.

There is thus a sense in which cultures can both enable and constrain learning. Indeed, they are likely to afford different opportunities for particular individuals and groups. It is to these issues that we now turn.

Opportunity

It has been said that 'education cannot compensate for society' (Bernstein, 1971) – and yet the opportunities which teachers and others aspire to create for their pupils make an important contribution to the meritocratic ideal to which most contemporary societies subscribe. However, the challenge of creating such opportunities through education is not to be underestimated.

Although there are substantial differences in Scotland, Wales, Northern Ireland and in England's regions, the UK as a whole is very wealthy in terms of global criteria – but at the same time there is significant inequality in the distribution of income and wealth. For instance, in 2018, households in the bottom 20 per cent of the population had on average an equivalised disposable income of £12,798, whilst the top 20 per cent had £69,126, and this inequality has grown during the COVID pandemic. The gap between the richest in society and the rest of the population widened between 2010 and 2020; the income share of the richest 1 per cent increasing from 7 per cent to 8.3 per cent (ONS, 2020). Such differences have existed for many centuries and tangible evidence of this is available in the contrasts of our buildings, estates and landscape in both urban and rural settings – or even in the windows of estate agents (also bearing in mind that increasing numbers of households do not own their homes). Indeed, it may seem extraordinary, but 4.3 million UK children (31 per cent) lived in poverty as defined by the Department for Work and Pensions (DWP, 2021). In many instances, these children are concentrated in particular communities in which 'cycles of disadvantage' (Rutter and Madge, 1976) are remarkably resistant to change (DCSF, 2009, Reading 5.4).

> **Expert Question**
>
> **Culture:** does the school support expansive learning by affirming learner contributions, engaging partners and providing attractive opportunities?
>
> This question contributes to a conceptual framework underpinning professional expertise (see Chapter 16).

In the case of the UK, there was a substantial rise in inequality during the 1980s and the incomes of top earners continued to race away (Sibieta, 2011). COVID exacerbated this gap, with the lowest wage earners much more likely to lose their jobs due to the lockdown (Montacute, 2020). Economists speculate about the causes of these trends and debate factors such as changes in employment opportunities, returns from high-level skills and education, regional differences and demographic patterns. The direct consequences of government policies on tax and benefits may moderate such structural factors, but the UK's recent experience is of a low level of inter-generational mobility (Blanden, Gregg and Machin, 2005). In other words, the circumstance of parents tends to be reproduced for their children.

> **Expert Question**
>
> **Consequence:** do assessment outcomes lead towards recognised qualifications and a confident sense of personal identity?
>
> This question contributes to a conceptual framework underpinning professional expertise (see Chapter 16).

In summary, affluence and poverty are both growing and becoming 'locked in' (Crawford et al., 2011; DCSF, 2009, Reading 5.4). The social differences in our societies tend to be reproduced from generation to generation. How then does this process of reproduction occur?

An illuminative analysis of this has been provided by a French sociologist, Pierre Bourdieu (e.g. see Bourdieu and Passeron, 1977). Whilst recognising exceptional cases, he argued that overall social status is significantly affected by three forms of 'capital' – each of which can be transferred from one generation to another. 'Economic capital' concerns access to material assets. 'Social capital' focuses on relationships in the family, community or wider society which offers contacts, networks and support. 'Cultural capital' relates to the understanding, knowledge and capabilities of individuals to act within particular social settings. The seeds of difference are sown in the ways in which young children are brought up (see Ball, 2003, **Reading 5.3**). For instance, Lareau (1989) contrasts the 'concerted cultivation' of middle-class families with the assumption of 'natural growth'. The latter causes less aware families to interact with their children in quite different ways – with particularly significant consequences for language development. Reay (2000) illuminates how mothers in different circumstances deploy 'emotional capital' to support their children, and she suggests that generational reserves are built up over time.

Families thus provide economic, social, cultural, linguistic and emotional resources. These affect the experiences, opportunities and expectations which are made available to the next generation.

These factors are particularly transparent in relation to school choice, with the private sector offering to reinforce advantages for the children of parents who can afford their fees. Sociologists fear that the quasi-market in schooling, which has been extended in England through the roll-out of independent academies, will further embed inequality (Ball, 2008). Whilst the Government promotes the 'freedom' of such schools from local authorities, the new structures of provision are expected by others to undermine education as a public good and render it as a 'market-controlled commodity' (Benn, 2011).

Using very large data-sets and innovative statistical techniques, it is now possible to measure the relative influence of neighbourhood, school, family and personal influences on a child's education (Rasbash et al., 2010). This shows that family and personal factors are by far the most significant, which puts the work of schools into perspective (see **Research Briefing 5.1** on p. 162).

It is absolutely clear then, that it is impossible for education to 'compensate for society'. And yet the particular needs of the pupils before us still have to be met, and this is a moral imperative as well as a professional responsibility. Whatever the nature of the overall context around us, teachers must focus on providing the best possible educational opportunities for their pupils. Indeed, beyond the overarching statistics, there are many examples of people whose lives have been transformed through the influence of teachers. One project to enhance home–school knowledge exchange is described in **Research Briefing 4.1** on p. 136, a synopsis of international evidence on improving learning outcomes through parental involvement is provided in EEF **Toolkit Evidence 4.1** summary on p. 135, and strategies to support effective parental engagement can be found in the EEF's recent guidance report (EEF, 2018b).

reflectiveteaching.co.uk/rtps6/part2_ch5

The resources which are available in a school make a big difference in the creation of learning opportunities, and we will distinguish four types here: people, buildings, equipment and materials.

Many people are involved in the life of a successful school and, for this reason collaboration and teamwork are needed, irrespective of status. Apart from the head and the teaching staff, there are many others, such as cleaners, midday meal supervisors, cooks, admin officers, teaching assistants and caretakers, who all have very important supportive roles to play. However, from the educational point of view, the expertise of classroom teachers is the key factor in determining the quality of provision. Teachers themselves are the most important resource, which puts a premium on the recruitment, development and retention of excellent staff. Class size is perceived as a major factor in determining practice and research has supported this proposition for many years (e.g. Glass, 1982; Pate-Bain et al., 1992; Blatchford and Russell, 2020).

Buildings are also an important influence on what goes on in schools. Most obviously, buildings constrain decisions about numbers and types of classes because of the number and nature of the classrooms which are available. This often affects class sizes and forms of curriculum and teaching organisation. The quality of the school environment will also be influenced by aesthetic considerations, and schools vary considerably in terms of the degree of consideration that is given to this issue. Reflective teachers are likely to be concerned about the quality of the learning environment within their classrooms, departments and school and will aim to maximise the learning potential of the spaces which they have available (see Chapter 8).

Equipment and materials enable teachers to provide learning experiences of various sorts. For example, for primary schools maintaining a broad and balanced curriculum across all subjects, the needs range from hall and playground requirements to instruments for music-making, artefacts for historical work and specific resources associated with curriculum progression in English, mathematics and science. In secondary school subject departments, equipment and materials are even more specialised and are likely to be tuned to particular exam syllabi as well as reflecting more generic educational objectives.

The most challenging form of equipment for schools to maintain relates to information technology. This is fast moving in terms of both hardware and software, and variation in provision between schools is often considerable.

UK schools have locally managed budgets in which income from national taxation is distributed annually on the basis of a formula. This allocates a certain amount for each pupil on roll, plus allowances in respect of social disadvantage or special educational needs. The way this is organised varies. For instance, in Scotland three-year budgets are managed through the thirty-two local authorities that are responsible for provision in their areas. The total cost of funding for schools is significant. For example, during 2019/20 schools in England had an expenditure of £51 billion. Secondary school spending per pupil in England (£6,000) was about 16 per cent higher than in primary schools (£5,200) in 2019–20, and spending on primary and secondary schools represented 80 per cent of overall spending (Sibieta, 2021).

Expenditure is the responsibility of the headteacher and governors. However, once fixed costs are taken out of the overall budget, school managers often have relatively small

reflectiveteaching.co.uk/rtps6/part2_ch5

sums to spend at their discretion. Indeed, the salaries of teachers and other staff often amount to around 75 per cent of the budget, followed by costs of building maintenance and school running costs. Only a relatively small percentage is left for books, equipment, materials and discretionary expenditure.

The key factor in school budgets remains the number of pupils on roll. Each school's position in the quasi-market for pupil enrolments in its area is thus crucial to its resource base – hence the pressure for performance in formal assessments and in developing a positive local reputation.

Resources thus structure the material conditions in which teachers work and the opportunities they can provide for pupils. However, the actions they take are also likely to be influenced by the degree of autonomy which they feel they have. For this reason, we now focus on the issue of accountability.

Accountability

Teachers are paid to provide professional services. However, the degree of accountability and external control to which they have been subject has varied historically.

In the nineteenth century, state provision for education was managed through 'payment by results'. Teacher salaries were dependent on the results of annual visits by inspectors to test pupils in reading, writing and arithmetic. Indeed, when introducing the Revised Code for Education of 1862, its proposer Robert Lowe made the famous boast that: 'If it is not cheap, it shall be efficient, if it is not efficient, it shall be cheap.' Although superseded in the first part of the twentieth century, the approach left a legacy in the form of imposed performance requirements. However, from the 1920s teachers began to develop greater professional autonomy (Lawn and Ozga, 1986). In particular, the independence of headteachers within their schools and of class teachers within their classrooms emerged to become established principles. After the Second World War, as professional confidence grew, this independence extended into the curriculum to the extent that, in 1960, the curriculum was described by Lord Eccles, Minister for Education, as a 'secret garden' into which central government was not expected to intrude. Such confidence was probably at a high point in the early 1970s.

In 1977, a speech at Ruskin College, Oxford, by Prime Minister Callaghan reflected a changing ideological, economic and political climate. This resulted in teachers coming under increasing pressure to 'increase their accountability' and to demonstrate competent performance against centrally defined criteria. These developments were presented by Margaret Thatcher's Conservative government during the 1980s as a necessary reduction in the influence of the 'producers' (seen as teacher unions, administrators and theorists) and thus to enable educational provision to be shaped by the 'consumers' (seen as parents and industry, though with little direct reference to children and young people themselves). Later, under Tony Blair's New Labour administration, the emphasis was in terms of applying modern personnel and performance management systems so that nationally prescribed curricula and pedagogies could be delivered – for instance, as set out in England through the National Curriculum and Literacy and Numeracy Strategies.

In the contemporary, devolved UK and in Ireland, a wide range of approaches is now evident. Each country has its national curriculum and inspection system but the form and role of these vary considerably.

With effect from 2014, England adopted a new National Curriculum which requires primary schools to focus on core knowledge in English, mathematics and science, whilst also expecting provision of a 'broad and balanced' education. Subject to these constraints, schools are to make their own judgements about the 'school curriculum' as a whole. Secondary schools have been particularly encouraged to leave the state system to become independent 'academies', for which the statutory requirements of the National Curriculum do not formally apply. In relation to assessment and qualifications, formal testing remains at age 11. GCSEs were 'reformed' to increase rigour and A Level exam syllabi continue to frame school provision but now with input from universities. The accountability measure for secondary schools was expanded to include progress in eight subjects, thus endorsing the value of a broad curriculum. League tables will continue to be produced – despite the technical difficulties of doing so (Leckie and Goldstein, 2009). The model in England remains one of schools being required to directly account for themselves to stakeholders, in competition with other schools in their locality. The direction of policy by successive governments has been to use market forces to hold schools to account.

England also retains a powerful interventionist capacity in the form of the Ofsted inspection system. Ofsted contracts teams of inspectors to make a structured report on every individual school in a regular cycle. Comparative data from schools serving similar socio-economic communities and baseline data from the school being inspected are used to evaluate levels of performance and improvement. The strongest sanction available to Ofsted is that a school be placed in 'special measures'. This means that it is deemed to have been failing to meet expected performance standards under the present management. Support or even an alternative leadership team may be provided. 'Failing schools' can be closed by order of the Secretary of State.

Scotland has taken a very different approach and, in 2011, established *Education Scotland* which aims to coordinate almost all of Scotland's provision for curriculum, pedagogy, assessment, leadership, self-improvement, professional development and inspection. It seeks to support quality and improvement by working 'in partnership alongside the full range of bodies and organisations active in Scottish Education'.

In addition to schools themselves, this includes local authorities, further and higher education, third sector organisations and parent groups. Improvement is thus expected to come from processes of personal and institutional self-development, local collaboration and a collective sense of national purpose.

In 2011, the General Teaching Council for Scotland (GTC S) was granted full independence from the government (effective April 2012) as a self-regulating, professionally led body – the first in the world. The establishment of the GTC S was strongly influenced by the model provided by the General Medical Council. It is thus based, at root, on trust in the teaching profession's capacity to regulate and improve its own professional standards.

reflectiveteaching.co.uk/rtps6/part2_ch5

England's Chartered College of Teaching was established in 2017 although its roots date back to the College of Preceptors in 1849, and the College of Teachers in 1998. In contrast to the GTC S, the Chartered College of Teaching (CCT) does not accredit teacher education courses, monitor professional standards, nor manage teacher induction. Instead, the CCT's mission is celebrating, supporting and connecting teachers through its membership, publications and professional development programmes (chartered.college/aboutus/).

The General Teaching Council for England (GTC E) published a policy paper on these issues just before its abolition (2011, Reading 5.5). The GTC E argued that accountability is by nature 'relational' because it is associated with actions by both the account-holder and the account-giver. Particular forms of accountability thus influence behaviour and provision. A question then arises about the effects of accountability in relation to overarching educational objectives. On this, the GTC E argued that in England there had been insufficient focus on teaching quality. Rather, the foundations of professional collaboration and enduring school improvement had been undermined by measurement of narrow, short-term performance and by punitive inspection. In place of this, they suggested, the teaching profession needs systems which support the development of expertise and record how professional responsibilities are discharged. Ultimately, the profession needs to regulate itself. In order to tackle this latter issue, The Chartered College of Teaching was established in 2017, with a focus on connecting teachers and enabling them to take pride in their profession, and providing the best possible education for children and young people through connecting teachers to research evidence.

> **Expert Question**
>
> **Warrant:** *are our teaching strategies evidence-informed, convincing and justifiable to stakeholders?*
>
> This question contributes to a conceptual framework underpinning professional expertise (see Chapter 16).

In Wales, the General Teaching Council for Wales (GTC W) was reconfigured and renamed to become the Education Workforce Council (EWC) in 2015. The EWC is the independent regulator for teachers and learning support staff in schools in Wales.

In Northern Ireland and Ireland, General Teaching Councils maintain professional standards of conduct and practice, register teachers and support professional development. Like the GTC E (and the former GTC W), they were established by legislation in the late 1990s and are largely reliant for core functions on income from annual teacher registration. However, since numbers of registered teachers are relatively small in Wales and Northern Ireland, this is challenging. It raises a question about the extent to which teachers should themselves pay for professional regulation or whether it should be funded by governments in the public interest.

The issue of accountability thus crystallises many issues concerning the relationship between education and society. Should education be a relatively autonomous system or should it be under tight forms of control? Should teachers simply carry out centrally determined instructions, or should they develop and exercise professional judgement? What, indeed, is the role of local democratic institutions in this? And who should pay for the accountability system? The history of our education system provides many fascinating instances of attempts to reconcile such dilemmas (Silver, 1980) and there are plenty of related current issues which a reflective teacher might consider.

In particular, though, and following the dialectical model of social change which we discussed at the beginning of this chapter (Readings 5.1 and 17.5), the issues of accountability, autonomy and control pose questions of a personal nature for reflective teachers. How should each individual act? To whom do you feel you should be accountable – to children, parents, colleagues, your headteacher, local or national government, the media, inspectors or yourself?

Reflective Activity 5.1

Aim: To review and explore the significance of ideology, culture, opportunity and accountability.

Evidence and reflection: Arrange to meet with a small group of work colleagues. In preparation, share out study of each section of Chapter 4 so that ideology, culture, opportunity and accountability are each covered.

In a meeting, each sub-group should explain the issues raised in their section of the chapter, and should relate them to your work context. How, in particular, is your school affected by the context in which it exists?

Extension: What other contextual factors are particularly significant in determining the circumstances of your school?

PEOPLE AND AGENCY

We now turn to the individual and personal factors which are the second element in the dialectical model that underpins this book. For instance, classroom life can be seen as being created by teachers and children as they respond to the situations in which they find themselves. Thus, as well as understanding something of the factors affecting the social context of schooling, we also need to consider how teachers and children respond. Such responses reflect subjective perceptions, beliefs, values, commitments, identities, life narratives and imagined futures. This is the exercise of agency and voice – and recognition that our actions are not simply determined by our circumstances.

We begin by focusing on teachers.

Teachers

The importance of high-quality teaching is now understood by governments across the world (Barber and Mourshed, 2007; OECD, 2005; Chetty, Friedman and Rockoff, 2014; Chapter 4). This has significantly increased the attention being given to teaching as a profession, and to the individuals within it.

reflectiveteaching.co.uk/rtps6/part2_ch5

Teachers are people who happen to hold a particular position in schools. No apologies are made for asserting this simple fact, for it has enormous implications, as we saw in the first chapter of this book. Each person is unique, with particular cultural and material experiences making up their 'biography' (Sikes, Measor and Woods, 1985). This provides the seedbed for their sense of 'self' and influences their personality and perspectives (Mead, 1934; Gu, 2007, Reading 1.1). The development of each person continues throughout life, but early formative experiences remain important. Indeed, because personal qualities, such as having the capacity to empathise and the confidence to project and assert oneself, are so important in teaching. Indeed, much of what particular teachers will be able to achieve in their classrooms will be influenced by them. Of even greater importance is the capacity to know oneself. We all have strengths and weaknesses, and most teachers would agree that classroom life tends to reveal these fairly quickly (Turnbull, 2007). Reflective teaching is, therefore, a great deal to do with facing such features of ourselves in a constructive and objective manner and in a way which incorporates a continuous capacity to change and develop.

The particularly human capability of being able to review the relationship of 'what is' and 'what might be' is one which teachers often draw on when considering their aims and examining their educational values and philosophies. While there has always been a good deal of idealism in commitment to teaching, there has also always been a concern with practical realism. Indeed, a very important factor which influences teachers' perceptions in the classroom is that the teacher has to 'cope', personally as well as professionally, with the classroom situation (Pollard, 1982; Woods, 1990; Sachs, 2003). For this reason, we would suggest that a fundamental element of classroom coping, or survival, is very deeply personal, for it involves teachers, with a particular image of their self, acting in the challenging situation which classrooms represent (Bennett, 2012). In this, it is important to remember that what it is possible to do in classrooms is constrained by the basic facts of large numbers of children, limited resources, compulsory attendance, curriculum and assessment frameworks and other external expectations which exist about what should and should not take place. The 'social work' role of teachers in supporting children, young people and their parents or carers in some communities is also considerable – particularly in primary schools (Webb and Vulliamy, 2002). The recent impact of COVID and lockdown has also highlighted the pressing need for schools to support children's mental health and wellbeing (e.g. Hurry et al., 2021).

In such circumstances, teachers face acute dilemmas between their personal and professional concerns and the practical possibilities (Berlak and Berlak, 1981; Eaude, 2012, Reading 16.3). They are forced to juggle their priorities as they manage the stress which is often involved (Cole and Walker, 1989; Dunham, 1992; Sikes, 1997) and as they come to terms with classroom situations.

And yet the espoused goal of contemporary policy is for the lightening of constraint on teachers so that they are enabled to exercise professional judgement in a wider range of circumstances. This is particularly significant in England where government ministers claim to value teacher judgement in respect of the 'school curriculum'. However, this rhetoric is in tension with how the national curriculum and statutory assessments are realised in practice, for example the over-specification of the core subjects; the incursions into pedagogy in the prescription of synthetic phonics for early reading; and statutory assessment processes which impact on the curriculum. The exceptions are extremely important qualifiers. Diversity of school provision will reflect innovation by teachers as they exploit new opportunities. Reflective teachers will of course want to consider the nature of this innovation and its social as well as educational consequences.

In recent years, considerable attention has been paid to providing stronger continuity in professional development, so that the situation of a trainee, newly qualified teacher, established teacher, experienced teacher and headteacher is now well defined. This may offer a sense of continuity for a career professional and will certainly enable governments to provide more systematic forms of support and direction. Arguably the most cogent UK example of such thinking is 'Teaching Scotland's Future' (Donaldson, 2010). The introduction in 2021 in England of the Early Career Framework and the revised suite of National Professional Qualifications for school leaders were also intended to offer a 'golden thread' of quality professional development for teachers as they move through their careers.

We also need to consider the position of teachers as employees. Teachers have legitimate legal, contractual and economic interests to maintain, protect and develop (Lawn and Grace, 1987). For example, as we saw in Chapter 1, teachers in maintained schools in England and Wales are contracted to work up to 1,265 hours per year 'directed time' over 195 working days. Morning and afternoon breaks count as directed time, and a midday break for lunch is also protected. Teachers may be required to undertake activities which are additional to basic classroom teaching such as attendance at staff planning meetings and parents' evenings, and extracurricular activities such as sport, clubs, choirs, orchestras and drama productions. Teachers working in schools designated as 'academies' may have particular contractual obligations and some have felt vulnerable to the whims of powerful headteachers. Given this context, surveys of working hours regularly record that teachers work far in excess of their contractual obligation and, in recent years, the reduction of teacher workload has become an educational policy priority in England.

Headteachers have a duty to manage the school's workforce with regards to their wellbeing, and a balance has to be struck between educational expectations and what is reasonable to ask of people who happen to earn their living from teaching. Many teachers also have significant family responsibilities, as well as other interests which may be important to them. Many teachers find employment protection, and more, from joining a union – such as the National Education Union.

Notwithstanding such considerations, teaching attracts people who have a sense of moral purpose. There is thus, in general terms across the profession, a principled commitment to providing high-quality education that meets the needs of learners. It is this value commitment which causes teachers to 'go the extra mile' on behalf of children and young people.

Pupils

As with the personal factors associated with teachers, the most important point to make about children and young people is that they are thinking, rational individuals (Corsaro, 2011; James, Jenks and Prout, 1998; Jones, 2009, Reading 1.5). Each one of the ten million UK school pupils has a unique 'biography', and the ways in which they feel about themselves, and present themselves in school, will be influenced by their understandings of previous cultural, social and material experience in their families and elsewhere (Bruner, 1986). Through their compulsory education, from age 5 to 16, most children develop a relatively clear sense of their identity as learners (Warin, 2010; Pollard and Filer, 1996, Reading 1.2). Indeed, preschool experience and social processes in the primary school lead them to perceive themselves as relative school failures or successes (for example, Francis, Tailor and Tereshchenko, 2019). The foundations of their 'learning disposition' and stance as a 'lifelong learner' become established, and there is no doubt that this is the crucial age phase for educational investment (Karoly, Greenwood and Everingham, 1998) with research showing a strong link between a high-quality early years education and later educational outcomes (Melhuish and Gardiner, 2020).

> **Expert Question**
>
> **Empowerment:** is our pedagogic repertoire successful in enhancing wellbeing, learning disposition, capabilities and agency?
>
> This question contributes to a conceptual framework underpinning professional expertise (see Chapter 16).

As children progress through secondary schools, with their complex systems of setting, banding, options and 'pathways', these self-perceptions are further reinforced or modified (see also Lawrence, 1987, Reading 6.6). At the point of leaving schooling and entering the worlds of college or work, children's life trajectories are thus likely to be well established. Teachers should therefore not lose sight of the fact that, in their daily work, they are shaping long-term life chances and identities, as well as working towards immediate targets for performance (Feinstein et al., 2008b, Reading 1.6).

Pupils at school embody, and are influenced by, a huge range of circumstances and prior experiences. These include factors such as sex, social class, race, language development, learning disposition, health and type of parental support. As we saw earlier in this chapter in the discussion of opportunities, patterns of advantage and disadvantage are very significant. However, such factors do not determine consequences.

The key issue is how children and young people respond to their circumstances – and in this, teachers can have a crucial role in supporting them.

Pupils have to survive in classroom situations in which they may well feel insecure (Jackson, 1968, Reading 6.1). Peer culture and the support of friends are considerable resources in this. However, this can also pose dilemmas in class when pupils attempt to please both their peers and their teacher. Creative strategies are called for and these may cover a range from conformity through negotiation to rejection. The agency of young learners is thus played out in the immediacy of the classroom and teachers therefore have unique opportunities to influence factors such as motivation as well as approaches to learning and subject knowledge (Rudduck and McIntyre, 2007; see also Reading 1.3).

Above all, though, we must never forget that children are placed in the role of 'pupils' for only part of each day. It is no wonder that families, friends, relationships, social media, film, computer games, music, fashion, sport etc. are important to them. A reflective teacher, therefore, must aim to work with an understanding of the culture of young people. Indeed, it is very unwise to try to do otherwise and, if connections can be made, then pupil culture can itself provide an excellent motivational hook into schoolwork.

reflectiveteaching.co.uk/rtps6/part2_ch5

Parents and carers can play a particularly important role in supporting the learning of children and young people. They are often thought of as supplementary teachers, with an advantageous one-on-one teaching ratio, and such support is certainly a major factor in pre-school development and early literacy. However, perhaps the most important role for parents and carers today is in providing a source of stable emotional support for children as they encounter new challenges in school. Reay (2000) has provided a fascinating analysis of this as a form of 'emotional capital'. Schools are increasingly pressured places, and there is a need for someone to really nurture the developing child from day to day, year to year.

It is not necessary to be well off financially to do this; indeed, the most valuable contributions are probably time, patience, understanding and affection. There is also an increasing understanding that all families and communities, including those that may seem disadvantaged, have 'funds of knowledge' that should be tapped to enhance children's learning (Moll and Greenberg, 1990). Social circumstances do, however, radically affect participation (Crozier and Reay, 2005; Ball, 2003, Reading 5.3; Vincent, 1996, 2000) and the voices of young people can sometimes be inadequately recognised (Crozier, 2000). However, if processes for supportive knowledge exchange between such parents and teachers could be established, the potential for enhancing learning is enormous (Hughes and Pollard, 2000; Desforges with Abouchaar, 2003).

> **Expert Questions**
>
> **Development:** does formative feedback and support enable learners to achieve personal learning goals?
>
> **Engagement:** do our teaching strategies, classroom organisation and consultation enable learners to actively participate in and enjoy their learning?
>
> This question contributes to a conceptual framework underpinning professional expertise (see Chapter 16).

> **Expert Question**
>
> **Connection:** does the curriculum engage with the cultural resources and funds-of-knowledge of families and the community?
>
> This question contributes to a conceptual framework underpinning professional expertise (see Chapter 16).

Reflective Activity 5.2

Aim: To consider the meaning and significance of 'agency', both for teachers and for learners.

Evidence and reflection: **Reflective Activity 5.1** reviewed circumstances, and this activity focuses on how people respond and act in relation to these. In particular, it is about the human spirit and the possibilities which always exist whatever the circumstances.

An interesting way of approaching this is to share one's educational biography with a colleague with whom one feels secure. Taking it in turns, take time to provide a narrative of how you moved through your education, meeting different teachers, growing up, finding some learning difficult but succeeding in others . . . Identify and focus on some key episodes or turning points which enabled you to progress. Explore, if you can, the actions you took and the encouragement or support you received from others.

Does consideration of such narratives and key moments enable you to see the significance of agency, in the form of your determination to succeed or the judgement by others to encourage you?

Extension: You might like to consider the learning of a small number of pupils you know at school. To what extent are they able to exercise agency in relation to their circumstances and goals, and might you be able to help?

CONCLUSION

The intention in this chapter has been to discuss the relationship between society as a whole and the people who are centrally involved in education. This is because school practices and classroom actions are influenced by the social circumstances within which they occur. However, it has also been argued that individuals can, and will, have effects on future social changes as they exercise their personal agency – though the degree of influence ebbs and flows depending on the roles occupied and at different phases of history.

A theoretical framework of this sort is important for reflective teachers because it establishes the principle that we can all 'make a difference' within our society. Professional commitment is therefore very important, and we should not accept an ascribed position as passive receptors of externally determined prescription. The provision of high-quality education is enhanced when social awareness complements high levels of teaching skills, and when individual responsibilities for professional actions are taken seriously.

This fundamental belief in the commitment, quality and constructive role of teachers underpins the book. The analysis is optimistic. High-quality education depends on the professionalism of teachers.

reflectiveteaching.co.uk/rtps6/part2_ch5

CHAPTER WEBPAGE

reflectiveteaching.co.uk offers additional professional resources for this chapter. For the chapter webpage, go to: **reflectiveteaching.co.uk/rtps6/part2_ch5**

The importance of the context in which teaching and learning takes place is immense, and this chapter merely touches the surface of the issues. However, the internet offers some really wonderful resources. Take a look, for instance, at **jrf.org.uk** where the Joseph Rowntree Foundation summarise their work on education. Or visit the website of the Sutton Trust, which specialises in attempts to improve social mobility – **suttontrust.com**. The Institute for Fiscal Studies also has a 'theme' focused on the economic importance of education, skills and human capital (**ifs.org.uk/research_areas/38**). And there are many more sources of evidence about the influence of our histories, economies, cultures, polities and social structures on the lives of communities, families and children.

The *Reflective Teaching* webpage for Chapter 5 provides a particularly strong set of *Reflective Activities*, with five times more than those printed in the text above. They are there to do a job, which is to help in relating wide-ranging societal factors to the lived experiences of individuals. As the chapter suggests, public issues lie behind many personal troubles, and we are all caught up in, and contribute to, our circumstances. The suggested activities suggest ways of exploring these relationships.

The pattern of further support in studying such issues continues, with three levels of guidance being provided.

1 On the chapter webpage, the *Further Reading* tab provides an overview of sources, following the structure of the chapter. It will be particularly useful if you have access to an education or social science library.

2 *Key Readings*, below, is a shorter list of recommended texts. It should suit those who have limited time but still have access to a library.

3 The edited excerpts from *Readings for Reflective Teaching in Schools* provide quick access to high-priority texts. A brief description of the contents for this particular chapter is indicated within the *Key Reading* list below.

KEY READINGS

We begin with the theoretical framework which informs this book, with its juxtaposition of social context and individual agency.

> Mills, C.W. (1959) *The Sociological Imagination.* Oxford: Oxford University Press. (**Reading 5.1**)

The Department for Education and Science exercised its own imagination to produce:

Teaching and Learning in 2020 Review Group (2006) *2020 Vision: Report of the Teaching and Learning in 2020 Review Group.* London: DfES. (**Reading 10.7**)

However, the use of evidence, even by government bodies, does have to be carefully checked. On this, see:

Benn, M. and Downs, J. (2016) *The Truth About Our Schools. Exposing the Myths, Exploring the Evidence.* London: Routledge.

For a comparative analysis of educational values in different countries, their effects on provision and on what seems possible, see:

Green, A., Preston, J. and Janmaat, J.G. (2006) *Education, Equality and Social Cohesion: A Comparative Analysis.* London: Palgrave. (see also **Reading 5.2**)

Devolution has enabled distinctive policies to develop in each part of the UK. For an authoritative account, see:

Mitchell, J. (2012) *Devolution in the United Kingdom.* Manchester: Manchester University Press.

For a comprehensive review of issues facing primary and secondary education in England see:

Alexander, R. (ed.) (2010) *Children, Their World, Their Education. Final Report and Recommendations of the Cambridge Primary Review.* London: Routledge.

The work of Pierre Bourdieu has influenced ways of understanding different forms of cultural, social and emotional capital, alongside the economic, through which social differences are perpetuated. See:

Bourdieu, P. and Passeron, J.C. (1977) *Reproduction in Education, Society and Culture.* London: SAGE.

Stephen Ball has documented policies and practices in the reproduction of social class and other forms of differentiation, with particular reference to secondary education. A collection is:

Ball, S. (2006) *Education Policy and Social Class.* London: Routledge. (see also **Reading 5.3**)

On the challenges of working in schools to overcome disadvantage, see:

Department for Children, Schools and Families (2009) *Breaking the Link between Disadvantage and Low Attainment.* Nottingham: DCSF Publications. (**Reading 5.4**)

An important international study of the consequences of inequality is:

Wilkinson, R. and Pickett, K. (2009) *The Spirit Level: Why Equality is Better for Everyone.* London: Penguin.

The contextual factors which affect education so significantly are the central focus of the field of Education Studies. See, for example:

Ward, S. (ed.) (2012) *A Student's Guide to Education Studies.* London: Routledge.
Bates, J. and Lewis, S. (2009) *The Study of Education: An Introduction.* London: Continuum.
Bartlett, S. and Burton, D. (2012) *Introduction to Education Studies.* London: SAGE.

To review the challenges and pleasures of being a teacher, see:

Day, C. and Gu, Q. (2010) *The New Lives of Teachers.* London: Routledge. (see also **Reading 1.1**)

For an understanding of modern childhoods and schooling, and an appreciation of the value of engaging with pupils, take a look at:

Blundell, D. (2012) *Education and Constructions of Childhood.* London: Continuum. (see also **Reading 1.5**)
Rudduck, J. and McIntyre, D. (2007) *Improving Learning through Consulting Pupils.* London: Routledge. (see also **Reading 1.3**)

The challenges of parents and teachers working together in partnership to support learners are explored in practical ways in:

Crozier, G. and Reay, D. (2005) *Activating Participation: Parents and Teachers Working Towards Partnership.* Stoke-on-Trent: Trentham Books.

Spend data from:

ifs.org.uk/uploads/2020--annual-report-on-education-spending-in-England-schools.pdf

reflectiveteaching.co.uk/rtps6/part2_ch5

RESEARCH BRIEFING 5.1
School, family, neighbourhood: which is most important to a child's education?

Children grow up in complex social environments. The influences on a child's development are many, and multi-layered. The school they go to, the family around them and the neighbourhood they grow up in are often highlighted as particularly important for children's educational achievements. But, which is the most important?

- Families account for 40 per cent of the overall variation between children in their academic progress during secondary schooling.
- The wider shared environments of primary school (9 per cent), secondary school (10 per cent), neighbourhood (2 per cent) and Local Education Authority (LEA) (1 per cent) account for a total of 22 per cent.
- Children themselves account for the remaining 38 per cent.

From a school effectiveness point of view it is interesting that the family effect is just as important as the child effect. However, this does not necessarily imply that interventions to improve child academic outcomes are best implemented at the family level. While primary and secondary schools appear less important than families, they still make reasonably substantial contributions; and it is at these levels that many educational policies are likely to be most effective. It is easier for governments to intervene in the running of schools than to change parenting practices within families.

The research
Our knowledge of the impact of schools, neighbourhoods and families comes from studies that look at each of these influences separately, and therefore little is known about their relative importance. For example, school effectiveness studies attempt to measure the importance of schools on children's academic progress, but nearly always ignore the role of family. Family research using siblings, on the other hand, attempts to quantify the importance of genetic and environmental family influences, but nearly always ignores the role of the wider shared environment of schools and neighbourhoods. Knowledge of the relative effects of schools, neighbourhoods and families is needed to help inform decisions about the allocation of government resources to programmes and policies that will support children's learning.

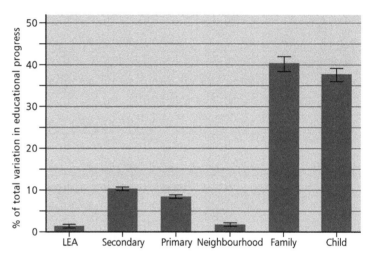

The importance of different influences on educational progress, with 95% credible intervals.

Research design
We follow half a million English school children through secondary schooling. We use cross-classified multilevel statistical models to estimate the impact of the different influences of children's complex social environments on their academic progress.

Our final model decomposes the variation in children's progress into effects attributable to six influences: Local Education Authorities (LEAs), secondary schools, neighbourhoods, primary schools, families and children. This is an improvement on previous school effectiveness studies because it differentiates, for the first time, between the effects of the family and of the pupil; and it is an improvement on previous family research because it estimates the influence of the family-shared environment separately from those of the wider shared environments of schools and areas. Thus, we unite school effectiveness studies and family research under a single framework and therefore disentangle the various influences on children's progress.

Further information
References for practitioners, journalists and policymakers
Leckie, G., Pillinger, R., Jenkins, J. and Rasbash, J. (2010). *School, family, neighbourhood: which is most important to a child's education?*
MethodsNews: Newsletter from the ESRC National Centre for Research, Summer, 4.
Leckie, G., Pillinger, R., Jenkins, J. and Rasbash, J. (2010). *School, family, neighbourhood: which is most important to a child's education? Significance*, 7, 67–72.

This work was carried out at the University of Bristol.

Chapter 6
Relationships
How are we getting on together?

Introduction	164

Enhancing classroom climate	165
Classroom climate and emotional security	166
Supporting children's confidence and self-esteem	169
Developing an inclusive classroom	170

Classroom relationships	172
Learning to establish and maintain positive relationships	172
Social and emotional learning and relationship skills	174
Rules and routines	175
Identifying routines and understandings	176
Being 'fair'	177

Relationships for learning	178
Curriculum and relationships	178
Pupil perspectives of teachers	181
Teacher and pupil actions	182
Patterns in pupil actions	183
Positive and negative cycles	184

Teacher thinking and professional skills	186
Teacher perspectives	186
Expectations of others and bias	187
Professional skills	188
Classroom authority	189

Conclusion	190

reflectiveteaching.co.uk/rtps6/part2_ch6

INTRODUCTION

Relationships underpin and enable both 'order' and 'learning' and are thus the foundation for success as a teacher. Further, good classroom relationships contribute enormously to the social and emotional learning of children – a factor which has been shown to make a tangible difference to learning outcomes (see EEF **Toolkit Evidence 6.1** on p. 193). At their best, teacher–pupil relationships are respectful and stable – part of the routine of classroom life. However, a 'good relationship' is not something which can be assumed. The skills and competencies that underpin effective relationships must be developed by children, ideally with explicit support from their teachers.

Classrooms tend to be potentially threatening to both teachers and pupils because of their very structures and purposes, as Waller's classic study of 'latent conflict' illustrated so vividly (1932). In simple terms, the teacher faces relatively large numbers of children and is expected to educate them, while each child faces the evaluative power of the teacher and is expected to learn (see Jackson, 1968, Reading 6.1). There are significant challenges for both parties, so that teachers and pupils put considerable efforts into developing ways of coping with the situation. It is not unusual for teachers or student teachers who lack negotiating skills to attempt to impose themselves. Although the strategy may work in the short term, it can have unfortunate side effects. Pupils are quick to discern when the expectations of them and the sense of order in the classroom are based more on the use of teacher power than on a sense of fairness and respect. How then, is a way forward found? There are two basic possibilities: either order is imposed by teachers using their power, or there is negotiation between teachers and pupils so that understanding ways of collaborating together are constructed. These understandings are the basis of 'good relationships'.

As we have seen, for instance in Chapter 1, teachers normally have a strong moral purpose and place great emphasis on establishing good relationships with children. We have a moral obligation to do our best to ensure each child feels welcome, cared for, respected and secure in school. We must also recognise that these early experiences of schooling can impact their future educational and life experiences. Many challenges faced by adults, such as mental health issues, criminality, and poor literacy and numeracy, can be traced back to early childhood experiences (World Health Organization, 2022).

If teachers attempt to unduly impose themselves, although the strategy may work in the short term it, can have unfortunate side effects. When teachers 'become angry' they may be seen by children as being unfair. Children can feel 'picked on', 'shown up' and humiliated – and such feelings do not create appropriate conditions for effective learning (Immordino-Yang and Damasio, 2007, Reading 6.2).

Fortunately, however, a shared sense of the moral order of the classroom, with social conventions, expectations and rules, and thus a sense of what is 'right', is the normal outcome of successful classroom negotiations. Such codes and principles of interaction have wider and longer-term significance in contributing to the social, ethical and moral

reflectiveteaching.co.uk/rtps6/part2_ch6

education of children. In a sense, good relationships and 'citizenship' in the classroom can act as a model for responsible, active citizenship in later life.

TLRP Principles

Three principles are of particular relevance to this chapter on classroom relationships as a foundation for learning:

Effective teaching and learning equips learners for life in its broadest sense. Learning should aim to help people to develop the intellectual, personal and social resources that will enable them to participate as active citizens, contribute to economic development and flourish as individuals in a diverse and changing society. (*Principle 1*)

Effective teaching and learning requires teachers to scaffold learning. Teachers should provide activities which support learners as they move forward, not just intellectually, but also socially and emotionally, so that once these supports are removed, the learning is secure. (*Principle 4*)

Effective teaching and learning fosters both individual and social processes and outcomes. Learning is a social activity. Learners should be encouraged and helped to work with others, to share ideas and to build knowledge together. Consulting learners about their learning and giving them a voice is both an expectation and a right. (*Principle 7*)

See Chapter 4

This chapter is structured in four main parts.

It begins with a consideration of 'classroom climate'. This includes specific sections on emotional security, self-esteem and inclusion. We move on to a detailed discussion of classroom relationships, how young children can be supported in developing relationship-building skills, and the roles of rules, routines and fairness. This understanding is then directly applied to teaching and learning processes through consideration of curriculum, teacher and pupil actions, and developmental cycles in class relationships over time. Finally, we discuss teacher expectations and professional skills – particularly for maintaining classroom authority.

Then, in Chapter 7, we focus more directly on managing classroom behaviour.

ENHANCING CLASSROOM CLIMATE

Before discussing classroom relationships in detail we will start by taking a broader view of the classroom and considering overall outcomes in terms of the classroom as an environment for learning. This is summarised through the concept of 'classroom climate'.

reflectiveteaching.co.uk/rtps6/part2_ch6

In this section, we will also review how the classroom environment can support pupil self-esteem and make inclusive provision for all children.

Classroom climate and emotional security

The influence of classroom environments on teachers and children has been a research topic for many years. One obvious question which emerged was how to define the 'environment'. In a classic study, Withall (1949) answered this by highlighting the 'socio-emotional climate' as being particularly significant.

Contemporary advances in neurobiology draw connections between social, emotional, cognitive and biological factors. For example, the authors of an article entitled 'We feel, therefore we learn' explain that:

> Modern biology reveals humans to be fundamentally emotional and social creatures. . . . The relationship between learning, emotion and body state runs much deeper than many educators realise. It's not that emotions rule our cognition, nor that rational thought does not exist. It is rather, that the original purpose for which our brains evolved was to manage our physiology, to optimise our survival and to allow us to flourish. . . . But there is another layer to the problem of surviving and flourishing, [for] as brains and the minds they support became more complex, the problem became not only dealing with one's own self but managing social interactions and relationships. . . . The physiology of emotion and its consequent processes of feeling have enormous repercussions for the way we learn. (Immordino-Yang and Damasio, 2007, pp. 3–9, Reading 6.2)

Put another way, the feelings which pupils develop about classroom life, about their teachers and about learning itself have profound educational implications (Hascher, 2003). We are unlikely to 'open up' for learning unless we feel personally secure.

Indeed, a systematic review of high-quality, international evidence on children's social and emotional learning by the Education Endowment Foundation has indicated its importance in providing a foundation for educational progress, on which skilled teachers can build (see **Toolkit Evidence 6.1** on p. 193).

Taking forward such ideas in their work on school and community networks, West-Burnham, Farrar and Otero (2007) have argued that 'all learning is relational' and that new ways of thinking about learning relations in local communities are necessary. In this perspective, relationships both within and beyond the school make social, emotional *and* cognitive contributions to learning. The significance of this is attested by the strength of the association of home circumstances and pupil outcomes, as we saw in Chapter 5. And yet, despite what is known about such relational factors, 'life in classrooms' remains dominated by the themes of 'crowds, praise and power' (Jackson, 1968, Reading 6.1).

There are thus good reasons why reflective teachers attend to the social and emotional dimensions of pupil experience. They are a foundation for the development of a sense of

Chapter 6 Relationships 167

belonging and they engender constructive approaches to learning which can set pupils up well for success in their school career and later life.

Attempts have been made to measure classroom climate by studying the perceptions of teachers and children (see Frieberg, 1999). Indeed, Fraser and Fisher (1984) developed a 'My Classroom Inventory' for teachers to use in their own classrooms (see Reflective Activity 6.1). This can give structured feedback on pupil feelings about classroom life and might be used to take a snapshot and identify areas for development. However, such techniques arguably fail to grasp either the subtleties of the interpersonal relationships to which many school teachers aspire, or the dynamic complexity of teacher–pupil interaction. Asking pupils to simply 'draw a picture of important things in their classroom' can also be extremely revealing, and may be more appropriate for younger children.

Reflective Activity 6.1

Aim: To 'measure' overall classroom environment at a particular point of time.

Method: Each child will need a copy of the inventory below. As a class (or in a group) pupils should be asked to circle the answer which 'best describes what their classroom is like'. The items could be read out in turn for simultaneous, but individual, responses. Scoring of answers can be done using the teacher's column. 'Yes' scores 3 and 'No' scores 1 except where reversed scoring is indicated (R). Omitted or indecipherable answers are scored 2.

There are five scales, made up by adding various items, as follows:

Satisfaction (S)	Items 1, 6, 11, 16, 21
Friction (F)	Items 2, 7, 12, 17, 22
Competitiveness (CM)	Items 3, 8, 13, 18, 23
Difficulty (D)	Items 4, 9, 14, 19, 24
Cohesiveness (CH)	Items 5, 10, 15, 20, 25

Follow-up: Mean scores for each scale will indicate the nature of the overall classroom climate and may raise issues for further consideration, particularly if repeated some time later. (It should be noted that the inventory reproduced here is a short form of a longer instrument and is not a reliable measure of the feelings of individuals.)

NAME. . . . .

What describes your classroom?	Circle your answer		
1 The pupils enjoy their school work in my class	Yes	No	
2 Children are always fighting with each other	Yes	No	
3 Children often race to see who can finish first	Yes	No	
4 In our class the work is hard to do	Yes	No	
5 In my class everybody is my friend	Yes	No	
6 Some pupils are not happy in class	Yes	No	R
7 Some of the children in our class are mean	Yes	No	
8 Most children want their work to be better than their friend's	Yes	No	
9 Most children can do their schoolwork without help	Yes	No	R

---

reflectiveteaching.co.uk/rtps6/part2_ch6

10	Some people in my class are not my friends	Yes	No	R
11	Children seem to like the class	Yes	No	
12	Many children in our class like to fight	Yes	No	
13	Some pupils feel bad when they don't do as well as the others	Yes	No	
14	Only the smart pupils can do their work	Yes	No	
15	All pupils in my class are close friends	Yes	No	
16	Some of the pupils don't like the class	Yes	No	R
17	Certain pupils always want to have their own way	Yes	No	
18	Some pupils always try to do better than others	Yes	No	
19	Schoolwork is hard to do	Yes	No	
20	All of the pupils in my class like one another	Yes	No	
21	The class is fun	Yes	No	
22	Children in our class fight a lot	Yes	No	
23	A few children in my class want to be first all of the time	Yes	No	
24	Most of the pupils in my class know how to do their work	Yes	No	R

Enduring insights on the social and emotional foundations of secure relationships are provided by the work of Rogers on counselling (1961, 1969, 1980). He suggested that three basic qualities are required if a warm, 'person-centred' relationship is to be established – acceptance, genuineness and empathy. If we apply this to teaching, it might suggest that acceptance involves acknowledging and receiving children 'as they are'; genuineness implies that such acceptance is real and heartfelt; whilst empathy suggests that a teacher is able to appreciate what classroom events feel like to pupils. Rogers introduced the challenging idea of providing 'unconditional positive regard' for his clients and perhaps this can also provide an ideal for what teachers should offer children and young people. Good relationships are, according to Rogers, founded on understanding and on 'giving'.

Rogers' three qualities have much in common with the three key attitudes of the reflective teacher, discussed in Chapter 3. Being able to demonstrate acceptance and genuinely empathise requires 'open-mindedness' and a 'wholehearted' commitment to the children in our care. It also necessitates 'responsibility' when considering the long-term consequences of our feelings and actions. However, this analysis is not really adequate as a guide to classroom relationships because additional factors are involved. For a number of reasons, the warmth and positive regard which teachers may wish to offer their class can rarely be completely 'unconditional'. In the first place, we are constrained by our responsibility for ensuring that the children learn adequately and appropriately. Second, the fact that teachers are likely to be responsible for relatively large numbers of pupils means that the challenges of class management and discipline must always condition our actions. Third, the fact that we ourselves have feelings, concerns and interests in the classroom means that we, too, need to feel the benefit of a degree of acceptance, genuineness and empathy if we are to give of our best.

reflectiveteaching.co.uk/rtps6/part2_ch6

Good relationships in classrooms and schools must then be based on each teacher having earned the respect of children and young people by demonstrating empathy and understanding *and* by establishing a framework of order and authority. It is a finely judged balance between two necessary elements.

If, as reflective teachers, we are to take full account of the social and emotional climate in our classrooms, we need a form of analysis which recognises this subtlety. It must recognise both the importance of interpersonal understandings and also the inevitable power struggle between teachers and pupils.

> **Expert Question**
>
> **Culture:** *does the school support expansive learning by affirming learner contributions, engaging partners and providing attractive opportunities?*
>
> This question contributes to a conceptual framework underpinning professional expertise (see Chapter 16).

Supporting children's confidence and self-esteem

Children often feel vulnerable in classrooms, particularly because of their teacher's power to control and evaluate. This affects how children experience school and their openness to new learning. Indeed, it is often suggested that children only learn effectively if their self-esteem is positive (Gill and Thompson, 2017; Roberts, 2002). A considerable responsibility is thus placed on teachers to reflect on how they use their power and on how this use affects children.

There are two basic aspects of this. First there is the positive aspect of how teachers use their power constructively to encourage, to reinforce appropriate child actions and to enhance self-esteem (Lawrence, 1987, Reading 6.6; Merrett and Wheldall, 1990, Reading 7.6). Indeed, the importance of maintaining 'high expectation' of children cannot be over-emphasised (Gipps and MacGilchrist, 1999, Reading 6.5). Second, however, there is the potential for the destructive use of such power. This particularly concerns the manner in which teachers act when 'rules' are broken or children's behaviour is challenging. This can be negative and damaging, but skilful and aware teachers will aim to make any necessary disciplinary points yet still preserve the dignity of each child. Activities are suggested below to monitor each of these aspects, starting with 'being positive'.

'Being positive' involves constant attempts to build on success. The point is to offer suitable challenges and then to make maximum use of the children's achievements to generate still more. This policy assumes that each child will have some successes. Sometimes a child's successes may be difficult to identify. Such difficulties often reveal more about the inability of an adult to understand and diagnose what a child is experiencing. As the psychologist Adler argued many years ago (Adler, 1927), irrespective of the baseline position, there is always an associated level of challenge – a target for learning achievement – which is appropriate and which can be the subject of genuine praise (Butt, 2011, Reading 14.3). It may range from correctly forming a letter of the alphabet to

> **Expert Question**
>
> **Authenticity:** *do learners recognise routine processes of assessment and feedback as being of personal value?*
>
> This question contributes to a conceptual framework underpinning professional expertise (see Chapter 16).

producing a vivid story; from sustaining personal lesson concentration to beginning to master the subject as a whole; from joining in sporting activities to breaking a school record etc. The appropriateness of the achievement is a matter for a teacher to judge, but the aim should be to encourage all children to accept challenges and achieve successes (Merrett and Wheldall, 1990, see also Chapter 10, p. 328 on lesson planning for differentiation).

This brings us to 'avoiding destructive action'. This is the second aspect of the teacher's use of power – the way in which control is used. All teachers would probably agree that a class of children has to be under control if purposeful and productive activities are to take place. However, a teacher's power can be exercised in many ways. In most situations teachers try to be calm, firm and fair and to separate the child from the behaviour – they act within the bounds of the working consensus and use positive statements and various types of legitimate 'routine censure' to maintain discipline.

A recommended way of enforcing authority, whilst at the same time protecting the self-esteem of each child, is to focus on the action or behaviour of the children rather than on the children themselves (Hargreaves, Hestor and Mellor, 1975; Robertson, 1996). The undesirability and negative effects of the behaviour can be discussed, reprimands can be firmly given, but the self-image of each child is left relatively intact. Each child, if they then conform, is able to do so with dignity. This will be discussed further in Chapter 7, where we focus on classroom management and other aspects of discipline and behaviour.

Thus, reflective teachers are likely to attempt to use their power positively and constructively, and they will be particularly aware of the model they provide and the potential damage to relationships which can be done by overhasty reactions to some classroom crises.

A further type of reflection on relationships concerns the degree of involvement by children, which brings us to the notion of what we have called the 'inclusive classroom'.

Developing an inclusive classroom

An inclusive classroom is one which is consciously designed to enable each child to act as a full participant in class activities and also to feel themselves to be a valued member of the class (Kershner, 2009, Reading 15.6). This is what all of us wish for but there is plenty of evidence that, in the context of curriculum pressures, relatively large class sizes and the requirements of many assessment procedures, it is difficult to achieve.

Classes also vary in the degree to which differences between children and their abilities are valued. Such differences between people must inevitably exist (see Pollard, 1987a, Reading 15.2), but a contrast can be drawn between classes in which the strengths and weaknesses of each child are recognised and in which the particular level of achievement of each child is accepted as a starting point (see, for example Thorne, 1993, Reading 15.5), and classes in which specific qualities or abilities are regarded as being of more value than others in absolute terms. Sadly, in the case of the latter, the stress is often on levels of attainment rather than on the effort which children may have made. Indeed, relative attainments become institutionalised through inflexible within-class or between-classes 'ability' grouping; the ethos becomes competitive rather than cooperative; and the success of some children is made possible only at the cost of the relative failure of others. The overall effect is to marginalise and exclude some children whilst the work of others is praised and regarded as setting a standard to which other children should aspire. This can have very negative consequences for children's perceptions of themselves as learners (Dweck, 1986, 2000, Reading 2.6).

One feature which often causes problems is that there are variations in both the quantity and quality of teacher attention that is given to different categories of children or in the expectations teachers have for different groups of children (Gipps and MacGilchrist, 1999, Reading 6.5). There are many categories around which such differentiation is often found (West and Pennell, 2003; see Chapter 15, p. 495) – for example: ability (e.g. Alur and Hegarty, 2002; Ireson and Hallam, 2001; Mortimore et al., 1988), gender (e.g. Delamont, 1990; Francis, 2000), race (e.g. Connolly, 1998; Troyna and Hatcher, 1992), social class (e.g. Rist, 1970; Sharp and Green, 1975; Reay, 1998) and SEND (Webster and Blatchford, 2013). Age could also be an important factor, particularly in the lower primary and in mixed-age classes. In addition, it is necessary to analyse and to be aware of the responses to school life of individual children. It is very understandable if teachers tend to deal first with children whose needs press most or whose actions necessitate an immediate response. However, the problem which then arises is that some other children may be consistently passed over (Collins, 1996). Skilled support staff can be deployed to assist the teacher in meeting the needs of all the children in a class. Croll and Moses (2000) provide a challenging analysis of this in relation to children with special educational needs, but we have a responsibility to ensure that teacher effort is distributed in proportion to the needs of all the pupils (Sharples, Webster and Blatchford, 2018).

> **Expert Question**
>
> **Inclusion:** *are all learners treated respectfully and fairly in both formal and informal interaction?*
>
> This question contributes to a conceptual framework underpinning professional expertise (see Chapter 16).

We would suggest that an inclusive classroom will produce better classroom relationships and more understanding and respect for others than one which emphasises the particular success of a few. Such issues are particularly significant when specific assessment knowledge is gathered. In the United Kingdom the outcomes of both teacher assessment and national testing now produce relatively formalised 'results' and must be handled very carefully if they are not to threaten the self-esteem of lower achieving children (Reay and Wiliam, 1999). Of course, children who are less academically successful may have considerable other strengths and achievements and these can be recognised and celebrated. Thus, there are some central questions about how children are valued which should be answered by a reflective teacher. Among them are those which are suggested in Reflective Activity 6.2. This time they take the form of a checklist.

> **Reflective Activity 6.2**
>
> *Aim:* To evaluate progress towards an inclusive classroom.
>
> *Evidence and reflection:* There are many indicators which might be considered. For instance:
>
> 1. Are children helped to learn to respect each other? Does any unnecessary and divisive competition take place? Which is emphasised most, the achievement of children or the learning efforts that are made?
> 2. How flexible and responsive are classroom organisational groupings? Do they reflect the diversity of children's capabilities?
> 3. In decisions about the curriculum, are the interests of each of the children recognised and given appropriate attention? Is the children's previous experience drawn on as National Curriculum requirements are adapted?
> 4. How are the products of the class represented – in classroom displays, in assemblies, in more public situations? Are there some children whose work features more often, and others whose work is seen less often?
> 5. How wide-ranging are the pupil achievements which are valued? Does every child experience at least some success to reinforce their self-belief and commitment to learning? Is formal assessment activity and its reporting handled sensitively?
>
> *Extension:* Having completed your review, what can you do to increase the sense of inclusion of all pupils? How could you develop the classroom climate to increase children's confidence as learners?

Overall then, teachers wishing to sustain an inclusive classroom will set out to provide opportunities for children to feel valued, to 'join in' and to believe in themselves as learners. At the same time they will attempt to eliminate any routines or practices which would undercut such aims by accentuating the relative weaknesses of some children (Putnam and Burke, 1992; McDermott, 1996; see also Clegg and Billington, 1994, Reading 8.3).

For more extensive elaboration of issues associated with inclusion, please see Chapter 15.

CLASSROOM RELATIONSHIPS

Learning to establish and maintain positive relationships

Positive relationships in education begin with the vital work done in early years settings which are characterised by high adult–child ratios, play-based activities, and often rely on a key-person approach where each child has a designated adult who greets them and supports them throughout the day. Personal, social and emotional development is at the heart of the curriculum, and the relationship with the key person is seen as important in helping the child move from the home setting, providing security for the child and acting as a link with the family. Children are supported to form new relationships with peers and adults in the setting and their developing skills in this area are assessed and supported directly.

Research has shown that children's peers make a significant contribution to each other's development (Ladd, 2005). The work of both Piaget and Vygotsky highlights the significance of interpersonal relationships in the development of young children's knowledge and skills (De Vries, 2000). Both Vygotsky and Piaget recognised that children's peer interactions are a key site for both cognitive and social development, a position widely held within education (e.g. Kutnick, Ota and Berdondini, 2008; Rogoff, 1990; Pellegrini and Blatchford, 2000), and that there are particular dimensions to interactions which support learning. Yet, it is suggested that merely providing children with opportunities to interact is insufficient for supporting the development of a learning environment which supports learning to take place. Of course, many children will learn, but we are concerned with developing an environment which supports all children to learn and for the opportunities to be maximised. In fact, a child's peer relationships are complex, and a number of issues may arise during interactions which hinder learning. Damon and Phelps (1989), drawing upon Piaget's work, state that while interactions are likely to lead to a level of understanding which could not have been reached through working alone, this requires equal power between the individuals. They note that complex understanding is gained through terms such as 'mutuality' and 'connectedness', where both partners are equally participative and they work together (Kutnick and Colwell, 2009). Where power is unequal, a number of issues arise, including that those who fear being mocked may not take the risk of joining the activity and become passive (Galton and Williamson, 1992), and that members of the dyad (pair) or group can become polarised by the group (because of gender or ability, for example) (Cowie and Rudduck, 1990).

Such issues highlight that learning with others can in itself act as an inhibitor to learning, as research has shown that young children with poor peer relationships have an increased risk of school failure (Janes et al., 1979; Kupersmidt and Coie, 1990). Such work suggests that for children to gain the greatest potential benefits from their interactions with their peers, they will need social competencies to benefit from their interactions and for these interactions to be supportive of learning.

As children move out of the early years their social and emotional development can become less of an explicit curriculum focus (see Chapter 9 for more discussion of this and variation across the UK regions) but primary teachers recognise social and emotional learning and support for behavioural needs as an important part of their role (van Poortvliet et al., 2021).

reflectiveteaching.co.uk/rtps6/part2_ch6

Social and emotional learning and relationship skills

The ability to establish and maintain good relationships can be seen as an aspect of social and emotional learning (SEL) and the primary school is an important site for developing this ability as children build relationships with peers and adults. Indeed, relationships in schools and children's sense of 'connectedness' have been found to be associated with children's mental health (Kidger et al., 2012 and Shochet et al., 2006 in Hurry et al., 2021) The EEF's guidance report on evidence-informed practice for 'Improving Social and Emotional Learning in Primary Schools (van Poortvliet et al., 2021) identifies both explicit teaching, and modelling integrated into the school day, as appropriate means to support children's SEL and relationship skills. They stress the importance of children being able to 'recognise, express and regulate their emotions' and to empathise with others as providing a foundation for relationships building. Communication skills are also important, and children need the opportunity to practice and reflect on 'relationship building' (van Poortvliet et al., 2021).

Van Poortvliet et al. suggest that teachers should support this development through explicit teaching as part of a planned curriculum, where progression in skills is part of the planning. Teachers should also 'integrate and model SEL skills through everyday teaching', for example by providing a model of good relationships between adults, by modelling relationship building and repair skills. They can also use opportunities that arise in the daily life of the classroom to draw attention to adults' or children's employment of SEL skills. Other useful teaching strategies include role-play, circle-time discussion, exploration of relationships in stories and the opportunity to discuss and practise skills in pair and group work with clear ground rules (van Poortvliet et al., 2021).

Research suggests that some children with SEND may need additional support with peer relationships (Cullen et al., 2020). However as in most areas, high-quality teaching that all children can access in the starting point for learning for all.

Children, and we as teachers, need to develop good relationship skills as a starting point for good classroom relations. As we move up the primary school, good classroom relationships are based on recognition of the legitimate interests of others and on a mutual exchange of dignity between the teacher and pupils in a class. There evolves, in other words, a reciprocal, but often tacit, recognition of the needs of the other in coping with classroom life (Pollard, 1985, Reading 6.3). In a classroom, shared understandings about working together will not just appear. To a very great extent, the development and nature of relationships will depend on initiatives made by teachers, as they try to establish the rules, understandings, routines and rituals, the working consensus, which will structure behaviour in their classrooms. Underpinning this process, classroom order and discipline should be based on good relationships and a sense of engagement in learning.

> ## Expert Question
>
> ***Relationships***: *are teacher–pupil relationships nurtured as the foundation of good behaviour, mutual wellbeing and high standards?*
>
> This question contributes to a conceptual framework underpinning professional expertise (see Chapter 16).

reflectiveteaching.co.uk/rtps6/part2_ch6

Rules and routines

A key aspect of providing a secure basis for children is to have clear boundaries and expectations. Children often expect adults to set boundaries and make expectations clear, and these may helpfully be expressed in a small number of formal, overt rules – tailored, of course, for the age of the children. Chaplain (2018, Reading 6.4) makes the important point that such overarching rules offer pupils a sense of personal and psychological safety. They should demonstrate and affirm that the classroom will be secure, thus contributing to the conditions for future learning (Immordino-Yang and Damasio, 2007, Reading 6.2). They also provide a foundational form of moral principles for interpersonal relationships in the classroom – and should be expressed in a forward looking, positive way.

Often, these rules can (and should) be derived from whole-school policy and practices. We might, for instance, promote three overarching rules on:

- treating others as we would want to be treated (e.g. respect, support, empathy);
- committing ourselves to learning in school (e.g. positive thinking, effort, resilience);
- behaviour in school and classroom (e.g. noise levels, movement, teacher respect).

The first few days and weeks with a class, the period of 'initial encounters' (Ball, 1981b), is a particularly important opportunity during which a teacher can take initiatives and introduce rules and understandings. Classroom routines enable us to operationalise overarching rules and apply their principles to concrete activities. Each teacher will have their own favoured routines and they will certainly vary by age of pupil. Examples of activities to be managed include:

- entering the classroom;
- getting attention;
- getting out materials;
- changing activities;
- transitions
- dealing with interruptions;
- keeping pupils on task.
- tidying up time;
- play time;
- changing for PE;
- story time;
- going home time.

Routines, in other words, are multi-purpose procedures which put rules and understandings into practice. When they are established, a switch-signal may be given (maybe a teacher announcement, a sound or hand-signal) and hardly anything needs to be said. But the expectations which are embedded in the routines do always need to be patrolled and maintained. If this is not done, then understandings will decay and children may take advantage of the situation. Routines are thus a major focus of negotiation as a working consensus develops.

Identifying routines and understandings

Awareness of routines and tacit understandings is particularly important for a trainee teacher who is likely to be working with children who have already established a set of understandings with their normal class teacher. Reflective Activity 6.3 is designed to help with this.

Reflective Activity 6.3

Aim: To identify the overt and tacit content of classroom rules, routines and understandings.

Evidence and reflection: Asking the pupils is an obvious first step. With care, this can be done either in discussion or might be introduced as a written activity. Young children might be asked to help an imaginary new pupil in school, perhaps using a puppet, by explaining how things should be done and correcting the puppet when they go wrong. Students usually enjoy such activities, and they may make it possible to increase awareness of tacit understandings. Another interesting method is to focus notes on key routines, for instance, at transitions points in classroom processes through the day. Try to identify the 'switch signals' and notice the way the teacher monitors the effectiveness of the routine and renegotiates or asserts if it begins to fray.

Extension: A further way to gather information on tacit expectations is to study the patterns which exist in what people do. Observation, using a notebook to record such patterns, is one possibility. A more explicit method is to record the events which lead to pupils being reminded of routines and rules. These could be noted during observation, or a video recording could be made of a session for later analysis.

Having developed an understanding of key expectations, we may of course wish to review and evaluate them. Do they enable us to fulfil our educational intentions and to teach in the ways which we favour? Which need reinforcement, or adjustment – and how might we prioritise such developments?

However, notwithstanding any future developments we may anticipate, a basic and prior requirement is that teacher actions are regarded as being fair.

reflectiveteaching.co.uk/rtps6/part2_ch6

Being 'fair'

In the negotiation of the working consensus and establishment of 'good relationships', there is nothing more important than being seen, by pupils, to have acted with fairness. This occurs because of their ultimate vulnerability to teacher power, and they therefore need to be assured that teachers will act reasonably. Children have to survive the challenges of the classroom – the crowds, praise and power, as Jackson (1968, Reading 6.1) put it.

If a teacher or student teacher acts without consideration of existing rules, routines and understandings this is likely to produce a negative response from the children.

Reflective Activity 6.4

Aim: To check that we are acting in ways which are regarded as being 'fair'.

Evidence and reflection: Again, the only really valid source of information on this is from the pupils themselves. Whilst it is possible to discuss the issue openly with them or to approach it through story or drama, it is probably less contentious and as satisfactory to watch and note their responses to teacher actions. This should be a continuous process for teachers who are sensitive to the way their children feel about school, but it is worthwhile to focus on the issue from time to time. Both verbal and non-verbal behaviour could be noted and interpreted – the groans and the expressions of pleasure, the grimaces and the smiles. From such information, and from the awareness to be gained from such an activity, it should be possible to analyse classroom actions in terms of the classification which is discussed below.

One obvious point to note here is that not all the children will feel the same about teacher actions. Patterns in such responses may be significant (see p. 183 below).

Extension: The feedback which this activity should produce could contribute to the smooth running of the classroom and to the maintenance of the working consensus. If rules and understandings which were previously established are being broken by a new teacher, then the children may become resentful if change is not explained. If classroom routines are not being maintained and enforced by the teacher, then the pupils may well consider the teacher to be 'soft' and may try some 'playing-up' at their expense.

The discussion above highlights the development of mutually shared understandings about classroom life and emphasises their legitimacy. This, whilst acknowledging the leadership role of the teacher, is the basis of a good classroom relationship.

RELATIONSHIPS FOR LEARNING

Perhaps the most important strategy in establishing good relationships with pupils is to establish some sort of connection with them as people (Gill and Thomson, 2017; Olson, 2014). Each of us welcomes recognition of our individuality and responds to a smile, a kind word or any other expression of interest – and so it is with children and young people in schools. Many teachers have these 'soft skills' and an authentic interest in the children for whom they have responsibility – after all, significant personal fulfilment in teaching comes through the success of others. If pupils feel this open, positive regard (Rogers, 1961) and compassion (Hart and Hodson, 2004), and understand that it has to be framed by the requirements of school, then the foundations for good relationships for learning exist.

Curriculum and relationships

Teaching can only be regarded as successful if the learners are learning. When this happens, both teachers and pupils feel fulfilled, and the quality of their relationship is enhanced. Good relationships thus contribute to the conditions which make learning possible, but are also reinforced by success.

> **Expert Question**
>
> **Engagement:** do our teaching strategies, classroom organisation and consultation enable learners to actively participate in and enjoy their learning?
>
> This question contributes to a conceptual framework underpinning professional expertise (see Chapter 16).

A major contribution to good classroom relationships is thus the provision of an interesting and appropriate curriculum, with suitable learning experiences and high-quality feedback. Issues concerning curriculum, pedagogy and assessment are thus never far away. However, the way in which such provision is made is particularly significant for the development of relationships.

Educationalists taking stock of such issues and looking to the future, such as those contributing to *2020 Vision* (Teaching and Learning Review Group, 2006, Reading 10.7), recommend a more 'personalised' curriculum in which learners are directly involved. Research on 'pupil voice' has made a valuable contribution to this (Rudduck and McIntyre, 2007, Reading 1.3; see also **Research Briefing 1.2**, p. 36).

It is thus valuable to consult children on how they feel about classroom activities. This information supplies a basic type of feedback on children's motivation and can be set alongside other diagnostic information about learning achievements and difficulties.

The method suggested in Reflective Activity 6.5 involves direct comparison between classroom activities in different areas of the curriculum. Such comparisons are useful because they often highlight hidden issues.

Reflective Activity 6.5

Aim: To gather information on how pupils feel about curricular activities which they undertake in school.

Evidence and reflection: One method is simply to ask them to compare two activities which you choose. This may be carried out verbally or, for older children, it may be worth structuring this at the beginning by suggesting notes are made under headings such as the ones below:

	Good things	Bad things
Activity 1		
Activity 2		
Activity 3, etc.		

There is no reason why even very young children cannot participate in discussions about the activities which they like and dislike. Fairly open questions might be used such as, 'Can you tell me about the things that you like doing best at school?' and 'Can you tell me about the things which you don't like doing?' These, if followed up sensitively by further enquiries to obtain reasons (and the results recorded), should soon show up the children's criteria and patterns in their opinions about your provision. The recording is important, for when there is no record to reflect on it is very easy to fail to fully appreciate the messages one may be being offered.

Observation is also key, particularly with younger children, and the use of careful observation notes can help you to spot patterns, for example children may exhibit more challenging behaviour when given less structured activities or when asked to work with others if they lack the skills to negotiate their role.

Extension: This activity should yield data of considerable importance for future planning and provision, and should be analysed to identify any patterns in the children's perspectives. If some children seem to be poorly motivated, to lack interest or to engage in distraction techniques, then the situation must be reconsidered and remedial measures taken.

Lesson Study 6.1 provides an example of how children's feelings about an area of the curriculum can affect their approach to learning – and, in particular, of how teachers can turn this around. The girls, who were uneasy about tackling maths, were re-engaged by teachers who carefully observed and listened, and then had the insight to introduce creative and experimental variety into the curriculum, as well as reassurance.

reflectiveteaching.co.uk/rtps6/part2_ch6

180   Part 2   Creating conditions for learning

LESSON STUDY 6.1

Creative pedagogy for girls learning mathematics in Reception

The school: Emmanuel CE Primary School is situated at the heart of the vibrant community of West Hampstead and provides an education for children between 3 and 11 years.

What we wanted the children to learn: We noticed that some girls, even as young as 5, had decided that mathematics was 'not for them'. Considering the consequence that this could have on their future school success, we aimed to find ways to re-engage these children and inspire their agency in learning mathematics. The focus chosen was that the children could perform, understand and demonstrate a simple subtraction. The engagement aim was for those reluctant girls to proactively choose to engage in mathematics activities without having to be directed to do so by their teacher.

What research is available: There is now a lot of research on listening to children's voices and taking their perspectives seriously, as discussed in Chapter 1 of this book. And psychologists emphasise the importance of motivation in learning (Chapter 2, p. 63). For this lesson study, we were inspired by oracy work with young children including the use of talk, rhyme, song and role-play games. We considered if something similar could be developed for mathematics to create narrative meaning for the mathematics being learned, as well as a motivation to engage and 'join in'.

What we discovered in our research lessons:
RL1: In the first lesson we tried singing number songs, and using props such as glove-puppets and play dough to act out a subtraction number song. We hoped that, by blending maths with singing and acting, girls would be more motivated to join in. During the lesson, we observed that while all children joined in with the song and modelling subtraction in the main whole class teaching session, some girls, including two of the pupils on which we were focusing, did not engage with the maths activities during the independent work time.

RL2: Taking into consideration what we had observed in the first lesson, in the second lesson we decided to use more craft activities such as 'drawing currant buns' and 'making necklaces with beads' both in the main teaching and independent work time. During the lesson, we observed that the consistent use of picture drawing activity both in the main teaching and as an independent activity helped most girls to consolidate their understanding of subtraction as 'taking away' and their abilities to demonstrate their subtractions with objects and number sentences. However, the second lesson was not successful at getting the girls to choose a maths activity independently. All three case pupil girls required teacher support to engage in an independent activity.

RL3: In the third lesson, we decided to return to using narratives to reinforce the girls' understanding of taking away and their ability to demonstrate a subtraction. However, this time we started by eliciting pupils' real-life experiences of taking away by asking them to tell a number story that involves subtraction. We then tried linking subtraction to the Year 6 Peter Pan production that reception children loved. We introduced two activities, Peter Pan capturing pirates and a Tinker Bell activity for which children needed to make up a taking away number story and demonstrate the subtraction through role play. The third lesson turned out to be much more successful at getting the girls to initiate thinking and verbalisation of maths throughout the lesson. In fact, all three case pupils independently chose a maths activity to work on. In these ways, the research lessons helped the girls achieve both the curriculum and engagement goals.

reflectiveteaching.co.uk/rtps6/part2_ch6

What pupils learned: In terms of direct pupil outcomes, all the girls met or exceeded our expectations in this lesson study cycle, including the three girls who we initially predicted would need to revisit the learning objectives.

What we learned: In particular, the more time we spent planning activities that intrinsically motivated the children, the greater the rewards we reaped in terms of their engagement and progress. For example, when maths was turned into a creative exercise, such as drawing, craft making, storytelling and acting, the girls' engagement was boosted. Making maths personal also seemed to help the girls engage. When the girls were asked to tell a subtraction story, they each brought their personal experience and knowledge into the understanding of mathematical concepts. When subtraction was linked to the school's summer drama production, this really captured the children's imaginations.

Additionally, however, we also learned that the use of visual and concrete resources for explicit teaching was crucial in helping the case pupils understand the concept of subtraction as taking away.

We learned key things about our case pupils and ways to support them in learning mathematics in the future. For example: Alice needs a lot of reassurance – as much from her peers as from adults and in terms both of work and play. She can benefit from 1:1 support to access the maths content. Anna is a much more capable mathematician than we had first thought. But like Alice, she also sought reassurance, often from adults, and was afraid of making a mistake.

From this lesson study cycle, we decided that we would try to build creativity into maths activities and would develop activities that allow for experimentation, a variety of approaches and also give children more time to think. We believe that this combination should give girls more confidence in approaching maths activities.

How we shared: We turned what we'd learned into a short report and shared it during a staff meeting. As a school, we decided to take the lessons learnt and really consider how we could engage girls like these in their maths learning throughout our school. This became a focus for the Maths Development Plan for the following year.

Pupil perspectives of teachers

Another aspect of pupil perspectives is their views on their own teacher. This is a fairly well researched issue and enquiry into it can yield good summary data on the way young people feel about the quality of relationships and education in their classroom. Obviously, for professional and ethical reasons, teachers should only collect such information in their own classroom, or with the permission of other people who may be concerned (Wilson and Powell, 2001).

Research has consistently shown that students like teachers who are kind, consistent, efficient at organising and teaching, patient, fair and who have a sense of humour. They dislike teachers who are domineering, boring, unkind, unpredictable and unfair. Strict/soft are two common constructs which children use, with 'strict but fair' often being positively valued. 'Softness' is usually regarded as a sign of weakness and can be associated with inconsistency which is linked to perceptions of unfairness.

Predictability is also usually important and children and young people are often expert interpreters of the 'moods' of their teachers. The boundaries and relationships children find in school should provide a sense of security and any unpredictability or inconsistency from teachers is a threat to this security. For some children this can be more challenging than

reflectiveteaching.co.uk/rtps6/part2_ch6

Part 2 Creating conditions for learning

for others and challenging behaviour may be a response to the lack of control children can feel when in an unpredictable situation where, because of the relative power structures, they have little control.

Teacher and pupil actions

Figure 6.1 provides a simple model for reflecting on the types of action which teachers and children make in classrooms when a working consensus exists.

The most important distinction is between actions which are bounded by the understandings that have been negotiated and those which are not. Five basic 'types of action' can be identified.

Figure 6.1 A classification of types of teacher and pupil classroom action

Teacher Acts			Pupil Acts	
Unilateral	Within the working consensus			Unilateral
Non-legitimate censure	Legitimate routine censure	Conformity	Legitimate routine deviance	Non-legitimate rule-framed disorder

Conformity. These actions, by teachers or children are 'as expected'. They are according to the tacit conventions and agreements of the working consensus.

Routine deviance. This is the type of mischief or petty misdemeanour which is accepted as being part of normal pupil behaviour. Talking at inappropriate times, 'having a laugh' and 'day dreaming' might be examples. Such activities are partly expected by teachers and are not normally intended as a challenge. They are thus within the bounds of the working consensus. It is important for support staff to also be aware of such boundaries.

Routine censure. This is the typical teacher response to routine deviance – a mild reprimand. It will be regarded by the pupils as legitimate, in so far as such a reprimand will not threaten the dignity of a child nor be employed inappropriately. Censures of this type are also within the bounds of the working consensus – they are expected. The teacher is doing their job.

Non-legitimate disorder. This is a type of pupil action which teachers dislike and find hard to understand. It often occurs when a child or a group of pupils seek to disrupt a classroom situation. They are particularly prone to do this if pupils perceive themselves to have been treated 'unfairly' or feel that their dignity has been undermined. Action of this type usually reflects the cultural rules of peer groups and can be used to build up a type of 'solidarity' or an alternative source of positive self-esteem.

Non-legitimate censure. This is the type of adult action which pupils dislike and cannot understand. It often occurs when a teacher loses his or her temper or feels under great

reflectiveteaching.co.uk/rtps6/part2_ch6

pressure. The effect of such actions is that the children feel attacked and unable to cope. They perceive teacher power being used without justification. Such actions lie outside the bounds of the working consensus and are likely to lead to a breakdown in relationships.

The central argument is that 'good relationships' are based on the existence of a negotiated sense of acceptability and fairness which teachers and children share.

Patterns in pupil actions

We suggested above that children's actions might range from conforming to rules, engaging in routine deviance and mischief or, by stepping beyond this, to acting in unilateral and disorderly ways.

These patterns are indeed commonly found in classrooms – as in other walks of life. After all, they simply reflect strategies of agreement, negotiation or challenge. Etzioni (1961), in a classic analysis of compliance, documented how these dimensions recur in most social settings as people interact together.

In a teacher-research study, Pollard (1985) identified three types of friendship groups among 11-year-olds. 'Goodies' were very conformist, fairly able, but considered rather dull. 'Jokers' liked to negotiate and 'have a laugh' with their teachers. 'Gang' group members were willing to disrupt classes, had low levels of academic achievement and were thought of as a nuisance. If we relate characteristic pupil actions to such types of pupil friendship group, then we can represent the range of behaviour, as indicated in Figure 6.2.

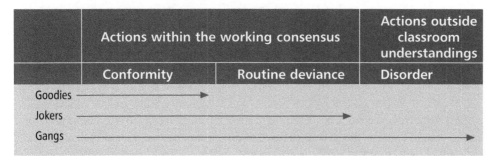

Figure 6.2 Parameters of pupil behaviour

Figure 6.2 simplifies significant complexities, but it does highlight some important social consequences of classroom relationships. If the quality of both interpersonal relationships *and* curriculum provision is high, then the parameters of pupil actions are likely to move to the left of the diagram and both behaviour and engagement are likely to improve. If interpersonal relationships are poor and curriculum provision is inappropriate, then the parameters are likely to move to the right of the diagram. The result is likely to be an increase in disruption, a decrease in learning and the growth of dissatisfaction with school. Overall, social differentiation and exclusion are likely to increase, as the teacher acts to deal with disruptive children – who may then become 'labelled' as such.

Positive and negative cycles

Changes in relationships with a class can be *felt* through day-to-day experience over a period of time in one's work with a class. They can also be represented for reflection. For instance, consider the model of a positive cycle of teaching and learning in Figure 6.3, a model seen from the pupil perspective.

In this model it is first suggested that teacher initiatives lead to learners enjoying a sense of their own dignity and value. Second, it is postulated that children are stimulated by the curriculum or learning activities provided for them by the teacher. These are judged to be interesting and appear likely to satisfy their interest-at-hand in learning. Third, the situation is regarded as being fair. There are two aspects of fairness here, relating to the way the children are ordered and controlled and to the nature of the tasks which they are presented with. Regarding the first, let us assume that the students and teacher are operating within established organisational and social frameworks and that thus they have both negotiated and both understand the parameters of permissible action.

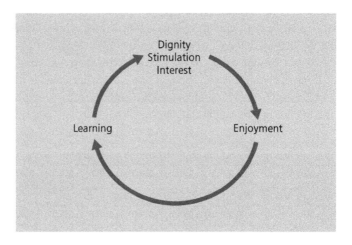

Figure 6.3 A positive cycle of teaching, learning and relationships

Order thus has a secure base. The other aspect of fairness concerns the appropriateness of the match between the task which the children are faced with and their ability and motivation to do it. If the task is well matched and attractively presented, then pupils are likely to accept its challenges and attempt to grapple with them vigorously. The result of the existence of this sense of dignity, stimulation and fairness is postulated in the model as being enjoyment and learning. This is brought about essentially because the children's interests are satisfied by teacher provision and action from the start. The further, and crucial, result of this child enjoyment and learning is that teacher interests are thereby satisfied. Order is maintained, instruction is effective and teacher self-esteem can flourish, with the likely result that the teacher will feel able to inject further energy and care with which to again project the dignity, stimulation and fairness to fuel another cycle. A cyclical process of reinforcement is created which can then spiral upwards into a higher and higher quality of learning experiences. Sometimes teaching goes just like this.

On the other hand, we must also recognise the existence of negative cycles which, instead of spiralling upwards, can lead to a decline into suspicion, hostility and unpleasantness. Again, this can be represented by a model seen from the child perspective (Figure 6.4).

In this model it is suggested that teacher initiatives threaten children's interests on three counts. First, they represent an affront to children's dignity as people. Teacher actions may be seen as being dismissive, high-handed or even aggressive. Second, the learning activities provided for the children are badly matched to the ability and concerns of the children. They are too hard, too easy or too disconnected from children's interests to provide significant motivational attraction. Third, teachers may be seen to be acting unfairly. In other words, they do not abide by negotiated understandings about their behaviour or that of the children.

> **Expert Question**
>
> **Relationships:** are teacher–pupil relationships nurtured as the foundation of good behaviour, mutual wellbeing and high standards?
>
> This question contributes to a conceptual framework underpinning professional expertise (see Chapter 16).

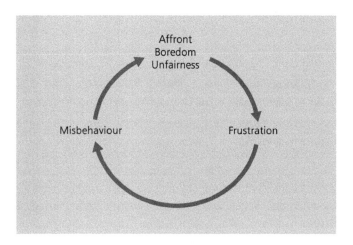

Figure 6.4 A negative cycle of teaching, learning and relationships

They use their power to act unilaterally. The children will, in a situation of this sort, feel and express a great deal of frustration. Their interests, far from being satisfied, are being ignored or threatened, while at the same time they are relatively powerless to defend themselves, and, in the primary school, required to remain in this situation for most of the school week. Work evasion and resistance through inappropriate behaviour, rather than learning, are a probable outcome.

Ironically, the further result of this, which completes the cycle, is likely to be damage to the teacher's interests. Order in the classroom will constantly be challenged if it is essentially oppressive. Attempts at instruction will not be matched by quality in learning if children have not been offered an appropriate motivation to learn. The children's deviant responses will constantly threaten the teacher's self-esteem and autonomy. Such resistance is likely to further reduce the teacher's enjoyment but increase the stress and the potential workload which that teacher faces.

Fortunately, there are not many classrooms where this situation endures, but it is worth being watchful and monitoring one's own provision. In such reflection on classroom relationships, if things seem to be deteriorating, it is tempting to perceive the causes of disruption as being exclusively to do with particular children. However, if we see behaviour as communicating something about the status quo, then reflection on our own actions in respect of the working consensus and the quality of curriculum provision may provide another set of issues for consideration. These issues are, to a great extent, within our own control as teachers.

TEACHER THINKING AND PROFESSIONAL SKILLS

Teacher perspectives

So far in this chapter, a number of suggestions have been made about how a teacher can take account of the perspectives, feelings and position of pupils. Now it is time to change the focus onto ourselves as teachers for, as was discussed in Chapter 5, the self-image of a teacher is just as important to maintain as the self-image of the child. Good teaching has never been easy, for to some extent it has always meant placing the learner's needs before our own. However, classroom relationships are a very special and subtle phenomenon. On the one hand, the nature of the working consensus is related to disciplinary issues and problems which are likely to confront the teacher. On the other hand, the quality of the relationships can, potentially, provide a continuous source of personal pleasure and self-fulfilment for a teacher. With young children we must also see ourselves as providing a model in how to build and maintain positive and rewarding relationships, which includes caring for ourselves.

If our own feelings as teachers are also an important factor in maintaining a positive working consensus, then ways of monitoring our feelings may be useful. Reflective Activity 6.6 suggests keeping a personal diary. This has been used by classroom researchers over many years (Dadds, 1995) and is a tried and tested way of reflexively taking stock of life as it unfolds. Talking with colleagues and friends can also be immensely valuable and supportive. The point is a simple one – to care for others, we must also look after ourselves (see also **Research Briefing 1.1** on teacher commitment and resilience, p. 35, and Turnbull, 2007).

Reflective Activity 6.6

Aim: To monitor and place in perspective our own feelings on classroom relationships.

Evidence and reflection: Probably the best way to do this is by keeping a diary. This does not have to be an elaborate, time-consuming one, but simply a personal statement of how things have gone and of how we felt.

The major focus of the diary in this case will obviously be on relationships. It is very common for such reflections to focus in more detail on particular disciplinary issues or on interaction with specific individuals. It should be written professionally, with awareness of ethical issues and the feelings of other classroom participants.

Diary-keeping tends to heighten awareness and, at the same time, it supplies a document which can be of great value in reviewing events.

Extension: Once a diary has been kept for a fortnight or so, you might set aside some time to read it carefully and to reflect upon it with a view to drawing reasonably balanced conclusions regarding yourself and your future planning for the classroom. It would be better still to discuss the issues which are raised with a colleague or friend.

Expectations of others and bias

The academic expectations of teachers for the learners in their charge have long been recognised as contributing to pupil achievements in school. The classic study of this, by Rosenthal and Jacobson (1968), suggested that a 'self-fulfilling prophecy' could be set up, in which children who were believed to be 'bright' would do well but, where negative expectations existed, then children would underperform. Indeed, although the ways in which teacher expectations influence pupil behaviour and attainment is highly complex, there is a broad consensus that high expectations can have a very positive effect (Gipps and MacGilchrist, 1999, Reading 6.5).

However, other research has shown differences in teachers' expectations of children from different social class backgrounds (e.g. Hartley, 1985; King, 1978; Sharp and Green, 1975), in relation to gender (Delamont, 1990), and race (Wright, 1992). Disability is another area where low expectations can limit children's potential to achieve. This raises a very important issue for reflective teachers who will want to ensure that they do not unwittingly favour some children over others. Two particularly comprehensive studies of links between expectations, behaviour and performance were carried out in London and considered differences in terms of gender, social class, race etc. (Mortimore et al., 1988; Tizard et al., 1988, see also Richardson, 2009, Reading 15.1).

Whilst teachers should aim to raise their expectations and look for positive points for potential development in their pupils, there are also dangers from the existence of negative expectations, which might include those with respect to attainment or more widely in terms of behaviour. For instance, stereotyping is the attribution of particular characteristics to

reflectiveteaching.co.uk/rtps6/part2_ch6

> **Expert Question**
>
> **Expectation:** *does our school support high staff and student expectations and aspire for excellence?*
>
> This question contributes to a conceptual framework underpinning professional expertise (see Chapter 16).

members of a group, and is often used negatively. Thus, sex-role stereotyping might be found, say, in an infant classroom, with girls being encouraged to become 'teacher helpers'. Perhaps they might also be encouraged to play domestic roles in the 'home corner', while boys engage in more active play such as using construction equipment. A further example might be holding culturally specific or institutionally sanctioned expectations about what a 'good learner' and positive forms of interaction look like in the classroom, expectations that can exclude groups of children (Bradbury, 2013). For example, behaviours like 'calling out' may be welcomed in some pupils and seen as disruptive from others.

Bias is a further source of unequal treatment of pupils. It might refer to images and ideas in books and in other resources which suggest the superiority or inferiority of certain groups of people (see Chapter 8). Unconscious bias is a term that helps emphasise the fact that we are all subject to thinking in terms of stereotypes and that this way of managing our response to the world operates outside of our conscious awareness. Thus to appreciate and remedy our own unconscious biases requires proactive examination of these biases and deliberate action to counter their effects, such as through carefully questioning the evidence base for any differences in how children are taught, responded to and supported within the classroom.

Educational procedures can also be biased in themselves. For example, there has been a longstanding debate about bias in intelligence tests and such questions are recurring with regard to aspects of national assessment procedures. This debate has focused on class, gender and cultural bias at various times and is closely associated with the ways in which disadvantages can be 'institutionalised'. The institutionalisation of disadvantage refers to situations in which social arrangements and procedures are established and taken for granted, despite the fact that they may systematically disadvantage a particular social group. Different forms of grouping students can have this effect if care is not taken (Francis et al., 2019). Epstein provided a particularly clear analysis of this with regards to racism (Epstein, 1993).

For a practical enquiry to try at this point, you could revisit **Reflective Activity 1.7**. This explores teacher perceptions of children in class and the possibility of patterned differences in the ways in which particular groups of children are viewed.

Professional skills

The specific ways in which teachers act, and their effectiveness, are a focus for professional learning and refinement over many years. An experienced teacher can seemingly act with minimal effort, and the extent of practice and reflection may not be apparent.

There are several levels at which such skills may be considered (Chaplain, 2017, 2018).

At the most basic, we might focus on non-verbal behaviour such as facial expression, use of eye contact, posture, gesture and movement. Pupils in classrooms monitor their teachers almost continuously for indications of their intentions or to pick up on changes in mood which might be of consequence. Thus, a skilful teacher is aware of, and manages, their non-verbal behaviour as a form of communication to pupils. It is thus possible, without saying a word, to convey confidence or anxiety, calmness or tension, satisfaction or displeasure through the ways in which we present ourselves.

Verbal capabilities represent another group of skills. Most obviously there is the capacity to project one's voice within a classroom environment. This is not necessarily to do with volume, but is certainly related to clarity in both the form and content of what is said. Pitching one's voice appropriately, so that it is not strained but can be heard, is extremely important and can be developed to improve effectiveness. When under pressure or anxious, people tend to speak more quickly and with a higher pitch – and this may need to be explicitly countered. Voice training should certainly be considered if difficulties are encountered. Through the *ways* in which we speak, we are also able to convey feelings of enthusiasm, confidence, concern etc. so that the form of the presentation will, hopefully, reinforce the substantive message we intend to communicate.

An equally important skill is the ability to listen to and interpret what is said by pupils and to understand the messages that are conveyed through their behaviour and body language. The most significant dimension of this is to maintain openness to what is said and communicated, rather than 'hearing what we expect to hear'. This is by no means easy. But it is an essential skill if an effective feedback loop from pupils to teacher is to be maintained. Without it, we cannot learn from pupil perspectives, and the appropriateness of our teaching, and the quality of our relationships with the children, will inevitably be impaired.

> **Expert Question**
>
> **Reflection:** *is our classroom practice based on incremental, evidence-informed and collaborative improvement strategies?*
>
> This question contributes to a conceptual framework underpinning professional expertise (see Chapter 16).

The ways in which teachers behave, speak and listen must, in aggregate, combine authority and accessibility. It is essential that pupils respect the role and knowledge of their teachers, that they feel secure in their ongoing respect and care, but also that they feel able to engage openly with them.

Expert teachers monitor this balance and are able, drawing on their professional skills, to make ongoing and contextually appropriate adjustments. In such ways, they establish classroom climates which are effective for learning.

Classroom authority

Teachers enact their role on behalf of parents and others in society more broadly. In that sense, the powerful position we hold is socially ascribed. But the main point of developing good relationships with the class as a whole is that this authority should be accepted by the children and young people themselves (Bennett, 2012, Reading 7.3). Only then, can the power of a teacher be converted into an authentic and practically useful 'authority'. Authority, in other words, is based on acceptance of the superior role of the teacher by those who are subject to them – on the legitimation of teacher power.

The understandings of the working consensus provide the moral foundation from which teacher power can be asserted and classroom authority can be established. Such authority is vital to the work of every teacher and we therefore refocus on it in Chapter 7, p. 201. There, in the context of managing pupil behaviour, we review the role of positive expectations, confident self-presentation, measured use of language and the development of a repertoire of strategies.

Classroom authority will be most secure when good relationships (as discussed in this chapter) are combined with constructive strategies for managing behaviour and building engagement (as discussed in Chapter 7).

CONCLUSION

Good relationships are intimately connected to pupil wellbeing, classroom learning and effective discipline. They give pleasure to the participants, provide a model for children's relationships in life and set a secure foundation for learning. No wonder that positive classroom relationships are a considerable source of teacher and pupil fulfilment.

Perhaps, too, an expectation of being caring towards each other may spread among the children and young people and be of longer-term benefit for society more generally.

We end this chapter with a note of caution, of particular relevance to trainee teachers.

There are sometimes children with whom very specific efforts to develop good relationships may need to be made. Such cases might include children who have seen dysfunctional relationships modelled at home; particularly able children who may become bored; children who find schoolwork difficult and who may become frustrated; children who have special educational needs; children who are new to the class or school; and children who have been upset by events in their lives over which they have little control, such as a bereavement, a breakup of their parents' marriage, parental unemployment or even sexual or physical abuse. Such children need very sensitive and empathic attention and may require special help to express their feelings, to place these in perspective, to realise that their teacher and others care about them and to feel that they have tangible and appropriate targets to strive for in their lives. Such care may enable a child to take control of the situation, with the support of their teacher, to the extent that this is possible.

However, teachers should guard against being amateur therapists. More experienced colleagues should be approached for support and advice. Child psychologists and social workers are available and they should also be invited to give advice if circumstances require their help.

reflectiveteaching.co.uk/rtps6/part2_ch6

CHAPTER WEBPAGE

reflectiveteaching.co.uk offers additional professional resources for this chapter. For the chapter webpage, go to: reflectiveteaching.co.uk/rtps6/part2_ch6

Everyone seems to be in favour of 'good classroom relationships', but not quite so many really understand how to achieve and sustain them. The fourteen *Reflective Activities* which can be accessed from the tab on the Chapter 6 webpage have been designed to complement the three parts of the text of the printed chapter, above. By trying some of them out, you will find that the chapter makes more sense in a practical way. You can try some you are interested in, or you could select some as a problem-solving strategy and to illuminate a challenge you are experiencing.

It is also worth taking some time to read the *Research Briefing* entitled *Education, Schooling and Learning for Life: How Meaning and Opportunity Build from Everyday Relationships* (Pollard and Filer, 2007). This describes Pollard's longitudinal study of children from age 4 to age 16, and shows how social relationships provide a foundation for learning, particularly in the evaluative contexts of schools.

The suggestions for study are quite developed for this chapter. Three levels of advice and information are again provided:

1 On the chapter webpage, *Further Reading* is a quite extensive overview of sources, following the structure of this chapter and requiring a library or on-line resources for follow up.
2 *Key Readings*, below, picks out a priority list of readings for further study.
3 *Readings for Reflective Teaching in Schools*, running in parallel to this book, provides short, edited extracts for major recommended readings. Some are highlighted below. It has been described as a 'mini-library' and is particularly convenient because of the immediate access which it provides.

KEY READINGS

The person-centred realism which characterises this chapter has many variants. Try, for instance:

> Gill, S. and Thomson, G. (2017) *Human-Centred Education. A Practical Handbook and Guide.* London: Routledge.
>
> Olson, K. (2014) *The Invisible Classroom: Relationships, Neuroscience and Mindfulness in School.* New York: Norton.
>
> Hart, S. and Hodson, V.K. (2004) *The Compassionate Classroom: Relationship Based Teaching and Learning.* Encinitas, CA: PuddleDancer Press.
>
> Rudduck, J. and McIntyre, D. (2007) *Improving Learning Through Consulting Pupils.* London: Routledge. (see also Reading 1.3)

One of a number of classic books by Carl Rogers on 'person-centred' theory is:

Rogers, C. (1969) *Freedom to Learn.* New York: Merrill.

Philip Jackson's classic text featuring 'crowds, praise and power' in classrooms is:

Jackson, P.W. (1968) *Life in Classrooms.* New York: Holt Rinehart and Winston. (Reading 6.1)

The interpretive, sociological analysis of classroom relationships which has informed much of this chapter is discussed in detail in:

Pollard, A. (1985) *The Social World of the Primary School.* London: Cassell. (Reading 6.3)

For helpful advice applying psychological knowledge on a wide range of issues in classroom relationships and management including professional social skills and classroom rules, routines and rituals, see:

Chaplain, R. (2017) *Teaching Without Disruption in the Primary School*, 2nd edn. London: Routledge.

General overviews of research on classroom relationships are provided by:

Watkins, C. (2004) *Classrooms as Learning Communities.* London: Routledge.
Pianta, R.C. (1999) *Enhancing Relationships Between Children and Teachers.* Washington, DC: American Psychological Association.
Ingram, J. and Worrall, N. (1993) *Teacher–Child Partnership: The Negotiating Classroom.* London: David Fulton.

On children's confidence and self-esteem, Lawrence provides a research review and practical ideas:

Lawrence, D. (1987) *Enhancing Self-esteem in the Classroom.* London: Paul Chapman. (Reading 6.6)

On children's social and emotional learning and wellbeing more generally:

Van Poortvliet, M., Clarke, A. and Gross, J. (2021) *Improving Social and Emotional Learning in Primary Schools* (Guidance report). London: Education Endowment Foundation.
Hurry, J., Bonell, C., Carroll, C. and Deighton, J. (2021) *The Role of Schools in the Mental Health of Children & Young People* (Presidential Roundtable Report). London: BERA.

The significance for learning of relationships within and beyond the school is described in:

West-Burnham, J., Farrar, M. and Otero, G. (2007) *Schools and Communities: Working Together to Transform Children's Lives.* London: Continuum.

reflectiveteaching.co.uk/rtps6/part2_ch6

TOOLKIT EVIDENCE 6.1
Social and emotional learning: often important, but never sufficient for progress

What is it?
There are three broad types of social and emotional learning approaches:

1. Universal programmes which generally take place in the classroom.
2. More specialised programmes which are targeted at students with particular social or emotional problems.
3. School-level approaches to developing a positive school ethos which also aim to support greater engagement in learning.

What does the evidence say?
On average, social and emotional learning interventions have an impact on attitudes to learning, social relationships in school, and attainment (up to four months' additional progress on average). However, not all interventions are equally effective at raising attainment. Benefits are more likely when approaches are embedded into routine educational practices, and supported by professional development and training for staff.

There is some evidence that social and emotional learning programmes may benefit disadvantaged or low-attaining pupils more than other pupils.

How sound is the evidence?
More research has been undertaken with younger children in primary schools and with older pupils in secondary schools, and more studies have evaluated the impact on disadvantaged or low attaining pupils.

What do I need to think about?
- Skills should be taught purposefully and explicitly linked to direct learning in schools, encouraging pupils to apply the skills they learn.
- The impact of social and emotional approaches on learning is not found consistently, so it is important to evaluate the impact of any initiative.

Links and further reading
Corcoran, R.P., Cheung, A.C., Kim, E. and Xie, C. (2018) 'Effective universal school-based social and emotional learning programs for improving academic achievement: A systematic review and meta-analysis of 50 years of research'. *Educational Research Review*, 25, 56–72. doi:10.1016/j.edurev.2017.12.001

The EEF Teaching and Learning Toolkit entry on 'Social and emotional learning': educationendowmentfoundation.org.uk/education-evidence/teaching-learning-toolkit/social-and-emotional-learning – see also the technical appendix for further references to the individual studies.

See also
Behaviour interventions (Toolkit Evidence 7.1)
Parental engagement (Toolkit Evidence 4.1)

Education Endowment Foundation

Chapter 7
Engagement
How are we managing behaviour?

| Introduction | 196 |

| Understanding classroom behaviour | 197 |

Children and young people 198
Providing an engaging environment 199
Progression in behaviou 200

| Establishing authority | 201 |

Expectations 202
Self-presentation 203
Language 204
Strategic repertoire 205

| Skills for engagement | 208 |

Gaining attention 208
Framing 209
With-it-ness 210

Overlapping 210
Pacing 211
Orchestration 211
Consistency 212

| Managing classroom episodes | 212 |

Beginnings 213
Development 214
Transitions 214
Endings 215
The unexpected 216

| Cycles of behaviour | 218 |

Towards engagement and independence 218
Managing challenging behaviour – avoiding a negative cycle 220

| Conclusion | 223 |

reflectiveteaching.co.uk/rtps6/part2_ch7

Part 2 Creating conditions for learning

INTRODUCTION

Behaviour management is vitally important in any classroom, because the teacher's intentions for learning cannot take place without a well-ordered classroom. Achieving a well-ordered classroom takes more than a simple behaviourist approach where teachers punish unwanted behaviour and reward desired behaviour. Far from it; for teachers to create an environment where children gain the most from their schooling, they need knowledge, skill, and effective behaviour management strategies as well as an understanding of how to meet the learning needs of all pupils. An important element of effective behaviour management is the process of supporting children to make positive choices that are conducive to learning.

Earlier, in Chapter 1, we discussed how emotive teaching can be. This is especially important to reflect upon when considering the behaviour of children. When children misbehave, it is important to remember that it is not necessarily the fault of the teacher but it is the responsibility of the teacher to act when misbehaviour occurs. Teachers after all have a statutory requirement to ensure that behaviour is managed effectively to ensure a good and safe learning for *all* children, as stated in Standard 7 (DfE, 2011b) of the standards for teaching in England.

'Good behaviour' is most easily obtained and maintained by establishing appropriate relationships (Chapter 6), providing clear expectations, using targeted approaches to meet the needs of individuals as well as ensuring that pupils are fully engaged in learning activities. *Improving Behaviour in Schools, A Guidance Report* by The Education Endowment Foundation (2019) considers that effective behaviour management requires positive learning relationships: teachers knowing and understanding their pupils is paramount to this. The focus of attention should therefore be directed to achieving a positive climate for learning. Teaching learning behaviours will reduce the need to manage misbehaviour so that more serious problems can be avoided. Using simple approaches and being consistent is also recommended by the EEF (2019). This is by no means easy since classrooms are complex places where events can unfold very quickly and are thus multi-dimensional and unpredictable (Doyle, 1977; Chaplain, 2017).

Although effective behaviour management is essential, teachers have to take care that classroom management does not become more important than learning itself. For example, even where teachers have control of the classroom pupils may remain unclear about the aims of learning tasks set for them. As Galton (1989) suggests, the consequence can be a sense of ambiguity and risk, which then undermines the quality of children's engagement with learning. Holt (1982) made this idea more controversial by suggesting that pupils 'learn to be stupid' in schools. They do this when teachers' requirements for conformity, with managerial rules, structure and order, override the pupils' need for understanding and engagement in high-quality learning tasks. The vital message for us is that classroom management is a necessary means to an end – but it is not the end itself (Holleran and Gilbert, 2015). TLRP's principles on pedagogy build on, and extend, this point.

reflectiveteaching.co.uk/rtps6/part2_ch7

> ## TLRP Principles
>
> Two principles are of particular relevance to this chapter on achieving an ordered classroom through pupil engagement:
>
> **Effective teaching and learning promotes the active engagement of the learner.** A chief goal of teaching and learning should be the promotion of learners' independence and autonomy. This involves acquiring a repertoire of learning strategies and practices, developing positive attitudes towards learning, and confidence in oneself as a good learner. (*Principle 6*)
>
> **Effective teaching and learning fosters both individual and social processes and outcomes.** Learning is a social activity. Learners should be encouraged and helped to work with others, to share ideas and to build knowledge together. Consulting learners about their learning and giving them a voice is both an expectation and a right. (*Principle 7*)

See Chapter 4

Before starting work in a new school, reflective teachers will ensure that they know and understand something about the ethos and values of the school they are about to join. At the very minimum, teachers are expected to read a school's behaviour policies and talk with mentors and other teaching and support staff about how those policies are put into practice.

This chapter has been structured into five sections. We begin by affirming the significance of behavioural issues both for teachers and policymakers, and also review some sources of professional support which are available. Next, we analyse how to establish classroom authority. We then focus on practical teaching skills for engaging pupils. We also look at how to manage typical classroom episodes. Finally, we consider positive and negative cycles, tying back to Chapter 6 on relationships. Drawing on EEF **Toolkit Evidence 7.1** (see p. 227), this section also addresses the use of specific forms of intervention to manage challenging behaviour.

UNDERSTANDING CLASSROOM BEHAVIOUR

There are a great many explanatory theories about children's behaviour, whether in or out of school. Three elements are typically posed:

Figure 7.1 Child, environment and behaviour

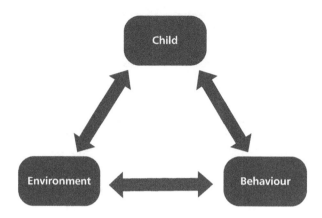

The terminology above is that of Chaplain (2018), who draws on the social learning theory of Bandura (1995). Bronfenbrenner (1979, Reading 8.1) has a similar conceptualisation (see Chapter 8, p. 232). Symbolic interactionist sociology would tend to speak of 'children', 'contexts' and 'strategic action'. Such nuanced distinctions can certainly be drawn. The basic point though, is that the actions taken by anyone relate both to the person they are and to the situation they are in.

From the teacher perspective then, to understand classroom behaviour, we must first appreciate the circumstances of the children and young people for whom we have responsibility; and we must then really think hard about the educational provision which we make for them in school. The latter constitutes the environment – the context, to which pupil behaviour is a response.

Children and young people

We need here to take stock of the issues raised in Chapters 1, 2 and 4 of this book, and to recognise that pupils in the same classroom may have very different home circumstances. Contemporary societies are seeing extreme differences in wealth and in the associated forms of cultural capital. Many families maintain a conventional, two-parent structure, whilst others sustain more diverse relationships. Some children will start school with great eagerness to learn, whilst others may feel deeply uneasy or even be frightened. As they get older, some pupils will receive significant support and interest from parents or carers, whilst others will find that their efforts may be treated as being of little consequence. Many will find that the language of instruction is their mother tongue and will be familiar with typical teacher discourse. Others may find that they need to adapt to the use of their second language in the school setting, or that some patterns of their home language are frowned upon at school.

It is very easy to succumb to stereotypes in seeking to make sense of the complexity of children's lives, but this really should be resisted. Being economically 'poor' does not denote a lack of commitment to one's children, just as being 'well off' certainly doesn't in itself produce valuable support. Each form of social difference – social class, gender, ethnicity, disability etc. – is simply a circumstance which needs to be understood. The question then, despite the patterns which research and experience might suggest, becomes: 'What do people make of their circumstances?' In summary, primary teachers need to do what they can to understand prior experiences of the children and young people they teach.

Providing an engaging and enabling environment

The school environment is crucial to establishing positive behaviour amongst pupils. Watkins has suggested that this is associated with proactive policies, a strong sense of community, teacher collaboration and promotion of pupil autonomy (2011, Reading 7.2). An 'Independent Report' (commissioned by the DfE, 2017c) by Tom Bennett, blogger and then government-appointed 'Behaviour Tsar', emphasised the importance of school culture in 'optimising behaviour'. From consultation with successful teachers, he picked out eight features of schools which are most effective in developing good pupil behaviour. Such schools feature:

- committed, highly visible school leaders, with ambitious goals, supported by a strong leadership team;
- effectively communicated, realistic, detailed expectations understood clearly by all members of the school;
- highly consistent working practices throughout the school;
- a clear understanding of what the school culture is – 'this is how we do things around here, and these are the values we hold';
- high levels of staff and parental commitment to the school vision and strategies;
- high levels of support between leadership and staff, for example, staff training;
- attention to detail and thoroughness in the execution of school policies and strategies;
- high expectations of all students and staff, and a belief that all students matter equally (DfE, 2017c, p. 7).

At the classroom level, there are four dimensions of the environment which teachers must review with particular care:

Curriculum: It is clearly crucial that pupils find the curriculum of interest. If they do, then that commitment will engender more engaged behaviour. If they don't, then they may seek diversions. This can be particularly tricky where basic skills need to be mastered over many years, and teacher creativity to find interesting ways of teaching these is imperative. Chapters 9 and 10 focus on curriculum.

Pedagogy: Pupils tend to be particularly aware of how they are being controlled – of the rules, routines and rituals of the classroom, the fairness which should underpin them and the security which they offer. Beyond this, they will hope for pedagogies which are participatory, make the subject matter interesting, support success in learning and enable fun, laughter and enjoyment. Chapters 11 and 12 address such issues.

Assessment: Anxiety about being judged by others is commonplace, and for some children school may be the first place in which they experience formal assessment. On the one hand, feedback which enables progress in learning is likely to be greatly welcomed. It indicates that the teacher has taken an authentic interest (see Chapter 13). On the other hand, the experience of more formal assessment (for example, Year 6 SATs) may not be a happy one, and certainly needs to be managed with great care (as discussed in Chapter 14).

Relationships with others: This dimension is essentially about relationships between peers, which can be fraught and challenging for some children. Feeling accepted by a peer group is very important for surviving in school and is manifested in 'having friends'. But children can also be unkind, and some children may become isolated or even be bullied. Teachers need to create classroom rules and a climate in which everyone is valued, but must then be watchful to ensure that the experienced environment lives up to these expectations (see Chapters 1 and 6).

> **Expert Question**
>
> *Engagement:* do our teaching strategies, classroom organisation and consultation enable learners to actively participate in and enjoy their learning?
>
> This question contributes to a conceptual framework underpinning professional expertise (see Chapter 16).

Where a classroom environment provides for such high-quality curriculum, pedagogy, assessment and relationships, poor behaviour is likely to be minimised.

Or, to put this another way, if poor behaviour arises, as well as thinking about the needs and perspectives of the child or children themselves, it is very valuable to review one's classroom provision. Might it be possible to engage the children more effectively?

Progression in behaviour

In principle, an effective teacher will expect to make progress during the school year in classroom control and the stability of pupil behaviour. And a similar progression may be experienced when a student teacher takes a class over a sustained period of time. It is helpful to try to see this positively in terms of 'leading learning activities', so that control itself is a by-product.

In his book *Teaching Without Disruption in the Primary School*, Chaplain (2017, see also Reading 6.4) presents a model that highlights some of the characteristic processes which are likely to be found in 'early encounters' and 'later stages' of the teachers' experience with children's behaviour over time. The model shows how the pressures of establishment of acceptable behaviour, and active negotiation, are gradually replaced by greater levels of trust by pupils and teachers. With this, most importantly, comes teacher encouragement for pupils to take more control of classroom situations and exercise more self-control. Of course, such agency remains framed by the understandings which have been established and honed over time. For example, for many teachers, a summer term, unless dominated by tests or examinations of one sort or another, is a time when they feel able to give pupils more freedom to explore their interests and potential.

Reflective Activity 7.1 invites a 'stock take' on classroom behaviour and engagement.

Reflective Activity 7.1

Aim: To understand pupil behaviour in our classroom circumstances.

Evidence and reflection: Reflect on the proposition that pupil actions relate both to the person they are and to the situation they are in (as discussed above).

Review pp. 199–200 and consider: How far do you really understand, and make connections with, the circumstances of your students' lives?

Do pupils feel engaged by the curriculum, pedagogy, assessment and relationships you are providing?

How are things going in terms of the *progression* of classroom relationships and behaviour over time?

It would be very valuable to discuss these issues with a colleague, so that there is an exchange of insights.

Extension: It would be excellent to make a visual recording of some periods of classroom practice to review and discuss in terms of the questions above.

Having developed a deeper understanding, the question becomes: What to do next? It is often helpful to map scenarios for consideration. Such analysis provides a foundation for successful behavioural strategies.

ESTABLISHING AUTHORITY

Establishing authority, not to be confused with taking an authoritarian approach, over a class is partly about self-belief, in the sense of acting with confidence as a teacher – and it is also partly about capability, in the sense of being professionally competent in the core pedagogical skills of teaching and, in particular, in being able to interpret and analyse classroom events as they develop so that adjustments are possible. Underlying these qualities, as we saw in Chapter 6, is the relationship which one develops with pupils and, in particular, being seen to act fairly.

The best teachers are competent, reflective and understanding – and thus become confident. Pupils respect these qualities and so trust their teacher. Bennett argues that these qualities are associated with justice, courage, patience, wisdom and compassion (2012, Reading 7.3) and suggests that there is a need for visualisation and self-belief. One has to 'take the stage'.

Part 2 Creating conditions for learning

The difficulty is that competence and understanding take time to develop – and whilst advice can support such processes, there is no substitute for direct experience. So trainee teachers face the difficult challenge of working on their competence and understanding, whilst groups and classes still need to be taught.

In this section, we focus on four issues which support the establishment of classroom authority – expectations, self-presentation, use of language and strategic repertoire.

Expectations

Children are, just like most of us, extremely good at sensing the beliefs, motivations and dispositions of others. Teachers who appear to presume that pupils are 'up to no good' and 'cannot be trusted' are likely therefore to engender similarly guarded responses. On the other hand, if a teacher is able to convey a set of expectations which presumes capability and projects realistic goals towards success, then it is likely that pupils will try to respond. Teachers therefore need to take control of their own expectations, and to review these carefully – particularly in relation to personal theories about pupil behaviour. Beliefs of any sort evolve in the light of experience, but can also be culturally and personally embedded. Indeed, as we saw in Chapter 1, p. 22, contrasting ideas of children as inherently 'good' or 'bad' have long histories within contemporary cultures – and may also be found within some staffrooms. To establish authority, teachers need to be cautious about unquestioned beliefs, in whatever form they may emerge. In the long term, neither being too 'soft' nor too 'strict' will work. The most realistic and effective strategy is to consistently convey presumption of the best from pupils, whilst watching carefully for signs of the worst.

> ### Expert Question
>
> **Expectation:** *does our school support staff and student expectations and aspire for excellence?*
>
> This question contributes to a conceptual framework underpinning professional expertise (see Chapter 16).

Expectations for behaviour in respect of classroom rules should thus be made explicit through discussion, giving children the opportunity to activate their agency by having a sense of ownership over the rules, and then reinforced. Whenever things begin to slide, or if established understandings are challenged, then such rules need to be reasserted. But the trick here is to achieve the reassertion in an incorporative way, without precipitating a negative reaction. As discussed in Chapter 2 on learning, it helps to 'credit' pupils with what they do, rather than focus on deficits and failures.

Setting high expectations about behaviour, as for learning, is thus an important foundation for establishing teacher authority (EEF, 2019). This is greatly helped if the expectations we seek to establish are congruent with whole-school policies and culture, and Reflective Activity 7.2 suggests ways of exploring this.

reflectiveteaching.co.uk/rtps6/part2_ch7

Reflective Activity 7.2

Aim: To explore and understand a school's policies and practices with regards to behaviour management.

Evidence and reflection: Answers to the following sequence of questions may be found by studying your school's behaviour policies and through talking to staff at various levels within the school.

1. What are the school's primary aims and values?
2. What principles about discipline and behaviour are derived from these?
3. What are the implicit and explicit 'school rules'?
4. What reinforcements and sanctions are accepted?
5. What are the greatest challenges in implementing the school's policies?
6. How can I appropriately reflect the schools' disciplinary principles and rules in my classroom organisation?
7. Where and in what way should I ask for support if things go wrong?

Add other questions to the list as they occur to you.

Extension: Having gathered information, the next process is to relate this to your own expectations and strategic repertoire for managing behaviour. How does the school support you, or qualify your original intentions?

Self-presentation

In this section, we consider self-confidence, judgement and various professional skills including an ability to 'act out' the teacher role.

Teachers who are able to project themselves so that pupils take for granted that they are 'in charge' have a valuable capability. There is an important element of self-confidence in this and student teachers, in particular, may sometimes find it difficult to enact the change from the student role to the teacher role. Perhaps this is not surprising, for a huge transition in rights and responsibilities is involved. The first essential, then, is to believe in oneself as a teacher; this can certainly take time to develop.

Judgement is needed about self-presentation because the process of establishing authority, as we saw in Chapter 6, is essentially one of negotiation between the teacher and the class. Authenticity is an important contribution to any negotiation and it is likely that, in the challenges of the classroom, attempts by novice teachers to bluff, and to pretend that they are hugely experienced, will be found out. Whilst necessary skills and understanding develop, it is therefore normally wise to progress carefully and 'with' the students if at all possible. This does not mean that one should not act the part and fulfil the 'teacher role' (see below) – indeed, the pupils will expect this. But it is best to recognise that establishing authority requires careful reflection on, and management of, the complementary roles and relationships between teacher and pupils.

reflectiveteaching.co.uk/rtps6/part2_ch7

Professional skills, as reviewed in Chapter 6, p. 188, come into their own here – for they are all related to demonstration of classroom competence. *Non-verbal skills* relate to such things as gesture, posture, movement, position in the room, facial expression etc. These will be actively interpreted by children. The intended impression might be one of confidence and competence, but the reflective teacher will need to consider how effectively this is achieved. How do you feel? How do you move within the classroom? *Voice control* is particularly crucial, for changing the pitch, volume, projection and intensity can convey meaning. If one's voice is to be used in this way then it will require some training and time to develop (Evans and Savage, 2018). Teachers, like singers and actors, can learn to use their diaphragm to project a 'chest voice', to breathe more deeply and speak more slowly so that their voice and their message are carried more effectively. And, of course, the skill of really *listening* to pupils and understanding what they have to say is also critical to the establishment of authority – for this is the basis of its legitimacy. Learning pupil names is extremely important to demonstrate that children are valued. It helps the build-up of confidence and establishes the groundwork for positive relationships with individual children.

The skills which have been reviewed above are necessary but are not sufficient. They have no substantive content or merit in their own right. A self-confident performer who lacks purpose and gets practical matters wrong (for example, has ill-defined objectives, mixes up children's names, plans sessions badly, loses books, acts unfairly etc.) will not be able to manage a class. A teacher has to be purposive as well as skilled and must understand the ends of education as well as the means.

Language

Sometimes, our primary purpose in speaking to pupils is to ensure that they correct some aspect of their behaviour. We may, quite simply, need to be assertive. But in so doing, as the adult and as the teacher, we also need to bear in mind our broader educational purposes. Every time we speak to pupils, for whatever purpose, we have educational opportunities. In relation to behaviour, the aim is to keep them 'on track' as effectively as possible as a means to educational ends.

Rogers (2011, p. 83) identifies seven ways in which language should be used to support good discipline:

1 keep corrective interaction as 'least-intrusive' as possible;

2 avoid unnecessary confrontation;

3 keep a respectful, positive tone of voice wherever possible;

4 keep corrective language positive where possible;

5 restore working relationships with a reprimanded pupil as quickly as possible;

6 follow up with children on matters beyond the classroom context;

7 if we need to communicate frustration, or even anger, do so assertively rather than aggressively.

reflectiveteaching.co.uk/rtps6/part2_ch7

In his final point, Rogers is warning teachers not to get 'out of control'. Pupils do have ways of describing this – the teacher has 'flipped', 'gone mad' or 'lost it'. This is the 'non-legitimate censure' discussed in Chapter 6, p. 182 – and the images of teacher insanity are not there by chance. Such uncontrolled use of power is a long way from establishing legitimated authority and respect.

Standing back from this a little, the basic point is that to establish our authority as teachers, even with the pressure of the busy classroom, we must carefully think about what we say and how we say it. In principle, teacher language to build good discipline should:

- *connect personally* with relevant pupil/s;
- *identify the behaviour* which needs to change;
- *encourage re-engagement* with curricular intentions;
- *minimise disruption* to others;
- *follow through* to ensure conformity.

For example:

- A simple, routine and individual primary classroom example might be: 'Bhavika' (teacher gains her attention with a neutral tone of voice and then sustains eye contact), 'that's enough talking for now', 'let's see if you can complete your story before playtime' (teacher watches beneficially, and makes that clear, to see that Bhavika goes back on task).
- In a routine whole-class, primary classroom situation the teacher might say: 'Now everybody' (gain attention, perhaps with a clap or other sign), 'we have been becoming rather noisy this afternoon and this isn't good for concentrating on our work', 'I'd like us to try really hard now so that we can all focus on what we have to learn', 'and then nobody will fall behind' (teacher presents the learning goals for the session and moves actively within the classroom to reinforce the request using proximity).

Put another way, measured and constructive assertiveness combined with provision of an interesting curriculum can sustain and reinforce good order – and thus help in the establishment of authority (Canter and Canter, 1992). Intemperate use of language can fuel poor discipline by undermining authority.

Although audio or video recordings never seem flattering, recording a lesson introduction or some other whole-class episode can be a useful way of seeing how much your verbal repertoire is developing.

Strategic repertoire

Experienced teachers are aware of a repertoire of strategies on which they can draw to establish and maintain appropriate pupil behaviour. Rogers (2011) reviewed a range of strategies and suggested that teachers should minimise their 'intrusion'. The proposal is closely tied to the existence of tacit classroom understandings, as described in Chapter 6.

reflectiveteaching.co.uk/rtps6/part2_ch7

Part 2 Creating conditions for learning

So good classroom relationships provide a sort of 'moral order' in the classroom which underpins behaviour. When this exists, it seems almost invisible – but don't be taken in! Teachers work continuously to maintain such relationships.

Teacher strategies become more intrusive when we feel the need to draw on our authority and assert our power. They are least intrusive when we are able to rely on the tacit understandings of the 'working consensus'.

Strategies identified by Rogers can be considered in three groups. These reflect *minimal, routine* and *assertive* levels of teacher action.

Minimal intrusion strategies

The efficacy of these strategies rests on the existence of well understood rules and good classroom relationships. Good behaviour can thus be achieved with simple reminders. Three of Rogers' minimal strategies are:

- Tactical ignoring – the teacher is aware of, but temporarily ignores, minor misdemeanours whilst focusing on and affirming positive behaviours. Pupils then come into line.

- Incidental language – reminders of classroom rules are given without attributing blame to anyone. Because rules are established and accepted, pupils self-adjust to conform. 'We have a rather messy classroom at the moment, and we can't go out if it's like that, can we?'

- Take-up time – after a rule reminder or request, the teacher moves away to give pupils time to cooperate. In so doing, she communicates trust (though she might also keep an eye on progress).

Routine strategies

This group of strategies reflects the ebb and flow of teacher–pupil interaction and the fact that relationships are always dynamic. A little jostling and testing of boundaries is thus to be expected. The strategies below are typical of those which teachers use to frame and control classroom situations, particularly when children or young people may have non-curricular activities in mind.

- Behavioural direction – expected behaviours are directly, positively and briefly communicated. 'All paying attention to me now, please.'

- Rule reminder – rather than 'picking on' a particular transgressor, the teacher reminds everyone of a rule. 'Now what are our rules about getting ready for PE?'

- Prefacing – with awareness of potential misbehaviour, this strategy can be used to anticipate and frame activities without being too heavy-handed. At appropriate moments, the teacher interacts with relevant pupils to show awareness, to nip unwanted aspects in the bud, and to redirect attention back to curricula goals.

reflectiveteaching.co.uk/rtps6/part2_ch7

Chapter 7 Engagement   207

- Distraction – this contrarian strategy involves deliberately drawing attention to something that is going well and thus by-passing something which might be problematic. With the class refocused, the difficulty fades away or can be quietly dealt with.

- Direct questions – such questions challenge pupils to justify themselves and to take responsibility. 'What should you be doing now? Where should you put the . . .?' Such questions may be the starting point for discussion and clarification of rules.

- Directed 'choices' – these are pupil options which are circumscribed by established rules and routines. 'Yes, you can go in the play area once you've finished your story.' 'When you have made notes on your homework, you can certainly go out for break.'

Assertive strategies

The strategies in this group depend on the teacher asserting their authority and 'standing up' to pupils in various ways. Whilst they are more categoric, they still make reference to established understandings and rules. However, they leave pupils in no doubt that the teacher is in charge.

- Blocking – this is an important strategy to maintain focus on important behavioural issues in the face of all sorts of distraction tactics which may be deployed by pupils. 'Hold on. Now let's get to the point about what really happened – and I'll hear you one at a time. John. . .'

- Assertion – this strategy calmly deploys verbal and non-verbal skills and draws on reserves of self-confidence to defend and promote a principle about behaviour which has been threatened. 'It is not OK to hit people in school, at any time at all.' 'Language of that sort is unacceptable.' The stance should be *non-aggressive* so that the teacher is clearly holding the moral high-ground. We thus demonstrate to the class as a whole that our action is responsible and legitimate – which erodes support for transgressors, re-asserts more routine expectations and gradually calms things down. It is quite possible, in some situations, that there may need to be a sequence of blocking and assertion moves as the complexity of pupil feelings, explanations and actions is worked through. Judgement is needed in what to block so that progress can be made, whilst also dealing with the issues which are felt to be important. From the pupil perspective, an overall judgement will eventually be made about the 'fairness' of the teacher in dealing with the incident.

- Command – a direct instruction. To be effective, a command needs to be delivered with clarity and confidence, and to be followed up immediately. 'Louise, put down the hose pipe NOW.' Eye contact, proximity and firm tone of voice will all convey the seriousness of teacher intentions. This strategy is one of direct intervention and should not be common in classroom use. If it is, it may be a sign that relationships are breaking down. The plight of a student teacher ineffectually demanding things

reflectiveteaching.co.uk/rtps6/part2_ch7

> **Expert Question**
>
> **Repertoire:** is our pedagogic expertise sufficiently creative, skilled and wide-ranging to teach all elements of learning?
>
> This question contributes to a conceptual framework underpinning professional expertise (see Chapter 16).

from an alienated class of children is not a comfortable experience. Thus, to be effective, commands still draw on mutual respect, for pupils will conform best when they trust the teacher.

We have reviewed a repertoire of strategies for managing behaviour. The moral foundation of these strategies rests, in all cases, on classroom relationships, as described in Chapter 6. Teachers' power is always circumscribed but, as responsible adults, we have the task of analysing and interpreting what is going on – and taking action if necessary. To do this, it is important to be able stand back a little.

> **Reflective Activity 7.3**
>
> *Aim:* To review the repertoire of strategies for managing behaviour which we typically use.
>
> *Evidence and reflection:* Brainstorm, perhaps with a group of colleagues, on the strategies which you use to manage behaviour – just get a list. Use the ideas above from Rogers, or harvest from other sources if this is helpful. Then maybe refine it a bit, to eliminate overlaps.
>
> Now see if you can sort your strategies into categories based on the degree of intrusion. Which rest on tacit understandings? Which contribute to routine patrolling? Which demand really assertive activity?
>
> *Extension:* Having expanded and analysed your strategic repertoire for managing behaviour, it is good to try it out. Acting mindfully, look for opportunities to experiment! In the light of your experience, refine your repertoire.

SKILLS FOR ENGAGEMENT

In this section, we look at a 'magnificent seven' of management skills which relate to the maintenance of classroom engagement: 'gaining attention', 'framing', 'with-it-ness', 'overlapping', 'pacing', 'orchestration' and 'consistency'. Such skills enable lesson plans to be put into action successfully (see Chapter 11, p. 320).

Gaining attention

This is often one of the first problems to confront a student teacher. With children in the classroom, talking, moving around, playing or whatever, how do you get them to stop what they are doing and turn their attention to you? Established teachers are likely to have at least one routine for this. Thus a single, sharp clap of the hands may cut through the noise and produce a short pause which creates an opportunity to take the initiative. In some primary contexts, teachers use a signal requiring children to raise one arm in silence and face the teacher. This has the considerable merit of making it very obvious which children are now paying attention, and which are not. Sadly, things are not always so simple and gaining attention often has to be worked for.

To understand why this is, it is worth considering what is at stake. When children or young people are milling about, talking and playing amongst themselves, they are free of adult constraints and able to indulge in all the excitements and diversions of peer culture. The switch signal given by the teacher is an interruption to this freedom. It is an assertion, based on the teacher's authority, that the time has now come for the children to assume the role of 'pupils' again. They are to set aside what they were previously doing, and must now accept the rules, routines and expectations of the classroom.

As with so many aspects of teaching, it is helpful to think of building up a repertoire of ways of gaining attention so that various strategies are available. Whilst a clear, firm command may be effective from time to time, is important to avoid uncontrolled shouting. Pitch of voice and speed of talking need to be watched. For student teachers, it is very good practice to study the strategies used by established teachers and to discuss their routines with them. Acting confidently, which such consultation will enable, will communicate competence so that, hopefully, success builds on success.

Gaining attention is a crucial test of authority. If we have earned the respect of the pupils as their teacher, and they know that we are likely to offer them an interesting curriculum, then they will normally pay attention when asked appropriately.

Framing

Understandings about classroom behaviour are not static. Indeed, even if an expected behaviour is well established, pupils are expert at gauging the degree to which they need to conform and the extent to which they might be able to 'get away' with something. To do this, they interpret the mood and intent of their teacher by monitoring their actions, statements and movements. For example, an active, purposeful entry to a classroom is a clear signal that a teacher 'means business' and will normally tighten the frame immediately. As long as something substantive and interesting follows, things should be fine. Conversely, acting rather casually, or withdrawing into conversation with a visiting adult, will usually cause behavioural expectations to weaken and may result in children relaxing in their approach to activities.

Framing thus indicates the extent to which situations or events are structured by expectations. It may apply in particular settings, or from moment to moment within a lesson. For instance, one might compare the strong frame which often exists in a hushed library, with the weak frame which often exists in classrooms during wet dinner breaks. For some purposes, such as during the introduction to a teaching session, one might want

reflectiveteaching.co.uk/rtps6/part2_ch7

the frame to be strong thus ensuring tight control and attention. On other occasions, such as for group problem-solving discussions, a weaker overall frame may be perfectly acceptable and may enable children to take initiatives which are necessary to fulfil learning objectives. Situations of difficulty often arise where strong framing is expected by a teacher but children act as if the framing is weak. If this happens, a teacher has to act quickly to redefine the rules in play.

The ability of a teacher to manage the strength of behavioural framing over time has a great deal to do with classroom discipline. It sustains expectations, and avoids a lurch from routine to routine. In particular, skilful management provides a means of pre-empting serious difficulties through giving clear expectations about acceptable behaviour. By its very nature, though, the development of such understandings cannot be rushed and frequently needs to be explicitly reviewed by teachers and children.

With-it-ness

This is a term coined by Kounin (1970, Reading 7.5) to describe the capacity of teachers to be aware of the wide variety of things which are simultaneously going on in a classroom. This is a constant challenge for any teacher and can be a particular strain for a new teacher until the skill is acquired.

Teachers who are 'with-it' are said to 'have eyes in the back of their head'. They are able to anticipate and to see where help is needed. They are able to nip trouble in the bud. They are skilful at scanning the class whilst helping individuals, and they position themselves accordingly. They are alert; they can pre-empt disturbance; and they can act fast. They can sense the way a class is responding, re-establish the framework of expectations if necessary and act to maintain a positive atmosphere.

Overlapping

This is another of Kounin's terms and it describes the skill of being able to do more than one thing at a time. This is similar to the popular term 'multi-tasking'. Most teachers work under such pressure that they have to think about and do more than one thing at a time. Decisions have to be made very rapidly. It has been calculated that over 1,000 interpersonal exchanges a day typically take place between each teacher and the children in their care. Frequently scanning the class, even whilst helping one individual, should enable the teacher to identify and reinforce appropriate behaviour or to anticipate and intervene at the first signs of trouble. As Kounin (Reading 7.5) points out, if children perceive that the teacher is 'with-it' enough to know what is going on, they are more likely to remain on task and achieve the appropriate learning objectives.

Pacing

Pacing involves making appropriate judgements about the timing and phasing of the organisation and content of teaching–learning sessions. Organisational decisions have to be made about when to begin and end an activity and how much time to leave for tidying up or a plenary discussion. It is very easy to get involved in activities, forget about the clock and suddenly find it is break time. More complex educational judgements are necessary in relation to learning activities and the various phases of a typical session. For example, the motivation generated at the start of an activity has to be sustained or managed throughout. There may also be a need for 'incubation' and 'developmental' phases in which children think about the activities, explore ideas and then tackle tasks. From time to time there might be a need for a 'restructuring phase' where objectives and procedures may need to be clarified further. Finally, there may be a 'review phase' for reinforcing good effort or for reflecting on overall progress. (For more detailed discussion on the pacing of content delivery, questions and answers etc. see Chapter 12, p. 375.)

In England, strict lesson structures were once imposed on teachers and learners through 'national strategies' for literacy and numeracy, but scope for flexibility and exercising judgement about pacing are vitally important. They depend crucially on being sensitive to how children are responding to activities. If they are immersed and productively engaged, then one might decide to extend a phase or run the activity into the next session. If the children seem to be becoming bored, frustrated or listless, then it is usually wise to retain the initiative, to restructure or review the activity or to move on to something new. If the children are becoming too 'high', excited and distracted, then it may be useful to review and maybe redirect them into an activity which calms them down by rechannelling their energies. As will be discussed in the next section, working with a class of individuals may involve being able to respond to many, if not all, of their responses at the same time.

Orchestration

We use the term 'orchestration' to refer to the way in which a teacher works with the whole class rather like a conductor controls an orchestra or a stand-up comedian 'plays' an audience. Whether the teacher is adopting whole-class, individual or group teaching strategies, part of their job is to maximise the time that all the individuals in the class are on task and paying attention. Involving all the children in the learning activities of a classroom involves developing the sensitivity to be able to 'read' how individuals or groups are responding and to be able to anticipate the most effective way of maintaining interest or re-engaging attention. Bored, listless behaviour might be engendered because a task is too easy or too difficult (see Chapter 10 on differentiation). On the other hand, some children may be highly motivated by an activity which others find tedious and dull. In all cases the teacher has to be aware of everything that is happening in their classroom and be prepared to act accordingly. This may involve a differentiated response in which some

reflectiveteaching.co.uk/rtps6/part2_ch7

children are allowed to continue with what they are doing whilst a new focus is found for others. Certainly, teachers have to be aware of a range of ways of motivating all the individuals in the class (Holleran and Gilbert, 2015).

Consistency

We identify one final, overarching skill for maximising learner engagement. This concerns the maintenance of consistency in the promotion of classroom rules, routines and expectations (EEF, 2019). Teacher inconsistency, if it occurs, reduces the integrity of the working consensus and the sense of fairness on which it is based. This, in turn, can lead to a variety of subsequent control difficulties and to risk-avoidance strategies so that new learning is compromised. Pupils will feel vulnerable unless they can rely on teacher consistency and fairness. However, with such security, children are more likely to open themselves up to the challenges and risks of new learning. Teacher consistency thus provides an underlying structure for high-quality pupil learning.

Reflective Activity 7.4

Aim: To investigate one's classroom management skills.

Evidence and reflection: Ask a colleague to observe you in a teaching session and to make notes on the way in which you manage the children. They could watch out for examples of gaining attention, framing, with-it-ness, overlapping, pacing, orchestration and maintaining consistency. Discuss the session together afterwards.

Alternatively, set up a video camera to record a session which you take. Analyse the playback in terms of the issues above.

Sometimes people only see what seems to be going wrong! If there is a danger that you are becoming negative about your management skills and judgements, then adopt the 'three to one rule'. This rule states that you can only identify one negative thing after you have identified three positives. When you run out of positives you have to stop. (This strategy also works with children who have been asked to evaluate their own work or that of others!)

Extension: Such analysis should increase self-awareness of management skills. Try to identify possible improvements which could be made. These can be practised and worked on. Give yourself time to develop your expertise.

MANAGING CLASSROOM EPISODES

'Flow' is a summary criterion which can be used to describe the consequences of classroom management over time. It highlights the degree of continuity and coherence

reflectiveteaching.co.uk/rtps6/part2_ch7

achieved in a learning session, and implies steady, continuous progression. The suggestion is thus that we should work with the children to develop a coherent sense of purpose within our classes; organise our classrooms in ways which are consistent with those purposes; and manage the children, phases and events so that learning objectives are cumulatively reinforced. Consistency and reinforcement of desirable behaviours can be important here, as Merrett and Wheldall (1990, Reading 7.6) emphasised.

In this section, we discuss five issues which pose particular management challenges to the flow of sessions. We discuss 'beginnings' of sessions; their 'development'; 'transitions' between phases of sessions or between sessions themselves; and the 'endings' of sessions. We also consider strategies for dealing with 'the unexpected'.

Beginnings

Just as for curriculum it is essential that pupils understand what they are expected to learn, so for behaviour it is helpful that there should be clarity concerning how they should behave.

The beginning of a session is often seen as important because of the way in which it sets a tone and clarifies intent. Simple strategies such as being in the classroom to receive the children help to establish that you are receiving them on your territory and, by implication, on your terms (Laslett and Smith, 1992).

The next important goals are usually as follows: introduce and interest the children in the planned activities; provide them with a clear indication of the learning objectives of the session and a clear understanding of what they are expected to do and how they can assess what they have done; and structure the activity in practical, organisational terms. See **Reflective Activity 11.2**.

Reflective Activity 7.5

Aim: To evaluate the beginning of a session and to consider areas for improvement.

Evidence and reflection: Video record a session you have taught or observe someone else's lesson. Consider what happened in terms of the following questions:

- How did the teacher attract the children's attention?
- Did the teacher explain the objectives of the session?
- What did the teacher use as a stimulus at the start of the lesson and how effective was this?
- Were the instructions to the class clear?

---

reflectiveteaching.co.uk/rtps6/part2_ch7

Part 2 Creating conditions for learning

- Did the children know why they were doing this activity?
- Did the children know what they were going to learn from it?
- Did the children understand the steps to success?
- Did the children know if any follow-up is expected?
- Did the children know on what criteria their work was to be assessed?
- Did the children know how this activity links with other work they had done or would do next?

Extension: What specific actions could be taken for improvement? What general skills need to be worked on?

Development

This issue calls for careful thought. However carefully the session begins, how does it develop? Pupils will expect to find some progression which will maintain their interest and engagement with curricular tasks. This is a clear example of how good behaviour can be seen as a product of good teaching – in this case, of appropriate curriculum planning (see Chapter 10).

Transitions

Transitions are a regular cause of control difficulties, particularly for trainee teachers. Difficulties often arise when expectations about behaviour concerning one activity have to be left behind and those of the new one have yet to be established. In these circumstances, a skilled teacher is likely to plan carefully, involve available support staff, take an initiative early and structure the transition carefully.

Expert Questions

Progression: does the curriculum-as-delivered provide an appropriate sequence and depth of learning experiences?

Engagement: do our teaching strategies, classroom rganization and consultation enable learners to actively participate in and enjoy their learning?

These questions contribute to a conceptual framework underpinning professional expertise (see Chapter 16).

For example, it would be a challenging prospect if a whole range of creative, artistic activities were in full flow when primary school children suddenly had to get changed for a physical education session in the hall. We would suggest that it is important to break down a transition such as this into three discrete stages. The skill lies in, first, anticipating problems before they arise; second, in pre-structuring the next phase; and, finally, in interesting the children in the next phase so that they are drawn through and into it. These principles (anticipate, pre-structure and engage) apply to any transition.

reflectiveteaching.co.uk/rtps6/part2_ch7

Reflective Activity 7.6

Aim: To monitor periods of transition in your own teaching.

Evidence and reflection: Consider a transition phase in your own teaching in the light of the following questions:

- Did you give an early warning of the transition?
- Did you give clear instructions for leaving existing work?
- Did you give the children clear instructions for the transition and for any movement that was necessary?
- Did you arouse the children's interest in the next phase?

Extension: Reviewing your performance as a whole, what are the major points for improvement? Do you see these as technical, as personal, or as associated with other factors? What might you try next time?

Endings

Ending a session is a further management issue and four aspects will be reviewed. The first is a very practical one. At the end of any session, equipment must be put away and the classroom must be tidied up ready for future sessions. The second aspect relates to discipline and control. Children can sometimes get a little excited at the end of a session when they look forward to whatever follows. This, combined with the chores of tidying up, can require a degree of awareness and firmness from the teacher. The procedures that are called for here are similar to those for transitions.

The two other aspects involved in ending sessions have more explicit and positive educational potential. One of these concerns the excellent opportunities which arise, for example in the plenary of a literacy lesson, for reviewing educational progress and achievements, for reinforcing good work and for contextualising activities which have been completed. This is complemented by the opportunities that also arise for asserting the membership of the class as a communal group. Shared experiences, teamwork and cooperation can be celebrated and reinforced through the enjoyment of poetry, singing, games, stories etc. Moreover, there are lots of very productive opportunities at the ends of sessions and even an odd space of unexpected time, perhaps waiting for a bell, which can be used constructively.

Overall, a carefully thought-out and well-executed ending to a session will contribute to the flow of activities by providing an ordered exit, by reinforcing learning and by building up the sense of 'belonging' within the class as a whole.

Reflective Activity 7.7

Aim: To review the end of a session and identify areas for improvement.

Evidence and reflection: Reflect back on a session you taught recently in the light of the following questions:

- Did you give early warning of the end of the session?
- Did you give clear instructions for tidying up?
- Did you reinforce those instructions and monitor the tidying up?
- Did you take opportunities to reinforce the educational achievements, efforts and progress made?
- Did you take opportunities to build up the sense of the class as a community?
- Did you praise the children for what they did well?
- Did you provide for an ordered exit from the room?
- How might you respond differently in future?

Extension: You could very usefully ask a mentor or an experienced colleague to observe your session and offer specific comments. Before you do, highlight the particular issues on which you want feedback. This might also be a good moment to do some reading about the principles of class management.

The unexpected

The unexpected is one of the most salient features of the classroom for trainee teachers (Doyle, 1977; Chaplain, 2017). It is difficult to predict children's reactions to questions or how they will respond to specific activities. Similarly, it is difficult to predict how long it will take for a class to complete an activity. These are skills which are acquired over time and with experience. However, in any classroom there is the continuous possibility of internal and external interruptions; for example, there may be changes in the normal schedule or a potential breakdown in equipment. Skilled teachers learn to plan ahead, to anticipate potential difficulties and to have a range of strategies for dealing with the unexpected. In this section we consider how teachers might deal with the unexpected in terms of both learning outcomes and 'crises'.

In line with a social constructivist approach to learning, teachers are encouraged to ask open-ended questions which can be interpreted and answered in a number of different ways (see Chapter 12, p. 375 for further discussion). As appropriate answers are not predetermined, teachers may be surprised by the children's responses. Where the answer is unexpected the teacher then faces the dilemma of wanting to acknowledge the legitimacy of the response without being drawn too far away from the teaching point being made. Consider, for example, the following situation. A teacher introduces her class of 7-year-olds to the subject of trees and what a healthy plant needs to grow. One child responds:

'Concrete'. At first this might seem an unusual response. However, on closer inspection it becomes clear that outside the school gates, oak trees can be observed 'growing out of concrete'. This is a clear example of a scientific misconception (Allen, 2014; McCrory and Worthington, 2018) Observation is one of the many important process skills which underpin scientific enquiry (National Curriculum for Science; DfE, 2013c) but can often cause cognitive dissonance, as we see here. As a skilled practitioner, the teacher praises and affirms the child for using their enquiry skills and then discusses or indeed demonstrates why this is incorrect, highlighting the correct conceptual knowledge. Being able to handle the unexpected in a way which reinforces children's prior learning and yet remains true to the original learning objective is the mark of a skilled teacher. (Note also the role of teacher knowledge in making this possible, as discussed in Chapter 9, p. 292.)

On a more practical level, a classroom 'crisis' is a clear example of the unexpected. Crises can come in many forms, from a child being sick or cutting a finger, to children (or perhaps a parent) challenging the teacher's authority and judgement. Despite the wide-ranging issues which are raised, there are three fairly simple principles which can be applied from the classroom-management point of view.

The first priority is to *minimise the disturbance*. Neither a child who is ill or hurt, nor a parent or child who is upset, can be given the attention which they require by a teacher who has continuing classroom responsibilities. Help from support staff, the school secretary, an ancillary helper, or other teacher should be called in either to deal with the problem or to relieve the class teacher so that they can deal with it. In this way disturbance to the classroom flow can be minimised and those in need of undivided attention can receive it. The school should have an identified procedure for how to handle crises. Of course, a student teacher usually has a full-time teacher upon whom to call.

The second step for handling a crisis is to *maximise reassurance*. Children can be upset when something unexpected happens and it may well be appropriate to reassert the security of their classroom routines and expectations. A degree of caution in the choice of activities for a suitable period might therefore be wise.

The third strategy, which is appropriate when a crisis arises, concerns *pausing for sufficient thought* before making a judgement on how to act. Obviously, this depends on what has happened and some events require immediate action. However, if it is possible to gain time to think about the issues outside the heat of the moment, then it may produce more authoritative and constructive decisions.

Reflective Activity 7.8

Aim: To monitor responses to a classroom crisis.

Evidence and reflection: After a crisis has arisen, a diary-type account of it and of how it was handled could be written. This might describe the event, and also reflect the feelings which were experienced as the events unfolded. It might be valuable to encourage children to record and talk about a similar account and reflection after the event, so that you can gain an insight into why they behaved as they did.

reflectiveteaching.co.uk/rtps6/part2_ch7

Part 2 **Creating conditions for learning**

The following questions might be asked:

- Did you inimize disturbance?
- Did you maximise reassurance?
- Did you make appropriate judgements on how to act?

Extension: Having examined your actions and the children's responses to the crisis it would probably be helpful to discuss the event and the accounts with a friend or colleague. An interesting reading would be David Tripp (1993) on 'critical incidents'.

CYCLES OF BEHAVIOUR

Towards engagement and independence

Here we revisit the discussion in Chapter 6, p. 178. Positive relationships between teacher and pupils are sustained if teachers act thoughtfully, constructively and fairly towards their pupils but also, most particularly, by the quality and appropriateness of the curriculum and educational experience which is on offer. Children are alert to this. They want to be interested and they want to learn. School can otherwise be 'so booooorrrrring. . .'. Pupil engagement will be high if tasks and activities are clearly introduced, appropriately chosen and well-matched to pupil needs. If this is done, success is possible and a sense of achievement can be gained.

So, to summarise, in terms of dealing with behavioural problems the most effective strategy is, without doubt, to try to prevent them from happening in the first place. Certainly, the incidence of inappropriate behaviour is likely to be significantly reduced by following some basic rules of thumb to improve pupil engagement (see Checklist 7.1).

Unfortunately, whilst such strategies should significantly reduce the incidents of misbehaviour, they may not prevent it in all circumstances. Consequently, a prudent teacher will develop in their repertoire a range of strategies for dealing with inappropriate behaviour . . . before it develops into anything worse.

Checklist 7.1

Aim: To pre-empt general misbehaviour and improve engagement.

1. Be clear about general class rules and what constitutes acceptable behaviour.
2. 'Catch 'em being good', and 'give credit' for appropriate behaviour.
3. Select tasks and activities that offer appropriate challenge and interest, but which also enable pupils to achieve success.
4. Have clear learning objectives and make sure pupils understand these.
5. Explain the activity or task clearly and be sure that everyone knows what to do and how to do it.
6. Be supportive of any problems encountered and provide feedback.
7. Show approval of appropriate work and reward effort.
8. Be consistent and be positive.

reflectiveteaching.co.uk/rtps6/part2_ch7

Lesson study 7.1 provides a good example of how teachers can be proactive in engaging children in worthwhile curricular activity, and thus avoid behavioural difficulties. Children who were becoming 'stuck' with their learning were helped to progress by breaking down and structuring collaborative tasks and by offering constructive feedback.

LESSON STUDY 7.1
Helping children who are 'stuck' to re-engage with their learning

The school: Caddington Village School is a semi-rural school in Central Bedfordshire. At the time of the lesson study, there were 550 pupils on roll, aged 3–13 years of age; 12 per cent of pupils were identified as having special educational needs or disabilities and 14 per cent were classified as disadvantaged.

What we wanted the children to learn: Existing school data identified a number of pupils who were 'stuck' with their learning. These learners included high-attaining children who were 'switched off', some pupils who appeared to be distracted and low-attaining pupils who were making very slow progress. We wanted the pupils who were stuck to understand that they needed to re-engage with the process of learning. We hoped that lesson study would help us to identify barriers and develop solutions that could be used by teachers across the age range and with pupils of differing abilities.

What research is available: This lesson study touches on both the issue of curricular differentiation (Chapter 10, p. 323) and appropriate selection from a pedagogic repertoire (Chapter 11, p. 355). Pupils were organised in groups, with progression in the ways in which these were structured (see Baines et al., 2017, Chapter 8, p. 248).

What we discovered in our research lessons:
RL1: In the first lesson we tried a radical change of classroom seating, trying out a range of attainment groupings and sizes. Challenging tasks were set for higher attaining pupils to solve independently from the very start of the lesson, thus enabling the teacher to work alongside less advanced pupils and provide modelling of tasks. The post-lesson discussion showed that only some pupils had responded to the challenging tasks well. The small grouping proved to be effective.

RL2: In the second lesson the challenging tasks were modified to make them more competitive and included 'rewards'. Specific responsibilities were given to the focus children, for example scriber, group leader, timekeeper and presenter. Tasks were given as 'personal challenges' and with time limits in order to focus and motivate all pupils in the group. Learning support assistants were deployed to work with pupils they would not normally work with, in order to promote independence in pupils who usually received support. The pupils responded to challenge and reward in a positive way: 'It makes me try harder, I know how to get merits.' Two of the research pupils worked to their full potential. Pupil 3 was a little slower to respond, and spent time observing other pupils before going on to use props to assist them.

RL3: In the third lesson we decided to build on the success we had in the second lesson. More particularly, we decided to steer the pupils who relied heavily on adult support towards more independent and self-directed learning. For them we developed a set of question cards which proved successful. The pupils were given three cards with a question mark printed on them. Each time a pupil asked an adult a question, a question card was taken away. The pupil then had to consider carefully the necessity of asking a question which in turn led to them becoming more independent.

What pupils learned: In relation to direct outcomes, all pupils in the study made at least expected progress in reading, writing and maths, and a number of them made accelerated progress over the course of the academic year (from November at the time of the lesson study to June results).

What we learned: Small groups of four worked well for collaborative pupil learning. It seemed to offer the right level of peer-to-peer support and an unintimidating space for challenge. And because the group is small enough to have 'nowhere to hide', all of the pupils have a specific role and task, and therefore must contribute to the group.

When pupils were challenged from the outset they engaged more eagerly with tasks; they did not have time to drift off task and remained motivated throughout the lesson.

Pupils valued having small, specific and timely rewards; they appreciated having a series of goals and derived satisfaction from regular praise and merits.

We also observed that many teachers were not providing an environment that facilitated learning. We launched a very simple, but effective initiative called 'See, Hear, Clear'. This required teachers to check that all pupils could see them, that all pupils could hear what was being said and that the desks were clear from clutter and distractions.

How we shared: The key findings were discussed at a staff meeting involving all staff. The following strategies were adapted across the school and promoted as good practice: give clear, one-step instructions using simple, specific and consistent language; produce a seating plan and vary the groupings from time to time – including where any learning support staff will be deployed; make some tasks competitive and give rewards and praise when goals are met; ask weaker pupils to explain their task back to an adult – to check they are clear and can work confidently; encourage higher level peer discussion by asking open questions; ensure easy access to practical resources; have clear success criteria that are shared and referred to frequently.

Managing challenging behaviour – avoiding a negative cycle

Although, hopefully, crises will be rare, there may be behavioural problems which gradually erode good relationships and threaten classroom order. In this section, we present them in terms of recurring challenges that even the most experienced teacher may have to deal with. The aim, of course, would be to anticipate undesirable behaviour and to 'nip it in the bud' so that it does not lead to a negative cycle (see Chapter 6, p. 184). Nevertheless, difficulties are bound to occur from time to time and prudent teachers are likely to want to think through possible strategies in advance so that they can act confidently in managing such situations.

The EEF Toolkit, which synthesises high-quality international evidence, suggests that specific behavioural interventions often do lead to improvements and are reflected in

reflectiveteaching.co.uk/rtps6/part2_ch7

academic progress too. The best results are achieved when particular issues or children with particular needs are targeted (see **Toolkit Evidence 7.1** on p. 227).

In routine circumstances, if behavioural problems seem to be emerging, it would be appropriate to consider the strategies listed below. Suggestions are offered for five progressive stages. The emphasis should remain on prevention, and you should bear in mind that, whilst the 1997 Education Act enables teachers to restrain pupils with 'such force as is reasonable in the circumstances' (Section 4), corporal punishment in any form is illegal.

1 If inappropriate behaviour occurs only once and seems relatively minor:
   - Indicate that you have noticed and disapprove of the behaviour – eye contact and a shake of the head.

2 If repeated:
   - Make sustained eye contact, use more emphatic non-verbal gestures.
   - Move towards the child.
   - Invite the child to participate – ask a question or encourage a comment, direct the focus onto work to be done.

3 If persistent, in addition to the responses above:
   - Name the child firmly and positively.
   - Move to the child.
   - Stop the action.
   - Find out the facts if the situation is ambiguous; avoid jumping to conclusions.
   - Briefly identify the inappropriate behaviour, comment on the *behaviour* (not the child), keep voice low and controlled, avoid nagging/lecturing.
   - Clearly state the desired behaviour, and expect a compliant response.
   - Distance the child from the situation – avoid a contagious spread, a public clash and an 'audience' which can encourage 'showing off'.
   - Focus on the principal individual involved; don't be drawn into discussion with a group – followers will conform if you control the leader.
   - Deal with the situation as quickly and neatly as possible; don't be drawn into long arguments; don't let the situation distract your attention from the rest of the class and the goals of your lesson.

4 If punishment is judged to be necessary:
   - Ensure that the punishments you consider are consistent with school policies and established classroom norms.
   - Be sure that the punishment you decide upon is appropriate and will be seen to be 'fair'.
   - Avoid indiscriminate punishment of class or group which would be deemed 'unfair'.
   - Be confident that you can implement the punishment as announced.

Part 2 Creating conditions for learning

5 Closure/after the event:

- Take those involved to one side, perhaps individually, and present them with 'the problem' – preserve their dignity, avoid 'supporters' chipping in.
- Encourage the child to identify what had been wrong, thus sharing responsibility.
- If you have acted inappropriately in any way, then apologise, so you are seen to be fair.
- Invite the child to draw up a 'contract' for the future.
- If privileges are to be withdrawn, show how they can be earned back.
- Provide new opportunities to earn praise.
- Conclude with 'peace terms' which are clear to all parties.

The point of all this is to be 'firm but fair'. You, as the teacher, are responsible and must take control. But you have to act appropriately and negotiate a new foundation for future conformity and a sustainable, positive relationship (see also Chapter 6).

Other problems can also exist in any classroom. These may be associated with an individual child who has particular difficulties. These need to be understood rather than lead to condemnation. To do this, it is important to record and analyse the behaviour and try to identify the possible causes before major action is taken. In keeping a diary of events, one might record the conditions, characteristics and consequences of the behaviour and thus produce evidence for future action.

Checklist 7.2

Aim: To record incidents of ongoing 'problem' behaviour.

Conditions: When exactly does the disruption occur?
- Is it random or regular?
- Is there a pattern with a particular child?
- Is there a pattern regarding a particular task?
- Is there a pattern with a particular teacher?

Characteristics: What exactly happens?
- Is it a verbal reaction?
- Is it a physical reaction?

Consequences: What are the effects?
- On the child, the teacher?
- On the class, the school?
- Do others join in, ignore, retaliate?

Such major, persistent problems are best discussed with other colleagues and a common strategy worked out in line with the school's behaviour policy. In most circumstances, this will also involve the parents, so that a consistent approach can be adopted.

reflectiveteaching.co.uk/rtps6/part2_ch7

Whether a problem is associated with an individual child or most of the class, a consistent, balanced, firm and constructive approach is essential and will, hopefully, provide security for pupils as well as support for the teacher. It must be remembered that children respond to situations and experiences. We, as teachers, structure such experiences. Thus, if students respond problematically, we must reflect on the experiences that we provide rather than simply trying to apportion blame elsewhere. As we have seen, teachers can be 'provocative' or 'insulative' (Hargreaves et al., 1975). Which are you? Can you find ways to manage behaviour which draw on and sustain a positive cycle in your classroom relationships?

> **Expert Question**
>
> **Reflection:** *is our classroom practice based on incremental, evidence-informed and collaborative improvement strategies?*
>
> This question contributes to a conceptual framework underpinning professional expertise (see Chapter 16).

For consideration of whole-school issues and a summary checklist of principles for classroom management deriving from the Elton Report, see the supplementary material for Chapter 7 on the chapter webpage at reflectiveteaching.co.uk.

CONCLUSION

This chapter has examined aspects of behaviour management which help to establish and sustain conditions for successful learning. Such issues are of great concern to us as teachers, because they underpin our effectiveness.

However, most of us gradually grow in confidence and competence with such challenges. Indeed, 'good discipline' is, above all, the product of professional expertise (see Chapters 1 and 16).

Student teachers should allow themselves time to learn, experiment and learn some more. We all make mistakes, but it is important to see these as learning opportunities. Direct experience is irreplaceable in developing competence, but there is also much to be said for sharing ideas, problems and successes through discussion with colleagues and mentors.

reflectiveteaching.co.uk/rtps6/part2_ch7

CHAPTER WEBPAGE

 reflectiveteaching.co.uk offers additional professional resources for this chapter. For the chapter webpage, go to: reflectiveteaching.co.uk/rtps6/part2_ch7

Chapter 7 provides a comprehensive review and good advice about classroom engagement, control and discipline, but that will only take on real meaning, in practical ways, if you are able to try out some of the recommended *Reflective Activities*. There are eight in the text above, but the chapter webpage offers double that number under the relevant tab. Again, these should be used selectively to investigate topics which are meaningful or valuable to you. Classroom engagement is bound to ebb and flow, and these activities will help to develop sensitivity to such processes and enable you to make appropriate responses in good time.

There is also a lot of material on the internet which may be helpful. For example, Bill Rogers, who features strongly in this chapter, has a number of thoughtful videos on YouTube. Why not try his 'Ensuring a Settled and Focused Class'? More radically, Peter Hutton has a YouTube TED Talk which speculates on, 'What If Students Controlled Their Own Learning?' and there is lots more besides. Don't overlook the YouTube channel called Behaviour2Learn, which pulls together material from various sources, including some funded from the English Department for Education.

For consideration of whole-school issues and a summary checklist for classroom management deriving from the Elton Report, see the supplementary material on the right-hand side of the chapter webpage.

Once again, three levels of advice and information for follow-up reading are available.

1 *Further Reading* on the chapter webpage is a general overview of sources, following the structure of this chapter. It should be helpful for essays, projects or looking at issues in depth, but you will need library access to follow up its recommendations.

2 *Key Readings*, below, is a more selective list, but still requires access to a library or some creative on-line work to find digital versions, if available.

3 *Readings for Reflective Teaching in Schools* provides short, edited extracts of particularly helpful texts. A brief description of the contents on engagement is indicated by the icons below.

KEY READINGS

For a sophisticated and influential analysis of classroom environments and engagement of pupils in learning tasks, see:

> Doyle. W. (1986). 'Classroom organization and management', in M.C. Wittrock (ed.), *Handbook of Research on Teaching* (3rd edn). New York: Macmillan. **(Reading 7.1)**

For a classic book which provide many original insights on classroom management, see:

> Kounin, J.S. (1970) *Discipline and Group Management in Classrooms.* New York: Holt Rinehart and Winston. **(Reading 7.5)**

There are many books which provide practical advice on classroom strategies to achieve good behaviour. For example:

> Bennett, T. (2015) *Managing Difficult Behaviour in Schools: A Practical Guide.* Unison. unison.org.uk/content/uploads/2015/04/On-line-Catalogue22970.pdf
>
> Holleran, G. and Gilbert, I. (2015) *A Teacher's Companion to Essential Motivation in the Classroom.* London: Routledge.
>
> Maynard, N. and Weinstein, B. (2019) Hacking School Discipline: 9 Ways to Create a culture of Empathy and Responsibility using Restorative Justice. Hack Learning Series.
>
> Rogers, B. (2015) *Classroom Behaviour: A Practical Guide to Effective Teaching, Behaviour Management and Colleague Support*, 4th edn. London: SAGE.
>
> Watkins, C. (2011) *Managing Classroom Behaviour.* London: ATL **(Reading 7.2)**

For a layered model for managing pupil behaviour, based on psychological research (**Reading 6.4**), see:

> Chaplain, R. (2017) *Teaching Without Disruption in the Primary School.* London: Routledge.

On 'positive teaching' see:

> Merrett, F. and Wheldall, K. (1990) *Identifying Troublesome Classroom Behaviour.* London: Paul Chapman. **(Reading 7.6)**

Being able to train and use one's voice effectively is essential to maintain classroom control, and this is the subject of:

> Evans, W. and Savage, J. (2018) *Using Your Voice Effectively in the Classroom.* London: Routledge.

reflectiveteaching.co.uk/rtps6/part2_ch7

Part 2 Creating conditions for learning

It is crucial to hold on to management issues in the context of broader educational objectives and with awareness of the overall effect on a classroom. On this, with a useful scale for analysing the 'working atmosphere', see:

Haydn, T. (2007) *Managing Pupil Behaviour.* London: Routledge.

Taking this even further, for a philosophical account see:

Straughan, R. (1988) *Can We Teach Children to be Good? Basic Issues in Moral, Personal and Social Education.* Buckingham: Open University Press.

From time to time, public concern is expressed about behaviour in schools. The outcome of one such episode led to the Elton Report (1989). Twenty years later, the Steer Report (2009) was the outcome of another period of concern. More recently, Tom Bennett undertook an independent review of behaviour in schools.

Department for Education and Science (1989a) *Discipline in Schools, Report of the Committee of Enquiry chaired by Lord Elton.* London: HMSO.

Steer, A. (2009) *Learning Behaviour: Lessons Learned, A Review of Behaviour Standards and Practices in Our Schools.* London: DCSF.

Department for Education (DfE) (2017c) *Creating a Culture: How School Leaders Can Optimise Behaviour.* Tom Bennett: Independent review of behaviour in schools. gov.uk/government/publications/behaviour-in-schools

reflectiveteaching.co.uk/rtps6/part2_ch7

TOOLKIT EVIDENCE 7.1
Behaviour interventions: sometimes necessary, but never sufficient for learning

What is it?
Behaviour interventions aim to improve learning in school by reducing challenging behaviour. This covers a wide range of approaches from tackling low-level disruption in the classroom to general anti-social activities, aggression, violence, bullying and substance abuse. The approaches themselves can be divided into three broad categories:
1. Developing a positive school ethos or improving discipline across the whole school, which also aims to support greater engagement in learning.
2. Universal programmes which seek to improve behaviour and generally take place in the classroom.
3. More specialised programmes which are targeted at students with specific behavioural issues.

What does the evidence say?
The average impact of behaviour interventions is four additional months' progress over the course of a year. Evidence suggests that, on average, behaviour interventions can produce moderate improvements in academic performance along with a decrease in problematic behaviours. However, estimated benefits vary widely across programmes.

School-level behaviour approaches are often related to improvements in attainment, but there is limited evidence to show that the improvements are actually caused by the behaviour interventions, rather than other school interventions happening at the same time.

Effect sizes are similar for targeted interventions matched to specific students with particular needs or behavioural issues and for universal interventions or whole-school strategies, though the impact does vary. Parental and community involvement programmes are often associated with reported improvements in school ethos or discipline so are worth considering as alternatives to direct behaviour interventions.

How sound is the evidence?
Overall, it is clear that reducing challenging behaviour in schools can have a direct and lasting effect on pupils' learning. This is based on a number of meta-analyses and robust studies of interventions in schools. The challenge is often in ensuring that changes in behaviour carry over into learning.

Closing the disadvantage gap
According to figures from the Department for Education (2019/20), pupils who receive Free School Meals are more likely to receive a permanent or fixed period exclusion compared with those who do not. The most common reason for exclusion is persistent disruptive behaviour. Pupil behaviour will have multiple influences, some of which teachers can directly manage though universal or classroom management approaches. Some pupils will require more specialist support to help manage their self-regulation or social and emotional skills.

How could you implement in your setting?
Behaviour interventions have an impact through increasing the time that pupils spend for learning effectively. This might be through reducing low-level disruption that reduces learning time in the classroom or through preventing exclusions that remove pupils from school for periods of time. If interventions take up more classroom time than the disruption they displace, engaged learning time is unlikely to increase. In most schools, a combination of universal and targeted approaches are likely be most appropriate:

- Universal approaches to classroom management can help prevent disruption – but often require professional development to administer effectively.
- Targeted approaches that are tailored to pupils' needs, such as regular report cards or functional behaviour assessments, may be appropriate where pupils are struggling with behaviour.

Across all approaches it is crucial to maintain high expectations for pupils and to embed a consistent approach across the school. Successful approaches may also include social and emotional learning interventions and parental engagement approaches. Evidence suggests that programmes delivered over two to six months seem to produce more long-lasting results. Whole-school strategies usually take longer to embed than individually tailored or single-classroom strategies.

reflectiveteaching.co.uk/rtps6/part2_ch7

228 Part 2 Creating conditions for learning

Behavioural interventions can require a large amount of staff time, compared with other approaches. Targeted or one-to-one approaches, delivered by trained school staff or specialists, will require additional staff time compared with universal approaches.

Alongside time and cost, school leaders should reflect on the impact of whole-school behaviour policies and support their staff to maintain a consistent approach. When adopting new approaches, school leaders should consider programmes with a track record of effectiveness. Improving classroom management may involve intensive training where teachers reflect on their practice, implement new strategies, and review their progress over time.

Links and further reading
Lee, A. and Gage, N.A. (2020) 'Updating and expanding systematic reviews and meta analyses on the effects of school wide positive behavior interventions and supports'. *Psychology in the Schools*, *57*(5), 783–804.
Reid, K. and Morgan, N.S. (2012) *Tackling Behaviour in your Primary School: A Practical Handbook for Teachers*. London: Routledge.
Education Endowment Foundation (EEF) (2019) *Improving Behaviour in Schools. A Guidance Report*.
educationendowmentfoundation.org.uk/education-evidence/guidance-reports/behaviour

See also
Parental engagement (Toolkit Evidence 4.1) educationendowmentfoundation.org.uk/education-evidence/teaching-learning-toolkit/parental-engagement
Social and emotional learning (Toolkit Evidence 6.1) educationendowmentfoundation.org.uk/education-evidence/teaching-learning-toolkit/social-and-emotional-learning

Education Endowment Foundation

reflectiveteaching.co.uk/rtps6/part2_ch7

Chapter 8
Spaces
How are we creating environments for learning?

Introduction	230

Environments for learning	231
What is a learning environment?	231
Formal and informal learning environments	232

Organising the classroom for learning	234
The classroom as a learning environment	234
Use of resources	235
Use of space	237
Use of time	239

Teaching and learning with technology	242

Managing pupils and adults	246
Organising pupils	246
Working with adults	253

Conclusion	255

reflectiveteaching.co.uk/rtps6/part2_ch8

INTRODUCTION

Pupils in schools routinely experience many 'learning spaces', yet how do spaces become effective learning environments? In this chapter we consider a number of key issues.

The core space for a teacher is, of course, the classroom, and a central concern of teachers in any phase of schooling is whether both the classroom and the class are organised in a manner that facilitates teaching and learning. For teaching and learning to succeed, it seems clear that the physical and human resources of the classroom need to be marshalled to reinforce the teacher's values, aims, curriculum and syllabus demands.

But classrooms are not the only spaces where pupils learn. Pupils spend most of their time in environments other than school, many of which have the potential to contribute to their learning. In addition to routine learning spaces such as home, street or park, institutions such as museums and nature reserves now offer more focused 'out of the classroom' learning experiences. Television, social media, apps and virtual learning environments often can play a significant role in supporting learning. Above all though, the home remains the most significant influence on pupils' attitudes, and is a resource for learning that might be further exploited (Mayall, 2009).

All of these spaces have 'affordances' for learning. The term, with its origins in Gestalt psychology, was first coined by Gibson (1977), in developing an ecological approach to perception. It has been widely adopted in education, particularly in relation to educational technologies (see Edwards, 2012, Reading 8.5), to express the inherent potential for learning which an environment or tool offers. For such potential to be realised, it has to be identified by the user. Thus, for example, a pencil may have affordance for drawing as a means of expression with variable use of line, shading and pattern – whilst another person may perceive it simply as a tool for writing. Even then though, it has important affordances, such as its susceptibility to a rubber for alterations. The other side of affordances is the idea of constraints – there are some things about an environment, space or tool that are likely to frame learning potential in particular ways. Reflective teachers need to be aware of the affordances and constraints of the environments and resources with which they work.

See Chapter 4

> ### TLRP Principles
>
> Two principles are of particular relevance to this chapter on learning environments:
>
> **Effective teaching and learning recognises the significance of informal learning.** Informal learning, such as learning out of school, should be recognised as at least as significant as formal learning and should therefore be valued and used appropriately in formal processes. (*Principle 8*)
>
> **Effective teaching and learning demands consistent policy frameworks with support for teaching and learning as their primary focus.** Policies at national, local and institutional levels need to recognise the fundamental importance of teaching and learning. They should be designed to create effective learning environments in which all learners can thrive. (*Principle 10*)

In this chapter we will see that not only is there a range of possible spaces for learning, but that each one has affordances and constraints for particular purposes. Exploiting the affordances and constraints of an environment can be achieved by good organisation and management. However, this should not be taken to imply rigidity because if the rules and routines of the classroom are clear and agreed, good organisation can increase freedom for a teacher or educator to teach and the learner to learn. In particular, it should give them more time to create a sense of 'learning community' (Watkins, 2004), to diagnose pupils' learning difficulties, to listen to pupils, and more generally to teach. This is preferable, in classrooms in particular, to having to spend too much time on 'housekeeping' (Hastings and Wood, 2001).

ENVIRONMENTS FOR LEARNING

What is a learning environment?

In considering the creation of a learning environment, with the learner at the centre, it is useful to begin by looking more generally at the complex 'layers' which exist within and around any learning space, and which can affect a person's development. The ecological systems theory of Bronfenbrenner (1979; 1993, Reading 8.1) provides a useful way to think about these layers. Bronfenbrenner represents a pupil at the centre, and layers of environment expanding in concentric circles, as shown in Figure 8.1. Immediately around the learner, he defines a layer comprising their own 'biology' and the relationships they have with their immediate surroundings. For example, a young person's peers may affect their beliefs and behaviour (and vice versa) and talking to their teacher may support their learning. The next layer is defined as the connections between the components of the previous layer; the relationship between a pupil's parents and their teacher would be included here. Beyond this lies the larger social system, over which the pupil has no power, but which may affect them. Parental work schedules are one example; a pupil has no role in them, but may be affected by increased pressure in the family home as a result of one parent being frequently absent. Finally, the outermost layer describes the wider cultural values, customs and laws within which the child is developing.

Thinking about a pupil's environment in this way makes it clear that no learning space can be considered in isolation. There are connections between the various settings and communities involved in a pupil's life. Of course, these interconnections change over time and the ways in which people, resources and space typically interact in early years and primary education have some similarities but are also distinct. Whilst recognising the significance of learning in a wide range of settings, it is important for an educator to understand what they can influence, manage and organise, and those influences to which they can only respond.

Sometimes a teacher will want to make a significant change to a pupil's immediate environment to support their learning. This could involve separating groups of pupils into

Figure 8.1
Bronfenbrenner's ecological theory (adapted from Bronfenbrenner, 1979)

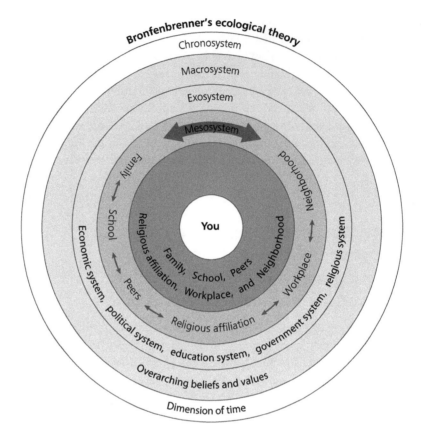

different teaching groups; it may involve talking to their parents to influence the learning environment at home to encourage homework completion; or it could involve rearranging the tables for group work. At other times, pupils may be encouraged to work in less formal learning environments.

Formal and informal learning environments

The classroom provides a structured and formal learning environment, which can be subject to a number of constraints. Less formal environments (such as museums, galleries and outdoor learning spaces) can present opportunities to work outside such constraints. These include:

- an immediate and novel context for learning;
- an alternative source of curriculum delivery, allowing repackaging of the curriculum through e.g. a museum's object collections;
- a chance to ensure that the curriculum does not restrict pupils' learning;

- objects and environments that can form the basis for enquiry and knowledge building, allowing pupils the chance to follow and explore their interests;
- the chance for pupils to develop wider engagement and knowledge building, through handling and questioning objects.

Working successfully within less formal environments can be a challenge for a teacher who is usually constrained by curriculum demands, and working off the school site in particular can involve extra organisation and risk assessment (a useful website which supports such planning is at schooltrip.com). Any use of a learning space outside the classroom by a teacher and their class needs to be considered from the pragmatic considerations of organisation, and from pedagogical perspectives on what will enable effective learning in these spaces. It is useful to note that such spaces can also provide distractions from learning. New technologies have particular affordances here. For example, apps or devices which allow instant communication in groups can enable collaborative group work and teacher support when working in different locations across extended outdoor sites – a great help on fieldtrips, for instance.

> **Expert Question**
>
> **Connection:** does the school curriculum engage with the cultural resources and funds-of-knowledge of families and the community?
>
> This question contributes to a conceptual framework underpinning professional expertise (see Chapter 16).

However, children's learning is not all intentional and planned. Children learn through everyday experience, from their peers in the playground, at home, and as part of their communities.

Peer group culture is important to children as part of adapting to school life (Davies, 1982). As children get older, the culture of the playground may start to mirror both academic achievement within school and social factors outside school, such as gender, social class and ethnicity. Some peer cultures favour school attainment and are likely to reinforce teacher efforts to engender a positive approach to learning. Other peer cultures derive meaning from alternative values, and children who are influenced by such cultures may approach school with minimal or even oppositional expectations. Such children will still be constructing understanding, but it may not be the type of understanding for which teachers would have aimed.

The interaction between home and school is also important for learning (Hughes and Pollard, 2000, see **Research Briefing 4.1**, p. 136). Indeed, many of children's experiences at home can have an influence on their learning. Children may watch many hours of television each week, or spend many hours on the computer or on their phones, and their play and lifestyles are influenced by these activities including through social media and the internet. Young people may identify with particular 'imagined communities' (Anderson, 1991), but also with virtual communities, which could include friends from school and beyond. As Buckingham (2000) has argued, digital media provide an alternative environment within which enduring questions are played out. How much they learn will depend on whether children are passive or active in their stance and how new cultural experiences are interpreted and used.

As well as the home, the wider community also has key opportunities for learning. A 'community' can mean different things, but usually refers to either a community of locality

Part 2 Creating conditions for learning

or a community of identity. Having said that, a locality can be important to someone's identity, and can provide a network of support and a sense of belonging. Collective identities can also be important to children, and may be based on wider regional variations or looser groupings. The way in which values, beliefs and common experience define such communities can be very important to pupils' learning.

Explicit opportunities provided for learning within a community can include youth clubs, toddler groups, education–business partnerships (which provide schools with links to local business), learning resource services such as libraries, and organisations like the Scouts, Brownies or Guides. Such activities may also be mediated by specialist informal educators who will explore and enlarge experiences.

ORGANISING THE CLASSROOM FOR LEARNING

The classroom as a learning environment

Organising the classroom environment is important, because research suggests that disorganised classrooms predict poor attainment and poor behaviour (Pointon and Kershner, 2000). Such research reinforces the view that the environment in a classroom should: be well organised; be aesthetically pleasing; stimulate pupils' interest; set high standards in the display and presentation of pupils' work; and be created in such a way that it is practical to maintain. Display should not be too simple nor too complex. Displays which appear chaotic can be detrimental to pupils' learning, and some research suggests that 20–50 per cent of the available wall space should be kept clear (Barrett et al., 2015). In addition, however, reflective teachers should aim to structure the environment so that opportunities are taken to reinforce their overall purposes, both in general terms, and for particular lessons/lesson activities. Research suggests that the physical aspects of the classroom environment interact with the teacher's intentions for learning, and that careful consideration of the interaction of these elements is necessary in creating an 'inclusive classroom' (Lucas and Thomas, 2000), especially for children with autism (Hanley et al., 2017).

In considering the physical environment of the classroom, you may find the questions in **Checklist 8.1** helpful.

Checklist 8.1

Aim: To examine the classroom environment.

1 *Design*. What are the main design features of the room, and how do they affect its aesthetic feel?
2 *Affordances*. What are the possibilities and constraints for active learning in the classroom? Can you move the tables to enable discussion? What are the possibilities and issues for display on walls, on windows, on flat surfaces, off the ceiling?

---

reflectiveteaching.co.uk/rtps6/part2_ch8

> 3 *Purposes*. Do displays stimulate and inform? Do they provide opportunities for pupils to interact with them, for example, by posing questions? Do displays only show finished products or do they also reveal processes and value hard work, for example, displaying drafts and then finished products. Do they provide a stimulus for discussion (such as thinking walls, or a periodic table in a chemistry lesson), sharing problems, or giving mutual support and advice? Do they provide a stimulus for structuring enquiry, from devising questions to testing ideas? Is there too much on display? Might this be a sensory distraction for pupils?
> 4 *Quality*. Do classroom displays show that the pupils' work is valued? Do they provide a model which pupils may apply to their own work? Is there a 'working wall' which enables ongoing contributions by pupils?
> 5 *Practicality*. Is the classroom environment as practical as it can be to maintain?

Other research examines the impact of environmental factors, such as classroom temperature, air quality, acoustics, wall colour and lighting on pupils' ability to engage in learning (Woolner et al., 2007; Winterbottom and Wilkins, 2007; Barrett et al., 2015). Using multilevel modelling to try to identify the impact of each of these factors, Barrett et al. (2015) provide advice to teachers and architects on classroom design. Although there is a limit to what individual teachers can do to control such factors, much of the advice is easily achievable at little cost. Maintaining good ventilation, preventing 'over-lighting' of pupils' workstations to avoid glare, ensuring pupils sit where they cannot see a 'glare spot' on the interactive whiteboard (IWB) are all worthwhile. Likewise, teachers should use blinds to minimise the chance of glare, they should ensure active ventilation of a classroom space, they should be conscious of and take measures to keep the classroom cool. To minimise noise, carpets are useful, as are small rubber feet on movable furniture to avoid scraping.

Improving physical conditions in classrooms does directly affect the daily experience of teaching and learning for both teachers and pupils, but evidence also suggests that it is less important for eventual outcomes than the quality of the activities which take place (see **Toolkit Evidence 4.1** on p. 135). The most important resource remains the teacher.

Use of resources

A good supply of appropriate resources is essential, given the importance of direct experience and practical activities to pupils' learning. In primary schools you are likely to find resources which support active learning experiences, and resources should:

- motivate, inspire and focus pupils' attention;
- provide a basis for discussion, or be designed to enable pupils to learn independently;

- explain, instruct, or demonstrate procedures and ideas;
- enable pupils to access information;
- enable pupils to learn in manageable steps;
- help pupils to recall, consolidate and extend their learning;
- support assessment of pupils' understanding, perhaps by providing a structure for recording responses.

In some ways, organising resources is a straightforward matter, but it also requires careful thought and attention to detail. For instance, it is all too easy to discover that the paint has dried out in a Year 1 classroom. Likewise, even with centrally managed resources, laptops or tablets may have run out of charge, the printer may have run out of ink, or devices may update themselves for five minutes before they can be used. It is also common in schools that shared resources are not put back where they are usually stored; a sense of collective responsibility for the care and use of such centralised resources is therefore essential.

When considering employing resources for pupils' learning, four possible criteria might be considered:

- *Appropriateness*. What resources are needed to support the learning processes which are expected to take place?
- *Availability*. What resources are available? What is in the classroom, the school, the community, businesses, libraries, museums? Are there cost, risk, time or transport factors to be considered?
- *Storage*. How are classroom resources stored? Which should be under teacher control? Which should be openly available to the pupils? Which are stored by the technician? Are they clearly labelled and safely stored? Has a risk assessment been undertaken?
- *Maintenance*. What maintenance is required? Is there a system for seeing that this is done? In the case of ICT and specialist equipment, where is the expertise and technical support located and how can this be accessed?

Reflective Activity 8.1

Aim: To plan resources to support specific learning activities.

Evidence and reflection: Identify the objective for a proposed lesson activity, then consider the resources and classroom organisation which are required, using the four criteria listed above as a starting point:

Activity:
Objectives:
Resources required:
- Appropriateness:
- Availability:
- Storage:
- Maintenance:

reflectiveteaching.co.uk/rtps6/part2_ch8

Extension: Together with another teacher analyse the classroom(s) in which you both teach most often. Each of you should have one or more particular learning activities in mind, and you should work together to analyse each other's classrooms. Share the problems and issues that are pertinent to your circumstances.

Use of space

The way a teaching space is organised has considerable impact on the teaching strategies that can be deployed, the attitude of the learners and thus the quality of learning. Space in a classroom is always limited; yet what space there is must be used in such a way that it allows a teacher to change organisational strategies, for instance between whole-class teaching, group work, or pair work, with associated implications for seating. The use of IWBs and laptops or tablets in classrooms also creates particular demands on classroom space. Such technologies enable exciting new forms of whole-class and individualised learning but should be deployed in relation to educational purposes rather than just because of their availability.

Because primary teachers tend to occupy the same classroom for all of their teaching, it is often possible to use space flexibly, and to move tables and desks as appropriate for the learning activity. When thinking about the most effective use of classroom space, consider developing a classroom plan, either on card, or by using classroom design software (see Figure 8.2 for a primary example and consider Reflective Activity 8.2). Using such a plan it is possible to explore the affordances and constraints of each teaching space when organising for teaching and learning. For primary pupils in particular, creating well-defined zones for 'play-based' and more formal learning activities is important. The way in which you use space can also impact upon pupils' sense of belonging and ownership. Using pupil-created work for displays or allowing pupils to personalise their locker or coat pegs can be useful strategies (Barrett et al., 2015).

Reflective Activity 8.2

Aim: To produce a classroom plan.

Evidence and reflection: A simple plan should be made of the fixed points in the classroom – walls, windows, doors, sinks, pegs, benches, gas taps etc. It is relatively easy to produce a plan 'to scale' on computer or by using squared paper. Major existing items of furniture should be represented by shapes to the same scale as the classroom plan. The furniture can be moved around on the plan to experiment with different classroom layouts.

Extension: Careful analysis is needed of the space requirements of each classroom activity and of each activity in relation to the others. It is therefore worth considering the arrangement of the classroom for very different types of activity – e.g. in for drama, and small group work or whole-class question and answer sessions.

reflectiveteaching.co.uk/rtps6/part2_ch8

Figure 8.2 Plan of a Key Stage 2 classroom

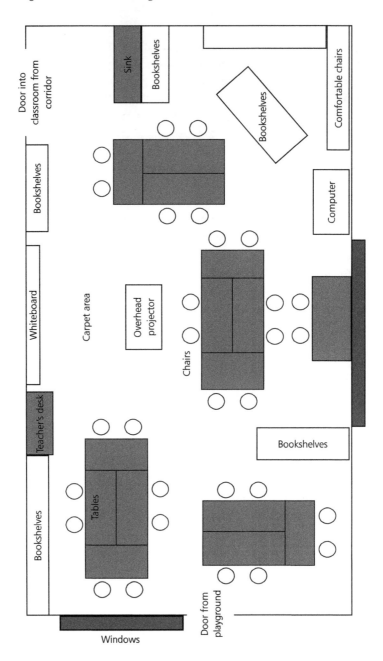

 When planning a classroom layout, it is important to consider how to promote and manage dialogue between the teacher and class and between pupils in groups and pairs (Mercer and Littleton, 2007, Reading 11.6). For example, IWBs can be effective tools to promote dialogic teaching at a whole-class level (Warwick et al., 2011). However, in this case the teacher must consider whether the screen is accessible to all pupils, and whether the classroom is organised to promote high-quality discussion at such a whole-class level with the IWB as a stimulus. Likewise, when trying to promote small group discussion, sitting in rows is not appropriate. It can be tempting to merely focus on the logistics of an activity, but if the classroom is not organised in such a way as to promote pupil talk, then a teacher may miss opportunities to support pupils' learning (Higgins, 2003).

Finally, whatever approach is taken to resource management or classroom layout, it is still important to have one eye on health and safety implications; it is easy for aisles to be blocked by bags, or for bottlenecks of pupils to build up in particular areas of the classroom.

> **Expert Question**
>
> **Dialogue:** *does teacher–learner talk scaffold understanding to build on existing knowledge and to strengthen dispositions to learn?*
>
> This question contributes to a conceptual framework underpinning professional expertise (see Chapter 16).

Use of time

Notwithstanding all the other dimensions of teaching, research has shown that the amount of time during which pupils are fully engaged in targeted instructional tasks is closely related to outcomes (Berliner, 1991, Reading 8.4; Heuston and Miller, 2011). This is affected by the length of the school year, day and timetabling, as well as by the effectiveness of classroom routines and organisation.

However well organised a classroom, and however good one's organisation of resources, when pupils start to use that space it can lead to a significant amount of 'evaporated time', and may require some re-analysis of the way in which space and resources, and pupils' use thereof, are designed and managed. For example, Campbell and Neill (1992) showed that almost 10 per cent is lost as 'evaporated time' in classroom-management activities. Minimising this evaporated time is important, but even within the remaining 'instructional' time, it is still important to ensure pupils are engaged and motivated for them to learn effectively (Goswami and Bryant, 2010). This is not necessarily always achieved. Findings from the Oracle study (Galton et al., 1999) showed considerable variations between different classrooms in the proportions of pupil time with high levels of engagement. Overall, Key Stage 1 pupils were task-engaged for about 60 per cent of classroom time, distracted for about 20 per cent of the time and organising themselves or being organised for the remaining 20 per cent. Hence, in this section, we consider two aspects: pupils' use of the space and resources to maximise the time available for curriculum activity, and the time actually spent in active learning.

Time available for curriculum activity. This is the remaining time in each teaching/learning session, once it has properly started, excluding interruptions and time to pack up at the end of the lesson. The time available is clearly related to a number of organisational strategies. The most obvious of these are the routine procedures which are developed within the classroom space that, for example, help to avoid queues and bottlenecks. These help to manage the pressure which might otherwise be placed on the teacher by the pupils and they contribute to producing a positive, structured classroom environment. Reflective

240 Part 2 Creating conditions for learning

Reflective Activity 8.3

Aim: To evaluate routine activities to maximise time for teaching and learning.

Evidence and reflection: Use this list as a starting point for considering the routines
that affect your lessons, and how you may improve your use of space and/or
resources to reduce wastage of time. The list is generic – you will need to add to
the list to match your type of classroom, your curriculum subject. Identify any
aspects of organisation you can deal with in advance of the lesson (for example,
moving the tables, or distributing resources before pupils enter the room). Can you
improve your own routines (for example, preventing bottlenecks by asking pupils to
unpack before putting their bags away, or by distributing resources around the
room)? Are you planning far enough ahead or practising crisis management (for
example, do you often find yourself hunting for resources in the cupboards)? Can
you actively involve pupils, giving them routine responsibility for specific aspects of
resource organisation (for example, giving automatic responsibility to particular
pupils to give out books or materials at the start of the lesson)?

Purpose of procedure	Procedure	Evaluation of procedure	Possible improvement
Entering the classroom			
Leaving the classroom			
Completing the registe			
Collecting in homework			
Issuing homework			
Distributing learning resources			
Collecting learning resources			
Going to the toilet			
Tidying up			

Extension: Teachers and teaching assistants build up a useful repertoire of strategies
for these organisational matters. A good extension would be to share and exchange
ideas with a 'critical friend'.

Activity 8.3 may be helpful in reviewing classroom organisation and procedures, thus
increasing the time available for curriculum activities.

Encouraging pupils to take on more responsibility for organising themselves, their
classroom and their resources is important, as it can enhance their learning time, reduce their
reliance on the teacher and give the teacher more time to focus on pupils' learning. Indeed,
the aim is for the classroom to run itself. For this to happen effectively, it is important to
ensure that the locations of all resources are labelled, or that resources are visible and

reflectiveteaching.co.uk/rtps6/part2_ch8

obvious, so that pupils can fetch them with ease where it is safe to so. Alternatively, a teacher may adopt different strategies to try to maximise time available for learning. These could include asking pupils to hand out resources to the rest of the class, or individuals or groups moving between workstations, with resources remaining fixed to such locations.

Time spent in active learning This is the second key issue. Whilst this can be assessed at any point, it may also be seen as providing summative information: a product of the overall learning environment which is provided for the pupils. Reflective Activity 8.4 helps in analysing the amount of time pupils spend actively learning.

Reflective Activity 8.4

Aim: To monitor an individual pupil to estimate active learning time.

Evidence and reflection: Watch a chosen pupil during a teaching/learning session. Judge the times at which:
1 the pupil is 'on task' (i.e. ***actively*** engaged in the given task and learning objectives);
2 the pupil is doing other necessary activities related to the task (e.g. logging into a computer, fetching equipment);
3 the pupil is 'off task' (i.e. appears distracted or disengaged).

Calculate the total amounts and proportions of learning time in each category:

'On-task' time   [. . . minutes], [. . . %]
'Task-management' time   [. . . minutes], [. . . %]
'Off-task' time   [. . . minutes], [. . . %]

Extension: Are there any changes in classroom organisation or management strategies which could help to maximise active learning time?

To maximise learning in which pupils are actively engaged, it is also important to ensure there is a *variety* of *stimulating* tasks over time. Teachers should try to avoid 'satiation' (i.e. letting the pupils get bored by monotonous or repetitive activities). Although such variety is closely related to the teaching and learning strategies a teacher employs, explicitly reflecting upon the planned activities to ensure variety is an organisational issue, the aim being to ensure that each pupil will remain engaged and motivated throughout (see Reflective Activity 8.5).

Reflective Activity 8.5

Aim: To evaluate the variety of learning objectives, tasks and activities, and the extent to which they engage pupils.

Evidence and reflection: This evaluation could be carried out by an observer who focuses on a particular pupil for a lesson or teaching episode. All activities should be recorded in terms of their motivational appeal, explicit purpose and what the

reflectiveteaching.co.uk/rtps6/part2_ch8

Part 2 Creating conditions for learning

pupil was required to do. Alternatively, tasks could be monitored, by the teacher, for a longer period. Some questions which might be asked could include:

a) Is there a planned highlight for each lesson or teaching episode?
b) Are there long sequences of the same type of task?
c) Is there variety between active and passive tasks?
d) Is there variety between pupils working alone, in small groups, and as a whole class?

Extension: Consider the findings from this exercise, and try to deduce the reasons for any patterns you identify. If you judge it appropriate, what could you do to increase the stimulus and variety of learning objectives, tasks and activities?

TEACHING AND LEARNING WITH TECHNOLOGY

As we have seen, the classroom environment consists of its physical environment and social systems, informed by the prevailing values and culture of the school. The ways in which resources are organised and used will reflect these interlinked elements. This is true too of IT resources, which are integral to teaching and learning. The organisation and use of technology can afford or constrain opportunities for learning. Pedagogy remains the most important element of teaching with IT resources, and the teacher's beliefs about IT resources are a fundamental part of this (Vidal-Hall, Flewitt and Wyse, 2020). We begin with some organisational considerations, but move swiftly to consider teachers' pedagogic intentions.

The general availability of technology in the classroom can be a strong determinant of whether it will be readily used by pupils to support their learning, or by teachers to support their teaching. The use of computer suites is decreasing because, although they may still be helpful for some purposes, they are not accessible at all times. Mobile devices have increasing potential for use too, though this also clearly raises coordination, technical and access issues among others. The increased affordability of tablets has been a strong driver in this respect. In any event, simply having technology in the classroom does not determine its effective use for pupils' learning.

'Digital technology can enhance educational outcomes, but only when it is informed by effective pedagogy' (Stringer, Lewin and Coleman, 2019). Stringer et al. (2019) also emphasise that technology should only be used if it addresses a particular learning need. As with many educational innovations, technology can be used well, or badly.

Much educational activity and associated learning takes place in the digital world, with many pupils using learning platforms to store their work, respond to learning tasks, complete homework and communicate with their teacher and their peers (Sutherland, Robertson and John, 2008; Facer et al., 2003). There are now many more user-friendly software and online resources for particular curricular purposes, and collaboration and exchange of ideas with colleagues and subject and sectoral associations will be helpful in identifying them. Many such apps and programmes are subject specific, such as maths or

reflectiveteaching.co.uk/rtps6/part2_ch8

language learning apps. Others are more generic but can offer the opportunity for dialogue and collaboration, such as learning platforms video conferencing and blogs. There has been, as Kress (2010, Reading 8.6) put it, a 'revolution in communication'.

Schools and the systems they operate within are relatively traditional places, and they can be profoundly challenged by new screen-based technologies and access to social media. Several authors have begun to write about the benefits of enabling pupils to use new technologies to help represent and enhance their thinking about more traditional bodies of knowledge. For example, Burn explores the benefits of using gaming technologies to enhance engagement with and understanding of literary texts (2021).

The COVID-19 pandemic and associated closure of schools, moreover, accelerated the need for teachers and educators to engage in a much more skilful way with increasingly high-quality educational software and online resources. Despite the challenges of relatively untrained teachers, and the digital poverty gap for some families, the ongoing use of blended and online learning seems set to remain a feature of education moving forward (Starkey et al., 2021). In short, the pandemic has shown schools that though the practical and technical issues are complex and uncertain given the rate of innovation, there clearly are potential opportunities from the use of new technologies.

With the increasing availability of smartphones and tablets this engagement between the teacher's pedagogical intentions and the pupils' everyday activity on such devices at home and elsewhere has generated more interest. The use of such devices – providing easy access to the internet, video and audio material, games for learning, applications with specific foci, social communication and e-books – contributes to the idea that their use for learning may be more 'natural', both in school and at home (Banister, 2004). The consequence is a shift in emphasis from 'teaching' to learning, and from the outcomes of teaching to the processes of learning. A note of caution concerning accessibility should be sounded here. Some researchers

> **Expert Question**
>
> **Connection:** *in what ways might the curriculum link with the cultural resources and funds-of-knowledge of families and the community?*
>
> This question contributes to a conceptual framework underpinning professional expertise (see Chapter 16).

have suggested that many pupils and parents see school and home as separate domains and the pandemic revealed that many have no access to devices or Wi-Fi at home (Starkey et al., 2021).

New technology also enables new processes of teaching and learning. Kennewell and his colleagues (2008) considered the practices of primary and secondary teachers using technology in the context of 'interactive' teaching approaches (Moyles et al., 2003). Here, the teachers might be characterised as being 'dialogic' in their orientation to teaching and learning, being advocates of the idea that communication is 'central to the meaning making process and thus central to learning' (Mortimer and Scott, 2007). So how does technology use 'fit' here?

The bottom line is that teachers are absolutely crucial to exploiting the potential of classroom technologies (Sutherland et al., 2008, see TLRP **Research Briefing 8.1** on p. 263).

A good example is that of the IWB, now familiar in many countries. IWBs provide a digital hub through which other technologies can be channelled, as orchestrated by the

> **Expert Question**
>
> **Culture:** does the school support expansive learning by affirming learner contributions, engaging partners and providing attractive opportunities?
>
> This question contributes to a conceptual framework underpinning professional expertise (see Chapter 16).

teacher and the pupils (see Beauchamp and Kennewell, 2013). Tools such as this offer a range of affordances and constraints for learning. These are determined by two things – the functionality of the device(s) and how both teachers and pupils see that functionality as providing opportunities for, or barriers to, learning. This relates substantially to the pedagogical perspective of the teacher (Warwick et al., 2011).

Consider a teacher who is committed to an interactive, dialogic pedagogy, with its emphasis on engaging pupils in active, self-regulated and collaborative learning (see dialogueiwb.educ.cam.ac.uk). As a result, the teacher's use of the IWB is often calculated to stimulate discussion, set the scene for collaborative group work or enable their pupils to 'take over' the use of the board in whole-class or group work. The teacher sees the board's multimodality (providing sound, text, still images and video) and ability to act as a 'hub' as providing the flexibility they need to teach according to their pedagogical intentions. In their classroom, a visitor might expect to see the whiteboard being used by the teacher or the pupils for:

- annotating still images, using input from pupil groups or talk pairs;
- revisiting resources – e.g. annotated pictures, audio recordings – to reignite understanding, reinforce learning and, through discussion, compare perspectives over time;
- creating or listening to sound files, sometimes associated with text or images;
- considering work from particular pupils, shown using the visualiser and annotated on the interactive whiteboard screen;
- group presentation of work, through the use of pictures, scanned objects, text etc.;
- groups working directly at the interactive whiteboard on tasks that contain multimodal elements;
- the use of the internet to pick up instantly on pupils' contributions to discussion;
- use of the interactive whiteboard with other resources, such as where simulations are used alongside actual group experiments in science;
- building pages of ideas from different groups in a plenary, in order to continue the trajectory of learning in the next lesson;
- communicating with other classes in the school or elsewhere through video links to support ongoing work.

None of these ideas are particularly technically challenging, but such uses of the whiteboard are unlikely to be seen in a classroom where the teacher has little concern with pupils being active and self-regulated in their learning, or with developing a collaborative learning ethos. In such classrooms, by contrast, the whiteboard might simply be used to present illustrations of a story being told by the teacher. Thus a teacher who adopts an interactive, dialogic pedagogy will perceive the affordances and constraints of particular hardware and software very differently from a teacher who favours a more didactic pedagogy. This does not mean that the teacher's role in teaching and organising learning is less in either case – but it is significantly different.

The same points apply to software packages, as Reflective Activity 8.6 explores.

> **Expert Question**
>
> **Dialogue:** *does teacher–learner talk scaffold understanding to build on existing knowledge and to strengthen dispositions to learn?*
>
> This question contributes to a conceptual framework underpinning professional expertise (see Chapter 16).

> **Reflective Activity 8.6**
>
> *Aim:* To consider the affordances and constraints of a particular piece of software.
>
> *Evidence and reflection:* Pick a particular program that you use a lot or that you encourage the pupil to use – it can be on any device. What do you consider to be the specific affordances for learning that it has? (Or, to put it another way, how does it help pupils to learn?) What are the particular constraints of the same program, in your view?
>
> *Extension:* Do you think that the pupils share your view of the affordances and constraints of the program? Whether 'yes' or 'no', what makes you think so?

The constraints on the uses of technology in classrooms derive not only from the pedagogic intentions of teachers or the availability of hardware and software, but from other features of the learners or the setting. The fundamental question for the teacher has to be: 'Will this use of technology in the lesson enhance the pupils' learning?' **Checklist 8.2** suggests pedagogical and practical considerations to consider.

> **Checklist 8.2**
>
> *Aim:* To consider the pedagogical and practical implications of the classroom use of technology.
> - Has online safety been considered? In particular, do all devices you plan to use have an appropriate firewall? Can pupils easily access the sites you want them to use?
> - Is some direct teaching in relation to online safety a necessary feature of the lesson? (See **gov.uk/government/publications/teaching-online-safety-in-schools**)
> - Have you considered how the use of technology may impact on the time management of your lesson (e.g. set-up time, time on task)?
> - Have you planned for the procedural aspects of technology use in the lesson (e.g. numbers of pupils to a device, physical placement of online resources, possible circulation of groups to a single resource such as the IWB)?

reflectiveteaching.co.uk/rtps6/part2_ch8

- Are any password systems, used to access devices, clear for the pupils?
- Are the devices fully charged? (This is a particularly important consideration where laptop or mobile device charging units may not be in your classroom.)
- Is the right version of the software that you plan to use actually on each of the devices the pupils will be using?
- Have you considered whether the pupils are able to store their own work in progress, and know how to do so?

MANAGING PUPILS AND ADULTS

Schools and classrooms need to be organised and managed in ways which are most appropriate for supporting the learning activities that have been planned. First, this involves consideration of school structures and policies, and the ways in which these impact on practical arrangements.

Grouping pupils by 'setting' may be established – and this reflects attempts to group pupils by their general attainment or performance in particular subject areas. Although in widespread use, the idea that groups can be established 'by ability' is normally inappropriate, for all the reasons rehearsed in Chapter 2, pp. 53–58. Whilst setting is common, evidence has accumulated over many decades which consistently shows that they have significant educational disadvantages for the confidence and attainment of low-attaining pupils (see EEF **Toolkit Evidence 15.1** on p. 508). Put starkly, setting within a year class is convenient for teachers, and it can benefit higher attaining pupils, but it is also divisive (see Chapter 15, p. 500 for detail of processes of differentiation and polarisation). As long ago as 1964, Brian Jackson wrote a critique entitled *Streaming: An Education System in Miniature*, which demonstrated perverse consequences of streaming in what was then, as now, an unequal society. Streaming and setting thus require very careful consideration before enactment. There may be overriding reasons to take them forward, but reflective teachers will also want to take proactive steps to mitigate their disadvantages.

However, pupils do, of course, need to be organised in various practically efficient ways. Below, we focus on the classroom level.

Organising pupils

Choices in organising pupils for teaching purposes should be made with regard to both pedagogical and practical considerations and with the overriding principle of 'fitness for purpose'. Pedagogical considerations include the general aims of the teacher that inform classroom ethos and procedures, as well as any particular learning objectives for the task and pupils. Practical factors include the number of pupils, the size of the room and the availability of resources.

Here we set out the three basic organisational choices available to us – whole class teaching, group work and individual work – identifying the main characteristics of each. For further discussion of the pedagogic strategies associated with each of these three forms of organisation, see Chapter 11.

Whole class teaching

This is a strong form of organisation for starting and ending a lesson; giving out administrative instructions; introducing or agreeing learning objectives, tasks and activities; the direct teaching of specific concepts and knowledge that the whole class needs to learn at the same time; demonstrating; and extending and reviewing work. Whole-class elements to lessons should be seen as part of the flexible repertoire that a teacher has with respect to pupil organisation, to be used as appropriate.

Whole-class activity is generally assumed to be teacher-centred, and what most whole-class activities have in common is that the teacher generally remains the focus of control. But there is a continuum of teacher dominance even when the whole class is involved in the same activity, and these sessions can be highly interactive (see, for example, Muijs and Reynolds, 2017, Reading 8.7). At one end of the continuum is the situation where the teacher talks and the pupils listen, take notes or copy from the board. At the other, the teacher may plan to give control of the activity to the pupils who may 'teach' by, for example, reporting what they have learned, demonstrating the result of an activity, offering solutions for problem-solving, discussing alternative or conflicting ideas, and asking questions.

Expert Question

Repertoire: *is our pedagogic expertise sufficiently creative, skilled and wide-ranging to teach all elements of learning?*

This question contributes to a conceptual framework underpinning professional expertise (see Chapter 16).

These activities can create a sense of class identity and shared endeavour. Again, it is the teacher's pedagogic framework that will determine how whole-class elements of lessons proceed; some will encourage pupils' active participation in *all* elements of a lesson, whilst others may be reticent to do so.

Using whole-class organisational procedures may give the teacher a chance to teach the class more directly and economically than when working with groups. For instance, they may be able to stimulate pupils' thinking by sharing lesson objectives, exploring ideas, asking more 'probing' questions, modelling quality answers and supporting review, assessment and reflection on their learning. Hopkins et al. (2000) weigh up the benefits of whole-class teaching and cooperative group work, considering just such ideas. However, whole class work can challenge both the teacher and the listener. It is difficult to match the instruction appropriately to pupils' differing needs. There is a tendency for teaching to be pitched in the 'middle', potentially failing those capable of more and those needing support. Whilst some believe that one of the strengths of whole-class teaching is that it 'pulls along' the less able, others recognise that engagement can be uneven, with some pupils 'opting out' even though they retain an apparent 'listening posture' (Cordon, 2000).

Some pupils may be reluctant to face the risks involved in contributing to the whole class, whilst the ability of listeners to remain focused on one speaker is limited and affected both by the listeners' motivation and the speaker's skill. There is evidence of teachers addressing questions only to pupils in a V-shaped wedge in the centre of the room, or to particular groups or individuals (Wragg, 2000). An awareness of these potential difficulties should help teachers to tailor the length and nature of whole-class elements of lessons to the learning needs of their pupils.

Group work

Group work is often recommended for developing social and language skills and as a means by which pupils can support, challenge and extend their learning together, as in computer-based problem-solving (Wegerif and Dawes, 2004), work on a creative task collaboratively or in any subject where practical work is beneficial. Group work can provide teachers with opportunities to observe pupils' learning more closely and, through questioning or providing information, to support them as they move forward. This approach draws particularly on social constructivist psychology (see Chapter 2 for a discussion of the theoretical understanding behind this approach). Work in small groups – 'the smaller the better' – is usually effective, according to a synopsis of international evidence by the Education Endowment Foundation (see p. 368).

Groups are likely to exist in some form in most classrooms. However, their form and function may vary considerably (Kutnick, Blatchford and Baines, 2002; Baines et al., 2017; Kutnick et al., 2008; see **Research Briefing 11.1**, p. 370). Five types of group work can be identified according to the purpose they are intended to serve:

- *Task groups*. The teacher decides on a group of pupils to work together on a particular task or learning objective. Pupils in the group may or may not normally sit or work together and are likely to be given specific group roles, such as recorder or researcher.

- *Teaching groups*. Groups can also be used for 'group teaching' purposes, where the teacher instructs pupils who are at the same stage, doing the same task, at the same time. This may be followed by the pupils working individually. Such a system can be an economical use of teacher instruction time and resources. The teaching may be directive or be based on a problem-solving activity.

- *Seating groups*. This is a very common form of grouping, where a number of pupils sit together around a table, usually in a four or six. Such an arrangement is flexible, allowing pupils to work individually and to socialise when appropriate. The central question for the teacher here is: 'If the pupils are not actually working together, is this arrangement beneficial to their learning?'

- *Collaborative groups*. This is used where there is a shared group aim, work is done together and the outcome is a combined product – perhaps in the form of a presentation, a model, completed experiment, story or problem solved. Importantly, it involves pupils working and talking together, sharing their ideas and explaining their reasoning (Mercer and Littleton, 2007, Reading 11.6). The collaboration can also lead to a number of different outcomes from individuals or pairs.

- *Reciprocal teaching.* This form of collaboration occurs when pupils work in pairs, one taking the role of 'teacher partner', offering evaluation and feedback. This approach is particularly evident in subjects like PE, drama and languages, which involve 'performance'. The teacher supports by intervening to develop the quality of the evaluation and feedback.

Interestingly, genuinely collaborative group work is rather rare in schools (Galton, 2007), despite the fact that it is probably the most productive form of group work for learning (see EEF **Toolkit Evidence 11.3** on p. 369). In particular, it requires rather more organisation on the part of the teacher than other forms of group work, together with a genuine commitment to the active involvement of pupils in their own learning. It is crucial that pupils share an understanding of the task and of the ground rules for their collaborative activity, and these need to be explicit (Baines et al., 2017).

Reflective Activity 8.7

Aim: To consider the pros and cons of group working.

Evidence and reflection: Either closely observe pupils working in groups in two lessons, or reflect on group work activities that you have initiated in your classroom over the last week. Use these questions as a starting point for your reflections:

- What were the successful elements of the group work?
- What was less successful?
- Can you identify why a particular group activity was successful or unsuccessful?
- What would you do differently next time?

Extension: Had the pupils in the groups been guided and trained in how to work productively for learning in this way? Do you consider that this would have enhanced the group work?

Teachers have identified a number of problems associated with group work. Some appear concerned about motivating the pupils and helping them to recognise that being in a group is for the purposes of work rather than a chance to 'just have fun'. The monitoring of group work can also pose problems, especially if the group is intended to work collaboratively on their own without a teacher. And the management of groups, in terms of numbers, membership and workspaces, may pose dilemmas.

Identifying criteria by which groups may be formed can help to clarify some of the key issues. Possible criteria may include:

- *Age groups.* These are occasionally used as a convenient way of grouping for some activities. They are much less useful as a basis for specific teaching points because of the inevitable spread of attainment interests and needs.

- *Attainment groups*. Groups based on attainment levels can be useful for setting up specific and well-matched tasks; Ireson and Hallam (2001) discuss this issue in some depth. They are divisive if used as a permanent way of grouping.

- *Interest groups*. It is important to enable pupils with shared interests to work together from time to time. There may be particular advantages for the social cohesion of the class when pupils are of different attainment, sex, race, social class.

- *Friendship groups*. These provide opportunities for social development. Awareness of the needs of any isolated and marginal pupils is necessary, as is some attention to the possibility that friendship groups can set up divisive status hierarchies among the pupils, or reinforce stereotypes about gender, race or abilities.

Group work most frequently fails where pupils do not have a clear sense of purpose and appropriate skills to work together effectively. The work of the *Thinking Together* group shows that pupils have to be taught how to talk productively in groups, developing their capacity to use what Barnes (2008) and Mercer (2000) call 'exploratory talk' (see thinkingtogether.educ.cam.ac.uk).

Lesson Study 8.1 is a direct illustration of how teachers can improve the structuring of collaborative group work by careful, reflective investigation of classroom practice.

LESSON STUDY 8.1

Helping children to develop skills for collaborative learning

The school: Richard Cobden is an inner city community school for pupils aged 3 to 11 year olds in the London Borough of Camden. English is an additional language for 96 per cent of pupils and 24 per cent have special educational needs.

What we wanted the pupils to learn: We wanted to improve the impact of Year 5 children's talk on learning, particularly for those who have difficulty engaging productively in collaborative activities. We wanted pupils to: develop better oracy skills to enable them to use group discussion to improve learning, and to develop a more positive approach to group learning in general.

What research is available: Our previous lesson studies in maths and reading showed that some children demonstrated limited use of language for explaining their reasoning and developing their thinking. This inhibited their ability to work collaboratively without significant adult support. Following training provided at a whole school INSET, we were introduced to the work of Neil Mercer, especially the *Thinking Together* project – see: Dawes, Mercer and Wegerif (2000), Littleton and Mercer (2013) and Dawes (2011) (see Chapter 12, p. 379).

What we discovered in our research lessons:
RL1: The first lesson tested how well the children were able to use the Group Talk protocols that had been set up in their class. Through observation, we found that they were good at taking turns, making eye contact with each other and being respectful. However, they were not good at really listening to what other children said. Therefore they couldn't link or build on each other's ideas or challenge each other's contribution. There wasn't really a learning discussion taking place and they were unable to reach agreement. Our focus children disengaged with the activity when it was not their turn to talk.

RL2: We explicitly taught and modelled three key skills for the children to use in the group discussion: speculating (and giving reasons); building on someone's ideas; and challenging someone's idea respectfully. These last two skills were chosen specifically to get the children to listen more carefully to what their peers were saying. We modelled each skill and provided some sentence prompts for the children to use to help them with a 'way in'. In the post-lesson discussion, the children all commented on how the modelling helped them to be clearer about how they could contribute to the discussion and the sentence starters gave them more confidence to do so. Our focus children demonstrated more engagement in discussion. Trying to build on an idea, or challenge it, had made them listen much more carefully.

RL3: We modelled the skills again and also focused on getting the children to identify when a particular skill was being used in the group discussion. Children were each given a particular skill to listen out for and had to indicate when they heard it. This reinforcement primed them for the final group activity. We had previously observed some of the quieter children making a really good point or suggestion, but quietly accepted one of the more confident children's opinions. We targeted adult support to two of the groups so that they could intervene at an appropriate moment to prompt, model and support quieter children to challenge respectfully, argue their point and finally to seek agreement. Afterwards, the children said they felt that the adult modelling ways of contributing to the discussion was really helpful. They felt that focusing on listening out for a particular skill really helped them to understand how this skill enabled children in the group to explain their thinking or to understand another child's point. They felt it helped them to work more respectfully together.

What pupils learned: In terms of direct pupil outcomes, we saw how the target children increased their participation in group discussions. The quality of their input improved as did their ability to remain engaged throughout activities. The class were better able to use group discussion to extend their thinking and they could identify the individual strategies they were using to do so.

> 'I like talk for learning because you share ideas and you can disagree or agree with other people. You start with something small and you can build upon ideas and think of things you never thought of before.'

> 'We use talk for learning in English, Maths, Science and all the topics we do at school. It's not just something we do, it's how we learn.'

> 'I think talk for learning is good. You can build on each other's ideas. If you disagree with someone you can question them, but in a polite way so you can challenge each other respectfully.'

What we learned: We found that children need to be explicitly shown what effective collaborative talk looks and sounds like. Specific skills need to be named and made visible through modelling, sentence prompts, skilful and well-timed adult intervention, and then reflected upon to become embedded and used by children. Teachers and children need to know that these skills have to be taught and learnt alongside the curriculum content and that we learn effectively together when we use them.

The study highlighted the impact of some children's 'approach to learning' on the outcomes of the group as a whole. Some anticipated they could progress, others felt more helpless. Sometimes, moods seemed to impinge too. We aim to increase our focus on developing positive attitudes to the 'ups and downs' of learning so that children can contribute to group activities with more resilience and resourcefulness.

How we shared: We have introduced a whole school approach to developing oracy skills to improve thinking and learning, particularly in group activities. Group talk protocols have been adopted in all classes and children are explicitly taught the necessary skills to enable them to explain their thinking, justify their opinions, challenge the opinions of others, seek clarification when needed and reach agreement with peers.

reflectiveteaching.co.uk/rtps6/part2_ch8

Individual work

Whether or not pupils are *seated* in groups, they spend a great deal of classroom time working individually. They may be learning via tasks which require them to work alone or demonstrating the results of their learning in individual outcomes. Individual work is thought to be particularly useful for developing pupils' ability to work independently and autonomously.

Working individually may be the dominant mode in many lessons, but does not mean that the pupils are working without support. The teacher's role in supporting activity and scaffolding learning (van de Pol, Volan and Beishuizen, 2012) is probably even more intense than it is when pupils are working in groups, but it does have the potential advantage that such support and scaffolding is targeted on the specific learning needs of an individual. As a result, it is likely to be highly productive for learning (see Chapter 12).

However, there are potential problems. A teacher who relies heavily on setting individual work in lessons may find that similar teaching points have to be explained on many separate occasions. An emphasis on working with each individual separately inevitably means that only a limited amount of time can be spent with any one pupil, and it has been shown that most of this time is spent monitoring pupils' work, rather than in developing their understanding (Galton et al., 1999). It is particularly important to think of individual work, as with whole-class work, as part of the repertoire of organisational alternatives open to a teacher at particular points in a lesson. So a teacher must ask themselves: What am I hoping to achieve by getting the pupils to work individually at this point in the lesson? Is this the best form of organisation for the task, or for my intended outcomes?

One further option is to encourage a form of peer tutoring, in which learners work in pairs or very small groups to support the learning of each other. This may happen informally between classmates, but can be beneficially developed further. EEF **Toolkit Evidence 13.2** (see p. 435) has shown that, typically, both the 'tutor' and 'tutee' benefit if this is done in appropriately structured ways. It is particularly effective for consolidating understanding.

Professional judgement is essential in ensuring that, whatever organisational strategy is being considered – whole-class, group or individual – it is consistent with learning goals and evidence of effectiveness. Each approach within the teacher's repertoire has a different purpose and specific potential. Whilst each has its justifiable place in the classroom, they should be used to fulfil educational purposes.

We now go on to consider how teachers can liaise and work with other adults, including parents and support staff, in and beyond the classroom.

Working with adults

Parents and carers

Involvement by parents and carers is particularly significant in work with young pupils. Whilst the most important support for learning offered by parents and carers is in the home, the educational benefits of home–school liaison are well documented (**educationendowmentfoundation.org.uk/education-evidence/teaching-learning-toolkit/parental-engagement**). Whilst classroom interventions have been shown to make a bigger difference to academic outcomes, there are a number of effective ways to work in partnership with parents that can support learning for pupils (Van Poortlviet, Axford and Lloyd, 2018). Examples of good practice include not only working in classrooms, but the institution of parent councils or forums.

A wide range of patterns of parental involvement exist, but we will identify three:

- *Parents as consumers*. Receiving the services of the school but maintaining a discrete separation of parent and teacher responsibilities (e.g. where involvement is through formal parents' evenings, and other 'managed' school events).

- *Parents as resources*. Providing a range of help, for example in support of the school or in providing direct assistance based upon their skills.

- *Parents as partners*. Recognised as a partner in each pupil's all-round development, e.g. discussing the curriculum and each pupil's response; contributing as parent governors; having open access to the classroom and regular informal contacts with teachers (Crozier and Reay, 2005).

If the interest and expertise of parents or carers is to be drawn on, perhaps three basic things need to be done. The first is to make time for adequate discussion with parents to find out what they have to offer and to help them engage with the school environment. The second is to think carefully about how they can be most educationally productive when they are in the school. Third, if parents and carers are to work in classrooms, it is necessary to negotiate clear ground rules on issues such as classroom roles, confidentiality and access to areas of the school such as the staff room. Finally, it is obviously crucial to discuss whether they will interact with their own child and, if so, what the ground rules will be.

> **Expert Question**
>
> **Reflection:** *is our classroom practice based on incremental, evidence-informed and collaborative improvement strategies?*
>
> This question contributes to a conceptual framework underpinning professional expertise (see Chapter 16).

It seems that parents and carers, teachers and pupils have mixed feelings on the question of parental involvement in classrooms. Pupils in one study expressed strong views about protecting the privacy of their home life and were against their parents coming into school (Edwards and Alldred, 2000). Some parents may feel anxious about working in a school because of their own 'bad' experiences of school; because they do not feel they have anything to offer the 'expert' teacher; or because they are unsure about how to relate to pupils in the school situation. Further, parents are often only available for short and specific periods of the day and may find it difficult to fit into school routines. Other parents may be resistant to approaches from a school or teacher, feeling that it is the teacher's job to do the teaching. Teachers may also have reservations, perhaps feeling vulnerable in case something happens in class which could undermine their status in the eyes of the parents; or having a more principled perspective that acknowledges parental help can become a socially divisive factor, giving greater advantages to comparatively advantaged middle-class pupils whose parents are most likely to participate in such schemes.

Despite such challenges, the clear message is that the creation of stronger partnerships between home and school are likely to be of considerable advantage to pupils' learning.

Support staff

Expert Question

Connection: does the curriculum engage with the cultural resources and funds-of-knowledge of families and the community?

This question contributes to a conceptual framework underpinning professional expertise (see Chapter 16).

The number of support staff in schools has increased considerably throughout the UK. For example, in 2012, 43 per cent of the mainstream school workforce in England comprised support staff, with over half being teaching assistants (TAs). Their duties were wide-ranging. Some 'Higher Level Teaching Assistants' regularly take over a full teaching role during teachers' planning, preparation and assessment time, and are involved in staff meetings and staff training. Many support staff are involved in other 'teaching-related' activities, for example recording pupils' progress and contributing to the assessment of pupils' work. Assistants, whatever their title, are often involved in working with pupils with learning and behaviour difficulties.

There is evidence that the work of TAs can enhance academic attainment, but it is mixed. In particular, effectiveness appears to depend on how TAs are deployed. If they are used simply to replace a teacher, perhaps to take a group with special needs, then the consequences may be negative. This evidence has been presented in EEF **Toolkit Evidence 8.3** on p. 262.

To study the issue in more depth, Blatchford, Russell and Webster (2011) assessed the impact of teaching assistants and their role in the English education system. Their conclusions are pertinent both nationally and internationally. When looking at results for 8,200 pupils over the five years to 2011, the authors found that, despite much innovative and effective practice, pupils who received the most support from TAs consistently made *less* progress than similar pupils who received less TA support. They argued that this is fundamentally a question of how TAs are used and prepared for their work, rather than any fault of the TAs themselves. They note 'a drift toward teaching assistants becoming, in effect, the primary [main] educators of lower-attaining pupils and those with special educational needs', and state that 'the more support pupils get from TAs, the less they get from teachers', separating these pupils from the teacher and the curriculum. Thus, they state, 'it is perhaps unsurprising then that these pupils make less progress'.

It seems that what is important is the way in which the school and the individual classroom teacher handles relationships with support staff (Sood, 2005) and prepares them for their role in the classroom. In particular, Blatchford et al. (2011) note the nature and extent of the pedagogical role of the teaching assistant as being at the heart of whether they will be effective in supporting pupil learning. They suggest schools might focus on three areas that can enhance the value TAs add to pupil learning:

- *Preparedness*. There should be a formal induction process for TAs, and more joint planning and feedback time for teachers and TAs.

- *Deployment*. TAs should not routinely support lower attaining pupils and those with Special Educational Needs and Disabilities (SEND), but be deployed in ways that allow them to 'add value' to teachers' own teaching.

- *Practice*. TAs should receive professional development to help them focus on understanding, rather than task completion, in their interactions with pupils (Webster, Blatchford and Russell, 2013).

It is particularly important for the individual teacher to note that the quality of classroom teaching and learning can be greatly enhanced if all the adults in a classroom plan together, so that they understand and carry out specific activities in a coordinated and coherent fashion. Certainly it is the case that that, whenever they are asked, teaching assistants of all kinds state that they greatly appreciate it when teachers work *with* them, sharing learning intentions and expectations of their classroom roles on a lesson by lesson basis (O'Brien and Garner, 2001). The skill and dedication of such support staff cannot be doubted, but their effective deployment in helping to promote pupils' learning is clearly the responsibility of the school and the class teacher.

CONCLUSION

In this chapter, two major points about learning spaces have been made.

First, all contexts and settings (whether directly experienced or virtual) provide conditions which influence learning. Some will enable learning to flourish, whilst others may inhibit such development. These differences in 'affordance' are similar to the patterns in any ecological context. So, when we organise our own classroom learning environments, we should consider the likely overall effect on our objective of supporting learning (Bransford et al., 1999, Reading 8.2).

Second, classrooms are far from being isolated entities. Rather, they are contextualised by many other influences on pupil lives. Among the most obvious are the school as a whole, the family and community. But these factors are also encompassed by wider cultural, economic, technological, social and political conditions.

reflectiveteaching.co.uk/rtps6/part2_ch8

Effective classroom organisation thus requires consideration of the physical environment, resources, technologies, structures, routines, processes and people that are intended to progress pupil learning. Such factors, as well as the organisation of pupils themselves, must be considered in relation to their capacity to enable or constrain learning.

Awareness of the range of influences on pupil learning and appropriate organisation of classroom provision is a hallmark of an expert teacher.

reflectiveteaching.co.uk/rtps6/part2_ch8

CHAPTER WEBPAGE

reflectiveteaching.co.uk offers additional professional resources for this chapter. For the chapter webpage, go to: reflectiveteaching.co.uk/rtps6/part2_ch8

The webpage resources for Chapter 8 may be particularly helpful for getting to grips with its underlying rationale. The elements within the chapter, such as the use of space, resources, technology, teaching assistants and the organisation of pupils may seem disparate. However, they are linked in that they all contribute to the nature of the learning environment which is created. Such environments have affordances which directly influence the types of learning that are developed. These may suit some learners, but not others. They may suit some learning goals, but not others. They may suit some teachers, but not others.

Trying out some of the *Reflective Activities* suggested for this chapter will give insights into how these issues play out in classrooms which you know well. Studying some of the suggested reading, for instance, on ecological psychology (see Bransford or Bronfenbrenner below), will fill out the rationale and help you in applying the same principles to other learning settings, spaces and environments in the future.

Three levels of advice for follow-up study are again provided.

1 *Further Reading* on the chapter webpage provides a wide-ranging review of sources and follows the structure of the chapter. It should be helpful for essays, projects or investigating issues in depth, but library access or some fortunate on-line searching is likely to be required.

2 *Key Readings*, below, is a list of selected highlights or 'essential reads', but it of course requires a good library.

3 *Readings for Reflective Teaching in Schools* provides short, edited extracts of many of the key readings, and acts rather like a mini-library. A brief indication of the contents for this chapter is provided below. This complementary book makes things very easy, but consultation with full versions of texts of particular interest is still recommended.

KEY READINGS

A powerful analysis of the design of learning environments is provided by:

Bransford, J., Brown, A. L., and Cocking, R. (eds) (1999) *How People Learn: Brain, Mind, Experience, and School*. Washington, DC: National Academy Press. (Reading 8.2)

For ground-breaking insights into how new technologies enable learner-centric contexts for learning, see:

Luckin, R. (2010) *Re-Designing Learning Contexts. Technology-Rich, Learner-Centred Ecologies*. London: Routledge.

Understanding of the conditions which enable learning, development and performance has been enhanced by ecological analyses which trace contextual influences. Classics are:

Baker, R.G. (1968) *Ecological Psychology: Concepts and Methods of Studying the Environment of Human Behaviour*. Stanford: Stanford University Press.

Bronfenbrenner, U. (1979) *The Ecology of Human Development: Experiments by Nature and Design*. Cambridge, MA: Harvard University Press. (Reading 8.1)

Influences on the development of children and young people have been extensively studied. A good summary is:

Corsaro, W.A. (2011) *The Sociology of Childhood*. London: SAGE.

There are many excellent studies of home–school relations:

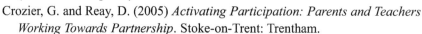

Rogoff, B., Goodman Turkanis, C. and Bartlett, L. (2001) *Learning Together: Children and Adults in a School Community*. Oxford: Oxford University Press. (see also Reading 2.10)

Crozier, G. and Reay, D. (2005) *Activating Participation: Parents and Teachers Working Towards Partnership*. Stoke-on-Trent: Trentham.

As all practitioners know, circumstances vary in different classrooms and judgement has to be applied to select appropriate forms of classroom organisation for the purposes which the teacher has in mind. For insights into these challenges and opportunities, see:

Hopkins, D., Harris, A., Singleton, C. and Watts, R. (2000) *Creating the Conditions for Teaching and Learning*. London: David Fulton.

Display within school and classroom environments can convey important messages. On this, see:

Andrew-Power, K. and Gormley, C. (2009) *Display for Learning*. London: Continuum (see also Reading 8.3)

The impact of physical factors on pupils' learning has become increasingly clear in recent years. For insights into these areas see:

Barrett, P., Zhang, Y, Davies, F. and Barrett, L. (2015) *Clever Classrooms. Summary report of the HEAD project*. Salford: University of Salford.

The classic paper on the effective use of time in classrooms is:

Berliner, D. (1991) 'What's all the fuss about instructional time?' in M. Ben-Peretz and R. Bromme (eds), *The Nature of Time in Schools: Theoretical Concepts, Practitioner Perceptions*. New York: Teachers College Press. (Reading 8.4)

For more general guidance on classroom organisation see:

Dean, J. (2008) *Organising Learning in the Primary School Classroom*. London: Routledge.

For insights into working with ICT across the curriculum, see:

Savage, J. and McGoun, C. (2015) *Teaching in a Networked Classroom*. London: Routledge.

Beauchamp, G. (2012) *ICT in the Primary School: From Pedagogy to Practice*. Harlow: Pearson.

Edwards, A. (2012) *New Technology and Education*. London: Continuum (Reading 8.5)

On the potential influence of technology and new media from beyond school, take a look at:

Facer, K. (2011) *Learning Futures: Education, Technology and Social Change*. London: Routledge.

Kress, K. (2012) *Literacy in the New Media Age*. London: Routledge. (see Reading 8.6)

On interactive and dialogic teaching, see:

Mercer, N. and Hodgkinson, S. (2008) (eds) *Exploring Talk in School*. London: SAGE. (Reading 11.6)

Muijs, D. and Reynolds, D. (2017) *Effective Teaching: Evidence and Practice*. London: SAGE. (Reading 8.7)

For a practical introduction to effective group work, including consideration of issues related to ability grouping, see:

Baines, E., Blatchford, P. and Kutnick, P. (2017) *Promoting Effective Group Work in the Classroom*. London: Routledge. (TLRP **Research Briefing**, p. 370)

Ireson, J. and Hallam, S. (2001) *Ability Grouping in Education*. London: SAGE. (see also Reading 15.4)

On teaching assistants, Sharples et al.'s guidance report has practical messages for classroom deployment, whilst Dillow records the experience of working in the role.

Sharples, J., Webster, R. and Blatchford, P. (2018) *Making Best Use of Teaching Assistants*, 2nd edn. EEF: London. Available at: educationendowmentfoundation.org.uk/education-evidence/guidance-reports/teaching-assistants

Dillow, C. (2010) *Supporting Stories: Being a Teaching Assistant*. Stoke-on-Trent: Trentham Press.

TOOLKIT EVIDENCE 8.1
The built environment of schools: focus on pedagogy not learning spaces

What is it?
Changing the physical conditions or the 'built environment', either by moving to a new school building or seeking to improve the structure, air quality, noise, light or temperature of an existing building or classroom. This should be distinguished from planning for effective interaction within a particular space (the learning environment).

What does the evidence say?
Overall, changes to the built environment of schools are unlikely to have a direct effect on learning beyond the extremes (i.e. once an adequate building standard has been achieved).

Most individual factors in the physical environment show a relationship with learning only at the extremes. If the noise levels are very high (such as under the flight path of an airport) then there can be a measurable detrimental effect on learning. Very warm (particularly above 30°C) and very humid conditions can cause a loss of concentration and drowsiness. Poor internal air quality can have a negative impact on attainment (reducing word recognition by 15 per cent in one study). Low air quality can occur due to the build up of carbon dioxide in poorly ventilated classrooms. Lighting in schools is usually adequate for reading and writing, the effects of colour on learning is unproven.

How sound is the evidence?
The research on the impact of the built environment on learning is generally weak, and is mainly based on correlational studies or drawn as inferences from wider environmental research. There are very few rigorous experimental designs, and this makes it hard to establish causal claims about the impact of physical changes in classrooms and schools.

What do I need to think about?
- Most environmental factors have an impact on learning in classrooms only at the extremes.
- Planning for effective use of existing space, and for effective teaching and learning using it is likely to be more productive than altering physical features.

Links and further reading
Woolner, P., McCarter, S., Wall, K. and Higgins, S. (2012) 'Changed learning through changed space. When can a participatory approach to the learning environment challenge preconceptions and alter practice?' *Improving Schools*, 15(1), 45–60.

The EEF Teaching and Learning Toolkit entry on 'Built environment': educationendowmentfoundation.org.uk/education-evidence/early-years-toolkit/built-environment – see also the technical appendix for further references.

See also
educationendowmentfoundation.org.uk/education-evidence/guidance-reports/digital?utm_source=/education-evidence/guidance-reports/digital

Education Endowment Foundation

TOOLKIT EVIDENCE 8.2
Digital technology: learning tool or toy to entertain?

What is it?
The use of digital technologies, such as computers, tablets, mobile and web-based technologies to support learning. Approaches in this area are very varied, but a simple split can be made between:
1. technology for pupils, where learners use technology in problem solving or more open-ended learning, as tools for learning; and
2. technology for teachers, such as interactive whiteboards or learning platforms or tutorial software, as tools for teaching.

What does the evidence say?
Overall, studies consistently find that digital technology is associated with moderate learning gains (on average an additional four months' progress). However, there is considerable variation in impact. Evidence suggests that technology should be used to supplement other teaching, rather than replace it.

It seems likely that different technologies can change aspects of teaching and learning interactions, such as by providing more effective feedback for example, or enabling more helpful representations to be used, or encouraging learners to take greater responsibility, or simply by motivating learners to practise more. There is some evidence that it is more effective with younger learners and studies suggest that individualising learning with technology (one-to-one laptop or tablet provision, or individual use of drill and practice) may not be as helpful as small group learning or collaborative use of technology. There is evidence that it is more beneficial for areas like writing rather than spelling and mathematics practice rather than problem solving.

How sound is the evidence?
There is extensive evidence across age groups and for most areas of the curriculum which shows positive effects. However, the variation in effects and the range of technologies available suggest that it is important think through *how* it will make a difference. The pace of technological change means that evidence is usually about yesterday's technology rather than today's, but average effects have remained consistent for some time, implying that general messages are likely to remain relevant.

What do I need to think about?
- Effective use of technology is driven by pedagogy. What are your learning and teaching goals?
- What will change in terms of learning? Will learners work harder, for longer, more efficiently or more effectively?
- Using technology confidently in an empty classroom is very different from using it fluently in your teaching with twenty-five pupils watching. Practice is essential.

Links and further reading
Higgins, S., Xiao, Z. and Katsipataki, M. (2012) *The Impact of Digital Technology on Learning: A Summary for the Education Endowment Foundation*. London: EEF. files.eric.ed.gov/fulltext/ED612174.pdf
Kaye, L. (2016) *Young Children in a Digital Age: Supporting Learning and Development with Technology in Early* Years London: Routledge.

The EEF guidance report on digital technology: educationendowmentfoundation.org.uk/tools/guidance-reports/using-digital-technology-to-improve-learning/

See also
Meta-cognition and self-regulated learning (Toolkit Evidence 2.1)
Collaborative learning (Toolkit Evidence 11.3)

Education Endowment Foundation

TOOLKIT EVIDENCE 8.3
Effective deployment of teaching assistants: supporting the teacher or helping pupils learn?

What is it?
Teaching assistants (also known as TAs or classroom support assistants) are adults who support teachers in the classroom. Teaching assistants' duties can vary widely from school to school, ranging from providing administrative and general classroom help to providing targeted support in a teaching role to individual pupils or small groups.

What does the evidence say?
Evidence suggests that TAs can have a positive impact on academic achievement. However, effects tend to vary between those studies where TAs provide general administrative or classroom support, which do not show any benefit, and those where TAs support individual pupils or small groups, particularly using targeted interventions where they have received training, which show consistent moderate positive benefits (up to three to five months' additional progress). Some negative effects have been recorded, particularly for pupils with Special Educational Needs and Disabilities (SEND). Here it seems likely that support from TAs has been substituted for rather than supplemented the teacher's role.

How sound is the evidence?
Overall, the level of evidence related to teaching assistants is limited. A number of systematic reviews of the impact of support staff in schools have been conducted. However, there are no meta-analyses specifically looking at the impact of TAs on learning.

Correlational studies looking at the impact of TAs providing general classroom support have shown broadly similar effects. One of the largest studies, conducted in England, suggests that on average low attaining pupils do less well in a class with a TA present, compared with a class where only a teacher is present. Intervention studies, including six randomised controlled trials conducted in England since 2011, provide a strong indication that TAs can improve learning if they are trained, supported and deployed carefully.

What do I need to think about?
- Are you sure your TA is supporting progress rather than simply managing a group?
- Do you brief your TA about their role so that they understand how to support learning?
- Are you sure your role is not being replaced? Are the most vulnerable pupils getting your full support?

Links and further reading
Webster, R., Russell, A. and Blatchford, P. (2015) *Maximising the Impact of Teaching Assistants*. London: Routledge.
Farrell, P., Alborz, A., Howes, A. and Pearson, D. (2010) 'The impact of teaching assistants on improving pupils' academic achievement in mainstream schools: A review of the literature'. *Educational Review*, 62(4), 435–48.

The EEF Guidance Report on TAs: educationendowmentfoundation.org.uk/tools/guidance-reports/making-best-use-of-teaching-assistants/

See also
Small group teaching (Toolkit Evidence 11.2)

Education Endowment Foundation

RESEARCH BRIEFING 8.1
Teaching and learning with new technology in the classroom

There is enormous potential in the use of technology for schools, college, university, workplace and lifelong learning.

TLRP's two major projects on the use of new technology in schools have contributed to these developments – one based on learning in nursery schools and the other focused on the teaching of specific subjects in secondary schools. In both instances, the research showed that the affordance of the technological tools to support effective learning is not drawn out consistently without teacher expertise guiding the learner on how to interpret and make sense of their experiences. Technology can enhance learning and complement teaching, but it is unlikely to replace the role of a more knowledgeable other in discussion, guidance and feedback.

Key findings:	Implications:
Equipment: New technological equipment is, in itself, not terribly useful in enhancing learning.	The key to enhancing learning concerns the use to which technological tools are put.
Guided interaction: Learners' encounters with new technology are enhanced when practitioners use guided interaction to support them.	Professional development should aim to enhance the capability of teachers and others in using new technology to scaffold new understanding.
Essential teaching: Effective teaching and learning with new technology involves building bridges between 'idiosyncratic' and 'intended' learning.	Authentic new knowledge is not embedded in the technology. Effective learning depends on teacher contributions to shape, amend or reinforce emerging understanding.
Multiple experiences: Providing experience of a broad range of new technologies promotes opportunities for learning.	Experience of many technologies builds confidence and positive attitudes to technology-enhanced learning and its use.
Formal and informal learning: There is a two-way exchange of knowledge between home and school use of new technology, which impacts on learning in school.	Students can be beneficially encouraged to build on their out-of-school learning within school, and to continue their school learning at home.

Among the 'subject design initiatives' underpinning the InterActive project were:

Learning to spell: 10–11-year-old pupils used WordRoot, a multimedia sound and word package, and the presentation package PowerPoint, to analyse the structure and etymology of 'hard words'. Pupils' spelling improved, as shown by paper and pencil tests.

Learning to write in a foreign language: 13–14-year-old pupils used drop-down menus in Word to support their writing in German. They wrote more in the foreign language and took more risks with grammar. Pupils' writing on paper was also enhanced after this exercise.

Learning mathematical proof: 13–14-year-old pupils used dynamic geometry software and presentation software to learn about geometrical proof. They worked in groups and presented their work to the class for feedback on the validity of the proofs they had produced.

Using computers for shared writing: 9–10-year-olds in pairs composed an extra chapter of Alice in Wonderland, writing direct to screen. Analysis of pupils' interactions and writing suggests that the computer affords a more visual way of conceptualising the narrative voice and structure of a text than pen and paper. This challenges traditional notions of the writing process.

Further information
Plowman, L. (2006) *Supporting Learning with ICT in Pre-school Settings*. TLRP Research Briefing 15. London: TLRP.
Sutherland, R. et al. (2006) *Using Computers to Enhance Learning*. TLRP Research Briefing 19. London: TLRP.
Sutherland, R., Robertson, S. and John, P. (2008) *Improving Learning with ICT*. TLRP Improving Learning series. London: Routledge.
These projects were directed from the University of Stirling and University of Bristol. reflectiveteaching.co.uk/books-and-resources/rts5/part2/ch8"

Part three

Teaching for learning

9   **Curriculum** What is to be taught and learned?   267

10   **Planning** How are we implementing the curriculum?   305

11   **Pedagogy** How can we develop effective strategies?   345

12   **Communication** How does use of language support learning?   371

13   **Assessment** How can assessment enhance learning?   403

This part supports the development of practice across the three classic dimensions of teaching – curriculum, pedagogy and assessment.

Chapter 9 starts us off with a review of curricular aims and design principles, before progressing to a review of national curricula in the UK and the role of subject knowledge. 'Planning' (Chapter 10) puts these ideas into action and supports the development and evaluation of programmes of study, schemes of work and lesson plans.

Chapter 11 offers ways of understanding the art, craft and science of pedagogy – and the development of a pedagogic repertoire. 'Communication' (Chapter 12) extends this with an introduction to the vital roles of talking, listening, reading and writing across the curriculum. Perhaps the core instructional expertise of the teacher lies in the skill of dialogic teaching?

Finally, this part concludes by demonstrating how assessment can be tied into teaching and learning processes in very constructive ways (Chapter 13). In short, through principled strategies for sharing goals, pupil engagement, authentic feedback, self-assessment and responsive teaching, excellent progress in learning can be made.

Chapter 9
Curriculum
What is to be taught and learned?

| Introduction | 268 |

| Principles for curriculum provision | 270 |

Knowledge, development and curriculum — 270
Aims and values — 271

| Elements of learning | 274 |

Knowledge — 275
Concepts — 278
Skills — 280
Attitudes — 282
A balanced curriculum — 284

| National curricula | 285 |

UK curricular structures — 287
Teaching, learning and national curricula — 289
Subject-based and integrated curricula — 290

| Subject knowledge for teachers | 292 |

Content knowledge — 292
Pedagogical content knowledge — 293
Curricular knowledge — 294
Applying subject knowledge — 295

| Conclusion | 299 |

Part 3 Teaching for learning

INTRODUCTION

The existence of national curricula is common across the world. Such provision ensures coverage of a specified range of knowledge, thus providing pupil entitlements and satisfying national aspirations in terms of the purposes of education for society as a whole. However, there is also awareness that centrally imposed requirements can inhibit local curricular adaption and, in particular, could stifle teacher innovation. All writers of curriculum texts make decisions about what to include and exclude and how to present issues and topics, which comes with the responsibility to ensure the selection and presentation is evidence-informed and inclusive including considering issues of bias and misrepresentation.

In this chapter we introduce enduring concepts and principles of curriculum design on which innovation and curriculum development can be based. We thus hope to equip the reflective teacher for career-long engagement with curricular issues.

See Chapter 4

TLRP Principles

Three principles are of particular relevance to this chapter on curricular requirements:

Effective teaching and learning equips learners for life in its broadest sense. Learning should aim to help people to develop the intellectual, personal and social resources that will enable them to participate as active citizens, contribute to economic development and flourish as individuals in a diverse and changing society. This implies adopting a broad view of learning outcomes and ensuring that equity and social justice are taken seriously. (*Principle 1*)

Effective teaching and learning engages with valued forms of knowledge. Teaching and learning should engage with the big ideas, facts, processes, language and narratives of subjects so that learners understand what constitutes quality and standards in particular disciplines. (*Principle 2*)

Effective teaching and learning demands consistent policy frameworks with support for teaching and learning as their primary focus. Policies at national, local and institutional levels need to recognise the fundamental importance of teaching and learning. They should be designed to create effective learning environments in which all learners can thrive. (*Principle 10*)

To begin, we briefly review three ways of thinking about 'curriculum':

- *The official curriculum*. This is the explicitly stated programme of learning and may incorporate a national curriculum which has been endorsed by government and any statutory requirements placed on schools. Such a course of study is likely

reflectiveteaching.co.uk/rtps6/part3_ch9

to have three elements. First, there will be the intended curriculum content. This will have been consciously planned and may be specified in terms of subject syllabi or broader areas of learning. Second, the official curriculum will normally require a particular sequence and progression, thus framing the content into scheduled programmes of study. Third, courses and other provision will be designed with the intention of challenging pupils appropriately and of enabling achievements to be recorded by teacher assessment, test or examination. While schools may develop their own assessment approaches, national assessment requirements also influence curriculum design. Curriculum activities that reflect school and community priorities are explicitly encouraged across the UK, although finding space in what can be a crowded curriculum can be a challenge. The official school curriculum thus reflects a historically specific combination of national requirements and local commitments and decisions.

- *The hidden curriculum.* This concept focuses attention on tacit learning during schooling. It highlights how children and young people come to understand such things as teacher and pupil roles and attitudes towards learning and schooling. Children may also acquire ideas about the ways boys or girls 'should' behave or how likely they are to be successful in different subjects. Children also learn about differences 'because' of being black or white, middle class or working class, and norms about sexual orientation or physical aspects related to people's characteristics may inadvertently be promoted. Such ideas reflect the way in which values are conveyed through the interaction and language associated with teaching and learning processes. The hidden curriculum is thus implicit within regular school procedures and curriculum materials, and can exert a powerful influence on pupils through its influence on self-image and expectations (see Jackson, 1968, Reading 6.1 for a classic study).

- *The experienced curriculum.* This way of conceptualising the curriculum draws attention to the parts of the curriculum, both official and hidden, which connect most meaningfully with children and young learners. Adults can plan all they like, and do so with the best of intentions, but what sense do learners actually make of this provision? It is this experienced curriculum that, by definition, has the most educational impact. Thinking about curricular provision from the perspectives of a deliberately wide range of learners is a helpful check when we review our planning, whether it is for a single lesson, series of lessons or even for a whole school.

The 'school curriculum', when seen as a whole, is thus considerably more than an aggregation of lessons. In England the Ofsted inspection framework stresses that judging 'quality of education' includes looking at curriculum in terms of 'the concepts of 'intent', 'implementation' and 'impact' to recognise that the curriculum passes through different states: it is conceived, taught and experienced' (Ofsted, 2019). The curriculum is thus the totality of the substantive provision and experience offered to pupils, as Male and Waters demonstrate (2012a and 2012b, Reading 9.1).

PRINCIPLES FOR CURRICULUM PROVISION

Knowledge, development and curriculum

The educational role of curricular provision relates to three basic, enduring considerations. They are fundamental to all curricular deliberation:

- the *nature of knowledge*;
- the *needs of learners*, and crucially;
- the *interactions* between them.

These elements were highlighted in the first chapter of an Expert Panel report on England's National Curriculum (DfE, 2011a). An edited version is reproduced below:

> Subject knowledge can be seen as representing the accumulated experience of the past and a representation of this for the future. The concepts, facts, processes, language, narratives and conventions of each subject constitute socially refined forms of knowledge – knowledge that is regarded as 'powerful' in our society (Young, 2008, **Reading 9.2**). Established knowledge is highly codified, with disciplines, associations, professions and specialist institutions. Many contemporary bodies of knowledge are more mobile, with innovation and change being characteristic features.

> However, education is also about the development of individual learners – in schools, as pupils. There are many dimensions to such development including the personal, social and emotional as well as the physical, neurological and cognitive. For young children in particular, such factors are of great significance because they provide the foundation for learning. The significance of the development of individuals over time has increasingly been recognised. Longitudinal research has demonstrated the lasting consequences of high-quality early learning experiences (Sylva et al., 2010) and a Foresight Report (Feinstein et al., 2008b, **Reading 1.6**) affirms the trajectories of 'learning through life' and the economic and wider benefits of such learning.

> Education can thus be seen, at its simplest, as the product of interaction between socially valued knowledge and individual development. It occurs through learner experience of both of these key elements. Education, through the school curriculum, mediates and structures these processes. The core expertise of teachers is to reach between and facilitate a productive interaction of knowledge and development. As James and Pollard (2012a and 2012b) put it, effective teaching 'engages with valued forms of knowledge' and also 'equips learners for life in its broadest sense'.

> Some people emphasise subject knowledge and discount the significance of more developmental aspects of education. And there are also many who foreground the development of skills, competencies and dispositions whilst asserting that contemporary knowledge changes so fast that 'learning how to learn' is all that is necessary. But these are unhelpful polarisations, for it is impossible to conceptualise 'learning to learn' except

in relation to some substantive purpose. Our position is therefore that *both* elements – knowledge and development – are essential considerations in relation to curricular provision.

The two elements are not, however, equally significant at every age. In particular, developmental aspects and basic skills are more crucial for young children, while appropriate understanding of more differentiated subject knowledge, concepts and skills becomes more important for older pupils. Curricular provision for early years, primary, secondary and further education is thus distinct, although the underlying issues endure.

The primary school curriculum must meet the needs of children at very different points in their educational trajectory. At the start of primary school, children make the transition from early years settings with curricula focused on early development and so the curriculum is implemented in a way that reflects the developmental needs of the children. However, young children also need to acquire knowledge with the help of their teachers. By age 11 children are preparing for another significant transition, with subject knowledge a greater focus as they move into the secondary school. Chapter 10, Planning, considers some of the ways in which the developmental needs of the children might have an effect on how we implement the curriculum.

Aims and values

When creating, adapting or implementing a curriculum, or any element within it, it is crucial to be very clear about the purposes the provision is expected to serve.

At a high level, legislation may define overall educational goals. For example, in England, Section 78 of the Education Act 2002 states that school curriculum should be 'balanced and broadly based' and should:

promote the spiritual, moral, cultural, mental and physical development of pupils at the school and of society, and prepare pupils at the school for the opportunities, responsibilities and experiences of later life.

This is a foundational statement for consideration of the school curriculum as a whole and represents value commitments about the nature of an appropriate 'education' which can be traced back to at least the 1944 Education Act. Similar high-level statements set expectations for the curricular frameworks in Scotland, Wales and Northern Ireland. They are essentially ethical, moral and political statements, which make transparent the values and ambitions to which a nation aspires. Reiss and White (2013) demonstrate the importance of an 'aims-based curriculum' in achieving coherence around educational purposes.

Historical study and international comparison (Meyer et al., 1992; National Foundation for Educational Research, 2011) reveal some common themes in relation to what can broadly be termed social, economic, personal, cultural and environmental goals. This can also be illustrated by comparison of the educational aims proposed within four sectoral reviews from England (see Figure 9.1).

reflectiveteaching.co.uk/rtps6/part3_ch9

Part 3 Teaching for learning

Expert Questions

Breadth: *does the curriculum represent society's educational aspirations for its citizens?*

Balance: *does the curriculum-as-experienced offer everything which each learner has a right to expect?*

These questions contribute to a conceptual framework underpinning professional expertise (see Chapter 16).

The representation in Figure 9.1 risks over-simplification, but does demonstrate some key points. First, it suggests that knowledge and skill, developed in age-appropriate ways, are of enduring importance in satisfying social and economic goals in all sectors. Of course, these are always prominent concerns for policymakers, industry and the media. Second, there is also a very strong emphasis on personal development in all sectors, which is often a particular commitment for parents and educationalists. The table also shows the awareness which exists about citizenship during schooling and it suggests that environmental concern is emerging. Sehgal Cuthbert and Standish argue that 'instrumental' aims for the curriculum are problematic, whether these are to address environmental, social, political or other problems, as they risk undermining the idea of education as a public good (2021).

In the case of the early years, in Figure 9.1, the particular importance of personal goals is further asserted by identifying *prime* and *other* areas for learning. Such factors remain crucial throughout 'primary' education but gradually give way to 'secondary' education's need to focus on knowledge and skill in preparation for formal examinations and the social and economic demands of the workplace.

Expert Question

Connection: *does the curriculum engage with the cultural resources and funds-of-knowledge of families and the community?*

This question contributes to a conceptual framework underpinning professional expertise (see Chapter 16).

It is appropriate for reflective teachers, schools and their stakeholders to deliberate on educational purposes on a regular basis. Whilst positions on social, economic, personal, cultural and environmental issues might be expected, the particular priorities, expression and provision should reflect the values, judgement, debate and resolution of each school community. In this way, specific connections can be created to the culture and aspirations of those served by each school (see also Chapter 10).

The outcomes of such deliberation on purposes should, of course, be published on websites and in school brochures. After all, the outcomes of education are of enormous significance and learners of any age, and their parents or carers too, have a right to expect that teachers will approach their work from a considered and morally justifiable position.

Further, without such clarity, it is not possible for a fully *coherent* and holistic curriculum to be offered (see Chapter 10) or for appropriately aligned and *congruent* assessment practices to be developed (see Chapters 13 and 14).

This brings us to the level of detailed application, where educational aims are chased through school policies and into specific programmes of study, lessons and everyday provision. This is likely to be of particular interest to student teachers, and is considered in some detail in Chapter 10. As we will see there, the existence of clarity and transparency in educational goals makes it more likely that intentions will be communicated to learners – and there is mounting international evidence that this is reflected in enhanced outcomes. Indeed, clarity informs evaluative review of provision and increases accountability.

reflectiveteaching.co.uk/rtps6/part3_ch9

Figure 9.1 A comparison of educational aims across sectors in England

	Expert Panel Report for the National Curriculum Review (DfE, 2011)	Early Years Review (Tickell, 2011)	Cambridge Primary Review (Alexander, 2010)	Nuffield 14–19 Review (Pring et al., 2009)
Social and Economic	Provide opportunities for participation in a broad range of educational experiences and the acquisition of knowledge and appreciation in the arts, sciences and humanities, and of high-quality academic and vocational qualifications. Satisfy future economic needs for individuals and for the workforce as a whole, including the development of secure knowledge and skills in communication, literacy and mathematics and confidence in acquiring new knowledge and skills	Communication and language; Expressive arts and design; Mathematics; Understanding the world	Exploring, knowing, understanding and making sense; Fostering skill	Knowledge and understanding; Practical capabilities
Personal	Support personal development and empowerment so that each pupil is able to develop as a healthy, balanced and self-confident individual and fulfil their educational potential	Personal, social and emotional development; Physical development	Wellbeing; Engagement; Empowerment; Autonomy	Personal fulfilment; Moral seriousness
Cultural	Appreciate national cultures, traditions and values, whilst recognising diversity and encouraging responsible citizenship		Empowering local, national and global citizenship; Celebrating culture and community	Community relatedness
Environmental	Promote understanding of sustainability in the stewardship of resources locally, nationally and globally		Promoting interdependence and sustainability	

> **Expert Questions**
>
> **Coherence:** *is there clarity in the purposes, content and organisation of the curriculum and does it provide holistic learning experiences?*
>
> **Congruence:** *are the forms of assessment fit for purpose in terms of overall educational objectives?*
>
> These questions contribute to a conceptual framework underpinning professional expertise (see Chapter 16).

Curricula vary in the extent to which they specify the pedagogy teachers should employ, with most national curricula leaving this to the professional judgment of the teaching profession. However, some national curricula do promote particular teaching approaches and this can prompt some resistance from teaching bodies. Particular examples in England (see Wyse and Bradbury, 2022) are the use of synthetic phonics to teach reading and the promotion of the study of grammar to support the teaching of writing (Wyse et al., 2022). Non-statutory guidance can also provide a softer way for governments to promote particular pedagogical approaches (for example, the promotion of the National Council for Excellence in Teaching Mathematics (NCETM)'s mastery approach to mathematics teaching through the DfE 'ready-to-progress' materials).

> **Reflective Activity 9.1**
>
> *Aim:* To examine statements of aims and values presented in National Curriculum and school documentation.
>
> *Evidence and reflection:* Are aims and values explicitly stated within the National Curriculum and school documentation at your disposal?
>
> If so, are the aims consistently supported by the stated underlying values? What vision of education do you derive from reading these statements?
>
> If not, can you derive some of the core aims and values from an examination of the curriculum advice presented in the documentation?
>
> *Extension:* How do the aims, values and vision connect with the particular communities that the school serves? To what extent do the explicit or implicit aims and values reflect your own views of what should inform an appropriate school curriculum? Is there anything missing? Is there anything that shouldn't be there? Why?

ELEMENTS OF LEARNING

This section discusses the building blocks of a curriculum for learning – knowledge, concepts, skills and attitudes. This framework derives from Her Majesty's Inspectorate (HMI) (1985, Reading 10.1) whose classic booklet, *The Curriculum from 5 to 16*, was designed to encourage and refine professional discussion of curriculum matters. They introduced the four elements in the following terms:

- *Knowledge.* Selections of that which is worth knowing and of interest. As HMI put it: 'The criteria for selecting content should be in the aims and objectives which a school sets for itself. That which is taught should be worth knowing, comprehensible, capable of sustaining pupils' interest and useful to them at their particular stage of development and in the future.'

- *Concepts.* The 'big ideas' which inform a subject, or generalisations which enable pupils to classify, organise and predict – to understand patterns, relationships and meanings, e.g. flow, change, consequence, temperature, refraction, power, energy.
- *Skills.* The capacity or competence to perform a task, e.g. personal/social (listening, collaborating, reflecting), physical/practical (running, writing, cutting), intellectual (observing, reasoning, imagining), communication (oracy, literacy, numeracy) etc.
- *Attitudes.* The overt expression of values and personal qualities, e.g. reliability, initiative, self-discipline, tolerance, resilience, resourcefulness etc.

Across the United Kingdom there are different national approaches to balancing these elements in curriculum design. England's 2014 national curriculum could be described as having a more knowledge-focused approach with emphasis on 'the essential knowledge that [children] need to be educated citizens' and with traditional subjects structuring the primary curriculum. Northern Ireland's curriculum (Council for the Curriculum Examinations and Assessment (CCEA), 2007) takes an explicitly skill-based approach, while Scotland's Curriculum for Excellence (2010) focuses on developing learners' 'capacities': the logic being that in a changing world there must be a strong focus on the skills and capabilities that set pupils up as lifelong learners from this first experience of formal education. The relative emphasis on knowledge and skills, particularly more generic skills or decontextualised skills, such as problem solving or managing information, is a contested area of curriculum design (comparison of another cross-curricular dimension in different national curricula can be located through Manyukhina and Wyse's blog: bera.ac.uk/blog/childrens-agency-what-is-it-and-what-should-be-done).

Knowledge

Understandings about the nature of knowledge underpin all curricula. Three basic positions are well established – with roots back to the philosophy, psychology and sociology of education.

1 There are those who argue that particular 'forms of knowledge' exist. These are thought to be distinguishable, philosophically, by the different ways of thinking and kinds of evidence which are employed in investigating them (Hirst, 1965; Peters, 1966). These forms are thought to be based on *a priori* differences, i.e. logical and inherent differences. Such a view has been referred to as 'rationalist' (Blenkin and Kelly, 1981) and is often used to legitimate the organisation of teaching into traditional curriculum subjects (Wilson, 2000, Reading 9.3).

2 There are those who emphasise the ways in which knowledge is socially constructed, and learned, by individuals and groups in interaction together and

with their environment, and by successively restructuring their understanding through these experiences (Berger and Luckmann, 1966; Light and Littleton, 1999). This view has resonance with the psychology of Piaget, Vygotsky and Bruner (see Chapter 2 and Readings 2.2, 2.3 and 9.5).

3 Knowledge can be seen in sociological terms as being defined by powerful groups who define certain types of understanding as being important or of high status. They may attempt to control access to some forms of knowledge, particularly those associated with power (Young, 1971; Bernstein, 1971), but they may also try to insist on the exposure of pupils to particular forms of knowledge which are deemed appropriate.

Of course, these views of knowledge are not discrete and any one person's perspective may draw on several of them, or even on them all. Michael Young (2008, Reading 9.2) makes an important distinction between 'powerful knowledge' (see position 1 above) and 'knowledge of the powerful' (position 3 above). The former is associated with specialist understanding which is capable of application in a wide variety of contexts. He argues that providing access to such powerful knowledge is the main purpose of schooling, whilst knowledge of the powerful must sometimes be challenged in democratic, egalitarian societies.

The important point is that the different emphasis which is placed on particular views of knowledge tends to reflect social values, and these *can* and often *do* influence the structure and content of the curriculum.

The call to decolonise the curriculum is an important recently re-emphasised example of the struggle to define the content of knowledge domains. This is seen most powerfully, although not exclusively, in the history curriculum, where for example we can ask whether black British history is taught as an integral part of British history or treated as a separate topic, and whether the central role and impact of colonisation is made clear in understanding the history of Britain from the sixteenth century onward. The existence of 'Black History Month' has provided a starting point for many primary schools in broadening their history curriculum and celebrating the achievements of black and minority ethnic individuals and groups. However, taken alone, a month devoted to this topic can be limiting in that it suggests that 'black history' is a specialist or niche interest, somehow separate from history proper.

Another recent tussle over control of what counts as important knowledge in the curriculum can be seen in the discussion of whether anti-capitalist material and viewpoints have a place in schools, with the UK government making an unprecedented move to prevent schools from using teaching materials produced by groups which oppose or seek to critique capitalism (see DfE, 2020c). Partly in response to criticism of this position, further guidance was issued in 2022 (DfE, 2022) removing this prohibition while introducing extensive guidance to teachers and schools on how they should approach 'political' issues in their curriculum and classrooms.

In developing England's National Curriculum implemented from 2014, government ministers were particularly influenced by the 'core knowledge curriculum' of E.D. Hirsch (1988), an American scholar. This sets out a specified sequence of topics to teach in each subject and promises thereby to enhance both standards and opportunities. Incremental progression was anticipated based on the logic of each subject, research and experience of typical learning sequences and comparison with the ordering of knowledge in successful jurisdictions internationally. The policy was caricatured in terms of proposing 'regurgitation of facts – as in the 1950s'. In an extreme form, such subject specification does indeed risk constraining the capacity of teachers to respond to specific pupil needs through the exercise of professional judgement. On the other hand, there is no doubt that, as TLRP's Principle 2 states, 'effective pedagogy engages with valued forms of knowledge' (see Chapter 4). To do this successfully, expert teachers have to master the content of each subject and consider the learning challenges associated with that domain, but they must also understand the specific needs and circumstances of their pupils and feel empowered to use their expertise to design appropriate classroom tasks and activities.

> ### Reflective Activity 9.2
>
> *Aim:* To consider the influence of views of knowledge on a part of a national or school curriculum.
>
> *Evidence and reflection:* This is a potentially large activity which needs to be made specific to keep it within bounds. We suggest that national or school documentation for a *single* subject is selected for study – history or geography may be good choices.
>
> Consider, how is knowledge viewed? To what extent is it seen as an established body of subject content and skills to be transferred to learners, and to what extent is knowledge seen as something to be created through experiential engagement in tasks and activities? Are any viewpoints, events or values left out? What alternative views might there be on what should be included? Can you see opportunities for synergies between these approaches?
>
> *Extension:* Is this view of knowledge consistent with the aims and values of the curriculum that you investigated in **Reflective Activity 8.1**?

Across the United Kingdom, despite differences in national approach, there is some consistency in how subjects provide the organisational frameworks for national curriculum requirements and in particular core statutory requirements. At primary school level, English or Language and Literacy and Mathematics and/or Numeracy are central. Each jurisdiction requires some form of digital literacy, ICT, computing or 'Technologies', whether conceived as a curriculum subject or as a cross-curricular skill. Science is found as a discrete subject, or as part of 'The World Around Us' or paired with technology. Health and wellbeing or personal development and physical education all have their place, as does some form of religious or moral education. In England, Personal, Social, Health and Economic education (PSHE) is statutory but no curriculum is specified while Relationships Education does have a specified statutory curriculum at primary level. The humanities, expressive arts and languages complete the picture with variations in emphasis.

This however, as we will see in due course, says little about the ways in which the curriculum of a school or classroom can or

> ### Expert Question
>
> *Progression:* does the curriculum-as-delivered provide an appropriate sequence and depth of learning experiences?
>
> This question contributes to a conceptual framework underpinning professional expertise (see Chapter 16).

should actually be presented to pupils and many variations emerge at the level of practice (Alexander, 2008a, Reading 12.3). In practice some primary schools take a topic-based approach to the delivery of the curriculum (see Chapter 10, Planning, for more discussion of this) while others maintain the separation of traditional subjects.

Concepts

Concepts enable the most important ideas and deep structure of knowledge and understanding in each subject to be presented in concise ways. This avoids long lists of curriculum content which sometimes bedevil attempts to represent a subject domain, and which can seem overwhelming to both teachers and pupils.

For example, in 2012 the Geographical Association proposed a curriculum for schools based on 'thinking geographically'. As they put it:

> A few large, organising concepts underlie a geographical way of investigating and understanding the world. These are high level ideas that can be applied across the subject to identify a question, guide an investigation, organise information, suggest an explanation or assist decision making. They are the key ideas involved in framing the unique contribution of geography as a subject discipline. The three main organising concepts for geography are place, space and environment. There are further basic ideas in geography that run across this overarching framework, such as connection, inter-relation, scale and change. Using these ideas carefully and accurately is a key component of what we mean by thinking geographically. (Geographical Association, 2012)

Such 'big ideas' reveal the powerful analytic core of subject disciplines. The potential of concepts in designing curriculum provision was specifically identified by Schools Council projects during the 1970s and early 1980s. For example, Elliott (1976) made the case in terms of:

> *The information explosion* – which generates new facts at such a rate that it is futile to try to keep up. An alternative is thus to select facts to support conceptual development.
>
> *Concepts for learning* – for new situations are rarely entirely novel and we are able to use our store of conceptual understanding to interpret and make sense of new experiences.
>
> *Concepts as organisers* – because they 'provide a map of knowledge' which breaks down the randomness of experience and enable us to understand it.
>
> *Concepts as anchorage points* – in providing stability for exploration of the subject and enabling cumulative understanding by learners.

Alan Blyth was one of the first serious researchers on primary education. He emphasised the need to maintain the integrity of school subjects in the teaching of young children. This philosophy was realised through a number of curriculum development projects, with *Time, Place and Society 8–13* (Blyth, 1976) providing an outstanding example. In the case of this integrated humanities work, the key concepts were: communication; power; values and beliefs; conflict and consensus; continuity and change; similarity and difference; causes and consequences.

The work of the Association for Science Education provides another example. Their *Principles and Big Ideas of Science Education* (Harlen and Bell, 2010) provides a comprehensive conceptual framework for teaching science and for curricular provision throughout schooling.

And the arts are, arguably, even better prepared for a conceptually based curriculum through the legacy of analysis and connoisseurship which distinguishes quality. Music and art have conceptual languages accumulated over hundreds of years. In some cases, such powers of discrimination have been codified – as in the case of dance and movement where Rudolf Laban (1879–1958) developed an exceptional analysis based on the concepts of body, effort, shape and space.

Through the provision of a robust and valid framework of key concepts, it is thus possible to maintain the integrity of subjects and their parent disciplines in very concise ways. The subject associations, which are often sub-divided in relation to particular sectors, play an invaluable role here.

Beyond the significance of concepts as a useful device in curriculum planning and provision, they really earn their place because of their capacity to illuminate and render accessible the deep structure of subject knowledge. This point has been made by scholars focusing from early years and through to higher education. Thus Aubrey (1994), in a classic collection of papers on the role of subject knowledge in the early years of schooling, emphasised 'the ways in which subject knowledge is acquired and the organisation of teaching to promote the learner's construction of meaning'. Research in higher education, such as that by Entwistle (2009) has documented 'ways of thinking and practising in the subject' (WTPS) and the development of 'deep understanding' through making transparent the conceptual frameworks of each discipline. 'Threshold concepts', which unlock disciplinary understanding, have been identified, as have the barriers posed by forms of 'troublesome knowledge' (Land, Meyer and Smith, 2008).

Nor should we perhaps fail to notice that this book on reflective teaching is itself explicit in offering a set of principles (Chapter 4) and a conceptual framework (Chapter 16) in an attempt to support deep understanding of teaching. Whilst providing practical guidance on 'how to survive in the classroom', the book also aspires to support professional analysis and the development of expertise throughout a career.

Challenges remain however and there is not always a consensus in research on what the relevant concepts are that might illuminate and render accessible the deep structure of subject knowledge. For example, the Department for Education (DfE) has produced guidance in Mathematics on 'ready-to-progress criteria' based on the 'most important conceptual knowledge and understanding' (DfE, 2020a) but without a clear evidence base for the concepts selected.

Concepts then, to return to HMI's definition, enable learners to classify, organise and predict – and to understand patterns, relationships and meanings within subjects. They are epistemological tools in support of high-quality, authentic learning.

reflectiveteaching.co.uk/rtps6/part3_ch9

Skills

Put simply, a skill is 'the capacity or competence to perform a task' (HMI, 1985, p. 38), but in the context of curriculum planning use of the term has become more complex. Several uses can be identified:

'Physical skills' normally refers to bodily coordination such as running, catching etc., and to fine motor skills such as writing, sewing, drawing or typing,

'Basic skills' usually refers to communication, literacy and numeracy, and sometimes includes the use of technology.

'Personal skills' is the most fundamental and typically includes capabilities such as self-awareness, reflection, thinking and problem solving; as well as interpersonal awareness, cooperation and leadership with others. 'Thinking skills' are discussed in Chapter 2.

'Study skills' tends to be a specific set of capabilities focused on managing one's own learning, such as observing, interpreting, classifying, memorising, prioritising.

'Subject skills' highlights particular capabilities required for learning in subject domains, such as mapping in geography, experimenting in science and empathising in drama.

Although skills identified in these classifications often overlap, the salient point is that there are sets of capabilities which complement and extend a curriculum that is expressed in terms of subject knowledge. An innovative project on this is that of *Opening Minds* promoted by the Royal Society of Arts (2013). This competence framework focused on citizenship, learning, relating to people, managing situations and managing information and 'emphasises the ability to understand and to do, rather than just the transmission of knowledge'.

One way of thinking about this is in terms of a classic distinction between declarative knowledge and procedural knowledge. If the former sets out that which is known, the latter describes how it is developed and used. This distinction between 'knowing that' and 'knowing how' was drawn by Gilbert Ryle (1945). His argument asserts the significance of skills, procedures and learning activities in the development of knowledge. He also shows how, in terms of moving beyond the dry recitation of facts towards application and relevance to life, capabilities to apply knowledge are vital. There is no doubt, then, that skills provide a distinct and valuable element of curriculum provision. Any gaps may affect the skills children leave the primary school with, as for example in the reduced emphasis on oral language skills in England's 2014 primary curriculum in comparison with earlier versions and when viewed internationally (Wyse and Anders, 2019).

However, as we have seen, bodies of knowledge and associated conceptual tools represent the accumulated understanding of our societies and therefore demand attention. Skills alone are unlikely to justify presentation as a complete curriculum. But skills add enormous value to engagement with subjects. Indeed, they support the development of subject knowledge, are realised through it and contribute to its transfer and application into practice.

reflectiveteaching.co.uk/rtps6/part3_ch9

Chapter 9 Curriculum

281

Systematic and embedded provision for skill development is thus a vital element of learning within any curriculum. It is often planned for and reviewed in cross-curricular terms, and such provision can be made at classroom, school or national levels – and most helpfully at all three.

When the National Curriculum was first introduced in England, the National Curriculum Council (NCC) published guidance on *The Whole Curriculum* (NCC, 1990) which drew teachers' attention to cross-curricular dimensions, skills and themes. Scotland's *Curriculum for Excellence* also provides a carefully developed skills framework offering 'Skills for Learning, Skills for Life and Skills for Work' (Scottish Government, 2009). Figure 9.2 illustrates the four 'capacities' which have been conceptualised and prioritised in Scotland. There is strong emphasis on the responsibilities of *all* educators to support such learning through all sectors and a framework of National Qualifications offers accreditation.

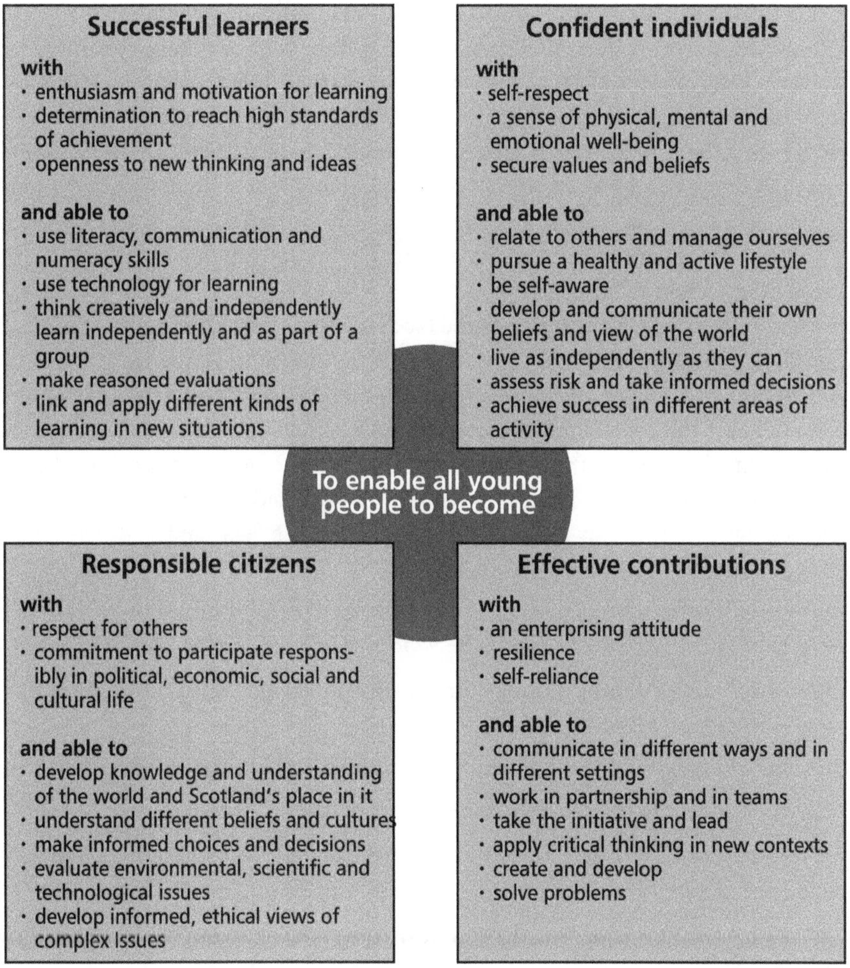

Figure 9.2 The four capacities of Scotland's *Curriculum for Excellence*

Successful learners

with
- enthusiasm and motivation for learning
- determination to reach high standards of achievement
- openness to new thinking and ideas

and able to
- use literacy, communication and numeracy skills
- use technology for learning
- think creatively and independently
- learn independently and as part of a group
- make reasoned evaluations
- link and apply different kinds of learning in new situations

Confident individuals

with
- self-respect
- a sense of physical, mental and emotional well-being
- secure values and beliefs

and able to
- relate to others and manage ourselves
- pursue a healthy and active lifestyle
- be self-aware
- develop and communicate their own beliefs and view of the world
- live as independently as they can
- assess risk and take informed decisions
- achieve success in different areas of activity

To enable all young people to become

Responsible citizens

with
- respect for others
- commitment to participate responsibly in political, economic, social and cultural life

and able to
- develop knowledge and understanding of the world and Scotland's place in it
- understand different beliefs and cultures
- make informed choices and decisions
- evaluate environmental, scientific and technological issues
- develop informed, ethical views of complex Issues

Effective contributions

with
- an enterprising attitude
- resilience
- self-reliance

and able to
- communicate in different ways and in different settings
- work in partnership and in teams
- take the initiative and lead
- apply critical thinking in new contexts
- create and develop
- solve problems

reflectiveteaching.co.uk/rtps6/part3_ch9

Attitudes

Attitudes were regarded by HMI as 'the overt expression, in a variety of situations, of values and personal qualities' (1985, p. 41). Examples given were honesty, reliability, initiative, self-discipline and tolerance which 'may be encouraged in the formal curriculum and the informal, and in the general life of the school'. Clearly, this affirms the significance of the 'hidden curriculum' to which we drew attention at the beginning of this chapter. Indeed, the process of induction of the young into the values of their society has always been one of the classic roles of schools. Important additions might include resilience and the sorts of positive mindsets that would provide a foundation for good mental health. The Northern Irish curriculum lists seventeen 'attitudes and dispositions' it seeks to foster, including 'moral courage', integrity, optimism and curiosity (CCEA, 2007).

Citizenship, attitudes to physical and mental health, sex and relationships education, exercise and diet are all important, and pressure has grown for schools to introduce children and young people to issues concerning environmental sustainability. Specific values and priorities thus reflect particular social, cultural and economic priorities. Over the years of a teacher's career, these will ebb and flow with changing governments and social norms. They may also vary depending on the particular circumstances and ambitions of the communities which a school serves, thus enabling local variation.

This brings us back to the issues raised in Chapter 2, p. 58). There, we saw how culture and language frame the interpretation of experience, and how attitudes are influenced by family, community, peers, school and the media. The overall effect is that children and young people form, or are socialised into adopting, attitudes which reflect the influence of significant others in their lives.

HMI also emphasised that schools should 'seek to promote positive attitudes through the attention they give to content and method' (1985, p. 41). Here we begin to focus on the educational issues which, in contemporary terms, might be termed 'dispositions to learn'. There is, after all, probably nothing more important for lifelong learning than the confidence of learners in tackling new learning challenges. In Chapter 2, again, we saw how important it is for learners to believe in their potential to learn and to improve – to adopt an 'incremental' theory of their own capability, as Dweck (1986, Reading 2.6) put it (see p. 56).

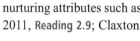

Claxton has cogently argued that it is possible to 'build learning power' in schools by nurturing attributes such as resilience, resourcefulness, reflection and reciprocity (Claxton, 2011, Reading 2.9; Claxton et al., 2011). As he puts it:

- *Resilience* covers aspects of the learner's emotional and experiential engagement with the subject matter of learning.
- *Resourcefulness* embraces the main cognitive skills and dispositions of learning.
- *Reciprocity* covers the social and interpersonal side of learning.
- *Reflectiveness* covers the strategic and self-managing sides of learning. (Claxton et al., 2011, p. 40)

Through such careful attention to learning itself, a 'supple learning mind' can be created (see Figure 9.3).

Reflectiveness

- Planning: working learning out in advance
- Revising: monitoring and adapting along the way
- Distilling: drawing out the lessons from experience
- Meta-learning: understanding learning, and yourself as a learner

Reciprocity

- Interdependence: balancing self-reliance and sociability
- Collaboration: the skills of learning with others
- Listening/Empathy: getting inside others' minds
- Imitation: picking up others' habits and values

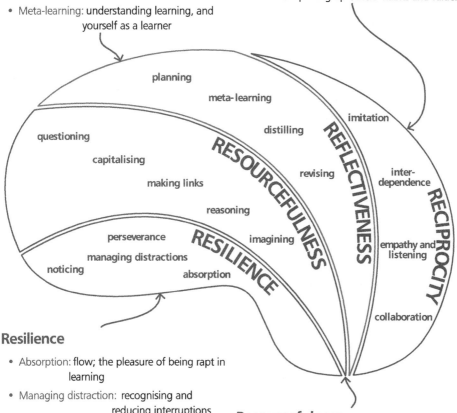

Figure 9.3 The supple learning mind (adapted from Claxton et al., 2011)

Resilience

- Absorption: flow; the pleasure of being rapt in learning
- Managing distraction: recognising and reducing interruptions
- Noticing: really sensing what's out there
- Perseverance: stickability; tolerating the feelings of learning

Resourcefulness

- Questioning: getting below the surface; playing with situations
- Making links: seeking coherence, relevance and meaning
- Imagining: using the mind's eye as a learning theatre
- Reasoning: thinking rigorously and methodically
- Capitalising: making good use of resources

reflectiveteaching.co.uk/rtps6/part3_ch9

> **Expert Question**
>
> **Engagement:** *do our teaching strategies, classroom organisation and consultation enable learners to actively participate in and enjoy their learning?*
>
> This question contributes to a conceptual framework underpinning professional expertise (see Chapter 16).

These attributes are closely associated with 'learning how to learn' (James et al., 2007, Reading 2.8) and are viewed by many as being essential for learning in the twenty-first century. For example, the *2020 Vision* report for the DfES in England (Teaching and Learning Review Group, 2006, Reading 10.7) anticipated the necessary characteristics of future teaching and aspired to 'design a new school experience'. Key elements were identified as assessment for learning, learning how to learn, pupil voice and engaging parents and carers in their children's education. Underpinning all this was a commitment to pupil engagement in a meaningful curriculum and authentic learning for life.

A balanced curriculum

The analytic power of the distinction between knowledge, concepts, skills and attitudes is particularly useful in curriculum design. A rounded curriculum will provide balance between them, ensuring that each has its place, and taking care to consider the age of the children. This is important for those who frame national curricular frameworks, but it is also an enormous help in the creation of the School Curriculum and in terms of classroom provision.

Reflective Activity 9.3 suggests a way of mapping the elements of learning within an area of curriculum provision.

> **Reflective Activity 9.3**
>
> *Aim:* To consider knowledge, concepts, skills and attitudes in schemes of work.
>
> *Method:* Select topics within a programme of study in a subject area. Working on your own or preferably with a colleague, identify and list the knowledge, concepts, skills and attitudes which are targeted for development.
>
> | TOPICS | Knowledge | Concepts | Skills | Attitudes |
> |---|---|---|---|---|
> | | | | | |
> | | | | | |
> | | | | | |
> | | | | | |
>
> *Follow-up:* How easy was it to identify elements in the four categories? Which were explicit, and which implicit?
>
> Has the activity led you to refine or extend your plans? How could the framework be used to take stock of pupil learning in your classroom?

From March 2020 the global pandemic led to long periods of school closure and the swift implementation of some form of online learning for most pupils. The impact of periods of lost learning has been that sections of the planned curriculum have been left unaddressed and there are gaps in children's developing knowledge and skills. In England, the DfE published guidance recognising that schools would need to modify their curricula 'substantially', emphasising the need to maintain a 'broad and balanced' curriculum as work is done to address these gaps (DfE, 2021b). The idea of key concepts is employed with schools asked to prioritise 'content' on which later learning depends.

The specification of a National Curriculum raises the question: 'Whose curriculum is it?' Any curriculum reflects values, views of knowledge and of learning. Reflective teachers will recognise that dominant opinions and influence can change over time and that they are not always clear-cut or coherent. Ambiguities and dissonances within and between the different agencies that govern education are also commonplace. Where teachers have views on such matters, perhaps based on study, experience, evidence and reflection, to make their voices heard in educational debates is a valuable professional contribution. Subject, phase or other professional associations are important vehicles for this.

NATIONAL CURRICULA

Structured national curricula have many attractions. For example:

> *Aims and objectives* for each stage of education can clarify what both pupils and teachers are expected to do (see p. 271 above).

> *Curriculum breadth and balance* can be considered 'as a whole' (see Chapter 10) and **Case Study 9.1** on p. 286.

> *Curriculum progression and continuity* can be planned and monitored both from class to class and on transfer between schools (see also Chapter 10).

> *Training and professional development* programmes for teachers can be tailored to known National Curriculum needs (see Chapter 17).

> *Resources* for teaching and learning programmes can be developed on a large scale and in organised, cost-effective ways (see Chapter 8).

> *Assessment and inspection* systems can be used to reinforce intentions (see Chapter 14).

> *Parents, employers and other stakeholders* have the opportunity to know and understand what is being taught and may be able to offer support more effectively (see Chapter 5).

> *Coherence, alignment* and improvement of the system as a whole can be developed through evaluation processes, research and refinement (see Chapter 4).

Expert Question

Balance: does the curriculum-as-experienced offer everything which each learner has a right to expect?

This question contributes to a conceptual framework underpinning professional expertise (see Chapter 16).

---

reflectiveteaching.co.uk/rtps6/part3_ch9

Part 3 Teaching for learning

However, there are a number of dilemmas in the design of national curricula. For example, how should the value of coherence and progression in subject knowledge be compared with the benefits of applied understanding through more integrated study or work focused on particular topics? How should the need to induct children into established bodies of disciplinary knowledge be balanced with the development of skills, including skills that support future learning? How can a National Curriculum framework guarantee curricular entitlements and guide the work of teachers whilst also enabling them to exercise professional judgement when responding to particular learning needs?

These questions illustrate the challenge posed by two of TLRP's principles. Effective teaching and learning 'engages with valued forms of knowledge' (Principle 2), but it also 'recognises the importance of prior experience and learning' (Principle 3) (see Chapter 4). The challenge of achieving a balanced curriculum is considerable, as a 2017 report by England's Chief Inspector of Schools made clear – see Case Study 9.1.

Case Study 9.1 'Balancing the Curriculum' (HMCI, 2017)

This text is extracted from a report by Amanda Spielman, the Chief Inspector of Schools in England. She was concerned that 'balance' in pupil learning experiences was being lost as the 2014 National Curriculum was implemented.

At the very heart of education sits the vast accumulated wealth of human knowledge and what we choose to impart to the next generation: the curriculum.

Balance is the constant challenge when schools plan. Choices need to be made about what to do when, how much depth to pursue, which ideas to link together, what resources to draw on, which way to teach, and how to make sure all pupils are able to benefit as each new concept, construct or fact is taught.

Most importantly, these decisions must be rooted in a solid consensus about what education should deliver for each pupil. What is the body of knowledge that a child needs so that they will flourish in the future and not be left behind?

There need be no tension between success on exams and tests and a good curriculum. Quite the opposite. A good curriculum should lead to good results. However, good examination results in and of themselves don't always mean that the pupil received rich and full knowledge from the curriculum. In the worst cases, teaching to the test, rather than teaching the full curriculum, leaves a pupil with a hollowed out and flimsy understanding.

Earlier this year, I commissioned a research programme to broaden our understanding of how curriculums are implemented in our schools. From first phase of the review, a striking conclusion is that there is little debate or reflection about the curriculum. Apart from the timetable, there was an absence of other tangible reference points to get to grips with the complex business of curriculum planning. It was evident that there is a lack of clarity around the language of the curriculum.

For example, the idea of 'skills' was liberally used in many contexts. Very rarely was it clear whether the meaning was subject-specific, for example reading skills. Other

---

reflectiveteaching.co.uk/rtps6/part3_ch9

uses included personal skills, such as the ability to work in a team, cognitive skills, such as critical thinking, or life skills, such as how to pay a bill or apply for a job. There were many other examples of terms where the meaning was woolly, such as progression, enrichment, questioning and repetition.

It is certainly possible that this ambiguity and lack of shared understanding expose competing notions of what curriculum means across the sector. However, the most likely explanation is that this arises from a weak theoretical understanding of curriculum. This was confirmed by school leaders, who said that there was a time when teachers were taught the theory that underpins curriculum planning. Over time, this competence across the sector ebbed away.

We have seen three important consequences of a reduced understanding of curriculum.

First, the primary curriculum is narrowing in some schools as a consequence of too great a focus on preparing for Key Stage 2 tests.

Second, school leaders have often misunderstood the purpose of Key Stage 3 and GCSE assessment criteria.

And third, the intended curriculum for lower-attaining pupils in some secondary schools is often associated with the qualifications that count in league tables but not with other knowledge they should be acquiring.

The challenge is deep. There is a serious risk of schools not fulfilling the promise and potential of the 2014 national curriculum or of academies not using their freedoms to achieve the same. School leaders need to recognise how easy it is to focus on the performance of the school and lose sight of the pupil. I acknowledge that inspection may well have helped to tip this balance in the past.

While the renewed attention to 'theoretical understanding' of curriculum in Spielman's report was welcome, the obvious omission from the account was that Ofsted itself had been partly responsible, for some years, for the lack of consideration of the whole curriculum due to its focus on 'the basics' of English and mathematics, and in particular school outcomes in statutory tests in these subjects. What's more, Spielman's views, which included suggested models for knowledge in schools' thinking about whole curriculum, were not informed by pupil-centred models (see bera.ac.uk/blog/what-next-for-curriculum).

UK curricular structures

Primary education

In the Early Years, national curricula emphasise children's development over curriculum content. Communication skills, physical development, and social and emotional development are central. These are complemented by a growing knowledge of and exploration of the world: the physical world, and shared cultural artefacts such as number, shape, space and music.

In primary education, there is some stability and similarity in UK systems – as there is around the world (Meyer and Kamens, 1992; DfE, 2011a). Subject areas and cross-curricular skills show remarkable consistency. In each country, the primacy of 'basic capability' in literacy and numeracy is emphasised. However, this is done in interestingly different ways.

In England's primary provision from 2014, exceptional priority was given by the Coalition Government to English, mathematics and science (deemed 'core subjects' and the focus of detailed, year-by-year programmes of study). 'Other foundation' subjects remain statutory but have very condensed content coverage and minimal assessment requirements. Whilst the core subjects are felt to be essential for future learning and work, other subjects are seen as contributing to a broad and balanced curriculum. Assessment and inspection arrangements reinforce this impression. However, the minimalist specifications for foundation subjects are intended to remove constraint from teachers and thus enable innovation. Official programmes of study are mainly concerned with knowledge and, to a lesser extent, with concepts. They almost exclusively leave consideration of subject-related and cross-curricular skills and attitudes to teachers. In principle, a unique 'school curriculum' can be constructed. However, each school must publish its curriculum on a year-by-year basis.

In Wales, from September 2022, primary schools will be responsible for their own curricula working within the Curriculum for Wales guidance (Education Wales, 2020). This highlights literacy, numeracy and digital competence as mandatory cross-curricular skills. Learning is organised into six areas such as expressive arts, science and technology and language, literacy and communication. Rather than provide detailed specifications of what should be taught in each area there is a more limited list of 'statements of what matters' in each area.

In Northern Ireland's primary curriculum, subjects are also set aside in favour of six 'areas of learning', and teachers are encouraged to 'integrate learning across the six areas to make relevant connections for children' (CCEA, 2007). *Gaeloideachas Primary Irish* and 'Aspects of Shared Cultural Heritage' is gaining impetus through new projects from 2016. Cross-curricular skills, thinking skills and personal capabilities are emphasised. Guidance is offered on broad approaches to teaching and 'ideas for connecting learning'. Thus, for example: 'Children learn best when learning is interactive, practical and enjoyable. Teachers should make use of a wide range of teaching methods, balancing whole-class, group and individual activities, to engage children in effective learning' (CCEA, 2007, p. 9).

Integrated approaches are also encouraged in Scotland's primary education, where the *Curriculum for Excellence* (CfE) has been carefully built around the aspiration that learners from 3 to 18 should achieve the 'four capacities' of 'successful learners', 'confident individuals', 'responsible citizens' and 'effective contributors' (see Figure 9.2). Eight 'curriculum areas' then structure programmes of expected 'experiences' and required 'outcomes' and reflect explicit consideration of the contribution of each area to the four

reflectiveteaching.co.uk/rtps6/part3_ch9

overall curricular purposes (see Scottish Government, 2006). Subjects are recognised as 'an essential feature of the curriculum, particularly in secondary school', but schools 'have the freedom to think imaginatively about how the experiences and outcomes might be organised and planned for in creative ways which encourage deep, sustained learning and which meet the needs of their children and young people' (Scottish Government, 2008). A 'refreshed narrative' on the CfE (Education Scotland, 2019) sought to make a more coherent overview of the curriculum while reviews of the CfE have suggested that the place of knowledge with respect to the capacities the curriculum aims to develop might be made clearer (OECD, 2015). In 2021 the OECD produced another report that, while recognising strengths in the CfE, also noted some areas for improvement, for example in relation to 'a common base of knowledge and skills' (OECD, 2021), a recommendation that could of course be in conflict with ideas such as a learner-centred curriculum which was explicitly built into the CfE.

In summary, within the UK's primary schools there are both similarities and differences in the particular curricular structures and requirements of each country, and these vary too over time, with digital competencies being a case in point. Whichever sector, country or area you work or study in, the important thing to note is that curriculum arrangements are social constructions. Although they may seem 'set in stone', they actually do change and teachers are likely to see quite a few in the course of a career. Whilst they reflect the history, culture, ideologies and political context of their construction, the basic elements of learning (knowledge, concepts, skills and attitudes) endure.

Teaching, learning and national curricula

TLRP's third principle states that: 'Effective teaching and learning recognises the importance of prior experience and learning'.

This poses a significant dilemma for highly structured national curricula: how can a specified curriculum, at one and the same time, set out a specific framework for required content and progression and yet remain flexible enough to draw on the interests, experiences, approaches to learning and physical and intellectual capabilities of individual children? Is there a risk that some pupils will feel excluded by the specified content? And how, if content is too specified, can innovation occur?

As we have seen, England's 2011 National Curriculum Review produced a tight specification of the core curriculum in terms of both content and structure. Detailed, year-on-year programmes of study were set out for core subjects building on the ideas of E.D. Hirsch (1988). To a large extent then, the curriculum for schools was placed in a linear form within core subjects – and this was, of course, backed up by formal assessment procedures.

There are several disadvantages in this approach. First, psychologists such as Bruner (1977, see Reading 9.5) suggest that children can learn most things at *most* ages if they are taught in meaningful ways and revisited at more advanced stages – thus coining the term 'spiral curriculum'. Some children, then, may experience and become interested in things which a linear National Curriculum does not anticipate – and teachers may feel constrained in following up those interests. Perhaps indeed, children's learning is driven by developmental considerations (e.g. Katz 1998; Pollard and Triggs, 2000) which subject-based national curricula may lack the flexibility to accommodate. Second, we now know that learners do not often acquire understanding in a simple, linear way, with a step-by-step progression (Gagné, 1965), as some behaviourist psychology might have had us believe. Other learning theorists, influenced by Vygotsky (see Chapter 2, p. 44, Reading 2.3) suggest that children learn when they are able to 'make sense' of some experience, particularly when they have an imaginative insight or are supported by more experienced or knowledgeable teachers, parents or peers (Tharp and Gallimore, 1988, Reading 11.4).

Nor do subject specialists suggest progression through a particular sequence of substantive knowledge without considerable flexibility. Building also on psychological understanding, the recommendation is that a curriculum specification should leave sufficient flexibility to enable teachers to use their judgement in support of *conceptual* development and application. Ernest made the point particularly clearly over thirty years ago in relation to mathematics. He wrote:

> One of the greatest dangers in stipulating a statutory curriculum in mathematics at (several) levels of attainment is that it becomes a barrier which may deny a youngster access to higher concepts and skills when he or she is ready for them. . . . The major flaw in this scheme (is) the mistaken assumption that children's learning in mathematics follows a fixed hierarchical pattern. . . . This is nonsense. (Ernest, 1991, p. 50)

Expert Questions

Breadth: *does the curriculum represent society's educational aspirations for its citizens?*

Balance: *does the curriculum-as-experienced offer everything which each learner has a right to expect?*

These questions contribute to a conceptual framework underpinning professional expertise (see Chapter 16).

The over-riding message is perhaps that learning is not always predictable or linear, and any curriculum that diminishes the opportunity for teachers to respond to pupil needs is less likely to promote meaningful learning.

At the classroom level, talking with pupils goes a long way in resolving this dilemma. Children and young people are perfectly capable of accepting that there is nationally expected curriculum coverage, but will welcome teacher efforts to make appropriate connections with their prior knowledge, emergent understanding and their experience. This is the only way through which a curriculum can, operationally, 'make sense' to learners.

Subject-based and integrated curricula

A subject-based curriculum is one which maintains high boundaries, distinction and specialisation between subjects. The resulting curriculum has been seen as being typical of secondary education. It has been called a 'collection curriculum' (Bernstein, 1971) because the learner acquires their overall education through the accumulation of understanding in different domains. Progression within each separate subject is intended

reflectiveteaching.co.uk/rtps6/part3_ch9

to be strong, though coherence of learning across subjects may be weaker. 'Cross-curricular themes' are often used to forge lateral links, but tend to be hard to sustain.

An integrated curriculum, on the other hand, is one which draws across subject boundaries to construct a more holistic and, it is hoped, meaningful focus for study (Turner-Bisset, 2000, Reading 10.3). For many years, this approach has been associated with primary education and, in particular, with provision for younger children. 'Topic work' is one classic manifestation and another rationale reflects beliefs about the value of 'play' itself (Central Advisory Council on Education (CACE), 1967, Reading 9.4).

To read a more extended discussion, including Pollard's resignation from a government role on this issue, see the supplementary material for Chapter 9 on reflectiveteaching.co.uk or the record made by Mary James (bera.ac.uk/bera-in-the-news/background-to-michael-goves-response-to-the-report-of-the-expert-panel-for-the-national-curriculum-review-in-england).

Arguments for the desirability of an integrated curriculum include the suggestion that the curriculum must draw on authentic pupil experiences (rather than 'artificial' subjects) if effective learning is to take place. A second argument proposes that a higher priority can be given to generic processes, key skills and attitudes if the emphasis on subject knowledge is lessened.

However, caricatures of differences between primary and secondary education do not stand, for there are many examples of exceptional integrated work in secondary education, and of skilful subject teaching in primary schools. Indeed, this is once again an example of an educational dilemma in which both positions have some merit. It is not surprising, therefore, that the best schools find ways of drawing on the strengths of each approach, with particular care given to supporting children during transitions where a change of emphasis in the curriculum is experienced, such as between early years settings and the primary school. The same principle can be applied at a classroom level by varying the ways in which curricular activity is presented to pupils.

The need for breadth in curriculum, to provide a range of learning experience, is well established. There has been a particular tendency in England for political concern to 'raise standards' in core subjects to drive out opportunities for quality engagement with languages, the arts and humanities.

And so we learn that, to offer an effective educational experience, the 'basics' have to be balanced with other curricular areas in responsive ways (see Chapter 10 for discussion of the principles of curriculum planning).

> **Expert Question**
>
> **Personalisation:** *does the curriculum resonate with the social and cultural needs of diverse learners and provide appropriate elements of choice?*
>
> This question contributes to a conceptual framework underpinning professional expertise (see Chapter 16).

The same dilemmas are faced in Scotland, Wales and Northern Ireland and, indeed, the Republic of Ireland, but at the time of writing government requirements are significantly less prescriptive than in England. Creative teachers in any setting will use their expertise to present the curriculum to pupils in meaningful ways. In so doing, the advantages and disadvantages of focusing on particular subjects or on integrating knowledge across them always has to be weighed. There are good arguments for both.

reflectiveteaching.co.uk/rtps6/part3_ch9

SUBJECT KNOWLEDGE FOR TEACHERS

Teachers with good subject knowledge are able to make more secure judgements about the *appropriate* teaching of knowledge, concepts, skills and attitudes. Indeed, international research studies such as the meta-analysis of Hattie (2009, Reading 4.6) suggest that the subject knowledge of teachers is an extremely important influence on pupil attainment. At primary level a challenge for teachers is having secure knowledge across a range of subjects. Perhaps the importance of subject knowledge is not surprising, but simply having a lot of specialist knowledge is *not* sufficient for effective teaching.

The most influential analysis of subject knowledge in education was provided by Shulman (1986, Reading 9.7). He identified three forms of subject knowledge:

- *Content knowledge* – knowledge of the subject held by the teacher.
- *Pedagogic content knowledge* – knowledge of how to use content knowledge for teaching purposes.
- *Curricular knowledge* – knowledge of curriculum structures and materials.

Content knowledge

Content knowledge refers to the kind of knowledge that teachers gain from their own schooling, university and college courses or from personal research and interest. It can be thought of as having two aspects, as defined by Schwab (1978):

- A foundational understanding of facts, concepts and principles of a subject and the way in which they are organised, and,
- Knowledge about why such knowledge is deemed important and is justified.

Knowledge of the social structure of Tudor England and of how various political influences affected the lives of people during this period would be an example of the former, while knowing how this knowledge has been arrived at through the use of primary and secondary evidence and an understanding of the relative validity of such evidence would be an example of the latter.

When planning for pupil learning, primary school teachers must draw on their knowledge of facts, concepts and principles from across all the subjects they teach as well as understanding the subject-specific processes through which these have been arrived at and how they can be justified – the main curricular challenge is one of breadth. The quote below from a reception teacher demonstrates how she drew on knowledge she had gained during her initial teacher education course when planning a lesson on counting:

> When I was planning this lesson I drew on my knowledge of the pre-requisites for counting: knowing the number names in order, one to one correspondence, the cardinal principle, being able to count objects that cannot be moved/touched and counting

reflectiveteaching.co.uk/rtps6/part3_ch9

objects that cannot be seen, e.g. sounds or beats. These developmental stages formed the progression and structure to the lesson.

Such knowledge is not always accessible from memory, and the reflective teacher will seek to refresh and develop their knowledge of topics before planning and teaching. For example, when planning to teach a topic on 'Egypt', one might research both ancient and modern Egypt, drawing on geographical and historical resources. Such sources might include schemes of work, textbooks, a library or the internet. Topics such as this may only be taught annually or even bi-annually and committed teachers will refresh and develop their subject knowledge each time they occur in order to invigorate their own interest and pass on enthusiasm to pupils. Subject leads can play an important role in supporting primary teachers' subject knowledge, developing and sharing a greater depth of knowledge in their subject, and drawing on support from subject associations.

To be a successful teacher of a subject requires two sorts of knowing – knowing the subject 'inside out' *and* knowing how best to present it so that it can be learned.

Pedagogical content knowledge

Pedagogical content knowledge is Shulman's (1986, Reading 9.7) second form of subject knowledge, which he described as 'subject matter knowledge *for teaching*'. It does not simply reflect understanding of a subject, or even of how to teach. Rather, it is knowledge of *how to combine both* in relation to a particular domain. It is thus a specific category of teacher knowledge and primary teachers must develop it across a range of different domains or subjects.

Teachers draw on their pedagogical content knowledge when deciding how they will introduce a new idea or develop pupils' knowledge or skills in relation to a specific aspect of a subject. For example, when teaching the scientific topic of 'our solar system', a primary teacher might decide to represent the sun and planets with different sized spheres and to take pupils out onto the school field in order to demonstrate the relative distances between objects in the solar system. When teaching about life in Victorian times, a teacher might borrow domestic artefacts from a local Victorian collection and ask pupils to consider for what purpose they were used. These teachers would not only have drawn on their knowledge of the subject matter and on their general knowledge of how children of a particular age learn; they would also have drawn on knowledge of how children learn in the particular subject. In science, much use is made of analogies since it is not always possible to demonstrate concepts concretely. Artefacts are often used for historical topics when trying to help children understand how people lived in earlier times.

Teaching another person what you know thus involves finding ways of *representing* subject matter to assist their learning, as well as being aware of the new representations that are subsequently developed. Our earlier discussion of concepts as significant elements of learning (see p. 278) resonates here. Shulman highlights new conceptual developments as 'transformations'. These transformations take many forms and are:

The most powerful analogies, illustrations, examples, explanations and demonstrations – in a word, the ways of representing and formulating the subject that make it comprehensible to others. (1986, p. 9)

With experience, teachers develop a 'representational repertoire' for the subject they teach which may itself enrich and extend their own subject understanding – it is a truism that a good way to understand something is to try to teach it. This repertoire is part of the result of 'thinking like a teacher' about a subject and is, of course, significantly helped by the teacher's own conceptual understanding. In any one lesson a teacher may use a number of different strategies of this kind. The successes and failures of our transformations in making learning meaningful for our pupils, individually and as a group, add to our knowledge – of the subject and of how it may be learned, in particular of subject-specific difficulties which pupils experience. Reflective Activity 9.4 is designed to help think about this.

Reflective Activity 9.4

Aim: To consider the idea of *transformations* when preparing to teach.

Method: For a particular lesson or series of lessons focus specifically on what you know about the content and what you want your pupils to learn about the content. If teaching materials are prescribed, review them in the light of your understanding of the subject matter.

How do you represent your personal understanding of this content? How might you make it meaningful for your pupils? Consider some ways in which you might *transform* the content. How might you introduce ideas/concepts/principles? How can you best move pupils from what is known or familiar to new knowledge? Are there any strategies, activities or tasks which seem particularly appropriate? What makes you think they will work? Are there parts of the learning where pupils may misunderstand or be misled? How might you avoid this? What language will you use? How will you approach any subject-specialist language?

If possible, discuss your ideas for *transformations* with another teacher or student teacher.

Follow-up: Teach the lesson and try out your *transformations*. How did they work? Is there anything from the lesson that you will to add to your representational repertoire?

Curricular knowledge

'Curricular knowledge' is Shulman's third form of teacher knowledge and perhaps the simplest. It relates to: programmes of study, syllabi, schemes of work, resources, technologies and instructional materials through which curricular objectives may be realised. The selection of such material is often structured by school policies, but rests on teacher judgement in respect of more specific activities and lessons. As teachers move between schools they may encounter different curricula and need to update their curricular knowledge so the ability to engage with these documents and to reflect on them using the ideas discussed above is important.

For most teachers, curricular knowledge is much easier to acquire than content knowledge or pedagogic content knowledge. Indeed, some would argue that, whilst curricular knowledge can be obtained from textbooks, the internet, or from school and National Curriculum documentation, the acquisition of content knowledge calls for sustained study and pedagogical content knowledge requires extensive experience and reflection.

Whilst there may be some truth in this view, confidence is enhanced by being clear about the nature of the expertise being developed. The elegance of Shulman's categorisation may help in this respect. In particular, for the reflective teacher, it should be possible to analyse the nature of the subject knowledge which one has in relation to the role one is required to fulfil. If there are discrepancies, then the new challenges can be faced.

> ## Expert Question
>
> **Coherence:** *is there clarity in the purposes, content and organisation of the curriculum and does it provide holistic learning experiences?*
>
> This question contributes to a conceptual framework underpinning professional expertise (see Chapter 16).

Applying subject knowledge

As we have seen, having decided what it is that pupils should learn, the reflective teacher draws on their subject matter knowledge and their pedagogical content knowledge in relation to a particular group of pupils in order to decide what they need to do in a lesson.

For example, when teaching the skill of overarm throwing, the teacher must be sure of what this involves – subject matter knowledge. They might decide that the best way to teach this would be by demonstrating it themselves before asking pupils to practise – pedagogical content knowledge. They will certainly want their pupils to try overarm throwing for themselves rather than just reading about it or watching a teacher demonstration since their syntactic knowledge of PE informs them that physical action is necessary for learning in this subject. The reflective teacher will consider the difficulty that some pupils might have with this and perhaps break the movement down into smaller actions for some pupils to practise – knowledge of pupils. Therefore, in order to decide what they need to do and what their pupils need to do in order to learn how to throw overarm, the reflective teacher draws on a number of categories of knowledge for teaching.

Pedagogical content knowledge might be considered to be the key to effective teaching and the reflective teacher will give careful consideration to how they 'represent and formulate the subject to make it comprehensible to others'. In the teaching of mathematics, the choice of examples (Watson and Mason, 2005), the use of representations (Drews and Hansen, 2007) and the making of connections (Askew et al., 1997) have all been found to be important aspects of pedagogical content knowledge. Teaching for mastery approaches emphasise the importance of variation in how concepts are presented and in how exercises

reflectiveteaching.co.uk/rtps6/part3_ch9

are sequenced in supporting pupils to see mathematical 'relationships and structure' (NCETM, 2017).

More generally, experienced teachers with thorough subject knowledge have been found to be more likely to adapt and modify textbooks and other published materials where they find the organisation of content and the representations of concepts unsatisfactory (Hashweh, 1987). Teachers with deep subject knowledge are also more likely to identify where learners might misunderstand, to recognise dawning insights and to see where connections might be made within the subject and with other subject areas.

Rowland et al. (2009) formalised this understanding through the development of what they call a 'knowledge quartet'. Their framework has its empirical origins in observations of trainee and beginning teachers teaching mathematics (Rowland et al., 2009). The 'quartet' highlights four aspects of subject knowledge.

Foundation – content knowledge in substantive and syntactic forms, which enables and circumscribes the available teaching repertoire.

Transformation – the capacity to re-present content knowledge in ways that are pedagogically powerful, as described above.

Connection – the expert teacher's awareness of the structures and sequencing of knowledge, so that particular elements can be related to a more holistic understanding.

Contingency – the teacher's capacity to respond to classroom events and pupil actions in ways which, though unexpected, still build towards understanding.

This work on mathematical content knowledge found that trainee and beginning teachers did not always use the most appropriate representations in their teaching and did not always make connections that would support the mathematical understanding of their pupils. However, when helped to reflect on the mathematical content of their teaching using the knowledge quartet framework as a tool, teachers often identified such limitations in their practice and suggested how they might make improvements (Turner, 2009).

Lesson Study 9.1 demonstrates each of the four aspects of the 'knowledge quartet' – content knowledge, transformational judgement, awareness of how to achieve connections between subject knowledge and children's understanding, and capacity to respond flexibly in purposive ways. It illustrates thoughtful teachers collecting and analysing evidence of their own practice to seek improvement in an area of curricular provision.

reflectiveteaching.co.uk/rtps6/part3_ch9

LESSON STUDY 9.1
Developing mathematical reasoning and verbalisation in Year 3

The school: Forest Dale Primary School is a community school in the London Borough of Croydon, providing education for boys and girls aged 4–11.

What we wanted the children to learn: The national Mathematics curriculum prioritises the development of higher order thinking – such as conceptual understanding, reasoning and problem solving. We therefore wanted our Year 3 pupils to develop rich use of mathematical language so that they could verbalise their capabilities. The focus of this lesson study cycle was 'angles' and the learning aim was for our pupils to maximally use mathematical language while identifying, explaining and applying in problem solving the mathematical properties of different kinds of angles.

What research is available: The teachers considered Orsay's *Verbal Reasoning & Mathematical Techniques* (2011) and the Gustin and Corozza's (2010) paper on 'Mathematical and verbal reasoning as predictors of science achievement'. In terms of the 'Knowledge quartet' (Chapter 9, p. 296), reading such specialist work informed their *foundational* knowledge and provided ideas for *transforming* it in pedagogically powerful ways. Drawing on their accumulated experience, they made judgements to achieve *connections* with children's understanding, and they remained responsive to any unfolding events and *contingencies*.

What we discovered in our research lessons:
RL1: In the first research lesson we wanted to try a sequence of interactive activities that would encourage children to take increasingly active control in their reasoning and verbalisation. We started with a sorting activity in which the pupils were challenged to first sort different angled shapes into correct categories and then to spot and correct any mistakes. Children's reasoning and verbalisation were prompted by the teacher's repeated use of the question 'How do you know?' The pupils could provide verbal explanations such as 'This angle is not an obtuse angle because it is less than 90 degrees' and were supported to record such reasoning in 'thought bubbles'. To further enhance their use of mathematical language, we next introduced a guessing game, 'Who am I?', in which the pupils were asked to pick an angle and describe its properties for their partners to guess what angle it was. With the support of teacher modelling and a vocabulary bank, the pupils could provide accurate descriptions such as 'I have an angle of greater than 90 degrees. What am I? or 'I have perpendicular lines. What am I?' We then progressed to a more independent visualisation activity. Pupils were asked to use angle shapes to create characters and draw an 'angle family'. They then wrote about their angle characters. The pupils enjoyed the freedom to imagine in this activity and created a variety of very interesting angle-featured characters such as Mr Right with a Square Head, Cat with Acute ears, and Mrs Obtuse.

In the post-lesson interviews, the pupils all said that they really enjoyed drawing and writing about imaginary angle characters. They also used accurate mathematical language to articulate what they had learned through the lesson.

reflectiveteaching.co.uk/rtps6/part3_ch9

> 'I learned about the angles. Acute angle has smaller than 90°. A right angle is exactly 90° (show with hands). Obtuse angle is bigger than 90°. A reflex angle is bigger than 90°.'

> 'I learned about right angles and perpendicular lines. Perpendicular lines are like this. One line is straight and one is connected to the bottom and it's also a right angle (Demonstrated a drawing).'

> 'I learned different angles. Right angles are like an L shape. Some can be the right way, some can be upside down. Obtuse angle is a fat angle, bigger than 90°. Acute angle is small, soft and fluffy, less than 90°.'

RL2: In the second lesson study session, we decided to raise the bar of challenge and embed them more in contexts of problem solving. We introduced a two-step investigation task to help pupils apply their knowledge of angles to shapes. As the first step, the pupils were given a range of shapes and asked to identify different types of angles within a shape. As the second step, the pupils were asked to work in pairs to draw shapes using given angles. They were also asked to explain why or why not some angles could fit within a shape, using thought bubbles. It was interesting to see that quite a number of children explored the relationship between right angles and the shape of triangles and came to the following conclusions through the investigation.

> 'It's possible to make a triangle with one right angle but it's not possible to make one with two right angles.'

> 'You can't do 2 right angles in the triangle. You'll need 4 sides. But a triangle has 3 sides.'

> 'You can't make a triangle with 2 right angles because you'll need 4 sides. You can make a triangle with 1 right angle.'

What pupils learned: In terms of direct pupil outcomes, the planned lesson study cycle enabled the learning objectives to be met or exceeded, thus providing a sound basis for future work on the Mathematics curriculum.

What we learned: Recapping previous learning and addressing misconceptions is valuable; carefully structured tasks and clear success criteria can make a big difference; paired work and collaborative discussion was beneficial; practical resources help, such as word banks for reference; explicit modelling of language, including examples of language good/bad use (with thought bubbles and verbal explanation), can be very beneficial; visualisation activities were very effective and provided a creative challenge.

How we shared: Since completion of the lesson study, we shared what we learned with colleagues through staff meetings. Colleagues particularly liked the visualisation strategies that we tried for eliciting in-depth mathematical reasoning and rich language use. We have now incorporated these across year groups.

reflectiveteaching.co.uk/rtps6/part3_ch9

CONCLUSION

National curricula provide a significant means of attempting to fulfil national objectives and of attempting to provide coherence and progression in the learning of pupils. They also clarify the aims and role of teachers. Even when, as in England, significant numbers of primary schools in the independent and academy sectors are formally exempt, national curricula influence exam boards and thus schools.

However, by the very act of setting out 'requirements', a 'framework' or a set of 'guidelines', the architects of national curricula select *particular* content for teaching, study, learning and assessment. This material tends to cater for the majority, but must inevitably be more suitable and interesting for some learners than for others. Children and young people with particular special needs, or coming from disadvantaged backgrounds, may not relate well to such curricula and alternative provision may suit them better.

Nor should we forget the clarification with which we began this chapter. The official curriculum of any country is a very different thing from the whole school curriculum, which includes the hidden curriculum and the curriculum-as-experienced by pupils. There is enormous scope for creativity, adaption and extension in the School Curriculum.

At the end of the day, teachers must use their expertise to manage a constructive interaction between the knowledge society deems to be important, and the specific needs of children and young people.

In the next chapter we focus on the practical implementation of the curriculum through whole school policies, programmes of study, schemes of work, lesson planning and evaluation.

reflectiveteaching.co.uk/rtps6/part3_ch9

CHAPTER WEBPAGE

reflectiveteaching.co.uk offers additional professional resources for this chapter. For the chapter webpage, go to: reflectiveteaching.co.uk/rtps6/part3_ch9

The chapter webpage for Chapter 9 has a great deal to offer. There are lots of *Reflective Activities* to support the practical exploration of curricular issues. You may also find it helpful to download some of the diagrams and figures. There are also links to the official websites of government education departments within the UK. These will enable you to check out any changes which may have taken place or study official documentation on curricular requirements. The set of four *Research Briefings* is also a bit special. It is focused on science education, and has been designed to provide a case study of the application of subject knowledge in an evidence-informed way.

As an example of the tensions and struggles which arise over national curricula, you may be interested to read the 'related article' entitled 'Teaching, Learning and National Curricula'. You will find it in the *Further Reading* section. This short article recounts what happened when Andrew Pollard, with his colleague Mary James, was asked to provide expert advice to Government on the production of a new National Curriculum for England. As you will see, it ultimately proved impossible to reconcile the views of the Secretary of State, Michael Gove, with an evidence-informed understanding of teaching and learning. Links to original documents are provided, including to an 'ioelondonblog' by Pollard which argued passionately that the proposed primary school curriculum was 'fatally flawed without consideration of the needs of learners'. This is the curriculum which, as this book goes to press, is still being experienced in English schools.

For following up curricular issues in more depth, three levels of support are provided.

1 *Further Reading* on the chapter webpage follows the structure of the chapter and provides an annotated bibliography covering key publications in the field. If you have access to a good library, it should be very helpful for projects and investigating issues in depth.

2 *Key Readings*, below, is a list of selected highlights or 'essential reads', but it of course it also requires library access or some fortunate web searching.

3 *Readings for Reflective Teaching in Schools* is an easy follow-up solution. It provides short, edited extracts of many of the *Key Readings*, and acts as a mini-library. A brief indication of some of the contents, linked to this chapter, is provided below.

Chapter 9 Curriculum

KEY READINGS

For a good introduction to significant thinkers on the school curriculum, take a look at:

Scott, D. (2008) *Critical Essays on Major Curriculum Theorists*. London: Routledge.

A balanced and highly influential overview of the nature, scope and design of school curricula is:

Her Majesty's Inspectors (1985) *The Curriculum from 5 to 16*. Curriculum Matters 2. An HMI Series. London: HMSO. (**Reading 10.1**) (available at **educationengland .org.uk**)

Extending common principles across primary and secondary education (**Reading 9.1**) are:

Male, B. and Waters, M. (2012a) *The Primary Curriculum Design Handbook*. London: Continuum.

Male, B. and Waters, M. (2012b) *The Secondary Curriculum Design Handbook*. London: Continuum.

The ways in which curriculum design has been developed in England, Northern Ireland, Scotland and Wales are described and analysed in:

Wyse, D., Baumfield, V., Egan, D., Hayward, D., Mulme, M., Menter, I., Gallagher, C., Leitch, R., Livingston, K. and Lingard, R. (2012) *Creating the Curriculum*. London: Routledge.

For sophisticated analysis and proposals on the primary curriculum, see:

Alexander, R. (ed.) (2010) *Children, Their World, Their Education. Final Report and Recommendations of the Cambridge Primary Review*. London: Routledge.

An alternative approach to curriculum design is explored in some detail in:

Reiss, M. and White, J. (2013) *An Aims-based Curriculum. The significance of human flourishing for schools*. London: UCL IOE Press.

The distinction between the 'knowledge of the powerful' and 'powerful knowledge for all' is drawn in Young's book below, and the argument is applied in the second volume:

Young, M. (2008) *Bringing Knowledge Back In*. London: Routledge. (**Reading 9.2**)
Standish, A. and Cuthbert, A.S. (2017) *What Should Schools Teach? New Disciplines, Subjects, and the Pursuit of Truth*. London: UCL IOE Press.

A wonderful book making the point that any curriculum must take full account of learning and developmental processes remains:

reflectiveteaching.co.uk/rtps6/part3_ch9

Bruner, J.S. (1966b) *Towards a Theory of Instruction.* Cambridge, MA: Harvard University Press. (see also **Reading 9.5**)

The classic argument for young children learning through direct experience was expressed in the Plowden Report:

Central Advisory Council for Education (CACE) (1967) *Children and their Primary Schools.* London: HMSO. (**Reading 9.4**)

A very strong case for developing personal capabilities, dispositions and skills through contemporary curricula has been presented through the works of Claxton, such as:

Claxton, G., Chambers, M., Powell, G. and Lucas, B. (2011) *The Learning Powered School: Pioneering 21st Century Education.* Bristol: TLO. (see also **Reading 2.9**)

How the school curriculum should represent the past and prepare for the future remains contentious. For a critical analysis, see:

Price, D. (ed.) (2017) *Education Forward: Moving Schools into the Future.* Horley: Crux Publishing.

Shulman provided the classic text analysing key dimensions of subject knowledge:

Shulman, L.S. (1986) 'Those who understand: knowledge and growth in teaching'. *Educational Researcher*, 15, 4–14. (**Reading 9.7**)

For an analysis of how the primary curriculum might be used to support the goals of social justice and climate action, see:

Kavanagh, A.M., Waldron, F. and Mallon, B. (eds.) (2021) *Teaching for Social Justice and Sustainable Development Across the Primary Curriculum.* Abington, Oxon: Routledge.

For a wonderful supply of ideas and innovation from UK subject associations, see the regular flow of practical journals on various subjects for teachers. These include:

British Journal of Religious Education (Professional Council for Religious Education)
British Journal of Teaching Physical Education (Physical Education Association of the United Kingdom)
Mathematics Teaching (Association of Teachers of Mathematics)
School Science Review and *Primary Science* (Association for Science Education)
Literacy (United Kingdom Literacy Association)
Teaching History and *Primary History* (The Historical Association)
The Journal of Design and Technology Education (Design and Technology Association).

In England, Ofsted has continued its focus on curriculum with the publication, from 2021 onwards, of a series of subject-specific research reviews. These have been well-received in some subjects, but contested in others, such as mathematics:

Ofsted Research Reviews, gov.uk/government/collections/curriculum-research-reviews
Gilmore, C., Trundley, R., Bahnmueller, J. and Xenidou-Dervou, I. (2021) 'How research findings can be used to inform educational practice and what can go wrong: The Ofsted Mathematics Research Review 202'. *Mathematics Teaching*, 278, 34–38.

Reference to official websites for UK countries that provide information about national curricula and links to subject can be found on **reflectiveteaching.co.uk**

Chapter 10
Planning
How are we implementing the curriculum?

Introduction	306

The school curriculum	307
Governance	307
Aims	307
Policies	308
Time frames for planning	308
Review	308

Long-term planning	308
Programmes of study	308
The early years – primary transition	310
Breadth and balance	311
Connection and coherence	311

Medium-term planning	313
Schemes of work	313
Progression	316
Relevance	319

Short-term planning	320
Lesson plans	320
Ensuring progress for all	328
Meeting children's needs	331

Evaluating curricular provision	333
Key evaluation questions	333
Tools to support the evaluation of teaching	336
What do you do in a lesson study?	336

Conclusion	339

reflectiveteaching.co.uk/rtps6/part3_ch10

INTRODUCTION

This chapter discusses the implementation of curriculum planning by moving through three successive levels of detail, considering the same issues which teachers or trainee teachers must review when planning their teaching. It then focuses on processes for evaluation and further development.

In case all this sounds over-structured, we must once again affirm the uniquely enriching role of the creativity and imagination of individual teachers in providing high-quality, responsive curriculum experiences for pupils in their classes. Qualities of experience which may be produced – excitement, surprise, awe, spontaneity, concentration, humour, amazement, curiosity, expression, to name but a few – are created through the rapport and interaction between a teacher and their class. From the pupil's point of view, this brings the curriculum 'alive'.

But it is easier to be imaginative and responsive if you are also secure. Good planning is thus enabling.

See Chapter 4

> ### TLRP Principles
>
> Two principles are of particular relevance to this chapter on providing high-quality curricular experiences:
>
> **Effective teaching and learning engages with valued forms of knowledge.** Teaching and learning should engage with the big ideas, facts, processes, language and narratives of subjects so that learners understand what constitutes quality and standards in particular disciplines. (*Principle 2*)
>
> **Effective teaching and learning recognises the importance of prior experience and learning.** Teaching and learning should take account of what the learner knows already in order to plan their next steps. This includes building on prior learning but also taking account of the personal and cultural experiences of different groups of learners. (*Principle 3*)

A valuable set of conceptual tools for thinking about the curriculum is embedded in the various sections of this chapter – breadth, balance, coherence, connection, relevance, ensuring progression and meeting the needs of all pupils. Most of these concepts derive from HMI (1985, Reading 10.1) and have been at the heart of national curriculum planning in each UK country for many years (Wyse et al., 2012).

The particular formulation of conceptual tools for analysing curricular provision offered here contributes to the holistic analysis of teacher expertise, which is the subject of Chapter 16.

THE SCHOOL CURRICULUM

There are many similarities in the curricula offered by schools, but also important differences of emphasis. The statutory requirements of the National Curriculum in each country assert pupil entitlements, but schools have significant scope to develop their own approach to curriculum whilst remaining constrained by assessment and inspection conditions and by parental expectations. Since 2014 only maintained schools in England are required to follow the National Curriculum; academies, free schools and private schools can create their own curricula.

Governance

The governing body of each school or multi-academy trust has legal responsibility for the curriculum and will receive and approve curricular proposals from the headteacher or senior leadership team. The governors should ensure that the review, development and articulation of the school's curriculum is carried out to a high standard.

Historically, the development of national curricula drew attention to the need for progression and coherence from year to year, but also for the responsibility on schools to provide a broad and balanced curriculum experience (see Male and Waters, 2012b, Reading 9.1 and p. 311 below). The increased autonomy in schools in England to create their own curricula has highlighted the need for the skills and knowledge required to design coherent curricula and Ofsted has made the curriculum offer of a school a greater focus of inspection (Spielman, 2018). The Curriculum for Wales (Education Wales, 2020) similarly requires the nurturing in schools of skills and knowledge to support local curriculum creation.

Aims

Irrespective of national requirements (see Chapter 9, p. 285), curriculum planning should be influenced by the overall philosophy and specific aims of a school. The longstanding central purpose of primary schools has been to ensure that children are literate and numerate, in addition to the commitment to learning across the whole curriculum. Many schools emphasise personal development and state their aim to ensure that each child achieves their potential and that each becomes a well-rounded, successful, caring and knowledgeable person. More recently, attention has been drawn to the role schools can play in supporting children's mental health and wellbeing, both through whole school approaches and by interventions that target children's 'social and emotional learning' and their development of 'resilience to stress' (Hurry et al., 2021). The effects of the COVID-19 pandemic have further reinforced the need to consider how young children's mental health and wellbeing can be supported in schools (Bunn and Lewis, 2021; Rose et al., 2021).

Policies

School policy statements reflect the overall philosophy and aims of a school but provide more detailed guidance for practical implementation. They are likely to address significant aspects of the life of the school (e.g. special educational needs and disability and equal opportunities) and may also frame the school's schemes of work for particular areas or subjects within the curriculum. They must be endorsed by school governors, with dates set for review.

Time frames for planning

In most schools, curriculum planning is managed in three time frames:

- long term (whole Key Stages);
- medium term (yearly, termly or half-termly);
- short term (fortnightly, weekly or for specific lessons or sequences of teaching).

Figure 10.1 provides a model of the links between national and school policies and the subsequent levels of curriculum planning. We will consider these levels in more detail through this chapter.

Review

Curriculum planning is not a once-and-for-all affair. The curriculum needs to be reviewed and revised from time to time to make sure it is relevant, up to date and enabling all children to achieve their potential. Good practice is to tie this review process closely in with school improvement planning.

LONG-TERM PLANNING

Programmes of study

Long-term planning of programmes of study must develop with awareness of national and organisational requirements.

In primary education, national curriculum frameworks provide guidance on the specific knowledge, concepts and skills which should be covered in each subject or area of learning. Sometimes this is organised by Key Stage, sometimes by year. More detailed

Chapter 10 Planning 309

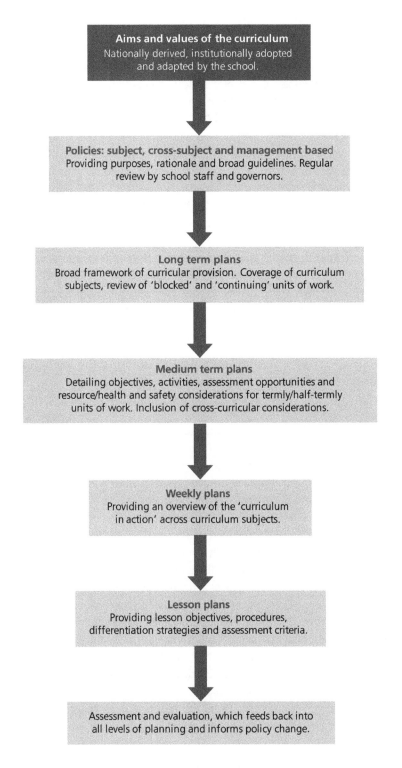

Figure 10.1
School philosophy, policies, schemes of work and teacher planning

reflectiveteaching.co.uk/rtps6/part3_ch10

requirements tend to be produced for core subjects such as English, mathematics, science and, increasingly, digital learning. For example in England, the primary school curriculum is tightly prescribed for these core subjects whilst other 'foundation subjects' (art and design, design and technology, geography, history, computing, music, physical education and foreign languages) focus only on 'essentials'. This is intended to leave scope for the development of particular school curricula as locally determined, although time for this remains a challenge.

While there is no longer a requirement for all schools in England to follow the National Curriculum, there are some statutory requirements on all schools, for example curriculum for relationships and sex education and health education (DfE, 2020c), and the requirement to provide religious education (DfE, 2010), although the content is at the discretion of schools and children, or parents have the option to opt out.

Some schools buy into and adapt commercially produced schemes of work which provide a programme of study with term-by-term progression. These can follow the national curriculum or may offer an alternative curriculum model. Some larger multi-academy trusts have their own trust-wide curricula and programmes of study. Whilst academies in England are not required to follow the National Curriculum, they must still respond to national systems for assessment which remain extremely influential.

The early years – primary transition

Many early years curricula are organised around wider areas of development, with a focus on language and communication, social and emotional development and physical development. This focus develops children's dispositions as learners, and their capabilities, allowing them to engage effectively with school and to learn with others. Child-centred, experiential learning, where the focus is on process over product, a developmentally appropriate curriculum, and the provision of a range of experiences and environments are accepted as best practice in early childhood education (OECD, 2004; Oberhuemer, 2005). Play-based learning presents challenges in planning. Key points of good practice when planning play include considering the individual needs of children, hence the need for knowledge of normative child development and where each child fits into this (Tassoni and Hucker, 2000).

As children move into the primary school, national curricula can offer a very abrupt change, but of course children's needs do not change overnight, and transition from a play-based early years curriculum to more formal learning with discrete lessons and subjects should be planned carefully. The best of early childhood practice can be drawn on to support planning in the primary school. Careful consideration should be given, particularly in the lower primary school, to fitting teaching to children's developmental stages and needs.

Breadth and balance

As we also saw in Chapter 9, p. 285, the requirement that the curriculum in England and Wales should be broad and balanced is longstanding; it was affirmed in the Education Act, 2002. It is expressed with reference to 'spiritual, moral, cultural, mental and physical development' and preparing pupils for 'the opportunities, responsibilities and experiences of adult life' (Parliament of the United Kingdom, 2002). Similar statements apply to Scotland, Northern Ireland and Wales. Taken seriously, breadth and balance address holistic questions about educational provision (see TLRP's first principle, Chapter 4). Thus, whilst the statutory curriculum contributes an important part, it should not be seen as the whole educational experience. This is the reason why most countries try to achieve balance in the knowledge, concepts, skills and attitudes which are expected across the curriculum as a whole, despite variations in emphasis, as we saw in the discussion of the different primary curricula across the UK in Chapter 9.

Inspection reports in all parts of the UK have, for decades, testified that children are likely to achieve most progress in the core skills or literacy and numeracy if they learn in a rich, broad and balanced curriculum which provides them with stimulating content to talk, read and write about and to explore mathematically, scientifically, socially or creatively. The same point is revealed by international evidence which found that a broad curriculum was a distinctive feature of high-performing jurisdictions (DfE, 2011a). Ofsted's 2019 inspection framework puts curriculum planning at the centre, focusing on the ambition of the curriculum and the intent that all learners have access to the full curriculum which should extend 'beyond the academic' and provide both for children's wider development and provide them space to develop their interests (2019).

However, it is sometimes necessary to have a concerted focus on certain aspects of the curriculum, particularly if children have for some reason fallen behind. Sustained efforts to keep cohorts of children together so that they are 'ready to progress' from year to year is again a feature of high-performing countries such as Singapore and Finland (DfE, 2011a).

> ### Expert Questions
>
> **Breadth:** *does the curriculum represent society's educational aspirations for its citizens?*
>
> **Balance:** *does the curriculum-as-experienced offer everything which each learner has a right to expect?*
>
> These questions contribute to a conceptual framework underpinning professional expertise (see Chapter 16).

Connection and coherence

Connection The concept of 'connection' draws attention to the extent to which curricular experiences are meaningful to pupils. For young children in particular it is vital that their experiences in school start from and build on their prior knowledge and experiences, as we saw in the discussion of how children learn in Chapter 2. Failure to make these links to existing knowledge and experience can allow misconceptions to remain and encourage rote learning without understanding.

The advent of national curricula has arguably improved provision of entitlements, but this success brings with it a degree of standardisation which may mean that, for some, the school curriculum simply fails to make connections with other parts of their lives. The extent of disengagement in schooling is disproportionately concentrated among children from poorer backgrounds, with lower outcomes at all ages. Curricular autonomy at its best allows schools the freedom to create a curriculum that is aspirational and meaningful and engaging for the community the school serves. Parents in some communities can also lack confidence in approaching those in schools. And yet, as one of TLRP's projects emphasised, there are 'funds of knowledge' (Moll and Greenberg, 1990) in all communities, and progress may be found if methods of 'home–school knowledge exchange' can be established (Hughes and Pollard, 2000, **Research Briefing 4.1** on p. 136). Curriculum innovation is thus an established response by schools to the problem of disengagement (Rawling, 2006), which becomes increasingly relevant at the upper end of the primary school. This innovation has been encouraged by governments across the UK, within the parameters of their national requirements, and is at the heart of the new Curriculum for Wales (2020).

An explicit attempt to explore the potential for greater connection between schools and their communities is the *Area Based Curriculum*, which was promoted by the Royal Society of Arts (RSA) (Thomas, 2010, Reading 10.4). This approach encourages teachers to begin with the formal curriculum through connections to the pupils' locality and lives outside school, and to expand their pedagogic repertoire to use resources, people and opportunities from beyond the classroom. The overall idea is to do everything possible to create authentic learning experiences that enable pupils to apply more abstract knowledge in ways which are contextually meaningful to them, and which allow them to build on their existing understanding.

The primary school model most common in the UK of a generalist teacher teaching across the curriculum also provides the opportunity to develop connections between subjects. This can be through cross-references or more directly within integrated curricula. Different approaches are discussed in Turner-Bisset (2000, Reading 10.3).

The Curriculum for Wales (2020) asks schools to develop their own curricula, drawing on what it calls their unique position to judge what is best for their pupils and in their context. It is explicit in asking schools to adopt an 'integrated approach' to teaching with traditional subject discipline grouped into 'areas of learning' and schools encouraged to select topics and activities that support pupils in making links between and within areas.

Coherence The concept of coherence refers to the extent to which the various parts of a planned curriculum relate meaningfully together to reinforce the knowledge, skills, concepts or content being learned. Coherence can be thought of across subjects, within a subject and in terms of planned progression over time. Examples of a lack of curricular coherence could be: a science topic that requires children to use mathematics they have not yet encountered; the premature introduction of more complex grammatical structures in writing; or the repetition without development of lessons on map reading in geography.

Clearly this is an important issue if we conceive of learning as a process of 'making sense' (Haste, 1987; Watkins, 2003). Indeed, Gestalt psychologists such as Lewin (1935) established the significance which developing an overarching frame of reference has on learning. People tend to enjoy learning more when they understand it as a whole. They feel more in control and are more willing to think independently and take risks. On the other hand, perceptions of incoherence can lead to feelings of frustration and to strategies such as withdrawal.

Coherence can also be thought of in terms of the coherence between the curriculum, different levels of planning and assessment systems in use. Incoherence here can lead to a narrowed curriculum or a wide gap between the intended and implemented curriculum.

The quality of the teacher's content knowledge and the pedagogic content knowledge are clearly significant variables in making connections between and within subjects and in achieving coherence, but coherence ultimately derives its force and 'impact' from the sense, or otherwise, that the *pupils* make of the curriculum which is provided.

> ### Expert Question
>
> **Connection:** *does the curriculum engage with the cultural resources and funds-of-knowledge of families and the community?*
>
> This question contributes to a conceptual framework underpinning professional expertise (see Chapter 16).

MEDIUM-TERM PLANNING

Schemes of work

Schemes of work provide a practical medium-term plan for each subject or area of learning (Jerome and Bhargava, 2016). If schools commit to publishing their year-by-year curriculum for parents, schemes of work are likely to underpin such documentation.

Schemes of work describe how the curriculum may be taught by individual teachers and thus, in aggregate, represent the work of the staff team as a whole. They are likely to incorporate, but may also adapt and supplement, the Programmes of Study of the National Curriculum. Schemes of work may draw on other published resources and are frequently modified in the light of both experience and curriculum initiatives. A key intention is that such schemes of work should give a clear view of how *progression* and *depth* in learning are provided in relation to each subject or area of learning. Teachers will also be concerned to ensure that the curriculum is presented in ways that are *relevant* to the pupils. We will return to these themes.

It is recommended that each scheme of work should address four basic issues:

- *What do we teach?* To outline knowledge, concepts, skills and attitudes to be developed, links between subjects and cross-curricular elements.

- *How do we teach?* To cover how the curriculum and learning processes are to be organised, units of work, learning activities and processes, forms of grouping to provide differentiation, resources needed, time allocations and opportunities for assessment. The pedagogy employed should be appropriate to the age of the pupils.

reflectiveteaching.co.uk/rtps6/part3_ch10

Part 3 Teaching for learning

- *When do we teach?* To address the issues of curriculum continuity and progression throughout appropriate Key Stages.

- *How do we know that children are learning?* To monitor progress and attainment, and to set future learning targets.

Expert Question

Coherence: *is there clarity in the purposes, content and organisation of the curriculum and does it provide holistic learning experiences?*

This question contributes to a conceptual framework underpinning professional expertise (see Chapter 16).

This level of planning is usually undertaken by class teachers, individually or in-year group teams, and with the support of subject specialists, although it may also be provided by a commercial scheme which is then adapted. It is likely to be updated, as with all planning, on the basis of teachers' views on the quality of activities, performance data and changes in school or year group organisation.

Schemes of work are thus each teacher's essential medium-term planning tool, but need to be developed in the light of the policies and priorities of the school as a whole. Without such plans we have little basis on which to define the purposes of teaching sessions, or to assess pupil progress.

There are many ways of setting out a scheme of work, but they tend to begin by recording the following:

Class/subject details: Brief details are provided of the year group, Key Stage, time period in which the work will be carried out, and the subject/curriculum areas encompassed in the plan. Medium-term plans may be shared with colleagues, and such details enable the context of the document to be understood.

Learning objectives: Objectives express what we intend the pupils to learn in terms of knowledge, concepts, skills and attitudes. More tangibly, 'learning outcomes' may also be used to state what the children will be 'able to do' as a result of the teaching and learning programme. Such statements may be used to formulate sequences or 'ladders' of success criteria on a gradient of complexity or 'difficulty'. Teachers and children can thus use these to review their progress and to help in understanding the level of challenge in a task. A further refinement could be to specify 'must', 'should' and 'could' criteria as a bridge between curriculum planning and assessment for learning (see Chapter 13).

Activities: This section indicates what the pupils will be doing in order to satisfy the stated objectives. Only a very brief description of activities is required at this stage of planning, and this may well be set out in a tabular form with each row being assigned for a lesson-by-lesson or week-by-week description of topics and activities. Other columns may record links back to objectives, necessary resources and key assessment points. For example:

reflectiveteaching.co.uk/rtps6/part3_ch10

Lesson/ Week	Topic/s	Activities	Link to objectives	Resources	Assessment
1					
2					
3					
Etc …					

This layout provides a holistic overview of the teaching programme and makes it possible 'at a glance' to review whether activities are appropriately varied and therefore likely to maintain pupil interest. It is also possible to begin to plan where differentiated support may be required for children of different attainment in the same class. With such planning, resources which need preparation or pre-ordering can be organised.

Reflective Activity 10.1 suggests learning more about schemes of work by working with a colleague.

Reflective Activity 10.1

Aim: To consider the quality of activities in schemes of work.

Evidence and reflection: Work with a colleague to compare the activities presented in a selection of schemes of work, either for your own class or for a specific age range. What are the strengths and weaknesses of the layouts used? Are the anticipated activities incremental in terms of pupil learning? What is the balance of types of activity? Are activities likely to enthuse and motivate pupils? Are outcomes clearly articulated? Is success in key learning points described?

Extension: Which activities would you replace, what with, and why?

When planning schemes of work, a reflective teacher should remember, as we saw in Chapters 2 and 9, that learning does not necessarily occur in a smooth, upward fashion. Unpredictable developments of insight and understanding may be experienced, just as occasional plateaus may occur and be needed. A reflective teacher thus needs to monitor activities closely to try to ensure the best balance, avoiding boredom from too easy tasks and frustration from tasks that are too hard, and aiming for both comfort from consolidation tasks and excitement from tasks that are challenging but not too daunting. The scheme of work is an excellent tool when taking stock of such issues.

Progression

Progression is a powerful concept in the analytic toolkit of reflective teachers (Haynes, 2010, Reading 10.6) – however, it is used in several significant ways.

First, in HMI's conception (1985), progression is linked to providing continuities in children's development as learners. They write:

> Children's development is a continuous process and schools have to provide conditions and experiences which sustain and encourage that process while recognising that it does not proceed uniformly or at an even pace. If this progression is to be maintained, there is a need to build systematically on the children's existing knowledge, concepts, skills and attitudes, so as to ensure an orderly advance in their capabilities over a period of time. Teaching and learning experiences should be ordered so as to facilitate pupils' progress, with each successive element making appropriate demands and leading to better performance.' (Her Majesty's Inspectors, 1985, p. 48)

> **Expert Question**
>
> **Progression:** does the curriculum-as-delivered provide an appropriate sequence and depth of learning experiences?
>
> This question contributes to a conceptual framework underpinning professional expertise (see Chapter 16).

This understanding of progression recognises variation, diversity and uncertainty in learning and urges teachers to adapt the curriculum in relation to pupils' existing knowledge.

Second, a rather more generic application can be illustrated through assessment where Scotland's system of curriculum levels and benchmarks provides an example of the sort of descriptors of understanding, skills and behaviour that can be used to support teachers to map children's progress within a curriculum area. The example below shows the key benchmarks for listening and talking within the Literacy and English curriculum, with the early level corresponding to the early years and the third level to early secondary schooling.

> Early level: As I listen and talk in different situations, I am learning to take turns and am developing my awareness of when to talk and when to listen.
> First level: When I engage with others, I know when and how to listen, when to talk, how much to say, when to ask questions and how to respond with respect.
> Second level: When I engage with others, I can respond in ways appropriate to my role, show that I value others' contributions and use these to build on thinking.
> Third level: When I engage with others, I can make a relevant contribution, encourage others to contribute and acknowledge that they have the right to hold a different opinion. I can respond in ways appropriate to my role and use contributions to reflect on, clarify or adapt thinking. (Education Scotland, 2017, tools for listening and talking)

A third, and rather different, emphasis comes from those who are concerned in the first place with the integrity of subject knowledge, for they tend to expect more specific progression in the substantive and logical dimensions of each domain. For example,

Hirsch's Core Knowledge Curriculum, which is based on *Cultural Literacy: What Every American Needs to Know* (1988) and which had a considerable influence on the latest version of the curriculum in England, orders information to be learned in great detail but leaves pedagogic implications for teachers to determine. The English review harvested national curricula from around the world and built up its programmes of study from a process of comparison, drafting and consultation about such knowledge (DfE, 2013a, 2013b), although the extent to which the consultation views were rigorously analysed and adopted remains questionable. So the outcome offers progression and very high expectations, but is primarily justified in subject terms rather than in terms of the learning of that subject knowledge.

In response to time lost in school during the COVID-19 pandemic, the DfE (2020b) published what it called 'ready-to-progress' criteria for primary mathematics; a document laying out the conceptual understanding and knowledge that children, it was suggested, needed in order to progress from year to year. This slimmed down version of the curriculum is suggested as identifying fundamental ideas that underpin later mathematics in much the same way as Hirsch's Core Knowledge Curriculum.

A final use of progression focuses at a more detailed level on the cognitive challenge of each curricular element. In Scotland, promotion of the concept of 'depth' gives particular prominence to this issue. We will explore it further below, when discussing Bloom's taxonomy of educational objectives in relation to planning learning tasks and activities.

In Lesson Study 10.1 we see how teachers encountered difficulties in their attempts to encourage disadvantaged children to talk about their learning. But we also see how they were able to move forward through 'scaffolding tasks', providing 'small, clear steps to success'. Providing supportive curricular progression of this sort can enable learners to break through and build confidence in meeting new challenges.

LESSON STUDY 10.1
Progression with disadvantaged 8-year-olds to 'Talk for Learning'

The school: Caddington Village School is a large, semi–rural school in central Bedfordshire for 5–13-year-olds; 12 per cent of pupils were identified as having special educational needs and 14 per cent as 'disadvantaged'.

What we wanted the pupils to learn: Through our focus on 'Talk for Learning', we aimed to develop pupils' speaking and listening skills and their ability to work with others.

What research is available: The EEF Teaching and Learning Toolkit suggests that developing 'meta-cognition and self-regulation' in pupils, along with giving focused 'feedback', secured high impact on pupils' progress for very low cost (see p. 434). This evidence summary is based on decades of contributing research, with Vygotsky's insights being among the most prominent (see Chapter 2, p. 44).

What we discovered in our research lessons:

RL1. Our first research lesson involved pupils working collaboratively to answer questions about a text. Pupils read the text aloud in groups, then selected a question from a pre-prepared bank for their partner to answer. Paired discussion then followed. Lesson success depended on pupils' collaboration and discussion skills. Unfortunately, although Case Pupil A was highly discursive, Case Pupil B was unresponsive. Thus, collaboration was unsuccessful. In the post-lesson pupil interview, Pupil B stated, 'I prefer working alone because I can work at my own speed.' However, he also acknowledged the potential benefits of collaborative working. In our post-lesson discussion we identified the long, rambling verbal responses of Pupil A and the poor listening skills of Pupil B. Establishing eye contact was an issue for both pupils.

RL2. In research lesson two, we introduced the PEE chain for reading, a process for enabling pupils to format their answers to questions about a text. Pupils were required to make a 'Point', provide an 'Example' to back up their point and then give additional 'Explanation' for clarification. This method proved successful for Pupil B but Pupil A lacked the understanding to apply it. Pupil A was challenged to shorten her responses – but unfortunately she 'clammed up' and could not speak. Whilst using friendship pairings helped Pupil B to engage in more animated talk for learning, he still preferred to work alone.

RL3. In this lesson we introduced a 'Talking-Lid' to enable Pupil A to record and hone her answers and to use a familiar text to instil personal confidence. Pupil B was engaged in a 'leader' role in the group. The introduction of the 'Talking-Lid' proved successful for Pupil A. In her pupil interview she stated, 'When I talk into the lid I realise how long my sentence is. If I keep on using it, I will get my sentences [length] down.' Giving Pupil B a leadership role proved highly successful. This could be seen in his response to the question, 'What can you do now that you couldn't do before?'; his answer was, 'Responding to my partner'. Both pupils showed deeper understanding and success when using the PEE chain.

What pupils learned: In terms of direct outcomes, pupils made expected or accelerated progress during the two years of the lesson study project. All finished 'at' or 'above' age-related expectations in reading, writing and maths.

What we learned: Through our research, we identified that learning can be achieved through scaffolding tasks with a set structure and small, clear steps to success. When introducing new skills, such as the PEE chain for reading, it was easier for pupils to learn when additional obstacles, such as unfamiliarity with the text, were removed. When given leadership roles, pupil participation levels improved significantly. For the able pupil, taking responsibility for the collective success of a task proved to be a motivator in itself. Friendship pairing was also more successful in generating better learning than other types of pairing.

When pupils saw the value of their learning and its meaning and relevance to their lives, they displayed higher levels of engagement. In addition, a resilient attitude to learning helped our case study pupils to be better learners. They learned from the mistakes they made rather than allowing them to be an inhibitor.

How we shared: We discussed our research with colleagues in staff meetings. Lesson study research is now built into our school improvement plan. Indeed, it has become an integral part of learning for staff, pupils and the wider school community.

Relevance

Relevance is of vital importance in the selection of content.

There is little doubt that children and young people learn most effectively when they understand the purposes and context of the tasks and challenges with which they are faced. When a pupil complains that an activity is 'pointless', is 'boring' or that they 'don't see what it's for', then the curriculum is failing to satisfy the criterion of relevance. When a young child struggles to connect what they are learning in school with their prior experience, knowledge and interests, again, the curriculum is not satisfying relevance.

> **Expert Question**
>
> **Relevance:** is the curriculum presented in ways which are meaningful to learners and so that it can excite their imagination?
>
> This question contributes to a conceptual framework underpinning professional expertise (see Chapter 16).

In such circumstances, motivation may fall and with it may go concentration, commitment and quality (see Watkins, 2003; Teaching and Learning Review Group, 2006, Reading 10.7; Pollard and Triggs, 2000). Progress and standards of work are thus likely to decrease unless the teacher can reconnect the activities and learning with the children's experience, or expand the children's experience in order to help them appreciate the curriculum. Indeed, even when an activity could have great relevance, this may not have been adequately explained to or appreciated by learners. One long-running finding regarding teaching has been that, very often, pupils have not known why they are doing an activity – hence the need to make learning 'visible' (Hattie, 2009, Reading 4.6; 2012, Reading 16.5).

A key consideration here is the value of incorporating practical activities, trips, visitors and first-hand experience into the teaching programme through the scheme of work. This should be done in ways which are appropriate to the age of the pupils, but is an essential part of curriculum provision. If this is ever doubted, try asking your pupils.

Reflective Activity 10.2

Aim: To explore the extent to which sharing learning intentions or success criteria influences feelings of engagement for pupils.

Evidence and reflection: The simple method here is to ask the pupils. Having taught a lesson, or seen one taught (pupils will often 'open up' more to someone who is not their own teacher), select a small group of children – ask them some or all of the following:

- What was the lesson mainly about?
- What did they think that they were supposed to be learning and what did they think that they learned?
- Do they see any connections with other work that they have done in the same subject?

320   Part 3 Teaching for learning

- Do they see any connections with work that they have done in other subjects?
- Did they enjoy the lesson?
- If the lesson was being taught again to a similar group how could it be improved?

Extension: Review what you have learned about the pupils' views. Share your findings with the class teacher if they were not 'your' pupils. What are the implications for the future?

SHORT-TERM PLANNING

Lesson plans

When planning individual lessons, reflective teachers will be aware of relevant programmes of study and schemes of work. They will also consider the existing understanding and motivation of their pupils so that specific objectives can be refined and provision can be differentiated (Lockyer, 2016). Finally, they should consider the age and experience of the children. Younger children will have shorter attention spans, a greater need to be physically active and need more adult attention.

Against this background, a particular learning session or sequence can be planned effectively. Of course, such plans provide a teacher with structure and security, and it should not be forgotten that the resulting confidence can be used to be responsive to the children during the session. Good planning underpins *flexibility*.

Lesson planning should be seen as a key process for teachers to ensure effective teaching and learning. This may or may not include producing written plans or more informal notes; in England teachers have been protected from the excess workload involved in producing formal written plans for every lesson (DfE, 2016). Whatever format it takes, the process of planning a lesson is likely to include consideration of:

a) context and previous assessment information;

b) learning intentions;

c) phases of the lesson;

d) learning tasks;

e) success criteria;

f) resources, ICT and safety;

g) supporting adults.

reflectiveteaching.co.uk/rtps6/part3_ch10

Each element is discussed in turn below.

a) *Context and previous assessment information.* In a written plan that may be accessed by others, it is helpful for an initial section to summarise basic organisational information such as:

- the class and any groups within it;
- the date and duration of the lesson/s;
- the subject/s and focus of the session/s.

Second, it is essential to take stock of, and carefully consider, the existing understanding of the learners and any potential barriers to learning. This may be from assessments in earlier lessons and should be recorded in an appropriate way.

- What are the present capabilities, knowledge and experience of the pupils?

b) *Learning intentions.* It sounds obvious, but it is important to be clear what pupils are expected to learn. Within the broader context of overall schemes of work, objectives for a lesson sequence or single lesson should be relatively focused. Clear learning intentions enable appropriate practical decisions to be made, for instance in selecting learning activities and tasks.

It is useful to give some thought to how learning intentions are expressed. One frequently used formulation adopts the opening phrase: 'By the end of this lesson pupils will be able to . . .' which certainly encourages precision. The things pupils 'will be able to do' should be observable so it is useful to select active verbs such as 'list, describe, compare, identify, explain, solve, apply, discuss, evaluate, demonstrate the ability to, or demonstrate an understanding of . . .'. Alternatively, objectives can be expressed more developmentally. Pupils might be expected, for example, to 'be aware of, have had practice in, been introduced to, have considered, developed the ability to, gained increased insight into, improved performance in, have considered, have an understanding of, begun to analyse . . .'. As well as general objectives for the class, we may want or need to define objectives for particular groups or individuals. Alternatively, objectives may be defined which all pupils are to be supported to meet, thus aiming for the class to be ready to move to the next lesson together, as discussed above. Further objectives can be set that it is hoped some pupils may meet without presupposing at the planning stage who will or won't do so. Rather than moving faster through the curriculum, these further objectives might explore a topic in greater depth.

> **Expert Question**
>
> **Congruence:** *are forms of assessment fit for purpose in terms of overall educational objectives?*
>
> This question contributes to a conceptual framework underpinning professional expertise (see Chapter 16).

As we saw in Chapter 1, it is good practice on appropriate occasions to consult with pupils and to share learning intentions (Rudduck and McIntyre, 2007, Reading 1.3), and also to discuss appropriate criteria to for judging success. Clarke (1998) coined the acronym 'WILF' (what I'm looking for) and has emphasised 'active learning through formative assessment' (2008), whilst Hattie (2009, 2012) has assembled international evidence on the significance of 'visible' teaching and learning (see Readings 4.6 and 16.5). Clear success criteria shared with pupils also help them to get a good fix on the object of their learning and what it will look and feel like when they have accomplished it. Thus, it can empower pupils to monitor, regulate and feedback on their own and each other's progress. Some years earlier, Gage and Berliner (1975) made a similar point by identifying the power of 'advance organisers'. This simply means offering learners a clear explanation of what is going to happen, why, and what is expected of them.

- Are the key learning objectives clear, and how will they be shared with pupils?

c) *Structure of the lesson/s.* Thinking through the structure of a lesson or lesson sequence is one of the most important aspects of planning. Of course it involves thinking about the specific pupils in the class, about what is appropriate given their age and the lesson objectives, but also, in particular, it requires the application of pedagogical content knowledge (see the discussion in Chapter 9, p. 294).

At primary level, two areas to consider are the age and attention span of the children.

Reflective Activity 10.3

Aim: To structure teaching and learning in a curriculum area.

Method: For a topic you plan to teach, think about how the knowledge might be presented and how teaching might be sequenced. Using your pedagogic subject knowledge and understanding of your pupils, what steps or 'chunks' might you plan for?

Identify possible tasks and activities. Experiment with the scheduling of activities to arrive at your first draft plan.

Examine the structure you are considering and identify where there will be teacher input, where pupil activity? What does the balance look like? Where are the opportunities for interaction?

Think about the ways in which your selection provides for progression (see p. 316), differentiation and personalisation (see pp. 328 and 332).

Think about time. How many sessions will you need? Have you got enough? How does the programme divide into lessons? Will you need to keep pupils together or is it possible to plan for fast and slow tracks?

Identify the elements of your proposed curriculum which are likely to be seen as highlights by the pupils. Do they come at appropriate places?

Are there opportunities for you to take stock with the pupils to share what has been achieved, what is working well and what barriers they are encountering?

Revise your programme as necessary.

Follow-up: Keep structure under review as you plan. Make it a focus of your evaluation and adjust your planning accordingly.

d) *Learning activities and tasks for 'mastery'*. A mark of good teaching is the ability to transform what has to be learned into manageable tasks and activities, which are matched in size, complexity and depth to learners' existing capabilities. In this way, pupils are both stimulated and able to cope – and thus they succeed. This approach has been promoted in recent years as 'mastery learning' and there is some long-established evidence to support this, particularly for lower attaining pupils (see EEF **Toolkit Evidence 10.1** on p. 343).

Judgements about progression and depth of cognitive challenge in tasks are particularly significant. Indeed, such judgements are probably the most important that a teacher makes. The international research, certainly says this. For example:

> Powerful and accomplished teachers are those who focus on pupils' cognitive engagement with the content of what it is that is being taught . . . (Hattie, 2012, p. 19, New Zealand, **Reading 16.5**)

> We have come to the conclusion, that the design of instructional and assessment tasks is the fundamental determinant of the quality of teaching and learning in the classroom. (Hogan, 2012, p. 103, Singapore, **Reading 4.2**)

> Our key point is that it is the intellectual demands embedded in classroom tasks that influence the degree of pupil engagement and learning. (Newmann, Bryk and Nagaok, 2001, p. 31, United States)

Central to the idea of cognitive challenge is the proposition that there are different forms of thinking. Bloom's *Taxonomy of Educational Objectives* (1956) identified six different kinds of thought processes: recall; comprehension; application; analysis; synthesis; evaluation.

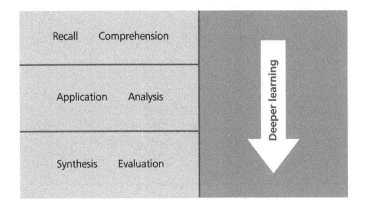

Figure 10.2 Bloom's taxonomy and deeper learning (adapted from Male and Waters, 2012a)

The taxonomy implies a hierarchy. Thus recall and comprehension are basic forms of knowing. Application and analysis come when knowledge is put to use. Synthesis and evaluation are only possible with deeper forms of understanding. Much of the work derived from Bloom is concerned with developing 'higher-order' and 'deeper' thinking in pupils through activity or teacher questioning.

Bloom's classification (or variations on it) has been used to analyse the range and variety of activities and tasks in both primary and secondary schools. For instance, in a study conducted in infant schools, researchers distinguished between five types of task demands:

Incremental: which introduces new ideas, concepts, procedures and skills which are acquired during a task.

Restructuring: which requires children to invent or discover for themselves, so that existing skills, knowledge and concepts are advanced.

Enrichment: through which, by using familiar ideas, concepts, procedures, knowledge and skills on new problems, learning is applied.

Practice: which reinforces ideas, concepts, procedures, knowledge and skills which are assumed to be already known.

Revision: which reactivates known skills, concepts, knowledge etc., which may not have been used for some time. (Bennett et al., 1984)

The study found that 60 per cent of tasks set in Language and Maths were intended as short-term practice, 25 per cent were 'incremental', 6 per cent were enrichment, 6 per cent were intended as long-term revision and only 1 per cent were intended as 'restructuring'. Practice tasks may be useful in confirming knowledge or skills, but one also has to consider at what point such tasks might become boring and counter-productive. A concern raised by the study is the comparative rarity with which pupils met with stimulating and demanding tasks.

> **Expert Question**
>
> **Expectation:** *does our school support high staff and pupil expectations and aspire for excellence?*
>
> This question contributes to a conceptual framework underpinning professional expertise (see Chapter 16).

The difficulty here is that there is a tendency for teachers and pupils to interact together in comfort zones. Routinised teaching produces drift in pupil learning and, through this mutual accommodation, everyone gets through the day (see Pollard, 1985). But such coping strategies are exactly the reason why inspectors, government ministers and others persist in challenging the profession to have 'high expectations'.

One way of approaching this is to review the stimulus and variety of tasks over time.

> **Reflective Activity 10.4**
>
> *Aim:* To evaluate the stimulus and variety of tasks and activities.
>
> *Method:* This evaluation could be carried out by an observer, by yourself or by involving the pupils.
>
> It can be carried out by focusing on a particular pupil for a relevant period, or on an analysis of whole-class or group provision.

Chapter 10 Planning 325

> The tasks in which pupils engage should be considered in terms of their motivational appeal, cognitive challenge and activity (write, read, talk, draw, listen, watch, move, sing etc.).
>
> Some questions which might be asked could include:
>
> - How were the pupils introduced to the activity?
> - Was there a motivational highlight?
> - Was the level of cognitive challenge appropriate?
> - How much writing were pupils required to do?
> - What is the balance between active and passive tasks?
> - What is the balance between collaborative and individual activity?
>
> *Follow-up:* Consider the findings from this exercise and try to deduce the reasons for any patterns you identify. How do you evaluate the results? Discuss your thoughts with others. If you judge it appropriate, what could be done to increase the stimulus and variety of activities and tasks?

Another decision in the planning of activities may be the grouping of pupils within the lesson. This may be temporary pairing or grouping for the purposes of group work or longer standing grouping which might be mixed attainment or based on prior assessments of attainment. Care should be taken when grouping pupils; research has highlighted some of the potential negative impacts of grouping by attainment. In particular, care should be taken that grouping does not lead to different levels of access to the teacher or curriculum, or to lower expectations of particular groups of pupils (Francis et al., 2018; Bradbury and Roberts-Holmes, 2017).

e) *Success criteria.* Assessment forms a vital element of every stage of planning. Without assessment and the consequent re-evaluation of planning, effective teaching cannot be developed and maintained. When preparing a lesson plan, it is good practice to think through and record appropriate *success criteria* for the lesson. Objectives are then much more likely to be borne in mind when explaining tasks, interacting with pupils and in providing feedback.

For example, a lesson objective for a Year 2 class might be:

- Pupils should be able to understand the operation of subtraction and its related vocabulary with numbers up to 20.

Success criteria should specify evidence of progress/success with respect to the objective. Of course, the anticipated outcomes will be influenced by the age of the pupils, by previous assessments of their capabilities, and by the precise nature of the activity. Thus, this objective is likely to lead to very different anticipated outcomes in a Year 1, Year 2 or Year 3 class. For example, anticipated outcomes for the above objective might lead to the following success criteria in a Year 2 lesson plan:

reflectiveteaching.co.uk/rtps6/part3_ch10

- Work demonstrates an understanding that subtracting zero leaves a number unchanged.
- In discussion, pupils demonstrate an understanding of the terms 'take away' and 'find the difference between'.

Such clarity of thinking at the planning stage allows the teacher to share with the pupils not only the broad lesson objectives but also to clarify specific expectations, targets and outcomes. Teacher feedback to pupils can be much more precise. Furthermore, if pupil involvement in assessing their own work is desirable, and Chapter 13, p. 421 argues strongly that it is, then explicating success criteria is a powerful tool in helping teachers to develop self-assessment as part of the pupil learning process (Clarke, 2001; Muschamp, 1994, Reading 13.4).

f) *Resources, ICT and safety.* The use of checklists (actual or mental depending on experience) is highly recommended for making absolutely sure that all the practical necessities for a successful lesson are in place. This is basic, but essential.

Safety considerations should be taken into account and there should be no short cuts in recording the issues anticipated and the provision made. If something does go wrong, such records assume considerable significance.

If the use of ICT is important for the lesson, a specific part of the lesson plan may be devoted to it. Clearly it would be impossible to outline how an interactive whiteboard was to be used in each phase of a lesson, though there may be phases of the lesson where its use by pupils, or its combined use with other resources for demonstration purposes by the teacher, merits a reference in the lesson plan. If pupils will have internet access during the lesson then online safety and opportunities to teach them how to stay safe online must be considered.

> **Expert Questions**
>
> **Authenticity:** do learners recognise routine processes of assessment and feedback as being of personal value?
>
> **Feeding back:** is there a routine flow of constructive, specific, diagnostic feedback from teacher to learners?
>
> **Development:** does formative feedback and support enable learners to achieve personal learning goals?
>
> These questions contribute to a conceptual framework underpinning professional expertise (see Chapter 16).

g) *Supporting adults.* Effective planning is essential to get the benefits from teaching assistants, volunteer parents or any one of a range of other adults who may be contribute to classroom work. It is important that the teacher shares the nature of lesson activities with any supporting adult, and makes it clear what their role will be within the lesson. Above all, however, it is also vital to share the learning intentions for an activity if the supporting adult is to play a full part in promoting learning (see Chapter 8, p. 253 for a fuller account of the effective use of adult learning support). Some teachers do this verbally, but many have a record to which supporting adults can refer that defines the lesson learning intentions, the activity and their role.

Research has shown the importance of considering the role of the teaching assistant (TA) in supporting high-quality teaching by the teacher (Webster and Blatchford, 2013). Key principles for effective deployment are that all pupils, particularly those who are lower attaining and have special educational needs and disabilities (SEND), should have equal access to the teacher, that TAs should be used to develop pupils' independence and TAs should be carefully briefed on the lesson and their role (Sharples et al., 2018).

The topics above are likely to feature in effective lesson plans, whatever variations there may be in their presentation. Degrees of detail will vary between the novice and more experienced teachers, between exploratory and established lessons and in relation to teacher confidence generally.

> ### Reflective Activity 10.5
>
>
> *Aim:* To review existing lesson planning.
>
> *Evidence and reflection:* For trainee teachers, we suggest that you select one lesson plan that you were responsible for creating. Review the plan in the light of the seven topics discussed above. To what extent does your plan reflect these elements and the issues associated with them? What might be done to improve your specific plan or the next plan in the teaching sequence? Compare your planning with that of another trainee or with another teacher in a different teaching team in your school. What are the similarities and differences? How might your planning be improved?
>
> *Extension:* Most teachers will agree that planning becomes more streamlined with experience. From the perspective of school inspectors, clearly stated objectives, task differentiation strategies and assessable outcomes are key features that are looked for in any plan.
>
> Review some lesson plans over at least three curriculum areas. Are these features clear in your planning?

There are, of course, numerous lesson plans available on the internet and as published materials. Whilst many materials are of high intrinsic quality, there are a lot of weaker publications. Any resource should therefore be carefully evaluated before use in school, with due consideration given to its appropriateness to *your school's* aims, *your objectives and methods*, and perhaps most importantly to the overall suitability for the specific needs, motivations and circumstances of *your pupils*.

We move now to consider two issues which underlie all elements of lesson planning. These concern how to meet the needs and ensure progress of all pupils. Two key approaches we will discuss are *differentiation* and *personalisation*. Put another way, they concern how we can design lessons which maximise meaningful connections between the knowledge to be taught and the children and young people who are to learn. A common issue across both will be how to adapt planning to learners' needs in a way that reduces rather than reinforces any pre-existing differences in attainment. This is an issue of equity as educational outcomes at primary level show clear patterns of underachievement in particular groups. Existing inequalities in educational outcomes have been exacerbated by school closures and disruption to learning during the COVID-19 pandemic (EEF, 2021).

Beyond the specific details of planning, what are the underlying issues?

reflectiveteaching.co.uk/rtps6/part3_ch10

Ensuring progress for all

An ambitious curriculum and careful planning are underpinned by the goal of ensuring progress for all pupils. Chapter 15 looks at how to support the needs of pupils with particular learning differences, special educational needs and disabilities. Here we consider strategies for adapting planning to ensure that teaching is carefully targeted to the prior understanding and needs of all pupils.

David Ausubel asserted:

> If I had to reduce the whole of educational psychology to just one principle, I would say this: 'The most important single factor influencing learning is what the learner already knows. Ascertain this and teach him accordingly'. (Ausubel, 1968, p. vi, cited in Hattie, 2012, **Reading 16.5**)

As we have seen in Chapter 2 and in TLRP's principle that 'effective pedagogy recognises the importance of prior experience and learning', learning is unlikely to take place if the cognitive challenge is too great or too small.

The concept of differentiation highlights the cognitive demands which a curriculum or an activity make of the learner (Haynes, 2012, **Reading 10.6**) and provides a means through which the teacher can approach adapting provision to meet the needs of all pupils. In terms of lesson planning, differentiation relates to the appropriateness, or otherwise, of particular tasks and activities to the learner's existing understanding and needs (Bartlett, 2016) and the forms of support that may be put in place to allow different pupils to access the teaching and to engage with it successfully. How well 'matched' are pupil and task given the planned level of support?

To achieve differentiation, teacher expertise is required at four key stages:

- establishing the intentions of the teacher and the pupil;
- identifying the pupil's existing knowledge, concepts, skills and attitudes;
- observing and interpreting the process by which the task is tackled;
- analysing and evaluating the outcomes from the task, so that appropriate plans can be made for future learning opportunities.

> **Expert Question**
>
> **Differentiation:** are curriculum tasks and activities structured appropriately to match the intellectual needs of learners?
>
> This question contributes to a conceptual framework underpinning professional expertise (see Chapter 16).

A mismatch could occur at any (or all) of the stages. To take an example at the first stage, a teacher could set a task for a particular purpose but, if this was not explained appropriately, then the pupil might misunderstand. Any task might be done 'wrongly', or it may be done 'blindly', i.e. without seeing the point of it. There could also be a mismatch at the second stage. The task may be too hard for a pupil because it requires certain knowledge or skills which they do not have. A mismatch at the third stage can be illustrated by a task which may be set with an instruction to use certain prompts or resources, or to present the outcome in a certain way.

reflectiveteaching.co.uk/rtps6/part3_ch10

However, the prompts and resources may not be necessary and may actually confuse the pupil, or the style of presentation may assume some skill which the pupil has not yet acquired. Additional problems could also arise from a mismatch at the fourth stage. Errors in pupils' work can provide important clues about misconception and where misunderstandings may have occurred, and teachers need the skills to gain information from children's responses that can be used to adapt teaching appropriately.

Various differentiation strategies can be used in lesson planning – and Kerry and Kerry (1997) identified no fewer than fifteen different methods. Here we will discuss differentiation by task, by outcome and by support.

Differentiation by task requires lesson plans in which, for all or part of the lesson, particular groups of children will be engaged in different activities. This may be because the pupils are grouped according to their attainment in a subject, or because it has been judged appropriate for particular children to focus on different topics. In such cases, the lesson plan should specify the particular groups, activities and objectives.

Differentiating by outcome calls for lesson plans in which the same basic task can be tackled in many ways – thus making it possible for pupils to respond in ways which are appropriate to their present level of knowledge, skill or understanding. A lesson plan might specify overall learning objectives but define differentiated outcomes in terms of what 'all', 'most' or 'some' pupils will be expected to accomplish.

Differentiating by support aims to ensure that as many pupils as possible access the same task and achieve the same learning outcome, with different levels and forms of support provided to children based on an assessment of their prior attainment and their needs.

The neat distinction between differentiation by task and outcome is, in reality, often blurred. And differentiation by support alone is challenging where differences in prior attainment are large.

It is worth bearing in mind that there are dangers in relying on differentiation by outcome too much because it can become a euphemism for 'just seeing how well they do'. It allows teachers to avoid going through the vital process of envisaging what success will look like.

Any form of differentiation must be examined critically to ensure that it does not magnify existing attainment gaps, for example, if the aimed at outcomes for 'all' children are not sufficiently ambitious. A key challenge in planning is balancing the need to start with learners' prior understanding, to ensure appropriate challenge and to aim to close rather than widen attainment gaps through ambitious goals and appropriate support. England's Early Career Framework highlights 'adaptive teaching' to meet children's needs without the 'artificial' creation of different tasks for different groups (DfE, 2019a).

However it is achieved, the cognitive challenge of tasks in your lessons should be matched to the cognitive needs of the learners in your class. Lesson Study 10.2 illustrates how work of this sort can be studied, refined and improved.

reflectiveteaching.co.uk/rtps6/part3_ch10

330 Part 3 Teaching for learning

LESSON STUDY 10.2

Differentiated teaching for attainment-based groups in Year 5

The school: Woodside Primary Academy is a primary school based in Walthamstow, North East London.

What we wanted the pupils to learn: Through this lesson study cycle, we aimed to develop better understandings about the learning needs of pupils in different classroom groups and to offer appropriately differentiated support. We chose to focus on 'Time'. More specifically we wanted to help pupils to understand the relationships between digital and analogue clocks and to be able to convert between time units and calculate time periods. For this lesson study cycle, we chose one pupil from each attainment group to focus on as our case pupils.

What research is available: The psychological insight that teaching must start from the learner's existing understanding is underscored by decades of research (e.g. Ausubel, 1968; Hattie, 2012). Specifically for this lesson study, we read an article by Latz et al. (2008) entitled 'Peer Coaching to Improve Classroom Differentiation'.

What we discovered in our research lessons:

RL1: For the first research lesson, we planned a range of practical and investigative tasks to find out about pupils' basic understandings in relation to the key areas of knowledge such as the analogue clock and time scale, similarities and differences between analogue and digital clocks, and AM and PM. Through close observation of the pupils, we were able to learn more about each group's prior knowledge and learning difficulties in relation to time. This led us to drop our initial expectation that the digital clock would be more difficult than the analogue clock. We also developed better knowledge about individual pupils and how they learned with partners and in groups. For example, we found that some pupils really enjoyed explaining things to others, whilst other pupils just copied answers from their peers.

RL2: The first change we made in the second lesson was to re-group the pupils so that they could work more productively together. We also placed more emphasis on the analogue clock. We started the lesson by getting the pupils to discuss the similarities and differences between an analogue and a digital clock. During this stage higher attainment (HA) pupils were involved as experts to support tasks at the lower attainment (LA) and medium (MA) tables. We then went on to focus on the analogue clock and time scale and got the pupils to practise labelling minutes on the clock and telling the time with 'minutes past' and 'minutes to'. As a final task, we asked the pupils to integrate their knowledge about the analogue and digital clocks to make a clock that could represent 24 hours and convert between the two. While the LA and MA pupils were working on these tasks, the HA pupils were put on more challenging tasks. But for the LA and MA pupils the lesson turned out to be quite difficult, especially for the LA pupils. We realised that we had probably been too ambitious with what we aimed to cover in one lesson.

RL3: In the third lesson, we readjusted the learning objectives for the LA and MA attainment sets to consolidate what was covered in the second lesson rather than moving on to new things. In particular we decided to give them more modelling about time scale and about reading time correctly with 'past' and 'to'. We also used real clocks to model change of minutes and other physical resources to contrast between 'past' and 'to'. In addition, we created more opportunities for repetition while at the same time reinforcing correct use of maths vocabulary both verbally and in writing. Only when we felt that the pupils had solidified their

---

reflectiveteaching.co.uk/rtps6/part3_ch10

understandings about analogue and digital clock, did we move on to conversion between the two. HA pupils, on the other hand, focused on adding on time to cross over date boundaries in this lesson. Through such differentiation across three successive lessons, more LA and MA pupils achieved the objectives of understanding and being able to convert between the analogue and digital time while the HA pupils achieved extended learning objectives for them.

What pupils learned: In terms of direct pupil outcomes, the pupils demonstrated a high level of engagement and enjoyment throughout the cycle. All pupils achieved the learning objectives set out for them in relation to 'Time' and reading clocks.

What we learned: The study emphasised the importance of learning about pupils' prior understandings, difficulties and misconceptions in relation to a new topic to inform lesson planning. For example, despite our expectations, the pupils seemed to have more difficulty with the analogue clock than the digital clock. Children approach learning in different ways. For example, the most confident enjoyed the opportunity to explain to a peer who didn't understand, but many other pupils needed careful modelling and scaffolding to secure their understanding. All pupils needed teacher assurance to feel secure about their learning, and most enjoyed practical working with concrete objects and resources.

We have changed our practice so that each time we move on to something new, we now aim to find out the children's strengths, weaknesses and difficulties before finally planning activities. We aim to create more opportunities in the future to observe the learning of our children, thus enabling better judgements – such as the need for a more balanced pace for covering the maths curriculum.

How we shared: We first shared our lesson plans and resources with colleagues of the same year group. These resources have now been built into the scheme of learning as resources for teaching 'Time'. With other colleagues, we also shared our findings about the necessity to keep a balanced pace of the mathematics curriculum. Across the whole school, we now agree that consolidation and repetition is important to ensure deep learning at each year level.

Meeting children's needs

Beyond the already challenging task of ensuring progression for all, what more might we need to consider when planning in order to meet the needs of all children? We might consider the role of the pupils' voices in planning and the importance of seeing themselves, their communities and their interests reflected in and broadened by curriculum provision.

'Personalisation' is an educational concept which reflects both cumulative international understanding about learning and contemporary commitment to reducing inequalities in outcomes. Whilst echoing the cognitive issues associated with differentiation, it extends and broadens these to also embrace the social, emotional and motivational dimensions of learning (see **Research Briefing 10.1** on p. 344).

The idea was cogently expressed by the Chief Inspector of Schools for England in a report setting out 'A Vision for Teaching and Learning in 2020'. She wrote:

Personalising learning means taking a more structured and responsive approach to each child's learning, so that all pupils are able to progress, achieve and participate. This will be evident in high-quality, challenging teaching that engages pupils and helps them to take ownership of their learning. Better assessment, whether of learning or for learning, will promote the progress of every child and young person. All children will experience an engaging curriculum that helps them to develop the knowledge, skills, understanding and attitudes they need to thrive throughout their lives. (Teaching and Learning Review Group, 2006, p. 41, **Reading 10.7**)

2020 Vision drew on a US research review (Bransford et al., 1999, **Reading 4.1**) to declare that:

Personalising learning is learner-centred and knowledge-centred . . .

Close attention is paid to learners' knowledge, skills, understanding and attitudes. Learning is connected to what they already know (including from outside the classroom). Teaching enthuses pupils and engages their interest in learning: it identifies, explores and corrects misconceptions. Learners are active and curious: they create their own hypotheses, ask their own questions, coach one another, set goals for themselves, monitor their progress and experiment with ideas for taking risks, knowing that mistakes and 'being stuck' are part of learning. Work is sufficiently varied and challenging to maintain their engagement but not so difficult as to discourage them. This engagement allows learners of all abilities to succeed, and it avoids the disaffection and attention-seeking that give rise to problems with behaviour.

. . . and it is assessment-centred

Assessment is both formative and summative and supports learning: learners monitor their progress and, with their teachers, identify their next steps. Techniques such as open questioning, sharing learning objectives and success criteria, and focused marking have a powerful effect on the extent to which learners are enabled to take an active role in their learning. Sufficient time is always given for learners' reflection. Whether individually or in pairs, they review what they have learnt and how they have learnt it. Their evaluations contribute to their understanding. They know their levels of achievement and make progress towards their goals.

> **Expert Question**
>
> **Personalisation:** does the curriculum resonate with the social and cultural needs of diverse learners and provide appropriate elements of choice?
>
> This question contributes to a conceptual framework underpinning professional expertise (see Chapter 16).

On this definition, personalised learning can be seen as a synoptic concept, drawing together many threads of good practice. However, it does this by particularly emphasising the engagement of 'children, young people and their parents as respected users of the education service, giving them choices about how they access learning, listening to what they think about the service they receive and even designing those services with them' (Teaching and Learning Review Group, 2006, p. 39).

The emphasis on engagement and on meeting the needs of individual learners can seem daunting until one realises that the needs of many children and young people are held in common. This is picked up elsewhere in this book, for instance on learning how to learn (Chapter 2), pupil consultation (Chapters 1 and 6), parental involvement and new technologies (Chapter 8), and assessment for learning (Chapter 13).

In the context of lesson planning, the concept of personalised learning can be used to review what has been planned and to pose questions for oneself regarding the likely efficacy of the provision. In addition to tasks being appropriately differentiated, will they really engage pupils, connect with their culture and expectations, and support their learning?

However it is achieved, personalisation should enable learners to identify with classroom activities in meaningful ways – a point which may have to be asserted (see **Research Briefing 10.1** on p. 344).

EVALUATING CURRICULAR PROVISION

In this section we begin by considering three generic questions which can be used to interrogate our own practice, with a particular focus on the application of subject knowledge in the curriculum. Addressing them will illuminate some issues on which personal improvement can be focused.

We then move on to consider 'lesson study' – a systematic approach to curricular improvement in collaboration with other colleagues. The latter has been used as a process to support high-quality teaching, learning and professional development.

These approaches illustrate, in different ways, TLRP's principle that 'pupil learning depends on teacher learning' (see Chapter 4, p. 123).

Key evaluation questions

All plans, at whatever level, should be open to modification and change depending on their success in aiding the development of learning in the classroom. A reflective teacher clearly understands the intimate links between the processes of planning, teaching, assessment and evaluation (see Figure 3.5, Chapter 3).

Three evaluation questions may be posed:

- Did pupils learn what was expected, and why?
- How did teacher knowledge support learning?
- How did classroom activities facilitate learning?

Question 1: Did pupils learn what was expected, and why?
'Assessment' and 'evaluation' are often confused because they are intricately entwined.

For example, the question, 'Did pupils learn what was expected?' focuses on both the learner and the teaching intentions. In order to answer the question, the reflective teacher needs assessment information on pupil performance. This information comes from formative assessment (see Chapter 13). *Assessment* thus involves collecting evidence about *how* pupils

Part 3 Teaching for learning

related to particular teaching/learning experiences and *what* (if any) knowledge, understanding or skills were developed. Evaluation, on the other hand, considers *why* the particular teaching and learning experience supported or did not support intended or unintended learning.

Assessment and evaluation thus go 'hand in hand' since it is not possible to consider the *why* without the *how* and the *what*. Evaluation of *why* pupil performance took the form it did is likely to lead to deeper analysis of teacher action – hence our other two questions.

Question 2: How did teacher knowledge support learning?
Evaluation of knowledge for teaching includes consideration of both content knowledge and pedagogical content knowledge (see Chapter 9, p. 292) and whether these were sufficient to support learning. The reflective teacher will have given some thought to these issues when planning. However, it may only be possible to fully answer this evaluation question after the teaching/learning has taken place. The reflective teacher will consider how well learning was supported by their knowledge of the subject and how to make this accessible to learners. Specific questions to ask include:

- Did I use appropriate and accurate language?
- Did pupils give responses to questions or make suggestions about which I was uncertain?
- Had I predicted what pupils would find easy or difficult and any misconceptions they might have?
- Did my explanations, choice of resources, modelling and/or demonstrations aid pupils' understanding of the content?
- Did I use the most appropriate examples and representations?
- Did I introduce ideas in an order which enabled understanding to be built?
- Did I make connections between ideas presented in the lesson and with pupils' learning more generally?

This is not intended to be a definitive list but gives an idea of the sorts of questions reflective teachers might ask which relate to their own knowledge for teaching.

The precise nature of evaluative questions to ask about their own knowledge for teaching will vary depending on the subject matter of the teaching/learning experience being evaluated. For example, in a religious education lesson a teacher might ask: 'Did the artefacts I used portray accurate information about the religious rites?' Of essence here is that the reflective teacher considers whether their pedagogical content knowledge facilitated learning. That is, did they know enough about not only the subject but also about how to teach the subject – so that pupils were able to learn?

The purpose of evaluating knowledge for teaching is not to identify limitations in teacher knowledge. Rather, it is to understand better how to meet the learning needs of pupils. Having evaluated our use of language, ability to respond to pupils, sequencing of content etc., this analysis can be used to inform our own learning and future teaching. Focusing on the way in which subject matter knowledge and pedagogical content knowledge supports learning, facilitates the development of knowledge for teaching (Turner, 2009). In this way future teaching and learning are enhanced.

reflectiveteaching.co.uk/rtps6/part3_ch10

Question 3: How did classroom activities facilitate learning?
The evaluation of classroom activities thus requires careful analysis of *how* children respond to activities, *what* they learn from them and *why* that learning takes place. Importantly, task completion should not be taken as a straightforward proxy for learning.

Certain pupil and/or teacher activities may facilitate learning of some types of subject content better than others, and understanding this is important if the teacher is to develop their repertoire of teaching strategies for particular subjects.

It is also necessary to focus on individual pupils. For example, analysis of an activity might suggest that some children learned from physically manipulating objects while explaining what they were doing, whilst other children learned from watching and listening. Yet other children may have failed to learn through listening, but then physically manipulated the objects and learned for themselves. There are many possibilities.

> **Expert Question**
>
> **Reflection:** *is our classroom practice based on incremental, evidence-informed and collaborative improvement strategies?*
>
> This question contributes to a conceptual framework underpinning professional expertise (see Chapter 16).

Analysis of *why* activities are successful for different types of content and with different pupils may lead to more generic pedagogical learning. Like the other two key evaluative questions, the answer to this question is only useful to the teacher if it leads to developments in their planning for teaching and learning. Provided that careful analysis is carried out, it is possible to learn about how to develop planning for teaching and learning both from activities that worked well and those that did not.

Reflective Activity 10.6

Aim: To evaluate a teaching session with particular reference to the appropriate application of subject knowledge.

Evidence and reflection:
1 Plan to teach a session involving some new learning. In doing so, consider: what you want pupils to learn; what knowledge you need in order to support their learning; and what classroom activities are most appropriate. Having thought about the possibilities be prepared to respond to pupil input.
2 Obtain some sort of record of what happens. For instance, you could set up a video, make an audio recording or ask a colleague to observe you. In the case of the latter, try to get your colleague to make detailed notes on what is said by both you and the children.
3 Teach the session.
4 Analyse what happened under headings of the three key evaluative questions:
   • Did pupils learn what was expected, and why?
   • How did teacher knowledge support learning?
   • How did pupil and teacher activities facilitate learning?

Extension: Discuss your findings with a colleague and consider the consequences of what you have learned.

Part 3 Teaching for learning

In the discussion of lesson study below, we see that this sort of evaluation activity can be made more systematic, collaborative and cumulative, and can lead effectively to improvements.

Tools to support the evaluation of teaching

Lesson study is a specific process that blends teacher creativity with scientific rigour to establish systematic processes for teacher learning about classroom practice. It has a long history in Japan, and has spread across Asia and into the West. It can be seen as a rigorous form of evaluation, with direct developmental implications.

The *creative* element is found in the fact that teachers work together to refine, innovate or create new teaching approaches or curricular designs. The *scientific* element is found in the ways in which these teachers gather from research evidence, information about teaching approaches that could be effective and then, equally systematically, gather evidence of their pupils' learning (from their observations as well as from the perspectives of the pupils themselves) as they try out, refine, re-try and re-refine their new teaching approaches. This process of trialling and refining is carried out over a cycle of mini group enquiries called 'research lessons' (RL). In these research lessons the group will study how the pupils are learning, in order to tease out ways of teaching the approach they are trialling that have the biggest effect on pupil learning.

Whatever teachers learn, they then make public. Learning and development do not remain the property of that classroom or school. Japanese teachers are culturally very collaborative and teacher knowledge is viewed with the same importance as medical knowledge in the West. Japanese teachers read the accounts of other teachers' lesson studies with interest as part of the literature they consult before engaging in their own classroom research. When they have completed a lesson study, they will also invite colleagues to their classrooms for 'open house' events where they teach their new approach or an aspect of their new curriculum *in public* in front of an invited audience from local schools or colleges, before discussing it with their guests (and their pupils).

Lesson study groups work best if they have several perspectives on the lesson and also include teachers with a range of experiences. A minimum of three is preferable, though in Japan such groups are often very much larger. Sometimes a lesson study group will include a teacher from outside the school who has particular expertise in the pedagogical or curriculum area under focus and who can bring this expertise to bear. Alternatively, the group may include a member who has participated in lesson studies that have successfully developed new approaches in similar aspects of teaching.

What do you do in a lesson study?

A lesson study involves collaboratively planning (in great detail) a lesson, teaching the lesson with colleagues present, and observing the pupil learning that occurs – and then, immediately afterwards, analysing the evidence collected by the group members. This is

reflectiveteaching.co.uk/rtps6/part3_ch10

Chapter 10 Planning

done over a number of 'research' lessons so that there is comparison, refinement and cumulation in the pedagogy which is adopted.

Lesson study has itself evolved over a long period and a number of deliberate steps have become established. These are:

1 Members of a lesson study group will draw up or agree to observe a protocol which ensures that the group come together as equals in learning and enquiry, and that whatever experience individual members bring to the process, it is treated with respect as an equal contribution to the group's collective endeavour.

2 The group will agree their focus – which can usefully be expressed as a research question – although it always takes a similar form: 'How can we teach X more effectively to Y in order to improve their learning?' (where X will be an aspect of curriculum or subject knowledge and Y will be a learner group such as 'Year 5' or 'boys in Year 4 who have fallen behind in narrative writing').

3 Members will investigate what is 'out there' in terms of evidence of successful approaches developed elsewhere in relation to their focus. They will meet to pool their research findings. They may also plan their first research lesson. They will need to agree whose class will be used. They will often identify a small number of 'case pupils' who will be the subject of particular attention in the lesson study. Case pupils represent or typify learner groups in the class. They may, for example, represent high, middle and lower attaining pupils.

4 When planning the research lesson, the lesson study group plans for the whole class but pays specific attention to the planned learning for the case pupils. The group predicts and sets out what they hope each case pupil will achieve by the end of the research lesson (very like success criteria) and they also list what they hope each of the pupils will be doing at each stage of the lesson.

5 One of the teachers then teaches the research lesson. The others observe the class taking note of everything that goes on but paying particular attention to the case pupils and noting what they do. Observation notes are made on copies of the lesson plan which the teachers use as an observation pro-forma.

6 After the lesson, the teachers interview a sample of pupils in order to ascertain their perspective on the research lesson – what worked more or less well and how it could be improved next time.

7 After the lesson and pupil interviews, the teachers discuss what they observed as soon as they can after the lesson is over – and preferably on the same day. The discussion should always adhere to the following structure:

a Sharing what each member observed of the *learning* of each of the case pupils compared with the predictions the group had made for the case pupil, and a discussion about why such differences may have occurred.

b Discussion about the *learning* of the class as a whole.

c The discussion will then turn to the lesson itself and the teaching – but this is after much discussion about the learning and is always based on observed evidence of the learning that took place.

reflectiveteaching.co.uk/rtps6/part3_ch10

d Discussion about what to do in the next research lesson to address issues from the one just taught.

8 The group then plans the next research lesson.

9 After a sequence of three or more research lessons, the group has usually had a chance to reassess some of the pupils whose learning they will now understand in much greater detail. They will also usually have agreed some changes to the teaching or to the lesson designs that are to be adopted in the future and shared with colleagues. And so progress is made.

Figure 10.3 summarises the lesson study cycle diagrammatically.

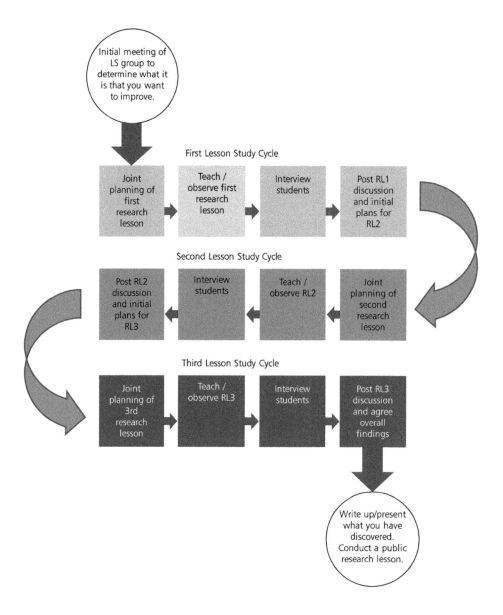

Figure 10.3 The lesson study cycle (adapted from Dudley, 2011)

Participating teachers tend to feel that, because the research lessons are jointly planned and analysed, they are the property of the group, rather than of the person who happens to teach the lesson. Therefore, if something goes wrong it is part of the whole group's learning and not something for the individual teacher to worry about. Teachers say that as a result of this they are more prepared to take risks and to tackle aspects of the curriculum or subjects which they feel least secure with (Dudley, 2011).

Furthermore, in a lesson study teachers are learning from and with each other while focused on a common endeavour – that of improving the learning of their pupils and the quality of their teaching. This helps even experienced teachers to see their classrooms, their teaching and their pupils' learning with fresh eyes. They thus become more aware of familiar or habitual practices that are not normally noticed but which, because they are suddenly more visible, can be changed and improved.

An ongoing lesson study programme of curriculum review and renewal can help a school to ensure that the structure and content of its curriculum is constantly evaluated and improved in terms of the learning and teaching that it generates. Furthermore, such improvements are passed on to other teachers and schools for further critique and adaption, thus generating a second wave of professional learning. In this way the curriculum is kept alive and appropriate progression, relevance, differentiation and personalisation are renewed.

CONCLUSION

Curriculum planning is a highly skilled activity underpinned by understanding of key principles (HMI, 1985, Reading 10.1; Hattie, 2012, Reading 16.5). Whilst it requires awareness of curriculum requirements at national level and of whole-school policies, this must be complemented by understanding of the prior knowledge of pupils, of subject knowledge and pedagogic knowledge.

As we have seen, these forms of expertise must be combined with sound practical organisation to deliver an interesting and appropriately challenging set of learning experiences. In the hands of a skilled and sensitive teacher, structure and purpose will be tempered by flexibility and intuition, and enriched by imagination and commitment.

CHAPTER WEBPAGE

reflectiveteaching.co.uk offers additional professional resources for this chapter. For the chapter webpage, go to: reflectiveteaching.co.uk/rtps6/part3_ch10

The webpage resources for Chapter 10 have been designed to directly support each step of curricula planning – from thinking about long-term intentions, to medium-term schemes of work and on to detailed, short-term lesson planning. The final stage, of course, is careful evaluation of curricular provision. To support work at each of these stages, you will find that there are reflective activities and detailed suggestions for Further Reading. The key point is to get into practicalities – given your aims, the characteristics of the learners and the curricular requirements, what will you actually do? To support you in answering that question, the chapter webpage provides four times more Reflective Activities than the printed book.

As may now be familiar to you, three levels of supplementary advice have been provided.

1. Supported by a good library, *Further Reading* on the chapter webpage will enable you to both deepen and broaden your understanding of curricula planning at each stage of provision. In so doing, it follows the structure of the chapter.

2. *Key Readings*, below, simplifies things further by suggesting some 'essential reads', but it of course also requires library access.

3. Short, edited extracts of many of the *Key Readings* are provided in *Readings for Reflective Teaching in Schools*. If you have it, you will see that it contains over 100 readings and acts rather like a mini-library. In respect of this chapter on curriculum planning, some readings are indicated by the icons below and a resumé for each of the relevant readings is provided on the chapter webpage.

KEY READINGS

For the classic statement of a planned whole curriculum framework and introduction to the conceptual tools of breadth, balance, coherence, progression, relevance and differentiation, see:

Her Majesty's Inspectors (HMI) (1985) *The Curriculum from 5 to 16*. HMI Series, Curriculum Matters No 2. London: HMSO. **Reading 10.1** (available at educationengland.org.uk)

Excellent overviews of curriculum planning issues, including the significance of breadth and balance, are provided in:

> Male, B. and Waters, M. (2012a) *The Primary Curriculum Design Handbook*. London: Continuum.
>
> Male, B. and Waters, M. (2012b) *The Secondary Curriculum Design Handbook*. London: Continuum. (**Reading 9.1**)

The importance of subject domains is addressed in Chapter 9, p. 292, and in Young (2008, **Reading 9.2**) and Wilson (2000, **Reading 9.3**). This is complemented by the case for study of topics across subjects and for cross-curricula planning. An exploration of different approaches to cross-curricular planning is given in Turner-Bissett and a committed argument is made by Hunter and Scheirer, whilst the Siraj-Blatchfords explore specific strategies for cross-curricula provision.

> Turner-Bissett, R. (2000) 'Reconstructing the primary curriculum', *Education 3–13: International Journal of Primary, Elementary and Early Years Education*. 28 (1), 3–8. (**Reading 10.3**)
>
> Hunter, R. and Scheirer, E.A. (1988) *The Organic Classroom: Organizing for Learning 7 to 12*. London: Falmer.
>
> Siraj-Blatchford, J. and Siraj-Blatchford, I. (1995) *Educating the Whole Child: Cross-curricular Skills, Themes and Dimensions*. Buckingham: Open University Press.

Establishing curricular connections and relevance for the lives of pupils is a constant challenge for teachers. To help in meeting this need there have been calls for more use of local resources within the curriculum and attempts to personalise provision in a range of ways.

> Thomas, L. (2010) *The RSA Area Based Curriculum: Engaging the Local*. London: RSA. (**Reading 10.4**)
>
> Teaching and Learning in 2000 Review Group. (2006) *2020 Vision: Report of the Teaching and Learning in 2020 Review Group*. London: DfES. (**Reading 10.7**)

On lesson planning, Haynes provides systematic, practical guidance, whilst Griffiths and Burns demonstrate the benefits of being absolutely clear about what pupils know already and about one's ultimate learning goals. Hattie draws implications from his exceptional synthesis of international evidence on effective lesson design and teaching practices.

> Haynes, A. (2010) *The Complete Guide to Lesson Planning and Preparation*. London: Continuum. (**Reading 10.6**)
>
> Griffiths, A. and Burns, M. (2014) *Teaching Backwards*. Carmarthen: Crown House.
>
> Hattie, J. (2012) *Visible Learning for Teachers: Maximising Impact on Learning*. London: Routledge. (**Reading 16.5**)

Part 3 Teaching for learning

Practical advice on how to achieve classroom differentiation for learning is offered in:

> Bartlett, J. (2016) *Outstanding Differentiation for Learning in the Classroom.* London: Routledge.

The link between curriculum planning and assessment is further elaborated in Chapter 13.

Systematic and open evaluation of lessons is key to improvement, as Hattie's work has shown, and the lesson study approach suggests practical ways of framing this in collaboration with colleagues. On this, see:

> Dudley, P. (2011) *Lesson Study: A Handbook.* Cambridge: Dudley. (Available at lessonstudy.co.uk)

For stimulating views on the principles that underpin curriculum planning and design, and stressing learner engagement, see:

> Egan, K. (1988) *An Alternative Approach to Teaching and the Curriculum.* London: Routledge.
>
> Eisner, E. (1996) *Cognition and Curriculum Reconsidered.* London: Paul Chapman.

reflectiveteaching.co.uk/rtps6/part3_ch10

TOOLKIT EVIDENCE 10.1
Mastery learning: developing a mindset for success?

What is it?
Mastery learning, originally developed by Benjamin Bloom in the 1970 and 1980s, breaks subject matter and learning content into units with clearly specified objectives which are pursued until they are achieved. Learners work through each block of content in a series of sequential steps. Contemporary approaches, such as 'maths mastery' emphasise whole class teaching, the development of fluency and deep subject knowledge.

Pupils must demonstrate a high level of success on tests, typically at about the 80 per cent level, before progressing to new content. Mastery learning can be contrasted with other approaches which emphasise coverage of the curriculum, without ensuring effective competence is achieved. Those who do not reach the required level are provided with additional tuition, peer support, small group discussions, or homework so that they can reach the expected level. Effective diagnosis of knowledge and skills helps to avoid unnecessary repetition and to maintain the right level of challenge.

What does the evidence say?
There are a number of meta-analyses of older research which indicate that, on average, mastery learning approaches are effective, leading to an additional five months' progress over the course of a school year compared with traditional approaches. Unusually however, the effects of mastery learning tend to cluster at two points with studies showing either little or no impact or an impact of up to six months' gain. This suggests that making mastery approaches work effectively may be challenging.

How sound is the evidence?
There is a large quantity of research on the impact of mastery learning, though much of it is quite dated. A more recent study in the US found that mastery learning approaches can increase learning by up to six months in maths for 13–14-year-olds, which is consistent with older studies. By contrast, a UK study by the EEF published an evaluation of the Mathematics Mastery programme in English schools showing one additional month's progress on average when compared with similar classes.

What do I need to think about?
- Overall master learning approaches appear to have potential, particularly for low-attaining pupils.
- Using the approach effectively is challenging and needs time to plan and prepare both content and teaching approaches.
- Setting clear objectives and consistently meeting these for all pupils is a key feature.

Links and further reading
Lessons of Mastery Learning by Thomas R. Guskey: uknowledge.uky.edu/cgi/viewcontent.cgi?article=1011&context=edp_facpub

The National Centre for Excellence in the Teaching of Mathematics (NCTEM) has support for 'maths mastery': ncetm.org.uk/teaching-for-mastery/

The EEF Teaching and Learning Toolkit entry on 'mastery learning': educationendowmentfoundation.org.uk/education-evidence/teaching-learning-toolkit/mastery-learning – see also the technical appendix for further references.

See also
Small group teaching (Toolkit Evidence 11.2)
Collaborative learning (Toolkit Evidence 11.3)

Education Endowment Foundation

RESEARCH BRIEFING 10.1
Personalising learning

In January 2004, David Miliband, then Schools Minister in England, suggested that personalised learning included: 'high expectation of every child, given practical form by high quality teaching based on a sound knowledge and understanding of each child's needs' (North of England Conference Speech). Building on this, the DfES *2020 Vision* expansively emphasised children 'taking ownership' of their learning:

> Personalising learning means taking a more structured and responsive approach to each child's learning, so that all pupils are able to progress, achieve and participate. This will be evident in high quality, challenging teaching that engages pupils and helps them to take ownership of their learning. All children will experience an engaging curriculum. (2006, p. 41)

However, the English teacher training agency was restrictively focused on performance and national standards:

> The term 'personalised learning' means maintaining a focus on individual progress, in order to maximise all learners' capacity to learn, achieve and participate. This means supporting and challenging each learner to achieve national standards and gain the skills they need to thrive and succeed. (TDA, 2007, p. 5)

TLRP analysed the concept of personalised learning as it emerged, and published a Commentary identifying four particular challenges.

Key TLRP questions and findings:	Implications:
Conceptualisation: Are the components of personalised leaning and the relationships between them empirically supported and sufficient? There is a tension between expansive interpretations and restrictive definitions. Personalisation could be about the development of learner identities and dispositions – but it could also be about more pupil assessment and target setting.	A really powerful concept sounds attractive, is intellectually coherent and practically robust. The many versions of 'personalised learning' could make implementation difficult, but also provide considerable scope for professional interpretation.
Authenticity: Is this initiative really about learning? Or is it, despite the title, still primarily about teaching and curriculum delivery? By drawing attention to the personal, and to learning rather than teaching, 'personalised learning' enlists a softer vocabulary than that of targets, performance and delivery. But can a simple reconciliation be achieved? It seems unlikely where high-stakes assessment remains.	Personalisation is in some tension with the commitment, in England, to regular and end of key stage assessment. The rhetoric may be perceived as an ideological 'smoke screen'. Things may be easier in Wales, Scotland and Northern Ireland.
Realism: Are the ambition and rhetoric over-reaching themselves? The school system has been subject to deep and wide change in recent years. There are questions about the system's ability to cope with further innovation. Nor is it safe to assume that practices which prove effective in some places will succeed in others.	The problem of scaling up is considerable and workforce reform introduces fresh challenges. Personalisation represents a huge challenge to the teaching profession. Whilst innovative schools show the way, can others follow?
Risks: What are the major difficulties likely to be and how can they be managed? The concept of personalised learning continues to be interpreted in many ways. The response of the profession is a major risk factor and concerns about workload are important. Personalisation challenges the mutual accommodations which often grow up in routine teacher–pupil classroom practices and calls for high expectations, positive responses and new forms of learner-aware pedagogy.	The profession should contribute actively to the definition of personalised learning. Continued constructive negotiation on workloads is likely to be necessary. Appropriate support for teachers will be needed. Government agencies should work to achieve consistency.

Further information
James, M. and Pollard, A. (2004) *Personalised Learning: A TLRP Commentary*. Swindon: ESRC. (Available on the chapter page for this book at reflectiveteaching.co.uk)
Sebba, J., Brown, N., Steward, S., Galton, M. and James, M. (2007) *An Investigation of Personalised Learning Approaches used by Schools* (Research Report RR843). London: DfES.

Chapter 11
Pedagogy
How can we develop effective strategies?

| Introduction | 346 |

Enacting pedagogy	347
The importance of teacher–pupil interaction	347
Analysing pedagogy	350

Pedagogy, knowledge and learning	350
The development of pedagogic principles	350
Perspectives on effective pedagogies	351

Enacting learner development	353
Building from prior learning	353
Analysing pedagogy	354

Pedagogic repertoire	355
Using talk for whole-class, small group and individual teaching	356
Scaffolding whole-class, small group and individual learning	359

Enacting a series of lessons	360
Chancing pedagogy over time	360
Analysing pedagogy	362

| Conclusion | 363 |

reflectiveteaching.co.uk/rtps6/part3_ch11

INTRODUCTION

Pedagogy was described by historian of education Brian Simon (1981) as: 'the act and discourse of teaching'. This compact definition summarises complex ideas related to how we might define pedagogy and think about teaching and learning.

The *act* of teaching is everything that teachers do while working with their pupils. Indeed, the major topics covered in earlier chapters of this book are all relevant – understanding how children learn, sustaining good relationships, behaviour and engagement, organising the classroom environment, curriculum content and implementation, etc. How then, do teachers pull all this together in what they actually do? To provide some insights on this, three sections of this chapter focus on examples of 'enactment' through classroom practice. The chapter also highlights the need for teachers to develop a *repertoire* of teaching strategies. Because all pedagogic approaches have strengths and weaknesses, teachers need to feel confident with a range of strategies so they can draw on whatever is judged to be most effective for particular educational purposes and learner needs.

The *discourse* of teaching can be seen as ranging widely, from professional debates such as whether it is appropriate for governments to prescribe teaching methods, to more practical matters such as lesson and curriculum planning, and to the vital role of teacher–pupil interaction in classrooms. This wider view of pedagogy recognises that teachers cannot avoid engagement with the ideas and values of their societies (Alexander, 2004). These are most immediately related to conceptualisations of children, learning, teaching and curriculum, but they also are influenced by patterns in teachers' beliefs, school cultures, public policies, histories of practice in education and, most particularly, in the nature and use of language.

Language is fundamental to pedagogy in so many ways. Indeed, human language is unique in its capacity to enable teaching and learning. It is through language that we pass to successive generations our prior learning. Oral language is also vital because it is the basis of written language (Wyse, 2017). The learning in early years settings that focuses very much on children's play, which is enacted through oral language, gradually becomes augmented by pupils' ability to write, something which is also fundamental to most learning in schools. Large-scale qualitative work on pedagogy, comparing primary education in different countries, has identified oral language, and views about how it should be represented in policy and practice, as fundamental to understanding pedagogy (Alexander, 2000).

We begin the chapter with an example that enables us to see 'pedagogy in action'. A short discussion of how thinking about pedagogy has developed is then provided, for its significance to the profession has not been fully established in the UK until relatively recently. Next, we focus on pedagogic judgements to support learner development, and we then return to the issue of pedagogic repertoire. This is illustrated in action by focusing on the use of talk to 'scaffold' student understanding through whole-class, small group and individual teaching. Finally, we look at the way in which pedagogy develops over time, as can be seen even through a case study of two teachers' work to change their teaching of writing.

In discussing pedagogy, we also acknowledge the crucial importance to pedagogy of *subject knowledge*, which we take to mean the concepts, knowledge and understanding, within and between domains of learning, on which teachers' subject-specific planning and teaching draws. For detailed discussion of subject knowledge, see Chapter 9, p. 292. Of course, this is complemented by the need for understanding about *learning*. Whatever aspirations or expectations may exist, it is essential to take account of the existing knowledge, experience and understanding of children and young people. For more detailed discussion of learning, see Chapter 2. Pedagogic expertise, as you can see, draws on a wide range of understanding and capabilities – which is what makes it so interesting.

The chapter is thus about classroom enactment as teachers deploy their understanding and expertise in practical situations. However, it also recognises some major issues of wider significance which frame and influence such processes. Therein lies the fascination and importance of pedagogy.

See Chapter 4

TLRP Principles

Two principles are of particular relevance to this chapter on teacher strategies and pedagogic repertoire:

Effective teaching and learning requires teachers to scaffold learning. Teachers should provide activities which support learners as they move forward, not just intellectually, but also socially and emotionally, so that once these supports are removed, the learning is secure. (*Principle 4*)

Effective teaching and learning promotes the active engagement of the learner. A chief goal of teaching and learning should be the promotion of learners' independence and autonomy. This involves acquiring a repertoire of learning strategies and practices, developing positive attitudes towards learning, and confidence in oneself as a good learner. (*Principle 6*)

ENACTING PEDAGOGY

The importance of teacher–pupil interaction

Case Study 11.1 focuses on a research project that reported a teacher's interaction with her class. The teacher was focused on developing her class's understanding of productive ways to talk when doing group activities.

reflectiveteaching.co.uk/rtps6/part3_ch11

Part 3 Teaching for learning

Case Study 11.1 Ground rules for talk in groups

A teacher of a Year 5 class had been working with her class to develop their understanding of working together in groups. The lesson, that the transcript below is taken from, was planned as a computer-based science investigation for the pupils to work together on. The lesson was the sixth in a series of lessons where the teacher had been encouraging the children to become more aware of how they talked and worked together.

Teacher: Before you go on to the next step on the computer what do you need to make sure that the whole group has done? Oh! More hands up than that. Emma?

Emma: Agreed.

Teacher: Agreed. The whole group needs to agree. *Teacher writes 'everybody agrees' on board.* OK one of my speech bubbles. I wonder what kind of things we might hear each other saying during today's lesson?

Teacher draws a speech bubble. Points to a child.

Boy: What do you think?

Teacher What do you think? *Teacher writes 'What do you think?' in speech bubble.* Anything else you might hear people saying as we have today's lesson? Kaye.

Kaye: What is your idea? *Teacher draws a speech bubble and writes 'What is your idea?' in it.*

Teacher: Brilliant! What's your idea? Ooh, Sydney.

Sydney: Why do you think that?

Teacher: Excellent. Well done. *Teacher draws a speech bubble and writes 'Why do you think that?' in it.* Any other things we might hear people say? Ruby.

Ruby: I'm not too sure on that idea. What do you think? Teacher draws a new speech bubble.

Teacher: Brilliant. Well done. What do we need to remember in our groups? Kiera?

Kiera: That everybody gets a turn to talk.

Teacher: Everybody gets a turn to talk. Teacher points to a child.

Girl: Everybody needs to share their opinions.

Teacher: Yeah – and are we all the same?

Class: No.

Teacher: Will there be someone in your group that perhaps wants to talk all the time?

Class: Yes.

Teacher: Will there be someone in your group who doesn't want to talk at all?

Class Yes!

Teacher: How are you going to get that person who doesn't want to talk at all to say something? Shane? What do you think? How are you going to get that person who sits there and doesn't say anything to say something in your group? Help him out Tyber.

Tyber: Ask them.

reflectiveteaching.co.uk/rtps6/part3_ch11

> Teacher: Ask them. Brilliant. What about that person who talks ALL the time? *Emphasises with actions.*
>
> Boy: Tell him to shut up.
>
> Teacher Ooh! Are you? I hope not because that's not positive language, is it? What could you do to help them out? Kiera.
>
> Kiera: Ask them and then ask somebody else and then ask the other person. *Teacher silences an interruption with a gesture.*
>
> Teacher: Brilliant. Making sure that you ask everybody in the group. Excellent. Kaye?
>
> (Mercer, 2005, p. 152)

The most important aspect of the pedagogy represented in this short extract of classroom dialogue is that it is not only the aims and practicalities of the lesson that are important to the teacher; it is her explicit focus on talk, and in this case on ground rules to help children benefit from collaborative talk in their groups.

The teacher's interaction in this example is consistent with the Initiation, Response, Feedback (IRF) style of teacher interaction that is common in whole-class discussions with a teacher. Ironically the teacher is encouraging the pupils to talk in ways that will be more productive for their learning in groups and yet the teacher uses a form of interaction that tends to result in short answers from pupils. However, this underlines another important aspect of pedagogy. Teachers need to be able to select from a repertoire of interaction styles that suit their intentions for pupils' learning in a given context. In this case, where one of the teacher's aims is to review and check that the class is thinking about the ground rules, the IRF pattern is appropriate for that aim. At other times it is vital for teachers to interact with pupils in a way that encourages them to give a more extended contribution to a discussion. Mercer's (2005) analysis of the example focuses on what he calls the temporal quality of the dialogue: the way the teacher is reminding children about experiences they have had in the recent past in order to be at least as productive in the forthcoming lesson that the teacher is introducing.

As Alexander (2000) made clear, there is a risk that oral language, as a focus in its own right as part of the curriculum, can be neglected in national curricula and in classroom discourse. One of the criticisms of England's 2014 national curriculum is that the recognition of the importance of oral language as part of the curriculum, represented as Speaking and Listening in previous versions of the national curriculum, appeared to have been lost somewhat. Neil Mercer's work has drawn attention to the importance of oral language as an explicit focus for teaching and pedagogy, and his research has included attention to how teachers' practice can evolve in order to support the development of pupils' talk.

reflectiveteaching.co.uk/rtps6/part3_ch11

Analysing pedagogy

> **Reflective Activity 11.1**
>
> *Aim:* To identify aspects of pedagogy in our teaching.
>
> *Evidence and reflection:* Make a short video or audio recording of you teaching your class in a whole-class session. Reflect on the key features of the way you interact with the class. For example, to what extent did you use the IRF pattern? To what extent did you encourage longer contributions from children? What might you change in your teacher–pupil interaction? Select a short example to discuss with the children in your class to see what they understand about the nature of aspects such as turn-taking; listening; putting forward points of view; etc.
>
> *Extension:* Work with a colleague to share short recordings of your teaching and/or observe each other teaching. Discuss you different ways of interacting with pupils.

PEDAGOGY, KNOWLEDGE AND LEARNING

The development of pedagogic principles

How is pedagogy represented in a selection of the literature? In the introduction to the TLRP commentary, *Professionalism and Pedagogy: A Contemporary Opportunity*, we are reminded that 'the relative lack of reference to pedagogy in educational discussion within the UK, compared with practice in many other successful countries, has been the focus of academic debate for the best part of thirty years' (GTC E, 2010, p. 4, **Reading 11.2**). The origin of concern about this lack is traced to Brian Simon's thought-provoking chapter written in the 1980s entitled 'Why No Pedagogy in England?' (Simon, 1981) (**Reading 11.3**). In this text, Simon also defines the term pedagogy as the 'science of teaching' (p. 124), arguing that although the concept of pedagogy has long been revered in many European countries, in England it had been shunned. The chief reason was argued to be:

> the practice and approach of our most prestigious educational institutions (historically speaking), the ancient universities and leading public schools. Until recently, and even perhaps today, these have been dominant, both socially and in terms of the formation of the climate of opinion. It is symptomatic that the public schools, in general, have until recently contemptuously rejected the idea that a professional training is in any way relevant to the job of a public schoolmaster. (p. 125)

The view that education of teachers was only needed for those teaching in the elementary schools meant that education 'as a subject of enquiry and study, still less a "science", has had little prestige in this country' (p. 128). Teachers in the public schools thus only needed a good knowledge of their subject rather than professional training. However, the challenges for teachers working in the elementary schools did eventually force school boards to take a more systematic approach and a science of teaching emerged which could be incorporated into teacher education. Hence, there began to be some recognition of the importance of pedagogy. Simon's challenging question has been revisited on numerous occasions from different perspectives, not least because the concept of pedagogy has continued to carry uncertain weight and meaning. It remains the case that teachers working in private schools are not required to have qualified teacher status, although many, of course, do. However, whilst Simon argued that the development of teaching was dominated by a concern with the individual differences between learners and groups of learners, and how to respond to them, he also offered an interesting, but contrasting, viewpoint:

> To develop effective pedagogy means starting from the opposite standpoint, from what children have in common as members of the human species; to establish the general principles of teaching and, in the light of these, to determine what modifications of practice are necessary to meet specific individual needs. (p. 141)

It was on the basis of Simon's appeal, to the establishment of 'general principles of teaching', that TLRP began its work on the principles which underpin effective teaching and learning (see Chapter 4).

The concept of pedagogy has thus, over the years, become transformed from Simon's notion of a science of teaching to a much more holistic idea, one which requires teachers to reflect on whether and how their pedagogy develops from established principles. We now review some of these developments.

Perspectives on effective pedagogies

Critical pedagogy In some parts of the world, educators have used the concept of pedagogy to challenge the status quo. One of the most well-known of those educators is the Brazilian, Paulo Freire, whose central argument in *Pedagogy of the Oppressed* (2000) is that pedagogy is the means by which the most oppressed people can be taught to reflect critically on their oppression and actively participate in liberation from it. Freire's notion of pedagogy is of teaching through which the oppressed learner becomes literate and gains the power of self-direction, rather than merely adopting the forms of education offered by the oppressor or, indeed, being filled up like an empty vessel.

Instead, he views the literacy process as a dynamic one in which 'reading the world always precedes reading the word, and reading the word implies continually reading the world' (Freire, 2000, p. 37). Education of this kind means making connections between language and life so that each illuminates the other. Freire's pedagogy, often referred to as critical pedagogy to indicate the expectation that some form of action will arise out of the stance being adopted, stems from very particular attitudes and values but resonates with educators in many different parts of the world.

reflectiveteaching.co.uk/rtps6/part3_ch11

Culturally relevant pedagogy There is a persistent need for teachers to develop pedagogy that is grounded on responding to a culturally diverse society and enabling students from minoritised groups to succeed. This means confronting deficit perspectives of learners and actively teaching in ways that value ethnic diversity and the knowledge and experience that all students bring to the classroom (Gay, 2010). Ladson-Billings (2021) demonstrates how teachers can confront deficit perceptions of learners by actively seeking examples of teaching that explicitly value cultural diversity and embed ways to build on local community knowledge and experience when designing learning experiences and activities for students. A framework for implementing culturally relevant pedagogy is offered by Brown-Jeffy and Cooper (2011, p. 71) based on five themes: identity and achievement, equity and excellence, developmental appropriateness, teaching the whole child, and student–teacher relationships. They argue that, 'simply stated, equity involves giving students what they need. It is not the same as equal opportunity' (p. 74). It requires teachers to be deeply reflective practitioners, supported by working in collaboration, developing respect for their students as a basis for teaching.

Theories of mind Meanwhile, other prominent educators, for example Jerome Bruner in the United States, have viewed pedagogy from the perspective of educational psychology with different consequences again. Bruner, strongly influenced by the work of Vygotsky, was interested in how theories of the human mind affect teachers' practice. In his analysis of 'folk pedagogy' (1996, Reading 11.1), he demonstrates that the way teachers perceive learners' minds affects how they teach, a powerful argument for a science of teaching which would enable us to understand the workings of the mind as clearly as possible. Drawing connections between 'models of mind and models of pedagogy' (1996, p. 53), he demonstrated how a theory of mind which holds that learners acquire knowledge through imitation will lead to a very different pedagogy from a theory of mind which privileges learning through inter-subjective exchange. Bruner is not arguing for one model over and above another; rather, he suggests that what is needed is the forging of different perspectives on learning into 'some congruent unity, recognised as parts of a common continent' (1996, p. 65). Echoes of Dweck and Sfard are clear (see Chapter 2).

Pedagogical discourse Deborah Britzman, an American critical ethnographer with a keen interest in teacher education, likewise argues the need for teachers to learn how theoretical perspectives inform their pedagogy. In *Practice Makes Practice: A Critical Study of Learning to Teach* (2003), she explored how it is not just important to identify and reflect critically on theoretical perspectives but also on different discourses that can crucially affect the way in which teachers, teaching and pedagogy are construed:

[E]very curriculum, as a form of discourse, intones particular orientations, values, and interests, and constructs visions of authority, power, and knowledge. The selected knowledge of any curriculum represents not only things to know, but a view of knowledge that implicitly defines the

---

Expert Questions

Repertoire: *is our pedagogic expertise sufficiently creative, skilled and wide-ranging to teach all elements of learning?*

Warrant: *are our teaching strategies evidence-informed, convincing and justifiable to stakeholders?*

These questions contribute to a conceptual framework underpinning professional expertise (see Chapter 16).

knower's capacities as it legitimates the persons who deem that knowledge important. This capacity to privilege particular accounts over others is based upon relations of power. (Britzman, 2003, p. 39)

Teachers therefore need to remain keenly aware of the way different discourses shape their thinking and that of their students. Discourses which characterise learners mainly in relation to categories in statutory assessments (e.g. 'not achieving the expected standard') need to be defamiliarised and challenged, as they were by the UK team who conducted the 'learning without limits' research (Hart et al., 2004, see Reading 1.4). The researchers and the teachers with whom they worked set out to explore what changed when students' potential achievements were viewed as 'limitless', modifying their perspective to 'formulate the teaching task not primarily in terms of opposition to something negative, but as one of commitment to something positive: transforming the capacity to learn' (Hart et al., 2004, p. 262).

Agency and pedagogy The repertoire of pedagogical approaches outlined in this chapter relies on teachers having the capacity to determine the approaches that they wish to adopt, and also the *affordances* to do so: something we call *agency*. Agency has been defined as the 'socially situated capacity to act' (Manyukhina and Wyse, 2011, bera.ac.uk/blog/childrens-agency-what-is-it-and-what-should-be-done). Teacher agency (see Priestley, 2015, bera.ac.uk/blog/teacher-agency-what-is-it-and-why-does-it-matter) has attracted more attention in scholarly work than children's agency, hence The Helen Hamlyn Centre for Pedagogy has initiated a strand of research on children's agency (HHCP, 2022, ucl.ac.uk/ioe/departments-and-centres/centres/helen-hamlyn-centre-pedagogy-0-11-years/research-themes/childrens-agency).

ENACTING LEARNER DEVELOPMENT

Building from prior learning

The example which follows exemplifies TLRP Principle 3, which links teaching to prior experience and learning and 'includes building on prior learning but also taking account of the personal and cultural experiences of different groups of learners' (James and Pollard, 2006, p. 8). In it, we see an early years trainee teacher, Siobhan, carrying out focused observations and analysis of an individual child, Alfie, and how both of these form part of her pedagogic practice. The case features the teaching of phonics as a method of learning to read, and illustrates how this approach can demotivate some children unless it is embedded in a rich, literacy environment (EEF **Toolkit Evidence 11.1**, p. 367).

354 Part 3 Teaching for learning

Case Study 11.2 Studying a child's reading development

Siobhan, an early years trainee teacher, conducts a study into 6-year-old Alfie's reading development over the course of a six-week school placement. At the start of the placement she collects evidence of the child's current attitudes to, and attainment in, reading from:

1 classroom observations of the child reading in a variety of situations;
2 reading to and with the chosen child;
3 a reading interview;
4 a running record;
5 observations and assessments of phonics lessons and guided reading lessons.

During the placement she continues to gather observational and assessment evidence from phonics and reading lessons and repeats the initial activities towards the end.

From her initial observations of the child reading in a variety of situations, Siobhan notes that Alfie frequently chooses to read during 'independent' time in the classroom, selecting a range of texts from *Beano* comics to factual books about dinosaurs and poetry books about monsters. He often engages other children in what he is doing, attempting to tell them what the book is about and asking them to read with him. He reads aloud to his peers in an excited and animated fashion, making sound effects and loud exclamations. It is evident that he has read many of the texts in the book corner. Siobhan elects to conduct a running record on a book about monsters and this he reads with confidence and fluency. Whether reading books with his peers, or on a one-to-one basis with an adult, Alfie enjoys the opportunity to share his enthusiasm and to discuss texts. In contrast, during phonics and guided reading sessions, Alfie appears distracted and not engaged in the content of the sessions or the books, only becoming so when phonics sessions contain images of monsters or when the content of the book in guided reading sessions captivates him. When asked about books he doesn't like reading, he states, 'the ones at guided reading are so boring'. His parents have contacted the school to say that the books that are being sent home are not engaging him and he has committed them to memory.

The reading interview elicits further information about Alfie's attitudes to reading. He confidently asserts, 'I like reading a lot' but with the caveat 'not when we have to read on the carpet and my legs get itchy and I can't see the pictures. I like seeing the pictures'. At home he reads with his older brother, and his dad sometimes. He makes frequent reference to his older brother and how he reads his 'chapter books', especially his monster books and also his *Beano* comics.

Analysing pedagogy

Siobhan's study enables her to make reflective observations about Alfie's learning and demonstrates how focused observations and analysis of an individual child are central to pedagogy (see Chapter 2 for further examples). Siobhan comments on the holistic nature of young children's learning and development and reveals how a teacher's pedagogy is

reflectiveteaching.co.uk/rtps6/part3_ch11

underpinned by knowledge of the individual learner, both in school and beyond, and their responses to a wide variety of classroom interactions. Alfie's keen interest in reading is not evident from his responses in guided reading and phonics sessions but is apparent through the observations Siobhan makes of him reading independently and with his peers and also from the comments he makes during the one-to-one reading interview. He benefits greatly from having adults and peers share his enthusiasm and read with him individually, and the impact on his self-esteem and his attitude to reading in contrast with his behaviours during more structured reading sessions is notable. Alfie's comments about his discomfort on the carpet and frustration about not being able to 'see the pictures' indicate the pedagogic value of listening to young children's individual voices and taking account of their physical and emotional needs. Finally, we see through the notable influence of Alfie's older brother on his reading, the crucial impact of home literacy experiences on school learning and the potential this has to fertilise learning and teaching.

> **Expert Questions**
>
> **Reflection:** *is our classroom practice based on incremental, evidence-informed and collaborative improvement strategies?*
>
> **Empowerment:** *is our pedagogic repertoire successful in enhancing wellbeing, learning disposition, capabilities and agency?*
>
> These questions contribute to a conceptual framework underpinning professional expertise (see Chapter 16).

> **Reflective Activity 11.2**
>
> *Aim:* To reflect from a learner's perspective on aspects of pedagogy.
>
> *Evidence and reflection:* Reflect back on a significant moment from your own early education, and what you remember about yourself as a learner. Recall what happened. To what extent were your values, attitudes, responses and prior knowledge taken into consideration by the teacher in this episode? What aspects of pedagogy might, or could, your teacher have been drawing on at this point?
>
> *Extension:* In the light of your current thinking about pedagogy, how might you have acted had you been in the teacher's position?

PEDAGOGIC REPERTOIRE

The idea of pedagogy is multifaceted and needs to be constantly refined through teachers' reflections on their classroom experience from their own and their students' perspectives. We need to question whether our pedagogic expertise is sufficiently creative, skilled and wide-ranging and whether our teaching strategies are evidence-informed, convincing and justifiable. Some aspects of pedagogy may appear to be more visible and, possibly, more urgent than others but ultimately all of them need to be in play. The pedagogical choices made by reflective teachers, and their agency, are also influenced by government's control of curriculum and increasingly pedagogy (for example see Wyse and Bradbury, 2021, in relation to government control over the teaching of reading).

A key step is to link the learning intentions of a lesson with appropriate teaching strategies. The planning of lessons is discussed extensively in Chapter 10 and particular emphasis is placed on differentiation and personalisation so that the cognitive and motivational appropriateness of planned activities can be maximised. Being able to draw on a range of strategies complements this by enabling the selection of effective teaching/learning processes. Overall intentions can then be shared with pupils (Hattie, 2012, Reading 16.5). In summary, to be most effective, aims and methods should be matched *and* understood.

> **Expert Questions**
>
> **Repertoire:** is our pedagogic expertise sufficiently creative, skilled and wide-ranging to teach all elements of learning?
>
> **Warrant:** are our teaching strategies evidence-informed, convincing and justifiable to stakeholders?
>
> These questions contribute to a conceptual framework underpinning professional expertise (see Chapter 16).

As Robin Alexander argues, 'teachers need a repertoire of teaching approaches from which they can select on the basis of fitness for purpose in relation to the learner, the subject-matter and the opportunities and constraints of context' (Alexander, 2008a, p. 109, Reading 12.3).

Alexander's analysis of pedagogic repertoire concentrates on three broad aspects: the organisation of interaction (see also Chapter 8, p. 249), talk for teaching and talk for learning (Alexander, 2008a).

We focus here on talk for teaching and on some of the research informing it. For those relatively new to teaching, it is pedagogy as craft, and talk as a key feature of that craft, which often makes the most immediate and pressing demands. We therefore explore this aspect of the pedagogic repertoire in some depth.

Using talk for whole-class, small group and individual teaching

As Alexander (2008a, Reading 12.3) stresses, choices about when, how and to what extent to interact with the whole class underpin a teacher's pedagogic craft. A paradox in teaching is that whilst teachers use talk as the main tool of their trade, many are not aware of the range of ways they *could* use it when interacting with students. Broadly speaking, as teachers we use talk to provide information, check understanding and maintain control. However, there is much we can also do such as link present activities to past experience, set up future activities, relate existing ideas to new educational frames of meaning and model ways of using language (Mercer and Littleton, 2007, Reading 11.6; see also Chapter 8). One interesting way of thinking about and reflecting on different teacher and learner interactions is to use categorisations such as those suggested by Mortimer and Scott (2007). They divide whole-class interactions into four types of communicative approach along two dimensions; the first representing a continuum between dialogic and authoritative talk and the second between interactive and non-interactive talk:

Interactive/dialogic: the teacher and students explore ideas, generating new meanings, posing genuine questions and offering, listening to and working on different points of view.

Non-interactive/dialogic: the teacher considers various points of view, setting out, exploring and working on the different perspectives.

Interactive/authoritative: the teacher leads students through a sequence of questions and answers with the aim of reaching one specific point of view.

Non-interactive/authoritative: the teacher presents one specific point of view. (Mortimer and Scott, 2007, p. 39)

The first two approaches allow for whole-class dialogue where the teacher engages pupils and elicits their ideas, gets extended responses and allows pupil contributions to shape the dialogue. However, in the second pair, through authoritative talk, the teacher pursues a direction or 'story', presents new information for children to consider and/or learn and is unlikely to seek extended contributions. We return to the concept of dialogic talk more extensively in Chapter 12, but in relation to pedagogy, a reflective teacher will consider the affordance these different types of whole-class interactions offer to particular learning situations.

The findings of one large investigation into classroom talk, the Observational Research and Classroom Learning Evaluation (ORACLE) research, showed that approximately 80 per cent of teachers' time, in Key Stage 2 classrooms, was spent in talk between the teacher and children – 56 per cent with individuals, 15 per cent with the whole class, 7 per cent with groups (Galton, Simon and Croll, 1980). Later, Galton et al. found that 'for the typical pupil, 75 per cent of all pupil–teacher exchanges are experienced as a member of the class, exactly as they were twenty years ago' (1999, p. 84). Interestingly, a similar large project, the Primary, Assessment, Curriculum and Experience (PACE) research, found that in Key Stage 1 classrooms, the proportion of whole-class work was also very high, with a lower figure for individual work (Pollard and Triggs, 2000). Robin Alexander built on this previous work to develop his ideas about dialogic teaching (e.g. Alexander, 2018). Reflective teachers may want to consider their own pedagogy in the light of such findings.

There has been a strong body of research in the past thirty years, both internationally and recently in the UK, which supports the view that by working in groups and interacting with others, students' academic performance and attitudes to learning can be improved. For example, EEF **Toolkit Evidence 11.2** (see p. 368) states: 'Small group teaching usually is effective. On average, it increased progress by about four months.'

Galton (2007) summarises the key benefits of training students to work in groups as follows:

First, the process promotes *independent thinking,* such that pupils gain a sense of control over their learning. Second, it can develop *speaking and listening skills*, allowing pupils to share feelings and ideas. Third, it can encourage *positive self-esteem*, allowing pupils to build confidence in their own abilities. Fourth, it can improve classroom *relationships*, enhancing pupils' sense of social responsibility. (Galton, 2007, p. 110)

Considerations about the organisation of collective and collaborative group work and activity between students are therefore part of a teacher's pedagogic repertoire, as the enactments in this chapter demonstrate.

An example of a project which also demonstrates how teachers aim to enhance the learning potential of pupils working in classroom groups (at Key Stages 1–3) is the SPRinG project (Baines et al., 2017). It began in 2000 and continues in a number of ways. It actively involved teachers collaborating with researchers in a programme designed to raise levels of group work during typical classroom learning activities and to enhance students' skills of listening, explaining, sharing ideas, building trust and respect, planning, organising and evaluating. The project also aimed to develop the skills of the teacher in group work through supporting, guiding, monitoring, fostering independence and providing classroom management. Findings from the study have important implications for pedagogy (see TLRP **Research Briefing 11.1** on p. 370). Involvement in SPRinG had positive effects on pupils' academic progress in relation to usual classroom practices. In Key Stage 1, benefits were seen in reading and mathematics. In Key Stage 2, group work benefited all types of knowledge in science but especially conceptual understanding and inferential thinking, while at Key Stage 3 the success depended on the type of topic but appeared to benefit higher cognitive understanding. Across the three Key Stages, pupils were more likely to sustain high-level interactions, engaging in more autonomous learning relative to comparison pupils, and teachers were more likely to monitor interactions between pupils and engage less in direct teaching.

Although such studies demonstrate the benefits of group work, a consistent finding in research since the 1970s is that whilst pupils may sit *in* groups they rarely work *as* groups (Alexander, 2008b) so that this arrangement is not as productive as it could be. Amongst factors which Galton (2007) identifies as causing teachers to desist from setting up group work are the perception of a loss of teacher control over the learning environment and the difficulty in ascertaining whether talk in groups is on-task. Issues that can impede effective group work are constructing tasks appropriate for the arrangement and the degree of structure required. Size and composition of groups can also create difficulties. (These aspects of group work will be discussed further in Chapter 12.)

> **Expert Questions**
>
> **Engagement:** do our teaching strategies, classroom organisation and consultation enable learners to actively participate in and enjoy their learning?
>
> **Dialogue:** does teacher–learner talk scaffold understanding to build on existing knowledge and to strengthen dispositions to learn?
>
> These questions contribute to a conceptual framework underpinning professional expertise (see Chapter 16).

Whatever the challenges in setting up effective group work, from a cognitive perspective, the social constructivist ideas of Vygotsky point to the benefits of establishing group work as part of a repertoire of strategies. In the same way that a more knowledgeable adult can help a student move through the zone of proximal development, so too more knowledgeable peers can support learning. However, it is not unusual to see teachers setting up group work and then almost immediately beginning to circulate and check understanding and give comments. Galton and Williamson (1992) found that when a teacher's intervention occurs too early in the group's deliberations, then students can quickly feel a loss of ownership and control over discussion. Judgements therefore need to be made about when it is appropriate to scaffold discussion. It is to this aspect of pedagogic craft that we now turn.

Scaffolding whole-class, small group and individual learning

Scaffolding is a term that is often used loosely to describe all kinds of support that teachers may offer (Pea, 2004). However, in the sense that the term was used by Wood, Bruner and Ross (1976) in their seminal paper, the concept offers much more than this. They described scaffolding as the support given to a less experienced learner by a more experienced adult or peer – which Tharp and Gallimore (1988) refer to as assisted performance (Reading 11.4). In scaffolding learning, teachers actively, temporarily and contingently provide learners with just the right amount of cognitive support to bring them closer to independence. Over time, an adult, or more experienced other, can reduce the degree of freedom to make a complex task more manageable for the student so that they can achieve independent competence. Their idea of scaffolding can thus be seen to develop the work of Vygotsky and the concept of the 'zone of proximal development' (ZPD) (see Chapter 2 and Reading 2.4).

Established conceptualisations of scaffolding see it as an interactive process occurring between teacher and student in which both participate actively and where learners are 'guided by others' (Stone, 1998, p. 351) to develop understandings that would be problematic for them to achieve unaided. Van de Pol, Volan and Beishuizen (2012) discuss literature around scaffolding and argue that its characteristics are threefold. The first of the characteristics is 'contingency', which suggests that the teacher's scaffolding approaches are tailored to the specific needs and current levels of performance of the learners. The second characteristic is 'fading', whereby scaffolding is gradually withdrawn according to the learner's developing understanding and competence. Third, transfer of responsibility occurs. In considering how, where and when to scaffold learning a teacher therefore needs to take into account:

- how approaches are tailored to the specific needs and current levels of performance of learners;
- how the level of scaffolding can be withdrawn depending on the learner's progress;
- how learners can take responsibility for their learning.

Teachers are often urged to use modelling as a way to scaffold learning. For example, it was a key feature of the recommended teaching sequence for writing in primary classrooms where teachers were encouraged to demonstrate the skills of an expert writer to the class. The basis for the approach was set out in the joint United Kingdom Literacy Association (UKLA)/Primary National Strategy (PNS) publication, *Raising Boys' Achievements in Writing* (2004). However, when a teacher models something in the classroom, the children should not be expected simply to imitate it. As Bruner says:

360   Part 3 Teaching for learning

[W]hat the teacher must be, to be an effective competence model, is a day-to-day working model with whom to interact. It is not so much that the teacher provides a model to *imitate*. Rather, it is that the teacher can become a part of the student's internal dialogue – somebody who respects what he wants, someone whose standards he wishes to make his own. (Bruner 1966b, p. 124)

Scaffolding, which includes modelling, is thus a dynamic interaction that needs to be finely tuned to the learner's ongoing progress. Support given by the teacher depends on the characteristics of the situation, for example the type of task and the responses of the student. Scaffolding strategies therefore need to be adapted for each classroom situation, which is what makes it a key part of teachers' pedagogic repertoire. It is also vital to remember that the teachers should always be looking to remove scaffolding so that students can demonstrate independence in their thinking.

ENACTING A SERIES OF LESSONS

Changing pedagogy over time

In Case Study 11.3, two teachers reflected on their teaching of writing in order to make changes in their classroom practice during the course of a year. The work was part of a research project that began with discussions and planning to make changes to classroom practice in relation to seven evidence-based principles for the teaching of writing (Wyse, 2017):

1 Increase the amount of time spent writing with an emphasis on the process of writing.

2 Create a supportive writing environment in the classroom (enthusiasm; scaffold learning; pupil independence; clear goals).

3 Develop pupils' skills, strategies and knowledge (planning, revising and editing; knowledge about creativity).

4 Teach pupils about 'self-regulation' (pupils reflect on their use of writing strategies).

5 Use assessment for learning techniques (adult feedback; assessment of learning feeding into teaching; encourage pupils' self and peer evaluation).

6 Teach keyboard use as well as handwriting.

7 Teach writing across the curriculum (different text structures for different purposes).

Expert Question

Repertoire: *is our pedagogic expertise sufficiently creative, skilled and wide-ranging to teach all elements of learning?*

This question contributes to a conceptual framework underpinning professional expertise (see Chapter 16).

The teachers reflected then wrote detailed plans about how they would change elements of their teaching of writing in relation to one or more of the principles. These processes of change were part of the overall study of the teachers' work.

reflectiveteaching.co.uk/rtps6/part3_ch11

Case Study 11.3 Teaching writing research project

The two teachers who are described in this case study had a passion for literacy and wanted to know how to teach it even better than their current practice. The teachers wanted to develop children as independent writers who knew how to write confidently for readers. They wanted to develop strategies to cultivate children's ownership, independence and autonomy, and for the children to appreciate and explore a wide range of genres, including storytelling and poetry.

The teachers decided to introduce *free-writing books* to their repertoire of teaching approaches. These were notebooks that the children could personalise and choose what they wanted to write about at certain times during the week, for up to half an hour at a time (Year 1), or two to three times a week (Year 3). These books were not marked, or judged in any way; the teachers did however read them. One of the teachers described them as flexible and organic. The children in her class were able to sit where they wanted to during free writing sessions to write alone, or collaboratively with a friend. One such session led to two of her children, who were interested in popular music, experimenting with their own song lyric. The teacher said, 'I've learnt more about them as writers from their free-writing books.' Another teacher experimented with playing music during free writing sessions. These were strategies that led to the teachers thinking about how to create the optimum learning environment within the classroom (evidence-based writing research Principle 1). One teacher stated:

> The success of free writing sessions . . . has been huge and universal! Self-declared reluctant writers have become enthusiastic about writing in this way. Children demand free writing whenever a gap arises in the timetable. Children eventually got used to the idea of writing whatever they wanted and the burden of thinking of an 'idea' lessened as children realised that they could write in ANY way, including random ideas, words, jokes, lists, and other informal texts. (Class teacher, Primary School 1)

Free writing had the biggest impact on children's views of themselves as writers, and as individuals with ideas, opinions and preferences.

The teachers also participated in a Centre for Language in Primary Education (CLPE) training day entitled 'The Power of Poetry', led by Michelle Rooney, where the teachers experienced writing poetry for themselves as well as suggestions for developing poetry in the classroom as part of their teaching repertoire. This led to a poetry unit of work being developed in one of the classrooms. Children were given the opportunity to write their own personal anthologies of poetry. A poetry corner and dedicated readings meant they became immersed in the genre whilst at the same time developing their poetry skills with confidence.

The teachers developed their subject knowledge through their different approaches to teaching. The metalinguistic knowledge, which they shared with their pupils, was rather different from the knowledge that is specified in the national curriculum, for example grammatical terms.

> Our classroom discussions [include] a purposeful, meta-awareness about language. The children in my class can confidently talk about the writing process, a process of which they have ownership. They can use language such as editing, publishing, purpose, audience and drafting with ease. (Class teacher, B Primary School)

reflectiveteaching.co.uk/rtps6/part3_ch11

> The teachers felt that it would be 'going backwards' to not use the seven research-based principles within their teaching and planning of writing in future. In our view one of the strongest statements of impact came from the teacher at Primary School 2.
>
> > I feel like I have created an overall ethos and style where the national curriculum can naturally slot into. I have control over the government guidelines, not vice versa.
>
> [The project in this case study was funded by the Sainsbury Family Charitable Trust.]

Analysing pedagogy

At the time that the teachers in the case study made changes to their practice, the teaching of writing was constrained by England's national curriculum of 2014, for example by the extensive requirement to teach grammatical terms. Their decision to adopt free-writing books within writing workshop style lessons required the teachers to have confidence that there was a good chance that the new pedagogy would result in improvements in their practice. This confidence was generated in part by the warrant given by the seven evidence-based principles that were central to the project. Although the changes in practice were about a quite specific area of the curriculum, the teaching of writing, there were also more general factors relevant to the teachers' new practices, for example professional autonomy and the confidence to innovate in spite of restrictions created by education policy. The professional development the teachers took part in organised by the CLPE also has a scholarly base, for example as seen in CLPE's work about the influence of the reader in the development of the writer (Barrs and Cork, 2001, Reading 12.5).

> **Reflective Activity 11.3**
>
> *Aim:* To explore how principles about pedagogy relate to our own planning and teaching.
>
> *Evidence and reflection:* Review a sequence of three lessons you have recently planned and taught. Identify as many different aspects of pedagogy as possible within and between the three lessons, explaining and justifying them in the light of what you have just read. What is the balance between the different aspects and how do you account for it? What challenges did the sequence present in terms of your subject knowledge?
>
> *Extension:* What implications are there for classroom interactions and teachers' scaffolding of students' learning in this series of lessons?

reflectiveteaching.co.uk/rtps6/part3_ch11

CONCLUSION

In this chapter we have explored interconnected aspects of pedagogy. As our readings, discussion and enactments show, pedagogy is a rich and fascinating concept, constantly being shaped and re-shaped by teachers. At times, some elements of pedagogy will appear more pressing than others. Nevertheless, how we teach and respond to learners will be crucially informed by our understanding of pedagogy as a whole. Whilst some ideas about teaching and learning endure, others change and are transformed, not only as new research is undertaken by teachers in classrooms or professional researchers but also because teaching and learning are human enterprises and hence are never static. No two teachers are the same; no two learning contexts are the same. We all need, therefore, to reflect on our pedagogy as and when our own understanding is further developed by experience. At all times, we need to juggle our concern with subject knowledge and the need to consider learners holistically. As the case study of Alfie above demonstrates, the importance of listening to students' individual voices cannot be underestimated.

reflectiveteaching.co.uk/rtps6/part3_ch11

CHAPTER WEBPAGE

reflectiveteaching.co.uk offers additional professional resources for this chapter. For the chapter webpage, go to: reflectiveteaching.co.uk/rtps6/part3_ch11

The chapter has had a special character because it is about 'enactment' – putting into practice powerful ideas such as 'prior learning', 'repertoire' and 'scaffolding'. That is why the chapter contains several case studies of teachers and learners at work in schools. As you will see, the Reflective Activities and guidance on further reading are designed to support this focus on enactment. If you were challenged to pick out the most powerful, single, pedagogic idea in Chapter 11, what would it be? For many, it might be that of the 'zone of proximal development' – the concept that highlights what a learner might be able to do in future, *if* appropriately supported. Suggested activities and readings are signalled on the chapter webpage, but it is also instructive to look further across the web. On Wikipedia, you can read a comprehensive description of ZPD, and learn about its origins and significance. Or you can turn to one of Sarah Wright's '30-second briefings' on the ZPD, hosted by the *Times Educational Supplement*. There is a good collection of videos on YouTube too.

As established, we offer three levels of suggestions for follow-up study.

1 *Further Reading* on the chapter webpage follows the structure of the chapter and guides you to closely linked research-based studies. With the support of a good library, it should be extremely helpful if you want to investigate issues in depth.

2 *Key Readings*, below, is a list of selected highlights or 'essential reads'. Most good educational libraries should have this material.

3 *Readings for Reflective Teaching in Schools* provides the simplest solution for anyone who is short of time or opportunity for library-based study. The edited extracts of many of the *Key Readings* are extremely convenient and some are indicated below. A brief description of the full contents for this chapter is provided on the chapter webpage, so you can see how it might fulfil your needs.

KEY READINGS

TLRP's overall school findings, including 'ten principles for effective teaching and learning', are discussed in Chapter 4 of this book. For a simple explanation of the idea of pedagogy seen as science, craft and art, and an exposition of 'conceptual tools' for tackling enduring educational issues, see:

Pollard, A. (ed.) (2010) *Professionalism and Pedagogy: A Contemporary Opportunity.* London: TLRP. (**Reading 11.2**) (see also Chapter 16)

Alexander's comparative analysis of pedagogic issues has generated a strong conceptual framework which is applicable to any setting. See:

> Alexander, R. (2000) *Culture and Pedagogy. International Comparisons in Primary Education*. Oxford: Blackwell.
>
> Alexander, R. (2008a) *Essays on Pedagogy*. London: Routledge. (Reading 12.3)

An influential application of a synthesis of global research is:

> Hattie, J. (2012) *Visible Learning for Teachers*. London: Routledge. (Reading 16.5)

A classic summary of research on teaching is provided in a US handbook, and many other overviews are also available:

> Anderson, P.M. (2008) *Pedagogy. A Primer*. New York: Peter Lang.
>
> Joyce, B., Weil, M. and Calhoun, E. (2009) *Models of Teaching*. New York: Pearson.
>
> Muijs, D. and Reynolds, D. (2017) *Effective Teaching*. London: SAGE. (Reading 8.7)
>
> Duran, D. and Topping, K. (2017) *Learning by Teaching. Evidence-based Strategies to Enhance Learning in the Classroom*. London: Routledge.

There are many excellent guides to practical teaching strategies and skills. Among the best are:

> Wassermann, S. (2017) *The Art of Interactive Teaching. Listening, Responding, Questioning*. London: Routledge.
>
> Kyriacou, C. (2009) *Effective Teaching in Schools: Theory and Practice*. Cheltenham: Nelson Thornes.
>
> Petty, G. (2009) *Teaching Today: A Practical Guide*. Cheltenham: Nelson Thornes.
>
> Sotto, E. (2007) *When Teaching Becomes Learning*. London: Continuum.

To explore the particular significance of dialogue in classroom pedagogy, see:

> Mercer, N. and Littleton, K. (2007) *Dialogue and the Development of Children's Thinking*. London: Routledge. (Reading 11.6)
>
> Phillipson, N. and Wegerif, R. (2017) *Dialogic Education. Mastering Core Concepts through Thinking Together*. London: Routledge.

There is a long tradition of thinking about teaching as a creative and organic process. This approach emphasises how teaching must connect with the learner as a person and with their construction of meaning. See:

> Bruner, J. (1996) *The Culture of Education*. Cambridge, MA: Harvard University Press. (Reading 11.1)
>
> Dixon, A., Drummond, M. -J., Hart, S. and McIntyre, D. (2004) *Learning Without Limits*. Maidenhead: Open University Press. (see also Reading 1.4)

reflectiveteaching.co.uk/rtps6/part3_ch11

Part 3 Teaching for learning

For consideration of more radical approaches to pedagogy, try:

Kincheloe, J.L. (2008) *Critical Pedagogy Primer*. New York: Peter Lang.
Leach, J. and Moon, B. (2008) *The Power of Pedagogy*. London: SAGE.

In one way or another, most of *Reflective Teaching*'s chapters are concerned with pedagogy and, for readings on more specific issues – such as relationships, engagement, behaviour, assessment etc. – please consult the relevant chapter.

reflectiveteaching.co.uk/rtps6/part3_ch11

TOOLKIT EVIDENCE 11.1
Phonics: cracking the written code

What is it?
Phonics is an approach to teaching reading, and some aspects of writing, by developing learners' phonemic awareness. This involves the skills of hearing, identifying and using phonemes or sound patterns in English. The aim is to systematically teach learners the relationship between these sounds and the written spelling patterns, or graphemes, which represent them. Phonics emphasises the skills of decoding new words by sounding them out and combining or 'blending' the sound-spelling patterns.

What does the evidence say?
Phonics approaches have been consistently found to be effective in supporting younger readers to master the basics of reading, with an average impact of an additional four months' progress. Research suggests that phonics is particularly beneficial for younger learners (4–7- year-olds) as they begin to read. Teaching phonics is more effective on average than other approaches to early reading (such as whole language or alphabetic approaches), though it should be emphasised that effective phonics techniques are usually embedded in a rich literacy environment for early readers and are only one part of a successful literacy strategy.

Qualified teachers tend to get better results when delivering phonics interventions (up to twice the effectiveness of volunteers or untrained staff), indicating that expertise is a key component of successful teaching of early reading.

How sound is the evidence?
Overall, the evidence base related to phonics is very secure. There have been a number of studies, reviews and meta-analyses that have consistently found that the systematic teaching of phonics is beneficial. Several robust studies of the use of phonics programmes in England have been published in recent years. The findings show that phonics approaches can be effective, but also underline the importance of high quality implementation.

What do I need to think about?
- The teaching of phonics should be explicit and systematic to support children in making connections between the sound patterns they hear in words and the way that these words are written.
- The teaching of phonics should be matched to children's current level of skill in terms of their phonemic awareness and their knowledge of letter sounds and patterns (graphemes).
- Phonics improves the accuracy of a child's reading but not their comprehension. How are you planning on developing wider literacy skills such as comprehension and vocabulary development?

Links and further reading
Resources to support literacy in primary schools from the Education Endowment Foundation:
educationendowmentfoundation.org.uk/support-for-schools/eef-regional-support/campaigns/north-east-primary-literacy-campaign

Melby-Lervåg, M., Lyster, S.A.H., and Hulme, C. (2012) 'Phonological skills and their role in learning to read: a meta-analytic review', *Psychological Bulletin*, 138(2), 322. idoi:10.1037/a0026744

The EEF Teaching and Learning Toolkit entry on 'phonics: educationendowmentfoundation.org.uk/education-evidence/teaching-learning-toolkit/phonics – see also the technical appendix for further references.

See also
Meta-cognition and self-regulated learning (Toolkit Evidence 2.1)
Reading comprehension (Toolkit Evidence 12.2)

Education Endowment Foundation

TOOLKIT EVIDENCE 11.2
Small group teaching and learning: instruction or interaction?

What is it?
Small group teaching is where one teacher or teaching assistant is working with two, three, four or five pupils. This arrangement enables teaching to focus exclusively on a small number of learners, usually on their own in a separate classroom or working area. This is often to support those who are falling behind, but it can also be used as a more general strategy to ensure effective progress, such as in mastery learning, or to teach more challenging topics or skills.

What does the evidence say?
Small group teaching usually is effective and, as a rule of thumb, the smaller the group the better. Groups of two have slightly higher impact than groups of three, but slightly lower impact compared with one-to-one tuition. Once group size increases above six or seven there is a noticeable reduction in effectiveness. On average, intensive small group teaching increased progress by about four months.

There is evidence that some small group teaching can be more effective than either one-to-one or teaching pairs of children. The variability suggests two things. First, the quality of the teaching in small groups may be as important, or even more important, than group size. Second, it is imperative to evaluate the effectiveness of different arrangements as the specific curriculum content being taught and composition of the groups may influence success.

How sound is the evidence?
The evidence is fairly limited and mainly relates to low-attaining pupils receiving additional support to catch up with their peers. More research has been undertaken into paired tuition than other kinds of small group teaching, so the evidence across varying sizes of groups and at different levels of intensity is not conclusive and mainly comes from single studies where multiple comparisons were made.

What do I need to think about?
- Small group tuition is most likely to be effective if it is targeted at pupils' specific needs. How will you diagnose pupils' needs accurately before adopting a new approach?
- One-to-one tuition and small group tuition are both effective interventions. However, the cost effectiveness of one-to-two and one-to-three indicates that greater use of these approaches may be worthwhile. Have you considered trying one-to-two or one-to-three as an initial option?

Links and further reading
Vaughn, S., Wanzek, J., Wexler, J., Barth, A., Cirino, P.T., Fletcher, J. and Francis, D. (2010) 'The relative effects of group size on reading progress of older students with reading difficulties'. *Reading and Writing*, 23(8), 931–56. doi:10.1007/s11145-009-9183-9.

The EEF Teaching and Learning Toolkit entry on 'Small group tuition': educationendowmentfoundation.org.uk/education-evidence/teaching-learning-toolkit/small-group-tuition?utm_source=/education-evidence/teaching-learning-toolkit/small-group-tuition&utm_medium=search&utm_campaign=site_search&search_term=small%20group – see also the technical appendix for further references.

See also
Effective deployment of teaching assistants (Toolkit Evidence 8.4)
Mastery learning (Toolkit Evidence 10.1)
Collaborative learning (Toolkit Evidence 11.3)

Education Endowment Foundation

TOOLKIT EVIDENCE 11.3
Collaborative learning: designing tasks for effective interaction

What is it?
Collaborative or cooperative learning is where pupils work together in a group small enough for everyone to take part in a joint task or activity that has been designed to support their learning. This can be either a task where group members do different aspects of the task but contribute to a common overall outcome (such as in jigsaw groups or team approaches), or a shared task where group members work together throughout the activity and take equal responsibility.

Some collaborative learning approaches also have mixed capability teams or groups working in competition with each other, in order to drive more effective collaboration. There is a very wide range of approaches to collaborative and cooperative learning involving different kinds of organisation and tasks to support classroom learning.

What does the evidence say?
Research indicates that impact of collaborative approaches on learning is typically positive, but it does vary so it is important to get the detail right. Effective collaborative learning requires much more than just sitting pupils together and asking them to work together. It needs planned and structured approaches with well-designed tasks to lead to benefit in learning outcomes. There is some evidence that collaboration can be supported with competition between groups, but this is not always necessary, and can lead to learners focusing on the competition rather than the learning it aims to support. Approaches which promote talk and interaction between learners tend to result in the best gains.

How sound is the evidence?
Evidence about the benefits of collaborative learning has been found consistently for over forty years and a number of systematic reviews and meta-analyses of research studies have been completed. In addition to direct evidence from research into collaborative learning approaches, there is also indirect evidence where collaboration has been shown to increase the effectiveness of other approaches such as mastery learning or digital technology. It appears to work well for all ages if activities are suitably structured for learners' capabilities and positive evidence has been found across the curriculum.

What do I need to think about?
- Pupils will need support and practice to work together; this does not happen automatically.
- Tasks need to be designed carefully so that working together is both effective and efficient, otherwise some pupils will try to work on their own.

Links and further reading
Hertz-Lazarowitz, R., Kagan, S., Sharan, S., Slavin, R., and Webb, C. (eds.). (2013) *Learning to Cooperate, Cooperating to Learn*. New York: Springer.

Collaborative learning professional development materials: education.gov.scot/improvement/learning-resources/dylan-wiliam-collaborative-learning/
The EEF Teaching and Learning Toolkit entry on 'Collaborative learning': educationendowmentfoundation.org.uk/education-evidence/teaching-learning-toolkit/collaborative-learning-approaches
– see also the technical appendix for further references.

See also
Meta-cognition and self-regulation (Toolkit Evidence 2.1)
Reading comprehension (Toolkit Evidence 12.2)
Peer tutoring (Toolkit Evidence 13.2)

Education Endowment Foundation

RESEARCH BRIEFING 11.1
Improving pupil group work

This project, SPRinG, was designed to develop principles and strategies to improve the quantity and effectiveness of group work. Teachers and researchers collaborated to develop children's capacity to work in groups (listening, explaining, sharing ideas, building trust and respect, planning, organising, evaluating) and to develop the role of the teacher in group work (support, guide, monitor, fostering independence, providing classroom management) (see the *Improving Practice* workbook by Baines et al., 2017, below).

An experimental design was used so that the success of the intervention programme could be evaluated against a control group who were not exposed to the intervention. Pupil progress in the experimental and control groups were monitored over a school year and measures of attainment, motivational, attitudinal and behavioural evidence were recorded.

Key findings:	Implications:
Integrating group work: Thoughtful and committed teachers successfully implemented structured group work into mainstream curriculum areas in primary and secondary schools and across the whole curriculum.	Children need to be *actively taught* group work skills and encouraged to appreciate supportive relationships. A whole-school approach to group work is desirable, with CPD on teaching strategies.
Pupil attainment: Involvement in structured group work had positive effects on pupil's academic progress and higher conceptual learning.	There is a need to rethink pedagogic strategies which favour teacher-led situations and individual work. The effectiveness of peer-based co-learning has been relatively neglected.
Pupil behaviour: Involvement in the structured group work had positive effects on pupil behaviour through an increase in active on-task interactions, more equal participation in learning, sustained interactions and higher level discussions.	Given the space and time to develop pupils' group-working skills, teachers can bring about a transformation in the learning environment.
Relationships: Personal relationships between teachers and the class and between pupils within the class improved, provided teachers take time to train pupils in the skills of group working.	Teachers were freed up to engage with learning rather than being sidetracked by classroom management. Beneficial groupwork strategies were also applied by children beyond the classroom.

Previous research had indicated that there can be positive learning and social effects of cooperative group work. But this evidence did not provide teachers with the basis for adopting group work for everyday classroom life. The SPRinG project was distinctive in providing a general programme that applies group work across the curriculum, over the school year and when a range of learning tasks may be undertaken simultaneously.

The main impetus for the SPRinG project was thus to address the wide gap between the potential of group work and its limited use in schools.

A new approach was needed in order to integrate group work into the fabric of the school day. We therefore embarked on an ambitious project in which we worked with teachers to develop a programme of group work that could be successfully integrated into school life. This programme was then systematically evaluated by examining pupil progress over a full school year, and in comparison with a control group in terms of attainment, motivation for group working, and within-group interactions.

Further information
Blatchford, P., Galton, M. and Kutnick, P. (2005) *Improving Pupil Group Work in Classrooms.* TLRP Research Briefing 11. London: TLRP.
Baines, E., Blatchford, P. and Kutnick, P. (2017) *Promoting Effective Groupwork in Primary Classrooms.* TLRP Improving Practice Series. London: Routledge.

This project involved the universities of London, Brighton and Cambridge.

Chapter 12
Communication
How does use of language support learning?

| Introduction | 372 |

| Characteristics of classroom communication | 373 |

| Speaking and listening | 374 |

Questioning, responding, instructing and explaining	375
Dialogic teaching and learning	378
Inter-thinking and group work	379
Creative talk	381

| Reading | 382 |

Teaching reading	383
Theories of reading	383
Reading and engagement	384
Reading across the curriculum	386
Reading multimodal texts	387
School values and reading	387

| Writing | 389 |

The relationship between reading and writing	390
Teaching writing	391
Researching writing	391

| Knowledge about language for communication | 393 |

Knowledge about grammar	393
Some differences between spoken and written language	393
English as an additional language	395

| Conclusion | 396 |

reflectiveteaching.co.uk/rtps6/part3_ch12

Part 3 Teaching for learning

INTRODUCTION

In this chapter we address speaking, listening, reading and writing as crucial forms of classroom communication between all teachers and their pupils, and consider some of the ways in which each is vital to learning. In order for teachers to deepen their understanding, we consider what it is helpful to know about spoken and written language, discussing some essential ideas about grammar, dialect and standard English. We show how teachers model, respond to and engage knowledgeably with the many varieties of language and modes of communication that are used in their classrooms every day. We focus on different kinds of texts that pupils may read or write, whether verbal, or visual. We also acknowledge that texts span a wide variety of modes including but not limited to traditional novels, graphic novels, pen and paper, text messages, digital media, and visual imagery. Furthermore, we outline some of the key features involved in supporting pupils who have English as an additional language (EAL).

The idea of communication always includes purpose, audience, context and style, a notion first drawn to teachers' attention by James Britton and colleagues in their classic research study, *The Development of Writing Abilities (11–18)* (Britton et al., 1975). Why are these four ideas so important for teachers and learners? Although for much of the time language is taken for granted, when we reflect on it we realise that these four elements are always in play. For example, communication in the playground often involves children talking together to negotiate how they play, and their choice of language is informed by the fact that they are with their peers in a very familiar context, hence, their talk will be informal in style. By contrast, in a whole-school assembly, communication could involve talk in a very formal style by an adult addressing an audience of pupils about the topic of road safety with a didactic purpose. In both instances, the purpose, audience, context and style determine the characteristics of the communication, as is the case in any authentic communicative interactions, whether spoken, written or visual.

See Chapter 4

TLRP Principles

Two principles are of particular relevance to this chapter on the use of language in teaching and learning:

Effective teaching and learning requires teachers to scaffold learning. Teachers should provide activities which support learners as they move forward, not just intellectually, but also socially and emotionally, so that once these supports are removed, the learning is secure. (*Principle 4*)

Effective teaching and learning fosters both individual and social processes and outcomes. Learning is a social activity. Learners should be encouraged and helped to work with others, to share ideas and to build knowledge together. Consulting learners about their learning and giving them a voice is both an expectation and a right. (*Principle 7*)

---

reflectiveteaching.co.uk/rtps6/part3_ch12

Chapter 12 Communication

These ideas about the social and interactive nature of communication underpin the whole of this chapter.

CHARACTERISTICS OF CLASSROOM COMMUNICATION

There are many aspects of classroom communication which have an impact on how effectively teachers and pupils communicate in early years, primary and secondary classrooms. For example, it is valuable to remember that high-quality communication is important across the whole curriculum, not just in English. The Bullock Report (DES, 1975) advocated the importance of paying attention to language across the curriculum to underline the argument that educationally productive talk is the responsibility of all teachers, not solely English teachers. Thirty-five years later, the final report of the Cambridge Primary Review (Alexander, 2010) emphasised high-quality talk as fundamental to effective teaching and learning, including the character, quality and uses of reading, writing and talk and the development of pupils' understandings of the distinct registers, vocabularies and modes of discourse of each subject. Alexander asserts, 'oracy must have its proper place in the language curriculum. Spoken language is central to learning, culture and life and is much more prominent in the curricula of many other countries' (2010, p. 24).

Language skills are fundamental to communication but the interpersonal nature of communication also calls for significant social skills and high-quality interactions with adults. Recent evidence reviews have demonstrated that language development is sensitive to environmental input, in particular from adult–child interaction (Law et al., 2017). In addition to verbal exchanges, a great deal of what we say is conveyed by non-verbal means. Tone, pitch, volume and how we project our voice are all part of the communication process. Non-verbal language, such as facial expression, effective eye contact, posture, gesture and interpersonal distance or space, is usually interpreted by others as a reliable reflection of how we are feeling (Nowicki and Duke, 2013). However, non-verbal signals may also confuse or contradict what we are trying to communicate. This may be particularly so in communication between people from different cultures and backgrounds. Siraj-Blatchford and Clarke argue that 'language involves more than learning a linguistic code with which to label the world or to refer to abstract concepts; language also involves learning how to use the code in socially appropriate and effective ways' (2000, p. 20).

> **Expert Question**
>
> **Coherence:** is there clarity in the purposes, content and organisation of the curriculum and does it provide holistic learning experiences?
>
> This question contributes to a conceptual framework underpinning professional expertise (see Chapter 16).

reflectiveteaching.co.uk/rtps6/part3_ch12

> **Reflective Activity 12.1**
>
> *Aim:* To investigate who speaks and how much during a lesson.
>
> *Evidence and reflection:* We recommend that you begin with an audio recording of part of a lesson. You may want to gather data on your own teaching.
> Now sit back, relax and listen . . . Consider:
> - How much speaking is there?
> - Who is doing the speaking?
> - Which pupils speak?
> - When does the teacher speak?
> - When do the pupils speak?
>
> Reviews of this kind can highlight the pattern of talk in a classroom. It can often reveal aspects which surprise us, because it is so difficult to be aware of how much we talk, to whom and when, whilst we are engrossed in the process of teaching itself.
>
> *Extension:* Having identified the pattern of talk, we need to decide whether what we do is consistent with our aims. You might like to see if you can develop the way you teach in the light of what you have learned in this activity. You could also use a similar approach to investigate different aspects of classroom interaction, e.g. teacher–pupil interaction in group work; pupil–pupil interaction, generally or in small group work. You will find suggestions for other observations in subsequent Reflective Activities in this chapter.

Since communication in classrooms is often focused on some meaningful topic, it requires appropriate cognitive capacities in addition to language and interpersonal skills. It requires knowing something about the subject under consideration and being able to think about and process what we want to communicate to others as well as what they are trying to communicate to us. Nor can the attitudes of the participants be forgotten: developing the cognitive relationship between them and the context itself is also very important if they are to remain motivated to learn. Furthermore, when pupils consciously examine these relationships, their meta-cognitive capacities will come into play (Whitebread and Pino Pasternak, 2010).

A great many skills and processes therefore are in play in good classroom communication. In this chapter, we focus chiefly on speaking, listening, reading and writing, but it is helpful to bear these other facets in mind.

SPEAKING AND LISTENING

As discussed in Chapter 11, teachers' pedagogic repertoire crucially includes classroom talk (Alexander, 2008a, Reading 12.3). In this chapter, classroom talk is defined as speaking and listening activities aimed at developing children's understanding about a topic (Khong, Saito and Gillies, 2019). We know that improving the quality of classroom talk can improve children's learning because learning is mediated by talk (Boyd, 2015). A recent study involving nearly 5,000 pupils in the United Kingdom (Alexander, 2018) found that children's academic achievement in maths and English improved if teachers achieved high levels of pupil participation in dialogue, encouraged elaboration, pupil to pupil questioning, and productive group work.

In classroom situations, teachers and pupils act as both speakers and listeners as they engage in classroom talk. In the following section we outline some of the key literature which informs teachers' thinking and practice, emphasising in particular the notion of achieving a strategic balance between authoritative and dialogic discourse (Mortimer and Scott, 2007). EEF **Toolkit Evidence 12.1** (see p. 401) suggests that communication and language approaches overlap with meta-cognitive development and demonstrate consistent gains in learning outcomes. This effect is measurable for all, but is particularly strong for younger and lower-attaining pupils.

Expert Questions

Repertoire: *is our pedagogic expertise sufficiently creative, skilled and wide-ranging to teach all elements of learning?*

Dialogue: *does teacher–learner talk scaffold understanding to build on existing knowledge and to strengthen dispositions to learn?*

These questions contribute to a conceptual framework underpinning professional expertise (see Chapter 16).

We begin by discussing the impact of teacher-initiated talk on pupils' learning, for example through questioning, responding, instructing and explaining, and then move on to discuss more overtly collaborative forms of spoken communication, whether between teachers and pupils or amongst small groups of pupils themselves.

Questioning, responding, instructing and explaining

How good are we at asking questions? Questions can be used for a wide range of purposes and are a vital tool for teaching and learning. They can be thought of in terms of the level of demand they make on children's thinking and can be broadly divided into two main categories: lower-order and higher-order questions. Lower-order questions are often closed or literal, requiring relatively brief, factual answers which are either right or wrong. They are less cognitively demanding (Sedova, Sedlacek, and Svaricek, 2016). Higher-order questions invite a range of possible answers and require children to apply, reorganise, extend, evaluate or analyse information. A useful way of thinking about categorising types of questions is Bloom's taxonomy (1956). This identifies six levels of cognitive processes: knowledge, comprehension, application, analysis, synthesis and evaluation (see also the discussion at p. 323). It also provides examples of questions which can elicit different types of thinking.

Asking questions can provide teachers with immediate feedback on pupils' thinking: on what they know and, most importantly, how they can improve its quality. Research,

> **Expert Questions**
>
> **Relationships:** are teacher–pupil relationships nurtured as the foundation of good behaviour, mutual wellbeing and high standards?
>
> **Engagement:** do our teaching strategies, classroom organisation and consultation enable learners to actively participate in and enjoy their learning?
>
> These questions contribute to a conceptual framework underpinning professional expertise (see Chapter 16).

however, shows that teacher-led patterns of talk are overwhelmingly prevalent (Mortimer and Scott, 2007) rather than interchanges which elicit higher-order thinking from pupils. Kyriacou and Issitt (2008) argue that when teachers' use of talk is linked to good learning outcomes, they use strategies other than closed question exchanges and help pupils appreciate the value of dialogue for learning. Moreover, Rojas-Drummond and Mercer's research (2003) shows that the most effective teachers are those who use question and answer sequences, not just to test knowledge but also to guide the development of children's understanding.

Questioning and response interactions have often been characterised as initiation–response–evaluation (IRE) (Cazden, 1988) or initiation–response–feedback (IRF). In the former, the teacher initiates an exchange by posing a question, the pupil responds with a brief answer and the teacher acknowledges the answer and moves on to the next question. In the context of IRE, teachers ask many questions but too often they are 'closed', requiring only short responses and not enough of the kinds of questions that get children thinking or encourage extended answers. Smith et al. (2004) found that in literacy and numeracy lessons, most of the questions asked were of a low cognitive level designed to funnel pupils' responses towards a required answer that the teacher already knows. In a worthwhile IRF exchange, on the other hand, the teacher makes an evaluation of the pupil's response, gives feedback or elaborates on the answer and this pattern then often becomes a more positive chain of interactions between a teacher and an individual pupil (Mortimer and Scott, 2007). The process can thereby help a class construct a common basis of knowledge and provide vital information about where learners are in their understanding (see Chapter 13). As Dawes (2004) suggests, learners benefit from having their ideas rephrased and elaborated. Critically though, the value of these exchanges depends on the quality of the feedback. Wells (1999) evaluates the IRF sequence and argues that the teacher's feedback can also be used to clarify, exemplify, expand, explain or justify a pupil's response and can help pupils to plan ahead for a task they are about to carry out or review and generalise from lessons they have already learnt. Wragg and Brown (2001) note the teacher's response should provide reinforcement, feedback and encouragement. It is important that all answers are considered and here non-verbal features of communication such as a teacher's body language, gesture and facial expression also come in to play. An atmosphere of trust in which pupils are not afraid of saying the wrong thing is essential.

In analysing the kinds of questions teachers use, Nystrand et al. (1997) (Reading 12.1) distinguish between test questions and authentic questions. Of course, test questions have their place, but they are retrospective rather than prospective and do not take forward pupils' thinking. Nystrand's findings about dialogically organised classrooms have made a particular contribution to understanding about the nature of classroom discourse and its effect on pupil learning. However, he argues that the relationship cannot be simply reduced to measuring 'authentic' versus 'recall and display' questions; the inappropriate use of authentic questions can be counter-productive and the skilful use of a lecturing style can, on occasion, be effective. A concise, clear exposition by the teacher may be a more efficient way of explaining the nature and purpose of the task and authentic questions, unrelated to the objective of the lesson, are unlikely to develop pupils' understanding. What matters most is not the frequency of particular types of exchange but how far pupils are treated as active participants in the construction of their own knowledge. Kim and Wilkinson (2019) highlight the role of pupil agency in the co-construction of knowledge with a more expert other in Nystrand's conceptualisation of dialogic instruction.

Diagnostic questions take time and thought to devise, but elicit valuable information about pupils' learning. Some whole-class questioning skills that have long been understood as being effective in eliciting thoughtful and informative responses include pausing, prompting, asking for further clarification and relating pupils' contributions to other relevant aspects of their learning (Perrot, 1982, Reading 12.2). In Wolf, Crosson and Resnick's (2004) research into talk about literary texts, effective strategies included: teachers reformulating and summarising what pupils say, providing opportunities for other pupils to build on these ideas; teachers encouraging pupils to put the main idea in their own words; and teachers pressing the pupils for elaboration of their ideas, e.g. 'How did you know that?' or 'Why?'. As well as those questions asked by teachers, Harlen (2006) highlights the importance of pupils asking questions because these can show what they neither know nor understand, demonstrating the limits of their understanding and the nature of their own ideas. Pupils can also gain satisfaction and motivation for learning when they are given the opportunity to investigate their own questions (Hodgson and Pyle, 2010).

Expert Question

Authenticity: *do learners recognise routine processes of assessment and feedback as being of personal value?*

This question contributes to a conceptual framework underpinning professional expertise (see Chapter 16).

Although it may seem an obvious point to make, pupils need to have time to answer questions. In the ORACLE study of group work in the 1980s, Galton and his colleagues found that that the average time teachers allowed children to respond was two seconds before either repeating the question, rephrasing it, redirecting it to another child, or extending it themselves (Galton, Simon and Croll, 1980). Without 'wait time', children will give less well-formulated answers than they may otherwise have done or even have no answer to give. According to Alexander (2008b), increasing the wait time from three to seven seconds resulted in an increase in: 1) the length of pupil responses; 2) the number of unsolicited responses; 3) the frequency of pupil questions; 4) the number of responses from less capable pupils; 5) pupil–pupil interactions; and 6) the incidence of speculative responses. Another shortcoming in teacher questioning is not distributing questions around the class. One strategy which Harrison and Howard (2009) propose to alleviate this is to have a no-hands-up policy. This conveys the message that all children are expected to have an answer and ensures that the child who thrusts their hand up enthusiastically is not always chosen.

>
>
> ### Reflective Activity 12.2
>
> *Aim:* To identify question and response patterns in a lesson.
>
> *Evidence and reflection:* For this activity you could either choose to audio/video record a lesson you teach or, with their agreement, observe a colleague's lesson. Choose three five-minute periods in the teaching sessions (e.g. at the beginning, middle and end) and note the questions asked. Identify the questions which are closed and those which are open. How many follow either an IRE or an IRF pattern? Were there opportunities for children to formulate their answers because they were given wait time?
>
> *Extension:* Were there opportunities for children to ask questions themselves, of you and of each other?

Dialogic teaching and learning

As discussed in Chapter 11, and above, research shows that teachers do the majority of speaking in the classroom. Drawing in the main on the theoretical ideas of Bakhtin and Vygotsky, however, a number of authors have advocated the potential of teacher–pupil communication which enables pupils to play a more active part in shaping classroom discourse. Wells (1999, see also **Reading 2.4**) formulates the concept of dialogic inquiry, in which knowledge is co-constructed by teachers and pupils as they engage in joint activities, stressing the potential of collaborative group work and peer assistance. Nystrand et al. (1997) describe dialogic instruction, characterised by the teacher's uptake of pupils' ideas, authentic questions and the opportunity for pupils to modify the topic, making a strong case for the effectiveness of dialogically organised instruction over a monologic approach. They argue that classroom talk should require pupils to think, not just to report someone else's thinking. More recently, Kim and Wilkinson (2019) defined dialogic teaching as an approach that uses talk to develop pupils' thinking, learning and problem-solving.

Whilst the term *dialogic teaching* is increasingly used in education discussions, it is helpful to be aware of its origins if it is to be understood and implemented. Alexander (2008a, **Reading 12.3**) argues that dialogic teaching demands a balance of speaking, listening, reading and writing; management of classroom space and time; a productive relationship between speaker and listener; and attention to the content and dynamics of talk itself. Dialogic teaching, he suggests, is characterised by five key criteria. It is:

- *collective*: teachers and children address learning tasks together, as a group or as a class;
- *reciprocal*: teachers and children listen to each other, share ideas and consider alternative viewpoints;
- *supportive*: children articulate their ideas freely, without fear of embarrassment over 'wrong' answers, and they help each other to reach common understandings;

- *cumulative*: teachers and children build on their own and each other's ideas and chain them into coherent lines of thinking and enquiry;
- *purposeful*: teachers plan and steer classroom talk with specific educational goals.

The main pedagogic implication for reflective teachers is an emphasis on the importance of social learning through teacher–pupil and pupil to pupil dialogue. A dialogic approach to teaching and learning requires teachers and pupils to build actively on each other's ideas, posing questions and constructing shared interpretations and new knowledge. For teachers, it involves using open-ended, higher-order questioning, feeding in ideas and reflecting on and interpreting pupils' contributions to a lesson. For learners, it encourages articulation and justification of personal points of view, appreciating and responding to others' ideas and taking turns in whole-class and group interactions (Mercer and Littleton, 2007, Reading 11.6). In contrast to a teacher-led, transmission approach, a dialogic pedagogy signals the co-presence of the teacher as a member of a community of learners, available to guide and coach the learner, modelling the exploratory nature of dialogue. However, as Mortimer and Scott (2007) discuss (see Chapter 11), teachers need to make decisions about where and when a transmissive approach may in fact be appropriate to guide learners.

In all this, we emphasise the need for teachers to be aware of the individuals in their classroom and how meaningful contexts and audiences for developing pupils' speaking and listening are key. Alexander (2018) stresses that ensuring the ethos and the conditions of the classroom, or classroom culture, are conducive is essential in order for dialogic teaching, and pupils' learning, to take place. Indeed, Kim and Wilkinson (2019) also highlight that dialogic teaching is not just about talk per se. Teachers must also consider the role of culture, and in particular the relationship between talk, classroom culture and the cultural backgrounds of the classroom community.

> **Expert Questions**
>
> **Engagement:** *do our teaching strategies, classroom organisation and culture enable learners to actively participate in and enjoy their learning?*
>
> **Dialogue:** *does teacher–learner talk scaffold understanding to build on existing knowledge and to strengthen dispositions to learn?*
>
> These questions contribute to a conceptual framework underpinning professional expertise (see Chapter 16).

> **Expert Questions**
>
> **Personalisation:** *does the curriculum resonate with the social and cultural needs of diverse learners and provide appropriate elements of choice?*
>
> **Relevance:** *is the curriculum presented in ways which are meaningful to learners and so that it can excite their imagination?*
>
> These questions contribute to a conceptual framework underpinning professional expertise (see Chapter 16).

Inter-thinking and group work

All forms of classroom communication call for particular types of awareness about the rules of communication. Pupil behaviour in small groups largely mirrors the discourse modelled by, and the expectations communicated by, their teachers (Webb et al., 2006). In communicating with pupils therefore, the reflective teacher needs to model appropriate discourse and expectations. In order to participate productively, the rules must be clear and each participant must understand and accept these rules. In the 'Thinking Together' project, Mercer and Littleton (2007, Reading 11.6) show how children and teachers collectively construct and agree some ground rules for good, productive discussion. Critically, these rules are not predefined and imposed but emerge from collective discussion and consideration and therefore can expose the particular concerns of children, taking account of their own perspectives of group work. Having been negotiated and agreed, ground rules can then be summarised and displayed so that they can be referred to by the children and the teacher when appropriate.

As discussed in Chapter 11, cooperative group work can, at its best, be a particularly good context for learning. It fits well with Vygotskyan ideas about the importance and meaningfulness of the social context in which the learner acts (see Chapter 2). In Johnson and Johnson's (1997) review of 378 studies, collaborative learning activities were shown to benefit learning and conceptual development, especially for complex tasks. So too, in a research survey for the Cambridge Primary Review (Howe and Mercer, 2007), talk in groups was shown to be good for children's learning. Mercer and Littleton (2007) argue that by talking together, pupils do more than interact: they 'interthink'. This means that they engage in collective thinking which enables them to share strategies, construct new strategies together, examine others' strategies and make decisions only once all group members are satisfied. It also helps them learn to think better on their own.

A series of *Thinking Together* projects, reported by Mercer and Littleton (2007), assessed the impact of dialogue-based intervention on pupils' educational attainment, indicating that pupils who had been taught using this approach made better, more rapid progress in both maths and science. Other school-based studies have provided convincing evidence for the educational value of talk in collaborative learning, but only when guided and organised by teachers (Kyriacou and Issitt, 2008; Howe, 2010; see also EEF **Toolkit Evidence 11.3** on p. 369).

What then is the role of the teacher in facilitating and contributing to group work and what kinds of interaction among pupils are necessary to achieve its potential? Clarity of goals, the appropriateness of the task, the composition of the group and the degree of help pupils have been given in developing group-work skills are significant. Baines et al. (2017) argue that teachers need to adapt grouping practices for different purposes and learning tasks and that adults should support and guide groups, monitoring progress in ways that encourage independence rather than directly teaching pupils. Above all, teachers should ensure that the talk used in group work is productive.

Mercer and Littleton (2007, Reading 11.6) characterise three different ways in which pupils in classrooms talk together as 'disputational', 'cumulative' and 'exploratory'. They argue that exploratory talk constitutes a powerful way for pupils to think and reason together. Its effectiveness is due to three main reasons. First, participants appropriate successful problem-solving strategies and explanatory accounts from each other; second, they jointly construct new, robust, generalisable explanations; and third, participation in external dialogue promotes internal dialogue. According to Mercer et al. (2004), in their study of science learning, pupils with experience of exploratory talk achieve significantly better than pupils without this experience.

> **Reflective Activity 12.3**
>
> *Aim:* To analyse and categorise an example of classroom talk.
>
> *Evidence and reflection:* After seeking and gaining permission, record a group discussion and make a transcript. Analyse the transcript, categorising the types of talk using Mercer and Littleton's three categories: disputational, cumulative and exploratory talk. (See **Reading 11.6** for examples.) Reflect on which of the three were most commonly in use. How would you account for this?
>
> *Extension:* With reference to Mercer and Littleton's ideas about interthinking, what might be the next steps in developing pupils' capacity to think together?

Creative talk

A key aspect of talking and listening is how it can encourage creative thinking and learning in the classroom (Cremin and Reedy, 2015). Reflective teachers work to extend pupils' abilities as speakers and listeners and help them express themselves effectively to create and critically evaluate their own work. Through creative talk, Cremin and Reedy argue, teachers can foster pupils' curiosity, capacity to make connections and express themselves, take risks and innovate. What do we mean by 'creative' talk? Some examples might be oral storytelling or drama techniques including role play, hot-seating and freeze-frame.

Oral storytelling and retelling is a powerful way for pupils to take ownership of their own narratives, enabling them to make choices about words and phrases. As Hardy (1977) argued, narrative is a primary act of mind. Cremin and Reedy (2015) write persuasively about the role oral narrative has in helping children make sense of the world, fostering the creative sculpting of language, imaginative engagement in learning and the confidence and competence it develops. Personal oral stories have their place in the curriculum. Rosen (1988) and Zipes (1995) have shown the significance of autobiography and of individual and collective memory in the formation of identity. In a book-making project with children in post-war Bosnia, Darvin (2009) discusses how, through storytelling, the social nature of this literacy event helped the children begin to explore the vital concepts of preservation, friendship and peace and to construct and see themselves in relation to others. In addition to personal oral narratives, Grainger, Goouch and Lambirth (2005) have shown how experience of retelling well-known and traditional tales can make a rich contribution to children's writing.

As with storytelling, drama incorporates the use of talk and self-expression and has been shown as a strong form of communication in its own right as well as a successful precursor to invigorate successful writing, allowing pupils to experience and explore situations with their teacher and peers and to organise their thoughts orally. According to Woolland (2010), drama can raise the self-esteem of even the most disaffected of children. Because it is rooted in social interaction, Winston (1998) argues that drama is a powerful way to help children relate positively to each other, experience negotiation, gain confidence and raise self-esteem.

In drama, a number of forms of talk are used – as well as gestures, facial expressions and movements – to create meaning. Learners adapt speech for different purposes and can reflect upon language choices to contribute to their growing command of the spoken word. In many classrooms, teachers use role play to offer pupils crucial opportunities to enact, imitate, imagine, confront, review and understand the social world they inhabit as well as to use their knowledge and understanding in different areas of the curriculum (Cremin, 2015).

There are many different drama conventions which can be exploited to promote creative talk and learning in the classroom (Neelands and Goode, 2000). A particularly effective strategy is hot-seating, in which pupils or teachers take on the role of a character to be questioned about their behaviour and motivation. Characters may be hot-seated individually, in pairs or in small groups. The technique is very effective for helping pupils to engage with characters, both fictional and real, and also for developing pupils' questioning techniques. Another useful strategy is freeze-frame, where the action in a play or scene is frozen, as in a photograph or video frame. This requires pupils to share and negotiate ideas, discussing as a group how best to convey a moment in time. Thoughts can then be interrogated through thought-tracking, where individuals in the freeze-frame are tapped on the shoulder and asked to speak their thoughts or feelings aloud. There are therefore multiple opportunities for pupils at all stages of schooling to deepen their learning through creative talk.

READING

In this next section, we turn our attention to reading as one of the main forms of communication through which pupils learn. Being able to read involves making meaning from texts; it is not simply a matter of learning to decode letters and words. Making meaning from texts enables people to construct and explore other worlds, whether real or imagined, to engage in debates and to encounter different forms of knowledge. From texts, readers learn how writers communicate with readers, and readers with writers.

Teaching children to read and ensuring young people acquire a habit of lifelong reading are amongst the highest aims to which any teacher aspires. Indeed, reading has both intrinsic and extrinsic benefits. It gives pleasure, but it also makes many other things possible. EEF **Toolkit Evidence 12.2** (p. 402) suggests that teaching programmes to enhance reading comprehension can significantly enhance pupil progress, and can 'unlock' learning for those who may have fallen behind.

How reading is taught is a much discussed and debated topic. Here, we focus on just a few issues that are helpful to think about. Reflective teachers, whether working with children in the early years, or at any stage thereafter, will constantly find reasons for reading (Cliff Hodges, 2010) and want to develop their own understandings about why reading is so important (Harrison, 2004, Reading 12.4).

There are many reasons why we read. However, if children learn to read but do not learn what reading is for, they will not make progress. Maryanne Wolf's thought-provoking book, *Proust and the Squid: The Story and Science of the Reading Brain*, reminds us why this is:

> Reading is one of the single most remarkable inventions in history; the ability to record history is one of its consequences. Our ancestors' invention could come about only because of the human brain's extraordinary ability to make new connections among its existing structures, a process made possible by the brain's ability to be shaped by experience. The plasticity at the heart of the brain's design forms the basis for much of who we are, and who we might become. (Wolf, 2008, p. 3)

If human beings are not genetically predisposed to read, but rather must actively learn how to do so, then there are extremely important implications for how reading is taught in the classroom:

> To acquire this unnatural process, children need instructional environments that support all the circuit parts that need bolting for the brain to read. Such a perspective departs from current teaching methods that focus largely on only one or two major components of reading. (Wolf, 2008 p. 19)

Wolf's point makes clear the need for teachers to approach reading from a wide variety of perspectives, ensuring that, at the same time as learning to decode text, children become increasingly aware of the many pleasures and purposes that reading might hold for them.

Teaching reading

The teaching and development of reading skills and knowledge are deeply rooted in approaches from which children and young people learn the social, cultural, aesthetic and practical pleasures of reading. Although the development of cognitive reading skills and knowledge involves teaching and learning how to decode written language, it includes much else besides (Meek, 1988). For example, it includes inference or prediction, both of which require knowledge about the distinctiveness of different texts such as picture books and recipes, or about different media, for example films and posters, as well as knowledge about the world. When pupils leave school, they need reading to be something they can use to learn and respond to an infinite variety of texts and media. Being able to read in versatile and sustained ways greatly enhances the scope of what people may be able to learn. So, what underlying principles can help all teachers to support their pupils' reading development?

Theories of reading

Theories are generalisations about an area of interest. They help us to frame and describe a phenomenon, like how children learn, or how we read (Unrau and Alvermann, 2013), and models of theory help teachers think about how reading skills operate. There are many

reflectiveteaching.co.uk/rtps6/part3_ch12

theories or models proposed to describe the reading process. Some focus on the cognitive skills and knowledge involved in decoding and understanding words and text (e.g. Hoover and Gough, 1990); others focus on the development of problem-solving skills involved in reading (e.g Holmes and Singer, 1961). Others focus on the motivational, cultural and contextual aspects of reading (e.g. Rosenblatt, 1978/1994; Ruddell and Unrau, 2013). Taken together, these theories can help teachers to support pupils' reading development by considering what factors are involved in learning to read and what teaching principles would support this.

Reader-response theory was proposed by Louise Rosenblatt, an American academic working with university pupils over several decades of the twentieth century. She developed ideas about reading that remain extremely valuable to teachers today (Rosenblatt, 1978/1994) because it reminds us that reading is more than decoding. She argues that reading forms a transaction between the reader and the text. Each transaction results in a unique reading. The uniqueness of the reading derives from the fact that readers bring with them their own prior knowledge which they use in their encounter with the text to make meaning. Her ideas chime with research into young people's *funds of knowledge* and the value of using what is learnt at home as a foundation of what is learnt in school in all areas of the curriculum (González, Moll and Amanti, 2005).

In addition to each reading being different depending on the individual reader, Rosenblatt also argues that what each reader gains from the reading depends on why they are reading. Readers will adopt different stances towards the text depending on whether they are reading for the feelings a text evokes or for the information it may yield, or both. For example, reading a text about First World War soldiers in the trenches may primarily generate what Rosenblatt calls an *aesthetic* response such as feelings of revulsion or fear, or it may generate an *efferent* response (from the Latin word *effere*, meaning to carry away), a response more concerned with information that remains after the reading (Rosenblatt, 1978/1994) such as details of how trenches were constructed or statistics about unsanitary conditions. Of course, a reader may also shuttle back and forth between aesthetic and efferent responses, the one informing the other. Because a text is never read in quite the same way by two readers, it can be very valuable for pupils in a classroom to make their individual readings available for discussion, learning to justify or modify their readings in the light of other people's. As well as what they learn from the reading, they are also learning about what it means to read *per se*, to question facts, interpret ideas and take up a critical position whilst the teacher, too, gains insight into how different pupils understand the same text.

Reading and engagement

National and international reports are clear about the need to do more than merely teach young people to decode text if they are to engage with and enjoy reading (Kirsch et al., 2002). What such reports argue strongly is the need for a culture of reading and the development of policies to promote literacy across the curriculum, and reading for many

reflectiveteaching.co.uk/rtps6/part3_ch12

Chapter 12 Communication

types of enjoyment, because motivation to read is fundamental to understanding text (Guthrie and Wigfield, 1999). There is a reciprocal relationship between reading attainment and positive dispositions to reading (Cremin and Moss, 2018). If choice is a key factor in promoting reader engagement (Clark and Pythian-Sence, 2008), we need to find ways to develop freedom of choice both within and beyond the curriculum. An ongoing and crucially important task for teachers is to be as familiar as possible with the breadth of literature available for children and young people and to know what the specific individuals we teach are reading, both at school and at home. Cremin et al. (2009) argue that opportunities for teachers to reflect on their own reading experiences and choices can help build confidence to use a wide range of literature. An example of this is the United Kingdom Literacy Association (2021) Teachers as Readers project.

In-depth surveys such as Hall and Coles' *Children's Reading Choices* (1999) are illuminating not just in terms of actual texts cited by young people but also what kinds of texts they enjoy. Contrary to the popular impression of young people's reading preferences, especially the assumption that boys prefer non-fiction, this survey found that between the ages of 10 and 14, '[o]verwhelmingly both boys' and girls' book reading at all ages is narrative fiction' (Hall and Coles, 1999, p. 85). Jerrim and Moss (2019), in an examination of data from thirty-five countries, found a 'fiction effect'; that reading children who read fiction had stronger skills than children who read other text types. If that is the case, and if such texts also enable readers not just to learn facts but to experience feelings, then classroom reading of literary and non-fiction narratives should be a vital part of every teacher's subject knowledge for teaching. Across the whole age range and curriculum, such reading offers young people different viewpoints from which to reflect on the world they live in. As Peter Hollindale argues, 'stories are very important. They take us across the bridge from the thinkable, where we are, to the imaginable, where we need to be' (2011, p. 110).

Hollindale draws on his own experiences as a child of reading about wildlife and the environment as having a major impact on his adult thinking and ideological bearings. He not only discusses narrative fiction but also non-fiction, which often combines strong narrative with powerful pictures. An example of this kind of narrative non-fiction is *Into the Unknown: How Great Explorers Found Their Way by Land, Sea and Air* (Ross and Biesty, 2011), which tells the stories of fourteen different journeys by explorers from all over the world. The stories comprise strong narratives, often drawing on the words used by the explorers themselves to communicate with other people, taken from journals, diaries and contemporary accounts. However, an equally important part of the text is the illustrations, diagrams and fold-out cross-sections of the craft or equipment the pioneers used. Embedded within the narratives and pictures are scientific, mathematical, historical and geographical ideas which encourage readers to think about how they contributed to these various explorers' achievements. Here, then, is an example of how reading enables communication in many different ways: visually, verbally and interactively.

> ## Expert Question
>
> ***Personalisation:*** *does the curriculum resonate with the social and cultural needs of diverse learners and provide appropriate elements of choice?*
>
> This question contributes to a conceptual framework underpinning professional expertise (see Chapter 16).

reflectiveteaching.co.uk/rtps6/part3_ch12

The extent to which young people's reading of texts such as these might shape their thinking and learning in different disciplines, beyond the mere gleaning of information – as scientists, mathematicians, historians and geographers – is under-explored. Margaret Mallett suggests that this is because 'for a long time informational kinds of reading and writing were relatively neglected. It was assumed that once children had learnt to read and write they could transfer these abilities to all aspects of literacy. Now we recognise that different kinds, or genres, of reading and writing require different strategies' (1999, p. 1). Many teachers are aware of different kinds of information texts and ways of reading them, due to critical studies by researchers such as Margaret Meek in her study, *Information and Book Learning* (1996), and are keen to help pupils understand ways of both reading and writing non-fiction.

> ## Expert Question
>
> ***Engagement:*** *do our teaching strategies, classroom organisation and consultation enable learners to actively participate in and enjoy this learning?*
>
> This question contributes to a conceptual framework underpinning professional expertise (see Chapter 16).

Reading across the curriculum

Reading across different subject areas places different demands on the reader in terms of the genre, text structures and critical evaluation (Shanahan, Shanahan and Misischia, 2011). Teachers who understand that there are many different ways of reading also know that different ways of teaching about reading are therefore required. Primary school pupils need to become familiar with, and be able to approach, historical texts differently from how they might approach a scientific text. For example, authentic texts in history lessons – whether imaginative, such as a picture books or novels, or real-life texts such as diaries, letters, accounts, memoires – have an audience, purpose, context and style which can (and must) be subject to scrutiny. Scholastic's *My Story* series is an example of series that provides journal type accounts of historical events. Texts like *D-Day* (Perrett, 2016) and *The Berlin Olympics* (Cross, 2012) provide place fictional characters in historical settings that provide cross-curricular learning opportunities. Primary resources like those provided by the National Archives provide opportunities to explore different text types like newspaper extracts, letters and transcripts. An example of these is the curated collection of texts about the Suffragettes (National Archives, 2022). These texts, used as part of both English *and* history lessons, could be read very differently. In English, the emphasis might be on the style of writing itself as an example of a certain type of non-fiction writing. It might also focus on the viewpoints represented by the writers and consider how the same events or places would have been differently represented had another figure in the account been writing them. In history, meanwhile, knowledge of the period in which the text was produced will be crucial to how the text is read and interpreted as historical evidence. History pupils therefore need to 'cultivate period-sensitivity' (Counsell, 2004, p. 1) to engage with texts, as well as using those very same texts to cultivate period-sensitivity. If the way texts are read is influenced by disciplinary perspectives, there is much to be gained by teachers working with different subject specialisms to explore distinctions and commonalities in the way knowledge is communicated.

> **Expert Question**
>
> **Coherence:** *is there clarity in the purposes, content and organisation of the curriculum and does it provide holistic learning experiences?*
>
> This question contributes to a conceptual framework underpinning professional expertise (see Chapter 16).

Reading multimodal texts

In some texts, for example *Ice Trap! Shackleton's Incredible Expedition* (Hooper and Robertson, 2000), which mingle narrative (the true story of how Shackleton's ship *Endurance* became trapped in the Antarctic ice in 1915) with non-narrative (for example information about pack ice and sledge dogs), visual images play a vital part in communicating both story and information. *Ice Trap!* is illustrated with large, vivid watercolour paintings, often taking up whole pages on their own, offering many different viewpoints of the Antarctic ice and life onboard ship. However, there are also scale drawings of maps and, at the end of the book, a timeline of the expedition with photographs taken by the ship's photographer, Frank Hurley. Inviting readers to compare the illustrations with the photographs requires analysis and interpretation, demonstrating the value of reading images as well as written text. At the same time, it is possible that the illustrations and pictures may well evoke emotions in the reader as they try to appreciate the horror, fear, courage or despair Shackleton and his companions may have felt when they realised they were trapped in the ice. Focusing on all modes, not just the verbal, develops pupils' explicit awareness of how ideas are communicated in multimodal texts so that they are better placed to analyse and interpret what is represented.

Increasingly too, written texts are complemented by, or flow from, other media such as film, cartoons, games, digital clips, blogs, tweets etc. Kress and van Leeuwen's book, *Reading Images: The Grammar of Visual Design* (2006), discusses how 'language, whether in speech or writing, has always existed as just one mode in the ensemble of modes involved in the production of texts' (Kress and van Leeuwen, 2006, p. 41; see also Kress, 2010, Reading 8.6).

School values and reading

What counts as reading is conveyed to pupils by the choices we make as teachers in terms of the literature we choose, how we teach reading, and what we choose to emphasise (Cremin et al., 2014). Teachers and their pupils become acculturated to schooled ways of doing things, including reading, so it can be instructive to step back for a while and consider how taken for granted some aspects of reading may quickly become. As teachers, it is valuable to reflect on the explicit and implicit messages we convey to pupils about reading both individually and as a school community. The messages they receive may depend on whether we discuss our own reading with them and make recommendations for

Part 3 Teaching for learning

books or magazines they might explore to support their learning. It may be that pupils are already familiar with novels, magazines or websites related to the topic we are teaching them and have funds of knowledge teachers can draw on in turn. Sometimes, we favour fiction over non-fiction, sending messages that the non-fiction is somehow inferior. In Case Study 12.1, experienced primary teacher Emma reflects on her interest in different kinds of reading and the implications for her pupils.

Case Study 12.1 Emma's reading and its influence on her teaching

My mother was a biology teacher and the paraphernalia of my childhood consisted of petri dishes, red biros, a formaldehyde preserved sheep heart and a trove of textbooks. My imagination was fired by the world of science and the marvels revealed within its diagrams and orbital cross-sections. My comfort with the informational realm would be a tremendous asset to me throughout my own primary education where there was a clear bias by class teachers towards topic work. Topics as varied as 'The Vikings', 'India' or 'Farms' were studied for an entire half term with teachers seamlessly embedding literacy, numeracy, history, music and all else comfortably within them. This may seem a little bizarre, archaic even in a modern primary classroom where subject areas are more discrete but I thrived within an environment which rewarded me for deep reading. To succeed I needed to engage with information in a very personal way. I learnt how to locate the marrow of a topic, some unique factoid which would elevate my writing and engage my teacher's attention.

I started to understand the rules which governed non-fiction books. The inaugural contents page which would set up my expectations as a reader and the terminal index provided me with easy access to the secrets within. Glossaries in particular hold a revered position in my memories. Upon reading a new word for the first time I would refer to the glossary to elucidate the meaning and then in my head I would roll the word around on my tongue manipulating it like a small child with a building block. Frustrated with the lack of similar signposts in fiction works I listed new words on the pasted down endpaper of fiction books.

My love of non-fiction led me towards reading biographies and autobiographies of famous people. Scientists, palaeontologists, inventors and artists. Learning the stories behind discoveries helped me to understand the wider political and social contexts of phenomena.

My reading diet further aided me in learning the nuances of emotive language. Words are global and like mythological shape-shifters able to traverse between the realms of fact and fiction. I knew what appealed to me and elicited an immediate response and I stored these techniques as part of my own narrative blueprint which would later become the hallmark of my own writing. It is something I advocate to all my pupils: the need to find a distinctive voice and a hook to capture the audience. I teach them how the mechanics of non-fiction texts perform an identical role to the beginning, middle and end of fiction tales and help them in writing powerful openings which demand attention.

My experience of working within primary education has shown me that sharing my love of reading is an unexpected and inspiring hook for pupils. The use of storytelling

---

reflectiveteaching.co.uk/rtps6/part3_ch12

devices especially has had a very powerful effect on my pupils. At the end of a recent Year 6 class on evolution and inheritance, my lesson objective was that pupils would recognise that fossils provide information about the evolution of living things. Beyond using non-fiction books to deepen the children's scientific knowledge and vocabulary I used a range of texts and modes to support their learning. I read them *Lightning Mary* (Simmons, 2019) that tells the story of the childhood of Mary Anning, a famous Victorian palaeontologist. The pupils were enraptured by the story of Mary's struggles growing up in poverty, her discoveries of fossils, and her difficulties being accepted by the scientific community as a woman. We used that National History Museum's online resources to learn more about her and to see some of her discoveries. Using story to support pupils' understanding of evolution opened up conversations about poverty, opportunity, and the role of women in science.

Real science is just as fantastic and enthralling as fantasy writing or science fiction. The ability to interweave difference text types and modes in the same seamless way as my teachers did in primary school has helped me to raise aspirations in my own classroom and create that 'buzz' which surely we all want to achieve?

Reflective Activity 12.4

Aim: To reflect on what messages we, as teachers, communicate about reading to learners.

Evidence and reflection: Make a list of the reading material you have recently included in your lessons. What reading matter is there on the walls relating to what you are teaching? Is any material in the classroom written by the pupils or is it formally published? What reading material related to your teaching is on your desk?

Extension: To what extent do you think your pupils perceive you, like Emma, as a teacher who reads?

WRITING

Writing lies on the other side of reading. Where reading might be considered a message getting activity, Clay (2001) proposed that writing is a message giving activity. It offers the ability to communicate outside real time, with people who are not present and whom we may or may not know. It has the potential to endure and thus not only affords the possibility of reflection, but also to extend beyond the present parameters of our lives.

The relationship between reading and writing

The American scholar, Robert Scholes, argues that young people need to acquire textual power by the end of their formal schooling, by which he means they need to become confident readers and writers of texts, who have the skills, knowledge and understanding to read for pleasure as well as interpret and take up critical positions towards texts and produce texts for others to do the same. To that end, he writes, we should 'perceive reading not simply as consumption but as a productive activity, the making of meaning, in which one is guided by the text one reads, of course, but not simply manipulated by it. . . . The writer is always reading and the reader is always writing' (Scholes, 1985, p. 8). His point is borne out by research conducted by Barrs and Cork into reading and writing at Key Stage 2 (Barrs and Cork, 2001, Reading 12.5). Barrs and Cork explored the effect on children's writing when high-quality literary texts were their starting point. Evidence from their research showed that children's writing was influenced by several pedagogical approaches, as well as the rich quality of the texts. These approaches included writing in role as characters to encourage empathy and alternative perspectives, reading aloud to hear the sounds and rhythms of the prose, and exploring ideas through drama before committing them to paper. Interesting outcomes may also arise from taking non-literary texts as prompts for writing. Jarman and McClune (2005), for example, have explored newspapers as a resource for extending reading and promoting engagement in the science classroom.

Reflective Activity 12.5

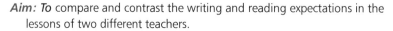

Aim: To compare and contrast the writing and reading expectations in the lessons of two different teachers.

Evidence and reflection: Join up with another teacher in your school and agree to observe one of each other's lessons with a particular focus on reading and writing. Make a note of all the reading material made available to the pupils during that lesson: writing that is part of the physical space in which the lesson takes place; writing prepared by the teacher before the lesson (e.g. PowerPoint slides or worksheets); published material (e.g. textbooks or class novel, noting with the latter whether photocopied sections or whole texts are used); writing done by the pupils, including the nature of the task, time allocated, what pupils are taught about how to accomplish it. Afterwards, discuss the commonalities and distinctions between reading and writing in your two lessons.

Extension: What might be the implications for pupils' reading and writing from the experiences the two of you offer them?

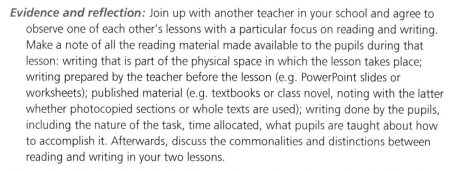

Teaching writing

Given the complexity of the writing process, all teachers need to make sure that pupils have sufficient time and support for whatever task they are set. For teachers of pupils in the early years and primary age, but also across the lifespan, this includes supporting pupils in the transcriptional as well as the compositional elements of writing (Bazerman et al., 2018). The transcriptional or secretarial element refers to features of the writing process such as the physical effort of writing, spelling, punctuation and legibility, whereas the compositional element includes the authorial considerations of capturing ideas, selecting words, adapting texts for a particular audience and using appropriate grammar and style. Throughout all phases of schooling, reflective teachers deepen pupils' understanding across various genres of writing, attending to both the transcriptional and authorial aspects of the writing process. We also need to help pupils learn what are some of the specific features of writing they will encounter across the curriculum, for example when writing about a science experiment as distinct from a historical explanation. They need encouragement to consider the audience for whom the writing is intended, to think about how its purpose will affect choice of style and format, and to judge the different ways in which the context of the writing affects any decisions they make about how their piece is to be written. Teachers may well offer scaffolding in the form of writing frames or paragraph structures. It is vital to remember that scaffolding is only ever intended to be a temporary form of support, to be dismantled once it is no longer needed (see also Chapter 11). As soon as pupils understand the purpose and diversity of paragraphing in the bigger picture of sustained pieces of writing, they need to be encouraged to write more independently, confident in their ability to make relevant stylistic choices to achieve particular effects.

> **Expert Question**
>
> **Personalisation:** *does the curriculum resonate with the social and cultural needs of diverse learners and provide appropriate elements of choice?*
>
> This question contributes to a conceptual framework underpinning professional expertise (see Chapter 16).

Researching writing

Writing develops across the lifespan. As adult writers, we continue to develop our authorial voice that is, no doubt, quite different from our writing as children, or indeed as college pupils. Researching writing is complex because writing is complex. It involves a wide range of skills – cognitive, motor, memory – and depends on audience, purpose, task and motivation (Bazerman et al., 2018). Graham (2018) proposed that writing development occurs when pupils become part of a writing community and involves a range of cognitive skills that interact with instruction and the writing culture of the classroom.

One very influential research study in the field of writing is Bereiter and Scardamalia's *The Psychology of Written Composition* (1987; Reading 12.6). A key idea is that of two models of composing: 'knowledge-telling' and 'knowledge-transforming'. Broadly, the capacity of writers' knowledge-telling is highly dependent on how much they know and can therefore write about. The main point, however, is developing knowledge through writing about it. In knowledge-transforming, on the other hand, the main aim is development of the text, the writer taking into consideration the audience, purpose, context and style in order to create a text which will have maximum impact, not just because of the knowledge the writer is offering, but because of the manner in which it is being represented textually. Teachers who share Bereiter and Scardamalia's ideas about these two models of composition also realise the potential benefit of seeing them as a two-stage process: first, the writer amasses knowledge then tackles the transformation, rather than trying to undertake both mental operations simultaneously.

Research which looks at writing as a form of design across a range of curriculum areas is a helpful way to conceptualise the task that faces pupils when they are learning to write. Undertaking research into pupils' reading and writing in modern foreign languages and English, Maun and Myhill (2005) explore the implications of multimodality for teaching writing. They argue that visual aspects of texts not only affect how they are read but also how writers make choices when writing. Thinking about text-making as design, not simply as writing, can help pupils to conceptualise it differently. It can also encompass a very wide variety of types of texts that young people need to learn how to write, not just verbal texts such as conventional story narratives but multimodal texts such as newspaper front pages or blogs (Bearne and Wolstencraft, 2007; Cremin and Myhill, 2012). Here, too, we need to ensure pupils develop a wide enough repertoire of genres, modes and technical proficiency to be able to make choices about how and what to communicate through their writing. Thinking about it as design is an approach that teachers and pupils often find helpful.

The best marking, feedback and assessment act as a form of high-quality communication in their own right. In particular, formative feedback on speaking and listening, reading or writing must be dialogic if it is to take effect. When teachers offer formative comments, whether orally or in writing, on young people's work, they act as an actual audience for the piece. To that end, it behoves them to respond genuinely as well as offering formative feedback. To be formative, however, the feedback needs to be acted on by learners in ways which make it clear that learning has taken place, not merely that learners are acting as automatons. Thus, at a very simple level, making changes to a draft along lines spelled out by the marker does not make the feedback formative; transforming the marker's feedback to the writer's own ends, does (see Chapter 13).

Expert Questions

Authenticity: *do learners recognise routine processes of assessment and feedback as being of personal value?*

Feeding back: *is there a routine flow of constructive, specific, diagnostic feedback from teacher to learners?*

These questions contribute to a conceptual framework underpinning professional expertise (see Chapter 16).

---

reflectiveteaching.co.uk/rtps6/part3_ch12

KNOWLEDGE ABOUT LANGUAGE FOR COMMUNICATION

Knowledge about grammar

Debates still rage about whether explicit knowledge about language, such as grammar, makes a difference to the quality of communication. Little evidence has been found to suggest that it does. However, it has been argued that research has not looked at instances where pupils are being taught about writing and about grammar simultaneously (Myhill et al., 2012). There remains no sure answer, but the discussion raises important questions about how language is perceived. Brian Cox and his committee, in their report for the National Curriculum for English in the United Kingdom (UK), stated that:

> Language is a system of sounds, meanings and structures with which we make sense of the world around us. It functions as a tool of thought; as a means of social organisation; as a repository and means of transmission of knowledge; as the raw material of literature; and as the creator and sustainer – or destroyer – of human relationships. It changes inevitably over time and, as change is not uniform, from place to place. Because language is a fundamental part of being human, it is an important aspect of a person's sense of self; because it is a fundamental feature of any community, it is an important aspect of a person's sense of social identity. (DES 1989b, para. 6.18)

If language is a fundamental part of being human, then it is important to teach young people something about how it works and a metalanguage for discussing it. They often find it intrinsically interesting (Crystal, 2002). If pupils are to learn about language from their teachers, we need to have some understanding of how the everyday language we use to communicate works. One of the concepts we need to teach about is grammar and why it is important in thinking about communication. Grammar comprises word order (syntax), word structure (morphology) and lexis (the vocabulary from which we select). Audience, context and purpose will always affect our grammatical choices.

> ### Expert Question
>
> **Balance:** *does the curriculum-as-experienced offer everything which each learner has a right to expect?*
>
> This question contributes to a conceptual framework underpinning professional expertise (see Chapter 16).

Some differences between spoken and written language

A crucial factor affecting our use of grammar is whether we are communicating in spoken or written language. For example, in a newspaper report about a football match we might have said that 'Beckham scored the goal'. A radio commentator, reporting live on the same match might have said, 'It's a goal, and Beckham the scorer'. Seen written down, the word

reflectiveteaching.co.uk/rtps6/part3_ch12

order of the radio commentary looks odd, but in the context of reporting a live football match when listeners cannot see for themselves what is happening, the crucial point to communicate is that a goal has been scored; who scored it will be of secondary importance. In a written report, however, there is time for a journalist to adjust the words into a more conventional written order. What needs to be understood about these two examples is that the radio commentator's grammar is not wrong, merely different because of the context, audience and purpose.

Understanding some of the differences between spoken and written language can be a valuable way for teachers to think about helping pupils develop their own communication skills. In spoken language, speakers typically: make use of stress patterns, pitch, speed and volume so listeners can hear what is meant; use gestures and body language to supplement what they say; repeat themselves, make false starts, hesitate, trail off without the listener necessarily losing the thread; interrupt each other or take turns; and link infinite numbers of clauses together (a pattern sometimes known as 'chaining') rather than speaking in sentences with clearly defined beginnings and endings. In *Learning to Write* (1993), Gunther Kress analyses children's speech and writing, drawing out some of the implications for teachers. Kress suggests several areas for consideration, all of which relate closely to the focus on audience, purpose, context and style within this chapter overall. We discuss three of these areas briefly.

First, when we speak, we do so for the most part in the physical presence of an audience (phone conversations being one exception). Speakers therefore adjust their talk depending on the immediate response they receive from the listener. When we write, we usually address an audience that is absent. Writers, therefore, need to develop the habit of explicitness in anticipation of how readers might respond. In much spoken language, the word order is often characterised by chaining (e.g. I went to the market *and* I bought some vegetables *and* I went for a coffee). Writing, however, tends to be more hierarchical, with main and subordinate clauses being used to signal to the reader what is key and what is of subsidiary importance (e.g. I went to the market *in order to* get some vegetables, *afterwards* going for a coffee). Writers therefore need to experience as wide a variety of sentence grammar in their reading as possible, with teachers drawing their attention to what different purposes syntax variety can serve, as and when appropriate.

Second, speakers make use of a range of intonation to communicate meaning to listeners. Writers, meanwhile, do not have that option very often. They need, therefore, to be able to use word order to suit their purposes instead. For example, if someone is standing beside a person they are teaching to toss a pancake, they will use intonation as well as words to explain how to move the pan, stress the danger, enjoy the fun. In a written recipe, much closer attention will be paid to word order, vocabulary and sequencing of instructions.

Third, in order to become as versatile a writer as possible, there is a need for an ever-expanding vocabulary. At a market stall I might say to the stallholder, 'One of those, please', indicating a punnet of strawberries. My speech would be minimal since pointing would do the rest. A description of strawberries on a menu to persuade a diner to select them for dessert might read 'Delicious, sun-ripened, locally picked, juicy strawberries', designed to persuade the diner to choose them without seeing or smelling them in advance.

Chapter 12 Communication 395

The more opportunities pupils are afforded to study the grammar and vocabulary of their own and other people's texts – whether spoken or written – and analyse how they work to achieve particular purposes and address audiences within specific contexts, drawing on particular styles, the greater the textual power that speakers as well as writers will acquire.

English as an additional language

Language is one of the most significant manifestations of identity and culture, and is thus of enormous significance for the self-respect of individuals and groups. Over 45 years ago the Bullock Report (1975) stated that:

> No child should be expected to cast off the language and culture of home as he [sic] crosses the school threshold, nor to live and act as though school and home represent two totally separate and different cultures which have to be kept firmly apart. (DES, 1975)

Bilingual and multilingual learners face two huge tasks in school: they need to learn to communicate in English as well as any other languages they speak, and they need to learn and communicate within the content of the curriculum. However, Sorace (2010) argues, the ability to communicate with two or more languages brings metalinguistic, cognitive and social advantages. It is essential, therefore, that teachers build on existing language capabilities, recognising the opportunities these bring to enhance the learning of all pupils.

Cummins (1996) adopted the metaphor of an iceberg to distinguish between basic interpersonal communicative skills (BICS) and cognitive and academic language proficiency (CALP). Children develop communicative skills first, in face-to-face, highly contextualised situations, but take longer to develop the cognitive and academic language proficiency that contributes to educational success. Cummins acknowledges that some interpersonal communication can impose considerable cognitive demands on a speaker and that academic situations may also require social communication skills. Generally speaking, children learning an additional language can become conversationally fluent in the new language in two to three years, but may take five years or longer to catch up with monolingual peers on the development of full language proficiency.

Multilingual children are experts in handling language because they become adept at 'trans-languaging' (switching between languages) (Smidt, 2016). Bilingual children are hearing two languages – or two distinct systems – which they have to internalise and respond to. Kuhl (2004) argues that at an early age neither language is likely to interfere with the other, so young children can acquire two languages easily. This does not lead to confusion; on the contrary, it has cognitive, metalinguistic and communicative advantages. Indeed, bilingual children

> ### Expert Question
>
> **Connection:** *does the curriculum engage with the cultural resources and funds-of-knowledge of families and the community?*
>
> This question contributes to a conceptual framework underpinning professional expertise (see Chapter 16)

reflectiveteaching.co.uk/rtps6/part3_ch12

outperform monolinguals in cognitive flexibility tasks (Bialystok, 2007) because they work constantly with two linguistic systems. These children have considerable language skills on which the teacher can build, and they are likely to have much to offer others, particularly with regards to the subject of language study. Having said this, even if the child may be skilled in language use, they may still need particular support and guidance to develop greater proficiency in the use of English at school, especially in terms of written English.

In Reese et al.'s (2000) large-scale study of emergent bilingual pupils in America, the importance of supporting pupils' languages was shown:

> [N]on-English speaking pupil success in learning to read in English does not rest exclusively on primary language input and development, nor is it solely the result of rapid acquisition of English. Both apparently contribute to pupils' subsequent English reading achievement . . . early literacy experiences support subsequent literacy development, regardless of language; time spent on literacy activity in the native language – whether it takes place at home or at school – is not time lost with respect to English reading acquisition. (Reese et al., 2000, p. 633)

> **Expert Question**
>
> **Inclusion:** *are all learners treated respectfully and fairly in both formal and informal interaction?*
>
> This question contributes to a conceptual framework underpinning professional expertise (see Chapter 16).

This means that the use of mother tongue or community languages should be positively encouraged in the classroom, both for children who are new to English and also as they become more fluent. Reflective teachers understand that it is unhelpful to conceive of 'multilingual children' as some kind of homogeneous group. Some children will have been born in this country and their parents may have insisted on a different first language in order to retain the child's sense of ethnic identity and community.

Consequently, the teacher needs to apply great sensitivity to these children: on the one hand, children learning English as an additional language should be encouraged to use spoken English at every possible opportunity; on the other, the teacher needs to employ teaching strategies which ensure that these same children do not begin to lose confidence in their language use because they perceive themselves as underperforming readers and writers. Because language use is closely linked with a person's identity, it requires sensitivity and perception by all who work with children (Blackledge, 1994, Reading 12.7).

CONCLUSION

In this chapter, we have discussed some important aspects of communication in the classroom. We have offered ideas about many of the ways in which teachers and learners communicate with one another. In particular, we have stressed what can be learnt by teachers and pupils when they attend to the audience, purpose, context and style of language use. Although there has been significant emphasis on oral communication, through speaking and listening, we have also shown some of the ways in which communication occurs through reading and writing in different modes. We have identified differences between spoken and written language in order to raise awareness of the interesting part they play in the choices we make when we communicate. Many of the young people with whom teachers work in classrooms are bilingual or multilingual, so understanding the advantages and challenges of working with English as an additional language is crucial to the role of any teacher. The Key Readings below offer further reading in all these broad areas for those interested in pursuing any of the ideas above further.

CHAPTER WEBPAGE

reflectiveteaching.co.uk offers additional professional resources for this chapter. For the chapter webpage, go to: reflectiveteaching.co.uk/rtps6/part3_ch12

The webpage resources for Chapter 12 are particularly strong in relation to advice for *Further Reading*. This follows the structure of the chapter, so covers the major characteristics of classroom communication, including speaking, listening, reading and writing.

One of the 'big ideas' discussed in the chapter is that of 'dialogic teaching' – the use of talk to extend pupils' thinking and improve understanding. Some of the best practice-based research on this has been done in Cambridge. Take a look, for instance, at thinkingtogether.educ.cam.ac.uk, which describes breakthrough work over a decade or more and also offers many resources for teachers. A strong exponent and analyst of this approach has been Robin Alexander who has web materials focused on the concept. For a neat summary, search on 'Alexander + dialogic teaching in brief'.

For those who find the concept of dialogic teaching challenging at this stage, you might want to focus on a direct communication skill such as the nature of the questions which we pose. Several of the *Reflective Activities* in this chapter relate to this and there is also a lot of useful material on the internet. One popular source remains the YouTube video by Ted Wragg on 'Types of Questions'.

Three levels of additional guidance are available.

1. As we have seen, with the support of a good library, *Further Reading* on the chapter webpage makes it possible to both deepen and broaden understanding of classroom communication issues. It follows the exact structure of the chapter, so finding appropriate sources for your interests should be straightforward.

2. *Key Readings*, listed below, provides an annotated shortlist of particularly helpful sources to study.

3. Short extracts of many of the Key Readings are provided in *Readings for Reflective Teaching in Schools*. Altogether, it contains over 100 readings and acts rather like a mini-library. For this chapter on Communication, a resumé for each of the relevant readings is provided on the chapter webpage. Some of the content is indicated by the icons below.

KEY READINGS

The classic government report on the significance of language across the curriculum is:

Bullock, A. (1975) *A Language for Life. Report of the Committee of Enquiry into Reading and the Use of English.* London: HMSO.

A National Oracy Project took this further by drawing on the experience of teachers and pupils to emphasise the centrality of talk for learning, see:

Norman, K. (ed.) (1992) *Thinking Voices: The Work of the National Oracy Project.* London: Hodder and Stoughton.

Such work provided foundations for more contemporary organisations such as The Communication Trust, and initiatives such as its 'What Works' online library of strategies to support pupils' speech, language and communication (including SEND provision). See also the work of Jean Gross, such as:

Gross, J. (2018) *Time to Talk. Implementing Outstanding Practice in Speech, Language and Communication.* London: Routledge.

Other important studies of classroom learning and language in primary classrooms are:

Edwards, D. and Mercer, N. (1987) *Common Knowledge: The Development of Understanding in Classrooms.* London: Methuen.
Webster, A., Beverage, M. and Reid, M. (1996) *Managing the Literacy Curriculum.* London: Routledge.

The cutting edge of understanding of effective teaching and learning through talk is now focused on 'dialogic teaching', about which Alexander, Mercer and Wegerif have made exceptional contributions. For summaries and applications, see:

Alexander, R. (2008) *Towards Dialogic Teaching: Rethinking Classroom Talk.* Cambridge: Dialogos. (see also **Reading 12.3**)
Mercer, N. and Littleton, K. (2007) *Dialogue and the Development of Children's Thinking.* London: Routledge. **(Reading 11.6)**
Phillipson, N. and Wegerif, R. (2017) *Dialogic Education. Mastering Core Concepts Through Thinking Together.* London: Routledge.

Approaches to reading are often controversial but there is no dispute about the educational priority that all pupils should achieve competence. For insights into some of the many debates about the teaching of reading, see:

Dombey, H. et al. (2013) *Teaching Reading: What the Evidence Says.* Leicester: UKLA.
Tennent, W. (2014) *Understanding Reading Comprehension.* London: Sage.
Harrison, C. (2004) *Understanding Reading Development.* London: SAGE. **(Reading 12.4)**

Cremin et al. illustrate the importance of analysing literacy in everyday life. And Styles and Arizpe also suggest the value of a broad appreciation of reading capabilities.

Cremin, T., Mottram, M., Collins, F., Powell, S. and Drury, R. (2016) *Researching Literacy Lives: Building Communities Between Home and School.* Oxford: Routledge.
Styles, M. and Arizpe, E. (2016) *Children Reading Pictures.* London: Routledge.

The approach to teaching reading which has informed this chapter is elaborated in:

> Cliff Hodges, G. (2016) *Researching and Teaching Reading: Developing Pedagogy Through Critical Enquiry*. Oxford: Routledge.

Writing is also essential for success in school and beyond. The books below offer fresh perspectives on writing across the full primary and secondary range:

> Bearne, E. and Wolstencroft, H. (2007) *Visual Approaches to Teaching Writing: Multimodal Literacy 5–11*. London: Sage/UKLA.
>
> Cremin, T. and Myhill, D. (2012) *Writing Voices: Creating Communities of Writers*. London: Routledge.

Knowledge about the English language is valuable to any teacher. For a fascinating overview, see:

> Crystal, D. (2002) *The English Language: A Guided Tour of the Language*. London: Penguin.

Excellent reviews of research, theory and practice on linguistic diversity are:

> Conteh, J. (2015) *The EAL Teaching book. Promoting Success for Multilingual Learners*. London: Sage.
>
> Bearne, E. and Marsh, J. (eds) (2007) *Literacy and Social Inclusion: Closing the Gap*. Stoke-on-Trent: Trentham Books.

To really drive home the significance of linguistic diversity, take a look at the Greater London Authority website, which provides information on the 40 per cent of pupils whose first spoken language at home was other than English, such as Bengali, Urdu and Somali:

londondatastore-archive.s3.amazonaws.com/visualisations/atlas/language-2011/atlas.html

TOOLKIT EVIDENCE 12.1
Speaking and listening activities: articulating and communicating for learning

What is it?
Speaking and listening approaches are based on the idea that language comprehension and reading skills benefit from explicit discussion of the content and/or processes of learning. Oral language approaches include:

- targeted reading aloud and discussing books with young children;
- explicitly extending pupils' spoken vocabulary;
- the use of structured questioning to develop reading comprehension.

Speaking and listening approaches have some overlap both with meta-cognitive approaches, which make talk about learning explicit in classrooms, and with collaborative learning, which promotes pupils' talk and interaction in groups. When learners articulate their thinking out loud it provides opportunities to use new vocabulary and language forms. If they can't describe and explain their thinking, they may not be able to understand when listening or reading, and will not be able to express their thoughts in written form.

What does the evidence say?
Overall, studies of speaking and listening interventions consistently show positive benefits for learning, including oral language skills, vocabulary use, reading comprehension and writing. On average, pupils who participate in these kinds of interventions make approximately six months' additional progress over the course of a year.

All pupils appear to benefit, but some studies show slightly greater effects for younger children and pupils from disadvantaged backgrounds (up to seven months' benefit). There is consistent evidence supporting reading to young children and encouraging them to answer questions and to talk about the story with a trained adult.

How sound is the evidence?
There is extensive and reasonably consistent evidence about the impact of speaking and listening interventions, including a substantial number of meta-analyses and systematic reviews. Although the majority of the evidence relates to younger children, there is also clear evidence that older learners, and particularly disadvantaged pupils, can benefit from a more explicit focus on speaking and listening.

What do I need to think about?
- How can you help pupils to articulate their thinking as part of teaching and learning activities?
- How will you match the speaking and listening activities to learners' current stage of development, so that it extends their learning *and* connects with the curriculum?

Links and further reading
Alexander, R. (2012) *Improving Oracy and Classroom Talk in English Schools: Achievements and Challenges*. In DfE Seminar on Oracy, the National Curriculum and Educational Standards (Vol. 20). robinalexander.org.uk/wp-content/uploads/2012/06/DfE-oracy-120220-AlexanderFINAL.pdf

Law, J., Charlton, J., Dockrell, J., Gascoigne, M., McKean, C. and Theakston, A. (2017) *Early Language Development: Needs, provision, and intervention for preschool children from socio-economically disadvantage backgrounds: A Report for the Education Endowment Foundation: October 2017*. Education Endowment Foundation and Public Health England. educationendowmentfoundation.org.uk/public/files/Law_et_al_Early_Language_Development_final.pdf

Marulis, L.M., and Neuman, S.B. (2010) 'The effects of vocabulary intervention on young children's word learning: A meta-analysis'. *Review of Educational Research*, 80(3), 300–35. doi:10.3102/0034654310377087

The EEF Teaching and Learning Toolkit entry on 'Oral language interventions': educationendowmentfoundation.org.uk/education-evidence/teaching-learning-toolkit/oral-language-interventions– see also the technical appendix for further references.

See also
Meta-cognition and self-regulated learning (Toolkit Evidence 2.1)
Collaborative learning (Toolkit Evidence 11.3)

Education Endowment Foundation

TOOLKIT EVIDENCE 12.2
Reading comprehension strategies: mastering the meaning of texts

What is it?
Comprehension-led approaches to improving reading focus on learners' understanding of the text. A range of techniques are taught explicitly which focus pupils' attention on comprehending the meaning of what is written, such as inferring the meaning from context, summarising or identifying key points, using graphic or semantic organisers, developing questioning strategies, and monitoring their own comprehension and identifying difficulties themselves.

What does the evidence say?
On average, reading comprehension approaches can improve learning by an additional six months' progress over the course of a school year. These approaches appear to be particularly effective for older readers (aged 8 or above) who are not making expected progress. Successful reading comprehension approaches carefully select activities for pupils according to their reading capabilities, and ensure that texts provide an effective, but not overwhelming, challenge.

Many of the approaches can be usefully combined with phonics, collaborative and peer-learning techniques. The use of techniques such as graphic organisers and drawing pupils' attention to text structures are likely to be particularly useful when reading expository or information texts. There are also some indications that computer-based tutoring approaches can be successful in improving reading comprehension, particularly when they focus on the development of strategies and self-questioning skills, though the evidence is less robust in this area.

It is important to remember that no particular strategy should be seen as a panacea, and careful diagnosis of the reasons why an individual pupil is struggling is very important when exploring possible intervention strategies.

How sound is the evidence?
There is extensive evidence in this area, from a range of studies over the last thirty years. A majority of studies were conducted in the United States, and focus on pupils aged 8–18 who are falling behind their peers or have difficulties with reading.

What do I need to think about?
- Effective diagnosis of reading difficulties is important in identifying possible solutions, particularly for older struggling readers.
- A wide range of strategies and approaches can be successful, but these need to be taught explicitly and consistently. How are you going to identify the strategies that will meet the needs of your pupils and how will these be reinforced?
- A key issue for teachers is identifying the level of difficulty for comprehension activities that is required to extend pupils' reading capabilities. How will you ensure the texts used provide an effective challenge?

Links and further reading
Shanahan, T., Callison, K., Carriere, C., Duke, N.K., Pearson, P.D., Schatschneider, C., and Torgesen, J. (2010) *Improving Reading Comprehension in Kindergarten through 3rd Grade: IES Practice Guide*. NCEE 2010-4038. What Works Clearinghouse. files.eric.ed.gov/fulltext/ED512029.pdf

The EEF Teaching and Learning Toolkit entry on 'Reading comprehension strategies': educationendowmentfoundation.org.uk/education-evidence/teaching-learning-toolkit/reading-comprehension-strategies – see also the technical appendix for further references.

See also
Meta-cognition and self-regulation (Toolkit Evidence 2.1)
Phonics (Toolkit Evidence 11.1)
Collaborative learning (Toolkit Evidence 11.3)

Education Endowment Foundation

Chapter 13
Assessment
How can assessment enhance learning?

Introduction	404

Assessment, learning and teaching	407
Guiding principles	407
Key ideas	409

Assessment for learning in the classroom	412
Sharing goals and identifying quality	414
Questioning and dialogue	416
Feedback	419
Self- and peer-assessment	421
Adjusting teaching and learning	425

Affirming assessment for learning	428

Conclusion	430

reflectiveteaching.co.uk/rtps6/part3_ch13

Part 3 Teaching for learning

INTRODUCTION

Assessment has a profound influence on learning. It can be used to build confidence, enhance self-esteem, and encourage young people to become learners who have a deeper understanding of progress and what action they might take to enhance their own learning. Equally, assessment experiences can reduce confidence, damage self-esteem, and encourage young people to become ever-increasingly dependent on their teachers and to see learning as a series of hoops to be jumped through just to get through the day. The choice about which experiences young people will have is largely ours, as teachers, and the awareness we have of what makes the difference between assessment as a force for good in learning and the kinds of assessment practice more likely to have a negative impact on learning.

If these seem startling claims, think about your own experience: perhaps you did well in one subject because it was clear what was required of you and each step was manageable. Alternatively, you might have disliked another subject and dropped it as soon as possible because everything seemed so confusing and difficult. Maybe you were motivated by the encouragement from one teacher, or humiliated by the comments from another. Possibly you know one of the many people who consider themselves failures because they got lower exam grades than they hoped for, or did not pass the '11-plus' test for secondary school selection; you might be one of the people who thinks they cannot do maths, or sing, or draw or whatever. More positively, you might have achieved something you never thought possible, and become confident that given effort and the right support you are able to succeed in many fields. As a teacher, you have undoubtedly helped others to learn and achieve, in formal and informal settings, and across a range of subjects, topics and tasks. Assessment is at the heart of all these scenarios.

The word 'assessment' comes from the Latin 'assidere' meaning 'to sit besides', and this broadens the conception of assessment to include collaborative activities, bringing to mind two people in dialogue, looking at something together, one person seeking to understand another's work and suggest improvements. We can also metaphorically sit beside ourselves, reviewing our progress, and planning our next steps. Sometimes, the words 'assessment', 'testing' and 'examinations' are used as if they were synonyms. They are not. Assessment is the process of gathering and using evidence for a specific purpose; principally, to inform learning. Tests and examinations are simply examples of ways in which evidence might be gathered, and there are many other ways; for example, observing children as they undertake tasks, using photographs of projects as they develop, or engaging children in conversation and listening carefully to their responses. What matters is that the process of assessment has a purpose in relation to pupils' learning. Evidence gathered should relate to that purpose, and crucially the evidence gathered should be used to promote further learning. What might this mean in practice?

reflectiveteaching.co.uk/rtps6/part3_ch13

Chapter 13 Assessment

Case Study 13.1 Observation in the early years

In the Early Years Centre, one member of staff commented that Jabari seemed to spend a lot of time on his own. The team agreed to a focused observation of Jabari during the 'Off to the Zoo' role play. This topic had been identified by the children following a discussion about their favourite animals. The children were:

- to plan a trip to the zoo;
- to use the picture map created by the teachers to plan which animals they would go to see and the route they would take around the zoo.

Soft toy animals were placed around the nursery and the group had to use the map to visit each animal, role playing a visit to the zoo.

The observation focused on identifying Jabari's interaction with others in his group and the extent to which Jabari took part. If Jabari withdrew from the activity, staff were invited to identify triggers for withdrawal.

During the observation, staff identified that Jabari began as an enthusiastic member of the group. As the children planned which animals they wanted to see, and used the picture map to decide the best route round the zoo, Jabari was listening carefully and looking interested. He said that he wanted to go to see the tigers but the other children did not pay attention to him, so he took a step back from the activity. He remained part of the group but did not contribute again.

Following the observation, the team discussed what had happened and agreed to involve the group of children in conversation. The member of staff asked the children to identify what happens in a good group discussion and created criteria for success with the children. Contributing, listening and responding were identified by the children as key aspects of good group discussion.

The children then began to discuss:

- 'What we saw at the zoo' and
- 'How we used the picture map'.

At the end of the group discussion, the member of staff asked the children to reflect on their discussion using the criteria established by the children: Who had contributed well? Who had listened well? Who had responded well? Every child in the group was invited to give feedback to another child in the form of two stars and a wish. Two things done well and one thing to improve for the next discussion.

The purposes of assessment in this scenario were

- to gather evidence to determine whether an impression of a child withdrawing from group work was accurate;
- to build children's understanding of what matters in group discussion that involves everyone.

reflectiveteaching.co.uk/rtps6/part3_ch13

The means of gathering evidence was observation. This was chosen as it was the method likely to offer insights on Jabari's engagement as part of the group. It was done in a way in which it was part of day-to-day learning in the Early Years Centre.

The evidence gathered was used to identify what next steps might be helpful to take forward each child's progression in interacting with other children. See Reading 13.3 for a range of ways to gather evidence of children's academic and development progress in the early years where assessment is integrated into learning.

Assessment that supports learning is referred to as 'Assessment for Learning' (AfL), a term that is often used interchangeably with 'formative assessment'. This chapter deliberately refers to 'Assessment for Learning' with a particular understanding of the term (as discussed on p. 407). In brief, AfL is a whole way of working involving learners and teachers that integrates assessment, learning and teaching. Activities associated with AfL not only provide information to be used for formative purposes, but also, and probably even more importantly, they are learning processes in themselves. Not only does AfL support the learning of whatever is being studied at the time, it also promotes learning how to learn. AfL is underpinned by a set of beliefs about learning, which when enacted establish a learning culture in the classroom and help develop learners' metacognitive skills and sense of responsibility.

See Chapter 4

TLRP Principles

Two principles are of particular relevance to this chapter on assessment for learning:

Effective teaching and learning needs assessment to be congruent with learning. Assessment should help to advance learning as well as determine whether learning has taken place. It should be designed and carried out so that it measures learning outcomes in a dependable way and also provides feedback for future learning. (*Principle 5*)

Effective teaching and learning promotes the active engagement of the learner. A chief goal of teaching and learning should be the promotion of learners' independence and autonomy. This involves acquiring a repertoire of learning strategies and practices, developing positive attitudes towards learning, and confidence in oneself as a good learner. (*Principle 6*)

There are three main sections to this chapter – 'assessment, learning and teaching', 'assessment for learning in the classroom' and 'affirming assessment for learning'. In the first section key issues, definitions and principles that concern the inter-relationships among assessment, learning and teaching are introduced and discussed. In the second, different ways of putting AfL into practice are considered in five groups. It is essential that both these sections are read together since 'doing' AfL divorced from a culture of learning and without understanding the underlying ideas and principles will not bring about the desired results; indeed, doing so could be detrimental to learning. The final section affirms an understanding of assessment for learning and explores how it differs from formative assessment in a little more depth.

The following chapter, Chapter 14, takes as its focus the closely related aspect of assessment in relation to achievement, and issues of evaluating learning outcomes.

Harlen et al. (1992, Reading 13.1) provides an overview of different types and purposes of assessment, and relates to both this chapter and Chapter 14.

ASSESSMENT, LEARNING AND TEACHING

Guiding principles

Three key principles about Assessment for Learning were generated through TLRP's *Learning How to Learn* project (James et al., 2007, Reading 2.8; see **Research Briefing 13.1** on p. 431):

- making learning explicit;
- promoting learning autonomy;
- focusing on learning (as opposed to performance).

'Making learning explicit' involves opening up and making very clear all phases and aspects of learning: what precisely is to be learnt, why it is important, what progress will look like and what counts as quality; exactly what pupils know and understand, and tellingly what misconceptions they hold; which aspects and parts of their work are evidence of high-quality learning, and how to improve elements that need strengthening. A classroom where learning is made explicit features rich dialogue focused on learning, among pupils and between the teacher and individuals. Exchanges go far beyond closed questions and very short answers, to open questions eliciting extensive responses, with in-depth probing leading to detailed explanation and considered reflection. When assessing children's work, learning cannot be made explicit by the occasional tick or an overall mark or grade, but rather by identifying particular strengths, pointing to specific points for improvement and, crucially, what action (next steps) might best be taken that would lead to improvement.

'Autonomous learning' refers to pupils taking responsibility for their learning and exercising some measure of independence. It does not mean that children work on their own, although there might be occasions when they decide that this is the most appropriate thing to do. For teachers to promote learning autonomy they must include some level of choice to pupils, and also support them to develop the skills and confidence to make those decisions. A key feature of autonomous learning is being able to evaluate your own work and progress, and decide on your next steps without having to be reliant on a teacher or someone else to tell you, so realistic self-assessment informed by knowledge of the intended learning and a clear idea of what quality would look like is crucial. Self-regulating learning is not something that can only be undertaken when a child reaches a certain age, it is an approach to learning that can be developed: pupils become more autonomous learners with guidance and through practice. This approach is very different from that of teachers asking children to self-assess using happy and sad faces. Strategies such as these encourage children to react to their work rather than engage deeply with how their learning might be enhanced.

The third principle, 'focusing on learning' (as opposed to performance), draws attention to the nature of the learning that is promoted and valued. It is learning with understanding at its core, and learning for its intrinsic worth and long-lasting value; rather than a mechanistic and utilitarian approach to getting marks in a test or examination after which the learning is soon forgotten, for example. This principle is closely linked to Carol Dweck's (2006, Reading 2.6) notion of a 'growth' mindset rather than a 'performance' mindset. Focusing on learning includes focusing on the process of learning, as well as the particular learning objective, so that through assessment for learning pupils become better learners.

As well as providing a useful aide memoire to the essential features of AfL, these three principles are very helpful in evaluating assessment for learning practices that are intended to support, and in checking on their actual effect. This is important because, as Mary James and her team made clear, 'if practices fail to serve the underlying principles such as making learning explicit and promoting learner autonomy, then they cease to be assessment for learning' (James et al., 2007, p. 215, Reading 2.8; see also **Research Briefing 13.2** on p. 437).

Another helpful reference point is the TLRP principles for effective teaching and learning discussed in Chapter 4. Principle 5, 'Effective pedagogy needs assessment to be congruent with learning', is obviously all about assessment, and stresses that assessment should enhance and advance learning as well as evaluating learning outcomes. This resonates with the third *Learning How to Learn* principle above, drawing attention to the learning process rather than performance per se.

> **Expert Question**
>
> **Congruence:** *are forms of assessment fit for purpose in terms of overall educational objectives?*
>
> This question contributes to a conceptual framework underpinning professional expertise (see Chapter 16).

The three principles derived from the *Learning How to Learn* project (making learning explicit, promoting learning autonomy and focusing on learning) resonate with Scotland's 'Curriculum for Excellence' capacities (see Chapter 9), particularly those of developing 'successful learners' and 'confident individuals'. The three principles (remembered by some through the mnemonic LEAF – Learning Explicit Autonomy Focus) serve well as aids to minute-by-minute decisions as well as more considered reflection on practice. Principled decision-making and evaluation are essential if damaging unintended consequences of misrepresentations of AfL are to be avoided, and the powerful benefits of authentic assessment for learning are to be realised.

Focusing on learning has a further dimension: children learn best in supportive communities. Research in early years education has consistently highlighted the importance of play (see Pyle, DeLuca and Danniels, 2017, Reading 2.9).

Reflective Activity 13.1

Aim: To apply principled reflection to the development of assessment for learning practices.

Evidence and reflection: Gather evidence and review a lesson in which practices regarded as assessment for learning were evident. To what extent: (a) was learning made explicit? (b) were learners encouraged to be autonomous? and (c) was there a focus on genuine learning (as opposed to performance simply to gain marks)?

Extension: Reflect on whether there were any harmful unintended consequences of the practices, and what could have been done differently to enhance the quality of learning.

Key ideas

Lying beneath any principles and practices are sets of beliefs, values, theories and ideas that shape our actions, whether or not we acknowledge or are even conscious of them. This section draws attention to conceptions of children and of learning, notions of ability and the interrelated aspects of roles, relationships, agency and identity.

Mary-Jane Drummond (2008) highlights the 'close and necessary relationship' between assessment and values, arguing that through the practice of assessment, educators make 'value-driven choices about children, about learning and achievements' (p. 3). She reminds us that over the years, children have been conceptualised in different ways, for example as empty vessels or blank sheets (John Locke), or as passing through stages of development (Jean-Jacques Rousseau and Jean Piaget). Some conceptualisations are essentially deficit models, whereby children are viewed as lacking, or yet to develop, the characteristics of a competent learner on the way to adulthood. By contrast, the image of pre-school children held by educators in Reggio Emilia, Italy, is of children as 'rich, strong and powerful' (quoted in Drummond, 2008, p. 9).

In terms of learning and achievement, the construction of curricula, learning activities and recording mechanisms based on pre-specified goals, sequenced steps and checklists reflect a view of children's learning as standardised, linear and predictable, rather than unique, complex and divergent. The 'Learning Stories' approach to assessment and recording developed in New Zealand (Carr, 2001, 2008; Carr and Lee, 2012) uses narrative to document children's learning not only for recording purposes but more importantly as a learning process in itself, shared with friends, teachers, parents and others. Building on the work of Wyse et al. (2016) that emphasised the importance of seeing curriculum, pedagogy and assessment as a coherent whole, Hayward et al. (2018) and IEAN (2020) explore how telling the story of progression through the curriculum is key to effective Assessment for Learning, allowing teachers and learners to see children's day-to-day activities as contributing to a longer term learning journey, making 'next steps' a far more meaningful concept. The IEAN (a network of researchers and policymakers from twelve nation states across four continents) explore the importance of progression for assessment for learning highlighting the central role of learner voice in the process. They argue for the importance of evidence of assessment for learning emerging within a particular theory of learning, socio-cultural theory (see Chapter 2). The theoretical context within which assessment for learning is situated is a factor crucial to its positive impact.

Mary James (1998, 2012) has explored the implications for assessment of three theories of learning (behaviourist, constructivist and socio-cultural; see Chapter 2), noting that beliefs about learning are often out of kilter with assessment practices. She advocated reviewing the methods we use for assessment to see the extent to which they align with beliefs and understandings about learning.

What teachers give attention to, and what they say, indicates to pupils what is valued. If feedback and comments are predominantly about presentation and quantity, rather than the learning intention and quality, these aspects will be seen as the most important. Crucially, if the highest attainment in the class is valued more than the greatest achievement by an individual, and if 'correct answers' appear to be more important than 'having a go', then most of the class will feel they can never succeed and will probably disengage, and the rich learning that comes through effort and risk-taking will be rare. Teachers' language reveals their perceptions of 'ability' and learning potential, and helps shape pupils' learning disposition and mindsets (Dweck, 2006, Reading 2.6). The idea of a 'growth' mindset as opposed to a 'fixed' mindset has been referred to above and in Chapter 2, and is further explored below and in Figure 13.1.

Whichever mindset is held has far-reaching repercussions for the disposition of both teachers and pupils. Teachers who ascribe to a fixed mindset try to ascertain pupils' abilities and then match their expectations to this supposed stable and constant entity. They may have fixed ability groups and although they may name the groups in ways not connected with ability, e.g. the red triangles and the green squares, children are keenly aware of the rank order of groups and judge their ability by where they perceive themselves to be in the group hierarchy. Pupils become concerned with how they appear to their peers and teachers, are anxious to look clever not stupid, believe that effort and challenges reveal inadequacies, and because they fear failure they often disengage completely since they would prefer to be thought of as lazy than stupid. By contrast, a growth mindset fosters effort, engagement, a willingness to tackle new and challenging tasks, and to view failure as part of a learning journey. When growth mindsets characterise a classroom, expectations are high, everyone tries, efforts are valued whatever the outcome, and, in the titles of two powerful books, learning is without limits (Hart et al., 2004; Swann et al., 2012, Reading 1.4).

> **Expert Question**
>
> **Validity:** in terms of learning, do the forms of assessment used really measure what they are intended to measure?
>
> This question contributes to a conceptual framework underpinning professional expertise (see Chapter 16).

Fixed Mindset	Growth Mindset
Intelligence is static	Intelligence is expandable
'I must look clever!'	'I want to learn more'
Avoids challenge	Embraces challenge
Gives up easily	Persists in the face of setbacks
Sees effort as pointless	Sees effort as the way forward
Ignores useful criticism	Learns from criticism

Figure 13.1 Fixed and growth mindsets

The roles and relationships of, and among, pupils and teachers that develop in classrooms are closely connected with the prevalent conceptions of children, learning and ability. It makes a huge difference whether children are regarded as rich, strong and powerful with unlimited possibilities for growth in diverse and complex ways, or of fixed potential with deficiencies yet-to-be remedied by inculcation with the knowledge necessary to succeed in tests. The inter-relationships between assessment practices on the one hand, and roles, relationships, autonomy, agency and identity formation on the other have been explored by a number of researchers (Pollard and Filer, 1999, Reading 14.7; Carr, 2001, 2008; Drummond, 2008, 2012; Stobart, 2008; Swaffield, 2011; Willis, 2011). Gordon Stobart's sketches of pupils illustrate powerfully how assessment 'creates' learners (2008, Reading 13.6). The essential argument is that the way assessment is practised shapes how learners view themselves (which has far-reaching consequences), has a strong influence on their development as successful learners (or not) and determines the culture and interactions of the classroom.

These questions contribute to a conceptual framework underpinning professional expertise (see Chapter 16).

> **Expert Questions**
>
> **Expectation:** does our school support high staff and pupil expectations and aspire for excellence?
>
> **Development:** does formative feedback and support enable learners to achieve personal learning goals?
>
> **Evidence:** what evidence might we gather to offer the best insights into the previous two questions?

> **Reflective Activity 13.2**
>
> *Aim:* To reflect on the influence of beliefs and related assessment practices on learner identity and self-efficacy.
>
> *Evidence and reflection:* Think about two contrasting individuals you know well (one of whom may be yourself) and consider whether there is any evidence that how they regard themselves has been shaped by their beliefs about learning and ability, and/or assessment practices they have experienced.
>
> *Extension:* Reflect on the influence you may have on the identity of children or adults you know by what you say and how you respond to them.

ASSESSMENT FOR LEARNING IN THE CLASSROOM

There have been great advances in the understanding and use of assessment to support learning in the last twenty-five years. Although there was a considerable amount of research, professional development and practice before that, in 1998 Paul Black and Dylan Wiliam published an academic article (Black and Wiliam, 1998a) and a summary booklet (Black and Wiliam, 1998b) that led to renewed interest and great activity in the field. Their work was influential because it (a) showed that assessment practice can lead to substantial increases in pupil learning, and (b) identified specific classroom practices.

Since then, there has been much development work and many other studies that have further deepened our knowledge and understanding. Most notable were the King's Medway Oxfordshire *Formative Assessment* project (Black et al., 2003), the *Learning How to Learn* project (James et al., 2007, see TLRP **Research Briefing 13.2** on p. 437), and work by Shirley Clarke (2005a, 2008, 2011, 2014), but there have also been many other projects, research studies and development programmes throughout the UK and around the world.

Whilst all this activity has added considerably to our knowledge about how assessment can support learning and has expanded the repertoire of classroom activities, it has also most importantly pointed out some difficulties. Assessment for Learning (AfL) is not a toolkit to pick and choose from, or a set of techniques that can be put in place almost mechanistically. Indeed, it has been found that when teachers apply the 'letter' rather than the 'spirit' of AfL (Marshall and Drummond, 2006) then it can do more harm than good. Rather, AfL rests on a set of beliefs about learning – notably that the learner has to be actively engaged and that learning is enhanced through working with others (a social constructivist perspective) and that, given effort, practice and the right support, everyone can achieve (a growth mindset) – and strategies will only be effective when conducted in congruence with these beliefs. Research has also produced sets of principles to guide practice, as discussed on p. 407.

The major features of AfL practice identified by Black and Wiliam (1998a, 1998b) have stood the test of time, and been affirmed by subsequent development and research work.

> **Expert Question**
>
> **Repertoire:** is our pedagogic expertise sufficiently creative, skilled and wide-ranging to support all elements of learning?
>
> This question contributes to a conceptual framework underpinning professional expertise (see Chapter 16).

In this chapter, these strategies are considered in five categories, but it should be remembered that they are interrelated. Since AfL is a coherent way of working, any grouping of the practices is to some extent artificial and slightly arbitrary. Also, since AfL is an integral part of learning and teaching, there are many connections with other chapters in this book, for example Chapter 4 on principles of effective teaching and learning, Chapter 6 on relationships and classroom climate, Chapter 10 on planning, Chapter 11 on teaching pedagogy and Chapter 12 on communication.

The approach which was developed in Scotland following the 1998 Black and Wiliam review, 'Assessment Is for Learning' (AiFL) (illustrated in Figure 13.2), is particularly interesting because of the way in which it integrated assessment principles into a national system reconciling a number of purposes (Hutchinson and Hayward, 2005). Scotland's 'Curriculum for Excellence' (see Chapter 9), and in particular its 'Framework for Assessment' (Scottish Government, 2011), built on AiFL and is backed by a *National Assessment Resource* (see also Reading 14.2). However, developing holistic, systematic provision and ensuring that policy rhetoric is matched with practical guidance and professional learning opportunities is extremely challenging (Spencer and Hayward, 2016), and the heightened summative assessment requirements of the 2016 National Improvement Framework for Scottish Education (see Chapter 14) may put further pressure on AfL practice in Scotland.

Finally, a reminder that it is essential to understand the underpinning beliefs and principles on which the practical strategies rest (see the 'Guiding Principles' section above), and to use these as a continual check on the implementation and effect of the practices.

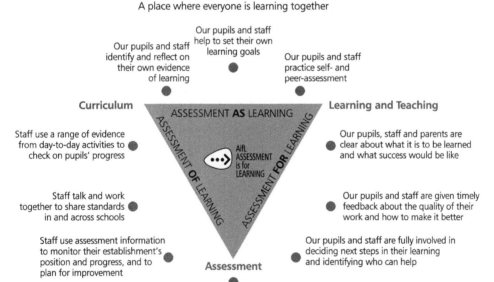

Figure 13.2
Scotland's 'Assessment is for Learning'

The work in Scotland represented an early attempt to bring greater attention to the relationship between curriculum, pedagogy and assessment. This issue, which is now of international interest, emerged from a concern that assessment, curriculum and pedagogy were too often treated as separate fields, yet all three were essential to learning. For a

Part 3 Teaching for learning

comprehensive overview of the curriculum, pedagogy and assessment relationship, see the editorial in Wyse et al. (2016), *The SAGE Handbook of Curriculum, Pedagogy and Assessment*.

Sharing goals and identifying quality

Mary Alice White wrote that adults might comprehend what the experience of school is like for pupils if they imagine being:

> on a ship sailing across an unknown sea, to an unknown destination. An adult would be desperate to know where he [sic] is going. But a child only knows he [sic] is going to school. . . . The chart is neither available nor understandable to him. . . . Very quickly, the daily life on board ship becomes all important. . . . The daily chores, the demands, the inspections, become the reality, not the voyage, nor the destination. (White, 1971, p. 340)

White is reminding us of the importance of helping children see the bigger picture and knowing how what they are learning today fits in with what they have learnt previously and will do in the future. Not only does this support constructivist learning (see Chapter 2), but it can also capture pupils' interest and increase motivation to learn.

Margaret Heritage (2008) recognised that to help children see a bigger picture, both teachers and learners would have to develop better understandings of progression in learning. She argues that:

> By its very nature, learning involves progression. To assist in its emergence, teachers need to understand the pathways along which pupils are expected to progress. These pathways or progressions ground both instruction and assessment. Yet, despite a plethora of standards and curricula, many teachers are unclear about how learning progresses in specific domains. This is an undesirable situation for teaching and learning, and one that particularly affects teachers' ability to engage in formative assessment. (p. 2)

In later work, Mosher and Heritage (2017) emphasise that progression is complex, children do not learn in linear pathways: they make progress, they regress, they make further progress as their thinking develops over time to new levels of sophistication. Hayward et al. (2018) worked with teachers to explore ideas of progression in learning in practice. They found that often teachers describe progression from the perspective of teaching: progression is the next topic or textbook. For Assessment for Learning to be successful, feedback has to focus on what action might best be taken to encourage progress in what matters in the curriculum.

Opening up learning begins by sharing the story, the narrative, of the learning journey children are on. From there, sharing learning goals, success criteria, notions of quality and information on how their work will be evaluated; all assist pupils to understand what they are trying to achieve. The word sharing is chosen with care. Involving children in contributing ideas about what they would like to learn is a crucial part of the idea of

reflectiveteaching.co.uk/rtps6/part3_ch13

Chapter 13 Assessment 415

sharing learning intentions, and young people who have a role to play in deciding what is to be learned are more likely to be motivated to learn. These are all elements of short-term planning – see Chapter 10, p. 320. These practices also help learning itself. Experiments by Frederikson and White (1997) showed that pupils' learning improved when they were involved in discussions about what they were learning, how their work would be assessed and what would count as good work. Moreover, the lower-attaining pupils made greater gains than the previously higher attainers, indicating that some pupils' previous lack of success may have been because they did not understand what was required.

It is now common practice for the teacher to announce the learning objective at the beginning of the lesson and to write it up so that it is visible and acts as a continual reminder of the aim of the lesson for everyone – pupils, teachers and learning assistants. More commonly, now, teachers also engage children in contributing to the identification of learning objectives. Referring to these throughout the lesson, and in a review at the end, helps keep the focus on what the pupils are learning, rather than what they are doing. Shirley Clarke (2008; 2014), who through her work with teachers over many years has really deepened understanding of the complexities and subtleties of sharing learning objectives effectively, advocates separating out objective, context, activity and success criteria. For example:

Learning objective:	To produce a travel brochure
Context:	For a place of pilgrimage
Activity (abbreviated):	Introduction, research, planning on paper, discussion, drafting brochure using ICT, self- and peer-assessment, producing final version
Success criteria:	The history of the place
	Features of special interest
	Reasons for visiting
	Places to stay
	Correct presentation

Source: Adapted from Clarke, 2008, p. 114.

Whilst it helps learners to know what they are aiming for, sometimes if it is only a statement by teachers at the beginning of a lesson, the approach can militate against a sense of excitement or surprise. A teacher might want to capture children's interest in any number of creative ways, leading to a statement of the learning objective part way into the lesson. In other cases, when pupils will be investigating or creating something it is inappropriate to give them the 'answer' before they begin. Here an understanding of different kinds of objectives is helpful. Elliott Eisner (2002) distinguished what he called 'curriculum' objectives from 'problem solving' and 'creative' objectives, and these categories suggest phraseology other than a statement of outcome – perhaps in the form of a question or a challenge.

Pupils can be helped to understand what they are aiming for by seeing examples of work generated previously. Single pieces can be discussed to reveal expectations, characteristics and indications of quality, but care must be taken to avoid giving the

reflectiveteaching.co.uk/rtps6/part3_ch13

impression that there is only one way, or that the model should be copied. Several examples could be looked at in sequence, but it can be even more powerful to compare two examples of differing quality as this helps reveal exactly what makes one piece more successful than the other and assists in making characteristics of quality explicit (Clarke, 2008; 2014). Examples do not of course have to be limited to written work: different kinds of products including models, artefacts, sound recordings and videos of action, can all be used. Sharing examples of high-quality work and analysing what makes them so can be very powerful, but multiple examples are needed so that pupils realise there are many possible and unique manifestations of excellence.

> ## Expert Question
>
> **Engagement:** *do our teaching strategies, classroom organisation and consultation enable learners to actively participate in and enjoy their learning?*
>
> This question contributes to a conceptual framework underpinning professional expertise (see Chapter 16).

Once learning goals have been shared, and notions of quality established, it is success criteria that help pupils understand what they are aiming for. Success criteria point out things to attend to, and may be closed instructions ('write down your calculation') or open-ended prompts ('use at least three ways of describing the person in your story, such as likes and dislikes, interests, personality, attitude to others etc.'). Although initially teachers will need to model appropriate success criteria, they are most effective when pupils help generate them. Ways of doing this include asking about key points to remember, comparing examples of products, presenting something that is incomplete, or the teacher 'doing it wrongly' and eliciting ways to improve a piece of work. Helping learners get into the habit and develop the skills of using success criteria enables them to aim for the best and continually improve.

Shared learning intentions, developing a sense of quality, and jointly creating success criteria all enable children to take responsibility for the quality of their work, individually and collectively, helping them to become more autonomous learners and assisting them in developing self-regulation. However, it is essential to note that these aspects of assessment for learning only come about when pupils are engaged in the process, as described above; they do not result from the mechanistic writing up of learning objectives. Also, it is crucial that the focus is kept on the learning intention, and that teachers do not unwittingly give the impression that other things (such as behaviour or presentation) are more important than the lesson's learning focus.

Questioning and dialogue

Questioning and dialogue are central to assessment for learning. It is through dialogue that pupils develop a sense of what they are aiming for, how to get there, and a sense of quality. Questioning and dialogue are integral to feedback and peer-assessment, and are key ways in which teachers ascertain what children have learned, giving insights into their comprehension and misunderstandings. There are many resonances with the research and issues discussed in Chapter 12, and some of the same authors are drawn on in this section.

reflectiveteaching.co.uk/rtps6/part3_ch13

Crucially for AfL, talk in the classroom not only assesses current understanding but is also an integral part of assessment that supports learning and is itself a thinking and learning process. For this to be the case, certain conditions must prevail, and pupils and teachers alike must learn how to engage in effective dialogue. These conditions are discussed below, preceded by a review of the meaning of dialogue.

The word 'dialogue' comes from Greek antiquity and can be interpreted as 'an exchange of meaning through speech'. So, the challenge is how to set up classroom talk, often stimulated by questioning, such that it can generate and distribute meaning and understanding. As we saw in Chapter 12, Robin Alexander (2004) identified five features of 'dialogic teaching':

- *collective* – pupils and teachers learning together rather than in isolation;
- *reciprocal* – pupils and teachers listening to each other, sharing ideas;
- *supportive* – pupils supported to voice ideas without feeling there is a single correct response;
- *cumulative* – pupils and teachers build on contributions to take thinking forward;
- *purposeful* – teachers plan and facilitate dialogue with particular goals in mind.

For 'meaning to develop through talk' there must first be opportunities for dialogue, in whole-class, small groups or pairs. Instead of what might be considered 'traditional' practice, where the teacher asks a closed question, one of the pupils with their hands up gives a short (often one-word) response, and the teacher declares it right or wrong, many ways of engaging more pupils more of the time have been developed. To encourage everyone to think about the issue, some teachers have introduced 'no hands up' (Black et al., 2003): every pupil is expected to be engaged and able to respond in some way, even if it is

> **Expert Question**
>
> **Dialogue:** *does teacher–learner talk scaffold understanding to build on existing knowledge and to strengthen dispositions to learn?*
>
> This question contributes to a conceptual framework underpinning professional expertise (see Chapter 16).

expressing a difficulty or doubt, and knows they can be called on to contribute at any time by the teacher or another pupil. Rather than the 'ping-pong' between teacher and volunteering pupils, whole-class discussions can become more like netball or basketball, where an issue is passed around the group. The next contributor can be selected at random (using named cards or lolly sticks) or nominated by teacher or pupils. Main points about questioning that supports learning are set out by Black et al. (2003).

Other techniques for increasing involvement in dialogue involve the use of small groups. Teachers working with Shirley Clarke (2008; 2011; 2014) have explored the practicalities of 'talk partners' in great depth. Key points include keeping discussions very focused and not too long (from five or ten seconds up to two or three minutes, depending on the task); and frequent changing of randomly selected partners. The quality of dialogue is enhanced by the establishment of protocols and ground rules (Mercer and Littleton, 2007, Reading 11.6), and the modelling of language use by teachers. Being able to engage in effective small-group dialogue is a very valuable skill in itself, and it needs to be practised and supported; making explicit the learning involved, explaining the value of

Part 3 Teaching for learning

being able to work with any partner, establishing success criteria and using these to reflect on what went well and how it could be improved should all be applied to the process.

Along with opportunities to engage, ways of working that enable educative, stimulating initiators of dialogue are required. Questioning is central, but the quality of ensuing dialogue is highly dependent on the nature of the questions. Closed questions used to check children's recall or speed of calculation have their uses, but they do not stimulate dialogue. Instead, open-ended questions, perhaps framed using Bloom's taxonomy or De Bono's 'thinking hats' (see Clarke, 2005a), are more fruitful. 'Why', 'how' and 'what' questions are more likely to lead to discussion than 'when' or 'where' questions, but much depends on the exact phrasing. The format of questions can also be varied with good effect. For example, dialogue can be stimulated by providing a question together with a range of answers, including answers that are definitely right, definitely wrong and ambiguous. Other approaches include asking whether and why pupils agree or disagree with a given statement; stating an answer and asking what the question could have been; and asking which statement/shape/object etc. is the odd one out and why; or using photographs to ask children to imagine what is going on.

Hogden and Webb (2008, p. 83) provide a list of generic questions that dialogue about a problem or task:

- Tell me about the problem.
- What do you know about the problem? Can you describe the problem to someone else?
- Have you seen a problem like this before?
- What is similar . . .? What is different . . .?
- Do you have a hunch? . . . A conjecture?
- What would happen if . . .? Is it always true that . . .?
- How do you know that . . .? Can you justify . . .? Can you find a different method?
- Can you explain . . . Improve/add to that explanation?
- What have you found out about . . .? What advice would you give to someone else about . . .?
- What was easy/difficult about this task?

Really good questions and prompts for dialogue often require thinking about in advance, and teachers find it helpful to keep a record of powerful questions, to share them with colleagues, and to plan together.

The final aspect of creating the conditions for dialogue concerns the ways teachers respond to pupils' contributions. Initially, they need to allow enough thinking time to produce responses beyond quick recall. Increasing 'wait/think time' even beyond one second takes practice as typically teachers rephrase, ask another question, give a clue, or redirect the question if there is not an immediate response. Dialogue is encouraged by teachers being seen to value all contributions, expected or not. 'As one Year 9 girl said, "When Miss used to ask a question, she used to be interested in the right answer. Now she

reflectiveteaching.co.uk/rtps6/part3_ch13

is interested in what we think."' (Hogden and Webb, 2008, p. 76). This is especially necessary when employing 'no hands up'. Teachers should take the time to carefully consider pupils' contributions, and in so doing model the use of thinking time to enhance dialogue.

> **Expert Questions**
>
> **Repertoire:** *is our pedagogic expertise sufficiently creative, skilled and wide-ranging to teach all elements of learning?*
>
> **Authenticity:** *do learners recognise routine processes of assessment and feedback as being of personal value?*
>
> These questions contribute to a conceptual framework underpinning professional expertise (see Chapter 16).

Feedback

A number of researchers have conducted meta-studies of the effects of feedback, including Kluger and De Nisi (1996) and Hattie and Timperley (2007). A contemporary summary of this international evidence is in EEF **Toolkit Evidence 13.1** on p. 434. The key message is that 'feedback is one of the most powerful influences on learning and achievement, but this impact can be either positive or negative' (Hattie and Timperley, 2007, p. 81). Burrell and Bubb's (2000) study of the feedback received by two children in the course of a day helps us understand why this should be so. Kluger and De Nisi reported an average effect size of 0.4 (quite substantial in educational terms) but they found that in over 40 per cent of cases the effect was negative. In other words, in two out of five instances feedback actually lowered performance. So clearly the nature of the feedback is crucial.

It is worth emphasising that authentic feedback has personal implications, and may or may not be welcomed. The quality of relationships and climate in the class is thus significant (see Chapter 6). Spendlove (2009, Reading 13.3) sees the establishment of an appropriate 'emotional environment for feedback' as being essential to an effective process so that pupils are open to learning and receptive to the messages which the feedback conveys (Immordino-Yang and Damasio, 2007, Reading 6.2).

Indicators of good practice can be elicited from the literature (Swaffield, 2008).

1 *Feedback should be timely and clear.* Feedback should be provided as promptly as possible, when the work to which it relates is fresh in the child's mind. The younger the learner, the greater the imperative that feedback is as immediate as possible, suggesting oral feedback whenever feasible. Oral feedback also has the advantage that the teacher can judge whether the message is being understood, and a fuller dialogue is possible. However, it is often not practical to feed back in this way especially when written work becomes lengthier and the overall quantity increases, hence the age-old practice of teachers marking or providing written feedback. Here again timeliness is important, as well as ensuring that the pupils can read and understand the comments.

2 *Use comments alone and avoid marks, grades or levels.* The latter all encourage the recipients to focus on performance ('what did I get?') rather than adopt a learning orientation ('what have I achieved and how can I improve my work still further?'). (There is a place for the occasional reference to grades or levels, but

these practices do not support learning and so are discussed in the following chapter, not this one.) It is important to note that it is only comments on their own that assist the focus on learning: if they are accompanied by marks or grades, pupils again just focus on those as signifiers of performance, and the learning potential of carefully crafted comments is lost (Butler, 1988). Smiley faces, stickers and stars all tend to function as marks or grades, turning children's attention to whether or not they were awarded a symbol of recognition and away from the specific qualities of their work. However, symbols or codes can be useful if they are understood to have a particular meaning, such as 'this point is a particularly good example of demonstrating the success criteria'. Some teachers have also adopted the use of a stamp to indicate that oral feedback has taken place, acting as a record and avoiding the impression that the teacher has not considered the work.

3 *Comments on work and possible improvement should be specific.* General comments such as 'good', 'well done' or 'you need to work harder' are little more than verbalised marks or grades and do not help the learner improve. Rather, the focus of feedback should be on particular qualities of the work, including information about success in relation to the learning objective and success criteria. Learning is likely to be enhanced if the focus is on the task (as opposed to the learner), and on process and progress (not the product). Comparison with others should be avoided, but instead comparisons should be made with the pupil's own previous work and with shared criteria. As well as acknowledging success, comments should be about next steps and provide specific advice on what and how to improve. This is most likely to support continued learning if couched in terms of questions or prompts rather than direct instruction.

4 *Pupils should respond to feedback.* The learning potential of high-quality feedback comments will only be realised if pupils take note and act on them. Children should therefore be expected to read (or listen) to feedback, to think about it, and to take some action that is challenging yet achievable. Improving the current piece of work in some way, while it is in progress, is the most meaningful response to feedback. Comments such as 'next time remember to . . .' are unlikely to be acted upon (even if they are remembered!) since they ask the pupil to do something that they are currently unable or disinclined to do at some indeterminate time in the future. Pupils require time to respond to feedback, which may (and most powerfully) be within the general flow of a lesson, and/or as a routine at the beginning of lessons.

5 *Make feedback and marking practice explicit and manageable.* To balance quality with manageability, teachers have to be selective about which pieces and aspects of work they mark in detail, ensuring that the focus and pupils rotate. Pupils need to know what to expect in terms of feedback and marking, and policy and practice need to be explained to parents.

Shirley Clarke strongly advocates the use of a visualiser to instantly share pupils' work, collectively reviewing and improving work in progress (Clarke, 2008, 2011). These

reflectiveteaching.co.uk/rtps6/part3_ch13

practices model the process of constant review and revision which learners can then adopt themselves. DeLuca et al. (2018) argue that the same approaches to feedback, approaches that are designed to build trust and to focus on improvement rather than judgement, are the same approaches that best support effective professional learning through collaboration amongst teachers.

> **Expert Question**
>
> **Feedback:** *is there a routine flow of constructive, specific, diagnostic feedback from teacher to learners?*
>
> This question contributes to a conceptual framework underpinning professional expertise (see Chapter 16).

> **Reflective Activity 13.3**
>
> *Aim:* To identify aspects of feedback practice to improve learning.
>
> *Evidence and reflection:* Choose one of the five points on pp. 419 and 420 (or work through all five in turn); consider your current practice in relation to the guidance given. What is working well, and what evidence supports your claim? What could be improved, and how? Try to improve at least one aspect of your practice.
>
> *Extension:* Talk with a colleague to get another perspective on feedback and marking practices. Consider the contributions of the examples discussed to making learning explicit, promoting learning autonomy, and focusing on learning (not performance).

Self- and peer-assessment

'All young people need to become their own best self-assessors,' declared Earl and Katz (2008, p. 90). The logic behind this is that everyone needs to be continually learning and adapting, becoming more autonomous, self-regulating, self-monitoring learners. The classroom strategies discussed in the sections above help pupils become more self-regulating learners. In particular, understanding the objective, and having a clear sense of success criteria and quality, enable learners to evaluate their own work. The feedback and marking comments they have seen modelled by teachers help pupils give feedback to themselves, essentially 'sitting beside' themselves reviewing their efforts (Muschamp, 1991, **Reading 13.4**). Self-assessment, as with so many other aspects of assessment for learning, needs support and practice, so to begin with the teacher initiates the activity. However, the aim is for pupils to take control so that they initiate repeated moments of self-assessment, integrating the practice into the continual process of working on a task. This is where the real power of self-assessment lies, not in 'marking' completed pieces of work.

The notion of 'mastery learning', promoted as part of contemporary curricular innovation in England (see also EEF **Toolkit Evidence 10.1** on p. 343), is practically strengthened when linked to self-assessment and self-regulated learning (see Chapter 2, p. 64). One approach to this, PEER, encourages children to Prove, Explain, Explore and Reapply, and thus progressively improve the quality of their work (see 'Mastery in the Classroom', **Case Study 13.2** on p. 423).

Similarly, peer-assessment is coming to be seen as 'co-operative improvement' (Clarke, 2011), rather than the swapping of books to be marked in the more traditional sense. Indeed, 'marks' of any kind may be more of a distraction than a help. If peers look at and discuss work together, with improvements being made immediately, there is little need for any marks to be made, much less comments written. Too often, especially for less competent writers, peer-assessment has become yet another literacy chore, limited by what can be expressed in writing, with consequent impoverishment of feedback.

Putting the focus on improvement also reduces the emphasis on judgement, and thus lessens some of the more sensitive aspects of peer-assessment, including possible threats to self-esteem and opportunities for bullying. Cooperating with a peer in order to make work even better helps pupils appreciate others' strengths and the value of another point of view, and can enhance learning autonomy by assisting the realisation that it can be very useful to seek another person's perspective. Peer-assessment should be focused, with the owner of the work indicating which particular aspect they are seeking help to improve and on how that improvement might best be realised.

> ### Reflective Activity 13.4
>
> *Aim:* To support pupil development as autonomous self-regulating learners.
>
> *Evidence and reflection:* Consider the opportunities that pupils already have in your classes to improve their learning through self- and peer-assessment. What are the strengths of current practice, and what might be possible negative consequences?
>
> *Extension:* Re-read about self- and peer-assessment (p. 421) and, if possible, explore other guidance on self- and peer-assessment. Evaluate what you have read against the three principles for AfL (making learning explicit; promoting learning autonomy; focusing on learning rather than performance). Decide what you can do in your practice to help pupils develop as more autonomous self-regulating learners. Discuss with a small group of pupils how practice in your classroom might improve.

An extension of self- and peer-assessment is to engage pupils in teaching each other, in other words passing responsibility at earlier stages of the teaching–learning process. This is most obviously possible across year groups, but can also be introduced with same-age peers who may have different forms of expertise or knowledge from which to draw. The act of adopting the teaching role is itself a learning experience. Findings from EEF **Toolkit Evidence 13.2** (p. 435) shows consistently strong and positive effects for both those in the tutor and tutee roles, particularly when used to consolidate learning rather than to introduce new material.

Case Study 13.2 Mastery in the classroom: the example of PEER

Mastery is based on the idea that with sufficient time and the right resources and support, tailored to individual children's needs, all children can succeed. Learning is therefore seen as a process in which individual children develop their capabilities over time. Progress needs to be reinforced through formative rather than summative assessment.

The PEER model (Prove, Explain, Explore, Reapply) is based on the fundamental principle that learning is a spiral process. The commitment is to 'mastery for all', where all children master knowledge, understanding and skills as their learning moves up the spiral. Mastery was originally theorised within education by Bloom and others in the 1960s and 1970s (e.g. Bloom, 1968) and is focused upon how teachers can best support each child to master a subject. It rejects the idea that 'ability' is a fixed characteristic and that only a small minority of 'talented' pupils are capable of mastery.

PEER is an assessment model consisting of four steps that continue in an upward spiral. Formative assessment is inbuilt as there is an emphasis on children explaining and proving their understanding. The four parts can be summarised as in the figure below:

Figure 13.3 The PEER assessment model to support mastery learning

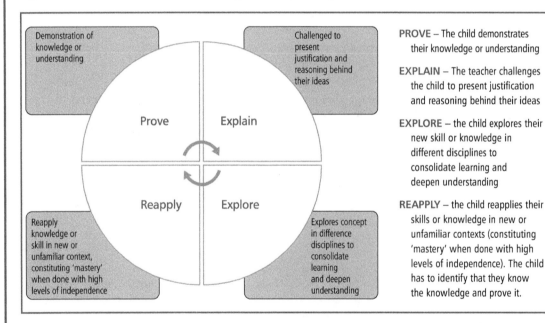

To illustrate how teachers can use this model in the classroom, an example of teaching Mathematics with a Year 3 class at Hallfield Primary School will be used.

Prove – The teacher aims for children to answer the question: how can you prove to me that you know your 4 × tables? Children can respond in any form that they choose, e.g. counting, using a number line or drawing diagrams. This allows the teacher to assess children's current understanding. This helps to inform the activity the teacher sets for each child in the next step.

Explain – To deepen the understanding of a group, the teacher challenges the children with questions: Can you represent 4 × 6 in different ways? Can you explain what 4 × 6 means? The teacher gives children a worksheet with the number sentence: 4 × 6. The sheet also contains the questions: 1. What does it mean?

2. How do you calculate it? One child wrote in response to the first question: 'It means get 6 groups of 4' and to the second question: 'You add 6 groups of 4'. Here the child developed and explained their understanding of the reasoning process behind multiplication.

Explore – Here the teacher aims for children to explore and search for patterns. For example, following on from the previous Explain activity, children work with a pinwheel designed and adapted by the teacher to further individual children's understanding. The pinwheel is divided into six sections: one has the number sentence 4 × 6 written in it and the other five sections have a question for the child in each. The child spins the pinwheel to arrive at a question. Examples of questions are: How do you write your calculation in words? What does your calculation look like on a number line? Will the product of your calculation be odd or even? How do you know?

Reapply – To solve a real-life word problem using knowledge of times tables. To use multiplication facts to derive other facts when solving problems, e.g. If a box of eggs has 6 eggs in it and if I buy 3 boxes, how many eggs will I have? I will have 18 eggs.

When planning like this, the PEER structure should be embedded in daily maths planning for times tables – this can be just a ten-minute starter every day whilst children are mastering their conceptual understanding of multiplication. Each day focuses on developing understanding from the previous day rather than simply learning by rote. Explicit teaching of reapplication and explanation skills improves outcomes for pupils. For example, children develop a much deeper understanding and conceptualisation of what is happening with multiplication and are able to articulate this for the equation 3 × 7:

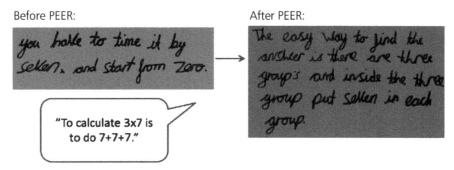

To understand the impact of the PEER model at Hallfield, and other primary schools which have adopted the model, four teachers at the school took part in an action research project supported by The Open University. The teachers' individual action research projects focused on understanding the impact on children's learning and teachers' understanding of Mastery and the PEER model. Pupil engagement with the PEER model led to children being reflective, fostering their autonomy and sense of self through a growing understanding of triangulating their knowledge base. By introducing PEER we have found that teachers are planning for activities that make vocabulary and reasoning of high importance, and as a result children are becoming more confident when explaining their ideas as they have the tools to do so. Examples of this are: vocabulary activities we explored with staff, asking for full sentences in subjects that can be accepting of one-word answers (maths – 60 instead of there are 60-minutes in an hour. I know this because . . .).

Hallfield Primary School is a large three-form entry primary school in the heart of central London. With over 500 children on roll, it is a diverse and vibrant community made up of 99 per cent minority ethnic backgrounds, speaking 39 different languages.

The PEER model was developed in 2015 by two Hallfield teachers, Georgina Nutton (then Deputy Head) and Remy Dyer (then Leader of Learning) in response to the 2014 National Curriculum. This requires schools to develop new assessment systems based on Mastery learning.

Chapter 13 Assessment

Adjusting teaching and learning

The most important factor influencing learning, according to Ausubel (1968), is what the learner already knows; therefore, the teacher should 'ascertain this and teach accordingly'. This seemingly simple yet powerful observation is a key element of assessment for learning with its notion of using assessment to match the next steps to the learner's current position. Examples of children's previous work in an area of the curriculum or a topic can provide useful information, but they should be checked against their current understanding as in the meantime children may have forgotten some things and grasped others. Conversations with learners can provide very helpful insights into their current thinking and point to where future growth might best begin.

There are a number of ways in which teachers can check pupils' understanding before starting on a new topic. A conversation with a group or a whole class can help begin to explore what children already know and understand. Concept maps can yield rich information, providing the pupils already know how to draw them. Children could be set a task designed to reveal knowledge and understanding and to highlight areas to be addressed, or given a quick quiz – orally, on paper or using ICT. A teacher in the King's Medway Oxfordshire *Formative Assessment* Project found that a discussion around an open question such as 'If plants need sunlight to make food, how come the biggest plants don't grow in deserts where it is sunny all the time?' (Black et al., 2003, p. 35) allowed all pupils to participate and enabled him to ascertain their starting point for the upcoming topic of photosynthesis. Another approach for gauging current understanding when pupils already have some knowledge is to ask them to set the questions for a class discussion. The questions themselves can help to reveal the breadth and depth of current knowledge as well as misconceptions and become a useful starting point for a further conversation. Some teachers give pupils a list of the items that will be part of the forthcoming topic and ask them to indicate their current understanding of each one, typically using 'traffic lights' (colouring items red, orange, green) or smiley faces (happy, neutral or sad). This technique can be very helpful in effectively directing what is always limited teaching time, but there are two necessary conditions. First, the items must be phrased in such a way that pupils' responses provide valid information (we don't know what we don't know about something – I may think that I understand 'sound' for example, but I may have many misconceptions of which I am unaware). Second, pupils must respond honestly, and are more likely to do so if they appreciate the purpose of the task and know the consequences of their responses. If a learning culture is well established in the classroom this is unlikely to be problematic, but may be more so if the emphasis has previously been on 'getting everything right' and being seen to 'be clever'.

Whichever approaches are used to explore children's current knowledge and understanding, the purpose is to provide information for the teacher to act on what they find out. The information gathered should be used to tailor subsequent lessons more closely to the needs of the children.

Having established the starting point, thought also needs to be given to the goal. This is often determined by the curriculum, particular topics or schemes of work. However, goals

reflectiveteaching.co.uk/rtps6/part3_ch13

must also be realistic, building from what children already know, understand and are able to do. Although it is always wise to have some learning intentions in mind, learning is not linear and predictable, so teachers need to be open-minded about unplanned worthwhile learning that may only become apparent during the process. It is also important to remember that within overall learning intentions, different children will progress at different rates and in different ways, and teachers should ensure that there are opportunities for every child to make progress. Real learning is a more complex process than planned learning

Some teachers involve the pupils in deciding what they are going to learn, a practice that increases their motivation and effort. However, the 'What do you want to learn?' question generally has to be guided to some extent since children are not aware of all the possibilities, nor of the constraints. One solution is to allow the pupils to select the context within which they explore concepts and skills determined by the teacher – for example, the skills of writing persuasively, calculating areas or exercising empathy could be learnt and practised in many different contexts. A second possibility is to allow elements of choice within a topic. For example, if the topic is Our Trip to the Zoo, before the topic begins the teacher might share with the class some of the areas for exploration. Why do different animals live in different parts of the world? Why are some animal species now endangered? What actions are zoos taking to support endangered species? In discussion with the class, the teacher might invite other areas for exploration, or within each topic area invite children to identify particular parts of the world where investigations might focus on particular animals of interest to the children.

Once the starting point and the goal have been ascertained, the actual learning journey needs to be planned, and once it is under way continual attention must be given to checking position, keeping track of progress and making necessary adjustments. Teachers should be checking learning and adjusting teaching minute-by-minute, lesson-by-lesson. There are many ways in which teachers can glean information about pupils' learning. For example:

- carefully phrased questioning that elicits important misunderstandings as well as understandings;
- listening attentively to what children say in response to questions and in discussion;
- observing pupils at work;
- checking written work and other tangible evidence;
- looking at responses on individual white boards;
- using 'ABCD' cards for every pupil to give a response to a multiple choice question;
- setting specifically designed tasks.

There are also ways in which children can be involved in gathering information about what is being learned. For example:

- asking children to generate ideas – how will we find out what we have learned in our topic?

Chapter 13 Assessment 427

encouraging children to generate criteria related to specific tasks that they can then use to reflect on their own work, e.g. we are going to make posters showing different animals in different parts of the world – what would a really good poster look like?

There are also many different adjustments a teacher can make in response to what they have found out about pupils' learning. In general terms this might involve speeding up or slowing down the learning journey, adding more steps or taking some out, refining the support whether that be from materials or people, setting different tasks, or changing working groups. The practical possibilities are endless, and range from rephrasing a question or providing a different illustration, to a complete rethink about the learning goal and ways to achieve it. Many adjustments are made almost instantaneously while others may be put into operation the next lesson or the next week. Continual monitoring and adjusting means the learning can be kept on track: if progress is checked only occasionally, much greater deviations might be found requiring a complete change of tack to get back on course.

Children too have an important role to play in monitoring progress and adjusting learning. The teacher has responsibility for the whole class, but no one knows better than the individual pupil whether they need some additional help or have grasped something and need to move on. Learners should have a number of strategies they can employ as necessary, such as asking a partner, drawing a diagram, using equipment, consulting reference material or expressing their understanding in a different way. Continual review and improvement is the essence of self-regulation, a key aspect of learning. In the discussion above, it will have been apparent in relation to self-assessment. When a learning culture is truly established in a classroom, learning is everyone's responsibility. Children and teachers both feel comfortable identifying what is going well in a lesson and what might be improved and regard it as their collective task to decide how to improve matters.

Teachers sometimes worry about deviating from set schemes of work. The important thing to remember is that learning is what matters. Schemes of work and plans are there to help not hinder learning; the aim is that pupils will have learnt, not that a pre-determined plan has been followed step by step. Reviewing a sequence of lessons at the end, thinking about what went well and what was less successful, will suggest changes that should be made to the plan for the next time the teacher teaches the same topic.

> ## Expert Question
>
> **Reflection:** *is our classroom practice based on incremental, evidence-informed and collaborative improvement strategies?*
>
> This question contributes to a conceptual framework underpinning professional expertise (see Chapter 16).

In summary, learning and teaching will be much more effective if the accuracy of the assumed starting point is checked, the appropriateness of the proposed finishing point questioned, and position and progress monitored throughout. Appropriate adjustments can then be made along the way, rather than when it is too late to rectify any problems.

reflectiveteaching.co.uk/rtps6/part3_ch13

> **Reflective Activity 13.5**
>
> *Aim:* To reflect on the ways in which teachers aid learning through minute-by-minute and lesson-by-lesson adjustments.
>
> *Evidence and reflection:* Think about times when you, or teachers you have observed, have adjusted teaching on the basis of pupils' learning. What provided the evidence of pupils' learning, or misunderstandings? What was the nature of the adjustments made?
>
> *Extension:* What experience do you have of when adjustments should have been made but were not? What was the result? How could the situation have been handled differently?

 Reading 13.2 from the Assessment Reform Group provides a succinct summary of characteristics of Assessment for Learning, as does **Research Briefing 13.2** on p. 437.

AFFIRMING ASSESSMENT FOR LEARNING

 The phrase 'Assessment for Learning' (AfL) can be found as the title of chapters, papers and books written by assessment experts first published over a quarter of a century ago (Black, 1986; James, 1992; Sutton, 1995). In recent years, the term has been used more and more commonly. Yet, despite several attempts to define AfL, it continues to be understood and interpreted in different ways. It is therefore a good idea to be clear in your own mind what you understand by Assessment for Learning, and to be alert to other interpretations. A key text is an Assessment Reform Group (ARG) pamphlet, *Beyond the Black Box* (ARG, 1999, Reading 13.2).

Mary-Jane Drummond's definition of assessment resonates with the 'sitting beside' notion of assessment referred to in the introduction to this chapter, and it highlights some very important features of AfL. She defined assessment as a process of teachers looking at pupils' learning, striving to understand it, and using that knowledge in the interests of pupils (Drummond, 2012). This is very close to the much-quoted definition of assessment for learning produced by the Assessment Reform Group:

> Assessment for Learning is the process of seeking and interpreting evidence for use by learners and their teachers to decide where the learners are in their learning, where they need to go and how best to get there. (ARG, 2002, p. 2)

Both Drummond and the ARG referred to assessment as a process (rather than an event), which involves the need for interpretation and the effort to understand on the part of the teacher, as well as the use of that knowledge. The ARG definition importantly cast learners (as well as teachers) as users of the information. Drummond made clear that the use should be in the interests of the pupils but did not go into specifics, whereas the ARG's definition referred

Chapter 13 Assessment 429

to present position, future goal and moving between the two. Unfortunately, some policymakers misinterpreted and distorted this second part of the ARG definition (Klenowski, 2009): they put the emphasis on frequent testing to assess pupil levels or grades and targeting the next level. This emphasis on performance hinders rather than helps real and sustained learning.

To address this damaging but influential misinterpretation of the definition of AfL, an international conference held in 2009 produced a position paper which included explanation and elaboration of what they called a 'second generation definition of Assessment for Learning' (Klenowski, 2009, p. 264). This read:

> Assessment for Learning is part of everyday practice by pupils, teachers and peers that seeks, reflects upon and responds to information from dialogue, demonstration and observation in ways that enhance ongoing learning. (Klenowski, 2009, p. 264)

This carefully thought through definition, based on evidence, encompasses many elements, each of which were explored in detail. It put pupils at the centre of the process, and stressed an enquiry process within everyday classroom activity. The elaboration brings out the depth and richness encapsulated in the definition so that it is worth quoting in full:

Expert Question

Authenticity: *do learners recognise routine processes of assessment and feedback as being of personal value?*

This question contributes to a conceptual framework underpinning professional expertise (see Chapter 16).

---

(1) 'everyday practice' – this refers to teaching and learning, pedagogy and instruction (different terms are used in different regions of the world but the emphasis is on the interactive, dialogic, contingent relationships of teaching and learning).

(2) 'by pupils, teachers and peers' – pupils are deliberately listed first because only learners can learn. Assessment for Learning should be pupil centred. All AFL practices carried out by teachers (such as giving feedback, clarifying criteria, rich questioning) can eventually be 'given away' to pupils so that they take on these practices to help themselves, and one another, become autonomous learners. This should be a prime objective.

(3) 'seeks, reflects upon and responds to' – these words emphasise the nature of AFL as an enquiry process involving the active search for evidence of capability and understanding, making sense of such evidence, and exercising judgement for wise decision-making about next steps for pupils and teachers.

(4) 'information from dialogue, demonstration and observation' – verbal (oral and written) and non-verbal behaviours during both planned and unplanned events can be sources of evidence. Observation of these during on-going teaching and learning activity is an important basis for AFL. Special assessment tasks and tests can be used formatively but are not essential; there is a risk of them becoming frequent mini-summative assessments. Everyday learning tasks and activities, as well as routine observation and dialogue are equally, if not more, appropriate for the formative purpose.

(5) 'in ways that enhance ongoing learning' – sources of evidence are formative if, and only if, pupils and teachers use the information they provide to enhance learning. Providing pupils with the help they need to know what to do next is vital; it is not

reflectiveteaching.co.uk/rtps6/part3_ch13

sufficient to tell them only that they need to do better. However, such help does not need to provide a complete solution. Research suggests that what works best is an indication of how to improve, so that pupils engage in mindful problem solving. (Third Assessment for Learning Conference, 2009; Klenowski, 2009, pp. 264–65)

This elaboration points to features that Sue Swaffield picked up when she made the case for distinguishing assessment for learning from formative assessment (Swaffield, 2011, Reading 13.5). She argued that AfL:

> is characterised by information being used to inform learning and teaching, its focus on learning conceived broadly, and actively engage progressively more autonomous pupils. It is distinctive in its timescale, protagonists, beneficiaries, the role of pupils, the relationship between pupil and teacher, and the centrality of learning to the process – all of which can but may not necessarily be features of formative assessment. (Swaffield, 2011, p. 433)

A classroom where authentic assessment for learning is practised has a particular culture and feeling, far removed from that generated by a relentless and narrow emphasis on scores and teaching to the test.

CONCLUSION

In focusing on assessment supporting learning, this chapter has sought to acknowledge the complexity of the relationship between curriculum, pedagogy, assessment and learning. It recognises the profound influence of assessment practices not only on the content of what is being learned, but even more importantly on the process of learning and on the learner's sense of self. Whilst it is a complex area, three research-generated guiding principles provided sound direction and useful checks for reflective practitioners.

Teachers should ask themselves continually whether their practices are:

Helping to make learning explicit – making clear the knowledge, understanding and skills that are the focus of each lesson, how this learning relates to the bigger learning journey children are undertaking and providing opportunities for pupils to demonstrate and articulate their learning.

Promoting learner autonomy – providing every opportunity and building an expectation for pupils to become increasingly more self-monitoring and resourceful in taking responsibility for and extending their learning.

Focusing on learning rather than performance – in other words, the type of learning that enhances an understanding and valuing of learning not for the sake of a mark or grade but for the development of valuable lifelong attitudes and skills, and for the joy and intrinsic reward of achieving something worthwhile through effort and persistence.

Teachers who are able to answer in the affirmative will likely be practising authentic assessment for learning that genuinely supports pupils in their learning, both for the present and the future.

CHAPTER WEBPAGE

reflectiveteaching.co.uk offers additional professional resources for this chapter. For the chapter webpage, go to: **reflectiveteaching.co.uk/rtps6/part3_ch13**

The webpage resources for Chapter 13 have been designed to directly support each step of curricula planning – from thinking about long-term intentions to medium-term schemes of work and on to detailed, short-term lesson planning. The final stage, of course, is careful evaluation of curricular provision. To support work at each of these stages, you will find that there are *Reflective Activities* and detailed suggestions for *Further Reading*. The key point is to get into practicalities – given your aims, the characteristics of the learners and the curricular requirements, what will you actually do? To support you in answering that question, the chapter webpage provides four times more *Reflective Activities* than the printed book.

As may now be familiar to you, three levels of supplementary advice have been provided.

1. Supported by a good library, *Further Reading* on the chapter webpage will enable you to both deepen and broaden your understanding of curricula planning at each stage of provision. In so doing, it follows the structure of the chapter.

2. *Key Readings*, below, simplifies things further by suggesting some 'essential reads', but it of course also requires a library.

3. Short, edited extracts of many of the *Key Readings* are provided in *Readings for Reflective Teaching in Schools*. If you have it, you will see that it contains over 100 readings and acts rather like a mini-library. In respect of this chapter on curriculum planning, a resumé for each of the relevant readings is provided on the chapter webpage.

KEY READINGS

Books that provide overviews of assessment tend to address issues covered in both this and the following chapter, and are included here. They are then followed by texts that are more focused on how assessment is integrated with teaching and learning.

Broadfoot's book is a very clearly written overview covering many aspects of assessment.

> Broadfoot, P. (2007) *An Introduction to Assessment*. London: Continuum.
> (Reading 14.1)

Part 3 Teaching for learning

A comprehensive and authoritative review of assessment to support learning by members of the Assessment Reform Group is:

Gardner, J. (ed.) (2011) *Assessment and Learning*. London: Paul Chapman.

In an eye-opening book, Drummond provides an important critical alternative to mechanistic approaches to assessment.

Drummond, M. (2012) *Assessing Children's Learning*. London: David Fulton.

An enquiring and reflective approach is encouraged in Swaffield's book in which leading figures in assessment explore the values, principles, research and practicalities of assessment.

Swaffield, S. (ed.) (2008) *Unlocking Assessment: Understanding for Reflection and Application*. Abingdon: Routledge. (see also **Reading 13.5**)

The wide-ranging TLRP *Learning How to Learn* project considered assessment in the classroom as well as issues at the whole school and network levels:

James, M., Black, P., Carmichael, P., Conner, C., Dudley, P., Fox, A., Frost, D., Honour, L., MacBeath, J., McCormick, R., Marshall, B., Pedder, D., Procter, R., Swaffield, S. and Wiliam, D. (2006) *Learning How to Learn: Tools for Schools*. London: Routledge.

James, M., Black, P., Carmichael, P., Drummond, M. J., Fox, A., MacBeath, J., Marshall, B., McCormick, R., Pedder, D., Procter, R., Swaffield, S., Swann, J., and Wiliam, D. (2007) *Improving Learning How to Learn: Classrooms, Schools and Networks*. London: Routledge. (see also **Reading 2.8**)

Black and Wiliam's influential review of research is summarised in:

Black. P. and Wiliam, D. (1998) *Inside the Black Box: Raising Standards through Classroom Assessment*. London: King's College.

Black and his colleagues at King's College have also published a series of subject and phase specific 'inside the black box' pamphlets.

'Inside the black box' was followed up by a pamphlet that described the key factors needed to put assessment for learning into practice in:

Assessment Reform Group (1999) *Assessment for Learning: Beyond the Black Box*. Cambridge: University of Cambridge, School of Education. (**Reading 13.2**)

Practice that developed from the Black and Wiliam review is reported in:

Black, P., Harrison, C., Lee, C., Marshall, B., and Wiliam, D. (2003) *Assessment for Learning: Putting It into Practice*. Buckingham: Open University Press.

Wiliam's book providing practical ideas and research evidence is written with US teachers in mind but is equally applicable in the UK.

> Wiliam, D. (2011) *Embedded Formative Assessment.* Bloomington, IN: Solution Tree Press. (see also **Reading 16.4**)

For practical guidance and ideas on developing assessment for learning practices as an integral part of learning and teaching, see:

> Blanchard, J. (2009) *Teaching, Learning and Assessment.* Maidenhead: Open University Press.
> Clarke, S. (2005a) *Formative Assessment in Action: Weaving the Elements Together.* London: Hodder and Stoughton.
> Clarke, S. (2005b) *Formative Assessment in the Secondary Classroom.* London: Hodder and Stoughton.
> Spendlove, S. (2009) *Putting Assessment for Learning into Practice.* London: Continuum. (**Reading 13.3**)

Ross Morrison McGill offers a practical account of the role of assessment and feedback in the cycles of teaching and learning which make up routine classroom life – and guidance on how to maximise their effectiveness:

> McGill, R.M. (2017) *Mark. Plan. Teach.* London: Bloomsbury.

An innovative and internationally acclaimed approach particularly for younger children links assessment practice with the formation of learning dispositions:

> Carr, M. and Lee, W. (2012) *Learning Stories: Constructing Learner Identities in Early Education.* London: SAGE.

The social processes influencing assessment in children's lives are the focus of:

> Filer, A. and Pollard, A. (2000) *The Social World of Pupil Assessment: Processes and Contexts of Primary Schooling.* London: Continuum. (**Reading 14.7**)

TOOLKIT EVIDENCE 13.1
Feedback: developing contingent teaching

What is it?
Feedback redirects or refocuses either the teacher's or the learner's actions to achieve a goal, by aligning effort and activity with an outcome. It is information given to the learner and/or the teacher about the learner's performance relative to specific learning goals. It should aim to (and be capable of) producing improvement in pupils' learning.

It can be about the learning activity itself, about the process of activity, about the pupils' management of their learning or self-regulation or about them as individuals (the least effective). This feedback can be verbal or written, or can be given through tests or via digital technology. It can come from a teacher or someone taking a teaching role, or from peers. It can be direct (to the learner) or vicarious (relevant feedback given to someone else).

What does the evidence say?
Feedback studies tend to show very high average effects on learning. However, feedback also has a very wide range of effects and some studies show that it can have negative effects and even hinder learning. It is therefore important to understand the potential benefits and the possible limitations of the approach. Research evidence about feedback was part of the rationale for Assessment for Learning (AfL). One evaluation of AfL indicated an impact of half of a GCSE grade per pupil per subject is achievable, which would be in line with the wider evidence about feedback.
Other studies reporting lower impact indicate that it can be challenging to make changes to feedback effectively in the classroom.

How sound is the evidence?
There are a substantial number of reviews and meta-analyses of the effects of feedback. Educational (rather than psychological or theoretical) studies tend to identify positive benefits where the aim is to improve learning outcomes in reading or mathematics or in recall of information.

What do I need to think about?
- Providing effective feedback is challenging. Research suggests that it should be specific, accurate and clear; should compare what a learner is doing right now with what they have done wrong before; should encourage and support further effort and be given sparingly so that it is meaningful; provide specific guidance on how to improve and not just tell pupils when they are wrong; and be supported with effective professional development for teachers.
- Feedback should be about complex or challenging tasks or goals as this is likely to emphasise the importance of effort and perseverance as well as be more valued by the pupils.

Links and further reading
Hattie, J. and Timperley, H. (2007) 'The power of feedback'. *Review of Educational Research*, 77(1), 81–112. doi:10.3102/003465430298487

The EEF Teaching and Learning Toolkit entry on 'Feedback': educationendowmentfoundation.org.uk/guidance-for-teachers/assessment-feedback see also the technical appendix for further references.

The EEF's review of marking: 'A Marked Improvement' educationendowmentfoundation.org.uk/education-evidence/evidence-reviews/written-marking

See also
Mastery learning (Toolkit Evidence 10.1)
Peer tutoring (Toolkit Evidence 13.2)

Education Endowment Foundation

TOOLKIT EVIDENCE 13.2
Peer tutoring: the best way to learn is to teach

What is it?
Peer tutoring includes a range of approaches in which learners work in pairs or small groups to provide each other with explicit teaching support. In cross-age tutoring, an older learner takes the tutoring role and is paired with a younger tutee or tutees. Peer-assisted learning is a structured approach for mathematics and reading with sessions of 25–35 minutes two or three times a week. In reciprocal peer tutoring, learners alternate between the role of tutor and tutee. The common characteristic is that learners take on responsibility for aspects of teaching and for evaluating their success. Peer-assessment involves the peer tutor providing feedback to children relating to their performance and can have different forms such as reinforcing or correcting aspects of learning.

What does the evidence say?
Overall, the introduction of peer tutoring approaches appears to have a positive impact on learning, with an average effect of approximately five additional months' progress in research studies. Findings have identified benefits for both tutors and tutees, and for a wide range of age groups. Though all types of pupils appear to benefit from peer tutoring, there is some evidence that children from disadvantaged backgrounds and low-attaining pupils may make the biggest gains.

Peer tutoring appears to be less effective when the approach replaces normal teaching, rather than supplementing or enhancing it, suggesting that peer tutoring is most effectively used to consolidate learning, rather than to introduce new material.

How sound is the evidence?
Peer tutoring has been extensively studied and a majority of studies show moderate to high average effects. High-quality reviews have explored the impact of peer tutoring at both primary and secondary level, and in a variety of subjects.

Though overall the evidence base related to peer tutoring is relatively consistent, some studies of peer tutoring have found lower average effects, suggesting that monitoring the implementation and impact of peer tutoring is valuable.

What do I need to think about?
- Is peer tutoring being used to review or consolidate learning, or to introduce new material?
- Are the activities sufficiently challenging for the tutee to benefit from the tutor's support?
- What support will the tutor receive to ensure that the quality of peer interaction is high?

Links and further reading
Topping, K. and Buchs, C. (2017) *Effective Peer Learning: From Principles to Practical Implementation*. London: Routledge.

Rohrbeck, C., Ginsburg-Block, M.D., Fantuzzo, J.W. and Miller, T.R. (2003) 'Peer-assisted learning interventions with elementary school pupils: A meta-analytic review'. *Journal of Educational Psychology*, 95(2), 240–57. doi:10.1037/0022-0663.95.2.240.

The EEF Teaching and Learning Toolkit entry on 'Peer-tutoring': educationendowmentfoundation.org.uk/education-evidence/teaching-learning-toolkit/peer-tutoring – see also the technical appendix for further references.

See also
Small group teaching (Toolkit Evidence 11.2)
Collaborative learning (Toolkit Evidence 11.3)

Education Endowment Foundation

RESEARCH BRIEFING 13.1
Promoting learning how to learn

TLRP's Learning How to Learn project, led by Mary James, makes a key contribution to the personalisation agenda (see p. 293). As *2020 Vision* puts it:

> Too many children drift into underachievement and disengagement and fail to make progress in their learning. Schools should consider how best to integrate 'learning how to learn' into the curriculum – focusing on the skills and attitudes pupils need to become better learners. (DfES, 2006, p. 21)

Learning How to Learn takes place alongside learning in subject areas – it must be about something. It builds on the explicitness, openness and reflexivity of Assessment for Learning, but goes further to engage with, and influence, the deeper principles and beliefs about learning and teaching held by teachers. INSET, workshops, questionnaire feedback, critical friendship and web-based support were offered to schools. Improvements in pupil learning were found to depend on teacher learning and reflective, classroom-focused, self-improvement activity. For this to succeed required support across the school and could be further enhanced by professional networks. Among the project's seventeen secondary and twenty-one primary schools was one of the top-performing schools in England, which had led on 'making learning explicit' and 'promoting learning autonomy'.

Key findings:	Implications:
Assessment for Learning: AfL helps teachers promote learning how to learn (LHTL) in ways which are in line with their own values, and reduces excessive performance orientation. But it is difficult to shift from reliance on specific techniques to practices based on deep principles.	Advice on AfL techniques is useful to teachers in the short term. But progressive professional development requires teachers to re-evaluate their beliefs about learning, the way they structure tasks, and the nature of their classroom roles and relationships.
Classroom enquiry: Classroom-focused enquiry by teachers is a key condition for promoting learner autonomy. Schools that embed LHTL make support for professional learning a priority.	School leaders need to create structures and cultures that focus on learning and support teachers in sharing and evaluating innovations in classroom practice.
New technology: Teachers are optimistic about the value of electronic tools for professional development purposes and networking, but they are not well-used.	There is much still to be done to provide resources, services and online environments that support knowledge creation about teaching and learning, and which align with teachers' professional development needs.
Professional networks: Educational networks are much talked about but little understood. They are subjective phenomena rather than objective structures and the way they are perceived varies according to a person's position.	Building network capacity is complex. It is best understood by analysing the roles and perspectives of those involved and the pathways by which they communicate.

School conditions that foster successful learning how to learn are represented below:

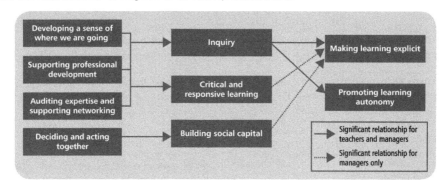

Further information
James, M. et al. (2006) *Learning How to Learn – in Classrooms, Schools and Networks*. TLRP Research Briefing 17. London: TLRP. (Available on the chapter page for this book at reflectiveteaching.co.uk).
James, M. et al. (2006) *Learning How to Learn: Tools for Schools*. TLRP *Improving Practice* Series. London: Routledge.
James M. (2007) *Improving Learning How to Learn*. TLRP *Improving Learning* series. London: Routledge.

This project was directed from the UCL Institute of Education.

RESEARCH BRIEFING 13.2
Assessment for learning

Many developments in formative assessment were stimulated by the work of the Assessment Reform Group, an offshoot of the British Educational Research Association, whose members have been closely engaged with TLRP. The Assessment Reform Group commissioned Black and Wiliam (1998b) to conduct a survey of research literature to answer the following questions:

- Is there evidence that improving formative assessment raises standards?
- Is there evidence that there is room for improvement?
- Is there evidence about how to improve formative assessment?

The answer to all three questions is 'Yes'. Indeed, formative assessment can produce substantial learning gains for all learners, with previously lower attainers improving even more than others. This means that the spread of attainment is reduced whilst attainment is raised overall. The formative assessment processes which lead to these improved performances also equip pupils for taking responsibility for their learning. This Research Briefing draws directly on Black and Wiliam's work.

Key findings:	Implications:
Feedback: Self-esteem and motivation are vital in successful learning. Feedback to any pupil should therefore be about the particular qualities of his or her work, with advice on what he or she can do to improve, and should avoid comparisons with other pupils.	Feedback should focus upon actual work, rather than the pupil. Rewards, such as gold stars, or grades, tend to result in children trying to find ways to obtain the rewards themselves, rather than thinking about their actual learning needs. Some may become reluctant to try new challenges for fear of failure.
Self-assessment: For formative assessment to be productive, pupils should be trained in self-assessment so that they can understand the main purposes of their learning and thereby grasp what they need to do to achieve.	Self-assessment is concerned with thinking about one's own performance in relation to clearly stated objectives. It is not, as some have interpreted self-assessment, checking work against an answer sheet. Self-assessment is a skill, which like any other skill needs training, coaching and practice.
Expressing understanding: Opportunities for pupils to express their understanding should be designed into any piece of teaching, for this will initiate the interaction whereby formative assessment aids learning.	Classroom practices should really enable children to demonstrate their understanding, and enable teachers to develop authentic insights into children's thinking.
Purposive dialogue: The dialogue between pupils and a teacher should be thoughtful, reflective, focused to evoke and explore understanding, and conducted so that all pupils have an opportunity to think and to express their ideas.	Sometimes the tasks we set mean that it is possible for children to get the right answers for the wrong reasons, and without carefully designed and conducted questioning and discussion these misconceptions may remain undetected, and so become a bar to later learning.
Congruence: Tests and homework exercises can be an invaluable aid to learning, but the exercises must be clear and relevant to learning aims.	Feedback on tests and homework should give each pupil guidance on how to improve, and each must be given opportunity and help to work at the improvement.

Assessment for Learning may seem simple, and elements like clarifying goals, providing feedback, encouraging self-assessment etc. can certainly be promoted. Expert practitioners of AfL argue, however, that the approach needs to draw on holistic and principled understanding of teaching and learning in classrooms. It is not just a set of techniques – but becomes an approach to classroom life! When sustained in authentic ways, AfL has the potential to transform classroom experience for both teachers and pupils, as well as underpinning very high standards of attainment.

Further information
Black. P. and Wiliam, D. (1998b) *Inside the Black Box: Raising Standards through Classroom Assessment*. London: King's College.
Black, P., Harrison, C., Lee, C., Marshall, B., and Wiliam, D. (2003) *Assessment for Learning: Putting It into Practice*. Buckingham: Open University Press.
James, M., Black, P., Carmichael, P., Drummond, M.-J., Fox, A., MacBeath, J., Marshall, B., McCormick, R., Pedder, D., Procter, R., Swaffield, S., Swann, J. and Wiliam, D. (2007) *Improving Learning How to Learn: Classrooms, Schools and Networks*. London: Routledge.

reflectiveteaching.co.uk/rtps6/part3_ch13

Part 3 Teaching for learning

Additional reading:

Danny Laveault and Linda Allal edit a book that brings together international examples that examine implementation of Assessment for Learning at three levels: policy enactment, professional learning of teachers and school leaders, and practices in classrooms and schools:

Laveault, D. and Allal, L. (2016) *Assessment for Learning: Meeting the Challenge of Implementation*. London: Springer.

Mike Carroll and Margaret McCulloch address a range of issues in primary education including understanding assessment:

Carroll, M. and McCulloch, M. (2018) *Understanding Teaching and Learning in Primary Education*. London: SAGE.

Dominic Wyse and colleagues reflect on all aspects of the primary curriculum including the relationship between curriculum and assessment:

Wyse, D., Baumfield, V., Egan, D., Hayward, D., Mulme, M., Menter, I., Gallagher, C., Leitch, R., Livingston, K. and Lingard, R. (2012) *Creating the Curriculum*. London: Routledge

For an in-depth exploration of Curriculum, Pedagogy and Assessment:

Wyse, D., Hayward, L. and Pandya, J. (2016) *The SAGE Handbook of Curriculum, Pedagogy and Assessment*, volumes 1 and 2. London: SAGE.

The importance of play in developing learning can be explored in:

DeLuca, C., Pyle, A., Valiquette, A. and LaPointe-McEwan, D. (2020) 'New directions for kindergarten education: Embedding assessment in play-based learning'. *Elementary Schools Journal*, 120(3), 455–79. doi:138.051.012.062.

Pyle, A., DeLuca, C. and Danniels, E. (2017) 'A scoping review of research on play based pedagogies in kindergarten education'. *Review of Education*, 5(3), 311–51.

UNICEF (2018) *Learning through Play: Strengthening Learning Through Play in Early Childhood Education Programmes*. Available at: **unicef.org/sites/default/files/2018-12/UNICEF-Lego-Foundation-Learning-through-Play.pdf** (accessed 4 January 2022).

Waters-Davies, J. (2022) *Introduction to Play*. London: Sage.

reflectiveteaching.co.uk/rtps6/part3_ch13

Part four

Reflecting on consequences

14 **Outcomes** How do we monitor pupil learning
achievements?   441

15 **Inclusion** How are we enabling learning opportunities?   481

Supplementary chapter at reflectiveteaching.co.uk
• Judgement Assessment without levels

This part draws attention to what is achieved, and by whom, in our classrooms. What are the consequences of what we do?

Chapter 14 reviews high stakes issues in the assessment of learning outcomes, with particular attention on how schools measure pupil achievement and manage accountability. Whilst some problems are raised, positive uses of summative assessment are also promoted.

'Inclusion' (Chapter 15) asks us to consider various dimensions of difference and also the ways in which routine processes differentiate between people. However, the emphasis is on accepting difference as part of the human condition and on how to build more inclusive classroom communities.

Chapter 14
Outcomes
How do we monitor pupil learning achievements?

| Introduction | 442 |

| Key issues | 444 |

The current context for thinking about assessment for improvement and accountability 444
National surveys of system performance 449

| Knowing about learning | 453 |

What might people want to know about children's learning? 453
How might trust be built in assessment information about learning? 455

| Who wants to know about children's learning over time? Summative assessment | 463 |

Guiding principles 463
Learners and parents/carers want to know about learning 466
Teachers and headteachers want to know about learning: understanding group, class and school progress to reflect on practice 468
School governors, school districts and local authorities want to know about learning: understanding progress at the level of governors, district or local authority responsible for education to reflect on practice 472
Politicians want to know about learning: the challenge of accountability C 473

| Conclusion | 475 |

Supplementary chapter at reflectiveteaching.co.uk
- **Judgement** Assessment without levels

442　　Part 4　Reflecting on consequences

INTRODUCTION

Children and young people go to school, of course, 'to learn' – this is often cited as a major goal of school teaching. Chapter 13 has presented principles and practices related to Assessment for Learning (AfL) and considered what really matters if assessment is to enhance learning. This focus of assessment is often called 'formative'.

This chapter discusses issues related to 'summative' uses of assessment information. Pupil achievements are of great interest to many people – beginning of course with the pupils themselves, but also their parents or carers, teachers and school leaders, employers and, at the end of schooling, admissions officers for the next stages of education or training, as well as politicians and the general public. Indeed, Newton (2007) identified no fewer than twenty-two different purposes of assessment, many of which concern summative assessment results. However, current thinking, as represented, for example, by the International Educational Assessment Network (IEAN) 2021 *Position Paper – Re-thinking Learner Progression in a Post-Covid World*, advocates use of all information obtained through assessment processes *as the basis for future learning*, whether in the same class or establishment or in another one in a subsequent stage of education, or indeed, of life. The multiple purposes for assessing learning are also associated with the technical complexities of evaluating diverse achievements – so some complicated issues and dilemmas do arise (Broadfoot, 2007, Reading 14.1).

The description, measurement and evaluation of learning are of importance to young people, their parents, their teachers, their early years setting or school, their communities and to politicians. The main purpose of any description, measurement or evaluation should be to enhance learning; be that for an individual child, a school, a community or a nation. All assessment evidence should identify and inform the next steps that should be taken to improve performance rather than to judge or categorise individual learners, schools or nations.

When assessment is used for summative purposes (or for formative purposes) it is important that there is good alignment between curriculum, pedagogy and assessment. Assessment should first seek to demonstrate what children and young people have learned, what they know, understand and can do, and to describe progress in terms of what matters in a planned curriculum. Approaches to assessment should be fair and manageable and should avoid undesirable consequences, such as narrow teaching to relatively limited, simplistic objectives which are easily tested. Evidence gathered should point to next steps, what further action might be taken to improve learning for an individual or group, to enhance the quality of teaching and learning in an early years setting or school or to focus attention and resources at the level of the nation to enable further progress in learning to be achieved.

To allow these issues to be explored in greater depth, this chapter falls into two main sections. In the first section, the focus is on the idea of knowing about young people's learning as a result of assessment. This part of the chapter considers what people might want to know and what action can be taken to optimise trust in assessment information about young people's learning. It therefore presents ideas, information and issues relating

reflectiveteaching.co.uk/rtps6/part4_ch14

to purposes of assessment, different types of assessment related to purposes (norm-referenced, criterion-referenced and 'ipsative'-referenced assessment) and validity, reliability and dependability of assessment processes.

The second part of the chapter addresses the question: who wants to know about learning? It considers ways in which a range of users of assessment information can use summaries of young people's learning to make future learning as rich and effective as possible. These groups of users of assessment information include learners themselves and their teachers, parents/carers, schools, education systems and governments.

Having assessment become a positive power in improving learning of individuals, communities or nations depends fundamentally on assessment being integrated with curriculum (what is to be learned) and pedagogy (the learning and teaching activities that enable learning to happen). Together, curriculum, pedagogy and assessment are the DNA of learning.

See Chapter 4

TLRP Principles

Two principles are of particular relevance to this chapter (see James and Pollard, 2006):

Effective teaching and learning needs assessment to be congruent with learning. Assessment should help to advance learning as well as determine whether learning has taken place. It should be designed and carried out so that it measures learning outcomes in a dependable way and provides feedback for future learning. (*Principle 5*)

Effective teaching and learning demand consistent policy frameworks with support for teaching and learning as their primary focus. Policies at national, local and institutional levels need to recognise the fundamental importance of teaching and learning. They should be designed to create effective learning environments in which all learners can thrive. (*Principle 10*)

This chapter: discusses some of the main issues in the assessment of pupils' learning; considers major approaches such as tasks and teacher assessment; discusses key uses of summative assessment information; and touches on methods of recording and reporting.

The four nations of the United Kingdom have different statutory arrangements for assessing pupils' learning outcomes, and there is a continuing history of change. There are also differences among subjects, and depending on the age and stage of the learner. For specific information on the current summative assessment requirements in Scotland, Wales, Northern Ireland and England respectively, please visit

education.gov.scot/

hwb.gov.wales/

ccea.org.uk/

gov.uk/government/organisations/department-for-education

reflectiveteaching.co.uk/rtps6/part4_ch14

For the Republic of Ireland, please see:

ncca.ie/en/

This chapter reviews issues and principles to assist the reflective teacher whatever the jurisdiction or context they work in.

KEY ISSUES

The current context for thinking about assessment for improvement and accountability

In recent years, in most parts of the world, the summative assessment of learning in educational thinking has become more and more associated with improvement and accountability. The main reason for this has been the concern of governments to introduce ways of 'measuring' educational outcomes – for performance comparisons of both schools and the educational system. From this perspective, measurement of outcomes informs accountability procedures and can be seen as forces for improvement.

However, such approaches to improvement have brought with them particular challenges. In comparing schools, governments tend to place particular emphasis on attainment in what are considered to be 'core' subjects, and particularly on standards of literacy and numeracy as measured by tests. Results from key assessments, commonly tests, are used as the basis for judgements about school quality, putting pressure on each school to perform well. Results are likely to inform parents' judgements when choosing schools for their children. Schools judged to be successful are often granted increased autonomy while those that are deemed to be less adequate or even 'failing' are put under intense pressure to improve. In England, schools which consistently underperform may be *closed*. The rationale for this is that each pupil has just a single opportunity in school and that all schools should provide a good education for all pupils all the time.

Schools and teachers are aware of the importance of tests, not only to the children but to the reputation of the school. In an attempt to raise test scores, often teachers teach to the test (Stobart, 2008, Reading 13.6), focusing time and attention on areas that are tested. Thus, the curriculum can be narrowed, where other areas of the curriculum such as art or music are squeezed out and children's educational experiences are more limited. This kind of effect is known as 'washback', and can lead to whole subjects (notably but not only the arts) being devalued, while even within the high-status subjects of mathematics and English key aspects such as investigations and oral capabilities receive very little attention. In other countries, such as Finland, accountability is very different. Schools which underperform will be *supported* to improve because of the entitlement of all communities to high-quality education in their locality. The way in which this dilemma is resolved reflects societal values and core assumptions about educational provision. It also reflects a view about the central function of assessment itself: to judge or to inform future learning.

A prominent use of assessment evidence particularly in England has been in relation to 'targets' expressed in terms of 'expected standards'. For primary schools these relate to English and maths, with new accountability measures implemented for the first time in 2016 when national curriculum levels were no longer used. Performance tables include measures of attainment and progress, expressed as percentages of pupils achieving the expected and higher than expected standards, pupils' average 'scaled scores' (ranging from 80 to 120), and progress scores (generally within the range -5 to $+5$). The progress measures compare pupils' Key Stage 2 results with those of other pupils nationally with similar prior attainment (i.e. Key Stage 1 results) and are deemed to be fairer since school 'progress' takes account of any increase in attainment by each of the pupils whether they are low, middle or high attainers, and schools with intakes with poor prior attainment can be recognised as doing a good job.

In Scotland, the 'National Improvement Framework for Scottish Education' (Scottish Government, 2016) includes national standardised assessments in primary and lower secondary schools. However, data from these tests are not collected. Instead, teachers are invited to use the information from tests as part of the evidence informing their professional judgement. Teachers' judgement of children's progress is collected. Assessment of pupils' progress is one of six 'key drivers of improvement' and is designed to provide evidence to assist with raising attainment and closing gaps in attainment across Scotland. A range of data is gathered, including the percentage of pupils achieving expected levels in literacy and numeracy at various ages, and school leavers' qualifications and destinations.

In Wales, there are radical changes planned to their approach to accountability within Curriculum for Wales. The approach adopted in 2016 schools in Wales has been overturned. Previously, schools were categorised into four groups – green, yellow, amber, red – that determined the level of support they received (ranging from up to four days for green to up to twenty-five days for red). A school's support category was determined using a range of performance measures, the school's self-evaluation, and an assessment of that self-evaluation, thus taking account of the quality of leadership, teaching and learning as well as attainment data. However, the 'washback' effect in schools was significant and assessment was seen by schools as having a negative impact on learning and on schools. Learning is at the heart of the proposed new approach to accountability with an emphasis on gathering information to inform future progress rather than to judge or categorise schools.

> At the heart of the evaluation and improvement arrangements is robust and continuous self-evaluation for all tiers of the education system. This, along with peer engagement will support learning and improvement, embed collaboration, build trust, drive self-improvement and raise standards for all our learners. (Welsh Government, 2019)

While each of the four jurisdictions of the UK has their own approach to performance and accountability measures that differ in detail, fundamentally they all seek to use a range of data to provide information for the various stakeholders (from the individual child and parent to national government), and to use the data to support improved learning for everyone.

reflectiveteaching.co.uk/rtps6/part4_ch14

In such ways, performance expectations and outcome data are hugely influential on school policies and practices as well as being central to accountability mechanisms. This is a worldwide trend, though 'England arguably has more data and more sophisticated data than any other jurisdiction in the world' (Earl et al., 2003, p. 385). National examinations, tests and related assessments of every pupil on many occasions during their school career have generated huge amounts of data, at the same time as developments in information technology have enabled largescale data storage, sophisticated analysis and detailed reporting. Alongside this, the high profile now given to accountability in education has spawned huge industries using assessment data for school improvement and accountability.

Teachers and headteachers use assessment data for school improvement. They have opportunities to mediate and explain information to pupils, parents and carers, to discuss data with colleagues, and are held accountable on the basis of the results of these data. Data can be extremely helpful in making informed decisions (Ofsted, 2008, Reading 14.4), but can also be misleading and misinterpreted. A basic understanding of data, their strengths, weaknesses and related issues, is therefore essential for all teachers.

Data derived from assessment are sometimes referred to as 'performance data', a term that encompasses:

- raw and aggregated attainment data;
- value-added data;
- contextual value-added data.

Attainment data can be generated by teacher assessment, tasks, tests and examinations, and typically attention is given to certain key indicators, for example, the attaining of a particular standard. When raw data from individual pupils are aggregated, other indicators are possible; for example, the percentage of pupils attaining national standards. Value-added data take account of the fact that pupils have differing starting points, and so two pupils with the same raw score at the end of a school stage could have made very different progress – or even none. Value-added data are applicable for both individuals and large groups of pupils and are particularly relevant when comparing schools whose pupils on intake were already attaining very differently. Contextual value-added data takes the notion further, by not only considering pupils' prior attainment but also taking account of other factors such as gender, ethnicity, special educational needs, and a proxy for social deprivation such as eligibility for free school meals. Many people regard contextual value-added data as being a much better measure of school performance than raw scores (Schagen and Hutchinson, 2003), although they do require understanding and care to interpret them appropriately.

Performance data may be aggregated, analysed and used to produce 'league tables' of schools. Where such tables exist, they often attract considerable media attention and are promoted as enabling parents to make judgements about 'good schools' and thus to inform choice of school. This, in turn, puts market pressure on schools to improve. However, the reliability of such analyses cannot be taken for granted, as Leckie and Goldstein have demonstrated (2009, see **Research Briefing 14.1** on p. 480). While the specific measures analysed by Leckie and Goldstein have been changed, the issues and cautions they raise remain pertinent, especially while new measures are being introduced and before research can be produced.

We have seen that the use of pupil assessment data to indicate school performance, whilst superficially attractive, also has many unintended consequences and may not be sufficiently dependable for the purposes to which it is put. As the introduction to this chapter made clear, assessment can be used for such purposes, but to do so weakens its contribution to other educational goals (see also Harlen et al., 1992, Reading 13.1). Using assessment data for accountability purposes can create problems if for example the media, the public and politicians do not understand the limitations of data and draw unwarranted inferences. These issues are discussed in Reading 14.5 by Mansell and James (2009).

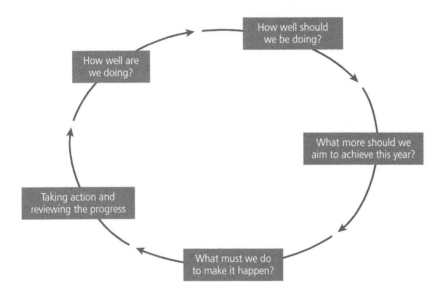

Figure 14.1
A five-stage cycle for school improvement

In a powerful argument, MacGilchrist (2003) stated that to seek school improvement simply through performance pressure was an approach which was 'past its sell-by date', and she urged more attention to the fundamental processes of teaching and learning themselves. This might be seen as a variation of the folklore that 'you can't fatten a pig by weighing it'. The Scottish curriculum and assessment system exemplifies a more holistic approach (see Scottish Government, 2011b, Reading 14.2).

reflectiveteaching.co.uk/rtps6/part4_ch14

> ### Reflective Activity 14.1
>
> *Aim:* To investigate the danger that high-stakes assessment distorts curriculum provision.
>
> *Evidence and reflection:* Talk to several teachers about the assessments their pupils undertake, in particular those that are reported publicly. Ask them about any concerns they may have. Enquire if it has been necessary to change curriculum provision to ensure that the children can perform respectably in important tests. Ask if public reporting of assessment results broadens, narrows or makes no difference to the curriculum which they provide.
>
> *Extension:* You could reflect on a potentially very significant dilemma here. A national curriculum often sets broad curriculum aims, whilst national assessment procedures test only a narrow range. Does one undermine the other?

Governments who are often concerned with global economic competition, including the effectiveness of the national workforce over the long term, use evidence from international comparative tests. Public education is funded by taxpayers who rightly expect good use of their considerable investment. In the long run the economic success of the country, including the pensions and welfare for its older citizens, is seen to depend on the education of youngsters. Governments across the world therefore pay great attention to international comparisons of school performance – particularly as portrayed through the Programme for International Student Assessment (PISA) and the Trends in International Mathematics and Science Study (TIMSS) and Progress in International Reading Literacy Study (PIRLS) (Sturman, 2012, **Reading 14.6**). The interpretation of such evidence can be controversial, but it is often boldly used for political purposes to 'blame' competing parties.

Any accountability mechanism based on summative assessment results can have unintended and negative consequences, which detract from the aim of improvement. For example, Bradbury and Roberts-Holmes (2018) have documented what they call 'the datafication' of primary and early years education. They argue that schools are becoming increasingly 'data obsessed' and risk losing sight of broader educational objectives. This phenomenon can be seen at all levels, from the single classroom to the nation state. It is particularly likely when the 'stakes' are high.

Whilst tensions created by assessment attempting to serve multiple purposes will always exist, difficulties can be identified and may be ameliorated by awareness and understanding of key issues discussed below (see also Broadfoot, 2007, **Reading 14.1**; Stobart, 2008, **Reading, 13.6**).

National surveys of system performance

In the discussion above, it will have been apparent how the outcomes of individual pupils are often aggregated and used as measures of the performance of schools or of national systems. This is common in 'neo-liberal' systems (see Chapter 5, Green and Janmaat (2011), Reading 5.2) where system-wide improvement is expected to come from competition between schools. However, as we have seen, it conflates assessment aims so that judgements about the learning of individuals become entangled in measures of school, local authority, sector or system effectiveness. As Harlen et al. (1992, Reading 13.1) argued, such conflation of aims can have unintended consequences.

An alternative approach is to rely on specific sources of information for each need. For instance, this was the practice in England in the 1970s and 1980s.

- Schools were responsible for the assessment of pupil performance. In primary education, a wide range of commercially available tests was commonly used – with a consequential lack of comparability across schools.

- Local authority advisers and inspectors in each local government area supported school improvement, and inspections by inspectors were significant accountability events.

- To achieve national monitoring on curricular and other issues, inspectors also carried out specific studies and published reports which drew on their extensive professional experience.

However, given the variation in provision and practice in different local authorities, monitoring of national performance prior to examinations at the end of schooling was a problem. This was solved from 1975–89 through the establishment of the Assessment of Performance Unit (APU) to monitor pupil achievement. Rather than tests being necessary in all schools, a sampling frame enabled selection of 1.5 per cent of all pupils at ages 11, 13 and 15 whose test results provided reliable evidence of national performance in selected subjects (including English and maths).

In Scotland, a similar national monitoring programme existed from 1983 until 2017. It used a nationally representative sample of pupils within primary and secondary schools who undertake assessment activities in a rolling programme to enable a focus on particular subjects, with a three-yearly cycle of surveys in English, maths and science. The system was refined over the years and the final survey, the Scottish Survey of Literacy and Numeracy, monitored performance at Primary 4, Primary 7 and Secondary 2. Results were not reported or recorded at pupil, school or local authority level. Rather, they were used to make judgements about national performance and to produce teaching and learning resources to support teachers in improving the quality of their provision.

National surveys of pupil performance can thus serve this particular purpose in cost-effective and efficient ways, and without unintended distorting effects on school practices.

There are, therefore, many ways to gather evidence at the level of the system and some approaches lead to more negative washback than others. It is important to remember that the 'what' and 'how' of teaching and learning are central daily concerns of teachers – reflective practitioners with values and beliefs who have to make decisions about practice within layered contexts of guidance, expectations and policy. When a professional's values and practices are misaligned for whatever reason, they can feel unease and stress. The *Learning How to Learn* project in England (James et al., 2007, Reading 2.8) investigated teachers' beliefs and practices through questionnaires and interviews and found 'many teachers felt constrained by a policy context that encouraged rushed curriculum coverage, teaching to the test and a tick-box culture' (pp. 215–16). Teachers' stress is increased by the importance and consequences of assessment results for many stakeholders, which in turn may have distorting effects on their teaching.

Ultimately, what matters most is pupils' experience of assessment: the early phases of the introduction of national assessment procedures in England and Wales brought enormous protests from primary teachers, many of whom provided illustrations of distressed children (Torrance, 1991). However, more representative samples of teacher opinion did not show the same level of concern (Pollard et al., 1994). Worries from parents were very strong in Scotland but were relatively small in England and Wales (Hughes, Wikeley and Nash, 1994). Evidence from children themselves on their experience of national testing mostly showed that many of them enjoyed it (Pollard et al., 1994). Indeed, in many classrooms the *early* assessment procedures seemed to have broadened the curriculum, such was its power, and to have been well received by children.

The longer-term picture appears to have changed as testing procedures have been narrowed and tightened by government agencies. Evidence of classroom practice suggests that teaching programmes are being attuned more closely to assessment requirements. The accountability stakes are high for schools in England, and primaries tend to focus on core subjects whilst secondaries are concerned for subjects within the EBacc (English Baccalaureate). The unintended consequence of such decisions is to limit the scope for some pupils to demonstrate other capabilities.

Similarly, there are dangers of stigma emerging from the overt form of some assessment procedures and categoric nature of the results – 'I'll be a nothing', as one child put it (Reay and Wiliam, 1999). Assessment can thus profoundly affect pupils' self-image and identity. Stobart (2008, Reading 13.6) cites not only Hannah, a 6-year-old who featured in Reay and Wiliam's research, but also Ruth, an 18-year-old who, far from being 'a nothing', was extremely successful in examinations. However, Ruth had developed a particularly instrumental approach to learning for tests, which did little to establish the habits of lifelong learning.

reflectiveteaching.co.uk/rtps6/part4_ch14

> # Reflective Activity 14.2
>
> *Aim:* To obtain direct evidence of pupils' feelings about routine assessment.
>
> *Evidence and reflection:* We suggest that you work with a group of pupils from your class and discuss with them examples of some assessments which you have made. Perhaps you could use some written work that has been produced and look at any comments and corrections which you made. How do the pupils feel about your responses?
>
> You could also self-consciously monitor your verbal feedback during a teaching session. Listen to your comments, observe the children's faces. How do they seem to respond? Are they delighted, wary, confused, anxious, angry, resigned?
>
> *Extension:* What ways of protecting young people's dignity can you develop, whilst still providing appropriate assessment feedback to them? Could you negotiate with the pupils to establish criteria by which their work will be evaluated? (See Chapter 13)

The ways in which assessment results influence the expectations that teachers have of pupils, pupils have of each other, and pupils have of themselves are still not yet fully researched. However, the PACE project (Pollard et al., 2000) suggested that pupil motivation, engagement and zest for learning in England were adversely affected by an overloaded curriculum and the extent of its assessment (see Figure 14.2, from the PACE project data archive). Despite the rise in measured standards, a significant number of children showed signs of developing negative dispositions towards learning. Harlen and Deakin Crick (2002) also found evidence of the negative impact of testing on pupils' motivation. Repeated testing, including practice tests, seems to undermine the self-image of lower-attaining pupils, which widens the attainment gap between pupils. As we will see in Chapter 15, it is likely that the socially differentiating effect of formal assessment will be reinforced by pupils' cultural responses, and the situation may polarise further (see Reading 15.2).

> **Expert Questions**
>
> **Expectation:** *does our school support high staff and pupil expectations and aspire for excellence?*
>
> **Inclusion:** *are all learners treated respectfully and fairly in both formal and informal interaction?*
>
> These questions contribute to a conceptual framework representing enduring issues and teacher expertise (see Chapter 16).

There is little doubt that national assessment procedures have long-term effects on pupils. In part, these may be seen as positive, in that the quality of teaching and learning may be enhanced.

Figure 14.2 A child's feelings about SATs (PACE data archive)

Reflective teachers will want, prudently, to watch for effects which could both damage the self-image and self-confidence of pupils and have other divisive effects. For that to happen, teachers need to have a deep understanding of how assessment can influence curriculum and pedagogy enhancing or negatively influencing learning.

KNOWING ABOUT LEARNING

The essence of assessment for summative purposes is not accountability but gathering evidence to reflect on children's learning and progress over time. When seeking to know about learning, it is crucial to ask:

What might people want to know about children's learning?

What action can be taken to optimise trust in assessment information about young people's learning?

Who will make use of the information and for what purposes?

What might people want to know about children's learning?

The interpretation of any assessment involves some form of comparison about performance in relation to something.

Performance can be judged in relation to:

- performances of others (norm referencing);
- specified, agreed standards (criterion referencing);
- an individual's previous performance (ipsative referencing).

Whilst the terms 'norm', 'criterion' and 'ipsative' may not be commonly used, the practices to which they refer are embedded in the assessment routines of almost all schools and they provide different kinds of knowledge about young people's learning.

Norm referencing With norm referencing, individual pupils are compared with others. Standardised tests and some types of national tests or examinations are norm referenced, providing a rank order of performance around the mean score achieved by a large random sample of a 'population' (e.g. all the children in a country of a particular age.). They are typically ranking the participants in terms of a kind of broad 'general ability' in the area being assessed (technically known as a 'latent trait') – e.g. a general reading or mathematical ability. They do not usually provide detailed information about specific elements in the reading or mathematical process, such as, for example, evaluation of an author's use of metaphor or the ability to do multiplication by two-digit numbers accurately.

reflectiveteaching.co.uk/rtps6/part4_ch14

Norm referenced assessment has often led to describing learners in terms of their ranking, and for much of the last century giving a class position was common ('she came third in the class in maths'). Performance can also be expressed in relation to the rest of the group with statements such as 'he's about average' and 'she's in the bottom third'.

Wanting to have a sense of how a pupil is doing in relation to others is understandable and is necessary when competition and selection are required. However, norm-referenced assessment results give no information about the specifics of what a pupil knows, understands and can do, nor do they identify particular difficulties or point to the appropriate next steps in learning. Categorisation can also have significant demotivating effects for weaker learners.

Criterion referencing Criterion-referenced assessment provides specific information about what a learner knows and can do in relation to pre-specified criteria – and this is irrespective of the performance of others. When criteria are made explicit, 'next steps' are implied through the criteria not yet grasped and those at the next level or stage. The kind of specific information referred to above, which can guide next steps in learning and teaching, relating to ability to evaluate an author's use of metaphor or to do multiplication by two-digit numbers accurately, comes from criterion-referenced assessment (whether in a carefully designed test or through the application of the teacher's professional judgement of classwork).

Criterion and norm-referenced approaches are interrelated in that the process of establishing criteria takes into account what it is reasonable to expect for pupils at a particular stage of progression in their learning journey. So, notions of norm-referencing do contribute to criterion referencing, for example in national testing or, in post-primary education, in public examinations such as 'A levels. Thus, both norm and criterion referencing are easily associated with notions of success and failure, whether this be judged in relation to others' performance, or the setting of particular standards, benchmarks or cut-off points in a criterion-referenced system.

Ipsative referencing The word 'ipsative' comes from Latin 'ipse' meaning 'self'. Although this is not a common term, teachers use ipsative-referenced assessment all the time as judgements are made about a pupil's performance in relation to their previous achievements. This works best for detailed assessment when the teacher knows the pupils well, can identify specific improvements, and guide next steps at an appropriate degree of 'stretch'.

Ipsative assessment is very supportive of learning, and seeks to motivate *all* pupils, however they are judged through norm- or criterion-referenced assessment. It is characteristic of very good day-to-day assessment for learning, as described in Chapter 13. However, occasional summative reflection on an individual learner's current stage of progress by both learner and teacher also contributes valuable information to motivating and guiding learning. Ipsative referencing is the most inclusive and enabling form of assessment, since it values and challenges those at both extremes of the attainment range and everyone in between (see also Chapter 15, Reading 2.6).

> **Expert Question**
>
> **Congruence:** are forms of assessment fit for purpose in terms of overall educational objectives?
>
> This question contributes to a conceptual framework representing enduring issues and teacher expertise (see Chapter 16).

In reflecting on the three bases for comparison, it may be helpful to think about the Olympic Games where ipsative, criterion and norm referencing are all in evidence. Ipsative referencing underpins preparation for the Games, as athletes strive to improve on their 'personal best'. Criterion referencing is then often used in relation to qualifying for an event, when athletes do, or do not, satisfy the standard. In the finals, the awarding of medals is norm-referenced as those who beat everyone else are acclaimed. Recognition is also sometimes given to athletes who produce their best ever performance, but it is the norm-referenced brilliance of gold medalists that gets paramount attention, rather than ipsative-referenced personal bests, no matter how remarkable these may be.

Reflective Activity 14.3

Aim: To consider the bases of comparison used in learning and teaching.

Evidence and reflection: Think of a pupil in your class whom you know well. Consider when it would be useful and appropriate to use norm, criterion and ipsative-referenced assessment. Now list all the different assessments that the pupil has experienced and identify the basis of comparison for each. How closely does what happens match what you thought would be useful and appropriate?

Extension: Be aware of the bases of comparison you are using and explore possibilities for prioritising forms most supportive of learning.

How might trust be built in assessment information about learning?

How do you know that you can trust an assessment outcome? Some endemic issues underlie this question, and we review these below (see also Mansell and James, 2009, Reading 14.5).

Information about young people's learning which may be summarised and reflected on by teachers and learners may derive from several types of assessment activity:

- Tasks and activities in day-to-day classwork, observed and responded to by the teacher.
- Non-statutory tests, designed by the teacher, or obtained from elsewhere.
- Statutory tests, which the state requires that pupils sit; and, in later stages of school, public examinations.
- National or international surveys of achievement.

There is an extensive range of technical literature about validity and reliability, much of which has been developed in relation to formal tests and examinations. In reading this literature, it can seem as if only such formal types of assessment have the cachet of 'serious', or 'scientific' methods. However, the discussion of validity, reliability and dependability which follows makes clear that the picture is far more complex. Every approach to assessment has advantages and disadvantages.

Validity This concept is of immense importance. In its traditional, technical meaning, it addresses the question: do assessments actually measure what they purport to measure? This is known as 'construct validity'. So, for example: 'is a whole-class spelling test a valid way of assessing pupils' ability to write effectively? The answer is 'probably not', because many other forms of knowledge, skill and understanding are involved in writing. What matters in writing is defined in the curriculum and what is defined in the curriculum is what is the focus for gathering evidence, i.e. assessment. If what a teacher wants to find out relates specifically to spelling, then a test might be deemed to have higher construct validity. But spelling is not writing and what a test measures and what matters in the curriculum should not be confused.

Tests can have other impacts that should be considered. For example, some children or young people do not perform consistently in stressful and somewhat artificial situations but may do better, or worse, when applying their knowledge of spelling in a more authentic writing activity.

Understanding of validity has thus evolved so that the answer to whether a test is valid would not be 'yes' or 'no', but rather that whilst some kinds of conclusions may be valid, others would not (Angoff, 1988).

The implication of this is that, whilst we are certainly interested in assessment results themselves, it is the inferences that we draw from them that make them so crucial. Results of assessment are used to make decisions, for example about: what matters most for a child to learn next; what to teach next; the quality of the progress that a pupil is making; appropriate next stages in terms of educational experience; levels of attainment reached; and, of course, the quality of schools and curricula. The quality of these decisions depends on the nature of the assessments on which they are based. As Dylan Wiliam puts it, 'validity is all about the interpretations that we can legitimately draw from assessment results' (Wiliam, 2011, p. 132).

Valid inferences depend on assessment purpose. The reflective teacher needs to be aware of important factors that can affect the legitimacy of inferences we may draw from the results of different types of assessment. For example, Drummond (2012) provides a radical critique of narrow forms of assessment. Illustrating her argument through work with young children, she insists that assessment data are not some form of objective 'evidence' but require interpretation to make sense of them in terms of a teacher's understanding of the child. Kane (2016) argues in a similar manner that test scores have to be interpreted. He asks: what does a score tell us about the knowledge/skills/abilities of the person(s) who achieved that score? The following example illustrates how different types of assessment raise issues about validity according to the purpose for which they are being used.

Suppose a pupil scores 80 per cent on a reading test. How do we interpret her score? What does it tell us about her reading abilities? If the test was designed as a norm-referenced standardised one, assessing a 'general' reading ability on the assumption that all the questions in some way test this general reading ability, the 80 per cent score tells us that the pupil has shown this general ability to a significant degree. Assuming that the

reflectiveteaching.co.uk/rtps6/part4_ch14

'standard', i.e. the average score of the population that had been sampled in the standardising process, is about 50 per cent, the 80 per cent score also tells us that this pupil ranks high among her peers in terms of the general reading ability tested. The 80 per cent score on its own does not tell us more than this. For example, it doesn't indicate what this pupil would need to do to improve her score on a later test to 90 per cent or 100 per cent.

Suppose, however, the test had been designed in a different, criterion-referenced way. It might then contain a number of questions on each of several important aspects of reading, such as:

(a) Literal recognition/understanding of the words/sentences;

(b) Making inferences based on the message of the text;

(c) Summing up the main purpose of the text; and the idea(s) the author is conveying and/or the author's standpoint in relation to them;

(d) Taking an evaluative position in relation to these purposes/ideas and justifying this;

(e) Commenting evaluatively on how effectively the author used language to pursue their purposes. (This is just one way of listing aspects of reading: it is not suggested that it is the only way.)

In this situation the test might give us for a particular pupil a profile of scores, e.g. for the five aspects listed, 85 per cent, 60 per cent, 55 per cent, 30 per cent and 20 per cent, or some other form of description of the extent of success in each category. Here the results achieved by this pupil can be interpreted in a quite different way. For example, they suggest that her abilities in relation to areas (d) and (e) are quite limited at present. If the purpose of assessment is to identify successes and areas where future action might be targeted, an assessment that would provide such a profile would be more useful.

The second example of a reading test described above gives us information which suggests that the pupil's abilities need to be boosted through teaching/discussion of *evaluation* of what is read in terms of critical thinking about the author's ideas and standpoint and in terms of awareness of language use. The pupil's 80 per cent or 20 per cent score on the norm-referenced test does not provide this kind of information that is directly useful to teaching – yet many countries/states using such tests claim that they have a diagnostic value and help improve learning/teaching.

Kane (2016) argues that validating a test must begin with this kind of spelling out the interpretation of the scores – what they tell us about what the participants know and can do. He then goes on to argue that validation also needs to consider whether the information that the scores give us is valuable for the purpose(s) to which the test may be put.

Other important issues are raised by this focus on purpose and on the use made of assessment information. Newton and Shaw (2014) and Newton and Baird (2016) extended the debate about the validity of an assessment to include 'social' impacts of assessment methods and use of results. Such 'social' impacts can include the wellbeing of the children and young people being assessed and the narrowing or distortion of curriculum and/or learning/teaching activities in contexts where assessments are 'high stakes'.

reflectiveteaching.co.uk/rtps6/part4_ch14

> **Reflective Activity 14.4**
>
> *Aim:* To identify the social impact of assessment.
>
> *Evidence and reflection:* Think about a group of children with whom you have worked. Can you identify occasions where there have been social impacts of assessment? If so, what might be done to reduce the social impact of assessment? If not, what prevented there being negative social impact?

Teacher professional judgement of evidence related to children's progress has the potential to have a high degree of validity. The curriculum sets out what matters in learning; teachers design learning and teaching opportunities to allow children to develop their knowledge, skills and understanding in relation to what matters; and evidence is gathered about how much and how well each child has progressed in all that matters. Teachers may use tests as one source of evidence but much of the information about progress will come from day-to-day activities where teachers use criteria to discern progress.

Criterion-referenced procedures, or tests at any stage of education, have the potential for high validity in that evidence gathered can reflect the specific learning that a programme of study offers to learners. However, as with all approaches to assessment, key issues have to be considered. For example: is the domain of learning being properly sampled? Is what matters in that area of learning being assessed by the procedure? In a portfolio of work, the specification of appropriate tasks and what each seeks to achieve is an important means of assuring validity. It has long been recognised that discussion among teachers, i.e. professional consensus, is an important strategy in the achievement of high validity (see, e.g. Pilliner, 1979).

It is worth noting that professional consensus is, in the end, also the basis of ensuring validity in norm-referenced assessment and in public examinations. The design of standardised tests and examinations typically involves a team of collaborating experts in the learning domain being assessed; and the steps taken by, for example, an examining body to make their tests rigorous and fair include a good deal of professional discussion among expert test designers.

The ultimate importance of consensus professional judgement in designing and interpreting the results of assessments – whether tests or other kinds of assessment activities – has important implications. Reflective teachers need to be aware that no one approach to assessment is intrinsically better than any other. The design and the interpretation of results in all approaches to assessment, whether based on teachers' professional judgment or on tests which a state or other authority requires their pupils to take, are open to rationale critique and interpretation. Professional learning communities among teaching colleagues are important for optimising the appropriateness and quality of assessments, sharing understandings of progression and reflecting on pupils' future learning needs and opportunities.

> **Reflective Activity 14.5**
>
> *Aim:* To consider the bases of comparison used in learning and teaching.
>
> *Evidence and reflection:* Think of a pupil in your class whom you know well. Consider when it would be useful and appropriate to use norm, criterion and ipsative referenced assessment. Now list all the different assessments that the pupil has experienced and identify the basis of comparison for each. How closely does what happens match what you thought would be useful and appropriate?
>
> *Extension:* Be aware of the bases of comparison you are using and explore possibilities for prioritising forms more supportive of learning.

Reliability If a form of assessment is deemed to be valid for a particular purpose, the next question becomes whether it can be used reliably and consistently. Many factors may influence the results of an assessment process. The reliability of assessment relates directly to the extent to which such factors are reduced. For example, differing states of health, concentration or motivation of young people may influence the quality of a child's performance. Time factors may also impact performance. For example, a primary mathematics test taken in a 'maths session' on a Monday morning may be very different from another group taking the same test last thing on a Friday after a PE lesson.

A number of factors can influence the reliability of assessment. For example:

- Is the language of the task sufficiently clear to be understood in the same way by all those being assessed?
- Are the judgments being made by the teacher or other assessor consistent? Does the same teacher on different occasions reach different conclusions about the same piece of work? Or do different teachers reach different conclusions?
- Are irrelevant factors interfering? A common problem arises when capabilities are interrelated – such as when the reading demand of a particular task may constrain some pupils' ability to demonstrate their understanding in drawing or music, number or history or some other domain. Assessment processes which conflate different attributes cannot always be avoided, and careful teacher judgement is often required in drawing conclusions.

Obtaining adequate reliability is particularly important when the stakes are high, for example, if information is to be used to allocate children to particular groups, or if information is being used to judge the quality of a teacher or a school. Care should be taken with issues of equity. For example, the Runnymede report (Joseph-Salisbury, 2020, p. 9) reports that 'racialised teacher expectations can impact upon the sets that pupils are put in, disciplinary procedures and teacher assessments'.

Reflective teachers understand that *all* assessment measures, no matter how professionally designed and administered.

> **Expert Question**
>
> **Validity:** in terms of learning, do the forms of assessment used really measure what they are intended to measure?
>
> **Reliability:** in terms of learning, to what extent can learners, teachers, headteachers and parents rely on the evidence of children's progress?
>
> These questions contribute to a conceptual framework representing enduring issues and teacher expertise (see Chapter 16).

Dependability Dependability is an overarching concept denoting the confidence which stakeholders have in the assessment system; how dependable they perceive the evidence to be. It reflects outcomes of the steps taken to achieve validity and reliability, and the perceived legitimacy of those outcomes. As Mansell, James and the Assessment Reform Group put it: 'Together, maximum validity and optimal reliability contribute to the *dependability* of assessments – the confidence that can be placed in them' (2009, p. 12, Reading 14.5).

The central dilemma is that validity and reliability are interrelated – so strengthening one aspect often weakens another.

- The quest for construct validity tends to lead in the direction of assessment procedures which are designed for routine classroom circumstances. They cover what matters in the curriculum and use a range of assessment techniques such as tasks, course work and continuous assessment. Such approaches resonate with assessment for learning, as discussed in Chapter 13.

- However, the pursuit of reliability tends to lead to simplification in assessment procedures and to narrowing the range of curriculum to be assessed. The result of this is often an emphasis on methods which can be tightly controlled, such as timed pencil and paper or ICT-based tests and examinations.

When the emphasis is on certification of pupil attainment and school accountability, politicians and the media stress this traditional view that 'tests and exams are reliable' and focus on tests and examinations. These 'users' of test or examination results are typically unaware of the reliability and Standard Error of Measurement issues described above as affecting their 'accuracy'. Nor are they conscious of the loss to validity of assessment if reliability is over-emphasised.

Reliability can be increased by using questions to which there is only one correct answer (as in multiple-choice questions), since such questions are likely to be marked accurately and consistently, and are increasingly marked electronically. However, multiple-choice questions can only assess certain kinds of learning outcomes so cannot be used to assess everything that is considered important, everything that matters. Art, music, drama, extended writing, speaking and listening, for example, require very different assessment arrangements and are more difficult to assess reliably than factual knowledge. Indeed, when National Curriculum assessment was first introduced in England, wide curriculum coverage was endorsed with authentic classroom tasks being used to assess 7-year-olds. However, such assessments were found to be both unmanageable and to have considerable problems of reliability (Shorrocks, 1991; Whetton, 1991). Consider, for example, Lee's interpretation of a mathematics task in Figure 14.3. Required to 'show your working', he did – but not as had been intended.

Statutory assessment in England has long been contentious. For example, although some argue that the Phonics Screening Check (PSC) is a necessary diagnostic tool, it has also provoked strong negative reactions because of its influence on the curriculum and in particular the way children are taught to read (e.g. see Wyse and Bradbury, 2022). A more recent development has been the Reception baseline assessment (gov.uk/guidance/reception-baseline-assessment). This was introduced with the intention to measure pupils' progress throughout their primary education. However, there is concern that this might impact negatively on curriculum and pedagogy in Reception classes, particularly in relation to play-based learning and its assessment through classroom observations of children's learning behaviour. The British Educational Research Association convened an expert group which recommended assessing a nationally representative sample of pupils rather than assessing all children in the country (bera.ac.uk/publication/high-standards-not-high-stakes-an-alternative-to-sats).

Expert Question

Dependability: *are assessment processes understood and accepted as being robust and reliable?*

This question contributes to a conceptual framework representing enduring issues and teacher expertise (see Chapter 16).

Figure 14.3 Lee 'shows his working'

Reflective Activity 14.6

Aim: To highlight dilemmas between construct validity and reliability.

Evidence and reflection: Focus on a specific objective for pupil attainment; for instance, one associated with children's mathematical understanding and computational competence with number. Consider how the competence and understanding of pupils across the country could be assessed with regard to the selected objective. Focus this, perhaps by imagining some individual children whom you know in different schools, or by discussion with teachers or student teachers working in different schools. Do you think your assessment method could reflect what is really involved in understanding and competence (construct validity), and yet be administered in standard and consistent ways by teachers wherever or whoever they are (reliability)?

Extension: Consider any test materials with which you are familiar. How do you feel that the test's designers have tried to resolve the validity/reliability dilemma? What compromises have they made? Do you think it is possible to devise assessment with high validity and high reliability for all subjects?

Decisions about forms of assessment should be related to the primacy of purpose. Thus, for example, in Chapter 13 (p. 404) we focused on the use of assessment to *support learning* itself (formative assessment) – a very different goal from the *measurement of attainment* (summative assessment) with which this chapter is concerned (see Reading 13.1). Reconciliation of the dilemmas posed by validity and reliability is much more likely if there is absolute clarity about such purposes – and this is the foundation on which confidence in an assessment system can grow. A robust and dependable assessment system will be one in which there is clarity about purposes.

However much care is taken with the technical aspects of assessment, it is worth bearing in mind that outcomes always reflect a series of *social* processes. For example, Filer and Pollard (2000, Reading 14.7) analysed pupils' assessment experiences throughout their primary schooling, and suggested that strict 'objectivity' is a myth. Pupil performance is crucially affected by the context of its production and social and cultural factors have considerable influence over its interpretation, meaning and consequence. A classic study of a similar sort is Becker's *Making the Grade* (1968), which will still have resonance for readers experiencing higher education.

Expert Question

Dependability: are assessment processes understood and accepted as being robust and reliable?

This question contributes to a conceptual framework representing enduring issues and teacher expertise (see Chapter 16).

Chapter 14 Outcomes 463

WHO WANTS TO KNOW ABOUT CHILDREN'S LEARNING OVER TIME? SUMMATIVE ASSESSMENT

Guiding principles

From learners to international communities, there is intense interest in learning progress. The second part of this chapter considers how different users of assessment information can use evidence to make future learning rich and effective. Users of assessment information include learners, their teachers, their parents/carers, schools, education systems and governments. This part of the chapter begins by identifying key principles that should inform the thinking of anyone who seeks to gather and use information about children's learning.

The ideas in this part of the chapter and the approaches suggested are guided by two crucial principles about use of assessment information which are emerging ever more clearly in international assessment debates:

- **The importance of an 'assessment culture'** where the focus shifts from summarising past attainment or creating 'performance data' to compare schools, areas and countries to one where assessment evidence is used to reflect on individual and group/class/school progress to inform future learning.

- **The need to ensure that learning is at the centre of all assessment activity.**

The rationale for these principles has been published in position papers produced by the International Educational Assessment Network (IEAN) in 2020 and 2021. IEAN is a network of internationally recognised assessment researchers and policy makers from twelve nations across four continents, who work collaboratively to tackle shared assessment challenges. The papers and information on the international network are available at iean.network/

It is worth reflecting on issues emerging from two IEAN papers as they indicate the 'direction of travel' of current international thinking about desirable assessment practice amongst both researchers and policy makers.

In *Rethinking Learner Progression for the Future*, IEAN (2020) argues that:

There is a need to rethink learning progressions and assessment to support better:

- the development and demonstration of a much wider range of achievements by all young people.
- learners' awareness and that of their parents/guardians, their teachers and all those with an interest in educational achievement that the journey through school education is a progression that builds continuously on previous learning.

Acknowledging young people's participation in a complex world, education systems must move beyond traditional paradigms of assessment (tests and examinations) and look towards progression-based approaches.

reflectiveteaching.co.uk/rtps6/part4_ch14

Part 4 Reflecting on consequences

Both researchers and policymakers recognise the importance of an integrated approach to curriculum and assessment. The focus for assessment is on how evidence might best be gathered and used to support learning progression. Also of interest is the reference to 'all' learners, the determination to promote a system that works for every child. However, perhaps of greatest significance is the focus on the changing role of the learner, from passive recipient to becoming an active participant in the learning process.

Reflecting on implications for summarising learning over time, the paper argues that:

There is a need for alternative ways to evaluate or make judgments about learning over time.

- Assessing learning progression over time requires ongoing evaluation. Teachers continuously make judgements about pupil progress which inform collaborative decisions about next steps and future learning.
- Focusing on what pupils can do and the progress they have made along a continuum is key.
- Traditional assessment methods such as numerical calculations of pupil performance are inappropriate when assessing a progression of learning.

The role of the teacher in gathering evidence of progression is central. In partnership with children and with other teachers, the process of assessment is built into the day-to-day activities of the learning environment, be that the early years setting, the outdoors learning environment or the classroom. The purpose of evidence gathering over time is to discern progress in what matters in the curriculum, identifying what children knew, understood and were able to do at one point in the year and what at a later point in the year, they now know, understand and can do, i.e. their progress, and building from that, what their most significant next steps might be. For this kind of evidence, test-based approaches are insufficient and numerical (or alphabetical) judgements are described as 'inappropriate'. Samples of children's work, photographs of their engagement in tasks, earlier and later drawings, recordings of music making are all ways of gathering evidence to show more meaningful evidence of progression.

Finally, the paper challenges many of the more traditional kinds of evidence emerging from assessment for summative purposes:

Assessments designed to provide summative information tied to particular ages or stages create an expectation that the pace of progression for most learners will be similar; they generally are not designed to measure the extent to which learners have progressed in their learning.

- We need to address the challenge of designing valid and reliable approaches to assessments that focus less on the learner's age and more on complex achievements which current tests and examinations typically do not reflect. Such assessments could include descriptions of personal capacities, based on observation of and interaction with learners. Progression frameworks that describe personal capacities, knowledge, and skills, while acknowledging the variability expected among learners, can provide a solid basis for assessment. A sharp focus on the purpose of assessment and the

reflectiveteaching.co.uk/rtps6/part4_ch14

learners involved, linked to clear progression frameworks, would provide a valid, reliable, and informative summative assessment at the end of a school career. Such assessment at different time points would also offer a measure of the degree and rate of progression of learners.
- There should also be a focus on making the information from jurisdictional assessments more useful to pupils and teachers, supporting their formative use as much as possible, utilizing descriptive language that focuses on what pupils are able to do and informs what they do next.

Amongst this group of international researchers and policymakers, the international direction of travel for the future of assessment is clear. Assessment purposes, whether for educators or for politicians, should have as their major function: to support learning progression.

Alison Peacock (2016), in *Assessment for Learning without Limits*, explores practical ways of how an assessment culture might be built with learning at its centre. An experienced headteacher and now CEO of the Chartered College of Teaching in England, Peacock builds her work from two research studies, *Learning without Limits* (Hart et al., 2004) and *Creating Learning without Limits* (Swann et al., 2012). She demonstrates the potential of how, by removing the barriers that emerge from children being labelled and categorised, young people can learn without limits. Assessment becomes the use of evidence to enhance learning rather than a source of judgement. By adopting an assessment culture built on the premise that every child can learn, these new approaches to assessment that are based on principles of collaboration, professional learning and inquiry can help to reduce inequity. In this study, children and adults work in partnership and the real-life stories in the book demonstrate how these strategies can transform both children's and their teachers' views of what it is possible to achieve.

Reflective Activity 14.7

Aim: To consider the practical implications of two IEAN guiding principles in practice.

Evidence and reflection: Two guiding principles to promote that all assessment is used to enhance children's learning are:

Change the assessment culture: Think about this principle in a context within which you are working or have worked. What is the assessment culture? What, if anything, would you like to change and why? What small steps might you begin to enhance the assessment culture?

Ensure that key learning and progression is at the centre of all assessment activity: Think about this principle in a context within which you are working or have worked. To what extent are learning and progression at the heart of all assessment activity? What evidence do you draw on to answer that question? What, if anything, might you change?

---

reflectiveteaching.co.uk/rtps6/part4_ch14

Learners and parents/carers want to know about learning

Learners and parents/carers are keenly interested in children's learning over time. Is progress being made? Are they making good progress?

The practical implications of gathering, reflecting on and sharing information on individual learners' progress are likely to vary according to the nature of the local curriculum developed by a school or a group of schools and local decisions about the particular purposes of these processes. Such purposes might include encouraging learners to reflect on their own learning, discussing with individual learners possible short-term and longer-term next steps, providing information for a subsequent teacher or sharing insights on progression in learning at home and in the early years setting or schools with parents/carers.

Parents and other carers are hugely significant in children's lives as, of course, is informal learning in non-school settings. For these reasons, if the teachers can inform, learn from and work with such significant others, the improvement in learning outcomes for pupils is likely to be considerable (Desforges, 2003; Goodall and Vorhaus, 2010).

However, the ways in which teachers report the progress of children and young people to parents are influenced by two seemingly contradictory sets of expectations.

The first makes the assumption that parents are *partners* with teachers in supporting the learning of each child (e.g. Hornby, 2011). Parents may thus be routinely invited into school, particularly in the early years. Parent–teacher discussions are likely to include consideration of the processes and progress of the pupil – perhaps illustrated by reference to their work.

The second expectation is based on an image of parents as *consumers* of education, having contracted with the school for the provision of educational services to their child (e.g. Chubb and Moe, 1990; Woods, Bagley and Glatter, 1998). They thus require a report of outcomes, through which the school can be held accountable for pupil progress.

Needless to say, most schools make provision which reflects elements of both these approaches. This is not surprising, for, whilst the partnership model is professionally acknowledged as contributing very constructively to pupil learning, the consumer model is increasingly underwritten by legal requirements. For example, for each pupil in England, annual reports to parents are required to include information about:

- achievements;
- progress;
- attendance.

Additional information is required for pupils who have undergone national assessments, including whether or not they have met the 'expected standard'. Such requirements feed the 'consumer' model of education. The partnership aspect is most clearly demonstrated by the inclusion within reports of targets for the future, and of advice about specific ways in which parents can help. In England, from 2014, maintained schools have been required to publish for parents a year-by-year curriculum plan. In principle, this enables parents to tune support for their children and could be very beneficial educationally.

However, it is by no means certain how this tension between partnership and consumerist models of home–school relationships will develop over time.

One of the most explicit ways of manifesting the partnership model is through the processes which a school adopts in reporting pupil achievements to parents. Annual written reports to parents may be legally required, but most schools offer much more in terms of formal and informal opportunities during the year. Consultation evenings, interim reports, home–school liaison notebooks, phone calls, emails, individual face-to-face discussions and so on can all strengthen the relationship between home and school, while also addressing parental expectations about access and information. Some of the best practice involves the pupils as active participants, for example through attending open days/evenings and contributing to written reports.

Reflective Activity 14.8

Aim: To develop an informative and constructive procedure for reporting to parents.

Evidence and reflection: This activity must be tailored to circumstances. Discuss with appropriate colleagues the aims and scope of a reporting exercise. If you are a student teacher, you might want to limit it to reflect a project which you have completed or build it into an end-of-term open day.

Consider the following questions:
- How can you best provide information to parents?
- How can you involve the children?
- How can you elicit information and support from parents?

Extension: Evaluate your reporting procedure. Did you find consumerist or partnership expectations from parents? How did the children benefit? What will you do when your next opportunity arises?

Teachers' approaches to identifying progress, and to sharing information with children and parents/carers and subsequent teachers, are likely to be influenced by school (or local authority or state) policies. Sometimes, such policies have led to time-consuming work for teachers which did not contribute effectively to children's future learning, e.g. extensive written reports or impersonal 'computer banks' of comments.

But what kinds of information sharing would help learning progression? Based on teacher interviews asking teachers what kinds of information they could use to support progression, Spencer and Hayward (2016) suggest that one practical approach to promote progression over time might involve:

- A manageable portfolio of work, representative of the key learning in the course/programme undertaken.

- Discussion with the learner to agree what evidence should be demonstrated in the portfolio, taking account of the learning aims of the locally planned curriculum and, where appropriate, how these relate to the national/state curriculum and cross-curricular competencies. Curriculum content may have a place in this discussion as context, but the focus should be on *what has been learned.*

- Discussion of progression based on the portfolio among teacher, learner and parents/carers and later between the learner (or, where appropriate, a group of learners) and a subsequent teacher, enabling the teacher to explore the children's learning through dialogue, as a basis for building on it.

There are circumstances where standardised testing, statutory or otherwise, is part of the school's assessment practice. Where this is the case, discussions should focus on the *learning* represented by the test score and should include positive description of success(es) and discussion of steps to improvement in learning. It is important also to set any information from tests in the context of wider evidence and to be open about the potential validity and reliability issues discussed above.

Teachers and headteachers want to know about learning: understanding group, class and school progress to reflect on practice

One approach to gathering evidence to identify the progress learners have made over a period of time (summative assessment) is based on teacher assessment where teachers make judgements about a pupil's performance based on wide knowledge developed in different contexts and over time. In England, the previous system of national curriculum levels was abandoned from 2014 in favour of a more substantive focus by schools on specific learning achievements in relation to programmes of study. Schools and local authorities have developed different approaches to 'assessment without levels': a research report from the (English) National College for Teaching and Learning (Lilly et al., 2014) found many examples but identified significant areas for development. The Standards and Testing Agency provides online 'teacher assessment guidance' and 'teacher assessment exemplifications' to support teachers in deciding whether a pupil is working towards, at, or at greater depth within, the expected standard for core subjects of the curriculum.

Tests and tasks can be used to inform teacher assessment, but the greatest value of teacher assessment is that a wide range of evidence is considered, thus increasing validity.

If teacher assessment is to be used for summative and comparative purposes, then the development of teachers' understanding of standards is crucial for its reliability. Further, once teachers have made provisional judgements, moderation is required to ensure fairness to pupils and that the data produced are useful. Teachers should discuss their assessments of pupils' work with other colleagues in the same school and in other schools, and systems of moderation involving the local authority help ensure the comparability of assessment across a wider area.

Non-statutory tests and tasks

There are many tests that teachers and schools can and do use on an optional basis. Some of these were developed to assist with the monitoring of progress between points of statutory assessment and are marked by the teachers of the pupils being tested. This activity itself gives teachers an insight into the statutory assessment process, helps them become more familiar with standards, and provides them with detailed information about each child's performance.

A variety of other externally produced tests are used routinely by schools, although in some cases the reasons for doing so may be questioned. Despite arguments about there being 'too much testing' in schools, teachers appear to do significantly more testing than is formally required. A number of reasons for using additional tests are given, and some, such as the diagnosis of specific reading difficulties, may be laudable. In the main, however, it seems that the high-stakes nature of statutory assessment has a knock-on effect. In particular, it is felt to be necessary to assess performance more regularly and at other ages.

However, even more serious than the overuse of tests is the false confidence which may be put in their results, as noted earlier in this chapter. Broadfoot (2007) argues further that educational assessment and the measurement of human achievement 'can never be objective since they are inevitably limited by the social nature of the assessment situation and the values and culture which overlay the interpretation of the quality of a given performance' (p. 28) (Reading 14.1). The issue of reliability is probably greater with non-statutory tests because of the lack of checks and safeguards associated with statutory tests. Filer and Pollard (2000, Reading 14.7) showed how 'objective' assessment practices depend on the contexts and social practices in which performance, judgement and interpretation of judgement are produced, and so are vulnerable to bias and distortion.

Teacher assessment

Evidence from tests is only useful if it is used, and too much time spent gathering evidence will limit the time available to use evidence to improve learning. Schools, as part of their continuing self-evaluation and improvement action, should hold themselves accountable for the extent to which their actions are making a positive difference to children's learning. The IEAN principles identified at the beginning of this part of the chapter are also relevant for teachers and schools as they engage in processes of self-evaluation and improvement of learning and progression. The kind of assessment culture in a school will determine how well teachers and headteachers are able to use assessment evidence to inform improvement. If teachers or headteachers feel themselves to be judged, their ability to improve will diminish. The focus of self-evaluation should be children's learning and what actions might be taken to improve every child's learning. The following list of examples exemplifies some of the types of self-evaluation:

- The professional learning communities in which school managers and staff are engaged are crucial contexts for discussion and self-evaluation. It is through interaction in learning communities with colleagues and, on occasion, with visitors from professional groups such as local authority support staff, inspectors and representatives of organisations responsible for testing and examinations, that teachers develop professional capacities. These professional capacities include shared understandings of the quality of pupils' work and ability to make well-founded professional judgements and to plan improvements in learning with pupils on the basis of them.
- Descriptions of the learning and progress of groups, classes and the school as a whole are the crucial evidence. These summaries of group/class/school success could be based directly on the individual portfolios and teachers' notes referred to in the section above on recording and reflecting on individual learners' progress. In any case, it is important that they should describe strengths and possible needs in relation to the learning aims of the locally planned subjects' curricula and cross-curricular skills/elements.
- As with individual pupils, consideration of test data (statutory or otherwise) should focus on what patterns of performance presented in terms of statistics mean in terms of curricular learning aims.
- Discussion of the quality of learning and progression and of appropriate steps to improvement should include consideration of evidence, e.g. from teachers' individual and collaborative self-evaluation activities, of the appropriateness of levels of challenge in the tasks pupils do in relation to desirable progress, the quality of the learning activities undertaken and pupils' motivation and engagement.
- It may be important, in developing and operating a self-evaluation system of the kind advocated, to explain advantages and disadvantages of statistical and more descriptive systems to parents/guardians and to elected representatives with a direct interest in the school.

Using evidence over time to support pupil progress

As we have repeatedly seen in this book, it is crucial to build on pupils' current knowledge and understanding (see also Butt, 2011, Reading 14.3). Thus, at the start of any unit of work teachers need to use assessment information to achieve a cognitive match (see Chapter 10, p. 320 on lesson planning). When meeting a new group of pupils, teachers are reliant on the assessment information provided by previous teachers, often at an earlier stage of schooling. As time passes, the dependability of records diminishes as pupils will have progressed in their learning, or perhaps forgotten certain things. Recorded information then has to be supplemented by more up-to-date evidence.

When teaching any lesson, teachers will use assessment information formatively to adapt their teaching depending on the children's responses. At the end of each lesson, they will be noting, probably on the plans themselves or in a daybook, things that need to be taken into account in the next lesson. These may apply to all or just some of the pupils and could be about the need to reinforce a particular concept or omit a planned activity since the learning objective it was designed to support is already well grasped.

Towards the end of a unit, the teacher may devise a particular assessment activity focusing on the key learning objectives for that unit and will use the last period of time to extend the work or review those objectives, as the need is demonstrated. After a unit of work has been completed, notes will again be made to inform both the future teaching of that unit to other groups, and the future teaching of related units to the same group of pupils.

Whilst notes are useful on a day-to-day basis, progress over time can be tracked using a simple three-category system that records whether a pupil is 'yet to reach', is 'meeting' or 'exceeding' expectations. Periodically the attainment of both individuals and groups can be compared with both their previous and target attainment, and judgements made about whether they are on an appropriate learning trajectory, falling behind or exceeding expectations. Different scenarios should lead to different actions to support learning – for example, reviewing expectations, providing additional support or extending the challenge. Similarly, when expectations for a unit of work have been set in terms of what 'all', 'most' and 'some' of the pupils should attain, recording names against each category enables pupil tracking but without recourse to levels or grades (see James, 2015). It is important to remember that, despite their apparent attractiveness, numbers are a very blunt instrument when trying to represent learning.

Using assessment information to support children for transfer and transition

Assessment information has a particular and important role in effective transition (moving from one class to another within the same school) and transfer (when pupils move from one school to another). In order that the next teacher and/or school can extend each pupil's present attainment, building on strengths and addressing weaknesses, it is vital that key information from the present teacher's knowledge is passed on in a manageable way and at times when the information can be used effectively. In England there is a Common Transfer File that must be used when a pupil moves to another school in England, Wales,

reflectiveteaching.co.uk/rtps6/part4_ch14

Scotland or Northern Ireland. In Scotland a process of profiling is used to support transfer and transition at key points.

Successful transfer and transition go far beyond the mere passing on of assessment information (Sutton, 2000, 2012). In particular, principled, professional conversation between past and future teachers at times of transition and transfer is extremely valuable in bringing documentary information to life. However, while this may be possible when a class moves from one teacher to another, it becomes much more difficult when pupils are transferring from many primary schools to a secondary school with different teachers for each subject. Transfer of assessment information and meetings between teachers are the two key strategies in what Galton, Gray and Rudduck (1999) termed the 'managerial/bureaucratic bridge'. They also identified four other 'bridges' used to span the gap – perhaps even more significant but harder to build than the first. These are the social/personal bridge; the curriculum bridge; the pedagogical bridge; and the learning-to-learn bridge. So, important though assessment information is in smoothing pupils' transitions and transfers, it is only one aspect of this crucial process.

School governors, school districts and local authorities want to know about learning: understanding progress at the level of governors, district or local authority responsible for education to reflect on practice

School governors, district or local authorities, as part of their continuing self-evaluation and improvement action, also have accountability responsibilities. If guided by the IEAN principles, they would hold themselves accountable for the extent to which their actions are making a positive difference to children's learning.

- In principle, the summaries of group/class/school success described above could form part of the evidence considered by governors/district/local authority staff in deciding on appropriate support that might be offered to particular early years settings or schools.

- Consideration of test data (statutory or otherwise) would focus on what patterns of performance presented in terms of statistics mean in terms of curricular learning aims.

- Discussion of the support which the governors/district/local authority could offer to schools would include discussion of the quality of learning and progression and of appropriate steps to improvement, e.g. drawing on schools' own self-evaluation reports. (Many local authorities in the four UK countries already collaborate with individual schools in deciding on support and action required following the school's self-evaluation.)

reflectiveteaching.co.uk/rtps6/part4_ch14

- The district or local authority has a particularly relevant role in making elected representatives aware of the advantages and disadvantages of statistical and more descriptive systems of evaluation as bases for helping schools improve learning.

Politicians want to know about learning: the challenge of accountability

Education is an area of real concern to policymakers. Internationally, politicians feel a responsibility to be able to demonstrate that education is serving the country well socially and economically. The kinds of desirable development in approaches to gathering and using assessment evidence described previously represent a growing worldwide reaction to the often-well-intentioned use in many jurisdictions of the results of standardised and national or state testing to demonstrate the effectiveness of an education system. The positive aim of using these test results is to inform teachers, schools, education authorities and parents/guardians about learners' progress and to improve the performance of individuals, schools and whole countries by providing comparative information about others' performance. However well-intentioned this use of performance data, it has had unintended negative consequences over a long period of time, including narrowing of the curriculum, learning aims and the range and quality of pedagogical experience for learners. The use of test evidence as the basis of judging the quality of a teacher, a school, a district or a nation led to an intense focus on test content and techniques. Indeed 'teaching to the test' has been a consistent, common problem in many parts of the world. For example, Rottenberg and Smith (1990), writing about experience in the United States, commented that 'As the stakes become higher, in that more hangs on the results, teaching becomes more "test like"'. Teaching to the test in whatever context typically not only focuses on a narrow part of the curriculum but also involves much test preparation concentrating on examination technique, question spotting, mark gaining and practice questions.

In terms of comparison of national systems, governments are concerned with global economic competition and the effectiveness of the national workforce over the long term. Public education is, after all, funded by taxpayers, who rightly expect good use of their considerable investment. In the long run, the economic success of the country, including pensions and welfare for its older citizens, is seen to depend on the education of youngsters. Governments across the world therefore pay great attention to international comparisons of school performance – particularly as portrayed through the Programme for International Student Assessment (PISA), the Trends in International Mathematics and Science Study (TIMSS) and the Progress in International Reading Literacy Study (PIRLS) (Sturman, 2012, Reading 14.6). Although many of these international tests gather data from pupils in secondary schools, they often washback into earlier years of education. They help to define what matters in the curriculum.

The interpretation of evidence from international tests can be controversial. The chapters in *The Intersection of International Achievement Testing and Educational Policy*,

reflectiveteaching.co.uk/rtps6/part4_ch14

edited by Louis Volante (2016), describe a wide range of differing uses of and responses to international assessment data across countries. Results are, however, often boldly used for political purposes to 'blame' competing parties or to support a current policy position or action in pursuit of an outcome desired by a government or organisation. Hayward, MacBride and Spencer (2016), in Volante's book, describe how the Minister responsible for education in Scotland interpreted the 2009 PISA results as demonstrating that 'for Scottish education, the tide has turned', while his counterpart in England argued that the very similar results there were a major concern and showed the need for sweeping curricular and assessment reform.

There are also examples of where evidence from international tests has been used positively, e.g. PISA data. 'The Learning Curve' is a project to collate, summarise and analyse international data on the performance of school systems. It is funded by Pearson and uses the expertise of the Economist Intelligence Unit (see The Learning Curve brunner.cl/?p=4737). Michael Barber, Pearson's Chief Education Adviser, argues that international benchmarking of education systems has become ever more prevalent and increasingly influential in shaping education policy at local, regional and national levels. As studies by PISA and TIMSS become more sophisticated and longitudinal time sequences develop, there is ever more to learn about what successful education systems look like and how success can be achieved. So, discussion and interpretation of findings has become more sophisticated and aware of complexities influencing performance. In the early days of international benchmarking, education ministers and other leaders tended to worry more about the media impact than the implications for policy. Increasingly now, there is a continuous dialogue among education ministers and top officials around the world about the evidence from international benchmarking and the implications for education reform. The November 2014 report from The Learning Curve cautioned against simplistic conclusions but identified a number of lessons in relation to education and skills for life, including:

- Approximately half of the economic growth in developed countries in the last decade came from improved skills.
- 'Basic skills' are not enough – abilities important for social interaction are very important.
- It is much more effective to learn skills early in childhood than adulthood, but skills decline in adulthood if not used regularly.

Nevertheless, no matter how well intentioned, accountability mechanisms based on results of international surveys can have unintended and negative consequences, which detract from the aim of improvement. These include devoting significant time and national effort to local standardised testing, in addition to the international testing, rather than to active improvement of curriculum and pedagogy, despite familiarity with the well-known folklore saying that 'you don't fatten a pig by weighing it'. Klenowski and Carter (2016) refer to substantial curriculum and assessment reforms arising from international comparisons using standardised testing programmes, but also to their unintended damaging impacts. Bradbury and Roberts-Holmes (2018) have documented what they call 'the datafication' of primary and Early Years education. They argue that schools are becoming increasingly 'data obsessed' and risk losing sight of broader educational objectives. This phenomenon can be seen at all levels, from the single classroom to the nation state. It is particularly likely when the 'stakes' are high. Whilst tensions created by assessment attempting to serve multiple purposes will always exist, difficulties can be identified and may be ameliorated by awareness and understanding of key issues discussed in this chapter (see also Broadfoot, 2007, Reading 14.1; Stobart, 2008, Reading, 13.6).

Understanding progress at national and government level

Government decision-makers, national and local, need to be aware of advantages and disadvantages of statistical and more descriptive systems of evaluation as bases for helping schools improve learning.

- National testing can provide relevant assessment data, but there should be public awareness of its limitations in terms of coverage of what matters in education and of the degree of uncertainty involved in terms of validity and reliability and, therefore, of accuracy of test results.
- Similar points apply to the results of a country's engagement with international achievement tests, such as PISA, TIMSS and PIRLS.
- Alternative approaches to evidence gathering can provide high-quality evidence for policymakers without undesirable 'washback' on curriculum coverage and the quality of learning and teaching, i.e. using sample surveys of achievement, rather than national testing of all pupils.
- In responding to data from any of the possible sources of test results or descriptions of learning, the focus of policy making should be the learning represented by the patterns of results for different groups.
- A national policy for educational improvement should give attention to the quality of learning and teaching and of school life in general, not just to test performance.

CONCLUSION

The assessment of pupils' learning is crucial, complex and increasingly controversial in some countries including England. First and foremost, it is of immense importance to the pupils themselves: their life-chances can be significantly affected, both through their results and by the shaping of their self-image and motivation. However, the process of assessing pupils' learning is complex and requires expert judgement. Assessment outcomes also often have implications for teachers and headteachers, as their work is increasingly judged based on pupil results in formal assessments.

Teachers, therefore, need a deep understanding of assessment so that they can make the best decisions for their pupils' learning, and engage in informed dialogue with colleagues, pupils, parents, policymakers and the public.

The introduction to this chapter argued that the description, measurement and evaluation of learning are of great importance. The importance of a supportive assessment culture and the need to have a relentless focus on learning are crucial factors in the creation of a constructive learning environment where assessment is used to inform everyone's learning. The aim should be to:

- assess learning in ways that demonstrate what children and young people are learning, have learned and point to what they might next most usefully learn;
- ensure that assessment is closely aligned to what matters in a planned curriculum which consists of well-researched and carefully thought out ideas of progression in learning;
- use fair and manageable assessment approaches which do not have undesirable consequences, such as narrow teaching to relatively limited, simplistic objectives which are easily tested.

We hope your engagement with the chapter has convinced you of the importance of having a deep understanding of assessment and has given you food for thought and reflection about the complexities of describing progress in learning over time.

CHAPTER WEBPAGE

reflectiveteaching.co.uk offers additional professional resources for this chapter. For the chapter webpage, go to: **reflectiveteaching.co.uk/rtps6/part4_ch14**

There are lots of ideas for further reading on the webpage resources for Chapter 14. To ease further study, they follow the structure of the chapter and address both the issues, successes and problems associated with various forms of summative assessment and national systems of comparison.

This is a good moment to become more familiar with international assessment systems, which provide an influential context for national policies within the UK. The most influential group are those managed by the OECD. The Programme for International Student Assessment (PISA) has evaluated outcomes from school systems in over eighty countries from 2000. The latest results, for 2018, will be found at **oecd.org/pisa**. In addition to the sweeps of the main study of performance of 15-year-olds (continuously of science, maths and reading) there are now also tests of broader capabilities and initiatives to support national Development and a Test for Schools.

Take a look also at the opposition to the power of the OECD tests, for instance, at: **theguardian.com/education/2014/may/06/oecd-pisa-tests-damaging-education-academics**. In this letter to a newspaper, academics from around the world set out both the problems with PISA and also offer constructive suggestions for future development.

A reflective teacher needs to be aware of the issues and dilemmas associated with a focus on pupil, school and national outcomes. The resources associated with this chapter should help.

1 *Further Reading* on the chapter webpage makes it possible to both deepen and broaden understanding of assessment issues.
2 *Key Readings*, listed below, provides an annotated shortlist of sources to study.
3 Additionally, short extracts of many of the *Key Readings* are provided in *Readings for Reflective Teaching in Schools*.

KEY READINGS

Books that provide overviews of assessment are listed in the key readings for Chapter 13 but are also relevant to this chapter. Readings given below are more focused on the summative purposes of assessment but may also relate to the issues discussed in the previous chapter.

For an excellent overview of a wide range of issues, policies and practices in assessment, see:

> Broadfoot, P. (2007) *An Introduction to Assessment.* London: Continuum. **(Reading 14.1)**

A TLRP commentary provides a succinct overview of key issues:

> Mansell, W. and James, M. with the Assessment Reform Group (2009) *Assessment in Schools: Fit for Purpose? A Commentary by the Teaching and Learning Research Programme.* London: TLRP. **(Reading 14.5)**

James' comprehensive book covers many timeless assessment issues:

> James, M. (1998) *Using Assessment for School Improvement.* Oxford: Heinemann.

Two pamphlets by the Assessment Reform Group are particularly pertinent:

> Assessment Reform Group (2002) *Testing, Motivation and Learning.* Cambridge: University of Cambridge Faculty of Education.

> Assessment Reform Group (2006) *The Role of Teachers in Assessment of Learning.* London: Institute of Education.

Drawing on the analysis of more than a dozen research projects a book that promotes the development of teacher assessment is:

> Gardner, J., Harlen, W., Hayward, L. and Stobart, G. with Montgomery, M. (2010) *Developing Teacher Assessment.* Maidenhead: Open University Press.

Stobart provides an insightful analysis of the effects of a variety of tests and assessment practices:

> Stobart, G. (2008) *Testing Times: The Uses and Abuses of Assessment.* Abingdon: Routledge. **(Reading 13.6)**

For a comprehensive discussion of the examination and testing regime in England and its consequences see:

> Mansell, W. (2007) *Education by Numbers: The Tyranny of Testing.* London: Politico Publishing.

For a principled guide to classroom assessment, including target setting, see:

> Butt, G. (2011) *Making Assessment Matter.* London: Continuum. **(Reading 14.3)**

Two useful booklets for helping to understand and use assessment and assessment data are:

> Swaffield, S. and Dudley, P. (2010) *Assessment Literacy for Wise Decisions*, 3rd edn. London: Association of Teachers and Lecturers. (see also **Reading 13.5**)

Ofsted (2008) *Using Data, Improving Schools.* London: Ofsted. (**Reading 14.4**)

For developed example of a national assessment system with strong alignment to curriculum objectives, see:

Scottish Government (2011b) *Principles of Assessment in Curriculum for Excellence Building the Curriculum 5. A Framework for Assessment.* Edinburgh: Scottish Government. (**Reading 14.2**)

A developed, sociological analysis of assessment practices is offered in:

Filer, A. (ed.) (2000) *Assessment: Social Practice and Social Product.* London: Routledge. (see also **Reading 14.7**)

Based on a review of research evidence and two new surveys The Independent Commission on Assessment in Primary Education (ICAPE) in England recommended the removal of high stakes testing, and a greater emphasis on formative assessment of children's learning. ICAPE Final Report available from: https://www.icape.org.uk

RESEARCH BRIEFING 14.1
School league tables: Are they any good for choosing schools?

Key findings
Each year the Government and the media publish league tables of schools' academic performances and encourage parents to use them when choosing a secondary school for their children. Our work showed that these tables are highly misleading when it comes to school choice.

- The most high-profile measure – the percentage of children getting five A* to C grades at GCSE – says more about the differences in schools' intakes than it does about the differences in their quality.
- Value-added measures are superior in that they adjust for these initial differences, but deriving from approximately 200 students per school, are so noisy that it is hard to statistically separate many schools' performances from one another.
- Just as with stocks and shares, schools' value-added past performances are not reliable indicators of their future performances and crucially it is these future performances which are relevant when choosing a secondary school.

More should be done by the Government and the media to communicate these important limitations to parents.

The research
Our work focused on a fundamental problem in using school league tables for school choice: school league tables report the past performance of secondary schools, based on children who have just taken their GCSE exams, whereas what parents want to know is how schools will perform in the future when their own children take the exams. Consider parents who chose a secondary school for their child in autumn 2012. Their child entered school in autumn 2013 and took their GCSE exams in 2018. Thus, the information parents needed when choosing was how schools were predicted to perform in 2018. However, at the time of our work, the most recent information available was the school league table for 2011. Thus, there was a seven year gap between the available information and what parents wanted to know. Much can happen in seven years.

Research design
We focused on the Government's 'contextual value-added' (CVA) league tables as the Government promoted these as being the most meaningful way to compare schools. Clearly, the more schools' CVA performances change over a seven year period, the less reliable school league tables will be as a guide to schools' future performances. We examined the official school league table data and showed that many schools which were performing in the top quarter of schools in 2002 were below average seven years later. We then proceeded to illustrate just how unreliable school league tables are by predicting schools' current performance using data from seven years previously. These predictions are so imprecise that almost no schools can be distinguished reliably from one another. This means that, for choosing a school, the league tables are essentially meaningless and, by not communicating this fundamental problem to parents, they are highly misleading.

References for practitioners, journalists and policymakers
Leckie, G. and Goldstein, H. (2009) 'School league tables: Are they any good for choosing schools?' *Research in Public Policy, Bulletin of the Centre for Market and Public Organisation*, 8, 6–9.
Goldstein, H. and Leckie, G. (2008). 'School league tables: what can they really tell us?' *Significance*, 5, 67–9.

This work was carried out at the University of Bristol. See Chapter 4

Chapter 15
Social justice
Can we enable all children to succeed?

Introduction	482

Inequality in society	483

Social differentiation in classrooms and schools	484
Curriculum	485
Pedagogy	486
Assessment	488
Curriculum, pedagogy and assessment	489

Polarisation through peer culture	489

Identity formation, perception and self-belief	492

Diversity and differentiation	494
Social class	495
Ethnicity	496
Gender	497
Sexuality	497
Age	498
Physical appearance	499
Disability	499
Learning capacity	500

Summary	501

Social justice and life-chances	501

Conclusion	502

reflectiveteaching.co.uk/rtps6/part4_ch15

Part 4 Reflecting on consequences

INTRODUCTION

This chapter is concerned with everyday classroom practice and the provision of opportunities for children to learn and thrive. It considers the issues which a reflective teacher faces when promoting social justice and inclusion for the children and young people they teach. The chapter explores social inequalities and some educational processes through which social advantages and disadvantages are reproduced. Awareness of these is a starting point in promoting social justice.

It is to the credit of the teaching profession that there is considerable awareness of inequalities and of how they can be tackled. However, promoting social justice is not at all easy. As we will see, hard-to-justify patterns of difference are commonly found when hard evidence is carefully considered.

We make two key assumptions in the chapter:

- Diversity amongst a class of learners is to be expected and welcomed.
- *All* learners have the right to achieve and to realise their abilities.

Such assumptions are embedded in enduring, global concerns about social justice and equity. For example, the 2030 Agenda for Sustainable Development and its Goals (SDGs) includes SDG3: *Ensure healthy lives, promote wellbeing for all at all ages;* and SDG4: *Ensure inclusive, equitable quality education and promote lifelong learning opportunities for all.* Other internationally recognised goals are relevant for addressing systemic issues of poverty and hunger, inequalities and inclusive societies.

See Chapter 4

TLRP Principles

Two principles are of particular relevance to this chapter on social justice and opportunities:

Effective teaching and learning equips learners for life in its broadest sense. Learning should aim to help people to develop the intellectual, personal and social resources that will enable them to participate as active citizens, contribute to economic development and flourish as individuals in a diverse and changing society. This implies adopting a broad view of learning outcomes and ensuring that equity and social justice are taken seriously. (*Principle 1*)

Effective teaching and learning fosters both individual and social processes and outcomes. Learning is a social activity. Learners should be encouraged and helped to work with others, to share ideas and to build knowledge together. Consulting learners about their learning and giving them a voice is both an expectation and a right. (*Principle 7*)

---

reflectiveteaching.co.uk/rtps6/part4_ch15

The chapter is divided into six sections. The first demonstrates the extent of inequality in society. As we focus on our own lives, this may not always be apparent but some stark facts bring it home. The second major section draws examples from across the book to show how the foundational 'message systems' of schools – curriculum, pedagogy and assessment – reflect and tend to reproduce social differences. Pupils of course respond to differential treatment as it arises, and some ways in which this is reflected, and may be polarised, within peer culture is the subject of the third section. Pupils' overall experience of school is a consequence of such differentiation and polarisation processes, and the fourth section considers the ways in which this influences pupil identity – their sense of 'who they are' and 'what it might be possible to become'. The fifth section is devoted to a review of the many dimensions of diversity and difference which exist, and to some illustrative research about each of these. Finally, in the last section, we return to the 'bigger picture' to consider the impact of all these issues on life chances.

INEQUALITY IN SOCIETY

Some of the inequalities in UK society are stark. For example, here are a dozen, each of which indicates the deep-seated problems that exist despite the apparent commitments of our modern, liberal democracies:

- The average wealth of households in Britain's richest decile is over 300 times greater than that of the poorest 10 per cent of families.
- In the last decade, the number of billionaires has more than doubled, but people using foodbanks has grown from 25,000 to over a million.
- Although women make up 51 per cent of the population, they form only 29 per cent of MPs, 25 per cent of judges and 24 per cent of FTSE 100 directors.
- On average, women spend more than twice as many hours as men doing unpaid work.
- Around 1.2 million women suffer domestic abuse a year and, every day, there are some 250 rapes or attempted rapes. Conviction rates are low.
- Adults identifying as lesbian, gay, bisexual and trans (LGBT) form approximately 3 per cent of the UK population. During schooling, they report significant amounts of bullying.
- Black workers with degrees earn 23 per cent less on average than White workers.
- Around 30 per cent of Pakistani, Bangladeshi and Black people live in overcrowded accommodation, while under 10 per cent of White people face the same challenges.
- In schools, Black Caribbean and Mixed White/Black Caribbean children have rates of permanent exclusion about three times that of the pupil population as a whole.

- Although over 4 million disabled people are in work, disabled people are almost twice as likely to be unemployed as non-disabled people.
- Almost half of the 4.5 million children living in poverty are in a family where someone is disabled.
- Of the 1.3 million children in England with Special Educational Needs and Disabilities (SEND), only a fifth succeed in getting a legally enforceable support plan. Almost half of all permanent exclusions from schools are of pupils with SEND.

It is clear that, whilst everyone shares the experience of growing up and learning through life, we do so in many different circumstances. The outcome is surprisingly high levels of inequality. To the extent that it can, the education system tries to challenge this – though, as we will see, this is by no means easy.

Research Briefing 15.1 on p. 508, produced by EuroHealthNet in 2020, summarises European patterns in health, education, inequality and wellbeing. The Network is committed to equity and social inclusion throughout life and uses research syntheses to influence policies of national governments and international agencies. As we can see from the EuroHealthNet briefing, education, health and wellbeing through life are inextricably linked together, with socio-economic status and its extremes of wealth and poverty being the 'number one' determining factor.

SOCIAL DIFFERENTIATION IN CLASSROOMS AND SCHOOLS

In this section, we reflect on some of the issues raised in earlier chapters which bear on social justice and processes of social differentiation within schools. The discussion is framed by the classic work of a sociologist, Basil Bernstein (1924–2000). Bernstein produced a very complex theory but, for our purposes here, some powerful, core ideas are highlighted.

Bernstein conceptualised three 'message systems' in schools – curriculum, pedagogy and assessment (see Bernstein, 1977). Together, he argued, these three aspects of school life provide a deep structure for pupil experiences. They thus influence the ways in which young people begin to think about themselves – their identities. The ways in which schools respond to difference, say in terms of social class, race, gender or sexuality, thus ripples on through its influence on pupils. The cumulative effect of whatever is done in the micro-world of everyday classroom interaction can have major implications for life chances in the future. In such ways, to a greater or lesser extent, schools contribute to the reproduction of many features of society from generation to generation – unless, of course, aware teachers are able to intervene!

You may notice that the chapters of this book reflect aspects of these three message systems, and it makes sense to now take stock of the effect of schools on social justice.

Despite value commitments and best efforts, we may find that there are intrinsic aspects of educational practice which mean that 'education cannot compensate for society' (Bernstein, 1970). In any event, it is right to try and, for many pupils, teachers and schools certainly do make a difference.

A starting point for making a difference is to clearly understand how processes of social differentiation work, and this chapter is intended to help in that. We begin then, with the first 'message system' – curriculum.

Curriculum

We saw in Chapter 9 how national curricula reflect aims and values as expressed by governments on behalf of society. These are then interpreted through successive stages and layers of implementation. Particular forms of knowledge, concepts, skills and attitudes feature more, or less, over time as political requirements ebb and flow and as the science of teaching and learning becomes better established. The key factor in making sense of all this is teacher professionalism which has tended to uphold an ideal of a 'balanced curriculum' as the foundation for a 'good education'.

Debates about how to teach the curriculum, through single, academic subjects or by deploying such knowledge through more integrated, practical work, are unlikely to cease – for each has an established rationale and value. However, the approach to the curriculum which is taken can have a differentiating effect when it transforms into tensions between Academic vs Vocational curricula. At this point, the social and economic status of different subjects comes into play and the subjects which young people choose to study at an advanced level can have a significant effect on their future employment. This is a very tangible form of curricular 'message'.

In Chapter 10, Planning, we looked at three levels of curricular planning – for the long, medium and short term. We saw how schemes of work need to provide for *progression* in subject matter, but also how this should be complemented by offering a *relevant* curriculum. As the argument was put there:

> There is little doubt that children and young people learn most effectively when they understand the purposes and context of the tasks and challenges with which they are faced. When a pupil complains that an activity is 'pointless', is 'boring' or that they 'don't see what it's for', then the curriculum is failing to satisfy the criterion of relevance. (p. ???)

This is of crucial importance for issues of social differentiation and social justice, for national curricula are rarely progressive. For example, after the 'Black Lives Matter' and 'Me Too' movements you might have expected to see more attention being paid to race and gender in a national curriculum. The English and History curricula might be a starting point, but ensuring the accessibility of all curricular subjects would be important. Sometimes this is done by teachers, particularly by schools adapting to serve their communities, but national curricula are so contested that they tend to lag behind.

reflectiveteaching.co.uk/rtps6/part4_ch15

The result is that the school curriculum can seem to be less relevant for some young people than it is for others. It is hard to motivate some groups, and academic performance suffers of course.

Pedagogy

We will draw across several chapters in considering pedagogy and the 'messages' it might convey.

Chapter 11 is a starting point, because it includes an important section on 'Pedagogy, Knowledge and Learning'. That discussion progresses to consider various perspectives on pedagogy: 'critical', 'culturally relevant', 'effective', etc. The point is that pedagogy can be thought about, and overtly or tacitly theorised, in very different ways. Many teachers have a commitment to promoting pupil agency, opportunities and 'potential' but find that this can be challenging to deliver in contemporary classroom conditions. Recent educational decision-makers, particularly in England, have been influenced by arguments for 'progression' in learning, and exam boards have introduced detailed subject-by-subject curriculum specification and assessment. There is a tension here though, for the pedagogic flexibility which is needed to respond to diverse pupil interests and needs can easily be jeopardised by statutory or assessment-driven curriculum requirements. Sadly, differences between students, when exposed by an inappropriate curriculum and pedagogy, often generate judgements about pupil deficits rather than a critique of the provision itself.

All pedagogies present 'opportunities to learn'. But what sort of opportunities are they? For whom are they most suitable? Whose successes do they enable? Whom do they constrain?

A very different example of the influence of pedagogy in providing opportunities is provided by the months of home learning which were required during the COVID pandemic of 2020–21. At various times during that period, schools were closed and 'home education' was called for. Many teachers struggled to provide meaningful, well-matched assignments across the curriculum, and many parents struggled to provide support and adequate digital resources. For a large number of pupils, this was a time of uncertainty and stress – with damaging consequences on learning, mental health and wellbeing. However, these difficulties were not experienced equally. Later research showed that pupils from poorer families were significantly more likely to have suffered badly from this experience. As a report from the Education Endowment Foundation put it:

> Research shows consistent patterns. Pupils have made less academic progress compared with previous year groups. There is a large attainment gap for disadvantaged pupils, which seems to have grown since the start of the pandemic. (EEF, 2021)

The point made about social differentiation is a simple one. The ways in which pupils are taught will suit them to different degrees. One method may be great for some, but not for others. Skilled teachers will have a repertoire of strategies at their disposal and will be sensitive to pupil needs in deploying them.

Managing pupil behaviour is one of the most important pedagogic tasks for any teacher, and this was the subject of Chapter 7. The underlying message of that chapter is that pupils normally present few behavioural problems if they are effectively *engaged* in the curriculum and other aspects of classroom life. To achieve this, teachers must both establish their classroom authority *and* provide a stimulating and appropriate curriculum. Processes involved in establishing authority are particularly prone to having socially differentiating effects, however unintended these may be. For example, Chapter 7 discussed teacher expectations, self-presentation in the classroom and the use of language. These are quite subtle aspects of interaction between teachers and pupils and it is terribly easy, in the ebb and flow of classroom life, for teachers to convey a differential valuing of some pupils over others.

For example, the amount and quality of attention given, such as feedback on students' efforts, is particularly important. If some pupils get more attention than others, this will certainly be noticed. Those who feel relatively neglected may become more disengaged, just as those receiving more support in their learning become more confident. This is one of the most significant ways in which 'expectations' are conveyed. They begin merely as tiny incidents in the school day, but they sow the seeds of beliefs about personal value and identity. Cumulatively, such differentiating effects build to affect self-image. So what to do?

The solution lies in trying to be very aware of any patterns in one's own behaviour and consciously committing to strategies which pro-actively seek to include and value each child. Because of the diversity which pupils bring, it is always possible to identify qualities to value, and the practice of overtly doing so will go a long way to demonstrating that all pupils are being respected and treated fairly. So, to establish authority, make a point of 'catching 'em being good'; make sure you pay attention to those on the periphery; introduce topics and experiences to draw in those who may find the curriculum challenging; be careful in the language you choose to use and think about the tone of voice adopted. Above all, try to take pleasure from, and see the best in, each child. Be particularly careful when you are feeling angry, frustrated, or tired! If you can establish authority with expectations with are both high and appreciative of all, then you will have created the interpersonal foundations of an inclusive relationship with your pupils.

Perhaps the most significant form of pedagogic differentiation used in primary schools concerns the management of classroom groups or year-group sets for teaching some subjects.

Grouping children by attainment is commonplace in the UK, and is often talked about, inaccurately, in terms of 'ability'. It is common that schools aim to teach mixed classes for many subjects, but opt for the creation of sets of pupils who are attaining at particular levels in highly structured subjects, such as Mathematics. There may also be more fine-grained setting at more advanced levels. Differentiation by attainment is thus organisationally convenient and is intended to make teaching easier by clustering together pupils with similar educational needs. Saljo and Hjorne (2009) describe categorisation in the school context as 'something people do to manage their daily chores' (p. 156), and it is likely to be done with the best of intentions for educational and organisational purposes.

reflectiveteaching.co.uk/rtps6/part4_ch15

However, longstanding research evidence shows that attainment-based grouping is not an effective way of raising attainment for most pupils (see **Toolkit Evidence 15.1**, p. 508; Ireson and Hallam, 2001, Reading 15.4). In summary, pedagogic practice and forms of school organisation may or may not be inclusive. Some pedagogic strategies may increase injustice by providing opportunities to some which are not available to, or suitable for, others.

Assessment

It is worth considering from first principles the interactive processes and potential consequences of classroom assessment. What we have are older and more knowledgeable teachers with socially ascribed authority to judge the performance of pupils. There is a power relationship here and the pupil is intrinsically vulnerable to the judgements made and fed back by the teacher. Furthermore, feedback typically takes place in public settings, so that the whole class, or year group even, is often able to form a view about who is 'good at' or 'struggles with' whatever is being learned. In due course, even parents come to know when reports are provided or examinations are faced. For pupils, the stakes are very high – and yet, to learn effectively, it is necessary to be open to trying things out, getting things wrong and trying again.

The experience of children who find learning difficult is thus likely to be very different from that of those who learn easily, and contrastive cycles of learning and behaviour, as discussed in Chapter 4, are commonplace in schools.

To avoid, or mitigate, such differentiating processes it is vital for teachers to use their power to greatest effect. This is one of the reasons why it is so important to focus on the quality of feedback which is provided to pupils in respect of their efforts. Feedback, be it in the form of a gesture, a spoken comment, annotated work, or a grade or mark, is at a relatively fine level of granularity in the teacher–pupil relationship – and yet it crucially accumulates to enable the learner to build a view of themselves.

Taking a more detailed look, in Chapter 13 five indicators of good practice in feedback were discussed:

1 Feedback should be timely and clear.
2 Use comments alone and avoid marks, grades or levels.
3 Comments on work and possible improvement should be specific.
4 Pupils should respond to feedback
5 Make feedback and marking practice explicit and manageable.

The idea is to connect directly with each learner's experience and to maximise their agency in the learning process. The particular benefit of accurate, timely and appreciative feedback is that it focuses pupil attention onto the specific, proximate learning for progress to be made.

Where teachers have the skills and understanding to provide such feedback, their pupils will almost certainly 'take off' and progress. Where teachers do not, then the outcome is likely to be far less good. Having said that, the same applies of course to the support offered to young people across the class or year group. Those who get good feedback should spiral up, whilst those who do not risk spiralling down.

The quality of feedback is as powerful in terms of social differentiation as it is in support of learning.

Curriculum, pedagogy and assessment

To summarise this section, we have illustrated each of the three 'message systems' which Bernstein saw as structuring school experience – curriculum, pedagogy and assessment.

Teachers may be aware of these underlying issues – but their consequences can be hard to counter. Curricular structure and content, teaching and grouping practices, and forms of assessment and evaluation tend to embed particular forms of differentiation.

One of Bernstein's many admirers summarised his analysis in respect of social class:

> Through a consideration of the inner workings of the types of educational practice, Bernstein contributed to a greater understanding of how schools reproduce what they are ideologically committed to eradicating – social-class advantages in schooling and society. Bernstein's analysis of the social-class assumptions of pedagogic discourse and practice is the foundation for linking micro-educational processes to the macro-sociological levels of social structure and class and power relations. (Sadovnik, 2001, p. 691)

Beyond social class, the 'message systems' of curriculum, pedagogy and assessment are equally powerful in respect of gender, ethnicity and sexuality – particularly when 'difference' becomes interpreted as 'deficit'.

We have focused on social differentiation and school experience, but a multiplier effect results from the ways in which pupils respond.

POLARISATION THOUGH PEER/ STUDENT CULTURE

When children and young people share similar experiences at school, particularly in relation to success or failure, friendships often form.

Indeed, whenever people of any age regularly experience being 'differentiated' by organisations or in other circumstances, they tend to bond together and provide each other with mutual support. Such friendship groups develop their own perspectives – ways of thinking about both themselves and other people.

For primary education, this process was first studied by Brian Jackson in 1964. His book on junior schools, *Streaming: An Education System in Miniature*, identified the

reflectiveteaching.co.uk/rtps6/part4_ch15

adverse effects of what he termed 'social learning'. Children placed in low streams devalued themselves, were likely to be disengaged from school and appeared more likely to become 'delinquent' in the future.

Similar processes occur even in fully mixed-ability classes when children become differentiated as awareness of performance becomes tangible. Successful pupils have progress to celebrate, but those who are less successful merely share a sense of disappointment or failure – perhaps with a lack of understanding too. Children who share experiences tend to bond together and, as they bond, the cultures of each group tend to be affirmed more strongly, particularly if there is rivalry or competition between groups.

In a study of mixed-ability classes by Pollard (1985) the strategies of 'Goodies', 'Jokers', and 'Gangs' were identified in later primary years. Goodies tended to conform to teacher wishes and 'be good' in most circumstances. They coped with school be keeping their heads down. Gang members often experienced relative failure at school and felt misunderstood. They often thought that teachers were unfair and, for mutual support and affirmation, they developed close friendships and were willing to challenge teacher authority at times. Jokers tended to be high-attaining children who also liked to 'have a laugh' at school. They got on very well with teachers, despite a fair degree of mischief or low-level deviance.

In sociological terms, such processes of bonding have been termed 'polarisation', for they ironically involve a reinforcement of the initial differentiation as the children or young people respond to it themselves. In a sense, it is a form of cultural coping strategy, developed in response to experience and circumstances. However, it is a strategy that can also easily reinforce differences and create educational exclusion, even if this is an unintended consequence.

If children reject school values over many years to protect their own pride and self-esteem, then this can have significant adverse effects. Pollard and Filer (1999) traced the 'school careers' of individual pupils and recorded the social influence of peer, family and teacher relationships as they formed increasingly differentiated and unique identities. Warin's book (2010), *Stories of Self*, is a similar longitudinal study of how children's identity and well-being develop as they negotiate school life.

This analysis, of how the effects of school differentiation are amplified by pupil culture, is summarised in Figure 15.1, and a more complete discussion is available in Pollard (1987a, Reading 15.2).

Figure 15.1
Differentiation–
polarisation
process and its
consequences

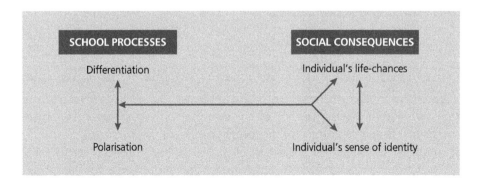

Chapter 15 Social justice   491

Polarisation has also been identified in relation to gendered cultures within primary school peer groups, and shows the overlapping of dimensions of difference. For example, Reay's study (2001) of girls' friendship groups in primary – 'Spice Girls', 'Nice Girls', 'Girlies' and 'Tomboys' – showed a range of responses to school circumstances, but highlighted the way this was overlain by cultures of femininity. As she put it, 'despite widely differentiated practices, all of the girls at various times acted in ways which bolstered boys' power at the expense of their own' (p. 153). Renold (2001) showed how dominant ideas about masculinity shape boys' dispositions to schooling, schoolwork and academic achievement. She found that, even in primary school, high-achieving boys felt the need to use 'disguise' to maintain an apparently masculine disdain for schoolwork, and wanted to differentiate themselves from girls. In such ways, pervasive cultural differences within our societies are reinforced by social processes within schools, classrooms and playgrounds.

Our challenge as teachers is to monitor the differentiating effect of our routine practices in relation to the polarising processes which may then occur within pupil cultures or as a result of pupil coping strategies. As we have seen, forms of setting, grouping, division, feedback and assessment are particularly relevant here.

The key processes lie in a chain, as classroom differentiation is reinforced by polarisation, and then begins to affect the self-image and self-esteem of individual pupils. Subsequent effects may be manifest in terms of participation, learning, attainment, exclusion and life-chances.

Reflective Activity 15.1

Aim: To reflect on common forms of social differentiation and polarization.

Evidence and reflection: Review the processes described in this section and read Pollard's article on 'social differentiation' in **Reading 15.2**. In that Reading, eight specific aspects of classroom differentiation are raised. Consider each in turn as they may apply to your own classroom.

- The official curriculum
- Classroom organisation and management
- Language
- Interpersonal relationships
- Teacher expectations
- Assessment
- The hidden curriculum
- Polarisation within pupil culture

Choose **one** issue for particular attention, and target developments in your practice which you think will help you to provide more equal opportunities for targeted students. Try out your ideas for, say, a week. As you do this, identify the things which

---

reflectiveteaching.co.uk/rtps6/part4_ch15

> go well and consider how you were successful. Think about the things which did not go so well. Consider the difficulties you encounter and alternative approaches you could try.
>
> *Extension:* You might like to consider the ways in which various forms of differentiation and polarisation may interconnect. A specific focus helps to make development work manageable, but is likely to highlight other issues for further exploration. Pace classroom development work, reviewing and planning as you go.

IDENTITY FORMATION, PERCEPTION AND SELF-BELIEF

Identity formation and self-confidence are strongly influenced by children's experiences of differentiation and polarisation at school.

To illustrate this, we draw on the work of Pollard and Filer (1996, 1999, 2007), which reported on a detailed longitudinal study of children progressing through twelve years of primary and secondary schooling. Experiences and relationships with teachers, peers, parents and siblings were recorded – with particular attention to effects on learning. Most children managed to attain and maintain viable social identities as classroom (and other) settings changed over time. For some, success come easily but, for others, survival was more of a struggle from year to year. The curriculum, for some of these children, was not easy to relate to and, with cumulative effects, they fell behind. Others were perhaps able to draw on home resources and, in any event, achieved more regular success. One way or another, the young people responded actively to the contexts they experienced, and gradually developed their personal, strategic biographies.

Analysis yielded a holistic understanding of learning and pupil identity. In particular, a cyclical model of learning and identity was presented (see Reading 1.2). This addressed five key questions: Where and when is learning taking place? Who is learning? What is to be learned? How supportive is the learning context? What are the outcomes? A more elaborated representation of this model is provided in Figure 15.2.

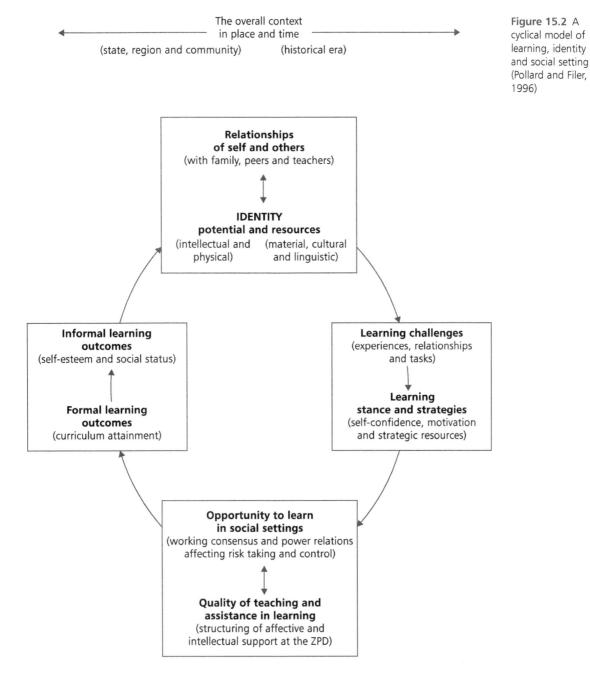

Figure 15.2 A cyclical model of learning, identity and social setting (Pollard and Filer, 1996)

494 Part 4 Reflecting on consequences

At the top of the model in Figure 15.2 there is reference to the overall context in place and time. This ecognizes that, in tackling school life, children are influenced by the ways of thinking, language and patterns of action which are experienced in their culture.

The model then represents learning in a cyclical process. The prior identity and confidence of the learner is a starting point, with which new learning challenges are faced by drawing on a repertoire of learning strategies. Hopefully, a positive learning stance is adopted (a sense of 'mastery') but some children will feel far less in control ('learned helplessness' in Dweck's terms – see p. 57, Reading 2.6).

The next stage is crucial for it is the primary responsibility of the teacher. What are the opportunities to learn? And what is the quality of teaching and learning? This is where high levels of social differentiation in routine classroom practices can have damaging implications. Or, seen another way, it is where inclusive strategies for teaching and learning may really make a positive difference. Indeed, there are many anecdotes about 'the teacher who changed my life'. When you read such stories, or listen to them, they are often about inspirational teachers who created new opportunities to learn and who provided exceptionally high-quality teaching which made a direct and meaningful connection with the learner.

And thus we move on to the outcomes. We may appreciate what is formally learned in curriculum terms, but success also enhances self-confidence and social status – just as failure diminishes them. And these, in turn, feed forward to identity and further cycles in the process of learning and becoming.

Expert Question

Consequence: how do assessment outcomes lead towards recognised qualifications and a confident sense of personal identity?

This question contributes to a conceptual framework representing enduring issues and teacher expertise (see Chapter 16).

A key point is that the acquisition of formal knowledge and skills cannot be divorced from learners' attempts to make personal meaning of themselves and of their lives. The form which the latter takes is primarily contingent on social, cultural and other contextual factors, and there are both continuities and variations of these as individuals progressively engage with new learning challenges.

The way in which social differentiation feeds forward into polarisation within peer culture and on to deeply personal cycles of learning should thus be apparent. This is the chain of connection, which links routine teacher work on curriculum, pedagogy and assessment to lifecourse trajectories and social justice. School experience influences the formation of 'identity'.

If the major inequalities of society are to be overcome, or moderated, the confidence and success of *all* children and young people must be nurtured. We, as teachers, have opportunities in our every day, routine practices to contribute to such ambitions.

DIVERSITY AND DIFFERENTIATION

The differences which make everyone unique should, of course, be acknowledged and celebrated. The challenge then, is to celebrate diversity whilst avoiding the damaging effects of social differentiation.

reflectiveteaching.co.uk/rtps6/part4_ch15

On the one hand, difference is simply a characteristic of being a person: a positive feature of the human condition to be recognised and celebrated. Human differences can also produce discomfort, even fear, especially when it is unfamiliar or considered abnormal. Thomas and Loxley (2007) explored these tensions in schools, arguing that: 'Whether difference is seen positively, as diversity, or negatively as deviance or deficit, depends on the mindset of the person or group of people who observe that difference' (p. 93) (Reading 15.3).

In this section we examine diversity as part of the human condition. To do so we introduce eight dimensions which are often used to recognise social differences: social class, ethnicity, gender, sexuality, age, physical appearance, disability and learning capacity. This list is only suggestive of the limitless dimensions of difference that may impact on educational and other experiences. Moreover, contemporary research often examines how social advantages and disadvantages associated with each category may be compounded by the advantages or disadvantages associated with another (e.g. Sewell, 1997; Plummer, 2000; Youdell, 2006; Alexander, 2010). Of course, consequences accumulate in school settings, as we discuss at the end of this chapter.

Whilst making what is essentially a moral case for social justice, it is also worth bearing the law in mind. The Equality Act 2010 of England, Wales and Scotland has extended the duties of teachers and schools so that key dimensions of difference (named as 'characteristics') are protected. This Act makes it unlawful to discriminate against a person on the basis of age, disability, race, sex, sexual orientation, gender reassignment, marriage and civil partnership, pregnancy and maternity or religion or belief. Similar legislation applies in Northern Ireland and the Republic of Ireland. (See Richardson, 2009, Reading 15.1, for underlying principles of the legislation and their implications for schools.)

Social class

Some commentators argue that social class provides the circumstances through which gender, race, ability, age and sexuality are played out. Indeed, inequalities of wealth, income and material opportunities remain highly significant in determining life-chances (Feinstein, Vorhaus and Sabates, 2008b, Reading 1.6) and there has been no 'withering away of class' in the lived experience of UK citizens. For example, for the last twenty years, there has been a consistent trend for the gap between the highest and lowest incomes to widen each year. One consequence was the fact that in 2018 there were 4.6 million children living in families experiencing poverty (Social Metrics Commission, 2019). However, at the same time, approximately 8 per cent of school-age children attended private schools. A UNICEF report (2021) compares children's material wellbeing in the UK with other 'economically advanced' nations and warns that child poverty is worsening. Recently, the UK government has committed to 'levelling up' and reducing geographical disparities of wealth is part of that ambition.

Not all definitions of class are based on income, wealth or economic capital; some focus more on status and level of education. The concepts of 'cultural capital' (Bourdieu and

Passeron, 1977) and 'social capital' (Coleman, 1988) were developed to describe the knowledge, attitudes and experiences which socialisation within a 'higher-class' family may offer, and which complements material wealth. One of their major insights into educational inequality is that children with social and cultural capital are likely to fare better in education than their otherwise comparable peers with less valuable social and cultural assets. For example, parents may deploy their economic, cultural, social and emotional capital by choosing to live in a particular area to access a favoured school and through the nature of the experiences and support which they provide for their children. Such strategies are manifestations of the process of 'social reproduction', in which one generation seeks to pass on the advantages of its social position to another (see, for instance, Connell et al., 1982).

Can we both affirm the diverse backgrounds and cultural resources which children embody whilst seeking to extend these by introducing new forms of knowledge?

Ethnicity

The term 'ethnicity' describes combinations of ancestry, heritage, religion, culture, nationality, language and region. As such, we all have ethnic identities. Globalisation and changing patterns of migration have challenged the idea that ethnicities are fixed. Cultures and social structures, compounded by differences of historical development, can make a considerable difference to people's experience, leading to much variation amongst ethnic groups.

> ### Expert Question
>
> **Inclusion:** *are all learners treated respectfully and fairly in both formal and informal interaction?*
>
> Such questions contribute to a conceptual framework underpinning professional expertise (see Chapter 16).

The population of the UK is, increasingly, ethnically diverse. Alibhai-Brown (2000) argued that Britain should adopt an approach which accepts the diverse contributions of different cultures and groups, past and present – including those White communities, rich or poor, which also feel excluded from significant aspects of modern society and which may harbour racism (see also Gay, 2010).

Racism is the term that describes processes in society which adversely affect people according to their identification as members of one ethnic group or another. Racism has a long history in the UK going back to the imperial past and beyond, and it has taken root in the discourse and structure of society. Racial prejudice is also reflected within the cultures of children and young people (Connolly, 1998; Troyna and Hatcher, 1992). Gillborn's (2008) analysis of research in the UK using Critical Race Theory offers, in his words, 'a damning critique of the racist nature of the education system'. Such prejudices may be further amplified by the social, cultural, legal and political structures that have developed over time.

In recent years, controversy about public statues of people associated with the Slave Trade has stimulated discussion of some of these issues. Some people defend public

reflectiveteaching.co.uk/rtps6/part4_ch15

endorsement despite the views of many in the Black community, whilst a growing number of others believe that moving controversial monuments to a museum better enables the full historical context to be presented.

In what ways might the curriculum reflect Britain's imperial past? If you were a pupil from a minority group with a post-colonial history, how would you feel about such a curriculum?

Gender

There is an accepted scientific basis for recognising two sexes: there are differences within the reproductive process and there is also evidence of genetic and neurobiological differences affecting some innate behaviours and brain functioning (Elliott, 2017). The term 'gender', on the other hand, describes the *social definition of sex roles* rather than the biological distinction itself. Indeed, masculinity and femininity should not be considered to be inherent biological properties, but as socially constructed products of society. They arise from, and condition, social processes.

'Sexism' is the operation of forces in society by which members of one sex obtain advantages over the other, because of and through their gender. *Patterns* of discrimination prompt us to ask questions such as how school life contributes to restrictive or enabling socialisation (Skelton and Francis, 2006).

This is a complex topic and, overall, girls do tend to perform better than boys when in school. Considerable attention has been paid to overcoming this gap by enhancing the performance of boys (for example, see Younger and Warrington, 2007).

Some subjects, particularly in secondary education, tend to be particularly favoured by boys and others by girls. For example, Archer and DeWitt (2017) studied young people's aspirations regarding science and the challenge of encouraging girls to take up STEM subjects.

We might ask ourselves: Do the ethos, curriculum and pedagogic practices of the school offer equitable support to both boys and girls?

Sexuality

In some communities there is still considerable social stigma associated with open expressions of sexuality and many teachers may be hesitant about addressing such issues. Yet the recognition and acceptance of such differences may be extremely important to the provision of equal opportunities for children, young people, teachers or parents who identify as lesbian, gay, bisexual or trans (LGB&T).

Discrimination against homosexuality has been common in the past, obliging many to work under the continual stress of pretence and secrecy. The notorious 'Section 28', which

reflectiveteaching.co.uk/rtps6/part4_ch15

Part 4 Reflecting on consequences

became part of the Local Government Act (1986), prohibited the 'promotion' of homosexuality in England and Wales, including 'the teaching in any maintained school of the acceptability of homosexuality as a pretended family relationship', and exerted a strong influence on the content of teaching about sexuality. The Act was repealed in 2003. However, cultural forces still exert huge influences on sexual identities and bullying directly and through social media is often reported. A research review (Hudson-Shard and Metcalf, 2016) concluded:

> Evidence shows young LGB&T people face a hostile environment – in education, at home and in wider society – at a stage in their lives when they are particularly in need of support and approbation. Experiences at this age have life-long implications for mental health and resilience. (2016: iv)

How, and at what age, should primary school pupils be introduced to sexuality as part of people's identity?

Age

The Universal Declaration of Children's Rights establishes the principle that children and young people should not be discriminated against because of their age. Research in the philosophy, history, psychology and sociology of childhood has repeatedly demonstrated how children's perspectives, activities and rights are structured, ignored or constrained by adults (Archard and MacLeod, 2002; James and James, 2004; Miller, 1997). Alternative conceptions of children as being either 'innocent' or 'corrupt' (Aries, 1962; Cunningham, 2006) can be found in popular culture and public policy, with the associated adult responses of both protection and moralising. Indeed, there is a discernible tension around whether the purpose of education is the protection or correction of children during childhood (Linklater, 2010).

In the past, teachers have been accused of constraining children because of a misplaced adherence to Piaget's conception of 'stages of development' (Walkerdine, 1984). Indeed, there remains a risk that linear assumptions of progress or achievement through schools' curricula could have a similarly limiting effect (Hart et al., 2004, see Reading 1.4) (see also Chapter 2, p. 24).

More commonly within the profession today, a view of children and young people as active agents, interacting, or co-creating their own childhoods is accepted (Dahlberg et al., 1999; Mayall, 2002; John, 2003). Indeed, longitudinal studies of educational experiences year-on-year have shown how children and young people negotiate their circumstances and act strategically to create and pursue their interests (see Pollard and Filer, 1999, for an analysis of 'pupil career').

One aspect of school experience that has received particular attention in the United Kingdom and in the United States is how the accident of birth date combined with the start of the school year produces age effects on academic attainment that can be traced throughout primary and secondary school (e.g. Crawford, Dearden and Maghir, 2007). In

reflectiveteaching.co.uk/rtps6/part4_ch15

particular, children who are young in their year can be disadvantaged when immaturity is misinterpreted as a lack of ability, producing an exclusionary effect within the classroom.

To what extent do you think the children in your class feel respected as learners?

Physical appearance

Physical appearance and perceptions of physical attractiveness have been found to have an important influence on our identities, behaviour and experiences, both in terms of what we expect for ourselves, and how others respond to us. A high proportion of children in the UK are overweight, with significant implications for long-term health (NHS Digital, 2020).

In the 1960s and 1970s social and psychological research focused on understanding teachers' expectations of pupils. Findings showed that children's attractiveness was significantly associated with how intelligent a teacher expected a child to be, how interested in education their parents were expected to be, how far the child was likely to progress in school and how popular they would be with their peers (Clifford and Walster, 1973; also Seligman, Tucker and Lambert, 1972). Subsequent research has continued to affirm a correlation between physical appearance, educational outcomes, self-esteem or motivating factors, and children and young people's standing within their peer group (for example, O'Dea and Abraham, 2000). For this reason, as well as impacting on teachers' expectations, physical appearance is also closely linked to developing a sense of identity.

Frances (2004) studied the social and psychological challenges encountered by children and young people who have facial disfigurements, which may be congenital (such as birthmarks or cleft lip) or acquired (burns or scars). She noted that those with visible differences felt a particular need to be affirmed and included.

What support might be offered to children with concerns about their appearance?

Disability

Understanding disability as a question of rights and opportunities has developed as a result of people with disabilities articulating a strong voice and rejecting society's traditional views of the disabled as inadequate, damaged, less than whole or less than fully human. The success of the Paralympic Games, following the Olympic cycle, has reflected this contemporary awareness.

Sociological studies have shifted the analysis of the nature and causes of disability from individualistic frames of reference to an examination of social policies and practice. Barton (2012) describes how this analysis 'provided a framework and language through which disabled people themselves can describe their experiences. Discrimination, exclusion and inequality can be named and challenged' (p. 115).

reflectiveteaching.co.uk/rtps6/part4_ch15

Recognising the voice of disabled people has been central to engaging with issues of human rights, respect and active citizenship, as exemplified by Peters in the extract below:

> People with disabilities have been called many things. I have labelled the worst name calling the 'in-words': *in*valid; *in*competent; *in*spirational. But I dream that I will be neither invalid nor inspirational. I want to be just an ordinary person who happens to use a wheelchair. I look forward to the day when it's ordinary to be different; the day when we recognise that our differences are what we all have in common. (Peters, 2012, p. 65)

However, *Scope*, the charity for disabled people, reports that prejudice remains strong, with a third of people perceiving deficiencies and failing to appreciate the *abilities* of the 14 million people in the UK who suffer from disabilities. Whilst many are elderly, some 8 per cent of children are also disabled. The care which they receive during their school days is vital to them. but it also provides an opportunity for other children to learn how to respect others.

From speaking with disabled children, how could their school experience be improved?

Learning capacity

For some children, learning is said to 'come easily', whilst for others the acquisition of the knowledge, concepts, skills and attitudes in the school curriculum or beyond is much more difficult. Psychologists, neuroscientists and geneticists study differences in the learning capabilities of individuals, and such abilities are likely to have very significant effects throughout a pupil's school career.

Adults also experience variations in their learning capacity – we tend to find it easier to learn things which are of intrinsic, personal interest. One can readily see then, how the factors we have reviewed above, such as social class, ethnicity or gender, can create conditions which may enable or constrain the particular types of learning which are possible in schools. Social, economic and cultural circumstances often have educational consequences.

> **Expert Question**
>
> **Personalisation:** *does the curriculum resonate with the social and cultural needs of diverse learners and provide appropriate elements of choice?*
>
> This question contributes to a conceptual framework underpinning professional expertise (see Chapter 16).

Understanding of differences and variations in the self-confidence and learning effectiveness of pupils is essential knowledge for any teacher in planning classroom provision. It enables targeted preparation to match pupil needs. Indeed, teachers tend to be very aware of 'brighter' and 'slower' pupils and many gradations in-between. Whilst such thinking may have a practical purpose in tuning provision, it is potentially dangerous if it leads to a reduction in expectations for some (Hart et al., 2004, see also Reading 1.4).

SUMMARY

In the discussion above we introduced eight dimensions which are associated with differences between people and with the opportunities that may or may not be made available. These dimensions interact in creating our individual identities. They affect our experiences inside and outside school, and influence the concepts, knowledge and frameworks we use to make sense of the world. As teachers, we have a responsibility to consider how our daily practices contribute to pupil experience and to social justice.

SOCIAL JUSTICE AND LIFE CHANCES

How then, do inequalities affect children in the long term?

It is now possible to objectively measure the consequences of social, economic and developmental inequalities within our education systems over time. This has been made possible by large scale 'cohort studies' in which researchers track the lives of thousands of people over many decades. For example, the National Child Development Study (NCDS) has been following the lives of around 17,000 children born in Britain in one week in 1958 (Elliott and Vaitilingam, 2008). Such longitudinal data has enabled analysis of the long-term consequences of early childhood and school experiences, and analysis has begun to identify factors that reinforce positive and negative developments in people's lives (Schoon, 2016; Elliott, 2013).

Another such project is the Millennium Cohort Study which tracks 19,000 children born between 2000 and 2002. It has documented many ways in which inequalities develop through childhood and adolescence. For example, as we saw earlier, obesity is now a major problem in the UK and, at the end of primary school one in three children are either overweight or obese (Fitzsimons and Benn, 2020). During secondary school, young people from poor families become even more likely to become obese than those from richer households – which is described by the researchers as a 'stark socioeconomic inequality'. This is something which teachers have to deal with in everyday classroom life as well as in sports activities, but teachers are not, of course, responsible for creating this inequality. Diet is strongly influenced by the affordability of different foods. Government regulation of food manufacturers, such as it is, seems to have limited impact.

The Millennium Cohort Study has also evidenced the difficulties faced by children and young people in respect of mental health and well-being. By early adolescence, one in six children reported high depressive symptoms, rising to one in four girls (Patalay and Fitzsimons, 2017). In 2020–21, the lockdowns, school closures and absences associated with the COVID pandemic made things considerably worse and the performance of primary-aged children was set back, particularly for those facing cramped homes and other disadvantages.

There are very considerable challenges then, but teachers should not give up! Feinstein et al. (2008b, Reading 1.6) drew again across a range of cohort studies in a Government

Foresight Study on 'learning through life'. They noted that, in addition to patterns of inequality, there are significant 'economic returns' to investment in education.

In an optimistic analysis of the 'wider benefits of learning' the researchers demonstrated how education can foster skills, confidence and qualifications which lead to many other benefits in later life and across society (see Figure 15.3).

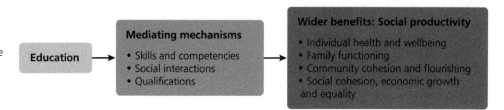

Figure 15.3
Mediating mechanisms for achievement of the wider benefits of learning (Feinstein et al., 2008b)

Feinstein et al. cite TLRP's 'evidence-informed principles' (see Chapter 4) as a means of improving teaching and learning practices. They argue that:

> Educational systems have a crucial role in equipping students and adults to withstand the economic, cultural and technological challenges they face in an increasingly globalised world. The fast pace of new technological developments and the intensification of economic pressures mean that the technical and academic skills of the working population are crucial for the UK economy. However, so are features of personal development such as resilience, self-regulation, a positive sense of self, and personal and social identity. The capability of individuals to function as civic agents with notions of personal responsibility, tolerance and respect depends on these wider features of identity which are strongly influenced by interactions with others in schools, workplaces, communities, neighbourhoods and through the media and other channels. (Feinstein et al., 2008b, p. 35)

CONCLUSION

In this chapter we have reviewed some of the processes and factors which reproduce inequalities despite the efforts of teachers to offer social justice. We considered the 'message systems' in schools (curriculum, pedagogy and assessment) over which teachers have only partial control. We looked at how the effects of differentiation by schools may be amplified by polarisation within peer cultures, and at how educational experiences influence the formation of identity and children' sense of capacity to learn. Eight dimensions of difference were considered and, finally, we drew on some findings from longitudinal cohort studies to see how inequalities may develop though the life-course. That is, of course, unless inspired teachers are able to offer children new visions and opportunities.

The implication of this chapter is thus to draw attention to the responsibilities on us as teachers. Certainly, our work contributes to our national economy, society and culture – but it does so though the lives of individual citizens. Each of these, the children in our care, deserves equal opportunities to participate and to succeed. We know, however, that there are significant, sustained patterns of difference both at entry and when leaving the education system. Inequalities remain deeply entrenched. In short, social justice has to be worked towards. However, whilst 'education may not be able to compensate for society' in an absolute sense, it can mitigate inequalities and it can generate new possibilities for many. It is our responsibility to try.

This is part of the moral case for education. Processes of teaching and learning represent opportunities to challenge social injustice. As we engage children and young people in new learning, so we challenge ourselves, as reflective practitioners, to create new possibilities for all our futures.

reflectiveteaching.co.uk/rtps6/part4_ch15

CHAPTER WEBPAGE

reflectiveteaching.co.uk offers additional professional resources for this chapter. For the chapter webpage, go to: reflectiveteaching.co.uk/rtps6/part4_ch15

For Chapter 15, the chapter webpage enables access to lots of material for classroom enquiries on issues associated with social justice and inclusion. There are three *Research Briefings*, for example, two of which illustrate the use of school-based action research by practitioners. The third one is focused on multi-agency working and, of course, teachers do increasingly have to liaise with other professionals as attempts are made to provide holistic care for children and families at risk of exclusion. To complement these resources, there are twenty suggestions for *Reflective Activities*. These echo the structure of the chapter.

Three levels of additional support are available:

1. As we have seen, with the support of a good library, *Further Reading* on the chapter webpage makes it possible to both deepen and broaden study of inclusion – in terms of difference, differentiation/polarisation, inequality and social justice.

2. *Key Readings*, listed below, provides quite an extensive annotated list of particularly helpful sources to study.

3. Short extracts of many of the *Key Readings* are provided in the mini-library, which is *Readings for Reflective Teaching in Schools* as indicated by the icons below. A resumé for each of the relevant readings is provided on the chapter webpage.

KEY READINGS

There is an enormous literature on topics such as diversity, social justice and inclusion, and the list below is indicative only. Consulting **reflectiveteaching.co.uk** will expand the suggestions.

We begin with books providing overarching perspectives on equality and difference. See, for example:

Arshad, R., Wrigley, T. and Pratt, L. (2012) *Social Justice Re-Examined. Dilemmas and Solutions for the Classroom Teacher*. London: Trentham.

Richardson, R. (2009) *Holding Together: Equalities, Difference and Cohesion*. Stoke-on-Trent: Trentham. (Reading 15.1)

Solar, J., Walsh, C. S., Craft, A., Rix, J. and Simmons, K. (2012) *Transforming Practice: Critical Issues in Equity, Diversity and Education*. Maidenhead: Open University Press.

Contemporary statistics and analyses are provided by many charities and other organisations working to reduce inequality. For instance:

The Joseph Rowntree Foundation maintains UK poverty statistics and works pro-actively to 'solve poverty'. No easy task, but they have a distinguished history of such work over 100 years. See Joseph Rowntree Foundation (2000) and: **jrf.org.uk**

The Equality Trust is a registered charity that works 'to improve the quality of life in the UK by reducing economic and social inequality'. See it at: **equalitytrust.org.uk**

The Child Poverty Action Group (CPAG) is a campaigning organisation, founded in 1965, which aims to: 'use our understanding of what causes poverty to campaign for policies that will prevent and solve poverty'. Their work is available at: **cpag.org**

The Sutton Trust carries out research and campaigns to reduce inequalities directly affecting or stemming from education. See: **suttontrust.com**

The analysis of how differentiation by teachers and schools is reinforced by polarisation within pupil culture can be traced through many sociological studies, including:

> Lacey, C. (1970) *Hightown Grammar: The School as a Social System.* Manchester: Manchester University Press.
> Pollard, A. (1985) *The Social World of the Primary School.* London: Cassell. (see **Reading 15.2**)

One of the best books tracing the formation of identity across the school years is that of Jo Warin. Through case studies of five children, she tracks the ways they negotiate their experiences and emphasises how schools and teachers can enhance identity development.

> Warin, J. (2010) *Stories of Self: Tracking Children's Identity and Well-being through the School Years.* Staffordshire: Trentham Books.

Eleanore Hargreaves offers many insights on how classroom life is experienced by children and on the benefits of teachers really 'listening' to pupil perspectives. See:

> Hargreaves, E. (2017) *Children's Experiences of Classrooms: Talking about Being Pupils in the Classroom.* London: SAGE.

Specific treatment of particular issues with regard to dimensions of difference is provided in books such as the following classic and contemporary studies.

The influence of social class reaches well beyond the classroom (see also Chapter 5) and excellent websites providing up-to-date data are available from the Sutton Trust and the Joseph Rowntree Foundation. See also:

> Evans, G. (2006) *Educational Failure and Working Class White Children in Britain.* Palgrave Macmillan: Basingstoke.
> Feinstein, L. Duckworth, K. and Sabates, R. (2008a) *Education and the Family: Passing Success Across the Generations.* Routledge: Abingdon.

On gendered experiences, and how these are reproduced, see:

> Renold, E. (2005) *Girls, Boys and Junior Sexualities. Exploring Children's Gender and Sexual Relations in the Primary School*. London: Routledge.
>
> Francis, B., Skelton, C. and Read, B. (2012) *The Identities and Practices of High Achieving Pupils: Negotiating Achievement and Peer Cultures*. London: Continuum.
>
> Jackson, C. (2006) *Lads and Ladettes in School: Gender and a Fear of Failure*. Maidenhead: Open University Press.
>
> Skelton, C. and Francis, B. (2009) *Feminism and 'The Schooling Scandal'*. London: Routledge.

For analyses of sexuality and education, see:

> Kehily, M.J. (2003) *Sexuality, Gender and Schooling. Shifting Agendas in Social Learning*. London: Routledge.
>
> Hudson-Sharp, N. and Metcalf, H. (2016) *Inequality among Lesbian, Gay, Bisexual and Transgender Groups in the UK: A Review of Evidence*. Slough: National Institute of Economic and Social Research.

On ethnicity and race, Walters offers an introduction, Connolly, and Troyna and Hatcher, are two classic empirical studies. Gillborn is a more advanced policy critique.

> Walters, S. (2011) *Ethnicity, Race and Education*. London: Continuum.
>
> Connolly, P. (1998) *Racism, Gender and Identities of Young Children: Social Relations in a Multi-ethnic, Inner-city Primary School*. London: Routledge.
>
> Troyna, B. and Hatcher, R. (1992) *Racism in Children's Lives: A Study of Mainly White Primary Schools*. London: Routledge.
>
> Gillborn, D. (2008) *Racism and Education: Coincidence or Conspiracy?* Abingdon: Routledge.

Given the performance pressures of recent years, many schools have returned to the practice of grouping children by attainment (often imprecisely termed 'ability'). The problems were documented many years ago, and remain. Alternative approaches are offered by 'learning without limits'.

> Jackson, B. (1964) *Streaming: An Education System in Miniature*. London: Routledge and Kegan Paul.
>
>
> Ireson, J. and Hallam, S. (2001) *Ability Grouping in Education*. London: SAGE. (see Reading 15.4)
>
> Hart, S., Dixon, A., Drummond, M.-J. and McIntyre, D. (2004) *Learning Without Limits*. Maidenhead: Open University Press. (see Reading 1.4)
>
>
> Swann, M., Peacock, A., Hart, S. and Drummond, M.-J. (2012) *Creating Learning Without Limits*. Maidenhead: Open University Press. (Reading 1.4)

Introductions to disabilities and special educational needs include:

> Thompson, J. (2010) *The Essential Guide to Understanding Special Educational Needs*. London: Longman.
>
> Wearmouth, J. (2011) *Special Educational Needs: The Basics*. London: Routledge.
>
> Thomas, G. and Loxley, A. (2007) *Deconstructing Special Education and Constructing Inclusion*. Buckingham: Open University Press. (Reading 15.3)

On the broader issues of understanding and improving life chances, see:

> Tucker, J. (ed) (2016) *Improving Children's Life Chances*. London: CPAG.

For a more sophisticated sociological account of the role of education in promoting life chances, see:

> Munro, L. (2019) *Life Chances, Education and Social Movements*. London: Anthem Press.

UK Cohort Studies are well represented by the Centre for Longitudinal Studies at IOE, University College London. See: **cls.ucl.ac.uk**

TOOLKIT EVIDENCE 15.1
Setting and streaming: balancing equity, 'ability' and efficiency

What is it?
Pupils with similar levels of performance are grouped together for teaching activities. This can be either for particular lessons on a regular basis ('setting' or 'regrouping'), or as a whole class ('streaming' or 'tracking'). The idea is to teach more effectively or more efficiently with a narrower range of attainment. Calling this approach 'ability grouping' is misleading. Pupils have not usually been given a test of their ability (potential), it simply reflects their current performance.

What does the evidence say?
Overall, although the average impact is zero, setting or streaming appears to benefit higher attaining pupils and to be detrimental to the learning of lower attaining learners. Low attaining learners who are set or streamed tend to fall behind by about one or two months per year, on average, when compared with the progress of similar students in classes with mixed attainment groups.

It seems likely that routine or regular setting undermines low attainers' confidence and discourages the belief that their learning can be improved through effort. Research also suggests that this kind of grouping can have a longer term negative effect on the attitudes and engagement of low attaining pupils. Summer-born children and those from disadvantaged backgrounds are more likely to be assigned to low attaining sets or groups.

Although the average impact of setting or streaming on low attaining pupils is negative, evidence suggests some approaches can be successful in the short term. For example, reducing the size of the lowest attaining groups in a class and assigning high-performing teachers to these groups can be effective, as can providing additional, targeted, catch-up support for those at risk of falling behind.

How sound is the evidence?
The evidence on setting and streaming is fairly consistent and has accumulated over at least thirty years of research.

What do I need to think about?
It is important to recognize that a measure of current attainment, such as a test, is not the same as a measure of potential or future capability.
  For pupils who are struggling to keep up with the rest of the class, flexible grouping within a class is preferable to setting or streaming.
  How will you monitor the impact of setting or streaming on learners' engagement and their attitudes to learning?

Links and further reading
Francis, B., Taylor, B. and Tereshchenko, A. (2019) *Reassessing 'Ability' Grouping: Improving Practice for Equity and Attainment*. London: Routledge.

Hallam, S., Ireson, J. and Davies, J. (2013) *Effective Pupil Grouping in the Primary School: a practical guide*. London: Routledge.

Macqueen, S.E. (2013) 'Grouping for inequity'. *International Journal of Inclusive Education*, 17(3), 295–309.
The EEF Teaching and Learning Toolkit entry on 'Setting or streaming': https://educationendowmentfoundation.org.uk/education-evidence/teaching-learning-toolkit/setting-and-streaming – see also the technical appendix for further references.

See also in the EEF Toolkit:
Mastery learning: educationendowmentfoundation.org.uk/education-evidence/teaching-learning-toolkit/mastery-learning

RESEARCH BRIEFING 15.1
Education, health and inequality

The number one factor that determines both health and educational outcomes is socio-economic status.

Health status during childhood and negative health conditions, such as chronic diseases or disabilities, affect school attendance, educational achievements, and the ability to perform well in class. Children's mental health, and social and emotional resilience influence academic performance. Anxieties, depression and other forms of mental ill-health are crucial factors undermining motivation and acquiring skills to learn, impacting educational success. Smoking, other emerging addictions, and poor nutrition and lack of physical activity have particularly strong negative impacts on educational outcomes.

Inequalities in health outcomes – such as life expectancy and healthy life years – strongly relate to childhood experiences in the earliest years. They are evident by the time children start school and extend through education. The academic performance gap between advantaged and disadvantaged children develops from as early as 10 years old and widens throughout students' lives. In Europe, by age 30, people with the lowest education levels can expect to live four to eight years less than people with the highest.

Education has a positive lifelong effect on health through increased employment opportunities and income, better living conditions, positive mental health and resilience, and (health) literacy. A well-educated population is better equipped with skills to adapt to the changing world of work, as well as the digital transformation. People with lower educational attainment have higher rates of premature mortality, morbidity, and functional and cognitive limitations, making healthy and active ageing difficult. Additionally, people with less- and low-quality schooling are more likely to experience employment difficulties, (in-work) poverty and social exclusion, and to receive insufficient and inadequate health support.

These health-education inequalities do not just affect the most disadvantaged people. They form a gradient across populations from all social classes. Investing in accessible and affordable quality education throughout the life-course, especially in early years, is an enabler to reduce inequalities across the gradient and break the cycle of poverty and its subsequent harmful effect on health and wellbeing. However, average government education spending represents only 4.6 per cent of GDP in EU states and has declined this century.

Evidence shows that investments in improved education also benefit healthier behaviours. School settings are important for promoting healthy behaviours and attitudes. For example, specific educational programmes to promote health and wellbeing have demonstrated reduced population rates of smoking and obesity, improved learning outcomes and wellbeing, plus reduced school absenteeism and drop-out.

A EuroHealthNet Policy Precis

Part five

Deepening understanding

16	**Teacher expertise** A holistic view	513
17	**Professional learning** How can we nurture career-long reflective teaching?	537
18	**Professionalism** How does reflective teaching contribute to society?	553

Supplementary chapters at reflectiveteaching.co.uk
- **Starting out** Learning as a newly qualified teacher
- **Improvement** Continuing professional development

This is the final and synoptic part of the book. It integrates major themes through discussion of teacher expertise and professionalism.

'Teacher Expertise' (Chapter 16) harvests and integrates powerful ideas from previous chapters into a holistic conceptual framework of enduring issues in teaching and learning. The chapter constructs a framework describing dimensions of expert thinking.

In Chapter 17, 'Professional Learning', we consider the ways in which teachers continue to learn as part of their professional role. Finally, in Chapter 18, 'Professionalism', we look at the bigger picture once more to consider the role of the teaching profession in our societies and suggest how reflective teachers can contribute to democratic processes.

Chapter 16
Teacher expertise
A holistic view

| Introduction | 514 |

| Educational aims | 520 |

Society's goals: an opportunity for discussion 520
Elements of learning 523

| Learning contexts | 524 |

Community context 524
Institutional context 525

| Classroom processes | 526 |

Processes for learners' social needs 526
Processes for learners' cognitive needs 528

| Learning outcomes | 529 |

Outcomes for continuing improvement in learning 529
Outcomes for certification and the lifecourse 530

| Using the conceptual framework | 531 |

Problem solving during initial training 531
Reflecting on professional commitment 531
Analysing teaching and learning 532
Supporting curriculum development 532

| Conclusion | 533 |

Supplementary chapters at reflectiveteaching.co.uk
- **Starting out** Learning as a newly qualified teacher
- **Improvement** Continuing professional development

reflectiveteaching.co.uk/rtps6/part5_ch16

INTRODUCTION

The main reason that teacher expertise is so important is that expert teachers have profound effects on the life chances of learners. As we saw in Chapter 4 of this book, it has been recognised internationally that 'teachers matter' (OECD, 2005; Sahlberg, 2012, Reading 4.3; Hattie, 2009, Reading 4.6) – a fact which TLRP's findings and principles embody and promote. As Dylan Wiliam argued, the quality of teaching has a far greater effect than differences caused by type of school. Indeed, 'there is a four-fold difference in the speed of learning between the most effective and least effective classrooms' (Wiliam, 2009, Reading 16.4). Research on effective primary teachers carried out in the United States, using ideas and research methods from economics, found that pupils taught by teachers who add high value to their pupils' test scores (known as high value-added or high VA) were on average more likely to attend college and earn higher salaries in adulthood (Chetty, Friedman and Rockoff, 2014). Understanding the very long-term effects of the work of teachers is some of the most challenging research to carry out because there are so many variables, and because longitudinal research is so expensive.

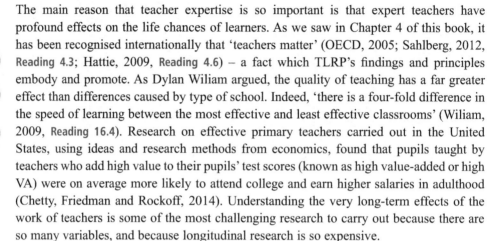

The influence of analyses of the 'effect-sizes' of different teaching and learning strategies (see, for instance, Hattie, 2012, Reading 10.7) is to be found throughout this book. Such findings offer important insights on high-quality teaching. However, specific findings also need to be integrated into teachers' routine practices and ways of thinking. This brings us to a discussion of the progressive development, and deepening, of teacher expertise.

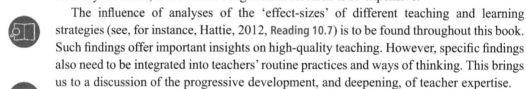

For extensive supplements to this chapter, see 'Deepening Expertise' at reflectiveteaching.co.uk.

See Chapter 4

> ### TLRP Principles
>
> **Effective teaching and learning depends on teacher learning.** The need for teachers to learn continuously in order to develop their knowledge and skills, and adapt and develop their roles, especially through classroom inquiry, should be recognised and supported. (*Principle 9*)
>
> **Effective teaching and learning demands consistent policy frameworks with support for teaching and learning as their primary focus.** Policies at national, local and institutional levels need to recognise the fundamental importance of teaching and learning. They should be designed to create effective learning environments in which all learners can thrive. (*Principle 10*)

The development of teacher expertise has been studied for many years, with the work of Dreyfus and Dreyfus (1986), Glaser (1999) and Berliner (2004) being particularly significant. Glaser (1999) identified three key 'cognitive stages' in the development of expertise – thus highlighting a transition from dependent to independent ways of thinking about classroom practice:

Externally supported > Transitional > Self-regulatory

Whilst this progression makes considerable sense, a further element of expertise lies in contextually appropriate judgement. In other words, it is not enough simply to accumulate a 'box of tricks' or to assemble 'teacher tips' – valuable though these may be. The key capability is to understand when and how to deploy such capabilities. Berliner (2004) picked out the significance of contextual judgement and of practice itself in his elaboration of five stages of teacher development (originally proposed by Dreyfus and Dreyfus, 1986). This is summarised by Eaude (2012, see Reading 16.3).

So far, the models of expertise that we have referred to are linear ones: in the simplest form the progression from novice to expert. However, there are many caveats to linear models. For example, people who begin initial teacher education and training arrive with a wide range of prior experiences and learning. Some start more expert than others yet they are all at the beginning of their formal training. Another important consideration is the ways in which professional learning takes place. For example, take the concept of teacher 'resilience'. Those teachers who have resilience are more likely to develop expertise because of their motivation to do so. This resilience is not only a fixed personal trait; it changes and fluctuates in non-linear ways and is dependent on professional relationships within and outside the work place (Gu, 2014). And although some types of expertise can be learned in a finite way, e.g. aspects of curriculum subject knowledge, other types of expertise are never fully learned because of the infinite possibilities for increasing expertise. The metaphor of spirals of learning, rather than linear or straight lines of learning, is helpful.

Another important aspect of expertise is knowledge about the possibilities for improving professional practice, and the role of research and other evidence to guide the development of knowledge. A teacher who does not seek to learn from other colleagues, or from other sources, about alternative practices, is less aware of possibilities than the teacher who seeks out colleagues' views and also reads more widely to update their knowledge about evidence-based practices. Teachers who are enthusiastic about professional development, and who may themselves undertake further study at master's and doctoral level, quickly find out that evidence-informed practice is complex for every topic of interest. For example, take the teaching of reading, a fundamental role of the primary school teacher. Although there are multiple high-quality research studies, there remain strong differences of interpretation and opinion, from researchers from teachers and from policy makers, about the best ways to teach reading (Wyse and Bradbury, 2022).

The trends in research on effective teaching and learning are not however like the swings of a pendulum, which some people argue represent an endless back and forth with no progress and no fundamental change. It is just that it takes decades of research in most cases to arrive at firm conclusions about what is likely to be effective or ineffective. The lengthy timescales for conclusive research findings do of course mean that while teachers continue to update their knowledge through practice, through reflection, and through wider reading, they also have to be confident to make decisions on what is most likely to help the pupils they are teaching at any given moment in a lesson, as part of their ongoing relationships with their pupils.

In summary, the development of teacher expertise occurs over time and is, in essence, concerned with acquiring more sophisticated ways of thinking about teaching and learning, including influenced by research, as well as the refinement of practical skills and curricular knowledge (Winch, 2012). From a reliance on generic rules for challenges such as classroom management, the expert teacher is able to 'read' a situation and draw intuitively on their repertoire of responses. The expert teacher has a repertoire of available strategies (see also Alexander, 2008a, Reading 16.3). This developmental process was first introduced in Chapter 3, when it was discussed simply as a career-long 'spiral of professional development' (see Figure 3.1, p. 80). From such foundations, this book has progressed, part by part, through educational intentions, conditions for learning, teaching processes and outcomes. Each chapter has focused on practical challenges, but has also been written with an eye to the cumulative development of teacher expertise. To that end too, TLRP's principles, powerful concepts and 'expert questions' for analysing teaching and learning in classrooms have been seeded through the chapters.

Principles, concepts and questions support the interpretation and understanding of classroom experience and of evidence. If we revisit our discussion in Chapter 3, p. 81 on 'evidence-informed practice', we can see just how vital such tools are. Figure 16.1, below, reproduces an earlier model (see p. 81) – but with one difference. Here, attention is drawn to how evidence has to be *interpreted and understood*. We must 'make sense' of our experience and of the information available to us.

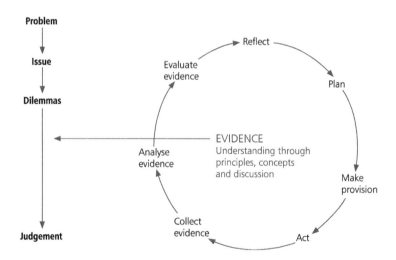

Figure 16.1
Principles, concepts and evidence-informed practice

For the development of high levels of expertise, what really matters are the frameworks and other sources for deeper understanding. Expertise is also related to the values which underpin professional judgement. For example, teachers make choices on the aspects of teaching that they wish to learn more about. Their values will direct their focus to some topics more than others. Indeed, their values will be part of how they select the kinds of schools they want to work in, including the kinds of head teachers that they want to work for.

Indeed, simple 'tips', 'toolkits' or lists of 'what works', whilst useful and worthy of careful attention, are not enough to achieve the highest quality of teaching. They can even be misleading. Hattie (2012, Reading 16.5) recognises this and proposes 'high-level principles' to integrate his otherwise fragmented lists of effective teaching strategies. James (2008, Reading 2.8) makes clear that improvement in pupil outcomes depends on the development of authentic teacher understanding. Put another way, as Bruner (1996, Reading 11.3) stated, 'a teacher's conception of a learner shapes the instruction he or she employs'. So, at the highest levels of professionalism, there is a key role for overarching, theorised *understanding* of learning and of teaching. Acknowledging this issue in relation to its 'Teaching and Learning Toolkit', the Education Endowment Foundation appropriately draws attention to a limitation of the toolkits:

> Because the Toolkits do not provide definitive answers, they should not be used in isolation. Your professional judgement and expertise is also needed to move from the information in the Toolkit to an evidence-informed decision about what will work best in your school. (**educationendowmentfoundation.org.uk/education-evidence/using-the-toolkits**)

Of course, TLRP's principles (see Chapter 4) promote a more holistic, multi-dimensional view of education, within which is nested appreciation of the need to achieve high standards in basic skills and subject knowledge. Indeed, the model of professionalism which underpins this book assumes that teachers will be concerned with issues such as the intrinsic quality of pupil learning experiences, the development of positive learning disposition and self-confidence, the fulfilment of potential and the provision of opportunities for all – as well as achieving very high standards in knowledge, skills and understanding.

Having seeded principles, concepts and questions in each chapter of the book, we are now able to harvest cumulatively from across the whole text and to offer an integrated, conceptual foundation for deepening expertise.

The conceptual framework (Figure 16.2) is simply a tool for thinking and for discussion that is based on the proposition that, in one way or another, teachers inevitably face issues concerning **educational aims, learning contexts, classroom processes** and **learning outcomes** (the rows) and they do so in relation to **curriculum, pedagogy** and **assessment** (the columns) (see also an online, featured version in 'deepening expertise' at reflectiveteaching.co.uk).

The 'expert questions' in each cell highlight the enduring issues which reflective teachers need to consider. As we have seen, this calls for evidence-informed professional judgement. The individual concepts that underpin the question in each individual cell in Figure 16.2 are also absolutely vital. If the concepts have sufficient validity then reflection about their applicability to teaching over time can contribute to the development of a professional language that is part of teacher expertise. Professional language that is evidence-informed in this way can also be used to challenge those who misunderstand the sophistication of education as a part of society and as an academic discipline in universities. Having said that, the specific meaning and use of the concepts is open to interpretation.

518   Part 5 Deepening understanding

ENDURING ISSUES		Curricular concepts
1 EDUCATIONAL AIMS	**1.1 Society's educational goals** What vision of 'education' is the provision designed to achieve?	**Breadth:** does the curriculum represent society's educational aspirations for its citizens?
	1.2 Elements of learning What knowledge, concepts, skills, values and attitudes are to be learned in formal education?	**Balance:** does the curriculum-as-experienced offer everything which each learner has a right to expect?
2 LEARNING CONTEXTS	**2.1 Community context** Is the educational experience valued and endorsed by parents, community, employers and civil society?	**Connection:** does the curriculum engage with the cultural resources and funds-of-knowledge of families and the community?
	2.2 Institutional context Does the school promote a common vision to extend educational experiences and inspire learners?	**Coherence:** is there clarity in the purposes, content and organisation of the curriculum and does it provide holistic learning experiences?
3 CLASSOOM PROCESSES	**3.1 Process for learners' social needs** Does the educational experience build on social relationships, cultural under-standings and learner identities?	**Personalisation:** does the curriculum resonate with the social and cultural needs of diverse learners and provide appropriate elements of choice?
	3.2 Processes for learners' emotional needs Does the educational experience take due account of learner views, feelings and characteristics?	**Relevance:** is the curriculum presented in ways which are meaningful to learners and so that it can excite their imagination?
	3.3 Processes for learners' cognitive needs Does the educational experience match the learner's cognitive needs and provide appropriate challenge?	**Differentiation:** are curriculum tasks and activities structured appropri-ately to match the intellectual needs of learners?
4 LEARNING OUTCOMES	**4.1 Outcomes for continuing improvement in learning** Does the educational experience lead to *development* in knowledge, concepts, skills and attitudes?	**Progression:** does the curriculum-as-delivered provide an appropriate sequence and depth of learning experiences?
	4.2 Outcomes for certification and the lifecourse Does the educational experience equip learners for adult and working life, and for an unknown future?	**Effectiveness:** are there improvements in standards, in both basic skills and other areas of curricular attainment, to satisfy society's goals?

reflectiveteaching.co.uk/rtps6/part5_ch16

Chapter 16 Teacher expertise

Pedagogic concepts	Assessment concepts
Principle: is our pedagogy consistent with established principles for effective teaching and learning?	**Congruence**: are forms of assessment fit for purpose in terms of overall educational objectives?
Repertoire: is our pedagogic expertise sufficiently creative, skilled and wide-ranging to teach all elements of learning?	**Validity**: in terms of learning, do the forms of assessment used really measure what they are intended to measure?
Warrant: are our teaching strategies evidence-informed, convincing and justifiable to stakeholders?	**Dependability**: are assessment processes understood and accepted as being robust and reliable?
Culture: does the school support expansive learning by affirming learner contributions, engaging partners and providing attractive opportunities?	**Expectations**: does our school support high staff and student expectations, and aspire to excellence?
Relationships: are teacher–pupil relationships nurtured as the foundation of good behaviour, mutual wellbeing and high standards?	**Inclusion**: are all learners treated respectfully and fairly in both formal and informal interaction?
Engagement: do our teaching strategies, classroom organisation and consultation enable learners to actively participate in and enjoy their learning?	**Authenticity**: do learners recognise routine processes of assessment and feedback as being of personal value?
Dialogue: does teacher–learner talk scaffold understanding to build on existing knowledge and to strengthen dispositions to learn?	**Feeding back**: is there a routine flow of constructive, specific, diagnostic feedback from teacher to learners?
Reflection: is our classroom practice based on incremental, evidence-informed and collaborative improvement strategies?	**Development**: does formative feedback and support enable learners to achieve personal learning goals?
Empowerment: is our pedagogic repertoire successful in enhancing wellbeing, learning disposition, capabilities and agency?	**Consequence**: do assessment outcomes lead towards recognised qualifications and a confident sense of personal identity?

Figure 16.2 A framework for teacher expertise: powerful concepts and expert questions

reflectiveteaching.co.uk/rtps6/part5_ch16

The framework is simply an analytic device for representing teacher expertise. It could be compiled and re-presented in different ways.

Review of the *columns* of curriculum, pedagogy and assessment are an important way of using the framework. For example, a classroom teacher, staff team or any other group of stakeholders in a school might want to focus on curriculum provision alone, in which case the 'expert questions' in that column would be effective probes for this, enabling considerations of curriculum aims, contexts, processes and outcomes (Chapters 8, 9 and 10 cover this ground too). Pedagogy could be similarly reviewed using the set of expert questions in its column (and Chapters 5, 6, 7, 11, 12 and 15 also focus on these issues). Assessment is the subject of the third column (which articulates directly with Chapters 13 and 14). On the version of the framework at reflectiveteaching.co.uk/deepening-expertise, more detail is available to enable focused consideration.

It is also worthwhile to think of the *rows*. If this is done, the interrelationship of provision for curriculum, pedagogy and assessment is reviewed in relation to each of the enduring issues concerned with aims, contexts, processes and outcomes. This is the approach taken in the remainder of this chapter. Alternatively, it is often insightful to explore connections between the concepts and questions in different parts of the framework. To help in this, reflectiveteaching.co.uk provides further ideas and information in relation to each cell.

For more information on how the conceptual framework was created, see the supplementary material for Chapter 16 on reflectiveteaching.co.uk

EDUCATIONAL AIMS

Society's goals: an opportunity for discussion

We start our review of the conceptual framework for deepening understanding by suggesting a discussion on aims and purposes. Reflective Activity 16.1 suggests an initial focus on national priorities. However, such concerns soon have to be transformed into practical action in schools and classrooms. What documentation on overall educational aims is available in your school?

> ## Reflective Activity 16.1
>
> *Aim:* To review national aspirations and consequential links between curriculum breadth, pedagogic principles and congruent assessment.
>
> *Evidence and reflection:* This activity challenges us to stand back and review our education system as a whole. Four questions might be posed, and could be tackled in discussion with colleagues.
>
> 1. Is there a broad consensus on educational purposes for schooling? An indication of this might be the nature of public debate about school provision. What aspects are taken for granted? Which are controversial?
>
> 2. How adequately do National Curriculum requirements represent educational goals on which there is broad agreement? For example, is the curriculum regarded as being sufficiently broad to provide an 'all-round education' and to foster positive attitudes to learning whilst also ensuring mastery of basic skills and enabling appropriate qualifications to be obtained?
>
> 3. Are favoured approaches to teaching justifiable in terms of established, evidence-informed principles, and what are the best sources of evidence? Do these approaches reinforce overall curricular intentions?
>
> 4. What sorts of assessment are significant in the school system in which you work? Are these congruent with overall curricular intentions?
>
> *Follow-up:* These questions are framed above in quite general terms, for consideration of wide-ranging issues across an entire school system. However, they can also be applied much more specifically, to a particular school, department or classroom. If this is done, they become powerful tools for stimulating reflection on overall educational purposes and provision. Our aims and methods should match of course, but do they?

Breadth: Is your professional knowledge sufficient in relation to what has to be taught and what you want to teach?

Principle: Is your pedagogic subject knowledge well founded in terms of what is known about effective teaching?

Congruence: Are you familiar with forms of assessment which will reflect your aims, and will not inadvertently distort pupil learning?

EDUCATIONAL AIMS
Society's goals

What vision of 'education' is the provision designed to achieve?	**Breadth:** Does the curriculum represent society's educational aspirations for its citizens?	**Principle:** Is our pedagogy consistent with established principles for effective teaching and learning?	**Congruence:** Are forms of assessment fit for purpose in terms of overall educational objectives?

Children and young people are our most precious asset. They come to embody our culture, and their values and capabilities will determine the ways in which our society will evolve over the twenty-first century. Education both reflects society and contributes to it including through the economy. Issues such as whether education reproduces social differences or provides new opportunities thus become very important. What vision of education should we adopt?

The Education Reform Act 1988, and its amendments, specifies official educational aims for England and Wales. Children are to be offered a 'balanced and broadly based curriculum' which:

- promotes the spiritual, moral, cultural, mental and physical development of pupils; and
- prepares pupils for the opportunities, responsibilities and experiences of adult life.

The law thus formally enshrines a rounded conception of education. However, pressure for short-term performance tends to narrow such goals – and thus we have a major issue of recent decades. Since the devolution of government in the countries of the UK that began in 1998 the national curricula in Northern Ireland, Wales, and Scotland became increasingly different in many respects from the national curriculum in England. The differences were increased when England's national curriculum of 2014 was introduced.

Curriculum concept: Breadth

There are many views about the areas of learning and experience which should be provided by schools (see Chapter 9). These encompass fields such as: arts and creativity; language and literacy; environment and society; modern languages; mathematics; science and technology; health and physical education; religious and moral education.

In England, very particular emphasis has been given to what are described by some as the 'core' subject areas of English, maths and science in primary education and to subjects in the EBacc in secondary. These are seen by some to be a too narrow focus on a limited range of subjects. Maintaining breadth in pupils' actual classroom experiences is a big challenge for teachers in any event, and is made difficult in such circumstances. Curriculum, assessment and accountability need to be fully aligned to reinforce breadth of provision.

Pedagogic concept: Principle

This aspect concerns the extent to which teachers' pedagogic judgement is informed by a deep understanding of learning and teaching and of the factors involved. TLRP's ten principles (see Chapter 4) is one way of representing these factors holistically so that their interconnectedness is emphasised. Such principles often underpin national recommendations but, at best, they should directly inform teacher expertise.

TLRP's principles form four groups. The first concerns the goals and moral purpose of education, knowledge to be learned and the prior experience of the learner. Three aspects of teacher expertise, in 'scaffolding' learning, assessment for learning and active engagement, form another. The role of social processes and informal learning feature next. Finally, the principles emphasise the significance of teacher learning and the need for consistent policy frameworks.

Assessment concept: Congruence

Assessment activity should support learning objectives – hence 'assessment for learning' (see Chapter 13).

TLRP's project on learning environments (Entwistle, 2009) studied ways in which assessment activity is aligned with learning objectives, appropriate for student backgrounds and fully supported institutionally. Assessment was thus seen as being much more than a narrow technical process, but woven into educational organisations, subjects and their practices. Such congruence supports learning because the learner can more easily understand and engage with available feedback. This work built on the concept of 'constructive alignment' (Biggs and Tang, 2011), which asks whether learning activities and forms of assessment are consistent and fit for their purpose.

Chapter 16 Teacher expertise

Case Study 16.1 Elements of learning

Integrating technology into a child-centred classroom environment

Vicky's nursery class was part of a primary school in the centre of a city in the southeast of England. Vicky was an experienced nursery teacher with strong beliefs in child-centred pedagogy. Her practice was also founded on her principles of the importance of play-based learning. Vicky agreed to take part in a research project that involved Charlotte the researcher working closely with Vicky over the course of a school year. The research design was one that requires the practitioner and researcher to work together on a new intervention that is collaboratively designed to improve an aspect of teaching. The researcher collects data about the implementation of the new intervention then researcher and participant reflect on the implications of the data and its analyses.

At the start of the research project Vicky was not particularly enthusiastic about the use of digital technologies as part of her teaching. She had an Interactive White Board (IWB), and a computer and tablets, available for use by the children but these digital resources were not built into her lesson/activity planning. In fact, at the start of the research Vicky was hostile to digital technologies, saying that they were something that 'sucked the life force'.

The first change that Vicky made, supported by Charlotte, was to explicitly plan for her interaction with children while the IWB and LearnPads were being used by the children during time they had for free play. For Vicky a key to her views beginning to change was that she could see an important role for her, which she described like this:

> The other big thing that has changed for me is understanding that my intervention is really, really important because first of all I saw this great social stuff happening and I thought OK but I don't really see my role in this social stuff happening . . . . But then reflecting again, when I was seeing this happening I understood that by moving in I could really, really extend what was happening and it was differentiated by virtue of these children leading and then I could extend [their learning]. (Vidal-Hall, Flewitt and Wyse, 2020, p. 8)

The changes in Vicky's practice happened gradually over the course of the year. She worked thoughtfully, on the basis of research, to adapt an area of her practice that she was not confident with.

In the end the aspect that seemed to result in a sustained and permanent change to Vicky's practice was when she could see that her beliefs about child-centred pedagogy could still be upheld while using digital tools with the children in her class. Consistent with other research about teachers' use of technology Vicky was able to regard the digital technology as tools rather than simply teaching resources with limited use. Her new understanding about pedagogy, and particularly her interaction with children while using digital tools, was the key to bringing congruence between her beliefs and her practice, which in turn unlocked more effective teaching and learning. Teacher beliefs and understanding are a vital aspect of curriculum and pedagogy.

Repertoire: The teacher developed her knowledge of digital tools and her pedagogy for using the tools. This resulted in improved teaching and learning.

For more information on this case study see Vidal-Hall et al. (2020). The research design used in the case study was Educational Design Research, a variant of 'close to practice research': see Wyse et al. (2020).

reflectiveteaching.co.uk/rtps6/part5_ch16

LEARNING CONTEXTS
Community context

Is the educational experience valued and endorsed by parents, community, employers and civil society?	**Connection**: Does the curriculum engage with the cultural resources and funds-of-knowledge of families and the community?	**Warrant**: Are the teaching strategies evidence-informed, convincing and justifiable to stakeholders?	**Dependablity**: Are assessment processes understood and accepted as being robust and reliable?

'Community' is associated with social relationships, cultures and histories and with a collective sense of place and identity (see Chapter 5). Some people and families may feel deeply embedded in their communities and benefit from extensive social networks; such social capital often brings status and advantage. Others, perhaps minority groups, may feel more marginal or even excluded. Such diversity is a very strong feature of contemporary life.

TLRP's research consistently showed the significance of informal, out-of-school learning: what happens within schools is enriched by understanding of what happened outside schools. Those in the community can thus help considerably, if constructive and trusting connections are made.

However, those beyond the school gate are also positioned as consumers. Parents, employers and others expect children to receive high-quality education. Forms of pedagogy and assessment have to be justified – hence the concepts of warrant and dependability.

Curriculum concept: Connection

'Only connect – live in fragments no longer,' wrote E.M. Forster. This thought can be applied to the meaningfulness and linkage of the curriculum with the communities which each school serves (see Chapter 10). TLRP's Home–School Knowledge Exchange project affirmed the knowledge of families and devised ways of drawing this into the curriculum. Outcomes in literacy and numeracy improved and transfer between Key Stages 2 and 3 was facilitated (Feiler et al., 2007; Winter et al., 2009). The Royal Society of Arts promotes an 'area based curriculum' (Thomas, 2010, Reading 10.4).

The underlying theme here is about the contextual meaningfulness of the curriculum. Whilst national frameworks exist, local adaption is likely to enhance both the perceived value of schooling and the quality of learning.

Pedagogy concept: Warrant

The word 'warrant' has several meanings associated with forms of authorisation and justification, ranging from the Royal Warrant to an arrest warrant. In relation to pedagogy, the concept of warrant challenges us to justify our practice to stakeholders such as parents, employers and learners themselves. We defined pedagogy earlier as 'the act and discourse of teaching' (Chapter 11). Further, it was suggested that maintaining a sound educational rationale and forms of reflective practice can support continuing improvement in the quality of professional judgements (p. 10). This is one clear way of fulfilling the responsibility, set out in the regulatory codes of conduct and practice for teachers in the four nations of the UK, for maintaining the quality of teaching.

Assessment concept: Dependability

How much confidence can we place in different forms of assessment (see Chapter 14)? Technically speaking, high dependability arises when an assessment is both valid and reliable – it measures what is intended and does so with high consistency. Consistent reliability is not easy to achieve. As TLRP's *Commentary on Assessment* pointed out (Mansell and James, 2009, Reading 14.5), it can be undermined by unfair or biased marking and by variations in standards applied by different teachers. Other studies have shown how differences in testing situations or in pupil preparation can affect performance. Electronic marking may achieve consistency in that respect, but struggles on some tests of validity. On the other hand, teacher assessment is likely to strengthen the validity of judgements made, but remains vulnerable to inconsistency unless moderation processes are taken extremely seriously.

For all these reasons, the dependability of school assessments always has to be worked for.

Institutional context

Case study 16.2 Children's rights to express their views

The UN Convention on the Rights of the Child (CRC) is an international treaty signed by all countries in the world apart from the United States. One of the 'articles' that details children's right says that children have the right of freedom of expression:

Article 12

1. States Parties shall assure to the child who is capable of forming his or her own views the right to express those views freely in all matters affecting the child, the views of the child being given due weight in accordance with the age and maturity of the child. (unicef.org.uk/what-we-do/un-convention-child-rights/)

The UN Convention applies to all children in all schools. A research study investigated the nature of the CRC and particularly Article 12 in two secondary schools and two primary schools. At the time not a single adult or child who was interviewed as part of the research had heard of the CRC nor of these rights to express their views.

At one of the secondary schools there was a school council that was made up of pupils whose role was to discuss things at the school that could be improved from their perspective. One of the older pupils on the school council who was also a head girl felt that although some things changed as a result of the views of the school council, for example some new lockers for children's possessions were installed, on matters that were deemed more important by the pupils nothing was done to make changes. A lack of action was combined with a lack of communication with the school council about any steps that had been taken to reflect the pupils' views.

The children in the primary schools did not have school councils as a mechanism for their participation. In one of the primary schools the children expressed their view that they were particularly concerned about the way they were treated by the teachers. The issues of behaviour, discipline and rights were all connected as part of this issue. For example, the children felt that although it was appropriate for teachers to tell them off if they broke the rules it was important that the teachers did not shout at them. The children also expressed the view that fair treatment was uni-directional: the children had to behave in certain ways to get some teachers' respect but the teachers did not see that they should behave in particular ways to get children's respect.

Expectations: Children's expectations about their education are in some ways different from teachers' expectations. It is important that teachers genuinely listen to their pupils and act on their views.

Professor Kay Tisdall has spent her career researching children's participation rights: ed.ac.uk/profile/kay-tisdall

See the research briefing about consulting pupils from the Chapter 16 page for this book at reflectiveteaching.co.uk, or consult Rudduck and McIntyre (2007, also Reading 1.3). Case Study 16.2 is drawn from Wyse (2001).

Part 5 Deepening understanding

CLASSROOM PROCESSES
Processes for learners' social needs

Does the educational experience take due account of learner views, feelings and characteristics?	**Relevance:** Is the curriculum presented in ways which are meaningful to learners and so that it can excite their imagination?	**Engagement:** Do our teaching strategies, classroom organisation and consultation enable learners to actively participate in and enjoy their learning?	**Authenticity:** Do learners recognise routine processes of assessment and feedback as being of personal value?

We all, at any age, value our dignity and appreciate it when our individuality is recognised. And we also, as part of our personal development, have to learn to appreciate the needs of others. Goleman (1996) called this 'emotional intelligence' – combining social empathy and skills with personal awareness and capacity to manage one's own feelings. Schools have always worked hard to support such development through curricular provision such as PSHE, drama and the arts.

Feelings about learning itself will directly affect outcomes. Pupils are expert at detecting teacher mood, respect and interest, and research demonstrates the importance of providing a consistent, positive classroom climate. Confidence to tackle new learning challenges is helped by interesting curricula, engaging activities and meaningful feedback. Pitching such learning experiences appropriately is crucial too, with anxiety arising if they are too challenging, and boredom if deemed too easy, repetitive or irrelevant. Such feelings are felt individually but are almost always strongly influenced by peer culture. John Holt's classic book, *How Children Fail* (1964), argued that underperformance is linked to such fear of failure.

Curriculum concept: Relevance

A key question when thinking about curriculum relevance is, how do we know what is relevant to the pupils we teach? An important part of the answer to this question involves finding out from pupils what they think is relevant to them. This can include directly surveying pupils but it also involves the more subtle and sophisticated skills of being a good listener including showing genuine interest in pupils' interests outside of primary schools. The idea of children's 'agency' is an important part of this, a concept that has been explored in more relation to the curriculum in England than in other countries (Manyukhina and Wyse, 2019; Wyse and Manyukhina, 2020).

After many years of relative neglect of curriculum studies, it was good to see the national inspectorate in England, Ofsted, take a renewed interest in the whole curriculum in primary schools. Their report (Ofsted, 2019) included the unexpected admission that too much of a focus on a limited number of measurable outcomes has negative consequences for the curriculum. It was also notable that Ofsted carried out some research, e.g. literature reviews and survey work with schools, to inform their new approach to inspecting school curricula.

One problem with the 2019 report was the lack of account of how and why the previously published research was selected to underpin Ofsted's conclusions. With regard to the primary curriculum, Ofsted's references to previously published work about curriculum are limited. Ofsted's conclusions about the kinds of curriculum designs that schools used, and *de facto* became recommended, were notable for their emphasis on knowledge and skills but not on pupils' agency (for an alternative reading see the blog by Wyse and Manyukhina, 2019, **bera.ac.uk/blog/ what-next-for-curriculum**, and more research related to this is available via the Chartered College of Teaching **theeducation.exchange/childrens-agency-and-the-curriculum/**).

reflectiveteaching.co.uk/rtps6/part5_ch16

Some of the first Ofsted curriculum reports published after the 2019 report were about separate subjects in the curriculum not about whole curriculum design in early years settings and primary schools. This overall emphasis on knowledge and on separate subjects, as important as these are, suggests an alliance with the ideology of England's knowledge-based national curriculum rather than a more open democratic attempt to critique and improve it. Evidence that a democratic approach to curriculum development that includes attention to pupils' and teachers' agency as a practical reality can be seen in national curriculum development in Ireland since 2020. The national curricula in all other countries in the UK do not have the same knowledge-based model that England has. The most serious consequence of Ofsted's approach is the missed opportunity to emphasise hildrenn's views and agency as a way to ensure curriculum relevance.

Pedagogy concept: Engagement

TLRP research on pupil consultation (e.g. Rudduck and McIntyre, 2007, Reading 1.3) and learner identities (e.g. Pollard and Filer, 2007, Reading 1.2) showed that, if pupils feel that they matter in school and are respected, then they feel more positive about themselves as learners. They can understand and manage their own progress better, and feel more included. The underlying driver here is termed 'agency' – the opportunity for self-directed action and fulfilment.

Young people become more engaged if their perspectives, concerns and experiences are taken seriously. The projects found that pupil contributions were invariably practical and constructive – and were thus also beneficial to teachers. Such feedback supported more open, collaborative and communicative relationships and thus had the potential to transform pedagogic strategies and enhance learning outcomes.

Assessment concept: Authenticity

Traditional assessments measure what a student can recall or do in the formal context of testing. By comparison, authentic assessment puts the emphasis on the meaningful application in *real-life situations* (Wiggins, 1989). Rather than being required to simply demonstrate performance for an artificial purpose, the learner has the opportunity to apply their growing knowledge and capability to genuine activity. The task, and feedback on it, is thus more personally meaningful. Authentic assessment is likely to affirm those who have the deeper levels of skill and understanding which are needed for application.

Overcoming the artificiality of school so that new knowledge can be grounded in the 'real world' is not easy. Project work is a long-standing strategy and new technologies provide wonderful resources. There are many contemporary initiatives to promote 'real-world learning', primarily because transfer of school learning consistently proves to be difficult.

reflectiveteaching.co.uk/rtps6/part5_ch16

Processes for learners' cognitive needs

Case Study 16.3 Time to talk

The slogan 'it's good to talk' has become a cliché, but that's because it's true. Projects such as TLRP's SPRinG and Cambridge's Thinking Together have demonstrated how effective pupil dialogue and discussion can boost children's attainment, enthusiasm and self-efficacy.

Examples published by Thinking Together show how teachers who are successful in teaching children to collaborate effectively model the kind of talk that is useful in discussion.

Here, a Key Stage 3 teacher introduces a maths activity to the whole class. The maths activity uses software called 'Function Machine', in which the children are asked to consider what operation might have been done to one number in order to end up with another. As well as deciding on the operation, the groups have to come up with a strategy for discovering it and for testing their ideas.

Teacher: OK. I'm going to put a number in. . .
Louis: One thousand?
Teacher: OK, Louis immediately said one thousand – is that a good number to put in?
Child: No.
Teacher: You're shaking your head – but why do you think it is not? . . . Shall we come back to you? You've got an idea but you can't explain it? OK, Louis had one thousand. Anybody think 'yes' or 'no' to that idea? . . . David.
David: Start off with an easier number.
Teacher: Start off with an easier number. By an easier number what kind of number do you mean?
David: Um. Something like – lower – five.
Teacher: Fine. A smaller number – a lower number – yes. Louis can you see that point of view?
Louis: Yes.
Teacher: If we put in a thousand we could end up with a huge number. If we put in five do you think it will be easier to work out what the machine has done?
Class: Yes.
Teacher: Everyone agree? OK, so I'm going to type in five to start with. . .

In this discussion the ground rules for talk are embedded in the teacher's demonstration of the activity. The language she uses is full of indicator words, such as 'what', 'how', 'if' and 'why' as she leads them through a line of reasoning. She accepts and discusses the challenges made by David and the class to Louis' suggestion, whilst respecting his contribution in initiating the discussion.

She demonstrates how to consider the validity of alternative suggestions, at the same time as seeking clarification. She invites others to speak so that as many people as possible feel able to join in the discussion. Finally, she ensures that an agreement is sought and reached. In this way, the teacher is demonstrating effective collaboration. The children are engaged in the discussion, motivated to participate and are real partners in the learning.

Dialogue: The teacher draws pupils into decision-making about an investigative strategy, respecting their ideas but leading their reasoning.

This case study is adapted with permission from Dawes and Sams (2004). See also TLRP's Commentary, *Assessment in Schools: Fit for Purpose* from the Chapter 16 page for this book at reflectiveteaching.co.uk

reflectiveteaching.co.uk/rtps6/part5_ch16

Chapter 16 Teacher expertise

LEARNING OUTCOMES
Outcomes for continuing improvement in learning

Does the educational experience equip learners for adult and working life, and for an unknown future?	**Effectiveness:** Are there improvements in standards, in both basic skills and other areas of curricular attainment, to satisfy society's goals?	**Empowerment:** Is our pedagogic repertoire successful in enhancing wellbeing, learning disposition, capabilities and agency?	**Consequence:** Do assessment outcomes lead towards recognised qualifications and a confident sense of personal identity?

What outcomes do we want from education?

We certainly need people who can contribute effectively in economic terms within the labour market. We also need citizens with social and global awareness in response to growing cultural diversity and the ecological challenge. We need those who will become good parents and contribute to their communities and civil society. And then there is the need for future technologists . . . and the arts . . . and so on, and so on. A review of the National Curriculum in England proposed an over-riding set of economic, social, cultural, personal and environmental goals (DfE, 2011a).

Whilst there is relative continuity in general priorities, specific needs and circumstances do change over time. An enduring priority is that learners should have self-confidence and a positive learning disposition. This relates to empowerment and 'agency' – the intrinsic, personal capacity to adapt to circumstances throughout the lifecourse.

Examinations are the traditional way of certifying capabilities in relation to summative attainment in mainstream school subjects. However, can innovative forms of assessment, such as portfolios, represent broader, developmental achievements.

Curriculum concept: Effectiveness

School performance is a major public issue and will always be a concern of parents, governors, local authorities, media and politicians (see Chapter 14). The quality of teaching is the single most important factor in realising pupil potential, a fact that is internationally recognised (OECD, 2005; Hattie, 2009). And the moral commitment of teachers to learners also calls for active monitoring of outcomes. Reviews of performance thus provide a valuable focus for systematic reflective and collaborative enquiry.

Inspection of schools is managed in different ways in each nation of the UK, but there appears to be an increasing focus on the quality of teaching and learning itself and, of course, on pupil outcomes. Significantly, the professional judgement of inspectors has the potential to tackle issues which numeric data cannot reach. For monitoring the performance of school systems internationally, performance in key subject areas is sampled, as is done in the OECD's PISA study.

Pedagogy concept: Empowerment

The first of TLRP's ten principles states that: 'Learning should aim to help people to develop the intellectual, personal and social resources that will enable them to participate as active citizens and workers and to flourish as individuals in a diverse and changing society' (see Chapter 4). So empowerment is the very stuff of 'education' in its broadest sense. But what does this mean in the classroom?

Dweck (2000, Reading 2.6) contrasted pupils with a 'mastery' orientation from those who develop 'learned helplessness'. Experiences of classroom life contribute to such self-beliefs. By creating opportunities for learners to take independent and successful action, teachers support the development of self-confidence and positive learning dispositions.

Assessment concept: Consequence

In taking stock of their work as a whole, teachers need to consider whether or not they have been able to enrich the lives of the learners in their care and increased learners' life-chances (see Chapter 15).

Are they better able to acquire the qualifications they will one day need to enter the labour market? We need to be sure that new knowledge, understanding and skills are secure. Indeed, it is crucial, that all students acquire good basic skills before they leave school. But have they also developed self-confidence and a strong sense of personal identity?

reflectiveteaching.co.uk/rtps6/part5_ch16

Outcomes for certification and the lifecourse

Case study 16.4 'Here's the keys, you're free now'

Tony Wilf was in his fifties, adjusting to the death of his wife, and had two young teenagers still at home. He wanted to look after them properly, and thought it would be nice to make home-made fish and chips.

'I couldn't remember how to do batter so I asked one of the old ladies next door, and she gave me this book,' he told researchers. 'But I could not read.' Tony ended up going to the chip shop because he felt too humiliated to ask the neighbour, or his children, to read the recipe out to him.

Tony had been unfortunate in his schooling. 'I was told time and time again by teachers, "you're thick, you don't understand". If somebody had said, "right, what's the problem?". . . that would have been fine.'

Tony had worked as an unskilled labourer for most of his life, and enjoyed learning from the older craftsmen, but he knew his literacy problems had stopped him from advancing.

It was forty years after leaving school that Tony was finally diagnosed with dyslexia. In fact, this came about because he was trying to help his daughter, Clare, with her own literacy.

Clare had trouble with her handwriting, so Tony decided to get a home computer to print out her work. 'So I went to "Computers for the Terrified". And it worked. I got into it, I really enjoyed that, and then something came up about "insert so and so after the third paragraph" and I thought, "what's a paragraph?" . . . so that's why I started coming back to doing the English. . .'

Tony's first English class didn't work out because he and the tutor got into arguments about his use of block capitals to write letters. His school experiences had left him unable to deal with not being listened to. Fortunately he tried again, and this time the tutor dealt with students as individuals. The use of coloured overlays designed for dyslexics led to a big improvement in Tony's reading. Apart from improving his basic skills, the courses provided a focus for his life: 'what I like about it, you know, everybody works as a group; nobody takes the Mickey out of anybody'.

Tony became interested in local history and started writing. 'It's as though I've been locked away for years and somebody's said, "well here you go, here's the keys, you're free now",' he said.

Empowerment: Supportive adult education opened new horizons for Tony, releasing his innate talents and interests.

Tony's case is adapted from Hodkinson et al. (2007). For more information on TLRP's *Learning Lives* project, see the research briefing on learning across the life course from the Chapter 16 page for this book at reflectiveteaching.co.uk. An accessible book of the project is: Biesta, Field, Goodson, Hodkinson and Macleod (2010). A comprehensive case for lifelong learning has been made by Schuller and Watson (2009).

USING THE CONCEPTUAL FRAMEWORK

The conceptual framework (Figure 16.2) represents the issues that teachers face on a day-to-day basis. It is offered as a tool to support professional reflection and deepen expertise. It is a reference point for many of the major questions that must be faced when practical classroom judgements are made.

The framework is an explicit tool for reflecting on theory and practice, as recommended by Timperley et al. in a wide-ranging international review of continuing professional development for teachers (2007, Reading 16.6).

In the 'Deepening Expertise' section of reflectiveteaching.co.uk, the framework is also available in a PDF format for you to download and explore.

Below are some ways in which the framework has been used.

Problem solving during initial training

Student teachers were introduced to the conceptual framework and 'expert questions' before going into schools – but at that stage it all seemed a bit complicated. During their time in school they were asked to identify their 'biggest challenge' and to relate it to the framework in discussion with a mentor. The *issues* underlying their *problems* became clearer. When back at college, these experiences were shared in group discussions with other students.

> Well, I was in survival mode at school really, but I did the exercise and began to see how the way the children were responding to me related to the curriculum I was providing and to the feedback I was giving them. Once I'd begun to realise how everything fits together, things started to drop into place. The framework is a good device for problem-solving. (Student Teacher)

Reflecting on professional commitment

Sally Brown had been teaching very successfully for twelve years in primary schools, and was respected as an excellent teacher. What was it that kept her in the classroom?

> I've been wondering about applying for management jobs for ages, but the framework showed me why I really prefer to be a hands-on teacher. I enjoy my classroom work immensely but I've found it hard to explain exactly what I do to other people, and even to myself! Now I feel I *can* explain. The framework gives a good overview of why teaching is difficult, but also why it is fascinating!' (Classroom Teacher)

reflectiveteaching.co.uk/rtps6/part5_ch16

Analysing teaching and learning

To start a discussion about effective teaching at a special school, each member of staff was asked to write about a successful lesson, describing and analysing what made it work.

Having shared their stories, the staff considered their practice in the light of the conceptual framework. How far were the concepts and questions reflected in narratives of experience? What changes would there have been if certain questions had been asked before planning the lesson?

> The framework offers a way of looking at our practice with a discerning eye, and to really discuss what we're doing. It reveals gaps, and then we collectively develop solutions. (Deputy Head)

Supporting curriculum development

A primary school redeveloped its approach to foundation subjects to make them more relevant and accessible to the children. The staff team used the conceptual framework to assess and evaluate the content, approach and effectiveness of their ideas.

> I feel the concepts in the framework reflect the important elements of a twenty-first century school curriculum. For me it asks the questions of why and how we are teaching rather than what – and it offers a structure to think about our provision. Pedagogy, it seems, has for some years not been as important a discussion topic as test results, but I think that effective pedagogy needs to be our principal concern. (Headteacher)

Reflective Activity 16.2

Aim: To explore using the conceptual framework to reflect on professional expertise.

Evidence and reflection: Consider each of the applications of the framework illustrated above. Do these approaches resonate with you – for problem solving, reviewing professionalism, analysing practice or curriculum development?

Select one of them and identify a particular issue which has challenged you. Does the framework help in reviewing this?

Extension: Use the framework when discussing a significant shared issue with a group of colleagues. Does it provoke new lines of discussion?

---

reflectiveteaching.co.uk/rtps6/part5_ch16

CONCLUSION

This chapter has presented a conceptual framework which, as a whole, represents the major dimensions of teacher expertise. The framework is organised around nine enduring issues associated with educational aims, learning contexts, classroom processes and learning outcomes. Each issue is explored in relation to curriculum, pedagogy and assessment. The chapter then provides examples of selected concepts, including some case study illustrations and a brief introduction to some of the research which underpins them. Links are also made back to chapters within the book.

The conceptual framework is offered as a contribution to the development of a shared professional language. It is a support for professional thinking and discussion together.

However, the framework also *celebrates* teacher expertise, for the truth is that, whilst it may seem complex, teachers work and succeed within this terrain all the time. Indeed, during a career, a great deal of professional fulfilment is derived from exploring the issues which the framework highlights.

The ongoing challenge, as part of the development of expertise, is to identify this expertise more explicitly and to find ways of representing it more clearly.

If this can be done, the profession may be seen as more self-confident as well as more effective. And the public may become even more appreciative of the skills, knowledge, understanding and moral commitment which good teachers embody, something that Alison Peacock of the Chartered College of Teaching has consistently reminded us all.

reflectiveteaching.co.uk/rtps6/part5_ch16

CHAPTER WEBPAGE

reflectiveteaching.co.uk offers additional professional resources for this chapter. For the chapter webpage, go to: reflectiveteaching.co.uk/books-and-resources/rts5/part5/ch16

Additionally, however, there is a whole section on the website on expertise – see: reflectiveteaching.co.uk/deepening-expertise. The Deepening Expertise section is being developed to provide links to websites which extend understanding and application of teacher expertise.

For example, Harry Fletcher-Wood has created a website on 'Improving Teaching' (improvingteaching.co.uk), which contains some incisive summarising blogs. Two of them are highly relevant to this chapter: 'What Makes Expert Teachers?' and 'Between Novice and Expert'. He picks out three characteristics of an expert teacher: they have detailed mental models; they recognise patterns; they think rapidly and accurately.

Of course, the conceptual framework introduced in this chapter is an explicit 'mental model' of teacher expertise, emphasising the range of knowledge and understanding on which it rests. In particular, it summarises and relates powerful concepts in relation to curriculum, pedagogy and assessment. The page at: reflectiveteaching.co.uk/deepening-expertise/conceptual-framework enables this framework to be manipulated, so that the rows and columns can be expanded and contracted to enable focus on particular dimensions or consideration of the whole.

Additionally, the chapter webpage provides an extended set of suggestions on *Further Reading*. And extracts from *Key Readings* are reprinted in *Readings for Reflective Teaching in Schools*.

KEY READINGS

Many of the Key Readings suggested for Chapter 3 on reflective practice are very relevant for this chapter, including, for example, Schön (1983, **Reading 3.2**) and Stenhouse (1975, **Reading 3.3**).

Key Readings for Chapter 4, on the principles of effective teaching and learning, are also highly pertinent to the enduring issues which have been identified. For example, see Dumont et al. for the OECD (2010, **Reading 4.4**) or Hattie (2009, **Reading 4.6**).

On continuing professional development through a career, the best summary of effective practice is Timperley et al. (2007, **Reading 16.6**).

We offer supplementary suggestions on the specific issue of expertise itself. For a philosophical overview of the nature of expertise, see:

> Winch, C. (2012) *Dimensions of Expertise: A Conceptual Exploration of Vocational Knowledge*. London: Continuum.

A completely different approach to the topic is provided by a compendium from practising teachers with 'hints and tips on how to be the best teacher you can be' – with interesting mapping of its contents to the conceptual framework provided in this chapter.

> Jones, R. (ed.) (2014) *Don't Change the Light Bulbs: A Compendium of Expertise from the UK's Most Switched-on Educators*. Carmarthen: Crown House.

Developmental accounts of how expertise evolves through the interaction of practice and analysis are provided by:

> Eraut, M. (1994) *Developing Professional Knowledge and Competence*. London: Routledge.
>
> Ericsson, K.A., Charness, N., Feltovich, P. and Hoffman, R.R. eds. (2006) *The Cambridge Handbook of Expertise and Expert Performance*. Cambridge: Cambridge University Press.
>
> Flook, J., Ryan, M. and Hawkins, L. (2010) *Professional Expertise: Practice, Theory and Education for Working in Uncertainty*. London: Whiting and Birch.
>
> Loughran, J. (2010) *What Expert Teachers Do: Enhancing Professional Knowledge for Classroom Practice*. London: Routledge.
>
> Shulman, L.S. (2004) *The Wisdom of Practice – Essays on Teaching, Learning and Learning to Teach*. San Francisco: Jossey Bass.

Two books which analyse and apply teacher expertise in primary school contexts are:

> Eaude, T. (2012) *How Do Expert Primary Classteachers Really Work? A Critical Guide for Teachers, Headteachers and Teacher Educators*. Northwich: Critical Publishing. (Reading 16.3)
>
> Sangster, M. (2012) *Developing Teacher Expertise: Exploring Key Issues in Primary Practice*. London: Bloomsbury Academic.

This is an exceptional chapter which integrates the 'expert questions' posed throughout the book into an overarching conceptual framework. To extend this journey, the internet offers many sources for deepening expertise further.

For an excellent guide to the use of the internet for education, see:

> Houghton, E. (ed.) (2012) *Education on the Web: A Tool-kit to Help You Search Effectively for Information on Education*. Slough: NFER.

Chapter 17
Professional learning
How can we nurture career-long reflective teaching?

Introduction	538

Understanding the 'professional' in career-long professional learning	540
Professionalism	540
Professional organisations	541

What do we know about how teachers learn?	542
What do we know about different approaches to teacher learning?	544

Engaging with professional learning policies	546
Policy as political	546
Central features of professional learning policies across the UK	547
What can we learn from looking across the four jurisdictions?	550

Conclusion	550

reflectiveteaching.co.uk/rtps6/part5_ch17

538   Part 5   Deepening understanding

INTRODUCTION

Across the UK teaching is considered to be a profession, rather than simply a job. Being part of a profession brings with it both contractual and moral obligations, and one of these obligations is that professionals should consider themselves as career-long learners. While most, if not all, teachers would agree wholeheartedly with that sentiment, the practicalities are a little more complex. Accessing and engaging in appropriate professional learning involves: being able to reflect critically on one's own learning priorities; understanding the development needs and priorities of one's own work context; understanding the wider national policy context and being able to adopt a critically reflective stance on that (see Chapter 3); ensuring that learning makes an impact on practice; engaging with relevant research evidence about teaching and learning; and, not least, finding time to engage meaningfully in professional learning activities. These elements can sometimes be in conflict with one another, or may seem out of balance, but this chapter aims to support you to both understand how teachers learn and the context within which teacher learning takes place.

See Chapter 4

> ## TLRP Principles
>
> Two principles are of particular relevance to this chapter on professionalism and professional learning:
>
> **Effective teaching and learning depends on teacher learning.** The need for teachers to learn continuously in order to develop their knowledge and skills, and adapt and develop their roles, especially through classroom inquiry, should be recognised and supported. (*Principle 9*)
>
> **Effective teaching and learning demands consistent policy frameworks with support for teaching and learning as their primary focus.** Policies at national, local and institutional levels need to recognise the fundamental importance of teaching and learning. They should be designed to create effective learning environments in which all learners can thrive. (*Principle 10*)

In talking about professional learning, it is worth saying a word or two about terminology, as this can vary across contexts. The term 'continuing professional development', or 'CPD' is perhaps most commonly used across the globe, and not just within teaching, but across a large number of professions. However, increasingly in teaching, we find the term 'professional learning' is favoured. While these terms are sometimes used synonymously, there is debate about the distinction between professional development and professional learning.

Often, the term 'professional development' is used to describe activities, or episodes of professional learning. For example, in their recent report for the Education Endowment

reflectiveteaching.co.uk/rtps6/part5_ch17

Foundation, Sims et al. (2021) define teacher professional development as 'structured, facilitated activity for teachers intended to increase their teaching ability' (p. 7), a somewhat narrow definition limited to only 'structured, facilitated' activity which precludes other forms of learning such as individual reading, teacher-initiated networks or mentoring conversations. In contrast, 'professional learning' might be seen to be a more holistic expression of the totality of a set of individual professional development experiences. Importantly, learning implies a change in knowing, and as Easton (2008, p. 756) argues, is rightly gaining more traction as a desirable facet of teacher professionalism:

> It is clearer today than ever that educators need to learn, and that's why professional learning has replaced professional development. Developing is not enough. Educators must be knowledgeable and wise. They must know enough in order to change. They must change in order to get different results. They must become learners, and they must be self-developing.

Suffice to say, that there is ongoing debate about the terms and their underpinning meaning, and that different contexts use different terms (sometimes to mean the same thing), but for the purpose of this chapter, professional learning will be the preferred term, unless quoting from other authors' work, in which case their original terminology will be used.

There are three parts to this chapter. The first explores professions and professionalism, by way of setting the scene for the expectation that teachers should engage in career-long professional learning. The second part of the chapter then looks at what we know about how teachers learn, before considering, in the third part, the policy contexts within which that learning takes place.

Reflective Activity 17.1

Aim: To reflect on how we define professional development and professional learning.

Evidence and reflection: Try to write your own definitions of professional development and professional learning. In what ways do they differ, if any? Now lay these definitions aside and engage with the rest of the chapter. When you've finished the chapter return to these definitions and see if there are any refinements you might want to make.

Extension: Use your refined definitions to consider what it is you think you have done over the past year that constitutes professional development or professional learning.

UNDERSTANDING THE 'PROFESSIONAL' IN CAREER-LONG PROFESSIONAL LEARNING

Professionalism

It is generally seen as uncontroversial that teachers should enact professionalism, owing to the fact that teaching is viewed as a profession. However, conceptualising 'professionalism' is a bit more controversial.

Eric Hoyle (1974) first drew the powerful distinction between 'restricted' and 'extended' professionalism.

- *Restricted professionalism* is often defined through sets of competence statements or benchmarks, and teachers' technical competence measured by the extent to which they are able to perform these competences. It positions teachers as technicians rather than as autonomous professionals, and limits the sphere of their responsibility to the class in front of them.
- *Extended professionalism* positions teachers as professionals capable of making reflective judgements in a range of different contexts, and also sees the remit of the teacher as going beyond simply delivering lessons to the pupils in front of them. It implies a commitment to the wider school community and to furthering one's own professional learning.

These ideas have been taken further in more recent years, and in particular, the work of Judyth Sachs has been very influential. Sachs (2001) distinguishes between managerial and democratic professionalism. Managerial professionalism she describes as having an emphasis on efficiency through management practices borrowed from business. Within this model, professional development (rather than learning) would be mandated centrally and be a means of ensuring greater compliance, and therefore efficiency. Democratic professionalism, on the other hand, Sachs describes as an approach which 'seeks to demystify professional work and build alliances between teachers and excluded constituencies' (p. 152). Crucially, professional learning under this model of professionalism would engage teachers in collaborative, critical and contextually relevant learning.

These contrasting models of teacher professionalism were considered by Menter et al. (2010) in a literature review commissioned by the Scottish Government. The review suggested that there are four conceptions of teacher professionalism evident in contemporary literature (Reading 17.2). This is summarised in Figure 17.1.

Figure 17.1
Models of teacher professionalism and practice

Restricted professionalism	Extended professionalism		
The effective teacher	The reflective teacher	The enquiring teacher	The transformative teacher

Menter and his colleagues argued that models of the 'effective teacher' had been favoured by many governments for the last thirty years and were underpinned by economic models of education which favour externally mandated accountability and performativity, thus establishing national systems of quality control and compliance. However, whilst these may be deemed necessary, they are not sufficient to move beyond the idea of the teacher as a functionary.

It seems that there is a broad tension here. Many teachers are committed to the concept of 'extended professionalism' and appreciate the trust and esteem which are enjoyed by colleagues in countries such as Finland. But some governments, despite their protestations that teachers are extremely important, are not yet prepared to really support the full development of the profession. There remains, as Onora O'Neill (2002) argued in her Reith Lectures, a crisis of trust in those who provide public services. It is clear from international evidence that this will have to change if overall standards of attainment are to improve. In particular, new relational models of accountability are needed, which recognise mutual responsibilities at all levels of the system. Teachers really do matter. Extended and democratic professionalism, with their capacity to support agency, innovation and collaboration, are the foundation of high-quality education in the modern world.

Professional organisations

The history of national General Teaching Councils has a very varied history across the jurisdictions of the UK. The most established is the General Teaching Council for Scotland (GTCS), which was founded in 1965 to register teachers, maintain professional standards and enhance the quality of teaching on behalf of all stakeholders. In 2012, the GTCS became fully independent of government, though debate on its future does occur from time to time. Over the years it has taken a more active role in shaping and supporting teachers' career-long professional learning, a role more recently shared with Education Scotland, the curriculum and inspection body. There are, of course, some boundary negotiations between the Educational Institute of Scotland (EIS) trade union and GTCS, but the two major teacher membership organisations are broadly complementary.

By contrast, the establishment of a General Teaching Council for England (1998–2011) was not fully endorsed by teacher unions, which left it vulnerable to closure. However, after widespread consultation, a Chartered College of Teaching was finally established in 2017. The College offers a research-informed, professional voice through its rapidly growing (voluntary) membership.

The General Teaching Council for Northern Ireland (GTC NI) has been in existence since 1998, having responsibility for maintaining a register of teachers, for regulating the profession and for providing advice to government on matters including career development.

In Wales, a General Teaching Council was established in 1998 but transformed into the Education Workforce Council (EWC) in 2015. The role as a regulator of professionalism and standards remains, and the EWC is also responsible for accrediting programmes of initial teacher education and for advising the Welsh Government on matters related to the wider education workforce.

reflectiveteaching.co.uk/rtps6/part5_ch17

Part 5 Deepening understanding

In addition to these profession-wide bodies, however, many primary teachers also seek support for their professional learning from subject associations such as the Association for the Study of Primary Education (ASPE), the National Primary Teacher Education Council (NaPTEC) and the United Kingdom Literacy Association (UKLA), thus supporting their disciplinary knowledge and identity. While many of these bodies claim UK-wide coverage, many also have national groups working specifically in each of the four jurisdictions of the UK.

WHAT DO WE KNOW ABOUT HOW TEACHERS LEARN?

In the past twenty years in particular there has been an upsurge in research on teacher professional learning and, as a result, we now have several important systematic reviews which synthesise the results of individual studies and draw conclusions about conditions most likely to enhance teacher professional learning.

Cordingley et al. (2005) undertook one of the first systematic reviews which concluded that teachers learn best when they learn collaboratively, engaging in reflection with colleagues on a sustained (rather than a one-off) basis. Since then, many other studies have lent support to these broad conclusions, adding other key elements that now seem key to effective professional learning. For example, Timperley et al. (2008, pp. 6/7) identified ten key principles which outline 'conditions for professional learning and development that impact positively on valued student outcomes', arising from a 'best evidence synthesis'. These principles are:

1 focus on valued student outcomes;

2 worthwhile content;

3 integration of knowledge and skills;

4 assessment for professional inquiry;

5 multiple opportunities to learn and apply information;

6 approaches responsive to learning processes;

7 opportunities to process new learning with others;

8 knowledgeable expertise;

9 active leadership;

10 maintaining momentum.

While a few years later, Stoll et al. (2012) identified nine key propositions about 'great professional development':

1 effective professional development starts with the end in mind;

2 effective professional development challenges thinking as part of changing practice;

3 effective professional development is based on the assessment of individual and school needs;

4 effective professional development involves connecting work-based learning and external expertise;

5 effective professional learning opportunities are varied, rich and sustainable;

6 effective professional development uses action research and enquiry as key tools;

7 effective professional development is strongly enhanced through collaborative learning and joint practice development;

8 effective professional development is enhanced by creating professional learning communities within and between schools;

9 effective professional development requires leadership to create the necessary conditions.

Reflective Activity 17.2

Aim: To consider the features of effective professional learning experiences.

Evidence and reflection: Think about some professional learning that you have done over the past year or so that you believe has had a positive impact on pupil learning. Now reflect on which features of that experience seem to align with those in the lists above.

Extension: Consider the extent to which certain conditions seem to be associated with professional learning that you believe makes a positive difference to your practice. Importantly, you should now think about how you might try to ensure that future professional learning can incorporate key conditions likely to enhance its effectiveness.

While there is clear commonality in key messages arising from these reviews, it is important to acknowledge that they can only tell us so much. Reviews of the literature are framed by particular questions that shape which evidence is selected for review. For example, Timperley et al. (2008) sought to 'consolidate the international and New Zealand evidence around the emerging knowledge base about how to promote teacher learning in ways that impact on outcomes for the diversity of pupils in our classrooms' (p. xxiii), while Stoll et al. (2011) asked the question: 'What makes great professional development which leads to consistently great pedagogy?' In addition to being shaped by the specific question, all such reviews are constrained by what literature already exists. That is, a systematic literature review can only draw conclusions from the research at its disposal, and that research may well be limited in scope. It is important, therefore, to bear in mind that there may well be other conclusions that could have been drawn had other research been available for review. In terms of teacher professional learning, this is often apparent in the kinds of research that link particular professional learning activities with gains in pupil

Part 5 Deepening understanding

learning; such studies tend to focus on pupil outcomes that are more easily measured, such as scores on maths tests, and they tend to avoid more subjective outcomes such as those in creative writing, expressive arts and personal and social development classes.

While it is important to recognise that such reviews have been based on a unique aim with an individual set of protocols, they do nonetheless provide some helpful general guidance in terms of key conditions likely to result in good professional learning. What they don't (and can't) do, however, is suggest the precise approaches that will serve to satisfy these key conditions in particular contexts. The next section of the chapter therefore explores how we might go about identifying approaches to professional learning that are fit for their intended purpose(s).

What do we know about different approaches to teacher learning?

The systematic reviews discussed above are unanimous in their conclusion that 'traditional' one-off presentation-type events are less likely to result in effective professional learning than opportunities that are collaborative, sustained and linked to real-life workplace challenges. With that in mind, we now move to explore how we might choose approaches that have the capacity to fulfil a range of different learning aspirations. It is important to note here, though, that we consider professional learning to be more of a process than a one-off event.

We often hear the phrase 'effective professional learning', and it is important to acknowledge that 'effective' is not an absolute measure, rather it is always contingent on context and learning aspirations; it means that the professional learning is fit for purpose. Kennedy (2014) identifies a spectrum of professional development models, organising them in relation to their capacity to support professional autonomy and teacher agency (Figure 17.2). Thinking about professional learning approaches in this way can help us to select approaches that are fit for purpose, and that therefore are more likely to result in the desired impact.

Figure 17.2
Spectrum of CPD models (Kennedy, 2014, p. 693)

Purpose of Model		Examples of models of CPD which may fit within this category
Transmissive	Increasing capacity for professional autonomy and teacher agency	Training models
		Models that address teacher 'deficits'
		Cascade model
Malleable		Award-bearing models
		Standards-based models
		Coaching/mentoring models
		Community of practice models
Transformative		Collaborative professional inquiry models

reflectiveteaching.co.uk/rtps6/part5_ch17

Kennedy (2014) describes transmissive as simply being inducted into the status quo whereas transformative learning provides a more 'supportive but challenging forum for both intellectual and affective interrogation of practice' (p. 344). While in many circumstances the aim of professional learning will undoubtedly be transformative, there are, of course, many things that might well be more suited to transmissive learning. For example, learning how to operate a new piece of technology might be better undertaken through a traditional face-to-face or online training mode, e.g. following a step-by-step film.

There are a number of different approaches to professional learning that might be deemed malleable in their purpose; that is, they could serve to promote either transmissive or transformative learning, depending on how they are implemented or engaged with. For example, mentoring is a common approach in the induction period for new teachers. Mentoring can be used to inculcate in the new teacher 'how things are done around here', thereby serving to train the new teacher into operating within the status quo. Mentoring can also be used in a much more transformative way where the learning between mentor and mentee is mutual, and where the mentor supports and challenges the new teacher in a journey of mutual professional growth. A useful source of further reading on coaching and mentoring from researchers and practitioners alike can be found in the CollectivED Working Papers series: **leedsbeckett.ac.uk/research/collectived/working-paper-series/**

Approaches that are more likely to result in transformative professional learning tend to involve an element of collaborative engagement and an element of inquiry; that is, a focus on the active development of contextually important knowledge as opposed to the passive transmission of more generic knowledge not specifically relevant to one's own practice context. There has been considerable focus in recent years in the research and development of approaches that can support transformative learning. Such approaches include lesson study (**tdtrust.org/what-is-lesson-study/**), practitioner inquiry (**gtcs.org.uk/professional-update/practitioner-enquiry.aspx**) and learning rounds or teacher rounds (**impact.chartered.college/article/teacher-rounds-putting-teachers-control-own-learning/**). These approaches support a more democratic conceptualisation of professionalism, as discussed earlier in the chapter, providing teachers with greater opportunity to exercise agency and to shape their learning in ways that will benefit their own 'problems of practice'.

Inevitably, teachers engage in a mixture of both externally or institutionally mandated and self-selected professional learning. In the past ten or twenty years, as technology has advanced, it has become easier and more commonplace for teachers to bypass the traditional gatekeepers of professional learning and to engage in what is sometimes termed 'teacher-initiated professional learning'. The lockdowns experienced in 2020 and 2021 as a result of the COVID-19 pandemic spurred exponential growth in such activity. As our worlds moved almost entirely online, seminars, conferences and workshops that traditionally would not have been accessible suddenly opened up a whole new world to teachers. Previous barriers such as physical location, timing and cost became much less problematic. In addition to organised events, teachers made much more use of online networking and communication than they had previously. That said, in a study of teachers' use of Twitter during the COVID-19 pandemic, Alwafi (2021, p. 11) found that while 'teachers interacted with people from both within and outside their academic disciplines, the majority of interactions were between people from the same discipline and country'. She concludes that teachers should be supported to increase their awareness of and engagement in professional networks, and that they should seek to develop greater intercultural communication competence in order to make the most of widely accessible global professional learning opportunities.

While the pandemic and related advances in our access to technology have no doubt increased professional learning opportunities for teachers, there is still a lack of research evidence exploring the specific learning gains possible through online teacher professional learning. Indeed, the lack of gatekeeping, while a bonus in terms of teacher autonomy and accessibility, means that quality assurance is much more problematic, and relies on teachers using critical judgement themselves in relation to the worth of such teacher-initiated professional learning. Pre-pandemic, Lantz-Andersson, Lundin and Selwyn (2018, p. 313) carried out a review of existing research into online teacher learning communities, raising a number of questions including what kind(s) of collegiality are developed in both formal and informal online professional communities, the power of often self-selected leaders to shape the community and 'whether teachers are actually working with (rather than working alongside) each other, [and] the extent to which online environments foster a sense of competition amongst participants or a desire to work primarily for the community's mutual benefit as opposed to enhancing one's own individual status and reputation'.

Whether engaging in formal or informal, planned or incidental, online or face-to-face and transmissive or transformative professional learning, the key message is that we must be conscious of selecting an approach that is fit for purpose and that we must apply our own critical scrutiny to our professional learning activities in order to ensure quality and fitness for purpose.

ENGAGING WITH PROFESSIONAL LEARNING POLICY

Policy as political

Professional learning is shaped by policy, and policy, as we know, is never neutral. As Tonna and Shanks (2017) assert, wider education reforms dictated by national governments can only be achieved if teachers adapt their practices, and they do this through professional learning. Professional learning is therefore a very powerful tool for achieving education reform.

Linked to this, policies which shape professional learning always reveal something about what a nation values in its teachers. For example, if teachers are positioned as technical operatives, then professional learning policies tend to list competences and provide externally mandated ways of ensuring that teachers can 'tick off' these lists of competences. On the other hand, if a nation wants teachers who are creative and autonomous, then professional learning policies will be much more likely to encourage a range of approaches and will encourage individuality and support teacher autonomy in choosing what, how and when to learn.

Teachers can, of course, contribute to the shaping of policy through general civic engagement such as taking an active role in local and national politics, but can also contribute to education policy discussion through more focused engagement with bodies such as teacher unions (see Chapter 18), national teaching councils and subject associations. In reality, however, Ball et al. (2011b, p. 633) reported that most newly qualified teachers (and probably many experienced teachers too) adopt a view borne out of the busyness of their job that: 'Policy comes from "them" – either SLT or "government" or both and is mostly something to be "followed", to be struggled with, to be "made sense of" or not, in less time than is really needed.' This suggests that in reality it is quite demanding to teach and to simultaneously engage critically and strategically in policy development. Nonetheless, understanding why things are the way they are allows a teacher to put a little critical distance between themselves and the 'regime' they work within. In relation to professional learning, it is then quite helpful for teachers to understand not only what policy levers exist that shape their professional learning, but also why they exist and how they can be used to best advantage. A good example of this is the case of professional standards. Used uncritically these can seem like lists of behaviours to be demonstrated and ticked-off, but used in a more developmental way, as a stimulus for talking about one's work, they can become a rich and useful source of ideas.

With this wider context of governance in mind, we now go on to look at some of the key features of teacher professional learning policies across the UK, examining both similarities and differences.

Central features of professional learning policies across the UK

In the past twenty years or so teacher professional learning has become increasingly enshrined in, and shaped by, national policies across and beyond the UK. Such policies include induction systems for newly qualified teachers, annual review and appraisal systems (often linked to ongoing registration requirements), preparation and qualifications for headship roles, and, perhaps most significantly in terms of their power to shape the professional learning discourse and practice, the publication of sets of professional standards. This chapter focuses on such policies in the UK context, but for readers interested in the wider global picture, the annual OECD 'Education at a Glance' publication provides interesting statistics on a whole number of education-related issues, including teachers and their professional preparation/learning (oecd-ilibrary.org/education/education-at-a-glance_19991487) and the OECD's Teaching and Learning International Survey (TALIS) provides more detailed analysis of specific elements of teachers' work (oecd.org/education/talis/).

Investing in systematic supported induction for newly qualified teachers has long been seen as an important means of both developing and retaining teachers in the system. All four jurisdictions of the UK have some sort of formal induction process in place, all of which are based around sets of professional standards (referred to as 'teacher competences' in Northern Ireland).

England

Early career teachers (the term now used in official policy to replace the term 'newly qualified teacher') working in England are required to undertake a two-year statutory induction period underpinned by the *Early Career Framework* (**gov.uk/government/publications/early-career-framework**). The framework sets out an entitlement to a two-year supported professional development experience which includes regular mentoring, and is clear that the assessment of early career teachers is based on the *Teachers' Standards* (DfE, 2011b, updated 2013 and 2021). These standards are firmly set within a wider legislative framework and are associated with not just the achievement of 'qualified teacher status' (QTS), but are also used within the mandatory induction period 'to assess the performance of all teachers with QTS who are subject to the Education (School Teachers' Appraisal (England) Regulations 2012' (p. 3). They are organised in two sections: part one listing specific competences under the heading of 'teaching' that a teacher must demonstrate, and part two entitled 'personal and professional conduct' listing behaviours that 'define the behaviour and attitudes which set the required standard for conduct throughout a teacher's career' (p. 14). The *Standards* portray a managerial perspective on professionalism within a top-down accountability framework. That is not to say, however, that teachers can't use the *Standards* as a stimulus for professional learning discussions, and indeed the *Early Career Framework*, while based on the *Standards*, encourages reflective dialogue.

Northern Ireland

Meanwhile, in Northern Ireland, early professional learning is conceptualised as a three-year period which includes induction and early professional development. It is viewed as a partnership between the Northern Ireland Education Authority and individual schools, and includes the provision of a named 'teacher tutor' to support early career teachers in schools. During the one-year induction period element of this process, new teachers are expected to use the GTC NI's *Teacher Competences* (GTC NI, 2011) as the basis of their development, and to present evidence of having met the competences in a portfolio.

The *Teacher Competences* are outlined in a document entitled 'Teaching: The reflective profession, incorporating the Northern Ireland Teacher Competences', which provides:

> a comprehensive discourse which sets out the ethical basis and moral purposes of our work, as well as a clear understanding of the practice of teaching. In providing a

common framework and language it will facilitate discussion and allow for teachers, acting in communities of practice, to more readily share experiences and understandings about the complex and value-laden process of education. (p. 6)

This document clearly portrays teachers as much more than technicians, and articulates a clearly developed position on how teachers are viewed in Northern Ireland, and their importance in the wider educational and societal context. This contrasts starkly with the more managerial and accountability-focused positioning evident in the English *Standards*.

Scotland

Scotland too has a mandatory induction period during which newly qualified teachers work towards meeting the *Standard for Full Registration*, having met the *Standard for Provisional Registration* during initial teacher education. Most newly qualified teachers in Scotland complete induction through the Teacher Induction Scheme, which entitles eligible ITE graduates to a one-year paid post in a school, with a reduced teaching timetable, support from a named 'supporter' (teacher mentor) and access to a programme of professional learning provided by the employing authority.

The *Standard for Full Registration* which newly qualified teachers are working towards during the induction year forms part of a suite of standards, the latest version of which was published in 2021: gtcs.org.uk/professional-standards/professional-standards-for-teachers/ While the suite contains separate standards for provisional and full registration, for career-long professional learning, for middle leadership and for headship, they all start with the same introduction which focuses on 'being a teacher in Scotland' and outlines the values and dispositions expected of teachers. There are parallels here with the introduction to the Northern Irish competences, although the Scottish version is much briefer.

Wales

Newly qualified teachers in Wales are also required to complete a statutory induction period during which they work towards meeting the *Professional Standards for Teaching and Leadership* (Welsh Government, 2018). As discussed earlier, Wales has an Education Workforce Council, rather than a Teaching Council, indicating its recognition of the wider staff group of education practitioners employed in schools and other education settings. Interestingly, however, the Welsh standards are published by the Welsh Government rather than the EWC, illustrating the complex overlap of responsibilities for teacher professional learning. The standards are organised around five key elements of a teacher's work: pedagogy, collaboration, innovation, professional learning and leadership. Similar to the Scottish professional standards, they are accompanied by an overarching statement of values and dispositions that 'drive all teachers to be the best they can be' (p. 3).

What can we learn from looking across the four jurisdictions?

It is clear that while the four jurisdictions of the UK share much in common, not least a UK-wide government, the operation of devolution settlements has led to increasing diversification in education policy, particularly between England and the other three jurisdictions. While each of the four jurisdictions has developed its own professional standards for teachers, and these are intimately connected with other policy levers, it is a useful exercise to look at professional standards from outside the particular nation in which you might currently be working as a teacher. This allows us not only to get a clearer idea of how teaching is positioned elsewhere, but also to reflect critically on how policy tools can help or hinder our own professional learning.

CONCLUSION

In drawing this chapter to a close, it is important to reiterate the central importance of career-long professional learning as a central element of teacher professionalism; it is a professional obligation and the means through which teachers continue to grow and to serve the children, young people and families with whom they work.

The chapter has explored the complexities of professional learning in terms of what constitutes 'good' professional learning, indicating that while it is possible to identify a number of conditions likely to result in good professional learning, so much depends on context and fitness for purpose. Part of the complexity of professional learning is that it serves such a wide range of purposes: it supports teachers to work better in their current workplace contexts, it helps them to develop knowledge and skills necessary to fulfil future career aspirations and it also serves as a tool through which governments and other national and supra-national bodies can enact reform. Considered and reflective engagement in career-long professional learning, then, is a fundamental aspect of being a teacher, and we hope that this chapter helps readers to understand its importance, its complexities and its possibilities.

reflectiveteaching.co.uk/rtps6/part5_ch17

CHAPTER WEBPAGE

reflectiveteaching.co.uk offers additional professional resources for this chapter. For the chapter webpage, go to: reflectiveteaching.co.uk/rtps6/part5_ch17

In England, the Chartered College of Teaching offers 'self-assessment toolkits' to support evidence-informed teaching (see: chartered.college/evidence-engagement). In Scotland, the General Teaching Council, has extensive resources on 'professional learning' and on 'research and practitioner enquiry' (see: gtcs.org.uk/professional-update/what-is-professional-learning.aspx).

Professional knowledge and support is available also by curricular subject and by age phase of schooling. For links to over twenty subject associations, go to: subjectassociations.org.uk

The chapter webpage provides an extended set of suggestions on *Further Reading*. And extracts from *Key Readings* are reprinted in *Readings for Reflective Teaching in Schools*.

KEY READINGS

Many of the books suggested as further reading for Chapters 3 and 5 will also be relevant here.

Eric Hoyle's classic paper on restricted and extended professionalism can be found in:

> Hoyle, E. and Megarry, J. (2005) *World Yearbook of Education 1980: The Professional Development of Teachers*. London: Routledge.

For a historically contextualised account of the development of teachers' professional agency, see:

> McCullough, G., Helsby, G. and Knight, P. (2000) *The Politics of Professionalism: Teachers and the Curriculum*. London: Continuum.

Stenhouse continues to have much to teach us on the role of the teacher in a democracy, and Sachs continues and extends the tradition.

> Sachs, J. (2003) *The Activist Teaching Profession*. Buckingham: Open University Press.
>
> Stenhouse, L. (1983) *Authority, Education and Emancipation*. London: Heinemann.

For penetrating analyses of how education policy is created in government and may be mediated by teachers, see:

Ball, S.J. (1994) *Education Reform: A Critical and PostStructural Approach.* Buckingham: Open University Press. (see also **Reading 17.7**)

Ball, S.J., Maguire, M. and Braun, A. (2011a) *How Schools Do Policy: Policy Enactments in Secondary Schools.* London: Routledge.

Action by reflective teachers within the democratic process calls for some knowledge of political structures and processes. For an excellent UK overview, see:

Leyland, P. (2012) *Constitution of the United Kingdom: A Contextual Analysis.* Oxford: Hart Publishing.

Of course, much of the philosophy which underpins this book as a whole was all set out a century ago by John Dewey:

Dewey, J. (1916) *Democracy and Education: An Introduction to the Philosophy of Education.* New York: Macmillan.

Chapter 18
Professionalism
How does reflective teaching contribute to society?

Introduction	554

Education and society	555
What should an education system be designed to do?	555
What can be achieved through education?	560

Addressing inequalities	561

Classroom teaching and society	563

Reflective teaching and the democratic process	566
Taking action	569
Professional and union organisation	570

Conclusion	571

reflectiveteaching.co.uk/rtps6/part5_ch18

INTRODUCTION

Historically, there is a strong tradition of civic responsibility among teachers in all parts of the UK, and the contribution to public life of socially aware professional educators has been very strong.

Indeed, teaching reflects moral purpose and has significant social consequences. For these reasons, commitments to educational quality and to social justice have been promoted by the UK General Teaching Councils. For example, the GTC NI's *Code of Values and Professional Practice* states:

> Teachers will, as reflective practitioners, contribute to the review and revision of policies and practices with a view to optimising the opportunities for pupils or addressing identified individual or institutional needs. (GTC NI, 2007, p. 44)

In our discussion of social contexts, Chapter 5, we introduced the idea of social development being based on a dialectical process, as individuals respond to and act within the situations in which they find themselves (Mills, 1959, Reading 5.1). Actions in the present are thus influenced by the past, but they also contribute to the future (see Archer, 1979, Reading 17.1). All teachers, as individuals, are members of society and we hope that reflective teachers will be particularly capable of acting in society to initiate and foster morally and ethically sound developments as 'imaginative professionals' (Power, 2008, Reading 17.5).

See Chapter 4

> ### TLRP Principles
>
> Two principles are of particular relevance to this chapter on professionalism and teachers' role in society:
>
> **Effective teaching and learning depends on teacher learning.** The need for teachers to learn continuously in order to develop their knowledge and skills, and adapt and develop their roles, especially through classroom inquiry, should be recognised and supported. (*Principle 9*)
>
> **Effective teaching and learning demands consistent policy frameworks with support for teaching and learning as their primary focus.** Policies at national, local and institutional levels need to recognise the fundamental importance of teaching and learning. They should be designed to create effective learning environments in which all learners can thrive. (*Principle 10*)

There are four parts to this chapter. The first part discusses the relationship between education and society, considering perspectives on the purpose of education and the implications for achieving such purposes. The second considers the role of education as a means of addressing inequality, and the associated responsibilities of the reflective teacher. The third part focuses on the actions that a reflective teacher could take as a citizen in trying to influence democratic processes of decision-making by local, regional and national governments, and the role of the professional associations in supporting teachers' work.

The Reflective Teaching website offers resources that will help with these issues: **reflectiveteaching.co.uk**

EDUCATION AND SOCIETY

Education has very often been seen as a means of influencing the development of societies. Two major questions have to be faced.

- What should an education system be designed to do?
- What can actually be achieved through education?

We will address these in turn and draw out some implications for reflective teachers.

What should an education system be designed to do?

The discussion below is structured in terms of five areas in which education has broad social significance (see Chapter 9 for a related discussion of educational aims). These areas of significance are:

- social justice;
- individual rights;
- environmental sustainability;
- wealth creation;
- cultural reproduction.

Social justice Contributing to social justice is a central purpose which is often identified for education systems. This concern influenced the 1944 Education Act as applied to England, Wales and Northern Ireland and, also, following disappointment in the divisions of grammar and secondary modern schools, the subsequent expansion of comprehensive schools from 1965. The issue features prominently in the educational goals which are set by many countries in Europe and across the world (for example, see the UN Sustainable Development Goal to 'ensure that all girls and boys complete free, equitable and quality primary and secondary education' by 2030) and has come to the fore post-pandemic, due to the highly visible gap between rich and poor. One critical point to make is that 'equality of opportunity' and the meritocratic ideal, which often lie behind policies on this issue, are concepts which are vulnerable to rhetoric. There is a significant difference between articulating a concern and really contributing to change. Paulo Freire, who was internationally recognised for his advocacy of a 'pedagogy of the oppressed' (Freire, 2000), also insisted on this need to face the structural inequalities of wealth, status and power which exist. If such issues are glossed over then the promotion of social justice through education policy is very unlikely to be successful.

A key issue remains the tail of underachievement in England which tragically affects almost 20 per cent of young people (see Chapter 5, p. 147). This phenomenon has been recognised and studied for many years. Rutter and Madge published their classic analysis of 'cycles of disadvantage' in 1976. The Centre for Wider Benefits of Learning has shown how underperformance can be identified in infancy which grows year on year so that trajectories can be mapped and, sadly, predicted (Feinstein et al., 2008a, Reading 1.6). In 2019, 53 per cent of children from poor backgrounds in England did not meet expected attainment at the end of primary, compared with just 32 per cent of pupils from affluent circumstances (DfE, 2019c); and there was a gap of almost 14 per cent for the Attainment 8 measure at GCSE (DfE, 2019b). There is no shortage of knowledge about this phenomenon (Clegg et al., 2016) which exists across all four UK nations (Machin, McNally and Wyness, 2013). At the root of such problems is the extent of inequality within UK societies. Wilkinson and Pickett's (2009) brilliant analysis of 'why more equal societies almost always do better' is one of many pieces of research to demonstrate the fundamental influence of cycles of advantage and disadvantage.

The concern for social justice through education can partly be seen as a desire to ensure that there is a legitimated system for fulfilling potential, certifying capabilities and allocating jobs in democratic societies, and thus for facilitating social mobility based on merit. However, we know too, that there are severe limits on the effectiveness of education in eroding structural inequalities.

However, having recognised the structural realities, we should also affirm that education can change lives and that futures cannot be entirely pre-determined. Indeed, learning depends on the quality of education, particularly through talk and interaction, far more that on wealth itself – it's just that patterns do tend to emerge.

Individual rights. As we saw in Chapter 9, supporting the personal development of pupils is a fundamental educational objective for teachers. In relation to 'education and society', this commitment is underpinned by international understanding about human rights.

Formal conventions on human rights were developed after the tragic experiences of the Second World War, and are thus based on deep and principled understanding of the need for moral and ethical standards (see Council of Europe, 1985, Reading 17.6). They still frame international law and set principles for the behaviour of governments and others in contemporary societies.

A clear exposition of the relationship between social structures and individual opportunities is contained in the Universal Declaration of Human Rights (United Nations, 1948). Article 1 of the Declaration states that:

> All human beings are born free and equal in dignity and rights. They are endowed with reason and conscience.

These rights are to be enjoyed, according to Article 2:

> Without distinction of any kind, such as race, colour, sex, language, religion, political or other opinion, national or social origin, property, birth or other status.

There then follow many articles dealing with rights and fundamental freedoms of movement, thought, religion, assembly, political participation, work, leisure and an adequate standard of living.

The implications for education of these provisions are made explicit in Article 26. It asserts that:

> Education shall be directed to the full development of the human personality and the strengthening of respect for human rights and fundamental freedoms. It shall promote understanding, tolerance and friendship among all nations, racial and religious groups.

Education was expected to have a crucial role in the dissemination of the UN Declaration across the world, for the document was to be 'displayed, read and expanded principally in schools and other educational institutions' in all member states.

Needless to say, the achievement of social justice and individual rights for all citizens remains a noble and appropriate goal. However, it is one which will probably always be with us for, as discussed earlier in this chapter, it is optimistic to think that educational provision alone can overcome structural inequalities in society. Indeed, the necessity of adopting a United Nations Convention on the Rights of the Child in 1989 underlines that fact. The general principles of the Convention focus on providing equal treatment, the child's best interests and giving appropriate weight to the views of the child.

Increasing numbers of schools are now seeking to achieve 'Rights Respecting School' status using the UN Convention on the Rights of the Child. The struggle to establish and maintain human rights may never be entirely overcome, but teachers, through their daily work, have tangible opportunities to make a difference to the lives of their pupils (Osler and Starkey, 2010).

Environmental sustainability. This educational goal has come to the fore in recent years as is crucial for the survival of life as we know it. There is now a growing international consensus on the increasing dangers of global warming and its significant effects on weather, sea levels, flora and fauna – and thence on food supply, energy policies, health and transport, housing etc. (Zhongming et al., 2021). Although politicians demonstrate concern and have established goals for carbon reduction, large-scale and sustained action has not been taken across all dimensions of contemporary societies. This lack of action has led to global marches with heavy involvement of school students in recent years, demonstrating young people's commitment to environmental issues.

As a result, it is likely that education will be required to give more prominence to environmental education so that the next generation can be better prepared for the future. This is already happening in some countries. For example, New Zealand expresses its educational vision in terms of 'young people who will seize the opportunities offered by new knowledge and technologies to secure a sustainable social, cultural, economic and environmental future for our country' (New Zealand Ministry of Education, 2012).

reflectiveteaching.co.uk/rtps6/part5_ch18

Wealth creation. One national priority for education is to contribute to economic goals. For instance, in the latter part of the Industrial Revolution in Great Britain, an important part of the argument for the establishment of an elementary school system was that it should provide a workforce which was more skilled and thus more economically productive. The idea became the linchpin of 'human capital' theory in the 1960s (Schultz, 1961) and many new nations, influenced by analyses such as Rostow's *The Stages of Economic Growth* (1962), put scarce resources into their education systems. The economics of education is still a flourishing area of policy and research.

In Britain, the links between education and economic productivity are constantly being drawn by governments, with particular attention to the standard of basic and vocational skills achieved in schools and to the proportion of young people acquiring advanced knowledge and skills in higher education. This aspiration has provided a rationale for education reforms for several decades – in good times and bad. For example, a Schools Minister for England stated:

> perhaps most important of all, we must ensure that more people have the knowledge and skills they need to succeed in a demanding economy. Here too, our long-term performance has lagged behind those of our international competitors. Our 15-year-olds are on average 3 years behind their peers in Shanghai in mathematics and we are the only OECD country whose young people do not have better levels of literacy or numeracy than their grandparents' generation. (Nick Gibb, speech at the Education Reform Summit, 2015)

As this example illustrates, concern for economic competitiveness has been fuelled by international comparisons between pupil achievement in Britain and that in other countries – most notably those in the Pacific Rim (e.g. Reynolds and Farrell, 1996; Oates, 2010; Jensen et al., 2016). The inference which is often drawn from such work is that British education is deficient in some way. For example, following publication of the Reynolds and Farrell study, 'interactive whole-class teaching' became a top priority in England, for this appeared to be the pedagogy which was contributing to pupil success and educational achievement in countries such as Singapore and Taiwan. Following publication of Oates's report, England's 2014 National Curriculum was reviewed to 'sequence core knowledge' in the same way as high-performing countries. It is very worthwhile to study other countries, and understanding about effective teaching and learning is accumulating globally, as TLRP's principles indicate in Chapter 4 (see also Hattie, 2009, Reading 4.6), but the economic imperative sometimes seems to alarm governments and leads to rather simplistic policy borrowing.

Cultural reproduction. Alternatively, there are those who would highlight the 'function' of education in the production and reproduction of a national culture.

Use of an education system for the production of a sense of shared national identity is common in many parts of the world, particularly where states have been established relatively recently or are growing rapidly. For example, in the United States through much of the twentieth century, the country was required to 'assimilate' and 'integrate' successive groups of new immigrants into an 'American culture'. The education system was seen as a vital part of the 'melting pot'. Of course, a highly questionable assumption here was that there was a single American culture, but the notion of the existence of a set of 'central values' was important in this period of the development of the United States. Pre-existing identities may be diminished by such use of education to develop or assert a national culture, and these costs are usually borne by minority or less powerful groups. The historical case of the education provided in the colonies of the British Empire provides a particularly graphic example of this last point (Mangan, 1993).

Following UK devolution, the unique culture and history of Scotland, Wales and Northern Ireland has been increasingly prominent. For example, the people of Wales preserve an important part of their culture through the teaching of Welsh in their schools, but, at the same time, their education system inducts Welsh children into the culture of the United Kingdom. In the unique position of Northern Ireland, the education system reflects strong historic and cultural links to England, but also looks towards the Republic of Ireland with its own independent traditions. Scotland, with its unique educational and political history, is wrestling to settle its position in relation to England and the UK – with echoes in its national *Curriculum for Excellence* (Education Scotland, 2019). In England too, debates about the curriculum have recently debated the necessity or otherwise of iconic cultural elements, recently involving the contentious term 'cultural capital'. This debate can be traced back to the influence of Arnold (1889) who helped to define the classical curriculum, in the phrase 'the best that has been thought and said', that remains influential today. Indeed, study of Shakespeare and key episodes in English history were deemed essential in the initial 1988 construction of the National Curriculum, and they remain prominent.

Schools also have direct connections to the specific communities in which they are located and to the families from which pupils come. This should be reflected in unique decisions on curricular priorities and in local adaption of national curricular requirements, as well as wider expectations placed on schools. Such tailoring of provision is designed to build on and extend existing learner and family experiences and understandings. These, of course, reflect the culture, language and funds of knowledge of each family and community (see Thomas, 2010, Reading 10.4).

Education thus plays a part in producing and reproducing culture at each of these levels, and schools have a unique role in managing the formative processes where local cultures and national expectations first meet, a role which contributed to the 2007 decision to make schools legally responsible for the promotion of local community cohesion (TDA, 2010).

Education policies and systems can thus be designed to emphasise and prioritise, in a variety of ways, economic production, cultural reproduction, social justice and individual rights. Environmental sustainability also needs to become a higher priority. Whilst such goals are not necessarily conflicting, various tensions and dilemmas are often posed. One issue concerns the rights of minority groups to maintain an independent culture and sense of identity within a majority culture, an issue which has come to prominence recently through the Black Lives Matter campaign. Another is the dilemma between the demands of individuals' development and those of economic production – or, indeed, of environmental sustainability. We raised such value concerns in Chapter 3 and argued that a reflective teacher should make informed and responsible judgements about them. The ways in which action might follow will be discussed further below.

We now move on to the second question: 'What can be achieved through education?'

What can be achieved through education?

There has been a long-running debate on the topic of the opportunities and limits for the influence of education on the development of societies. Some people, such as Coleman, Coser and Powell (1966), Jenks (1972) and Bowles and Gintis (1976), argued that education can make little difference to social development. Although coming to the issue from different theoretical perspectives, they argue that educational processes reflect and reproduce major features of existing society, particularly with regard to distinctions related to social class. The suggestion is that relationships of power, wealth, status and ideology are such that education should be seen as a part of the dominant social system, rather than as an autonomous force within it.

Others, such as Berger and Luckmann (1967), may be seen as taking a more idealistic theoretical position. They argue that, since our sense of reality is 'socially constructed' by people as they interact together, there is, therefore, scope for individuals to make an independent impact on the course of future social development. For a tangible example, the consequences of the agreements on Human Rights could be considered within schools and classrooms, as suggested by Osler and Starkey (2010). Thus, there *is* potential for education to influence change.

We have here the competing positions of those who believe in social determinism ranged against those who believe in individual voluntarism. As we have already seen, education is very often expected to bring about social and economic developments and it is an area which tends to attract idealists. However, we also have to recognise that the major structural features of societies are extremely resistant to change. What is needed then is a theoretical position which recognises the importance of action and of constraint. Such a position would accept that education has a degree of relative autonomy and would thus legitimate action by individuals to contribute to future social development.

Such a theoretical framework is provided by what we call the dialectic of the individual and society (see Chapter 4 for a full discussion and, in particular, Reading 5.1). As Berlak and Berlak (1981) put it:

> Conscious creative activity is limited by prevailing social arrangements, but human actions and institutional forms are not mere reflections of them. (p. 121)

The clear implication is that people can make their own impact on history but must do so in whatever circumstances they find themselves. If this theoretical framework is adopted, social developments can be seen as the product of processes of struggle and contest between different individuals and groups in society. Such processes are ones in which education must, inevitably, play a part.

Our answer to the question of what education can actually achieve must thus be based on a guarded and realistic optimism – as Power suggests, we need 'the imaginative professional' (2008, Reading 17.5). The dialectical model of the influence of individuals and social structures recognises constraints but asserts that action remains possible. This places a considerable responsibility on a reflective teacher whose professional work is both shaped by, and contributes to, society.

The next section considers recent evidence on educational inequality, and the role of the reflective teacher in taking action to narrow the gap for those pupils suffering disadvantage.

ADDRESSING INEQUALITIES

In line with the call to action detailed above, the issue of inequality in education has often been a key motivator for those entering the profession and frequently shaped the way teachers work. However in recent decades inequality has also become a key driver for policy, funding and educational debate, expanding its focus into a wider number of priorities and increasingly focusing on 'intersectionality', the overlap between multiple inequalities as the lived experience of many children and young people.

Perhaps the greatest focus in the inequalities agenda has been placed on the poverty gap. There is an ever-growing body of evidence to corroborate the enduring gap in terms of academic achievement for pupils from ages 4 to 18 and beyond and the impact of this gap on life chances (for example, Sammons, Toth, and Sylva, 2015; Wyness, 2017; Andrews, Robinson and Hutchinson, 2017). Other authors foreground the additional challenges faced by working class pupils (Reay, 2018). This challenge led to the introduction of the Pupil Premium grant for schools in England, a fund schools were directed to use specifically to narrow the attainment gap. Significant investment was also made in the establishment of the Education Endowment Foundation (EEF), whose goal is to make evidence available to teachers so that they can more effectively address this stubborn attainment gap. Despite numerous initiatives, reports and research studies, that gap remains (Farquharson, McNally and Tahir, 2022). The need for reflective teachers to engage with the evidence on the experiences of children and young people living in poverty, and to draw on the increasing body of knowledge about the most effective teaching strategies for these pupils, has never been more pressing.

For deprived pupils with SEND, educational outcomes are particularly low and recent research has shown a symbiotic relationship between poverty and special needs, in that children with SEND are more likely to live in poverty and therefore experience an achievement gap (Shaw et al., 2016). However, there is reason for the reflective teacher to be optimistic about the possibility of tailoring teaching to better support pupils with SEND, not least because of things like the concrete guidance on supporting the needs of pupils with SEND provided by the EEF (Davies and Henderson, 2020); strong research into the best ways to deploy Teaching Assistants (see **maximisingtas.co.uk/resources.php**); and a growing body of knowledge around specific needs, such as autism and dyslexia.

Problems with inequalities have come to the fore in relation to the experience of black and minority ethnic pupils, thanks to the Black Lives Matters movement. There has also been significant debate about the extent of and potential solutions to racial inequality (Tickly, 2022). A significant body of knowledge exists around the educational underachievement of certain minority ethnic groups (for example, Demie and McLean, 2017) but there remains relatively little evidence on strategies to tackle this at a systemic

562   Part 5   Deepening understanding

level. In the absence of such evidence, schools and individual teachers have begun to explore 'decolonising the curriculum' (Moncrieffe et al, 2020), and review recruitment and promotion processes (Tereshchenko, Mills and Bradbury, 2020).

The experiences of Lesbian, Gay, Bisexual, Transgender and Queer (LGBTQ) pupils have also been more widely understood in the last decade (for example, Bradlow et al., 2017), and these pupils' particular disadvantages are now championed by organisations like LGBTQEd. Gender gaps also remain prevalent in particular subjects and age phases (for example, see Younger and Warrington, 2007) and teachers in some Scandinavian countries have been at the forefront of research into the impact of 'gender neutral' schools (Shutts et al., 2017).

Teachers have begun to tackle many of these issues at school level, exploring diversifying the curriculum, ensuring that resources, such as books and other texts, reflect the communities they teach and the issues their pupils face in their daily lives, and adapting classroom practice based on emerging evidence of what makes a difference to the learning of disadvantaged pupils. It is the responsibility of the reflective teacher to understand the particular needs of both the cohort and the individual pupils whom they work with, to remain abreast of good practice and research material that addresses their needs, and to work with colleagues to test changes to practice that might support the closing of the educational gap. Organisations like the Education Endowment Foundation and the Chartered College of Teaching offer an ever-evolving range of evidence and good practice guidance, which can support the reflective teacher in tailoring their practice to make a greater difference to the pupils they teach.

Reflective Activity 18.1

Aim: To explore strategies to tackle of educational inequality in your own context.

1 *Identify underachievement:* Use school level performance data to identify an underperforming group in your school. This analysis could explore gender, ethnicity, deprivation or any other educational disadvantage.

2 *Explore the evidence:* Referring to the literature base in this chapter, work with a group of colleagues to review evidence of the challenges this particular group of pupils faces, and to explore ideas which may help support them to catch up with their peers.

3 *Plan and implement an intervention:* Decide on a change to practice that you and your colleagues will implement, and which draws on the evidence base for successful strategies for the particular group you have identified. Decide what success will look like and how you will evidence or measure success.

4 *Analyse impact:* Review the evidence of the impact of your intervention and decide on next steps. This could mean continuing or even extending the intervention, tweaking it and retesting it, or abandoning it and rethinking your approach.

Extension: Prepare a short presentation or report on your project and share this with colleagues to stimulate debate about wider changes in practice in your school.

reflectiveteaching.co.uk/rtps6/part5_ch18

CLASSROOM TEACHING AND SOCIETY

As we have seen, one implication of the adoption of a dialectical model of the relationship between individuals and society is that it highlights the possible consequences, for the 'macro' world of society, of actions, experiences and processes which take place in the 'micro' world of the classroom. In Chapter 3, we raised this issue with the assertion that 'reflective teaching implies an active concern with aims and consequences as well as with technical efficiency' and we must pick up the themes again here. One of the most important issues concerns the influence of a reflective teacher's own value commitments.

In Chapter 3, p. 100, we argued that reflective teachers should accept democratically determined decisions but should act both as responsible professionals and as autonomous citizens to contribute to such decision-making processes. The 'imaginative professional' (Power, 2008, Reading 17.5) is called for.

We also suggested that attitudes of 'open-mindedness' and 'responsibility' are essential attributes. Open-mindedness involves a willingness to consider evidence and argument from whatever source it comes. It is thus the antithesis of closure and of habituated or ideological thinking.

Focusing on English examples, National Curriculum expectations around the teaching of personal, social, health and economic education and (PHSE) have enabled teachers to support children and young people through the formal curriculum to review both their personal agency and the social processes that underpin society, and also to explore global issues. The rationale for this provision relates to the development of children's responsibilities in a liberal democracy.

In recent years Ofsted, the English inspectorate, has placed considerable emphasis on the responsibility of schools to teach social, moral, spiritual and cultural (SMSC) education, which encompasses a wide range of teaching, including pupils' mental health and wellbeing, the promotion of social cohesion, and the reduction of extremism. Since the pandemic threw a particular spotlight on mental health and wellbeing, schools have been welcomed the opportunity to tackle this issue. The British Educational Research Association (BERA) published an extensive overview of relevant research and practice (bera.ac.uk/publication/the-role-of-schools-in-the-mental-health-of-children-young-people), and schools can also draw on EEF-funded work by van Poortvliet, Clarke and Gross' (2019) practical guidance report for the Education Endowment Foundation.

In the political context for these issues there are tensions and contradictions. For example, the responsibility for the teaching of Sex and Relationships Education (SRE) within the PHSE curriculum has caused particular political conflicts in certain faith communities in England. Another contentious issue has been the responsibility for schools to promote community cohesion enshrined in law in 2007. This responsibility can place teachers in vulnerable positions, despite their best intentions, for example the Oldham Trojan Horse Scandal in 2013, a scandal involving claims of an alleged conspiracy that there was an organised attempt to introduce an Islamist ethos into several schools in Birmingham, England. These allegations led to several teachers and school leaders being

Part 5 Deepening understanding

temporarily given lifetime bans, until these were overthrown in 2017 (Holmwood and O'Toole, 2018).

At the same time that government rhetoric has praised teacher autonomy and the exercise of their professional judgement, the professional work of teachers has continued to be directed from the Department for Education (DfE), including through strong prescription of the curriculum, enforcement through inspection procedures and sanctions to ensure *compliance*. Unfortunately, successive governments have not yet acted on the idea that teachers and teacher-educators should be treated as active, thinking, value-driven professionals with whom partnerships to develop the educational system should be created. In the past teachers have been cast as the core 'problem' (HMCI, 1995). This point is illustrated by evidence from the Primary Assessment Curriculum and Experience (PACE) project, which explored the impact of the introduction of the National Curriculum from as far back as 1988. A major conclusion was that changes in curriculum, assessment and pedagogy were mishandled in many ways because of the lack of sincere attempts to work with teachers (Osborn et al., 2000; Pollard et al., 2000). From 1997, Labour governments maintained similar policies, with the result being that there was considerable professional disengagement leading to recruitment and retention problems. From 2010 the Coalition Government increased control of education, albeit with its own particular priorities ranging from 'core knowledge' to synthetic phonics and statutory assessment changes. The Conservative government of 2014 continued to enact policies which took little account of teachers' views, or the views of other education experts. The plans to introduce baseline testing into Reception classes is an example of government control of education.

Case Study 18.1 illustrates the possible effects of the position into which teachers have been placed – and the contrastive strategies of retreat and activism.

Case Study 18.1 Responding to circumstances: strategies of retreat or activism?

This case study illustrates the pressures which teachers often feel under through an anonymous letter sent to the *Times Educational Supplement* in October 2017. But this is contrasted with a 'clarion call' to action in the interests of maintaining educational quality and preserving professional commitments (Berry, 2016). Can you empathise with these positions? And how might you move forward yourself?

Dear TES,

I have just typed up my resignation and I am getting ready to go to the post office and send it recorded delivery as we speak.

Every single word I typed lifted some weight off my shoulders. This might sound dramatic, but I feel free. I feel free from the shackles of teaching. Having always wanted to be a teacher since I made registers for teddies and made them do spelling tests in my bedroom as a child, I feel lied to. Teaching was not and is not the profession I thought it would be. I know lots of happy teachers, but, sadly, I was not one of them.

Something just didn't 'click'. Maybe I was horrified at the thought of never being able to please everyone. Whether it was the child in the class who just wanted to get on with their work who couldn't get a minute of my attention because of the numerous behaviour problems I had to deal with, or the head of department who was told to nitpick the tiniest of errors or be at the mercy of the senior leadership team. Or perhaps it was the constant scrutiny, the constant feeling of 'I am just not good enough'. Or even the disapproving looks from parents at parents evening, that feeling that their child is failing, because of you.

None of that is true. I was a great teacher; I still am. But, as of now, there is no way I could continue. It's not healthy. No more driving home from work, laying in bed at night, spending Sunday worrying about what I might have done wrong, what I haven't done at all, and what I need to do.

Teaching made me hate my subject. It was box-ticking for the sake of box-ticking. My passion had gone. How is a teacher meant to teach when what they are teaching is boring even them?

Jon Berry has published a book called: *Teachers Undefeated: How Global Education Reform Has Failed to Crush the Spirit of Educators* (Berry, 2016). He argues that teachers invariably go to great lengths to do the best for their students. As he explains:

> They do so despite clumsy interventions from governments who have no idea how difficult they have made school life. They do so despite the fact that they are pressurized into producing dubious outcomes and are over-scrutinized in every aspect of their professional lives.

Jon Berry explains how political and economic circumstances play out in our classrooms on a daily basis. He discusses possibilities for collective resistance to policies that reduce the enjoyment of learning to a succession of test rehearsals and exam preparation. The book is filled with testimony from teachers who still bring energy, creativity and commitment to everything they do.

Teaching is, as we have seen, a profession which is informed by value-commitments as well as knowledge, skill and judgement. Although self-preservation has to take precedence when the chips are down, teacher resilience and agency has succeeded, over may decades and generations of teachers, in defending and promoting educational quality.

We can thus see that the relationship between teacher and society in England has dramatically changed since the inception of the National Curriculum following the Education Reform Act of 1988. From a position of some public esteem and professional recognition, could the role of the teacher now simply be cast as being to comply with centrally defined frameworks? Perhaps not, but as Simco (2000) argues, there is a danger that acceptance of compliance could eventually lead to the teaching profession retreating from consideration of aims, values and their associated pedagogies. This would be deeply damaging, for engagement with underpinning values remains essential to the moral foundations of teaching as a professional vocation. Nor should we ever forget how policy

reflectiveteaching.co.uk/rtps6/part5_ch18

is actually created, and the influence that remains with teachers. As Bowe and Ball with Gold (1992, Reading 17.7) argue, policy is not formed solely through political struggles and through the construction of legislation and official documents. Its operational reality is formed in the 'context of practice' – where it is often reformulated and 'mediated' through the application of professional judgement (see also Osborn et al., 2000; Chapter 3, p. 100).

Scotland, Northern Ireland, Wales and England have developed in increasingly distinctive ways and provide some important contrasts as, indeed, does the Republic of Ireland. The basic truth is that, whatever a government may attempt to determine, there are some contentious issues in education that cannot be avoided. In addition to questions about educational outcomes and standards, these include issues concerning individual dignity, equality and freedom, and the influence of sexism, racism and other forms of discrimination based on social class, age, disability or sexual orientation. These are issues upon which, we would argue, children have rights that socially responsible teachers should not compromise. We take this to constitute a 'bottom line', a value commitment to the fundamental rights of citizens in a democratic society and a necessary underpinning for a reflective professional.

REFLECTIVE TEACHING AND THE DEMOCRATIC PROCESS

In our discussion of 'reflective teaching' (see Chapter 3), we suggested that, in addition to professional responsibilities to implement democratically determined decisions, teachers as citizens also have responsibilities to act to influence the nature of such decisions. Teachers have rights and it is perfectly reasonable that they should be active in contributing to the formation of public policy. In terms of Bowe et al.'s model (1992, Reading 17.7), this is about teacher engagement in the 'context of influence'.

An exceptional example of pressure group activity in Education was the campaign orchestrated by the Cambridge Primary Review in England. This was founded on the discontent of many primary school educators with the degree of state control to which they had been subject. The National Curriculum prescribed *what* to teach and National Strategies told them *how* to teach. Standardised assessment tests (SATs) measured pupil performance whilst the inspection regime held schools to account. The groundswell of concern from phase-based associations was strong. These included NPT (the National Primary Trust), NPH (the National Primary Headteachers' Association), NAPE (the National Association for Primary Education), ASPE (the National Association for the Study of Primary Education), NaPTEC (the National Primary Teacher Education Conference) and CASE (the Campaign for the Advancement of State Education). Professional associations such as the National Union of Teachers (NUT), National Association of Schoolmasters Union of Women Teachers (NASUWT) and Association of Teachers and Lecturers (ATL) were also extremely active, though the most influential on government was probably the National Association of Head Teachers (NAHT).

The Cambridge Primary Review team was able to harvest, shape and represent a lot of this concern (Alexander, 2010). They obtained funding from an educational charity, consulted in meetings with practitioners across the country, liaised with stakeholder organisations and commissioned reviews of research evidence on a structured range of contemporary topics. These strategies legitimated the voice which they were then able to articulate. Journalistic help was recruited and press releases were issued on a wide range of issues and with considerable success in securing coverage. Civil servants were consulted on proposals as they emerged and lobbying took place of politicians in both the government and opposition parties. This was just as well, as the Labour government fell in May 2010, soon after publication of the review report. The Coalition government appeared to be better disposed to the basic thrust of the review. In particular, it was claimed that the extent of state control of schools and of professional practice was to be rolled back. Whilst this headline outcome was consistent with the proposals of the Review, it is noticeable that other aspects of the education policies of the Coalition showed disregard for the evidence and stakeholder opinion which had been marshalled. Perhaps at that point the Review's proposals were too complex, put too stridently, or just inconsistent with the predilection of Ministers – it is hard to tell.

The review delivered a coherent message about an issue of widespread professional and public concern. It was timely in publishing its findings in the run up to an election, and it made many proposals which were broadly consistent with the stated policies of an incoming government. However, where the politicians wished for other outcomes, the review was quietly bypassed.

This example suggests that there is both luck, judgement and vulnerability in pressure group activity and that, whilst some things may be achieved, compromises often have to be accepted. Even with significant resources and expertise, it also sometimes appears to be an uphill struggle to get decision-makers to simply understand all the dimensions of important educational issues. However, when the dust settled in England, the work of the Cambridge Primary Review was significant – not least by establishing conditions for the National Curriculum Review which followed it (DfE, 2011a) and the policy development of opposition parties.

Pressure group activity and collective action by individuals can thus both bring about new policy priorities and lead to a reappraisal of existing positions. This is an essential feature of democratic decision-making and we would suggest that reflective teachers have both the right and responsibility to contribute to such processes. Reflective Activity 18.2 suggests learning about these processes by studying in depth a single example of political activity and decision-making.

reflectiveteaching.co.uk/rtps6/part5_ch18

> **Reflective Activity 18.2**
>
> *Aim:* To investigate processes of political activity and decision-making with regard to the assessment reform agenda.
>
> *Evidence and reflection:* Working with a small group of colleagues, explore contemporary debates on primary assessment, by connecting to blogs, website, lobbying organisations and political debates online. A good place to start could be the More Than A Score campaign: **morethanascore.org.uk/** or responses of teaching unions or the British Educational Research Association (BERA).
>
> Newspapers can provide useful sources of easily retrievable information, particularly in terms of policymakers' responses to reform campaigns. Some, such as *The Times*, publish an index and this is particularly helpful. The BBC's and the *Guardian's* websites are also particularly good. Comments or threads on Twitter or within Facebook groups may also provide a useful source of information about public opinion, or that of teachers and policymakers.
>
> You may also find events or debates available online which you can either attend or watch retrospectively. These will give you an opportunity to hear directly from those directly seeking to effect change.
>
> Having gathered a variety of evidence about primary assessment, an attempt should be made to classify this evidence so that the competing positions are identified. From this point, it may be possible to gather policy statements directly from the participants, by email, social media, discussion, interview or library search.
>
> Finally, the decision-point can be studied. Were the public arguments influential? To what extent were decisions influenced by public debate e.g. social media? What interests seem to have prevailed when decisions were taken?
>
> *Extension:* Having studied an example of political influence on decision-making, it is worth taking stock of what has been learned. Did you feel that the political debate reflected appropriate educational concerns? Could educationalists have made more constructive contributions? In what format could their voices be more powerful?

We are conscious, though, that this is a book which is primarily designed to support student teachers during teacher education and training – and that activities to influence wider policies may seem inappropriate. We include them because such activity is a logical consequence of taking professionalism and reflective teaching seriously – and because some preparation for such activity is perfectly possible before taking up a full-time teaching post. One of the most important aspects of this is to demystify the democratic process. Investigation of the history of an issue might be followed up by small groups of students or teachers, by taking an educational issue as a case study, or indeed, by facing a real current issue.

Taking action

There is a tendency to regard decision-making as something done by 'them' – an ill-defined, distant and amorphous body. In fact, decisions in democracies are taken by elected representatives. The connection between the ordinary citizen and decision-makers can thus be much more close, direct and personal. The individual teacher interested in influencing change now has multiple opportunities to engage with public and political debate. This could involve attending local union meetings, responding to consultations or contributing to the public debate via social media platforms. Many educational issues have dedicated online campaigns with which the interested teacher can engage and to which they can contribute both their support and time to enable collective action. Or, even more locally, you could ask to attend a meeting of the governing body of your school. The names of school governors or Trustees and their associated responsibilities will be available on your school website.

At national level, lists of elected representatives, such MPs, MSPs, Assembly Members and Councillors, are available on the internet. Such lists can help you to identify and contact those who have a particular interest in education and those who have a particular degree of influence over decisions, for example those sitting on education committees at council or parliament level. It is essential to prepare a case well. This requires at least three things:

- appropriate factual information about the issue;
- good educational arguments in support of whatever is being advocated;
- an understanding of the interests and political circumstances affecting those whom it is hoped to influence.

A great deal of factual information can be gathered from newspapers, by visiting the websites of national, regional or local government agencies and through online discussions, blogs and social media. Face-to-face discussion should be sought with people who are involved locally with the issue under consideration. Sources within your school should be one starting-point. It is always worth checking key facts from a number of sources.

To develop coherent educational arguments, the research literature is an important resource (on reflectiveteaching.co.uk, see suggested Further Reading on the chapter pages of this book). Almost all significant educational topics have been researched at some time, and there is much to learn from the experience of others. Of course, one would certainly wish to discuss the issues under consideration with colleagues, and to build a really secure understanding.

Regarding the interests of those whom one wishes to influence, a good place to start is with any published policy statements or manifestos. This could be followed up by discussion and by making judgements regarding the pressures and constraints that they face. It is important to remember that not many politicians enjoy being forced to change course, but most are open to persuasion if they have not previously taken up a hard, public position.

Representative democracy is designed as a system which links decision-making with the views of a majority. It follows that the most successful type of campaigning is likely to be one which is broadly based – one which is produced by an alliance of interested parties bringing concerted pressure to bear on policymakers.

Reflective teachers may thus wish to act with others if and when they wish to influence public policy. Obvious places to look for allies are: other colleagues, perhaps through sectoral or subject associations, trade unions or the General Teaching Councils; parents and the importance of parental support cannot be overestimated; other workers in the public services; local community and interest groups who may be directly or indirectly affected by the issues under consideration; and existing national pressure groups such as those listed earlier in this section.

Other important issues to consider when getting your message out include: carrying out a review of the types of media which attract a large audience for educational issues (Twitter, Facebook, online petitions, press, radio, television etc.); holding discussions with people who have had experience of managing publicity to learn from them; preparing press releases and considering suitable images for photographic or filming purposes; and identifying and supporting a spokesperson for press follow-up.

Finally, even if your campaign is heard and taken on board, be alert to the possibility of policies being 'watered down' as attention moves onto new issues.

Professional and union organisation

Some professions have very long histories. For instance, law and medicine have served enduring needs for social order and personal health. However, from the Enlightenment and Industrial Revolution onwards, many other professional groups emerged as new demands for specialised expertise developed – teaching, engineering, accountancy and nursing were amongst these. Today, our complex modern societies depend on a very wide range of highly organised professions.

The rationale for professional groups has a strong dimension of fostering collaboration to provide valued services to others, but professional groups also often act to promote and defend the interests of their members – just as trade unions do. Indeed, trade unions were legitimised in the 1860s in response to the employment conditions of the industrial revolution and as a necessary defence of employee interests. 'Unity is strength', as the expression goes, whether you are a doctor or a low-paid cleaner on the minimum wage. Because of this appeal to both the public good and members' interests, there is often some tension in the actual practices of both trade unions and professional associations.

In Scottish education, the distinction in functions is relatively clear, with the Educational Institute of Scotland (EIS) having defended the employment interests of teachers since its foundation in 1847. On the other hand, the General Teaching Council for Scotland (GTC S) was founded in 1965 to register teachers, maintain professional standards and enhance the quality of teaching on behalf of all stakeholders. Since 2012, GTC S has become fully independent of government, though debate on its future does occur from time to time. There are, of course, some boundary negotiations between the EIS and GTC S, but the two major teacher organisations are broadly complementary.

reflectiveteaching.co.uk/rtps6/part5_ch18

In England, the situation is more complex. For many years there has been a number of trade unions with relatively little cooperation between them. In 2017, two important unions merged to form the National Education Union, with almost half a million members. Some other unions have more members from primary, secondary, further or independent sectors; and others cater for the particular circumstances of headteachers. Further mergers would be a logical response to the growth of direct control by government in recent decades. As teacher unions compete for members, contributions to public debates are often fragmented and it is hard for a positive public impression of the profession to form.

The establishment of a General Teaching Council for England (1998–2011) was not fully endorsed by teacher unions, which left it vulnerable to closure. However, after widespread consultation, a Chartered College of Teaching was finally established in 2017. The College aims to provide a research-informed, professional voice through its growing membership, publications and professional development programmes.

In Northern Ireland, the General Teaching Council remains financially vulnerable but is strategically of great importance as teaching continues its struggle to establish itself as an esteemed profession. Despite the relatively small number of teachers working in Northern Ireland, English teacher unions are represented in addition to those with large memberships from the Republic of Ireland.

In Wales, a General Teaching Council was established in 1998 but transformed into the Education Workforce Council (EWC) in 2015. The role as a regulator of professionalism and standards remains, and the EWC is also responsible for accrediting programmes of initial teacher education and for advising the Welsh Government on matters related to the education workforce.

As the brief narrative above reveals, for specific contextual reasons, the situation is complex and varied in each part of the UK. Arguably, a collective, independent organisation to regulate and improve teaching quality and to celebrate and promote teacher expertise is necessary in each country. This should complement the workplace concerns of the unions. To maximise effectiveness, teachers with a sense of history will no doubt encourage their unions to cooperate and even merge where possible.

CONCLUSION

Education is inevitably concerned not just with 'what is' but also with what 'ought to be' (Kogan, 1978). We hope that this book will help teachers and student teachers to develop not only the necessary skills of teaching but also the awareness and commitment which will ensure their future contribution as extended and imaginative professionals.

reflectiveteaching.co.uk/rtps6/part5_ch18

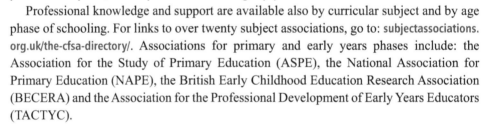

 reflectiveteaching.co.uk offers additional professional resources for this chapter. To see these, go to: reflectiveteaching.co.uk/rtps6/part5_ch18

Three levels of additional guidance are available.

1 *Further Reading* on the chapter webpage follows the exact structure of the chapter and suggests additional published sources of information or analysis on each topic.
2 *Key Readings*, listed below, is a selective, annotated shortlist of particularly helpful resources.
3 Short extracts of many of the *Key Readings* are provided in *Readings for Reflective Teaching in Schools*.

 Within the teaching profession, there are many associations and initiatives which provide guidance and assistance on professional matters – and these are often accessible online. For example, the largest professional association in the UK, the National Education Union (a merger of the NUT and ATL) provides Trainee Advice (see: **neu.org.uk/help-and-advice/trainee-advice**) on starting to work in schools. In England, the Chartered College of Teaching offers a range of resources to support evidence-informed teaching (see: **chartered.college/publications/**). In Scotland, the General Teaching Council has extensive resources on 'professional learning' and on 'research and practitioner enquiry' (see: **gtcs.org.uk/professional-update/what-is-professional-learning.aspx**).

 Professional knowledge and support are available also by curricular subject and by age phase of schooling. For links to over twenty subject associations, go to: **subjectassociations.org.uk/the-cfsa-directory/**. Associations for primary and early years phases include: the Association for the Study of Primary Education (ASPE), the National Association for Primary Education (NAPE), the British Early Childhood Education Research Association (BECERA) and the Association for the Professional Development of Early Years Educators (TACTYC).

There are also specific organisations addressing the needs of teachers and pupils from particular minority groups, for example: Women Ed, the BAMEed Network and LGBTEd, to name but a few.

 Whilst most teacher-led organisations have their roots in professional practice, many also contribute evidence and experience in relation to public debates on education policy. This is very evident, for example, in the deliberations of the House of Commons Select Committee on Education. To see this, take a look at: **committees.parliament.uk/committee/203/education-committee/**. You will find the same pattern in relation to lobbying on education policy issues in Wales, Ireland and Scotland.

KEY READINGS

Many of the books suggested as further reading for Chapters 3 and 5 will also be relevant here.

An excellent overview of key dimensions of professionalism, including a paper by Sally Power on 'the imaginative professional' (**Reading 17.5**) is:

> Cunningham, B. (ed.) (2008) *Exploring Professionalism*. London: Institute of Education.

Eric Hoyle's classic paper on restricted and extended professionalism can be found in:

> Hoyle, E. and Megarry, J. (2005) *World Yearbook of Education 1980: The Professional Development of Teachers*. London: Routledge.

For a historically contextualised account of the development of teachers' professional agency, see:

> McCullough, G., Helsby, G. and Knight, P. (2000) *The Politics of Professionalism: Teachers and the Curriculum*. London: Continuum.

On the structural relationships between education and society, with fascinating comparative and historical dimensions, see:

> Archer, M. (1979) *The Social Origins of Educational Systems*. London: SAGE. (**Reading 17.1**)

Interconnections between social structures and pedagogic practices are illustrated in the work of Paulo Freire, such as:

> Freire, P. (2000) *Pedagogy of the Oppressed*. London: Continuum.

Stenhouse continues to have much to teach us on the role of the teacher in a democracy, and Sachs continues and extends the tradition. Wrigley et al. demonstrate what is possible in schools across the world:

> Sachs, J. (2003) *The Activist Teaching Profession*. Buckingham: Open University Press.
> Stenhouse, L. (1983) *Authority, Education and Emancipation*. London: Heinemann.
> Wrigley, J., Thompson, P. and Lingard, R. (eds) (2012) *Changing Schools: Alternative Ways to Make a World of Difference*. London: Routledge.

The United Nations Convention on Children's Rights is an important international statement. For an excellent account of both it and its implications for the UK, see:

> Newell, P. (1991) *The UN Convention and Children's Rights in the UK*. London: National Children's Bureau.

For a child-focused account and more general guidance on Human Rights education, see:

Alderson, P. (2000) *Young Children's Rights*. London: Jessica Kingsley.
Osler, A. and Starkey, H. (2010) *Teachers and Human Rights Education*. Stoke-on-Trent: Trentham Books. (see also **Reading 17.6**)

For penetrating analyses of how education policy is created in government and may be mediated by teachers, see:

Ball, S.J. (1994) *Education Reform: A Critical and Post-Structural Approach*. Buckingham: Open University Press. (see also **Reading 17.7**)
Ball, S.J., Maguire, M. and Braun, A. (2011a) *How Schools Do Policy: Policy Enactments in Secondary Schools*. London: Routledge.
Cunningham, P. (2011) *Politics and the Primary Teacher*. London: Routledge.

Action by reflective teachers within the democratic process calls for some knowledge of political structures and processes. For an excellent UK overview, see:

Leyland, P. (2012) *Constitution of the United Kingdom: A Contextual Analysis*. Oxford: Hart Publishing.

Of course, much of the philosophy which underpins this book as a whole was all set out a century ago by John Dewey:

Dewey, J. (1916) *Democracy and Education: An Introduction to the Philosophy of Education*. New York: Macmillan.

Acknowledgements

I am honoured to have been invited by Andrew Pollard to take a leading role in the development of this most influential research-based textbook for trainee teachers. Thanks also to Steve Higgins who went beyond his author role in checking all the EEF materials. In addition to Andrew and Steve I'd very much like to acknowledge Alison Baker and Helen Tredget from Bloomsbury for their outstanding work and for their support.

Dominic Wyse
June 2022

For permission to reproduce figures or text, thanks are due to:

- The Teaching and Learning Research Programme for Figure 4.1, Ten evidence-informed educational principles for effective teaching and learning, James, M. and Pollard, A. (2006) *Improving Teaching and Learning in Schools: A Commentary by the Teaching and Learning Research Programme*.

- Georgina Nutton and colleagues at Hallfield Primary School and Amelia Hempel-Jorgensen of the Open University for Case Study 13.2 'Mastery in the Classroom'.

- The Scottish Government for Figure 13.2, Scotland's Assessment is for Learning, from Learning and Teaching Scotland (2007) *Assessment is for Learning*.

- Bloomsbury Publishing for Figure 15.2 from © Pollard with Filer, 1996, *The Social World of Children's Learning*, Continuum Publishing, an imprint of Bloomsbury Publishing Plc.

- The Government Office for Science for Figure 15.3, Mediating mechanisms for achievement of the wider benefits of learning, from Feinstein, L., Vorhaus, J. and Sabates, R. (2008b) *Learning Through Life: Future Challenges*. Foresight Mental Capital and Wellbeing Project.

- The Teaching and Learning Research Programme for Figure 16.2, from A framework for teacher expertise: powerful concepts and Expert questions, from Pollard, A. (ed.) (2010) *Professionalism and Pedagogy: A Contemporary Opportunity*.

- Aileen Kennedy for Figure 17.2 from Understanding CPD: The need for theory to impact on policy and practice. *Professional Development in Education, 40*(5), 336–51.

- Steve Higgins and the Education Endowment Foundation for summaries of sixteen strands of their Teaching and Learning Toolkit.

Acknowledgements

- The Teaching and Learning Research Programme for Research Briefings on: Teacher careers, Education and neuroscience, Consulting pupils, New technology, Personalised learning, Pupil group work, Learning how to learn, and Assessment for learning and Developing inclusion.

- George Leckie and Harvey Goldstein, and the Graduate School of Education, University of Bristol, for two Research Briefings: 14.1 School league tables: are they any good for choosing schools? and 5.1 School, family, neighbourhood: which is most important to a child's education?

reflectiveteaching.co.uk

Bibliography

Adler, A. (1927) *The Practice and Theory of Individual Psychology*. New York: Harcourt.
Ainscow, M., Booth, T. and Dyson, A. (2006) *Improving Schools, Developing Inclusion*. London: Routledge.
Alderson, P. (2000) *Young Children's Rights*. London: Jessica Kingsley.
Alexander, C. and Shankley, W. (2020) 'Ethnic inequalities in the state education system in England'. In Byrne, B., Alexander, C., Khan, O., Nazroo, J. and Shankley, W., Ethnicity (eds) *Race and Inequality in the UK: State of the Nation*. Bristol: Policy Press.
Alexander, R.J. (2000) *Culture and Pedagogy. International Comparisons in Primary Education*. Oxford: Blackwell.
Alexander, R.J. (2004) 'Still no pedagogy? Principle, pragmatism and compliance in primary education'. *Cambridge Journal of Education*, 34 (1), 7–34.
Alexander, R.J. (2006) *Towards Dialogic Teaching: Rethinking Classroom Talk*. Cambridge: Dialogos.
Alexander, R.J. (2008a) *Essays on Pedagogy*. London: Routledge.
Alexander, R.J. (2008b) *Towards Dialogic Teaching: Rethinking Classroom Talk*. Cambridge: Dialogos.
Alexander, R.J. (ed.) (2010) *Children, Their World, Their Education. Final Report and Recommendations of the Cambridge Primary Review*. London: Routledge.
Alexander, R. (2018) 'Developing dialogic teaching: Genesis, process, trial'. *Research Papers in Education*. doi:10.1080/02671522.2018.1481140.
Alexander, R.J., Rose, J. and Woodhead, C. (1992) *Curriculum Organisation and Classroom Practice in Primary Schools: A Discussion Paper*. London: Department of Education and Science.
Alibhai-Brown, Y. (2000) *Who Do We Think We Are? Imagining the New Britain*. London: Allen Lane.
Allal, L. (2012) 'Pedagogy, didactics and the co-regulation of learning'. In James, M. and Pollard, A. (eds) *Principles for Effective Pedagogy. International Responses to the UK TLRP*. London: Routledge.
Allen, V. (2014) *Understanding and Supporting Behaviour through Emotional Intelligence. A Critical Guide for Secondary Teachers*. St Albans: Critical Publishing.
Althusser, L. (1971) 'Ideology and the ideological state apparatus'. In Cosin, B.R. (ed.) *Education, Structure and Society*. Harmondsworth: Penguin.
Alton-Lee, A. (2003) *Quality teaching for diverse students in schooling: Best evidence synthesis June 2003*. Wellington, New Zealand: Ministry of Education.
Alur, M. and Hegarty, S. (2002) *Education and Children with Special Educational Needs*. London: Paul Chapman Publishing.
Alwafi, E. (2021) 'Tracing changes in teachers' professional learning network on Twitter: Comparison of teachers' social network structure and content of interaction before and during the COVID-19 pandemic'. *Journal of Computer Assisted Learning*, Special Issue Article, 1–13. doi:10.1111/jcal.12607.

American Psychological Association (1997) *Learner-centred Psychological Principles: A Framework for School Reform and Redesign*. New York: APA.

Anderson, B. (1991) *Imagined Communities: Reflections on the Origin and Spread of Nationalism*. London: Verso.

Anderson, P.M. (2008) *Pedagogy. A Primer*. New York: Peter Lang.

Andrew-Power, K. and Gormley, C. (2009) *Display for Learning*. London: Continuum.

Andrews, J., Robinson, D. and Hutchinson, J. (2017) *Closing the Gap? Trends in Educational Attainment and Disadvantage*. August 2017. London: Education Policy Institute.

Andrews, J., Perera, N., Eyles, A., Heller Sahlgren, G., Machin, S., Sandi, M. and Silva, O. (2017) *The Impact of Academies on Educational Outcomes*. London: Education Policy Institute.

Angoff, W.H. (1988) 'Validity: An evolving concept'. In Wainer, H. and Braun, H.I. (eds) *Test Validity*. Hillsdale, NJ: Lawrence Erlbaum Associates.

Archard, D. and MacLeod, C.M. (2002) *The Moral and Political Status of Children*. Oxford: Oxford University Press.

Archer, L. and DeWitt, J. (2017) *Understanding Young People's Science Aspirations: How Students Form Ideas about 'Becoming a Scientist'*. London: Routledge

Archer, M. (1979) *The Social Origins of Educational Systems*. London: SAGE.

Aries, P. (1962) *Centuries of Childhood*. Harmondsworth: Penguin.

Armstrong, M. (1980) *Closely Observed Children*. London: Writers and Readers.

Arnold, M. (1889) *Reports on Elementary Schools 1852–1882*. London: Macmillan.

Arnot, M. and Barton, L. (eds) (1992) *Voicing Concerns: Sociological Perspectives on Contemporary Education Reforms*. Wallingford: Triangle.

Arshad, R., Wrigley, T. and Pratt, L. (2012) *Social Justice Re-Examined. Dilemmas and Solutions for the Classroom Teacher*. London: Trentham Books.

Asbury, K. and Plomin, R. (2014) *G is for Genes: The Impact of Genetics on Education and Achievement*. Chichester: Wiley Blackwell.

Askew, M., Brown, M., Rhodes, V., Wiliam, D. and Johnson, D. (1997) *Effective Teachers of Numeracy: Report of a Study Carried out for the Teacher Training Agency*. London: University of London, King's College.

Assessment Reform Group (ARG) (1999) *Assessment for Learning: Beyond the Black Box*. Cambridge: University of Cambridge, School of Education.

Assessment Reform Group (ARG) (2002) *Testing, Motivation and Learning*. Cambridge: University of Cambridge, Faculty of Education.

Assessment Reform Group (ARG) (2006) *The Role of Teachers in Assessment of Learning*. London: Institute of Education.

Atkinson, T. and Claxton, G. (eds) (2000) *The Intuitive Practitioner: On the Value of Not Always Knowing What One Is Doing*. Buckingham: Open University Press.

Aubrey, C. (1994) *The Role of Subject Knowledge in the Early Years of Schooling*. Lewes: Falmer Press.

Ausubel, D.P. (1968) *Educational Psychology: A Cognitive View*. New York: Holt, Rinehart and Winston.

Baines, E., Blatchford, P. and Kutnick, P. (2017) *Promoting Effective Group Work in the Primary Classroom. A Handbook for Teachers and Practitioners*. London: Routledge.

Baker, R.G. (1968) *Ecological Psychology. Concepts and Methods of Studying the Environment of Human Behaviour*. Stanford, CA: Stanford University Press.

Ball, S. (1981a) *Beachside Comprehensive*. Cambridge: Cambridge University Press.

Ball, S. (1981b) 'Initial encounters in the classroom and the process of establishment'. In Woods, P.F. (ed.) *Pupil Strategies*. London: Croom Helm.

Ball, S. (1990) *Politics and Policy Making in Education: Explorations in Policy Sociology*. London: Routledge.

Ball, S. (2003) 'The More Things Change: Educational Research, Social Class and "Interlocking" Inequalities'. Professorial Inaugural Lecture, Institution of Education, University of London, 12 March.

Ball, S. (2006) *Education Policy and Social Class*. London: Routledge.

Ball, S.J. (1994) *Education Reform: A Critical and Post-Structural Approach*. Buckingham: Open University Press.

Ball, S.J., Maguire, M. and Braun, A. (2011a) *How Schools Do Policy. Policy Enactments in Secondary Schools*. London: Routledge.

Ball, S.J., Maguire, M., Braun, A. and Hoskins, K. (2011b) 'Policy actors: Doing policy work in schools'. *Discourse: Studies in the Cultural Politics of Education*, 32(4), 625–39. doi:10.1080/01596306.2011.601565.

Bandura, A. (1995) *Self-efficacy in Changing Societies*. New York: Cambridge University Press.

Banister, J. (2004) *Word of Mouse: The New Age of Networked Media*. Berkeley, CA: Agate.

Barber, M. and Mourshed, M. (2007) *How the World's Best Performing School Systems Come Out on Top*. London: McKinsey and Company.

Barnes, D. (2008) 'Exploratory talk for learning'. In Mercer, N. and Hodgkinson, S. (eds) *Exploring Talk in School*. London: SAGE.

Barrett, P., Zhang, Y, Davies, F. and Barrett, L. (2015) *Clever Classrooms. Summary Report of the HEAD Project*. Salford: University of Salford.

Barrow, R. (1984) *Giving Teaching Back to Teachers*. Brighton: Wheatsheaf.

Barrs, M. and Cork, V. (2001) *The Reader in the Writer: The Link Between the Study of Literature and Writing Development at Key Stage 2*. London: Centre for Language in Primary Education.

Bartlett, J. (2016) *Outstanding Differentiation for Learning in the Classroom*. London: Routledge.

Bartlett, S. and Burton, D. (2012) *Introduction to Education Studies*. London: SAGE.

Barton, L. (2012) 'Response'. In Arnot, M. (ed.) *The Sociology of Disability and Inclusive Education: A Tribute to Len Barton*. London: Routledge.

Bates, J. and Lewis, S. (2009) *The Study of Education: An Introduction*. London: Continuum.

Bazerman, C., Applebee, A., Berninger, V., Brandt, D., Graham, S., Jeffery, J., Matsuda, P.S., Murphy, S., Wells Rowe, D.W., Schleppegrell, M. and Campbell Wilcox, K. (2018) *The Lifespan Development of Writing*. Champaign, IL: National Council of Teachers of English. https://wac.colostate.edu/books/ncte/lifespan-writing/

Bear, M., Connors, B. and Paradiso, M.A. (2020) *Neuroscience: Exploring the Brain, Enhanced Edition: Exploring the Brain*, 4th edn. Burlington, MA: Jones & Bartlett Learning.

Bearne, E. and Marsh, J. (eds) (2007) *Literacy and Social Inclusion: Closing the Gap*. Stoke-on-Trent: Trentham Books.

Bearne, E. and Wolstencroft, H. (2007) *Visual Approaches to Teaching Writing: Multimodal Literacy 5–11*. London: SAGE/UKLA.

Beauchamp, G. (2012) *ICT in the Primary School: From Pedagogy to Practice*. Harlow: Pearson.

Beauchamp, G. and Kennewell, S. (2013) 'Transition in pedagogical orchestration using the interactive whiteboard'. *Education and Information Technologies*, 18(2), ACM Digital Library.

Becker, H.S. (1968) *Making the Grade. The Academic Side of College Life*. New York: Wiley.

Benn, M. (2011) *School Wars. The Battle for Britain's Education*. London: Verso.

Benn, M. and Downs, J. (2016) *The Truth About Our Schools. Exposing the Myths, Exploring the Evidence*. London: Routledge.

Bennett, N., Desforges, C., Cockburn, A. and Wilkinson, B. (1984) T*he Quality of Pupil Learning Experiences*. London: Lawrence Erlbaum.

Bennett, T. (2012) *Teacher: Mastering the Art and Craft of Teaching*. London: Bloomsbury.

Bennett, T. (2015) *Managing Difficult Behaviour in Schools: A Practical Guide*. Unison. unison.org.uk/content/uploads/2015/04/On-line-Catalogue22970.pdf

Bennett, T. (2017) *Creating a Culture: How School Leaders Can Optimise Behaviour*. London: DFE.

Bereiter, C. and Scardamalia, M. (1987) *The Psychology of Written Composition*. Hillsdale, NJ: Lawrence Erlbaum Associates.

Berger P. L. and Luckmann, T. (1966) *The Social Construction of Reality: A Treatise in the Sociology of Knowledge*. New York: Doubleday Garden City.

Berlak, A. and Berlak, H. (1981) *Dilemmas of Schooling*. London: Methuen.

Berliner, D. (1991) 'What's all the fuss about instructional time?' In M. Ben-Peretz and R. Bromme (eds) *The Nature of Time in Schools: Theoretical Concepts, Practitioner Perceptions*. New York: Teachers College Press.

Berliner, D. (2004) 'Describing the behaviour and documenting the accomplishments of expert teachers'. *Bulletin of Science, Technology and Society*, 24(3), 200–12.

Bernstein, B. (1970) 'Education cannot compensate for society'. *New Society*, 387, 344–47.

Bernstein, B. (1971) 'On the classification and framing of educational knowledge'. In Young, M.F.D. (ed.) *Knowledge and Control*. London: Collier Macmillan.

Bernstein, B. (1977) *Class, Codes and Control*, vol. 3. London: Routledge & Kegan Paul.

Berry, J. (2016) *Teachers Undefeated. How Global Education Reform Has Failed to Crush the Spirit of Educators*. London: Trentham Books.

Bialystok, E. (2007) 'Cognitive effects of bilingualism: How linguistic experience leads to cognitive change'. *International Journal of Bilingual Education and Bilingualism*, 10(3), 210–23.

Biesta, G., Field, J., Goodson, I., Hodkinson, P. and Macleod, F. (2010) *Improving Learning through the Lifecourse*. London: Routledge.

Biggs, J. and Tang, C. (2011) *Teaching for Quality Learning at University: What the Student Does*. Maidenhead: Open University Press.

Black, H. (1986) 'Assessment for learning'. In D. Nuttall (ed.) *Assessing Educational Achievement*. London: Falmer Press.

Black, P. and Wiliam, D. (1998a) 'Assessment and classroom learning'. *Assessment in Education*, 5(1), 7–74.

Black, P. and Wiliam, D. (1998b) *Inside the Black Box: Raising Standards through Classroom Assessment*. London: King's College.

Black, P., Harrison, C., Lee, C., Marshall, B. and Wiliam, D. (2003) *Assessment for Learning: Putting It into Practice*. Buckingham: Open University Press.

Black-Hawkins, K. and Florian, L. (2012) 'Teachers' craft knowledge of their inclusive practice'. *Teachers and Teaching: Theory and Practice*, 18(5), 567–84.

Blackledge, A. (ed.) (1994) *Teaching Bilingual Children*. Stoke-on-Trent: Trentham.

Blakemore, C. (2000) 'It makes you think'. (December) *Independent on Sunday*.

Blanchard, J. (2009) *Teaching, Learning and Assessment*. Maidenhead: Open University Press.

Blanden, J., Gregg, P. and Machin, P. (2005) *Intergenerational Mobility in Europe and North America*. London: The Sutton Trust.

Blatchford, P. and Russell, A. (2020) *Rethinking Class Size: The Complex Story of Impact on Teaching and Learning*. London: UCL Press.

Blatchford, P., Galton, M. and Kutnick, P. (2005) *Improving Group Work in Classrooms: A New Approach to Increasing Engagement and Learning in Everyday Classroom Settings at Key Stages 1, 2 and 3*. TLRP Research Briefing 11. London: TLRP.

Blatchford, P., Russell, A. and Webster, R. (2011) *Reassessing the Impact of Teaching Assistants*. London: Routledge.

Blenkin, G.M. and Kelly, A.V. (1981) *The Primary Curriculum*. London: Harper and Row.

Blishen, E. (1969) *The School That I'd Like*. Harmondsworth: Penguin.

Bloom, B.S. (1956) *Taxonomy of Educational Objectives*. New York: David McKay.

Bloom, B.S. (1968) 'Learning for mastery'. *Evaluation Comment (UCLA-CSIEP)*, 1(2), 1–12.

Blundell, D. (2012) *Education and Constructions of Childhood*. London: Continuum.

Blyth, A. (1976) *8–13: Place, Time and Society: Curriculum Planning in History, Geography and Social Science*. London: Schools Council.

Boas, G. (1966) *The Cult of Childhood*. London: Warburg Institute.

Bolster, A. (1983) 'Towards a more effective model of research on teaching'. *Harvard Educational Review*, 53(3), 294–308.

reflectiveteaching.co.uk

Bourdieu, P. and Passeron, J.C. (1977) *Reproduction in Education, Society and Culture*. London: SAGE.

Bowe, R., Ball, S. and Gold, A. (1992) *Reforming Education and Changing Schools*. London: Routledge.

Bowles, S. and Gintis, H. (1976) *Schooling in Capitalist America*. London: Routledge.

Boyd, M.P. (2015) 'Relations between teacher questioning and student talk in one elementary ELL classroom'. *Journal of Literacy Research*, 47(3), 370–404. doi:10.1177/1086296X16632451.

Bradford, H. and Wyse, D. (2020) 'Two-year-old and three-year-old children's writing: The contradictions of children's and adults' conceptualisations'. *Early Years*. doi:10.1080/09575146 .2020.1736519.

Bradbury, A. (2013) *Understanding Early Years Inequality: Policy, Assessment and Young Children's Identities*. London: Routledge.

Bradbury, A. and Roberts-Holmes, G. (2017) *Grouping in Early Years and Key Stage 1: 'A Necessary Evil?'* London: National Education Union.

Bradbury, A. and Roberts-Holmes, G. (2018) The Datafication of Primary and Early Years Education. London: Routledge.

Bradlow, J., Bartram, F., Guasp, A. and Jadva, V. (2017) *School Report: The Experiences of Lesbian, Gay, Bi and Trans Young People in Britain's Schools in 2017*. London: Stonewall.

Bransford, J.D., Brown, A.I. and Cocking, R.R. (eds) (1999) *How People Learn: Brain, Mind, Experience and School*. Washington, DC: National Academy Press.

Breakwell, G. (1986) *Coping with Threatened Identities*. London: Methuen.

Bridges, D. (2009) *Evidence-based Policy. What Evidence? What Basis? Whose Policy?* TLRP Research Briefing 74. London: TLRP.

British Educational Research Association (BERA) (2012) *Background to Michael Gove's response to the Report of the Expert Panel for the National Curriculum Review in England*. London: BERA. Retrieved 28 August 2015 from https://www.bera.ac.uk/promoting-educational-research/issues/ background-to-michael-goves-response-to-the-report-of-the-expert-panel-for-the-national-curriculum-review-in-england

Britton, J., Burgess, T., Martin, N., McLeod, A. and Rosen, H. (1975) *The Development of Writing Abilities (11–18)*. London: MacMillan Education.

Britzman, D.P. (2003) *Practice Makes Practice: A Critical Study of Learning to Teach*. Albany, GA: State University of New York.

Broadfoot, P. (2007) *An Introduction to Assessment*. London: Continuum.

Bronfenbrenner, U. (1979) *The Ecology of Human Development: Experiments by Nature and Design*. Cambridge, MA: Harvard University Press.

Bronfenbrenner, U. (1993) 'Environments as contexts of development'. In Gauvain, M. and Cole, M. (eds) *Readings on the Development of Children*. New York: Freeman.

Brophy, J.E. and Good, T.L. (1974) *Teacher–Student Relationships*. New York: Cassell.

Brown, M.E. and Precious, G.N. (1968) *The Integrated Day in the Primary School*. London: Ward Lock Educational.

Brown, S. and McIntyre, D. (1993) *Making Sense of Teaching*. Buckingham: Open University Press.

Brown-Jeffy, S. and Cooper, J.E. (2011) 'Toward a conceptual framework of culturally relevant pedagogy: An overview of the conceptual and theoretical literature'. *Teacher Education Quarterly*, Winter 2011.

Bruner, J.S. (1966a) *The Process of Education*. Cambridge, MA: Harvard University Press.

Bruner, J.S. (1966b) *Towards a Theory of Instruction*. Cambridge, MA: Harvard University Press.

Bruner, J.S. (1977) *The Process of Instruction*. Cambridge, MA: Harvard University Press.

Bruner, J.S. (1986) *Actual Minds, Possible Worlds*. Cambridge, MA: Harvard University Press.

Bruner, J.S. (1990) *Acts of Meaning*. Cambridge, MA: Harvard University Press.

Bruner, J.S. (1996) *The Culture of Education*. Cambridge, MA: Harvard University Press.

reflectiveteaching.co.uk

Bruner, J.S. (2006) *In Search of Pedagogy I and II: The Selected Works of Jerome S. Bruner, 1957–1978 and 1979–2006.* London: Routledge.

Buckingham, D. (2000) *After the Death of Childhood: Growing up in the Age of Electronic Media.* Cambridge: Polity Press.

Buckingham, D. (2008) *Youth, Identity and Digital Media.* Cambridge, MA: MIT Press.

Buckingham, D. (2013) *Media Education: Literacy, Learning and Contemporary Culture.* London: Wiley.

Bunn, S. and Lewis, S. (2021) 'Children's mental health and the COVID-19 pandemic' (No. 653). *UK Parliament POST.*

Burn, A. (2021) *Literature, Videogames and Learning.* London: Routledge.

Burn, K. and Childs, A. (2016) 'Responding to poverty through education and teacher education initiatives: A critical evaluation of key trends in government policy in England 1997–2015'. *Journal of Education for Teaching*, 42(4), 387–403.

Burn, K., Hagger, H. and Mutton, T (2015) *Beginning Teachers' Learning: Making Experience Count.* St Albans: Critical Publishing.

Burnett, C. and Merchant, G. (2020) *Undoing the Digital. Sociomaterialism and Literacy Education.* London: Routledge.

Burrell, A. and Bubb, S. (2000) 'Teacher feedback in the reception class: Associations with pupils' positive adjustments to school'. *Education 3–13*, 28(3), 58–64.

Butler, K.A. (1998) *Learning and Teaching Style: In Theory and Practice.* Columbia: Learner's Dimension.

Butt, G. (2011) *Making Assessment Matter.* London: Continuum.

Calderhead, J. (1994) 'Competence and the complexities of teaching'. *Mimeo.* ESRC seminar series on teacher competence.

Callaghan, J. (1976) 'Towards a national debate'. *Education*, 148(17), 332–33.

Campbell, C. (2011) *How to Involve Hard-to-reach Parents: Encouraging Meaningful Parental Involvement with Schools.* Nottingham: NCSL. dera.ioe.ac.uk/12136/1/download%3Fid%3D15 6367%26filename%3Dhow-to-involve-hard-to-reach-parents-full-report.pdf

Campbell, J. and Neill, S.R. St J. (1992) *Teacher Time and Curriculum Manageability at Key Stage 1.* London: AMMA.

Canter, L. and Canter, M. (1992) *Assertive Discipline: Positive Behaviour Management for Today's Classroom.* Santa Monica, CA: Canter and Associates.

Carr, M. (2001) *Assessment in Early Childhood Settings.* London: Paul Chapman.

Carr, M. (2008) 'Can assessment unlock and open the doors to resourcefulness and agency?' In Swaffield, S. (ed.) *Unlocking Assessment: Understanding for Reflection and Application,* 36–54. Abingdon: Routledge.

Carr, M. and Lee, W. (2012) *Learning Stories: Constructing Learner Identities in Early Education.* London: SAGE.

Carr, W. and Kemmis, S. (1986) *Becoming Critical: Knowing Through Action Research.* London: Falmer.

Carroll, M. and McCulloch, M. (2018) *Understanding Teaching and Learning in Primary Education.* London: SAGE.

Carter, C. and Nutbrown, C. (2016) 'A pedagogy of friendship: young children's friendships and how schools can support them'. *International Journal of Early Years Education*, 24(4), 395–413.

Cassen, R., McNally, S. and Vignoles, A. (2015) *Making a Difference in Education. What the Evidence Says.* London: Routledge.

Cazden, C. (1988) *Classroom Discourse: The Language of Teaching and Learning.* Portsmouth, NH: Heinemann.

Central Advisory Council for Education (CACE) (1967) *Children and Their Primary Schools.* London: HMSO.

Chaplain, R. (2017) *Teaching Without Disruption in the Primary School.* London: Routledge.

Chaplain, R. (2018) *Teaching Without Disruption in the Secondary School*. London: Routledge.

Chetty, R., Friedman, J.N. and Rockoff, J.E. (2014) 'Measuring the impacts of teachers II: Teacher value-added and student outcomes in adulthood'. *American Economic Review*, 104(9), 2633–79.

Children in Scotland (2018) *GTCS: The Review of the Professional Standards (Values) (2017–20)*. Available at: https://childreninscotland.org.uk/ gtcs-the-review-of-professional-teaching-standards-2018/

Choi, Á. and Jerrim, J. (2016) 'The use (and misuse) of PISA in guiding policy reform: The case of Spain'. *Comparative Education*, 52(2), 230–45.

Chubb, T.E. and Moe, T.M. (1990) *Politics, Markets, and America's Schools*. Washington, DC: Brookings.

Clark, C. and Phythian-Sence, C. (2008) *Interesting Choice: The (Relative) Importance of Choice and Interest in Reader Engagement*. London: National Literacy Trust.

Clarke, S. (1998) *Targeting Assessment in the Primary Classroom*. London: Hodder and Stoughton.

Clarke, S. (2001) *Unlocking Formative Assessment: Practical Strategies for Enhancing Pupils' Learning in the Primary Classroom*. London: Hodder and Stoughton.

Clarke, S. (2005a) *Formative Assessment in Action: Weaving the Elements Together*. London: Hodder and Stoughton.

Clarke, S. (2005b) *Formative Assessment in the Secondary Classroom*. London: Hodder and Stoughton.

Clarke, S. (2008) *Active Learning through Formative Assessment*. London: Hodder and Stoughton.

Clarke, S. (2011) *The Power of Formative Assessment: Self-belief and Active Involvement in the Process of Learning* (DVD). Shirley Clarke Media.

Clarke, S. (2014) *Outstanding Formative Assessment: Culture and Practice*. London: Hodder and Stoughton.

Clarricoates, K. (1987) 'Child culture at school: a clash between gendered worlds?' In Pollard, A. (ed.) *Children and Their Primary Schools*. London: Falmer.

Claxton, G. (1999) *Wise Up: The Challenge of Lifelong Learning*. London: Bloomsbury.

Claxton, G. (2002) *Building Learning Power*. Bristol: TLO.

Claxton, G. (2004) *Building 101 Ways to Learning Power*. Bristol: TLO.

Claxton, G. (2011) *Building Learning Power: Helping Young People Become Better Learners*. Bristol: TLO.

Claxton, G. (2013) 'School as an epistemic apprenticeship: The case of building learning power'. In *School as an Epistemic Apprenticeship: The Case of Building Learning Power. 32nd Vernon-Wall Lecture*, 1–27. Leicester: The British Psychological Society.

Claxton, G. Chambers, M., Powell, G. and Lucas, B. (2011) *The Learning Powered School: Pioneering 21st Century Education*. Bristol: TLO.

Clay, M.M. (2001) *Change Over Time in Children's Literacy Development*. Portsmouth, NH: Heinemann.

Clegg, D. and Billington, S. (1994) *The Effective Primary Classroom: Management and Organisation of Teaching and Learning*. London: David Fulton.

Clegg, N., Allen, R., Fernandez, S., Freedman, S. and Kinnock, S. (2016) *Commission on Inequality in Education*. Available at: https://www.smf.co.uk/wp-content/uploads/2017/07/ Education-Commission-final-web-report.pdf

Cliff Hodges, G. (2010) 'Reasons for reading: Why literature matters'. *Literacy*, 44(2), 60–68.

Cliff Hodges, G. (2016) *Researching and Teaching Reading: Developing Pedagogy Through Critical Enquiry*. Oxford: Routledge.

Clifford, M.M. and Walster, E. (1973) 'The effect of physical attractiveness on teacher expectations'. *Sociology of Education*, 46(2) (Spring), 248–58.

Cobley, S., McKenna, J., Baker, J. and Wattie, N. (2009) 'How pervasive are relative age effects in secondary school education?' *Journal of Educational Psychology*, 101(2), 520–28. doi:10.1037/ a0013845.

reflectiveteaching.co.uk

Coe, R., Aloisi, C., Higgins, S. and Major, L.E. (2014) *What Makes Great Teaching? Review of the Underpinning Research*. London: Sutton Trust.

Coffield, F., Mosley, D., Hall, E. and Ecclestone, K. (2004) *Learning Styles and Pedagogy in Post-16 Learning: A Systematic and Critical Review*. London: LSDA.

Cole, M. and Walker, S.E. (1989) *Teaching and Stress*. Buckingham: Open University Press.

Coleman, J.S. (1988) 'Social capital in the creation of human capital'. *American Journal of Sociology*, 94 (Supplement), 95–120.

Coleman, J.S., Coser, L.A. and Powell, W.W. (1966) *Equality of Educational Opportunity*. Washington, DC: US Government Printing Office.

Collarbone, P. (2009) *Creating Tomorrow: Planning, Developing and Sustaining Change in Education and Other Public Services*. London: Continuum.

Collins, J. (1996) *The Quiet Child*. London: Cassell.

Collins, R. (1977) 'Some comparative principles of educational stratification'. *Higher Education Review*, 47(1), 1–27.

Connell, R.W., Ashden, D.J., Kessler, S. and Dowsett, G.W. (1982) *Making the Difference: Schools, Families and Social Division*. Sydney: Allen and Unwin.

Connolly, P. (1998) *Racism, Gender and Identities of Young Children: Social Relations in a Multi-ethnic, Inner-city Primary School*. London: Routledge.

Conteh, J. (2015) *The EAL Teaching Book. Promoting Success for Multilingual Learners*. London: SAGE.

Coolahan, J., Drudy, S., Hogan, P. and McGuiness, S. (2017) *Towards a Better Future: A Review of the Irish School System*. Irish Primary Principals Network and the National Association of Principals.

Cooper, H. and Hyland, R. (eds) (2000) *Children's Perceptions of Learning with Trainee Teachers*. London: Routledge.

Corcoran, R.P., Cheung, A.C., Kim, E. and Xie, C. (2018) 'Effective universal school-based social and emotional learning programs for improving academic achievement: A systematic review and meta-analysis of 50 years of research'. *Educational Research Review*, 25, 56–72. doi:10.1016/j.edurev.2017.12.001.

Cordingley, P., Bell, M., Evans, D. and Firth, A. (2005) 'The impact of collaborative CPD on classroom teaching and learning. What do teacher impact data tell us about collaborative CPD?' In *Research Evidence in Education Library*. London: EPPI-Centre, Social Science Research Unit, Institute of Education.

Cordingley, P., Bell, M., Rundell, B., Evans, D. and Curtis, A. (2003) *The Impact of Collaborative CPD on Classroom Teaching and Learning*. London: EPPI-Centre.

Cordon, R. (2000) *Literacy and Learning through Talk: Strategies for the Primary Classroom*. Buckingham: Open University Press.

Corsaro, W.A. (2011) *The Sociology of Childhood*. London: SAGE.

Council for the Curriculum Examinations and Assessment (CCEA) (2007) *The Northern Ireland Curriculum*. Belfast: CCEA.

Council of Europe (1985) *Teaching and Learning about Human Rights in Schools, Recommendation No. R (85) 7 of the Committee of Ministers*. Strasbourg: Council of Europe.

Counsell, C. (2004) *History and Literacy in Y7: Building the Lesson Around the Text*. London: John Murray.

Cowie, H. (2012) *From Birth to Sixteen. Children's Health, Social, Emotional and Linguistic Development*. London: Routledge.

Cowie, H. and Ruddock, J. (1990) 'Co-operative group work in the multi-ethnic classroom'. In *Learning Together, Working Together*. Vol. 4. British Petroleum Service on behalf of the Co-operative Group Work Project, Division of Education, University of Sheffield: Sheffield.

Cowie, H. and Wallace, P. (2000) *Peer Support in Action: From Bystanding to Standing By*. London: SAGE.

Crawford, C., Dearden, L. and Meghir, C. (2007) *When You Are Born Matters: The Impact of Date of Birth on Child Cognitive Outcomes.* London: Institute for Fiscal Studies.

Crawford, C., Johnson, P., Machin, S. and Vignoles, A. (2011) *Social Mobility: A Literature Review.* London: BIS.

Cremin, T. (2009) *Teaching English Creatively.* London: Routledge.

Cremin, T. and Moss, G. (2018) 'Reading for pleasure: Supporting reader engagement'. *Literacy,* 52(2), 59–61. doi:10.1111/lit.12156.

Cremin, T. and Myhill, D. (2012) *Writing Voices. Creating Communities of Writers.* London: Routledge.

Cremin, T. and Reedy, D. (2015) *Teaching English Creatively.* London: Routledge

Cremin, T., Mottram, M., Collins, F., Powell, S. and Drury, R. (2016) *Researching Literacy Lives: Building Communities Between Home and School.* Oxford: Routledge.

Cremin, T., Mottram, M., Collins, F., Powell, S. and Safford, K. (2009) 'Teachers as readers: Building communities of readers'. *Literacy,* 43(1), 11–19. doi:10.1002/trtr.1893.

Cremin, T., Mottram, M., Collins, F., Powell, S. and Safford, K. (2014) *Building Communities of Engaged Readers: Reading for Pleasure.* London: Routledge.

Croll, P. and Moses, D. (2000) *Special Needs in the Primary School.* London: Cassell.

Cross, V. (2012) *My Story: The Berlin Olympics.* London: Scholastic.

Crozier, G. (2000) *Parents and Schools: Partners or Protagonists?* Stoke-on-Trent: Trentham.

Crozier, G. and Reay, D. (eds) (2005) *Activating Participation: Parents and Teachers Working Towards Partnership.* Stoke-on-Trent: Trentham Books.

Crozier, G., Reay, D. and Clayton, J. (2010) 'The socio-cultural and learning experiences of working-class students in higher education'. In David, M. (ed.) *Improving Learning by Widening Participation in Higher Education.* London: Routledge.

Crystal, D. (2002) *The English Language: A Guided Tour of the Language.* London: Penguin.

Cullen, M.A., Lindsay, G., Hastings, R., Denne, L., Stanford, C., Beqiraq, L., Elahi, F., Gemegah, E., Hayden, N., Kander, I., Lykomitrou, F. and Zander, J. (2020) *Special Educational Needs in Mainstream Schools: Evidence Review.* London: Education Endowment Foundation.

Cummins, J. (1996) *Negotiating Identities: Education for Empowerment in a Diverse Society.* Los Angeles, CA: CABE.

Cunningham, B. (ed.) (2008) *Exploring Professionalism.* London: Institute of Education.

Cunningham, H. (2006) *The Invention of Childhood.* London: BBC Books.

Cunningham, P. (2011) *Politics and the Primary Teacher.* London: Routledge.

Curriculum Council for Wales (CCW) (1991) The Whole Curriculum in Wales. Cardiff: CCW.

Dadds, M. (1995) *Passionate Enquiry and School Development: A Story about Teacher Action Research.* London: Falmer.

Dahlberg, G., Moss, P. and Pence, A. (eds) (1999) *Beyond Quality in Early Childhood Education and Care: Postmodern Perspectives.* London: RoutledgeFalmer.

Damon, W. and Phelps, E. (1989) 'Critical distinctions among three approaches to peer education'. *International Journal of Educational Research,* 58, 9–19.

Darling-Hammond, L. (1996) *The Right to Learn: A Blueprint for Creating Schools that Work.* San Francisco: Jossey-Bass.

Darling-Hammond, L. (2007) *Testimony Before the House Education and Labor Committee on the Re-authorization of the NCLB legislation.* 10 September.

Darling-Hammond, L. (2017) 'Teacher education around the world: What can we learn from international practice?' *European Journal of Teacher Education,* 40(3), 291–309.

Darling-Hammond, L., Barron, P.D., Pearson, A., Schoenfeld, E. et al. (2008) *Powerful Learning. What We Know About Teaching for Understanding.* San Francisco: Jossey-Bass.

Darling-Hammond, L., Flook, L., Cook-Harvey, C., Barron, B. and Osher, D. (2020) 'Implications for educational practice of the science of learning and development'. *Applied Developmental Science,* 24(2), 97–140.

Bibliography

Darvin, J. (2009) 'Make books, not war: Workshops at a summer camp in Bosnia'. *Literacy*, 43(1), 50–59.

Davies, B. (1982) *Life in the Classroom and Playground*. London: Routledge and Kegan Paul.

Davies, K. and Henderson, P. (2020) *Special Educational Needs in Mainstream Schools: Guidance Report*. London: EEF.

Dawes, L. (2004) 'Talk and learning in classroom science'. *International Journal of Science Education*, 26(6), 677–95.

Dawes, L. (2011) *Creating a Speaking and Listening Classroom*. London: Routledge.

Dawes, L. and Sams, C. (2004) *Talkbox: Speaking and Listening Activities for Learning at Key Stage 1 (Ages 6–8)*. London: David Fulton.

Dawes, L., Mercer, N. and Wegerif, R. (2000) *Thinking Together: A Programme of Activities for Developing Speaking, Listening and Thinking Skills for Children Aged 8–11*. Birmingham: Imaginative Minds.

Dawkins, R. (1978) *The Selfish Gene*. London: Granada.

Day, C. and Gu, Q. (2010) *The New Lives of Teachers*. London: Routledge.

Day, C., Kington, A., Stobart, G. and Sammons, P. (2006) 'The personal and professional selves of teachers: Stable and unstable identities'. *British Educational Research Journal*, 32(04), 601–16.

Day, C., Sammons, P., Stobart, G., Kington, A. and Gu, Q. (2007) *Teachers Matter: Connecting Work, Lives and Effectiveness*. Maidenhead: Open University Press.

De Vries, R. (2000) 'Vygotsky, Piaget, and education: a reciprocal assimilation of theories and educational practices'. *New Ideas in Psychology*, 18 (2–3), 187–213.

De Vries., Jochen, P., de Graf, H. and Nikken, P. (2016) 'Adolescents' social network site use, peer appearance-related feedback, and body dissatisfaction: Testing a mediation model'. *Journal of Youth and Adolescence*, 45, 211–24.

Deakin Crick, R. (2006) *Learning Power in Practice*. London: Paul Chapman.

Dean, J. (2008) *Organising Learning in the Primary School Classroom*. London: Routledge.

Delamont, S. (1990) *Sex Roles and the School*. London: Routledge.

DeLuca, C., Chapman-Chin, A.E.A., LaPointe-McEwan, D. and Klinger, D. (2018) 'Student perspectives on assessment for learning'. *The Curriculum Journal*, 29(1), 77–94. doi:10.1080/0 9585176.2017.1401550.

DeLuca, C., Pyle, A., Valiquette, A. and LaPointe-McEwan, D. (2020) 'New directions for kindergarten education: Embedding assessment in play-based learning'. *Elementary Schools Journal*, 120(3), 455–79. doi:138.051.012.062.

Demie, F. and McLean, C. (2017) *Black Caribbean Underachievement in Schools in England*. Schools Research and Statistics Unit, Lambeth Education and Learning.

DePalma, R and Atkinson, E. (eds) (2009) *Interrogating Heteronormativity in Primary Schools: The Work of the No Outsiders Project*. Stoke on Trent: Trentham Books.

Department for Children, Schools and Families (DCSF) (2009) *Breaking the Link between Disadvantage and Low Attainment*. Nottingham, DCSF.

Department for Education (DfE) (2010) *Religious Education in English Schools: Non-statutory Guidance 2010*. London: DfE. Available at: https://assets.publishing.service.gov.uk/government/uploads/system/uploads/attachment_data/file/190260/DCSF-00114-2010.pdf

Department for Education (DfE) (2011a) *The Framework for the National Curriculum. A Report by the Expert Panel for the National Curriculum Review*. London: DfE.

Department for Education (DfE) (2011b) *Teachers' Standards: Guidance for School Leaders, School Staff and Governing Bodies*, July 2011 (introduction updated June 2013, latest terminology update December 2021). London: DfE. Available at: https://assets.publishing.service.gov.uk/government/uploads/system/uploads/attachment_data/file/1040274/Teachers__Standards_Dec_2021.pdf

Department for Education (DfE) (2012) *Guidance for Local Authorities and Schools on Setting Education Performance Targets for 2012*. London: DfE.

Department for Education (DfE) (2013a) *The National Curriculum in England Key Stages 1 and 2 Framework*. London: DfE.

Department for Education (DfE) (2013b) *The National Curriculum in England Key Stages 2 and 3 Framework*. London: DfE.

Department for Education (DfE) (2013c) *The National Curriculum in England: Science Programmes of Study*. London: DfE. Available at: https://www.gov.uk/government/publications/national-curriculum-in-england-science-programmes-of-study

Department for Education (DfE) (2014) *Cyber Bullying – Advice for Headteachers and Staff*. London: DfE.

Department for Education (DfE) (2015) *The Special Educational Needs and Disability Code of Practice: 0 to 25 Years*. London: DfE.

Department for Education (DfE) (2016) *Reducing Teacher Workload: Planning and Resources Group Report. Report About Eliminating Unnecessary Workload for Teachers Regarding Lesson Planning, Including Principles and Recommendations*. 26 March 2016. London: DfE. Available at: https://www.gov.uk/government/publications/reducing-teacher-workload-planning-and-resources-group-report

Department for Education (DfE) (2017a) *Secondary Accountability Measures Guide for Maintained Secondary Schools, Academies and Free Schools*. London: DfE.

Department for Education (DfE) (2017b) *Preventing and Tackling Bullying: Advice for Headteachers, Staff and Governing Bodies*. London: DfE.

Department for Education (DfE) (2017c) *Creating a Culture: How School Leaders Can Optimise Behaviour*. Tom Bennett: Independent review of behaviour in schools. London: DfE. gov.uk/government/publications/behaviour-in-schools

Department for Education (DfE) (2019a) *Early Career Framework*. London: DfE. Available at: https://assets.publishing.service.gov.uk/government/uploads/system/uploads/attachment_data/file/978358/Early-Career_Framework_April_2021.pdf

Department for Education (DfE) (2019b) *Key Stage 4 Performance 2019* (revised). London: DfE. Available at: https://assets.publishing.service.gov.uk/government/uploads/system/uploads/attachment_data/file/863815/2019_KS4_revised_text.pdf

Department for Education (DfE) (2019c) *National Curriculum Assessments at Key Stage 2 in England, 2019* (revised). London: DfE. Available at: https://assets.publishing.service.gov.uk/government/uploads/system/uploads/attachment_data/file/851798/KS2_Revised_publication_text_2019_v3.pdf

Department for Education (DfE) (2020a) *Mathematics Guidance: Key Stages 1 and 2*. London: DFE.

Department for Education (DfE) (2020b) *Teaching Mathematics in Primary Schools*. London: DfE. Available at: https://www.gov.uk/government/publications/teaching-mathematics-in-primary-schools

Department for Education (DfE) (2020c) *Guidance. Plan Your Relationships, Sex and Health Curriculum*. London: DfE. Updated 17 February 2022. Available at: https://www.gov.uk/guidance/plan-your-relationships-sex-and-health-curriculum

Department for Education (DfE) (2021a) *ITT Core Content Framework*. London: DfE.

Department for Education (DfE) (2021b) *Teaching a Broad and Balanced Curriculum for Education Recovery*. November 2021. London: DfE. Available at: https://www.gov.uk/government/publications/teaching-a-broad-and-balanced-curriculum-for-education-recovery

Department for Education (DfE) (2022) *Guidance. Political Impartiality in Schools*. 17 February 2022. London: DfE. Available at: https://www.gov.uk/government/publications/political-impartiality-in-schools/political-impartiality-in-schools

Department for Education and Science (DES) (1975) *A Language for Life (The Bullock Report)*. London: HMSO.

Department for Education and Science (1989a) *Discipline in Schools, Report of the Committee of Enquiry, Chaired by Lord Elton*. London: HMSO.

reflectiveteaching.co.uk

Department for Education and Science (DfES) (1989b) *English for Ages 5–16*. London: HMSO.

Department for Education and Skills (2003a) *Excellence and Enjoyment: A Strategy for Primary Schools*. London: DfES.

Department for Education and Skills (2003b) *Every Child Matters*. London: DfES.

Department for Education and Skills (2004) *Personalised Learning: Adding Value to the Learning Journey through Primary School*. London: DfES.

Department for Education and Skills (DfES) (2006) *The Five Year Strategy for Children and Learners: Maintaining the Excellent Progress*. London: DfES.

Department for Work and Pensions (DWP) (2011) *A New Approach to Child Poverty. Tackling the Causes of Disadvantage and Transforming Families' Lives*. London: DWP.

Department for Work and Pensions (DWP) (2021) 'Households below average income, statistics on the number and percentage of people living in low income households for financial years 1994/95 to 2019/20', Table 4_5db.

Desforges, C. with Abouchaar, A. (2003) *The Impact of Parental Involvement, Parental Support and Family Education on Pupil Achievement and Adjustment: A Literature Review*. London: DfES.

Devine, D. (2003) *Children, Power and Schooling. The Social Structuring of Childhood in the Primary School*. Stoke-on-Trent: Trentham.

Dewey, J. (1916) *Democracy and Education: An Introduction to the Philosophy of Education*. New York: Macmillan.

Dewey, J. (1933) *How We Think: A Restatement of the Relation of Reflective Thinking to the Educative Process*. Chicago: Henry Regnery.

Dillow, C. (2010) *Supporting Stories. Being a Teaching Assistant*. Stoke-on-Trent: Trentham Books.

Dixon, A., Drummond, M.J., Hart, S. and McIntyre, D. (2004) *Learning Without Limits*. Maidenhead: Open University Press.

Dochy, F., Segers, M. and Buehl, M. (1999) 'The relation between assessment practices and outcomes of studies: The case of research on prior knowledge'. *Review of Educational Research*, 69(2), 145–86.

Doddington, C. and Hilton, M. (2007) *Child-Centred Education: Reviving the Creative Tradition*. London: SAGE.

Doharty, N. (2019) '"I FELT DEAD": Applying a racial microaggressions framework to Black students' experiences of Black History Month and Black History'. *Race, Ethnicity and Education* 22(1), 110–29.

Dombey, H. (2013) *Teaching Writing: What the Evidence Says*. Leicester: UKLA.

Donaldson, G. (2010) *Teaching: Scotland's Future. Report of a Review of Teacher Education in Scotland*. Edinburgh: Scottish Government.

Donaldson, M. (1978) *Children's Minds*. London: Fontana.

Donnelly, M. and Kilkelly, U. (2011) 'Participation in healthcare: the views and experiences of children and young people'. *The International Journal of Children's Rights*, 19(1), 107–25.

Dowling, J.E. (1999) *Neurons and Networks: An Introduction to Behavioural Neuroscience*. Cambridge, MA: Harvard University Press.

Doyle, W. (1977) 'Learning the classroom environment: An ecological analysis'. *Journal of Teacher Education*, 28(6), 51–54.

Drews, D. and Hansen, A. (2007) *Using Resources to Support Mathematical Thinking*. Exeter: Learning Matters.

Dreyfus, H.L. and Dreyfus, S.E. (1986) *Mind Over Machine*. New York: Free Press.

Drummond, M.J. (2008) 'Assessment and values: A close and necessary relationship'. In Swaffield, S. (ed.) *Unlocking Assessment: Understanding for Reflection and Application*. Abingdon: Routledge.

Drummond, M.J. (2012) *Assessing Children's Learning*. London: Routledge.

Dudley, P. (2011) *Lesson Study: A Handbook*. Cambridge: Dudley. Available at lessonstudy.co.uk

Dumont, H., Istance, D. and Benavides, F. (2010) *The Nature of Learning. Using Research to Inspire Practice.* Paris: OECD.

Dunham, J. (1992) *Stress in Teaching.* London: Routledge.

Dunn, J. (1988) *The Beginnings of Social Understanding.* Oxford: Blackwell.

Duran, D. and Topping, K. (2017) *Learning by Teaching. Evidence-based Strategies to Enhance Learning in the Classroom.* London: Routledge.

Dweck, C.S. (1986) 'Motivational processes affecting learning'. *American Psychology*, 41, 1040–48.

Dweck, C.S. (2000) *Self-Theories: Their Role in Motivation, Personality and Development.* Hove: Psychology Press.

Dweck, C.S. (2006) *Mindset. The New Psychology of Success.* New York: Ballantine.

Earl, L. and Katz, S. (2008) 'Getting to the core of learning: using assessment for self-monitoring and self-regulation'. In Swaffield, S. (ed.) *Unlocking Assessment: Understanding for Reflection and Application*, 90–104. Abingdon: Routledge.

Earl, L., Watson, N., Levin, B., Leithwood, K., Fullan, M. and Torrance, N. with Jantzi, D., Mascall, B. and Volante, L. (2003) *Watching and Learning 3: Final Report of the External Evaluation of England's National Literacy and Numeracy Strategies.* Toronto: Ontario Institute for Studies in Education.

Easton, L.B. (2008) 'From professional development to professional learning'. *Phi Delta Kappa*, 89(10), 755–58.

Eaude, T. (2012) *How Do Expert Primary Class-teachers Really Work? A Critical Guide for Teachers, Headteachers and Teacher Educators.* Northwich: Critical Publishing.

Eaude, T. (2018) *Developing the Expertise of Primary and Elementary Classroom Teachers. Professional Learning for a Changing World.* London: Bloomsbury.

Education and Employers, *Tes*, UCL Institute of Education, the National Association of Head Teachers and the Organisation for Economic Cooperation and Development Education and Skills (2018) *Drawing the Future: Exploring the Career Aspirations of Primary School Children from Around the World.* https://www.educationandemployers.org/wp-content/uploads/2018/01/DrawingTheFuture.pdf

Education Endowment Foundation (EEF) (2018a) *Metacognition and Self-regulated Learning: Guidance Report.* London: EEF.

Education Endowment Foundation (EEF) (2018b) *Working with Parents to Support Children's Learning.* London: EEF. https://educationendowmentfoundation.org.uk/public/files/Publications/ParentalEngagement/EEF_Parental_Engagement_Guidance_Report.pdf

Education Endowment Foundation (EEF) (2019) *Improving Behaviour in Schools. A Guidance Report.* London: EEF. https://educationendowmentfoundation.org.uk/education-evidence/guidance-reports/behaviour

Education Endowment Foundation (EEF) (2021) *Best Evidence on Impact of Covid-19 on Pupil Attainment.* https://educationendowmentfoundation.org.uk/guidance-for-teachers/covid-19-resources/best-evidence-on-impact-of-covid-19-on-pupil-attainment (accessed February 2022).

Education Scotland (2017) *Benchmarks: Literacy and English.* June 2017. Available at: https://education.gov.scot/nih/Documents/LiteracyEnglishBenchmarks.pdf

Education Scotland (2019) *Scotland's Curriculum for Excellence.* Available at: http://scotlandscurriculum.scot/

Education Wales (2020) *Curriculum for Wales.* Available at: https://hwb.gov.wales/curriculum-for-wales

Edwards, A. (2012) *New Technology and Education.* London: Continuum.

Edwards, D. and Mercer, N. (1987) *Common Knowledge: The Development of Understanding in Classrooms.* London: Methuen.

Edwards, R. and Alldred, P. (2000) 'Children's understanding of home–school relations'. *Education 3–13*, 28(3), 41–45.

Egan, K. (1988) *An Alternative Approach to Teaching and the Curriculum*. London: Routledge.

Egan, K. (2010) *An Imaginative Approach to Teaching*. London: John Wiley and Sons.

Eisner, E. (1996) *Cognition and Curriculum Reconsidered*. London: Paul Chapman.

Eisner, E. (2002) *The Arts and the Creation of Mind*. New Haven and London: Yale University Press.

Elliott, G. (1976) *Teaching for Concepts. Place, Time and Society 8–11*. London: Schools Council.

Elliott, J. (1991) *Action Research for Educational Change*. Buckingham: Open University Press.

Elliott, J. (2013) *The Power and Perils of Narrative. Making the Best Use of the British Birth Cohort Studies*. London: UCL IOE Press.

Elliott, J. and Vaitilingam, R. (2008) *Now We Are 50*. London: Centre for Longitudinal Studies, Institute of Education.

Elliott, Z. (2017) *Sex Differences: A Land of Confusion*. New York: Lulu.

Entwistle, N. (2009) *Teaching for Understanding at University*. London: Palgrave Macmillan.

Epstein, D. (1993) *Changing Classroom Cultures: Anti-Racism, Politics and Schools*. Stoke-on-Trent: Trentham Books.

Eraut, M. (1994) *Developing Professional Knowledge and Competence*. London: Routledge.

Eraut, M. (2007) 'Learning from other people in the workplace'. *Oxford Review of Education*, 33(4), 403–22.

Ericsson, K.A., Charness, N., Feltovich, P.J. and Hoffman, R.R. (eds) (2006) *The Cambridge Handbook of Expertise and Expert Performance*. New York: Cambridge University Press.

Ernest, P. (1991) *The Philosophy of Mathematics Education*. London: Falmer.

Etzioni, A. (1961) 'A basis for the comparative analysis of complex organisations'. In Etzioni, A.A *Sociological Reader on Complex Organisations*. New York: Holt, Rinehart and Winston.

Evans, G. (2006) *Educational Failure and Working Class White Children in Britain*. Basingstoke: Palgrave Macmillan.

Evans, G. (2007) *Early Career Learning at Work*. Research Briefing 25. London: TLRP.

Evans, W. and Savage, J. (2018) *Using Your Voice Effectively in the Classroom*. London: Routledge.

Ewing, R. and Manuel, J. (2005) 'Retaining quality early career teachers in the profession: New teacher narratives'. *Change: Transformations in Education*, 8 (1), 1–16.

Eyre, C. (2017) *The Elephant in the Staffroom. How to Reduce Stress and Improve Teacher Wellbeing*. London: Routledge.

Eysenck, H.J. and Cookson, C.D. (1969) 'Personality in primary school children: Ability and achievement'. *British Journal of Educational Psychology*, 39(2), 109–22.

Facer, K. (2011) *Learning Futures. Education, Technology and Social Change*. London: Routledge.

Facer, K., Furlong, J., Furlong, R. and Sutherland, R. (2003) *Screenplay: Children and Computing in the Home*. London: Routledge.

Farquharson, C., McNally, S. and Tahir, I. (2022) *Education Inequalities. IFS Deaton Review of Inequalities*. Available from https://ifs.org.uk/inequality/education-inequalities/

Farrell, P., Alborz, A., Howes, A. and Pearson, D. (2010) 'The impact of teaching assistants on improving pupils' academic achievement in mainstream schools: A review of the literature'. *Educational Review*, 62(4), 435–48.

Feiler, A., Andrews, J., Greenhough, P., Hughes, M., Johnson, D., Scanlan, M. and Yee, W. (2007) *Improving Primary Literacy: Linking Home and School*. London: Routledge.

Feinstein, L., Duckworth, K. and Sabates, R. (2008a) *Education and the Family: Passing Success Across the Generations*. Abingdon: Routledge.

Feinstein, L., Vorhaus, J. and Sabates, R. (2008b) *Learning Through Life: Future Challenges. Foresight Mental Capital and Wellbeing Project*. London: The Government Office for Science.

Feucht, F.C., Lunn Brownlee, J. and Schraw, G., (2017) 'Moving beyond reflection: Reflexivity and epistemic cognition in teaching and teacher education'. *Educational Psychologist*, 52(4), 234–41.

Filer, A. (ed.) (2000) *Assessment: Social Practice and Social Product*. London: Routledge.

Filer, A. and Pollard, A. (2000) *The Social World of Pupil Assessment: Processes and Contexts of Primary Schooling*. London: Continuum.

Fisher, R. (2008) *Teaching Thinking. Philosophical Enquiry in the Classroom*. London: Continuum.

Fitzsimons, E. and Benn, D. (2020) *Obesity Prevalence and its Inequality from Childhood to Adolescence*. London: Center for Longitudinal Studies, IOE University College London.

Flavell, J.H. (1970) 'Developmental studies of mediated memory'. In Reese, H.W. and Lipsett, L.P. (eds) *Advances in Child Development and Behaviour*. New York: Academic Press.

Flavell, J.H. (1979) 'Metacognition and cognitive monitoring'. *American Psychologist*, 34(10), 906–11.

Flitton, L. (2010) *Developing the Use of Talk as a Tool for Learning: From Classroom Analysis to School Development*. Unpublished Masters thesis: University of Cambridge.

Flitton, L. and Warwick P. (2012) 'From classroom analysis to whole school professional development: Promoting talk as a tool for learning across school departments'. Available at: http://www.tandfonline.com/doi/abs/10.1080/19415257.2012.719288 (accessed 9 November 2013).

Flook, J., Ryan, M. and Hawkins, L. (2010) *Professional Expertise: Practice, Theory and Education for Working in Uncertainty*. London: Whiting and Birch.

Florian, L. and Linklater, H. (2010) 'Preparing teachers for inclusive education: using inclusive pedagogy to enhance teaching and learning for all'. *Cambridge Journal of Education*, 40(4), 369–86.

Flückiger, B., Dunn, J. and Stinson, M. (2018) 'What supports and limits learning in the early years? Listening to the voices of 200 children'. *Australian Journal of Education*, 62(2), 94–107.

Fokkens-Bruinsma, M. and Canrinus, E.T. (2012) 'Adaptive and maladaptive motives for becoming a teacher'. *Journal of Education for Teaching*, 38(1), 3–19.

Frances, J. (2004) *Educating Children with Facial Disfigurement: Creating Inclusive School Communities*. London: RoutledgeFalmer.

Francis, B. (2000) *Boys, Girls and Achievement: Addressing the Classroom Issues*. London: RoutledgeFalmer.

Francis, B., Skelton, C. and Read, B. (2012) *The Identities and Practices of High Achieving Pupils: Negotiating Achievement and Peer Cultures*. London: Continuum.

Francis, B., Taylor, B. and Tereshchenko, A. (2019) *Reassessing 'Ability' Grouping: Improving Practice for Equity and Attainment*. London: Routledge.

Francis, B., Archer, L., Hodgen, J., Pepper, D., Taylor, B. and Travers, M. C. (2017) 'Exploring the relative lack of impact of research on "ability grouping" in England: A discourse analytic account'. *Cambridge Journal of Education*, 47(1), 1–17.

Francis, B., Craig, N., Hodgen, J., Taylor, B., Tereshchenko, A., Connolly, P. and Archer, L. (2020) 'The impact of tracking by attainment on pupil self-confidence over time: Demonstrating the accumulative impact of self-fulfilling prophecy'. *British Journal of Sociology of Education*, 41(5), 626–42.

Francis, R., Taylor, R., Hodgen, J., Tereshchenko, A. and Archer, L. (2018) *Dos and Don'ts of Attainment Grouping* (Report), UCL Institute of Education: London.

Fraser, B.J. and Fisher, D.L. (1984) *Assessment of Classroom Psychosocial Environment: Workshop Manual*. Bentley: Western Australia Institute of Technology.

Fray, L. and Gore, J. (2018) 'Why people choose teaching: A scoping review of empirical studies, 2007–2016'. *Teaching and Teacher Education*, 75, 153–63.

Frederiksen, J.R. and White, B.J. (1997) 'Reflective assessment of students' research within an inquiry-based middle school science curriculum'. Paper presented at the Annual Meeting of AERA Chicago.

Freire, P. (2000) *Pedagogy of the Oppressed*. London: Continuum.

Frieberg, H.J. (1999) *School Climate: Measuring, Improving and Sustaining Healthy Learning Environments*. London: Psychology Press.

Frijda, N.H. (2001) 'The laws of emotion'. In Parrott, G.W. (ed.) *Emotions in Social Psychology*. Hove: Psychology Press.

Gage, N. and Berliner, D.C. (1975) *Educational Psychology*. Boston: Houghton Mifflin.

Gagné, R.M. (1965) *The Conditions of Learning*. New York: Holt, Rinehart and Winston.

Gallard, D. and Cartmell, K.M. (2015) *Psychology and Education*. London: Routledge.

Galton, M. (1989) *Teaching in the Primary School*. London: David Fulton.

Galton, M. (2007) *Learning and Teaching in the Primary Classroom*. London: Paul Chapman.

Galton, M. and Williamson, J. (1992) *Group Work in the Primary Classroom*. London: Routledge.

Galton, M., Gray, J. and Rudduck, J. (1999) *The Impact of School Transitions and Transfers on Pupil Progress and Attainment*. London: DfEE.

Galton, M., Simon, B. and Croll, P. (1980) *Inside the Primary Classroom*. London: Routledge and Kegan Paul.

Galton, M., Hargreaves, L., Comber, C., Wall, D. and Pell, A. (1999) *Inside the Primary Classroom: 20 Years On*. London: Routledge.

Gardner, J. (ed.) (2011) *Assessment and Learning*. London: Paul Chapman.

Gardner, J., Harlen, W., Hayward, L. and Stobart, G. with Montgomery, M. (2010) *Developing Teacher Assessment*. Maidenhead: Open University Press.

Gay, G. (2010) *Culturally Responsive Teaching: Theory, Research, and Practice*, 2nd edn. New York: Teachers College Press.

Geographical Association (2012) *Thinking Geographically. Response to the Consultation on the National Curriculum Review*. London: Geographical Association.

Gibson, E.J. (1977) 'The theory of affordances'. In Shaw, R. and Bransford, J. (eds) *Perceiving, Acting and Knowing*. Hillsdale, NJ: Lawrence Erlbaum.

Giddens, A. (1984) *The Constitution of Society: Outline of the Theory of Structuration*. Berkeley, CA: University of California Press.

Gilchrist, G. (2018) *Practitioner Enquiry. Professional Development with Impact for Teachers, Schools and Systems*. London: Routledge.

Gill, S. and Thomson, G. (2017) *Human-Centred Education. A Practical Handbook and Guide*. London: Routledge.

Gillborn, D. (2008) *Racism and Education. Coincidence or Conspiracy?* Abingdon: Routledge.

Gillis, J.R. (1997) *A World of Their Own Making: Myth, Ritual, and the Quest for Family Values*. Cambridge, MA: Harvard University Press.

Gilmore, C., Trundley, R., Bahnmueller, J. and Xenidou-Dervou, I. (2021) 'How research findings can be used to inform educational practice and what can go wrong: The Ofsted Mathematics Research Review 202'. *Mathematics Teaching*, 278, 34–38.

Gipps, C. and MacGilchrist, B. (1999) 'Primary school learners'. In Mortimore, P. (ed.) *Understanding Pedagogy and Its Impact on Learning*. London: Paul Chapman.

Glaser, R. (1999) 'Expert knowledge and processes of thinking'. In McCormick, R. and Paechter, C. (eds) *Learning and Knowledge*. London: Paul Chapman.

Glass, G.V. (1982) *School Class Size, Research and Policy*. Beverley Hills, CA: SAGE.

Goldstein, H. and Leckie, G. (2008) 'School league tables: What can they really tell us?' *Significance*, 5, 67–69.

Goleman, D. (1996) *Emotional Intelligence: Why It Can Matter More than IQ*. London: Bloomsbury.

González, N., Moll, L. and Amanti, C. (eds) (2005) *Funds of Knowledge: Theorizing Practices in Households, Communities and Classrooms*. Mahwah, NJ: Lawrence Erlbaum Associates.

Good, T. and Brophy, J. (2008) *Looking in Classrooms*. Boston: Pearson.

Goodall, J. and Vorhaus, J. (2010) *Review of Best Practice in Parental Engagement*. London: DfE.

Goswami, U. (2008) *Cognitive Development. The Learning Brain*. Hove: Psychology Press.

reflectiveteaching.co.uk

Goswami, U. and Bryant, P. (2010) 'Children's cognitive development and learning'. In Alexander, R.J. et al. (eds) *The Cambridge Primary Review Research Surveys*. London: Routledge.

Gove, M. (2014) 'I refuse to surrender to the Marxist teachers hell-bent on destroying our schools: Education Secretary berates "the new enemies of promise" for opposing his plans'. *The Daily Mail*. Available at: http://www.dailymail.co.uk/debate/article-2298146/I-refuse-surrender-Marxist-teachers-hell-bent-destroying-schools-Education-Secretary-berates-new-enemies-promise-opposing-plans.html (accessed 23 January 2018).

Graham, S. (2018) 'A revised writer(s)-within-community model of writing'. *Educational Psychologist*, 53(4), 258–79. doi:10.1080/00461520.2018.1481406.

Grainger, T., Goouch, K. and Lambirth, A. (2005) *Creativity and Writing: Developing Voice and Verve in the Classroom*. London: Routledge.

Gramsci, A. (1978) *Selections from Political Writings*. London: Lawrence and Wishart.

Green, A. and Janmaat, J. (2011) *Regimes of Social Cohesion: Societies and the Crisis of Globalization*. Basingstoke: Palgrave Macmillan.

Green, A., Preston, J. and Janmaat, J.G. (2006) *Education, Equality and Social Cohesion. A Comparative Analysis*. London: Palgrave.

Griffiths, A. and Burns, M. (2014) *Teaching Backwards*. Carmarthen: Crown House.

Grimmett, P.P. and MacKinnon, A.M. (1992) 'Craft knowledge and the education of teachers'. *Review of Research in Education*, 18(1), 385–456.

Grospietsch, F. and Mayer, J. (2019) 'Pre-service science teachers' neuroscience literacy: Neuromyths and a professional understanding of learning and memory'. *Frontiers in Human Neuroscience*, 13, 20.

Gross, J. (2018) *Time to Talk. Implementing Outstanding Practice in Speech, Language and Communication*. London: Routledge.

GTC E (2010) 'Pedagogy matters'. In Pollard, A. (ed.) *Professionalism and Pedagogy: A Contemporary Opportunity*. London: TLRP.

GTC E (2011) *Teaching Quality: Policy Papers*. London: GTC E.

GTC NI (2007) *Teaching: The Reflective Profession*. Belfast: GTC NI.

GTC NI (2011) *Teaching: The Reflective Profession*, incorporating the Northern Ireland Teacher Competences. Belfast: GTC NI. Available at: https://gtcni.org.uk/cmsfiles/Resource365/Resources/Publications/The_Reflective_Profession.pdf

GTC S (2012) *Scotland's Code of Professionalism and Conduct*. Edinburgh: GTC S.

GTC S (2018) *Review of the Professional Standards: The Experiences of Children and Young People*, September 2018. Available at: https://childreninscotland.org.uk/wp-content/uploads/2022/01/Children-In-Scotland-Review-of-Professional-Standards.pdf

GTC S (2021) *Standard for Provisional Registration*. Available at: https://www.gtcs.org.uk/wp-content/uploads/2021/09/standard-for-provisional-registration.pdf

Gu, Q. (2007) *Teacher Development: Knowledge and Context*. London: Continuum.

Gu, Q. (2014) 'The role of relational resilience in teachers' career-long commitment and effectiveness'. *Teachers and Teaching: Theory and Practice*, 20, 502–29.

Guskey, T.R. (2007) 'Closing achievement gaps: Revisiting Benjamin S. Bloom's "Learning for Mastery"'. *Journal of Advanced Academics*, 19(1), 8–31.

Gustin, W.C. and Corazza, L. (2010) 'Mathematical and verbal reasoning as predictors of science achievement'. *Roeper Review*, 16(3), 160–62.

Guthrie, J. T. and Wigfield, A. (1999) 'How motivation fits into a science of reading'. *Scientific Studies of Reading*, 3(3), 199–205. doi:10.1207/s1532799xssr0303_1.

Hagger, H. and McIntyre, D. (2006) Learning Teaching from Teachers – Realizing the Potential of School-Based Teacher Education. Maidenhead: Open University Press.

Hall, C. and Coles, M. (1999) *Children's Reading Choices*. London: Routledge.

Hallam, S., Ireson, J. and Davies, J. (2013) *Effective Pupil Grouping in the Primary School: A Practical Guide*. London: Routledge.

reflectiveteaching.co.uk

Halpin, D. (2001) 'Hope, utopianism and educational management'. *Cambridge Journal of Education*, 31(1), 103–18.

Halsey, A.H. (1986) *Change in British Society*. Oxford: Oxford University Press.

Hamilton, L. and Corbett-Whittier, C. (2013) *Using Case Study in Education Research*. London: SAGE.

Hampson, S.E. (1988) *The Construction of Personality: An Introduction*. London: Routledge.

Hanley, M., Khairat, M., Taylor, K., Wilson, R., Cole-Fletcher, R. and Riby, D.M. (2017) 'Classroom displays – Attraction or distraction? Evidence of impact on attention and learning from children with and without autism'. *Developmental Psychology*, 53(7), 1265–75. doi:10.1037/dev0000271.

Hardy, B. (1977) 'Towards a poetics of fiction: An approach through narrative'. In Meek, M., Warlow, A. and Barton, G. (eds) *The Cool Web*. London: Bodley Head.

Hargreaves, A. (1998) 'The emotional practice of teaching'. *Teaching and Teacher Education*, 14(8), 835–54.

Hargreaves, A. (2007) *The Persistence of Presentism and the Struggle for Lasting Improvement*. Inaugural lecture. London: Institute of Education.

Hargreaves, D.H., Hester, S.K. and Mellor, F.J. (1975) *Deviance in Classrooms*. London: Routledge and Kegan Paul.

Hargreaves, E. (2017) *Children's Experiences of Classrooms: Talking about Being Pupils in the Classroom*. London: SAGE.

Harlen, W. (2006) 'Teachers' and children's questioning'. In Harlen, W. (ed.) *ASE Guide to Primary Science*. Hatfield: Association for Science Education.

Harlen, W. and Bell, D. (2010) *Principles and Big Ideas of Science Education*. London: Association for Science Education.

Harlen, W. and Deakin Crick, R. (2002) 'A systematic review of the impact of summative assessment and tests on students' motivation for learning' (EPPICentre Review). *Research Evidence in Education Library. Issue 1*. London: EPPI Centre, Social Science Research Unit, Institute of Education.

Harlen, W., Gipps, C., Broadfoot, P. and Nuttall, D. (1992) 'Assessment and the improvement of education'. *Curriculum Journal*, 3(3), 217–25.

Harrison, C. (2004) *Understanding Reading Development*. London: SAGE.

Harrison, C. and Howard, S. (2009) *Inside the Primary Black Box: Assessment for Learning in Primary and Early Years Classrooms*. London: GL Assessment.

Hart, S. (2000) *Thinking Through Teaching*. London: David Fulton Publishers.

Hart, S. and Hodson, V.K. (2004) *The Compassionate Classroom: Relationship Based Teaching and Learning*. Encinitas, CA: PuddleDancer Press.

Hart, S., Dixon, A., Drummond, M.-J. and McIntyre, D. (2004) *Learning Without Limits*. Maidenhead: Open University Press.

Hartley, B.L. and Sutton, R.M. (2013) A stereotype threat account of boys' academic underachievement. *Child Development*, 84(5), 1716–33.

Hartley, D. (1985) *Understanding the Primary School*. London: Croom Helm.

Hascher, T. (2003) 'Well-being in school – why students need social support'. In Mayring, P. and Von Rhoeneck, C. (eds) *Learning Emotions: The Influence of Affective Factors on Classroom Learning*. Frankfurt: Peter Lang.

Hashweh, M.Z. (1987) 'Effects of subject matter knowledge in the teaching of biology and physics'. *Teaching and Teacher Education*, 3, 109–20.

Haste, H. (1987) 'Growing into rules'. In Bruner, J.S. and Haste, H. (eds) *Making Sense: The Child's Construction of the World*. London: Methuen.

Hastings, N. and Wood, C.K. (2001) *Reorganising Primary Classroom Learning*. Buckingham: Open University Press.

Hattie, J. (2009) *Visible Learning. A Synthesis of Meta-Analyses Relating to Achievement*. London: Routledge.

Hattie, J. (2012) *Visible Learning for Teachers: Maximising Impact on Learning*. London: Routledge.

Hattie, J. and Timperley, H. (2007) 'The power of feedback'. *Review of Educational Research*, 77, 81–112.

Haviland, J. (1988) *Take Care, Mr Baker!* London: Fourth Estate.

Hay McBer Consultancy (2000) *Research into Teacher Effectiveness: A Model of Teacher Effectiveness*. London: DfEE.

Haydn, T. (2007) *Managing Pupil Behaviour*. London: Routledge.

Hayes, D., Mills, M., Christie, P. and Linguard, R. (2006) *Teachers and Schooling Making a Difference*. Sydney: Allen and Unwin.

Haynes, A. (2010) *The Complete Guide to Lesson Planning and Preparation*. London: Continuum.

Hayward, L., MacBride, G. and Spencer, E. (2016) 'Scotland: The intersection of international achievement testing and education policy'. In Volante, L. (ed.) *The Intersection of International Achievement Testing and Education Policy*. Oxford: Routledge.

Hayward, L., Jones, D. E., Waters J., Makara, K., Morrison-Love, D., Spencer, E., Barnes, J., Davies, H., Hughes, S., Jones, C., Nelson, S., Ryder, N., Stacey, D., Wallis, R., Baxter, J., MacBride, G., Bendall, R., Brooks, S., Cooze, A., Davies, L., Denny, H., Donaldson, P., Hughes, S., Lewis, I., Lloyd, P., Maitra, S., Morgan, C., Pellew James, S., Samuel-Thomas, S., Sharpling, E., Southern, A., Stewart, S., Valdera-Gil, F. and Wardle, G. (2018) *Learning about Progression: CAMAU Research Report*. Glasgow: University of Glasgow; Carmarthen: University of Wales Trinity Saint David.

Heilbronn, R. (2010) 'The nature of practice-based knowledge and understanding'. In Heilbronn, R. and Yandell, J. (eds) *Critical Practice in Teacher Education: A Study of Professional Learning*. London: Institute of Education.

Heine, S.J. (2011) *Cultural Psychology*. New York: W.W. Norton & Company.

Heinz, M. (2015) 'Why choose teaching? An international review of empirical studies exploring student teachers' career motivations and levels of commitment to teaching'. *Educational Research and Evaluation*, 21(3), 258–97.

Helen Hamlyn Centre for Pedagogy (HHCP) (2022) 'Children's agency'. Available at: ucl.ac.uk/ioe/departments-and-centres/centres/helen-hamlyn-centre-pedagogy-0-11-years/research-themes/childrens-agency

Hellige, J.B. (1993) *Hemispheric Asymmetry: What's Left and What's Left*. Cambridge, MA: Harvard University Press.

Her Majesty's Inspectors (HMI) (1985) *The Curriculum from 5 to 16. Curriculum Matters 2*. An HMI Series. London: HMSO.

Heritage, M. (2008) *Learning Progressions: Supporting Instruction and Formative Assessment*. Washington, DC: Council of Chief State School Officers.

Hertz-Lazarowitz, R., Kagan, S., Sharan, S., Slavin, R., and Webb, C. (eds) (2013) *Learning to Cooperate, Cooperating to Learn*. New York: Springer.

Heuston, B. and Miller, H. (2011) *Academic Learning Time: The Most Important Educational Concept You've Never Heard Of*. Salt Lake City, UT: Waterford Institute.

Higgins, S. (2003) *Does ICT Improve Learning and Teaching in Schools?* Nottingham: British Educational Research Association.

Higgins, S. and Katsipataki, M. (2015) 'Evidence from meta-analysis about parental involvement in education which supports their children's learning'. *Journal of Children's Services*, 10(3), 1–11. doi:10.1108/JCS-02-2015-0009.

Higgins, S., Xiao, Z. and Katsipataki, M. (2012) *The Impact of Digital Technology on Learning: A Summary for the Education Endowment Foundation. Full Report*. London: Education Endowment Foundation. https://eric.ed.gov/?id=ED612174

Higgins, S., Katsipataki, M., Kokotsaki, D., Coleman, R., Major, L.E. and Coe, R. (2013) *The Sutton Trust-Education Endowment Foundation Teaching and Learning Toolkit*. London: Education Endowment Foundation.

Hirsch, E.D. (1988) *Cultural Literacy: What Every American Needs to Know*. New York: Houghton Mifflin.

Hirst, P.H. (1965) 'Liberal education and the nature of knowledge'. In Archambault, R.D. (ed.) *Philosophical Analysis and Education*. London: Routledge.

HMCI (1995) *The Annual Report of Her Majesty's Chief Inspector of Schools*. London: HMSO.

HMCI (2017) *HMCI's Commentary. Ofsted's Chief Inspector, Amanda Spielman, Discusses Findings from Recent Research into the Primary and Secondary Curriculum. 11 October*. London: Ofsted.

Hodgson, C. and Pyle, K. (2010) *Assessment for Learning in Science: A Literature Review*. Slough: NfER.

Hogan, D. (2012) 'Yes Brian, at long last, there is pedagogy in England – and in Singapore too'. In James, M. and Pollard, A. (eds) *Principles for Effective Pedagogy. International Responses to the UK TLRP*. London: Routledge.

Hogan, D., Chan, M., Rahim, R., Kwek, D., Aye, K.M., Loo, S. C., Sheng, Y. and Luo, W. (2013) 'Assessment and the logic of instructional practice in Secondary 3 English and Mathematics classes in Singapore'. *Review of Education*, 1(1), 57–106.

Hogden, J. and Webb, M. (2008) 'Questioning and dialogue'. In Swaffield, S. (ed.) *Unlocking Assessment: Understanding for Reflection and Application*, 73–89. Abingdon: Routledge.

Holleran, G. and Gilbert, I. (2015) *A Teacher's Companion to Essential Motivation in the Classroom*. London: Routledge.

Hollindale, P. (2011) *The Hidden Teacher: Ideology and Children's Reading*. Stroud: Thimble Press.

Holmes, E. (1911) *What Is and What Might Be*. London: Constable and Co. Available at: http://www.educationengland.org.uk/documents/holmes/whatis.html (accessed 29 June 2021).

Holmes, J.A. and Singer, H. (1961) *The Substrata-Factor Theory: Substrata Factor Differences Underlying Reading Ability In Known-Groups at The High School Level*. Berkeley, CA: University of California.

Holmwood, J. and O'Toole, T. (2018) *Countering Extremism in British Schools?: The Truth about the Birmingham Trojan Horse Affair*. London: Policy Press.

Holt, J. (1964/1982) *How Children Fail*. London: Penguin.

Hooper, M. and Robertson, M.P. (2000) *Ice Trap! Shackleton's Incredible Expedition*. London: Frances Lincoln.

Hoover, W.A. and Gough, P.B. (1990) 'The simple view of reading'. *Reading and Writing: An Interdisciplinary Journal*, 2(2), 127–60. doi:10.1007/BF00401799.

Hopkins, D., Harris, A., Singleton, C. and Watts, R. (2000) *Creating the Conditions for Teaching and Learning*. London: David Fulton.

Hornby, G. (2011) *Parental Involvement in Childhood Education: Building Effective School–Family Partnerships*. London: Springer.

Houghton, E. (ed.) (2012) *Education on the Web: A Tool-kit to Help You Search Effectively for Information on Education*. Slough: NFER.

Howard-Jones, P. (ed.) (2007) *Neuroscience and Education: Issues and Opportunities. A TLRP Commentary*. London: TLRP.

Howard-Jones, P.A. (2014) 'Neuroscience and education: Myths and messages'. *Nature Reviews Neuroscience*, 15(12), 817–24.

Howe, C. (2010) *Peer Groups and Children's Development*. Oxford: Wiley-Blackwell.

Howe, C. and Mercer, N. (2007) *Children's Social Development, Peer Interaction and Classroom Learning*. The Primary Review: Research Survey 2/1b.

Howe, M.J.A. (1990) *The Origins of Exceptional Abilities*. London: Blackwell.

Hoyle, E. (1974) 'Professionality, professionalism and control in teaching'. *London Educational Review*, 3(2).

Hoyle, E. and Megarry, J. (2005) *World Yearbook of Education 1980: The Professional Development of Teachers*. London: Routledge.

reflectiveteaching.co.uk

Huberman, M. (1993) *The Lives of Teachers*. London: Cassell.

Hudson-Sharp, N. and Metcalf, H. (2016) *Inequality Among Lesbian, Gay Bisexual and Transgender Groups in the UK: A Review of Evidence*. London: National Institute of Economic and Social Research.

Hugdahl, K. (1995) *Psychophysiology: The Mind–Body Perspective*. Cambridge, MA: Harvard University Press.

Hughes, M. and Pollard, A. (2000) 'Home–school knowledge exchange and transformation in primary education'. *ESRC Project L139251078*. Bristol: University of Bristol.

Hughes, M., Wikeley, F. and Nash, T. (1994) *Parents and Their Children's Schools*. Oxford: Blackwell.

Hughes, M., Desforges, C., Mitchell, C. and Carre, C. (2000) *Numeracy and Beyond: Applying Mathematics in the Primary School*. Buckingham: Open University Press.

Hughes, M. et al. (2008) *Supporting Primary–Secondary Transfer through Home–School Knowledge Exchange*. TLRP Research Briefing. London: TLRP.

Hunter, R. and Scheirer, E.A. (1988) *The Organic Classroom: Organizing for Learning 7 to 12*. London: Falmer.

Hurry, J., Bonell, C., Carroll, C. and Deighton, J. (2021) *The Role of Schools in the Mental Health of Children & Young People*. British Educational Research Association. Available at: https://www.bera.ac.uk/publication/the-role-of-schools-in-the-mental-health-of-children-young-people

Hutchinson, C. and Hayward, L. (2005) 'The journey so far: Assessment for Learning in Scotland'. *Curriculum Journal*, 16, 225–48.

Hyland, T. (2011) *Mindfulness and Learning: Celebrating the Affective Dimension of Education* (vol. 17). New York: Springer Science & Business Media.

Immordino-Yang, M.H. and Damasio, A. (2007) 'We feel, therefore we learn. The relevance of affective social neuroscience to education'. *Mind, Brain and Education*, 1(1), 3–9.

Ingram, J. and Worrall, N. (1993) *Teacher–Child Partnership: The Negotiating Classroom*. London: David Fulton.

Inhelder, B. and Piaget, J. (1958) *The Growth of Logical Thinking from Childhood to Adolescence*. New York: Basic Book.

International Educational Assessment Network (IEAN) (2020) *Rethinking Learner Progression for the Future: A Discussion Paper*. Available at: https://www.iean.network/gallery/iean-learner-progression-discussion-dec2020v2.pdf

International Educational Assessment Network (IEAN) (2021) *Position Paper: Imperatives for a Better Assessment Future During and Post Covid*. Available at: https://iean.network/gallery/iean-assessment-imperatives-covid-may2021.pdf

Ireson, J. and Hallam, S. (2001) *Ability Grouping in Education*. London: SAGE.

Jackson, B. (1964) *Streaming: An Education System in Miniature*. London: Routledge and Kegan Paul.

Jackson, B. and Marsden, D. (1962) *Education and the Working Class*. London: Ark.

Jackson, C. (2006) *Lads and Ladettes in School: Gender and a Fear of Failure*. Maidenhead: Open University Press.

Jackson, P.W. (1968) *Life in Classrooms*. New York: Holt, Rinehart and Winston.

James, A. and James, A.L. (2004) *Constructing Childhood: Theory, Policy and Social Practice*. Hampshire: Palgrave Macmillan.

James, A., Jenks, C. and Prout, A. (1998) *Theorising Childhood*. Cambridge: Polity Press.

James, D. and Biesta, G. (2007) *Improving Learning Cultures in Further Education*. London: Routledge.

James, M. (1992) 'Assessment for learning'. Paper presented at the Annual Conference of the Association for Supervision and Curriculum Development (Assembly session on 'Critique of Reforms in Assessment and Testing in Britain') held at New Orleans, LA, April.

James, M. (1998) *Using Assessment for School Improvement*. Oxford: Heinemann.

James, M. (2005) 'Insights on teacher learning from the Teaching and Learning Research Programme (TLRP)'. *Research Papers in Education*, 20(2), 105–8.

James, M. (2012) 'Assessment in harmony with our understanding of learning: Problems and possibilities'. In Gardner, J. (ed.) *Assessment and Learning*, 2nd edn., 187–205. London: SAGE.

James, M. (2015) 'Assessing without levels: From measurement to judgement'. Available at: https://www.researchgate.net/.../Mary_James3/...Assessing_without_levels.../Assessing...

James, M. and Pollard, A. (2004) *Personalised Learning: A TLRP Commentary*. Swindon: ESRC.

James, M. and Pollard, A. (2006) *Improving Teaching and Learning in Schools: A Commentary by the Teaching and Learning Research Programme*. London: TLRP.

James, M. and Pollard, A. (2012a) *Principles for Effective Pedagogy. International Responses to Evidence from the UK Teaching and Learning Research Programme*. London: Routledge.

James, M. and Pollard, A. (2012b) 'TLRP's ten principles for effective pedagogy: Rationale, development, evidence, argument and impact'. *Research Papers in Education*, 26(3), 275–328.

James, A. and Prout, A. (2003) *Constructing and Reconstructing Childhood: Contemporary Issues in the Sociological Study of Childhood*. London: Routledge.

James, M., McCormick, R., Black, P., Carmichael, P., Drummond, M-J., Fox, A., MacBeath, J., Marshall, B., Pedder, D., Procter, R., Swaffield, S., Swann, J. and Wiliam, D. (2007) *Improving Learning How to Learn: Classrooms, Schools and Networks*. London: Routledge.

James, M., Black, P., Carmichael, P., Conner, C., Dudley, P., Fox, A., Frost, D., Honour, L., MacBeath, J., McCormick, R., Marshall, B., Pedder, D., Procter, R., Swaffield, S. and Wiliam, D. (2006) *Learning How to Learn: Tools for Schools*. London: Routledge.

Janes, C.L., Hesselbrock, V.M., Meyers, D.G. and Penniman, J.H. (1979) 'Problem boys in young adulthood: Teachers' ratings and twelve-year follow-up'. *Journal of Youth and Adolescence*, 8, 453–72.

Jarman, R. and McClune, B. (2005) '*Space Science News: Special Edition*: A resource for extending reading and promoting engagement with newspapers in the science classroom'. *Literacy*, 39(3), 121–28.

Jenks, C. (1972) *Inequality: A Reassessment of the Effect of Family and Schooling in America*. New York: Basic Books.

Jensen, B., Sonnemann, J., Roberts-Hull, K. and Hunter, A. (2016) *Beyond PD: Teacher Professional Learning in High-performing Systems*. Washington, DC: National Center on Education and the Economy.

Jerome, L. and Bhargava, M. (2016) *Effective Medium-term Planning for Teachers*. London: SAGE.

Jerrim, J. and Moss, G. (2019) 'The link between fiction and teenagers' reading skills: International evidence from the OECD PISA study'. *British Educational Research Journal*, 45(1), 181–200.

Jeynes, W.H. (2018) 'A practical model for school leaders to encourage parental involvement and parental engagement'. *School Leadership & Management*, 38(2), 147–63.

John, M. (2003) *Children's Rights and Power: Charging Up for a New Century*. London: Jessica Kingsley.

Johnson, D.W. and Johnson, F. (1997) *Joining Together: Group Theory and Group Skills*. Boston: Allyn and Bacon.

Jones, P. (2009) *Rethinking Childhood: Attitudes in Contemporary Society*. London: Continuum.

Jones, R. (ed.) (2014) *Don't Change the Light Bulbs: A Compendium of Expertise from the UK's Most Switched-on Educators*. Carmarthen: Crown House.

Joseph Rowntree Foundation (2000) *Poverty and Social Exclusion in Britain*. York: JRF.

Joseph-Salisbury, R. (2020) *Race and Racism in English Secondary Schools*. London: Runnymede Perspectives.

Joyce, B., Weil, M. and Calhoun, E. (2009) *Models of Teaching*. New York: Pearson.

Kagan, J. (1964) 'Information processing in the child: Significance of analytic and reflective attitudes'. *Psychological Monographs*, 78(1), 1–37.

reflectiveteaching.co.uk

Kallick, B. and Zmuda, A. (2017) *Pupils at the Center: Personalized Learning with Habits of Mind*. Alexandria, VA: ASCD.

Kane, M. (2016) 'Explicating validity'. *Assessment in Education: Principles, Policy and Practice*, 23(2), 198–211.

Karoly, L.A., Greenwood, P.W. and Everingham, S. (eds) (1998) *Investing in Our Children: What We Know and Don't Know about the Costs and Benefits of Early Childhood Intervention*. New York: RAND.

Katz, L. (1998) 'A development approach to the curriculum in the early years'. In Smidt, S. (ed.) *The Early Years: A Reader*. London: Routledge.

Kavanagh, A.M., Waldron, F. and Mallon, B. (eds.) (2021) *Teaching for Social Justice and Sustainable Development Across the Primary Curriculum*. Abington, Oxon: Routledge.

Kaye, L. (2016) *Young Children in a Digital Age: Supporting Learning and Development with Technology in Early Years*. London: Routledge.

Kehily, M.J. (2003) *Sexuality, Gender and Schooling. Shifting Agendas in Social Learning*. London: Routledge.

Kennedy, A. (2014) 'Understanding CPD: The need for theory to impact on policy and practice'. *Professional Development in Education*, 40(5), 336–51.

Kennewell, S., Tanner, H. et al. (2008) *Interactive Teaching and ICT. Research Briefing 33*. London: TLRP.

Kerry, T. and Kerry, C. (1997) 'Differentiation: Teachers' views of the usefulness of recommended strategies in helping the more able pupils in primary and secondary classrooms'. *Educational Studies*, 23(3), 439–57.

Kershner, R. (2009) 'Learning in inclusive classrooms'. In Hick, P., Kershner, R. and Farrell, P. (eds) *Psychology for Inclusive Education: New Directions in Theory and Practice*. Abingdon: Routledge.

Kettle, B. and Sellars, N. (1996) 'The development of student teachers' practical theory of teaching'. *Teaching and Teacher Education*, 12(1), 1–24.

Khong, T., Saito, E. and Gillies, R. (2019) 'Key issues in productive classroom talk and interventions'. *Educational Review*, 71(3), 334–49. doi: 10.1080/00131911.2017.1410105.

Kim, M. and Wilkinson, I.A.G. (2019) 'What is dialogic teaching? Constructing, deconstructing, and reconstructing a pedagogy of classroom talk'. *Learning, Culture, and Social Interaction*, 21, 70–86.

Kimbrough, K. (2015) *Classroom Dilemmas: Solutions for Everyday Problems*. Lanham, Maryland: Rowman and Littlefield.

Kincheloe, J.L. (2008) *Critical Pedagogy Primer*. New York: Peter Lang.

King, R. (1978) *All Things Bright and Beautiful? A Sociological Study of Infants' Classrooms*. Chichester: Wiley.

Kirsch, I., de Jong, J., LaFontaine, D., McQueen, J., Mendelovits, J. and Monseur, C. (2002) *Reading for Change: Performance and Engagement across Countries*. Paris: OECD Development.

Kirschner, P.A. and Hendrick, C. (2020) *How Learning Happens: Seminal Works in Educational Psychology and What They Mean in Practice*. London: Routledge.

Klenowski, V. (2009) 'Assessment for Learning revisited: An Asia-Pacific perspective'. *Assessment in Education: Principles, Policy and Practice*, 16(3), 263–68.

Klenowski, V. and Carter, M. (2016) 'Curriculum reform in testing and accountability contexts'. In Wyse, D., Hayward, L. and Pandya, J. (eds) *The Sage Handbook of Curriculum, Pedagogy and Assessment*. London: SAGE.

Kline, P. (1991) *Intelligence: The Psychometric View*. London: Routledge.

Kluger, A.N. and De Nisi, A. (1996) 'The effects of feedback interventions on performance: A historical review, a meta-analysis, and a preliminary feedback intervention theory'. *Psychological Bulletin*, 119, 254–84.

Knopik, V.S., Neiderhiser, J.M., DeFries, J.C. and Plomin, R. (2016) *Behavioral Genetics*, 7th edn. New York: Worth Publishers, Macmillan Learning.

Kogan, M. (1978) *The Politics of Educational Change*. London: Fontana.

Kohlberg, L. (1976) 'Moral stages and moralization: The cognitive-developmental approach'. In Lickona, T. (ed.) *Moral Development and Behavior*. New York: Holt, Rinehart and Winston.

Kosslyn, S.M. (2005) 'Mental images and the brain'. *Cognitive Neuropsychology*, 22(3), 333–47.

Kounin, J.S. (1970) *Discipline and Group Management in Classrooms*. New York: Holt, Rinehart and Winston.

Kress, G. (1993) *Learning to Write*. London: Routledge.

Kress, G. (2010) 'The profound shift of digital literacies'. In Gillen, J. and Barton, D. (eds) *Digital Literacies*. London: TLRP TEL.

Kress, G. (2012) *Literacy in the New Media Age*. London: Routledge.

Kress, G. and van Leeuwen, T. (2006) *Reading Images: The Grammar of Visual Design*. London: Routledge.

Kuhl, P. (2004) 'Early language acquisition: Cracking the speech code'. *Nature Neuroscience*, 5, 831–43.

Kupersmidt, J.B. and Coie, J.D. (1990) 'Preadolescent peer status, aggression, and school adjustment as predictors of externalizing problems in adolescence'. *Child Development*, 61, 1350–63.

Kutnick, P. and Colwell, J. (2009) 'Relationships and dialogue enhancement: The relational approach'. In C. Howe and K. Littleton (eds) *Educational Dialogue: Understanding and Promoting Interaction*. London: Routledge.

Kutnick, P., Blatchford, P. and Baines, E. (2002) 'Pupil groupings in primary school classrooms: Sites for learning and social pedagogy?'. *British Educational Research Journal*, 28(2), 187–206.

Kutnick, P., Ota, C. and Berdondini, L. (2008) 'Improving the effects of group working in classrooms with young school-aged children: facilitating attainment, interaction and classroom activity'. *Learning and Instruction*, 18(1), 83–95.

Kyriacou, C. (2009) *Effective Teaching in Schools. Theory and Practice*. Cheltenham: Nelson Thornes.

Kyriacou, C. and Issitt, J. (2008) *What Characterizes Effective Teacher–Pupil Dialogue to Promote Conceptual Understanding in Mathematics Lessons in England in Key Stages 2 and 3?* EPPI-Centre Report no. 1604R. Social Science Research Unit: UCL Institute of Education.

Lacey, C. (1970) *Hightown Grammar. The School as a Social System*. Manchester: Manchester University Press.

Ladd, G.W. (2005) *Children's Peer Relations and Social Competence*. New Haven, CT: Yale University Press.

Ladson-Billings, G. (2021) *Culturally Relevant Pedagogy. Asking a Different Question*. New York: Teachers College, Columbia University.

Land, R., Meyer, J.H.F. and Smith, J. (eds). (2008) *Threshold Concepts within the Disciplines*. Rotterdam: Sense Publishers.

Lantz-Andersson, A., Lundin, M. and Selwyn, N. (2018) 'Twenty years of online teacher communities: A systematic review of formally-organized and informally-developed professional learning groups'. *Teaching and Teacher Education*, 75(3), 302–15. doi:10.1016/j.tate.2018.07.008.

Lareau, A. (1989) *Home Advantage: Social Class and Parental Intervention in Elementary Education*. London: Falmer.

Laslett, R. and Smith, C. (1992) *Effective Classroom Management: A Teacher's Guide*. London: Routledge.

Latz, A.O., Speirs Neumeister, K.L., Adams, C.M. and Pierce, R.L. (2008) 'Peer coaching to improve classroom differentiation'. *Roeper Review*, 31(1), 27–39.

reflectiveteaching.co.uk

Lave, J. and Wenger, E. (1991) *Situated Learning: Legitimate Peripheral Participation.* Cambridge: Cambridge University Press.

Laveault, D. and Allal, L. (2016) *Assessment for Learning: Meeting the Challenge of Implementation.* London: Springer.

Law, J., Charlton, J., Dockrell, J., Gascoigne, M., McKean, C. and Theakston, A. (2017) *Early Language Development: Needs, Provision, and Intervention for Preschool Children from Socio-Economically Disadvantage Backgrounds: A Report for the Education Endowment Foundation: October 2017.* Education Endowment Foundation and Public Health England. educationendowmentfoundation.org.uk/public/files/Law_et_al_Early_Language_Development_final.pdf

Lawn, M. and Grace, G. (eds) (1987) *Teachers: The Culture and Politics of Work.* London: Falmer.

Lawn, M. and Ozga, J. (1986) 'Unequal partners: Teachers under indirect rule'. *British Journal of Sociology of Education*, 7(2), 225–38.

Lawrence, D. (1987) *Enhancing Self-esteem in the Classroom.* London: Paul Chapman.

Lazarus, R.S. (1991) *Emotion and Adaption.* Oxford: Oxford University Press.

Lazarus, R.S. (1999) *Stress and Emotion: A New Synthesis.* London: Free Association Books.

Leach, J. and Moon, B. (2008) *The Power of Pedagogy.* London: SAGE.

Leckie, G. and Goldstein, H. (2009) 'The limitations of using school league tables to inform school choice'. *Journal of the Royal Statistical Society: Series A.*, 172, 835–51.

Leckie, G., Pillinger, R., Jenkins, J. and Rasbash, J. (2010a) 'School, family, neighbourhood: Which is most important to a child's education?' *MethodsNews: Newsletter from the ESRC National Centre for Research*, Summer, 4.

Leckie, G., Pillinger, R., Jenkins, J. and Rasbash, J. (2010b) 'School, family, neighbourhood: Which is most important to a child's education?' *Significance*, 7, 67–72.

Lee, A. and Gage, N.A. (2020) 'Updating and expanding systematic reviews and meta-analyses on the effects of school-wide positive behavior interventions and supports'. *Psychology in the Schools*, 57(5), 783–804.

Lees, S. (1993) *Sugar and Spice: Sexuality and Adolescent Girls.* Harmondsworth: Penguin.

Levin, B. (2008) *How to Change 5000 Schools.* Cambridge, MA: Harvard Education Press.

Lewin, K. (1935) *A Dynamic Theory of Personality.* New York: McGraw-Hill.

Leyland, P. (2012) *Constitution of the United Kingdom: A Contextual Analysis.* Oxford: Hart Publishing.

Light, P. and Littleton, K. (1999) *Social Processes in Children's Learning.* Cambridge: Cambridge University Press.

Lilly, J., Peacock, A., Shoveller, S. and Struthers, d'R. (2014) *Beyond Levels: Alternative Assessment Approaches Developed by Teaching Schools.* Research report. Nottingham: National College for Teaching & Leadership.

Lindon, J. and Trodd, L. (2016) *Reflective Practice and Early Years Professionalism: Linking Theory and Practice*, 3rd edn. London: Hodder.

Lingard, B., Hayes, D., Mills, M. and Christie, P. (2003) *Leading Learning: Making Hope Practical in Schools.* Maidenhead: Open University Press.

Linklater, H. (2010) *Making Children Count? An Auto-ethnographic Exploration of Pedagogy.* Unpublished PhD thesis, University of Aberdeen, Scotland.

Linklater, H. (2013) 'Teaching and the individuality of everybody'. *FORUM*, 55(1), 85–94.

Littleton, K. and Mercer, N. (2013) *Inter-thinking: Putting Talk to Work.* Abingdon: Routledge.

Lockyer, S. (2016) *Lesson Planning for Primary School Teachers.* London: Bloomsbury.

Longfield, A. (2017) *On Measuring the Number of Vulnerable Children in England. Children's Commissioner's Report on Vulnerability.* London: Children's Commissioner.

Loughran, J. (2010) *What Expert Teachers Do: Enhancing Professional Knowledge for Classroom Practice.* London: Routledge.

reflectiveteaching.co.uk

Lucas, D. and Thomas, G. (2000) 'Organising classrooms to promote learning for all children'. In Clipson-Boyles, S. (ed.) *Putting Research into Practice*. London: David Fulton.

Luckin, R. (2010) *Re-Designing Learning Contexts. Technology-Rich, Learner-Centred Ecologies*. London: Routledge.

Luehmann, A.L. (2007) 'Identity development as a lens to science teacher preparation'. *Science Education*, 91, 822–39.

Mac an Ghaill, M. (1994) *The Making of Men: Masculinities, Sexualities and Schooling*. Buckingham: Open University Press.

MacGilchrist, B. (2003) *Has School Improvement Passed Its Sell-by Date?* Inaugural lecture. London: Institute of Education.

MacGilchrist, B., Myers, K. and Reed, J. (2004) *The Intelligent School*. London: SAGE.

Machin, S., McNally, S. and Wyness, G. (2013) 'Educational attainment across the UK nations: performance, inequality and evidence'. *Educational Research*, 55(2), 139–64.

Macqueen, S.E. (2013) 'Grouping for inequity'. *International Journal of Inclusive Education*, 17(3), 295–309.

Male, B. and Waters, M. (2012a) *The Primary Curriculum Design Handbook*. London: Continuum.

Male, B. and Waters, M. (2012b) *The Secondary Curriculum Design Handbook*. London: Continuum.

Mallett, M. (1999) *Young Researchers: Informational Reading and Writing in the Early and Primary Years*. London: Routledge.

Mangan, J.A.E. (1993) *The Imperial Curriculum: Racial Images and Education in the British Colonial Experience*. London: Routledge.

Mansell, W. (2007) *Education by Numbers: The Tyranny of Testing*. London: Politico Publishing.

Mansell, W. and James, M. with the Assessment Reform Group (2009) *Assessment in Schools: Fit for Purpose? A Commentary by the Teaching and Learning Research Programme*. London: TLRP.

Manyukhina, Y. and Wyse, D. (2019) 'Learner agency and the curriculum: A critical realist perspective'. *The Curriculum Journal*, 30(3), 223–43.

Manyukhina, Y. and Wyse, D. (2021) 'Children's agency: What is it and what should be done?' BERA blog post, 1 March 2021. Available at: bera.ac.uk/blog/childrens-agency-what-is-it-and-what-should-be-done

Marks, R. (2016) *Ability-grouping in Primary Schools: Case Studies and Critical Debates*. St Albans: Critical Publishing.

Marsh, J. (2005) *Popular Culture, New Media and Digital Literacy in Early Childhood*. London: Routledge.

Marsh, L. (1970) *Alongside the Child*. London: Black.

Marshall, B. and Drummond, M.J. (2006) 'How teachers engage with assessment for learning: Lessons from the classroom'. *Research Papers in Education*, 21(2), 133–49.

Marulis, L.M., and Neuman, S.B. (2010) 'The effects of vocabulary intervention on young children's word learning: A meta-analysis'. *Review of Educational Research*, 80(3), 300–35. doi:10.3102/0034654310377087.

Marzano, R.J. (2009) *Designing and Teaching Learning Goals and Objectives*. Bloomington: Solution Tree.

Maslow, A.H. (1954) *Motivation and Personality*. New York: Harper and Row.

Maun, I. and Myhill, D. (2005) 'Text as design, writers as designers'. *English in Education*, 39(2), 5–21.

Mayall, B. (1994) *Negotiating Health: Children at Home and Primary School*. London: Cassell.

Mayall, B. (2002) *Towards a Sociology for Childhood: Thinking from Children's Lives*. Milton Keynes: Open University Press.

Mayall, B. (2009) 'Children's lives outside school'. In Alexander R (ed.) *Children, Their World, Their Education*. London: Routledge.

Maylor, U., Smart, S., Kuyok, A.K. and Ross, A. (2009) *Black Children's Achievement Programme Evaluation.* Institute for Policy Studies in Education, Research Report DCSF-RR177. London: Department for Children, Schools and Families.

Maynard, N. and Weinstein, B. (2019) *Hacking School Discipline: 9 Ways to Create a Culture of Empathy and Responsibility Using Restorative Justice.* Hack Learning Series.

Maynard, T. and Furlong, J. (1993) 'Learning to teach and models of mentoring'. In McIntyre, D., Hagger, H. and Wilkin, M. (eds) *Mentoring: Perspectives on School Based Teacher Education.* London: Kogan Page.

McCrory, A. and Worthington, K. (2018) *Mastering Primary Science.* London: Bloomsbury.

McCullough, G., Helsby, G. and Knight, P. (2000) *The Politics of Professionalism: Teachers and the Curriculum.* London: Continuum.

McDermott, R.P. (1996) 'The acquisition of a child by a learning disability'. In Chaiklin, S. and Lave, J. (eds) *Understanding Practice.* Cambridge: Cambridge University Press.

McGill, R.M. (2017) *Mark. Plan. Teach.* London: Bloomsbury.

McGrath, J., and Coles, A. (2016) *Your Teacher Training Companion: Essential Skills and Knowledge for Very Busy Trainees* (2nd edn.). London: Routledge. doi:10.4324/9781315731926.

McGregor, D. (2007) *Developing Thinking; Developing Learning: A Guide to Thinking Skills in Education.* Maidenhead: Open University Press.

McGuinness, C. (1999) *From Thinking Skills to Thinking Classrooms.* Research Report 115. London: DfEE.

McLaughlin, C., Black Hawkins, K., Brindley, S., McIntyre, D. and Taber, K. (2006) *Researching Schools. Stories from a Schools–University Partnership.* Maidenhead: Open University Press.

McNally, J. and Blake, A. (eds) (2010) *Improving Learning in a Professional Context. The New Teacher at School.* London: TLRP.

McNiff, J. (1988) *Action Research: Principles and Practice.* London: Routledge.

McPherson, A. and Raab, C.D. (1988) *Governing Education: A Sociology of Policy since 1945.* Edinburgh: Edinburgh University Press.

Mead, G.H. (1934) *Mind, Self, and Society.* Chicago, IL: University of Chicago Press.

Meek, M. (1988) *How Texts Teach What Readers Learn.* Stroud: Thimble Press.

Meek, M. (1996) *Information and Book Learning.* Stroud: Thimble Press.

Meighan, R. (1978) 'The learner's viewpoint'. *Educational Review*, 30(2).

Meighan, R. and Siraj-Blatchford, I. (1981) *A Sociology of Educating.* London: Cassell.

Melby-Lervåg, M., Lyster, S.A.H., and Hulme, C. (2012) 'Phonological skills and their role in learning to read: a meta-analytic review'. *Psychological Bulletin*, 138(2), 322. doi:10.1037/a0026744.

Melhuish, E. and Gardiner, J. (2020) *Study of Early Education and Development (SEED): Impact Study on Early Education Use and Child Outcomes up to Age Five Years.* London: Department for Education.

Mental Health Foundation (2017) *Children and Young People.* London: Mental Health Foundation.

Menter, I., Elliot, D., Hall, J., Hulme, M., Lewin, J. and Lowden, K. (2010) *A Guide to Practitioner Research in Education.* Maidenhead: Open University Press.

Menter, I., Hulme, M., Elliot, D., Lewin, J. et al. (2010) *Literature Review on Teacher Education in the 21st Century.* Edinburgh: The Scottish Government.

Mercer, N. (1992) 'Culture, context and the appropriation of knowledge'. In Light, P. and Butterworth, G. (eds) *Context and Cognition: Ways of Learning and Knowing.* Hemel Hempstead: Harvester Wheatsheaf.

Mercer, N. (1995) *The Guided Construction of Knowledge: Talk amongst Teachers and Learners.* Clevedon: Multilingual Matters.

Mercer, N. (2000) *Words and Minds: How We Use Language to Think Together.* London: Routledge.

Mercer, N. (2005) 'Sociocultural discourse analysis: Analysing classroom talk as a social mode of thinking'. *Journal of Applied Linguistics*, 1(2), 137–68.

Mercer, N. and Hodgkinson, S. (eds) (2008) *Exploring Talk in School*. London: SAGE.

Mercer, N. and Littleton, K. (2007) *Dialogue and the Development of Children's Thinking*. London: Routledge.

Mercer, N., Hennessy, S. and Warwick, P. (2019) 'Dialogue, thinking together and digital technology in the classroom: Some educational implications of a continuing line of inquiry'. *International Journal of Educational Research*, 97, 187–99.

Mercer, N., Dawes, L., Wegerif, R. and Sams, C. (2004) 'Reasoning as a scientist: Ways of helping children to use language to learn science'. *British Educational Research Journal*, 30(3), 359–77.

Merrett, F. and Wheldall, K. (1990) *Identifying Troublesome Classroom Behaviour*. London: Paul Chapman.

Meyer, J.W. and Kamens, D.H. (1992) 'Conclusion: Accounting for a world curriculum'. In Meyer, J. W., Kamens, D. H. and Benavot, A. with Cha, Y.K. and Wong S.Y. (eds) *School Knowledge for the Masses: World Models of National Primary Curricular Categories in the Twentieth Century*. London: Falmer.

Meyer, J.W., Kamens, D.H. and Benavot, A. with Cha Y.K. and Wong S.Y. (eds) (1992) *School Knowledge for the Masses: World Models of National Primary Curricular Categories in the Twentieth Century*. London: Falmer.

Millar, R., Leach, J., Osborne, J. and Ratcliffe, M. (2006) *Improving Subject Teaching: Lessons from Research in Science Education*. London: Routledge.

Miller, J. (1997) *Never Too Young: How Young Children Can Take Responsibility and Make Decisions*. London: Save the Children.

Mills, C.W. (1959) *The Sociological Imagination*. New York: Oxford University Press.

Mitchell, J. (2012) *Devolution in the United Kingdom*. Manchester: Manchester University Press.

Mitchell, N. and Pearson, J. (2012) *Inquiring in the Classroom. Asking the Questions that Matter about Teaching and Learning*. London: Continuum.

Moll, L.C. and Greenberg, J.B. (1990) 'Creating zones of possibilities: Combining social contexts for instruction'. In Moll, L.C. (ed.) *Vygotsky and Education*. Cambridge: Cambridge University Press.

Moncrieffe, M., Asare, Y., Dunford, R., Harper, J., Biggs, S., Patel, B., Brooks, E., Klein, U., Wisker, G., Whilby, A. and Sibanda, F. (2020) *Decolonising the Curriculum: Teaching and Learning about Race Equality*. Centre for Learning and Teaching. Brighton: University of Brighton.

Montacute, R. (2020) *Social Mobility and COVID-19: Implications of the COVID-19 Crisis for Educational Inequality*, April 2020. London: The Sutton Trust.

Morange, M. (2001) *The Misunderstood Gene*. Cambridge, MA: Harvard University Press.

Mortimer, E.F. and Scott, P.H. (2007) *Meaning Making in Secondary Science Classrooms*. Maidenhead: Open University Press.

Mortimore, P., Sammons, P., Stoll, L., Lewis, D. and Ecob, R. (1988) *School Matters: The Junior Years*. Wells: Open Books.

Morton, J., and Frith, U. (1995) 'Causal modelling: A structural approach to developmental psychopathology'. In Cicchetti, D. and Cohen, D.J. (eds) *Manual of Developmental Psychopathology*. Volume 1. New York: Wiley, 357–90.

Moses, I., Berry, A., Saab, N. and Admiraal, W. (2017) 'Who wants to become a teacher? Typology of student-teachers' commitment to teaching'. *Journal of Education for Teaching*, 43(4), 444–57.

Mosher, F. and Heritage, M. (2017) *A Hitchhiker's Guide to Thinking about Literacy, Learning Progressions, and Instruction*. CPRE Research Report #RR 2017/2. Philadelphia: Consortium for Policy Research in Education. Available from: http://repository.upenn.edu/cpre_researchreports/97

Moss, P. and Petrie, P. (2005) *From Children's Services to Children's Spaces: Public Policy, Children and Childhood*. London: Routledge.

Moyles, J., Hargreaves, L., Merry, R., Peterson, F. and Esarte-Sarries, V. (2003) *Interactive Teaching in the Primary School: Digging Deeper into Meaning*. Buckingham: Open University Press.

Moyles, J.R. (ed.) (2005) *The Excellence of Play*. Maidenhead: Open University Press.

Muijs, D. and Bokhove, C. (2020) *Metacognition and Self-Regulation: Evidence Review*. London: Education Endowment Foundation.

Muijs, D. and Reynolds, D. (2017) *Effective Teaching: Evidence and Practice*. London: SAGE.

Munro, L. (2019) *Life Chances, Education and Social Movements*. London: Anthem Press.

Muschamp, Y. (1991) 'Pupil self-assessment'. *Practical Issues in Primary Education*, no. 9. Bristol: NPC SW.

Muschamp, Y. (1994) 'Target setting with young children'. In Pollard, A. and Bourne, J. (eds) *Teaching and Learning in Primary Schools*. London: Routledge.

Myhill, D., Jones, S., Lines, H. and Watson, A. (2012) 'Re-thinking grammar: The impact of embedded grammar teaching on students' writing and students' metalinguistic understanding'. *Research Papers in Education*, 27(2), 139–66.

Nash, R. (1976) *Teacher Expectations and Pupil Learning*. London: Routledge.

National Academies of Sciences, Engineering, and Medicine (2018) *How People Learn II: Learners, Contexts, and Cultures*. Washington, DC: The National Academies Press. doi:10.17226/24783.

National Archives (2022) *Cats and Mice: What Tactics Were Used By Suffragettes, Police and Government*. Available from https://www.nationalarchives.gov.uk/education/resources/cats-and-mice/

National Audit Commission (2001) *Tackling Obesity in England*. London: The Stationery Office.

National Curriculum Council (NCC) (1990) *The Whole Curriculum*. York: NCC.

National Council for Excellence in Teaching Mathematics (NCETM) (2017) 'Five big ideas in teaching for mastery'. Available at: https://www.ncetm.org.uk/teaching-for-mastery/mastery-explained/five-big-ideas-in-teaching-for-mastery/

National Foundation for Educational Research (NFER) (2011) *Report on Subject Breadth in International Jurisdictions. Review of the National Curriculum in England*. London: DfE.

National Research Council (1999) *Improving Learning: A Strategic Plan for Education Research and its Utilisation*. Washington, DC: National Academy Press.

Neelands, J. and Goode, T. (eds) (2000) *Structuring Drama work: A Handbook of Available Forms in Theatre and Drama*, 2nd edn. London: David Fulton.

Neimi, H., Toom, A. and Kallioniemi, A. (eds) (2012) *Miracle of Education: The Principles and Practices of Teaching and Learning in Finnish Schools*. Rotterdam: Sense Publishers.

Newell, P. (1991) *The UN Convention and Children's Rights in the UK*. London: National Children's Bureau.

Newmann, F., Bryk, A. and Nagaoka, J. (2001) *Authentic Intellectual Work and Standardized Tests: Conflict or Coexistence*. Chicago, IL: Consortium on Chicago School Research.

Newton, P. (2007) *Techniques for Monitoring the Comparability of Examination Standards*. London: Qualification and Curriculum Authority.

Newton, P. and Shaw, S. (2014) '21st century evaluation'. In Newton, P. and Shaw, S. *Validity in Educational and Psychological Assessment*, 183–226. London: SAGE.

Newton, P.E. and Baird, J. (2016) 'The great validity debate'. *Assessment in Education: Principles, Policy & Practice*, 23(2), 173–77.

New Zealand Ministry of Education (2012) *The New Zealand Curriculum Online*. Available at: http://nzcurriculum.tki.org.nz (accessed February 2013).

Nguyen, H.T. (2012) 'What role do race, ethnicity, language and gender play in the teaching profession?' *Race Ethnicity and Education*, 15(5), 653–81.

NHS Digital (2020) 'Childhood overweight and obesity'. Statistics on Obesity, Physical Activity and Diet. Available at: https://digital.nhs.uk/data-and-information/publications/statistical/statistics-on-obesity-physical-activity-and-diet/england-2020# (accessed 11 February 2022).

reflectiveteaching.co.uk

Nias, J. (1989) *Primary Teachers Talking: A Study of Teaching at Work*. London: Routledge.

Nias, J., Southworth, G. and Campbell, P. (1992) *Whole-school Curriculum Development in the Primary School*. London: Falmer Press.

Nias, J., Southworth, G. and Yeomans, R. (1989) *Staff Relationships in the Primary School: A Study of Organisational Cultures*. London: Cassell.

Norman, K. (ed.) (1992) *Thinking Voices: The Work of the National Oracy Project*. London: Hodder and Stoughton.

Nowicki, S. and Duke, M.P. (2013) 'Accuracy in interpreting nonverbal cues'. In Hall, J.A. and Knapp, M.L. (eds) *Nonverbal Communication*, 441–70. Berlin and Boston: De Gruyter Mouton. doi:10.1515/9783110238150.441.

Nuthall, G. (2007) *The Hidden Lives of Learners*. Wellington: NZCER Press.

Nystrand, M., with Gamoran A., Kachur, R. and Prendergast, C. (1997) *Opening Dialogue: Understanding the Dynamics of Language and Learning in the English Classroom*. New York: Teachers College Press.

Oates, T. (2010) *Could Do Better. Using International Comparisons to Refine the National Curriculum in England*. Cambridge: Cambridge Assessment.

Oberhuemer, P. (2005) 'Conceptualising the early childhood pedagogue: policy approaches and issues of professionalism'. *European Early Childhood Education Research Journal*, 13(1), 5–16.

O'Brien, T. and Garner, P. (2001) *Untold Stories: Learning Support Assistants and Their Work*. Stoke-on-Trent: Trentham Books.

O'Dea, J. and Abraham, S. (2000) 'Improving the body image, eating attitudes and behaviours of young male and female adolescents'. *International Journal of Eating Disorders*, 28, 42–57.

Office for National Statistics (ONS) (2020) *Household Income Inequality, UK: Financial Year Ending 2020*. London: ONS.

Ofsted (2008) *Using Data, Improving Schools*. London: Ofsted.

Ofsted (2011) *ICT in Schools 2008–11*. London: Ofsted.

Ofsted (2019) *The Education Inspection Framework*. Available at: https://www.gov.uk/government/publications/education-inspection-framework

Olson, K. (2014) *The Invisible Classroom: Relationships, Neuroscience and Mindfulness in School*. New York: Norton.

O'Neill, A. (2002) *A Question of Trust. The Reith Lectures*. London: BBC.

Opie, I. and Opie, P. (1959) *Children's Games in Street and Playground*. Oxford: Oxford University Press.

Organisation for Economic Co-operation and Development (OECD) (2004) *Starting Strong: Curricula and Pedagogies in Early Childhood Education and Care. Paris: Directorate for Education*. OECD. Available at: https://www.oecd.org/education/school/31672150.pdf

Organisation for Economic Co-operation and Development (OECD) (2005) *Teachers Matter: Attracting, Developing and Retaining Effective Teachers*. Paris: OECD.

Organisation for Economic Co-operation and Development (OECD) (2011) The Nature of Learning. Using Research to Inspire Practice. Paris: OECD.

Organisation for Economic Co-operation and Development (OECD) (2015) *Improving Schools in Scotland: An OECD Perspective*. Paris: OECD. Available at: https://www.oecd.org/education/school/Improving-Schools-in-Scotland-An-OECD-Perspective.pdf

Organisation for Economic Co-operation and Development (OECD) (2021) *Scotland's Curriculum for Excellence: Into the Future. Executive Summary*. OECD iLibrary. Available at: oecd-ilibrary.org/sites/1043bd5d-en/index.html?itemId=/content/component/1043bd5d-en

Orsay, J. (2011) *Verbal Reasoning and Mathematical Techniques*. Lexington, KY: Osote.

Osborn, M., McNess, E. and Broadfoot, P. with Pollard, A. and Triggs, P. (2000) *What Teachers Do. Changing Policy and Practice in Primary Education*. London: Continuum.

Osler, A. and Starkey, H. (2010) *Teachers and Human Rights Education*. Stoke-on-Trent: Trentham Books.

Papert, S. (1980) *Mindstorms: Children, Computers and Powerful Ideas*. New York: Basic Books.

Parker-Rees, R. and Leeson, C. (eds) (2015) *Early Childhood Studies*. London: SAGE.

Parliament of the United Kingdom (2002) *Education Act 2002*. Available at: https://www.legislation.gov.uk/ukpga/2002/32/part/6/crossheading/general-duties-in-respect-of-the-curriculum?view=plain

Pashler, H., McDaniel, M., Rohrer, D. and Bjork, R. (2008) 'Learning styles: Concepts and evidence'. *Psychological Science in the Public Interest*, 9(3), 105–19.

Patalay, P. and Fitzsimons, E. (2017) *Mental Ill-health among Children of the New Century*. London: Centre for Longitudinal Studies, IOE University College London.

Pate-Bain, H., Achilles, C., Boyd-Zaharias, J. and McKenna, B. (1992) 'Class size does make a difference'. *Phi Delta Kappa*, November, 253–55.

Pea, R.D. (2004) 'The social and technological dimensions of scaffolding and related theoretical concepts for learning, education and human activity'. *Journal of the Learning Sciences*, 13, 423–51.

Peacock, A. (2016) *Assessment for Learning without Limits*. London: McGraw Hill Education.

Pellegrini, A.D. and Blatchford, P. (2000) *The Child at School: Interactions with Peers and Teachers*. London: Arnold.

Perrett, B. (2016) *My Story: D-Day*. London: Scholastic.

Perrot, E. (1982) *Effective Teaching: A Practical Guide to Improving Your Teaching*. London: Longman.

Perry, E. and Francis, B. (2010) *The Social Class Gap for Educational Achievement: A Review of the Literature*. London: RSA Projects. Available at: thersa.org/discover/publications-and-articles/reports/the-social-class-gap-for-educational-achievement-a-review-of-the-literature.

Perry, N. and Ercikan, K. (2015) 'Moving beyond country rankings in international assessments: The case of PISA'. *Teachers College Record*, 117(1), 1–10.

Perry, T., Lea, R., Jørgensen, C.R., Cordingley, P., Shapiro, K. and Youdell, D. (2021) *Cognitive Science Approaches In The Classroom: A Review Of The Evidence*. London: Education Endowment Foundation. https://educationendowmentfoundation.org.uk/education-evidence/evidence-reviews/cognitive-science-approaches-in-the-classroom

Peters, R.S. (1966) *Ethics and Education*. London: Allen & Unwin.

Peters, S.J. (2012) 'The heterodoxy of student voice: Challenges to identity in the sociology of disability and education'. In Arnot, M. (ed.) *The Sociology of Disability and Inclusive Education: A Tribute to Len Barton*. London: Routledge.

Petty, G. (2009) *Teaching Today. A Practical Guide*. Cheltenham: Nelson Thornes.

Phelan, J.C., Link, B.G. and Tehranifar, P. (2010) 'Social conditions as fundamental causes of health inequalities: Theory, evidence, and policy implications'. *Journal of Health and Social Behavior*, 51(1), S28–S40.

Phillipson, N. and Wegerif, R. (2017) *Dialogic Education. Mastering Core Concepts through Thinking Together*. London: Routledge.

Piaget, J. (1926) *The Language and Thought of the Child*. New York: Basic Books.

Piaget, J. (1950) *The Psychology of Intelligence*. London: Routledge and Kegan Paul.

Piaget, J. (1951) *Play, Dreams and Imitation*. New York: Norton.

Piaget, J. (1961) 'A genetic approach to the psychology of thought'. *Journal of Educational Psychology*, 52, 51–61.

Pianta, R.C. (1999) *Enhancing Relationships Between Children and Teachers*. Washington, DC: American Psychological Association.

Pilliner, A.E.G. (1979) 'Norm referenced and criterion referenced tests: An evaluation'. In Jeffrey, A.W. for the Scottish Education Department (ed.) *Issues in Educational Assessment*. Edinburgh: Her Majesty's Stationery Office.

Plowman, L. (2006) *Supporting Learning with ICT in Pre-school Settings*. TLRP Research Briefing 15. London: TLRP.

Plummer, G. (2000) *Failing Working Class Girls*. Stoke-on-Trent: Trentham Books.

Pointon, P. and Kershner, R. (2000) 'Children's views of the primary classroom as an environment for work and learning'. *Research in Education*, 64, 64–77.

Pol, J. van de, Volan, M. and Beishuizen, J. (2012) 'Promoting teacher scaffolding in small group work: A contingency perspective'. *Teaching and Teacher Education*, 28(2), 193–205.

Polanyi, M. (1962) *Personal Knowledge. Towards a Post-critical Philosophy*. London: Routledge.

Pollard, A. (1982) 'A model of coping strategies'. *British Journal of Sociology of Education*, 3(1), 19–37.

Pollard, A. (1985) *The Social World of the Primary School*. London: Cassell.

Pollard, A. (1987a) 'Social differentiation in primary schools'. *Cambridge Journal of Education*, 17(3), 158–61.

Pollard, A. (1987b) 'Primary school teachers and their colleagues'. In Delamont, S. (ed.) *The Primary School Teacher*. Lewes: Falmer.

Pollard, A. (2007) 'The UK's Teaching and Learning Research Programme: Findings and significance'. *British Educational Research Journal*, 33(5), 639–46.

Pollard, A. (ed.) (2010) *Professionalism and Pedagogy: A Contemporary Opportunity*. London: TLRP.

Pollard, A. and Filer, A. (1996) *The Social World of Children's Learning: Case Studies of Pupils from Four to Seven*. London: Cassell.

Pollard, A. and Filer, A. (1999) *The Social World of Pupil Career: Strategic Biographies through Primary School*. London: Cassell.

Pollard, A. and Filer, A. (2007) *Education, Schooling and Learning for Life*. Research Briefing 23. London: TLRP.

Pollard, A. and James, M. (2004) *Personalised Learning: A Commentary by the Teaching and Learning Research Programme*. Cambridge: TLRP.

Pollard, A. and Oancea, A. (2010) *Unlocking Learning: Towards Evidence-informed Policy and Practice in Education*. London: BERA. Available at: bera.ac.uk/researchers-resources/publications/uk-strategic-forum-for-research-in-education-sfre-final-report

Pollard, A. and Triggs, P. (2000) *What Pupils Say: Changing Policy and Practice in Primary Education*. London: Continuum.

Pollard, A., Broadfoot, P., Croll, P., Osborn, M. and Abbott, D. (1994) *Changing English Primary Schools? The Impact of the Education Reform Act at Key Stage One*. London: Cassell.

Power, S. (2008) 'The imaginative professional'. In Cunningham, B. (ed.) *Exploring Professionalism*. London: UCL IOE Press.

Price, D. (ed.) (2017) *Education Forward: Moving Schools into the Future*. Horley: Crux Publishing.

Priestley, M. (2015) 'Teacher agency: What is it and why does it matter?'. BERA blog post, 3 September 2015. Available at: bera.ac.uk/blog/teacher-agency-what-is-it-and-why-does-it-matter

Pring, R. (2010) *The Philosophy of Educational Research*. London: Continuum.

Pring, R., Hayward, G., Hodgson, A., Johnson, J., Keep, E., Oancea, A., Rees, G., Spours, K. and Wilde, S. (2009) *Education for All: The Future of Education and Training for 14–19 Year Olds in England and Wales*. London: Routledge.

Pryor, J. and Torrance, H. (1996) 'Teacher–pupil interaction in formative assessment: Assessing the work or protecting the child?' *The Curriculum Journal*, 7(2), 205–26.

Putnam, J. and Burke, J.B. (1992) *Organising and Managing Classroom Learning Communities*. New York: McGraw Hill.

Putnam, R.D. (1995) 'Bowling alone: America's declining social capital'. *Journal of Democracy*, 6(1), 65–78.

Pyle, A., DeLuca, C. and Danniels, E. (2017) 'A scoping review of research on play based pedagogies in kindergarten education'. *Review of Education*, 5(3), 311–51.

Qualifications and Curriculum Authority (QCA) (2007) The Big Picture of the Curriculum. London: QCA.

reflectiveteaching.co.uk

Quigley, A. (2016) *The Confident Teacher. Developing Successful Habits of Mind, Body and Pedagogy*. London: Routledge.

Raphael-Read, L. (1996) 'Working with boys: a new research agenda'. *Redland Papers*, 3. Bristol: University of the West of England.

Rasbash J., Leckie G., Pillinger R. and Jenkins J. (2010) 'Children's educational progress: Partitioning family, school and area effects'. *Journal of the Royal Statistical Society*, 173(3), 657–82.

Rawling, E. (2006) 'A shift in the zeitgeist? Are we witnessing the return of curriculum development?' *Nuffield Review of 14–19 Education*, Working Paper. Oxford.

Reay, D. (1998) *Class Work: Mothers' Involvement in Children's Schooling*. London: University College Press.

Reay, D. (2000) 'A useful extension of Bourdieu's conceptual framework? Emotional capital as a way of understanding mothers' involvement in their children's education?' *Sociological Review*, 48(4), 568–85.

Reay, D. (2001) '"Spice Girls", "Nice Girls", "Girlies" and "Tomboys": Gender discourses, girls' cultures and femininities in the primary school classroom'. *Gender and Education*, 13(2), 153–66.

Reay, D. (2018) 'Miseducation: Inequality, education and the working classes'. *International Studies in Sociology of Education*, 27(4), 453–56.

Reay, D. and Wiliam, D. (1999) '"I'll be a nothing": Structure, agency and the construction of identity through assessment'. *British Educational Research Journal*, 25(3), 343–54.

Reese, L., Garnier, H., Gallimore, R. and Goldenberg, C. (2000) 'Longitudinal analysis of the antecedents of emergent Spanish literacy and middle-school English reading achievement of Spanish-speaking students'. *American Educational Research Journal*, 37(3), 622–33.

Reid, I. (1998) *Class in Britain*. Cambridge: Polity.

Reid, K. and Morgan, N.S. (2012) *Tackling Behaviour in your Primary School: A Practical Handbook for Teachers*. London: Routledge.

Reiss, M. and White, J. (2013) *An Aims-based Curriculum. The Significance of Human Flourishing for Schools*. London: UCL IOE Press.

Renold, E. (2001) 'Learning the "hard" way: Boys, hegemonic masculinity and the negotiation of learner identities in the primary school'. *British Journal of Sociology of Education*, 22(3), 369–86.

Renold, E. (2005) *Girls, Boys and Junior Sexualities. Exploring Children's Gender and Sexual Relations in the Primary School*. London: Routledge.

Reynolds, D. and Farrell, S. (1996) *Worlds Apart? A Review of International Surveys of Educational Achievement Involving England*. London: OFSTED.

Richards, M. and Light, P. (eds) (1986) *Children of Social Worlds*. Oxford: Blackwell.

Richardson, J. (1998) 'We're all here to learn'. *Journal of Staff Development*, 19(4), 49–55.

Richardson, R. (1990) *Daring to Be a Teacher*. Stoke-on-Trent: Trentham Books.

Richardson, R. (2009) *Holding Together. Equalities, Difference and Cohesion*. Stoke-on-Trent: Trentham.

Richardson, R. (2011) *Changing Life Chances: Practical Projects and Endeavours in School* [ebook]. Institute of Education Press.

Richardson, R. and Miles, B. (2008) *Equality Stories: Recognition, Respect and Raising Achievement*. Stoke-on-Trent: Trentham.

Riding, R.J. and Rayner, S. (1998) *Cognitive Styles and Learning Strategies*. London: Fulton.

Rist, R. (1970) 'Student social class and teacher expectations'. *Harvard Education Review*, 40, 411–51.

Roberts, R. (2002) *Self-esteem and Early Learning*. London: Paul Chapman.

Robertson, J. (1996) *Effective Classroom Control: Understanding Teacher–Pupil Relationships*. London: Hodder and Stoughton.

Robertson, S. and Dale, R. (2009) 'Aliens in the classroom: When technology meets classroom life'. In Sutherland, R., Robertson, S. and John, P. (eds) *Improving Classroom Learning with ICT*. London: Routledge.

Robinson, G., Sleigh, J. and Maines, B. (1995) *No Bullying Starts Today*. Portishead: Lame Duck.

Rogers, B. (2011) *Classroom Behaviour: A Practical Guide to Effective Teaching, Behaviour Management and Colleague Support*, 3rd edn. London: SAGE.

Rogers, B. (2015) *Classroom Behaviour: A Practical Guide to Effective Teaching, Behaviour Management and Colleague Support*, 4th edn. London: SAGE.

Rogers, C.R. (1961) *On Becoming a Person*. London: Constable.

Rogers, C.R. (1969) *Freedom to Learn*. New York: Merrill.

Rogers, C.R. (1980) *A Way of Being*. Boston, MA: Houghton Mifflin.

Rogoff, B. (1990) *Apprenticeship in Thinking: Cognitive Development in Social Context*. Oxford: Oxford University Press.

Rogoff, B., Goodman Turkanis, C. and Bartlett, L. (2001) *Learning Together: Children and Adults in a School Community*. Oxford: Oxford University Press.

Rohrbeck, C., Ginsburg-Block, M.D., Fantuzzo, J.W. and Miller, T.R. (2003) 'Peer-assisted learning interventions with elementary school pupils: A meta-analytic review'. *Journal of Educational Psychology*, 95(2), 240–57. doi:10.1037/0022-0663.95.2.240.

Rojas-Drummond, S. and Mercer, N. (2003) 'Scaffolding the development of effective collaboration and learning'. *International Journal of Educational Research*, 39, 99–111. doi:10.1016/S0883-0355(03)00075-2.

Rose, S., Twist, L., Lord, P., Rutt, S., Badr, K., Hope, C. and Styles, B. (2021) 'Impact of school closures and subsequent support strategies on attainment and socio-emotional wellbeing'. London: Education Endowment Foundation. Available at: https://educationendowmentfoundation.org.uk/projects-and-evaluation/projects/nfer-impact-of-school-closures-and-subsequent-support-strategies-on-attainment-and-socioemotional-wellbeing-in-key-stage-1

Rosen, H. (1988) 'The irrepressible genre'. In Maclure, M., Phillips, T. and Wilkinson, A. (eds) *Oracy Matters*. Milton Keynes: Open University Press.

Rosenblatt, L.M. (1978/1994) *The Reader, the Text, the Poem: The Transactional Theory of the Literary Work*. Carbondale and Edwardsville, IL: Southern Illinois University Press.

Rosenthal, R. and Jacobson, L. (1968) *Pygmalion in the Classroom*. New York: Holt, Rinehart and Winston.

Ross, S. and Biesty, S. (2011) *Into the Unknown: How Great Explorers Found Their Way by Land, Sea and Air*. London: Walker Books.

Rostow, W.W. (1962) *The Stages of Economic Growth*. Cambridge: Cambridge University Press.

Rottenberg, C. and Smith, M.L. (1990) *Unintended Effects of External Testing in Elementary Schools*. Conference of the American Educational Research Association. Boston, April.

Rowe, N., Wilkin, A. and Wilson, R. (2012) *Mapping of Seminal Reports on Good Teaching*. Slough: NFER.

Rowland, S. (1987) 'Child in control: Towards an interpretive model of teaching and learning'. In Pollard, A. (ed.) *Children and Their Primary Schools*. London: Falmer.

Rowland, T., Turner, F., Thwaites, A. and Huckstep, P. (2009) *Developing Primary Mathematics Teaching: Reflecting on Practice with the Knowledge Quartet*. London: SAGE.

Royal Society, The (2011a) *Neuroscience, Society and Policy. Brain Waves Module 1*. London: The Royal Society.

Royal Society, The (2011b) *Neuroscience: Implications for Education and Lifelong Learning*. Brain Waves Module 2. London: The Royal Society.

Royal Society, The and The British Academy (RS & BA) (2018) *Harnessing Educational Research*. Royal Society. Retrieved from https://royalsociety.org/topics-policy/projects/royal-society-british-academy-educational-research/

Royal Society of Arts, The (RSA) (2013) *Opening Minds: The Competence Framework*. London: RSA.

Rubin, Z. (1980) *Children's Friendships*. London: Fontana.

Ruddell, R.B. and Unrau, N.J. (2013) 'Reading as a motivated meaning-construction process: The reader, the text and the teacher'. In Alvermann, D.E., Unrau, N. and Ruddell, R.B. (eds) *Theoretical Models and Processes of Reading*, 6th edn., 1015–68. Newark, DE: International Reading Association. doi:10.1598/0710.38.

Rudduck, J. and Flutter, J. (2004) *Involving Pupils, Improving School*. London: Continuum.

Rudduck, J. and McIntyre, D. (2007) *Improving Learning through Consulting Pupils*. London: Routledge.

Ruthven, K. (2005) 'Improving the development and warranting of good practice in teaching'. *Cambridge Journal of Education*, 35(3), 407–26.

Rutter, M. and Madge, N. (1976) *Cycles of Disadvantage*. London: Heinemann.

Ryle, G. (1945) 'Knowing how and knowing that'. *Proceedings of the Aristotelian Society*, 46, 1–16.

Sachs, J. (2001) 'Teacher professional identity: Competing discourses, competing outcomes'. *Journal of Education Policy*, 16(2), 149–61. doi:10.1080/02680930116819.

Sachs, J. (2003) *The Activist Teaching Profession*. Buckingham: Open University Press.

Sadovnik, A.R. (2001) *Prospects: The Quarterly Review of Comparative Education*, vol. XXXI, no. 49, 687–703. Paris: UNESCO: International Bureau of Education.

Sahlberg, P. (2012) *Finnish Lessons: What Can the World Learn from Educational Change in Finland?* Boston, MA: Teachers' College Press.

Saljo, R. and Hjorne, E. (2009) 'Symptoms, categories, and the process of invoking labels'. In Daniels, H., Lauder, H. and Porter, J. (eds) *Knowledge, Values and Educational Policy: A Critical Perspective*. London: Routledge.

Sammons, P.M., Toth, K. and Sylva, K. (2015) *Background to Success: Differences in A-Level Entries By Ethnicity, Neighbourhood and Gender*. Oxford: University of Oxford.

Sangster, M. (2012) *Developing Teacher Expertise: Exploring Key Issues in Primary Practice*. London: Bloomsbury Academic.

Sarasin, L.C. (1999) *Learning Style Perspectives: Impact in the Classroom*. Madison, WI: Atwood Publishing.

Savage, J. and McGoun, C. (2015) *Teaching in a Networked Classroom*. London: Routledge.

Sawyer, R.K. (2006) *The Cambridge Handbook of the Learning Sciences*. Cambridge: Cambridge University Press.

Schagen, I. and Hutchison, D. (2003) 'Adding value in educational research – the marriage of value-added measures for school improvement data and analytical power'. *British Educational Research Journal*, 29(5), 749–65.

Schmidt, W. and Prawat, R. (2006) 'Curriculum coherence and national control of education. Issues or non-issue?' *Journal of Curriculum Studies*, 38(6), 641–58.

Scholes, R. (1985) *Textual Power*. New Haven, CT: Yale University Press.

Schön, D.A. (1983) *The Reflective Practitioner: How Professionals Think in Action*. London: Temple Smith.

Schön, D.A. (1987) *Educating the Reflective Practitioner*. San Francisco, CA: Jossey Bass.

Schoon, I. (2016) *Human Development in Context: The Study of Risk and Resilience*. London: UCL IOE Press.

Schuller, T. and Watson, D. (2009) *Learning through Life*. London: NIACE.

Schultz, T. (1961) 'Investment in human capital'. *American Economic Review*, 51, 1–17.

Schunk, D.H. and Zimmerman, B.J. (eds.) (2012) *Motivation and Self-Regulated Learning: Theory, Research, and Applications*. London: Routledge.

Schwab, J. (1978) 'Education and the structure of the disciplines'. In Westbury, I. and Wilkof, N.J. (eds) *Science Curriculum and Liberal Education*, 229–72. Chicago, IL: University of Chicago Press

Scott, D. (2008) *Critical Essays on Major Curriculum Theorists*. London: Routledge.

Scottish Government (2006) *A Curriculum for Excellence: Building Curriculum Series*. Edinburgh: The Scottish Government.

Scottish Government (2008) *A Curriculum for Excellence: Building the Curriculum 3*. Edinburgh: The Scottish Government.

Scottish Government (2009) *A Curriculum for Excellence: Curriculum Guidelines*. Edinburgh: The Scottish Government.

Scottish Government (2010) *Supporting Children's Learning: Code of Practice*. Edinburgh: The Scottish Government.

Scottish Government (2011) *Principles of Assessment in Curriculum for Excellence. Building the Curriculum 5. A Framework for Assessment*. Edinburgh: The Scottish Government.

Scottish Government (2016) *National Improvement Framework for Scottish Education*. Edinburgh: The Scottish Government.

Sebba, J., Brown, N., Steward, S., Galton, M. and James, M. (2007) *An Investigation of Personalised Learning Approaches used by Schools (Research Report RR843)*. London: DfES.

Sedgwick, F. (1988) *Here Comes the Assembly Man*. London: Falmer Press.

Sedova, K., Sedlacek, M. and Svaricek, R. (2016) 'Teacher professional development as a means of transforming student classroom talk'. *Teaching and Teacher Education*, 57, 14–25. doi: 10.1016/j.tate.2016.03.005.

Sehgal Cuthbert, A. and Standish, A. (eds.) (2021) What Should Schools Teach? 2nd. edn. London: UCL Press.

Seligman, C.F., Tucker, G.R. and Lambert, W.E. (1972) 'The effects of speech style and other attributes on teachers' attitudes towards pupils'. *Language in Society*, 1, 131–42.

Sewell, T. (1997) *Black Masculinities and Schooling. How Black Boys Survive Modern Schooling*. Stoke-on-Trent: Trentham.

Sfard, A. (1998) 'On the two metaphors of learning and the dangers of choosing just one'. *Educational Researcher*, 27(2), 4–13.

Shanahan, C., Shanahan, T. and Misischia, C. (2011) 'Analysis of expert readers in three disciplines: History, mathematics, and chemistry'. *Journal of Literacy Research*, 43(4), 393–429. doi:10.1177/1086296X11424071.

Shanahan, T., Callison, K., Carriere, C., Duke, N.K., Pearson, P.D., Schatschneider, C. and Torgesen, J. (2010) *Improving Reading Comprehension in Kindergarten through 3rd Grade: IES Practice Guide*. NCEE 2010-4038. What Works Clearinghouse. files.eric.ed.gov/fulltext/ED512029.pdf

Sharp, R. and Green, A. (1975) *Education and Social Control*. London: Routledge.

Sharples, J., Webster, R. and Blatchford, P. (2018) *Making Best Use of Teaching Assistants*, 2nd edn. London: Education Endowment Foundation. Available at: https://educationendowmentfoundation.org.uk/education-evidence/guidance-reports/teaching-assistants

Shaw, B., Bernardes, E., Trethewey, A. and Menzies, L. (2016) *Special Educational Needs and Their Links to Poverty*. London: Joseph Rowntree Foundation.

Shayer, M. and Adey, P. (eds) (2002) *Learning Intelligence: Cognitive Acceleration Across the Curriculum from 5 to 15 Years*. Maidenhead: Open University Press.

Shoffner, M. (2009) 'The place of the personal: Exploring the affective domain through reflection in teacher preparation'. *Teaching and Teacher Education*, 25(6), 783–89.

Shorrocks, D. (1991) *The Evaluation of National Curriculum Assessment at Key Stage One, Final Report*. Leeds: University of Leeds.

Shulman, L.S. (1986) 'Those who understand: Knowledge and growth in teaching'. *Educational Researcher*, 15, 4–14.

Shulman, L.S. (2004) *The Wisdom of Practice – Essays on Teaching, Learning and Learning to Teach*. San Francisco: Jossey Bass.

reflectiveteaching.co.uk

Shutts, K., Kenward, B., Falk, H., Ivegran, A. and Fawcett, C. (2017) 'Early preschool environments and gender: Effects of gender pedagogy in Sweden'. *Journal Of Experimental Child Psychology*, 162, 1–17.

Sibieta, L. (2011) *Inequality in Britain: An Explanation of Recent Trends*. London: Institute for Fiscal Studies.

Sibieta, L. (2021) *2020 Annual Report on Education Spending in England: Schools*. London: Institute for Fiscal Studies.

Siegler, R.S. (1997) *Emerging Minds: The Process of Change in Children's Thinking*. Oxford: Oxford University Press.

Sikes, P. (1997) *Parents Who Teach: Stories from Home and School*. London: Cassell.

Sikes, P., Measor, L. and Woods, P. (1985) *Teacher Careers: Crises and Continuities*. London: Falmer.

Silver, H. (1980) *Education and the Social Condition*. London: Methuen.

Simco, N. (2000) 'Learning to comply: The impact of national curricula for primary pupils and primary trainee teacher on the ownership of learning'. *Forum*, 42(1), 33–38.

Simon, B. (1981) 'Why no pedagogy in England?' In Simon, B. and Taylor, W. (eds) *Education in the Eighties*. London: Batsford Educational.

Simon, B. (1985) *Does Education Matter?* London: Lawrence and Wishart.

Simon, B. (1992) *What Future for Education?* London: Lawrence and Wishart.

Sims, S., Fletcher-Wood, H., O'Mara-Eves, A., Cottingham, S., Stansfield, C., Van Herwegen, J. and Anders, J. (2021) *What are the Characteristics of Teacher Professional Development that Increase Pupil Achievement? A Systematic Review and Meta-analysis*. London: Education Endowment Foundation. Available from: https://educationendowmentfoundation.org.uk/education-evidence/evidence-reviews/teacher-professional-development-characteristics

Siraj-Blatchford, I. and Clarke, P. (2000) *Diversity and Language in the Early Years*. Buckingham: Open University Press.

Siraj-Blatchford, J. and Siraj-Blatchford, I. (1995) *Educating the Whole Child: Cross-curricular Skills, Themes and Dimensions*. Buckingham: Open University Press.

Skelton, C. (2001) *Schooling the Boys. Masculinities and Primary Education*. Buckingham: Open University Press.

Skelton, C. and Francis, B. (2006) *The SAGE Handbook of Gender and Education*. London: SAGE.

Skelton, C. and Francis, B. (2009) *Feminism and 'The Schooling Scandal'*. London: Routledge.

Skinner B.F. (1953) *Science and Human Behaviour*. New York: Macmillan.

Skinner B.F. (1968) *The Technology of Teaching*. New York: Appleton.

Slee, P. (2017) *School Bullying. Teachers Helping Students Cope*. London: Routledge.

Sluckin, A. (1981) *Growing Up in the Playground*. London: Routledge and Kegan Paul.

Smidt, S. (2016) *Multilingualism in the Early Years*. London: Routledge.

Smith, A. (2007) 'Children and young people's participation rights in education'. *The International Journal of Children's Rights*, 15(1), 147–64.

Smith, F., Hardman, F., Wall, K. and Mroz, M. (2004) 'Interactive whole class teaching in the National Literacy and Numeracy Strategies'. *British Educational Research Journal*, 30(3), 395–411.

Smith, P. (2014) *Understanding School Bullying: Its Nature and Prevention Strategies*. London: SAGE.

Social Metrics Commission (2019) *Poverty in the UK: A Guide to the Facts and Figures*: London: Full Fact.

Solar, J., Walsh, C.S., Craft, A., Rix, J. and Simmons, K. (2012) *Transforming Practice. Critical Issues in Equity, Diversity and Education*. Maidenhead: Open University Press.

Solomon, J. (1987) 'New thoughts on teacher education'. *Oxford Review of Education*, 13(3), 267–74.

reflectiveteaching.co.uk

Bibliography

Sood, K. (2005) 'Working with other professionals'. In Cole, M. (ed.) *Professional Values and Practice: Meeting the Standards*. London: David Fulton.

Sorace, A. (2010) 'Two languages, one brain: Advantages of bilingualism across the lifespan'. Available at: bilingualism-matters.org.ppls.ed.ac.uk

Sorden, S.D. (2012) 'The cognitive theory of multimedia learning'. In Irby, B.J., Brown, G., Lara-Alecio, R. and Jackson, S. (eds) *Handbook of Educational Theories*, 1–22. Charlotte, NC: Information Age Publishing.

Sotto, E. (2007) *When Teaching Becomes Learning*. London: Continuum.

Spencer, E. and Hayward, L. (2016) 'More than good intentions: Policy and assessment for learning in Scotland'. In Laveault, D. and Allal, L. (eds) *Assessment for Learning: Meeting the Challenge of Implementation*. London: Springer.

Spendlove, S. (2009) *Putting Assessment for Learning into Practice*. London: Continuum.

Spielman, A. (2018) *HMCI Commentary: Curriculum and the New Education Inspection Framework*. Available at: https://www.gov.uk/government/speeches/hmci-commentary-curriculum-and-the-new-education-inspection-framework

Standish, A. and Cuthbert, A.S. (2017) *What Should Schools Teach? New Disciplines, Subjects, and the Pursuit of Truth*. London: UCL IOE Press.

Starkey, L., Shonfeld, M., Prestridge, S. and Cervera, M.G. (2021) 'Special issue: Covid-19 and the role of technology and pedagogy on school education during a pandemic'. *Technology, Pedagogy and Education*, 30(1), 1–5, doi:10.1080/1475939X.2021.1866838.

Steer, A. (2009) *Learning Behaviour: Lessons Learned, a Review of Behaviour Standards and Practices in Our Schools*. London: DCSF.

Stenhouse, L. (1975) *An Introduction to Curriculum Research and Development*. London: Heinemann.

Stenhouse, L. (1983) *Authority, Education and Emancipation*. London: Heinemann.

Stobart, G. (2008) *Testing Times: The Uses and Abuses of Assessment*. London: Routledge.

Stoll, L., Harris, A. and Handscomb, G. (2012) *Great Professional Development which Leads to Great Pedagogy: Nine Claims from Research*. National College for School Leadership. https://assets.publishing.service.gov.uk/government/uploads/system/uploads/attachment_data/file/335707/Great-professional-development-which-leads-to-great-pedagogy-nine-claims-from-research.pdf

Stone, C.A. (1998) 'The metaphor of scaffolding: Its utility for the field of learning disabilities'. *Journal of Learning Disabilities*, 31, 344–64.

Straughan, R. (1988) *Can We Teach Children to be Good? Basic Issues in Moral, Personal and Social Education*. Buckingham: Open University Press.

Stringer, E., Lewin, C. and Coleman, R. (2019) *Using Digital Technology to Improve Learning: Guidance Report*. London: Education Endowment Foundation (EEF).

Sturman, L. (2012) 'Making best use of international comparison data'. *Research Intelligence*, 119 (Autumn/Winter). London: BERA.

Styles, M. and Arizpe, E. (2016) *Children Reading Pictures*. London: Routledge.

Sutherland, R. et al. (2006) *Using Computers to Enhance Learning*. TLRP Research Briefing 19. London: TLRP.

Sutherland, R., Robertson, S. and John, P. (2008) *Improving Classroom Learning with ICT*. London: Routledge.

Sutton, R. (1995) *Assessment for Learning*. Salford: RS Publications.

Sutton, R. (2000) *Undoing the Muddle in the Middle*. Salford: RS Publications.

Sutton, R. with K. Gregory and J. Gray (2012) *Successful Student Transition*. Winnipeg, MB: Portage & Main Press.

Sustain (2006) *Changing Diets, Changing Minds*. London: Sustain.

Swaffield, S. (ed.) (2008) *Unlocking Assessment: Understanding for Reflection and Application*. Abingdon: Routledge.

reflectiveteaching.co.uk

Swaffield, S. (2011) 'Getting to the heart of authentic assessment for learning'. *Assessment in Education: Principles, Policy and Practice*, 18(4), 433–49.

Swaffield, S. and Dudley, P. (2010) *Assessment Literacy for Wise Decisions*. London: Association of Teachers and Lecturers.

Swaffield, S. and MacBeath, J. (2005) 'Self-evaluation and the role of a critical friend'. *Cambridge Journal of Education*, 35(2), 239–52.

Swann, M., Peacock, A., Hart, S. and Drummond, M.J. (2012) *Creating Learning Without Limits*. Maidenhead: Open University Press.

Sylva, K., Melhuish, E., Sammons, P., Siraj-Blatchford, I. and Taggart, B. (2010) *Early Childhood Matters. Evidence from the Effective Pre-school and Primary Education Project*. London: Routledge.

Sylva, K., Sammons, P., Chan, L.L., Melhuish, E., Siraj-Blatchford, I. and Taggart, B. (2013) 'The effects of early experiences at home and pre-school on gains in English and mathematics in primary school: A multilevel study in England'. *Zeitschrift für Erziehungswissenschaft*, 16(2), 277–301.

Tabachnick, R. and Zeichner, K. (eds) (1991) *Issues and Practices in Inquiry Oriented Teacher Education*. London: Falmer.

Tanner, J.M. (1978) *Education and Physical Growth*. London: University of London Press.

Tassoni, P. and Hucker, K. (2000) *Planning Play and the Early Years*. Oxford: Heinemann.

Taylor, A. (2017) *Character Education: A Bibliography of Recent Research, Reports and Resources*. Slough: NFER.

Teaching and Learning in 2020 Review Group (2006) *2020 Vision: Report of the Teaching and Learning in 2020 Review Group*. London: DfES.

Tennent, W. (2014) *Understanding Reading Comprehension*. London: SAGE.

Tereshchenko, A., Mills, M. and Bradbury, A. (2020) *Making Progress? Employment and Retention of BAME Teachers in England*. London: UCL Institute of Education.

Tharp, R. and Gallimore, R. (1988) *Rousing Minds to Life: Teaching, Learning and Schooling in Social Context*. New York: Cambridge University Press.

Thomas, A. and Pattison, H. (2007) *How Children Learn at Home*. London: Continuum.

Thomas, G. and Loxley, A. (2007) *Deconstructing Special Education and Constructing Inclusion*. Buckingham: Open University Press.

Thomas, L. (2010) *The RSA Area Based Curriculum: Engaging the Local*. London: RSA.

Thompson, J. (2010) *The Essential Guide to Understanding Special Educational Needs*. London: Longman.

Thompson, M. (1997) *Professional Ethics and the Teacher*. Stoke-on-Trent: Trentham.

Thorndike, E.L. (1911) *Human Learning*. New York: Prentice Hall.

Thorne, B. (1993) *Gender Play: Girls and Boys in School*. Buckingham: Open University Press.

Tickell, C. (2011) *The Early Years: Foundations for Life, Health and Learning*. London: DfE.

Tikly, L. (2022) 'Racism and the future of antiracism in education: A critical analysis of the Sewell Report'. *British Educational Research Journal*, 48, 469–87. doi:10.1002/berj.3776.

Timperley, H. (2011) *Realising the Power of Professional Learning*. Maidenhead: Open University Press.

Timperley, H., Wilson, A., Barrar, H. and Fung, I. (2007) *Teacher Professional Learning and Development. Best Evidence Synthesis Iteration [BES]*. New Zealand: Ministry of Education.

Timperley, H., Wilson, A., Barrar, H. and Fung, I. (2008) *Teacher Professional Learning and Development: Best Evidence Synthesis Iteration*. NZ Ministry of Education and University of Auckland.

Tizard, B. and Hughes, M. (1984) *Young Children Learning: Talking and Learning at Home and School*. London: Fontana.

Tizard, B., Blatchford, P., Burke, J., Farquhar, C. and Plewis, I. (1988) *Young Children at School in the Inner City*. London: Lawrence Erlbaum.

reflectiveteaching.co.uk

Tomlinson, P. (1999a) 'Conscious reflection and implicit learning in teacher preparation: implications for a balanced approach'. *Oxford Review of Education*, 24 (4), 533–44.

Tomlinson, P. (1999b) 'Conscious reflection and implicit learning in teacher preparation: Recent light on old issues'. *Oxford Review of Education*, 25(3), 405–25.

Tonna, M.A. and Shanks, R. (2017) 'The importance of environment for teacher professional learning in Malta and Scotland'. *European Journal of Teacher Education*, 40(1), 91–109. doi:10.1080/02619768.2016.1251899.

Topping, K. and Buchs, C. (2017) *Effective Peer Learning: From Principles to Practical Implementation*. London: Routledge.

Torrance, H. (1991) 'Evaluating SATs: The 1991 pilot'. *Cambridge Journal of Education*, 21(2), 129–40.

Training and Development Agency for Schools (TDA) (2007) *Professional Standards for Teachers in England from 2007*. London: TDA. Available at: https://www.rbkc.gov.uk/pdf/Excellent%20teacher%20standards.pdf

Training and Development Agency for Schools (TDA) (2010) *Promoting Community Cohesion: The Role of Extended Services*. Available at: https://dera.ioe.ac.uk/1279/7/3dec48eb-7335-4ec4-97c1-3e70307283b5_Redacted.pdf

Tripp, S.D. (1993) 'Theories, traditions, and situated learning'. *Educational Technology*, 33(3), 71–77.

Troyna, B. and Hatcher, R. (1992) *Racism in Children's Lives: A Study of Mainly White Primary Schools*. London: Routledge.

Tucker, J. (ed) (2016) *Improving Children's Life Chances*. London: CPAG.

Turnbull, J. (2007) *9 Habits of Highly Effective Teachers. A Practical Guide to Empowerment*. London: Continuum.

Turner, F. (2009) 'Growth in teacher knowledge: Individual reflection and community participation'. *Research in Mathematics Education*, 11(1), 81.

Turner-Bisset, R. (2000) 'Reconstructing the primary curriculum'. *Education 3–13: International Journal of Primary, Elementary and Early Years Education*, 28(1), 3–8.

UNICEF (2018) *Learning through Play: Strengthening Learning Through Play in Early Childhood Education Programmes*. Available at: unicef.org/sites/default/files/2018-12/UNICEF-Lego-Foundation-Learning-through-Play.pdf (accessed 4 January 2022).

UNICEF (2021) *Prospects for Children in 2022: A Global Outlook*. New York: UNICEF.

United Kingdom Literacy Association (2004) *Raising Boys' Achievements in Writing*. London: UKLA.

United Kingdom Literacy Association (2021) *Teachers as Readers Building Communities of Readers*. London: UKLA. Available at: https://ukla.org/ukla_resources/teachers-as-readers-building-communities-of-readers-research-projects-resources-and-evaluations/

United Nations (1948) *Universal Declaration of Human Rights*. New York: United Nations.

United Nations (1989) *Convention on the Rights of the Child*. New York: United Nations.

Unrau, N.J. and Alvermann, D.E. (2013) 'Literacies and their investigation through theories and models'. In Alvermann, D.E., Unrau, N. and Ruddell, R.B. (eds) *Theoretical Models and Processes of Reading*, 6th edn., 47–90. Newark, DE: International Reading Association. doi:10.1598/0710.02

Van Poortlviet, M., Axford, N. and Lloyd, J. (2018) *Working with Parents to Support Children's Learning: Guidance Report*. London: Education Endowment Foundation.

Van Poortvliet, M., Clarke, A. and Gross, J. (2019) *Improving Social and Emotional Learning in Primary Schools*. Guidance Report. London: Education Endowment Foundation.

Van Poortvliet, M., Clarke, A. and Gross, J. (2021) *Improving Social and Emotional Learning in Primary Schools*. Guidance Report. London: Education Endowment Foundation.

Vaughn, S., Wanzek, J., Wexler, J., Barth, A., Cirino, P.T., Fletcher, J. and Francis, D. (2010) 'The relative effects of group size on reading progress of older students with reading difficulties'. *Reading and Writing*, 23(8), 931–56. doi:10.1007/s11145-009-9183-9.

Vidal-Hall, C., Flewitt, R. and Wyse, D. (2020) 'Early childhood practitioner beliefs about digital media: Integrating technology into a child-centred classroom environment'. *European Early Childhood Education Research Journal*. doi:10.1080/1350293X.2020.1735727.

Vincent, C. (1996) *Parents and Teachers: Power and Participation*. London: Falmer.

Vincent, C. (2000) *Including Parents? Education, Citizenship and Parental Agency*. Buckingham: Open University Press.

Volante, L. (ed.) (2016) *The Intersection of International Achievement Testing and Education Policy*. Oxford: Routledge.

Vygotsky, L.S. (1962) *Thought and Language*. Cambridge, MA: Massachusetts Institute of Technology.

Vygotsky, L.S. (1978) *Mind in Society: The Development of Higher Psychological Processes*. Cambridge, MA: Harvard University Press.

Walker, M. (2017) *Why We Sleep: The New Science of Sleep and Dreams*. London: Allen Lane.

Walkerdine, V. (1983) 'It's only natural: Rethinking child-centred pedagogy'. In Wolpe, A.M. and Donald, J. (eds) *Is There Anybody There from Education?* London: Pluto Press.

Walkerdine, V. (1984) 'Cognitive development and the child-centred pedagogy'. In Henriques, D. (ed.) *Changing the Subject: Psychology, Social Regulation and Subjectivity*. London: Methuen.

Walkerdine, V. (1988) *The Mastery of Reason: Cognitive Development and the Production of Rationality*. London: Routledge.

Waller, W. (1932) *The Sociology of Teaching*. New York: Russell and Russell.

Walters, S. (2011) *Ethnicity, Race and Education*. London: Continuum.

Walton, J. (ed.) (1971) *The Integrated Day: Theory and Practice*. London: Ward Lock.

Ward, S. (ed.) (2012) *A Student's Guide to Education Studies*. London: Routledge.

Warin, J. (2010) *Stories of Self: Tracking Children's Identity and Wellbeing through the School Years*. Stoke-on-Trent: Trentham Books.

Warwick, P., Hennessy, S. and Mercer, N. (2011) 'Promoting teacher and school development through co-enquiry: Developing interactive whiteboard use in a "dialogic classroom"'. *Teachers and Teaching: Theory and Practice*, 17(3), 303–24.

Wassermann, S. (2017) *The Art of Interactive Teaching. Listening, Responding, Questioning*. London: Routledge.

Waters-Davies, J. (2022) *Introduction to Play*. London: Sage.

Watkins, C. (2003) *Learning: A Sense Maker's Guide*. London: ATL.

Watkins, C. (2004) *Classrooms as Learning Communities*. London: Routledge.

Watkins, C. (2011) *Managing Classroom Behaviour*. London: ATL.

Watson, A. and Mason, J. (2005) *Mathematics as a Constructive Activity. Learners Generating Examples*. London: Routledge.

Watters, A. (2021) *Teaching Machines: The History of Personalized Learning*. Cambridge, MA: MIT Press.

Wearmouth, J. (2011) *Special Educational Needs. The Basics*. London: Routledge.

Webb, N.M., Ing, M., Nemer, K.M. and Kersting, N. (2006) 'Help seeking in cooperative learning groups'. In Newman, R.S. and Karabenick, S.A. (eds) *Help Seeking in Academic Settings: Goals, Groups and Contexts*, 45–88. Hillsdale, NJ: Lawrence Erlbaum Associates.

Webb, R. and Vulliamy, G. (2002) 'The social work dimension of the primary teachers' role'. *Research Papers in Education*, 17(2), 165–84.

Webster, A., Beverage, M. and Reid, M. (1996) *Managing the Literacy Curriculum*. London: Routledge.

Webster, R. and Blatchford, P. (2013) *The Making a Statement project: Final Report: A Study of the Teaching and Support Experienced By Pupils with a Statement of Special Educational Needs in Mainstream Primary Schools (Report)*. London: UCL Institute of Education.

Webster, R., Blatchford, P. and Russell, A. (2013) 'Challenging and changing how schools use teaching assistants: findings from the Effective Deployment of Teaching Assistants project'. *School Leadership & Management: Formerly School Organisation*, 33(1), 78–96.

reflectiveteaching.co.uk

Webster, R., Russell, A. and Blatchford, P. (2015) *Maximising the Impact of Teaching Assistants. Guidance for School Leaders and Teachers*. London: Routledge.

Wegerif, R. and Dawes, L. (2004) *Thinking and Learning with ICT: Raising Achievement in Primary Classrooms*. London: RoutledgeFalmer.

Weiss, S. and Kiel, E. (2013) 'Who chooses primary teaching and why?' *Issues in Educational Research*, 23(3), 415e432. Available at: http://www.iier.org.au/iier23/weiss.html (accessed 12 September 2016).

Wells, G. (1999) *Dialogic Inquiry: Towards a Socio-cultural Practice and Theory of Education*. New York: Cambridge University Press.

Welsh Government (2018) *An Introduction to the Professional Standards for Teaching and Leadership*. Available at: https://hwb.gov.wales/api/storage/932d8940-56f5-4660-aa85-afb4e87560a9/an-introduction-to-the-professional-standards-for-teaching-and-leadership.pdf

Welsh Government (2019) *Draft Evaluation and Improvement (Accountability) Arrangements for Wales*. February 2019. Cardiff: Welsh Government. Available at: gov.wales/sites/default/files/publications/2019-02/draft-evaluation-and-improvement-accountability-arrangements-for-wales.pdf

Wenger, E. (1999) *Communities of Practice. Learning, Meaning and Identity*. Cambridge: Cambridge University Press.

Wertsch, J.V. (1985) *Vygotsky and the Social Formation of Mind*. Cambridge, MA: Harvard University Press.

Wertsch, J.V. (1991) *Voices of the Mind: A Socio-cultural Approach to Mediated Action*. Cambridge, MA: Harvard University Press.

West, A. and Pennell, H. (2003) *Underachievement in Schools*. London: RoutledgeFalmer.

West-Burnham, J., Farrar, M. and Otero, G. (2007) *Schools and Communities: Working Together to Transform Children's Lives*. London: Continuum.

Whetton, C.E.A. (1991) *National Curriculum Assessment at Key Stage One: 1991 Evaluation, Report 4*. Slough: NFER.

White, J. (1978) 'The primary teacher as servant of the state'. *Education 3–13*, 7(2), 18–23.

White, M.A. (1971) 'The view from the student's desk'. In Silberman, M.L. (ed.) *The Experience of Schooling*, 337–45. New York: Rinehart and Winston.

Whitebread, D. and Pino Pasternak, D. (2010) 'Metacognition, self-regulation and meta-knowing'. In Littleton, K., Wood, C. and Kleine, J. Staarman (eds) *International Handbook of Psychology in Education*. Bingley: Emerald.

Wiggins, G. (1989) 'A true test: Toward more authentic and equitable assessment'. *Phi Delta Kappa*, 70(9), 703–13.

Wiliam, D. (2009) *Assessment for Learning: Why, What and How?* Inaugural lecture, UCL Institute of Education, 24 January.

Wiliam, D. (2011) *Embedded Formative Assessment*. Bloomington, IN: Solution Tree Press.

Wilkinson, R. and Pickett, K. (2009) *The Spirit Level. Why Equality Is Better for Everyone*. London: Penguin.

Willingham, D. (2010) *Why Don't Students Like School?* New York: Jossey Bass.

Willingham, D.T. (2021) *Why Don't Pupils Like School?: A Cognitive Scientist Answers Questions About How the Mind Works and What it Means For the Classroom*. Chichester: John Wiley & Sons.

Willis, J. (2011) 'Affiliation, autonomy and assessment for learning'. *Assessment in Education: Principles, Policy and Practice*, 18(4), 399–415.

Willis, P.E. (1977) *Learning to Labour: How Working Class Kids Get Working Class Jobs*. Farnborough: Saxon House.

Wilson, C. and Powell, M. (2001) *A Guide to Interviewing Children*. London: Routledge.

Wilson, E.O. and Lumsden, C.J. (1981) *Genes, Mind and Culture*. Cambridge, MA, and London: Harvard University Press.

Wilson, E. (ed.) (2017) *School-based Research. A Guide for Education Students*. London: SAGE.

Wilson, J. (2000) *Key Issues in Education and Teaching*. London: Cassell.

reflectiveteaching.co.uk

Winch, C. (2012) *Dimensions of Expertise: A Conceptual Exploration of Vocational Knowledge*. London: Continuum.

Winston, J. (1998) *Drama, Narrative and Moral Education: Exploring Traditional Tales in the Primary Years*. London: The Falmer Press.

Winter, J., Andrews, J., Greenhough, P., Hughes, M., Salway, L. and Yee, W. (2009) *Improving Primary Mathematics: Linking Home and School*. London: Routledge.

Winterbottom, M. and Wilkins, A. (2007) 'Lighting and visual discomfort in the classroom'. *Journal of Environmental Psychology*, 29, 63–75.

Withall, J. (1949) 'The development of a technique for the measurement of social–emotional climate in classrooms'. *Journal of Experimental Education*, 17, 347–61.

Wolf, M. (2008) *Proust and the Squid: The Story and Science of the Reading Brain*. Cambridge: Icon Books.

Wolf, M.K., Crosson, A.C. and Resnick, L.B. (2004) 'Classroom talk for rigorous comprehension instruction'. *Reading Psychology*, 26(1), 27–53.

Wood, D. (1997) *How Children Think and Learn. The Social Contexts of Cognitive Development*. London: Wiley-Blackwell.

Wood, D., Bruner, J.S. and Ross, G. (1976) 'The role of tutoring in problem solving'. *Journal of Child Psychology and Psychiatry*, 17(19), 89–100.

Woods, P. (1990) *The Happiest Days? How Pupils Cope with School*. London: Falmer.

Woods, P.A., Bagley, C. and Glatter, R. (1998) *School Choice and Competition: Markets in the Public Interest*. Hove, UK: Psychology Press.

Woolland, B. (2010) *Teaching Primary Drama*. Harlow: Pearson Education.

Woolner, P., Hall, E., Higgins, S., McCaughey, C., Wall, K. et al. (2007) 'A sound foundation? What we know about the impact of environments on learning and the implications for Building Schools for the Future'. *Oxford Review of Education*, 33(1), 47–70.

Woolner, P., McCarter, S., Wall, K. and Higgins, S. (2012) 'Changed learning through changed space. When can a participatory approach to the learning environment challenge preconceptions and alter practice?' *Improving Schools*, 15(1), 45–60.

World Health Organization (2022) *World Mental Health Report: Transforming Mental Health for All*. Available at: https://www.who.int/publications/i/item/9789240049338

Wragg, E.C. (2000) *Class Management*. London: Routledge.

Wragg, E.C. and Brown, G. (2001) *Questioning in the Primary School*. London: Routledge.

Wright, C. (1992) *Race Relations in the Primary School*. London: David Fulton.

Wrigley, J., Thompson, P. and Lingard, R. (eds) (2012) *Changing Schools. Alternative Ways to Make a World of Difference*. London: Routledge.

Wyness, G. (2017) *Rules of the Game: Disadvantaged Students and the University Admissions Process*. London: Sutton Trust.

Wyse, D. (2001) 'Felt tip pens and school councils: Children's participation rights in four English schools'. *Children and Society*, 15, 209–18.

Wyse, D. (2017) *How Writing Works: From the Invention of the Alphabet to the Rise of Social Media*. Cambridge: Cambridge University Press.

Wyse, D. and Anders, J. (2019) 'Primary education curricula across the world: Qualitative and quantitative methodology in international comparison'. In Suter, L.E., Smith, E. and Denman, B.D. (eds) *The SAGE Handbook of Comparative Studies in Education*. London: SAGE.

Wyse, D. and Bradbury, A. (2022) 'Reading wars or reading reconciliation? A critical examination of robust research evidence, curriculum policy and teachers' practices for teaching phonics and reading'. *Review of Education*, 10(1), e3314. doi:10.1002/rev3.3314.

Wyse, D. and Manyukhina, Y. (2019) 'What next for curriculum?' BERA blog, 10 April, https://www.bera.ac.uk/blog/what-next-for-curriculum

Wyse, D. and Manyukhina, Y. (2020) *Children's Agency and the Curriculum*. The Education Exchange from The Chartered College of Teachers. Available from: https://theeducation.exchange/childrens-agency-and-the-curriculum/

Wyse, D. and Rogers, S. (eds) (2016) *A Guide to Early Years and Primary Teaching*. London: SAGE.

Wyse, D., Hayward, L. and Pandya, J. (eds) (2016) *The Sage Handbook of Curriculum, Pedagogy and Assessment*. London: SAGE.

Wyse, D., Brown, C. Oliver, S. and Poblete, P. (2020) 'Education research and educational practice: The qualities of a close relationship'. *British Educational Research Journal*. doi:10.1002/berj.3626.

Wyse, D., Hayward, L., Higgins, S. and Livingston, K. (2014) 'Editorial: Creating curricula: aims, knowledge, and control, a special edition of the *Curriculum Journal*'. *The Curriculum Journal*, 25(1), 2–6. doi:10.1080/09585176.2014.878545.

Wyse, D., Selwyn, N., Smith, E. and Suter, L. (eds) (2017) *The BERA/SAGE Handbook of Educational Research*. London: SAGE.

Wyse, D., Aarts, B., Anders, J., de Gennaro, A., Dockrell, J., Manyukhina, Y., Sing, S. and Torgerson, C. (2022) 'Grammar and writing in England's national curriculum: A randomised controlled trial and implementation and process evaluation of Englicious'. London: UCL Faculty of Education and Society.

Wyse, D., Baumfield, V., Egan, D., Hayward, D., Mulme, M., Menter, I., Gallagher, C., Leitch, R., Livingston, K. and Lingard, R. (2012) *Creating the Curriculum*. London: Routledge.

Yeager, D.S. and Dweck, C.S. (2020) 'What can be learned from growth mindset controversies?' *American Psychologist*, 75(9), 1269–84. doi:10.1037/amp0000794.

Yosso, T.J. (2005) 'Whose culture has capital?' *Race, Ethnicity and Education*, 8(1), 69–91.

Youdell, D. (2006) *Impossible Bodies, Impossible Selves: Exclusions and Student Subjectivities*. Dordrecht: Springer.

Young, M. (2008) *Bringing Knowledge Back In*. London: Routledge.

Young, M.F.D. (ed.) (1971) *Knowledge and Control*. London: Collier Macmillan.

Younger, M. and Warrington, M. (2007) 'Closing the gender gap? Issues of gender equity in English secondary schools'. *Discourse: Studies in the Cultural Politics of Education*, 28(2), 219–42.

Zeichner, K. and Liston, D. (1996) *Reflective Teaching: An Introduction*. Mahwah, NJ: Lawrence Erlbaum Associates.

Zhongming, Z., Linong, L., Wangqiang, Z. and Wei, L. (2021) *AR6 Climate Change 2021: The Physical Science Basis*. Available at: https://www.ipcc.ch/report/ar6/wg1/

Zimmerman, B.J. (1990) 'Self-regulated learning and academic achievement: An overview'. *Educational Psychologist*, 25(1), 3–17.

Zipes, J. (1995) *Creative Storytelling: Building Communities, Changing Lives*. London: Routledge.

Index

The letter *f* after an entry indicates a page with a figure.

2020 Vision: Report of the Teaching and Learning in 2020 Review Group) Teaching and Learning in 2020 Review Group) 160, 284, 331–2, 341
2030 Agenda for Sustainable Development 482

ability 53, 55, 56, 171
    groups 171, 487, 489–90
    labels 53, 54*f*–5
    mixed ability groups 490
    setting 246
Ability Grouping in Education (Ireson, J. and Hallam, S.) 259, 506
Ability-grouping in Primary Schools: Case Studies and Critical Debates (Marks, R.) 33
academies 110, 125, 143, 148, 151
acceptance 168
accommodation 42
accountability 150–3
actions, 182–3
Activating Participation: Parents and Teachers Working Towards Partnership (Crozier, G. and Reay, D.) 161, 258
active engagement 108*f*, 118–19
active learning, time spent in 241–2
Activist Teaching Profession, The (Sachs, J.) 103, 551, 573
activities 314–15, 320, 323, 335
Acts of Meaning (Bruner, J.) 75
Adler, A. 169
adolescence 26, 27
adults, working with 253–5
affective development 39
affordances 230–1
AfL (assessment for learning). *See* assessment for learning
age 171, 498–9
age groups 249
agency 49, 353
AiFL (Assessment is for Learning) 412*f*
Aims-based Curriculum. The Significance of Human Flourishing for Schools, An (Reiss, M. and White, J.) 301
Alderson, P. 574
Alexander, R. 115, 119, 128, 134, 160, 301, 356, 365, 377, 378–9, 398, 399, 417

Allal, L. 118–19
Aloisi, C. 133
Alternative Approach to Teaching and the Curriculum, An (Egan, K.) 342
Alwafi, E. 545–6
analysis 317*f*
analytical skills 93
Anderson, P.M. 365
Andrew-Power, K. 258
Anning, M. 389
application 317*f*
APU (Assessment Performance Unit) 449
Archer, M. 573
'area based curriculum' 125, 312, 524
ARG (Assessment Reform Group) 116, 428–9, 432, 437, 478
Arizpe, E. 399
Arnold, M. 559
Arshad, R. 504
Art of Interactive teaching. Listening, Responding, Questioning, The (Wassermann, S.) 365
arts, the 279
ASPE (Association for the Study of Primary Education) 542, 566, 572
assertion 207
assertive strategies 207–8
Assessing Children's Learning (Drummond, M.) 432
assessment 83–4, 151, 171, 200, 316, 325–6, 332, 333–4, *see also* assessment for learning
    authenticity 519*f*, 527
    Bernstein, B. 484, 489
    concepts 519*f*, 522, 524, 527, 529
    congruence 519*f*, 522
    consequence 519*f*, 527
    data 445–8
    dependability 460, 519*f*, 524

622 Index

development 519*f*
evidence gathering 464
expectations 519*f*
feeding back 519*f*
formative 430, 462
for improvement and accountability 444–8
inclusion 519*f*
inferences from 456
Phonics Screening Check 117, 460–1
Reception baseline 461
reliability 459, 460
social differentiation 488–9
social impacts 457
social processes 462
statutory 460–1
summative. *See* summative assessment
teachers' judgement 458
transfer and transition 471–2
trusting 455–63
types 455
validity 456–8, 460, 519*f*
Assessment and Learning (Gardner, J.) 432
'Assessment and the logic of instructional practice in Secondary
    3 English and Mathematics classes in Singapore' (Hogan,
    D., Chan, M., Rahim, R., Kwek, D., Aye, K. M., Loo,
    S. C., Sheng, Y. and Luo, W.) 133
assessment for learning (AfL) 16, 108*f*, 115–17, 406–7, 403–38
    see also assessment
    adjusting teaching and learning 425–8
    affirming 428–30
    autonomous learning 407–8
    in the classroom 412–28
    definitions 428–30
    feedback 419–21
    focusing on learning 407, 408
    formative 430, 462
    goal sharing 414–16
    International Education Assessment Network 409–10
    James, M. 410
    learning and teaching 407–11
    'Learning Stories' approach to 409
    making learning explicit 407
    Peacock, A. 465
    PEER model 421, 423*f*–4
    peer-assessment 422
    Phonics Screening Check 117, 460–1
    quality identifying 414–16
    questioning and dialogue 416–19
    Reception baseline 461
    research 412, 437–8
    self-assessment 421, 422
Assessment for Learning: Beyond the Black Box (ARG) 428,
    432
Assessment for Learning: Putting It into Practice (Black,
    P., Harrison, C., Lee, C., Marshall, B. and Wiliam, D.)
    432
Assessment for Learning without Limits (Peacock, A.) 465

*Assessment in Schools: Fit for Purpose? A Commentary by the
    Teaching and Learning Research Programme* (Mansell,
    W. and James, M. with ARG) 478
Assessment is for Learning (AiFL) 412*f*
Assessment Literacy for Wise Decisions (Swaffield, S. and
    Dudley, P.) 478
Assessment Performance Unit (APU) 449
Assessment Reform Group (ARG) 116, 428–9, 432, 437, 478
Assessment: Social Practice and Social Product (Filer, A.)
    479
assimilation 42
assisted performance theory 66
Association for Science Education 279
Association for the Professional Development of Early Years
    Educators (TACTYC) 572
Association for the Study of Primary Education (ASPE) 542,
    566, 572
Association of Teachers and Lecturers (ATL) 566
ATL (Association of Teachers and Lecturers) 566
attainment data 446
attainment groups 250, 487–8
attention, gaining 208–9
attitudes 275, 282–4
Aubrey, C. 279
Australia 128
Ausubel, D. 113, 328
authentic questions 376–7
authority 189–90
    establishing 201–8
Authority, Education and Emancipation (Stenhouse, L.) 551,
    573
autonomous learning 407–8
Aye, K. M. 133

Bahnmueller, J. 303
Baines, E. 259
Baird, J. 457
Baker, R.G. 258
Ball, S. 160, 566
Ball, S.J. 552, 574
Barrett, L. 258
Barrett, P. 258
Barrs, M. 390
Bartlett, J. 342
Bartlett, L. 258
Bartlett, S. 161
basic interpersonal communicative skills (BICS) 395
basic skills 280
Bates, J. 161
Baumfield, V, 301
Bearne, E. 400
Beauchamp, G. 259
BECERA (British Early Childhood Education Research
    Association) 572
Becker, H.S. 462
Beginning Teachers' Learning: Making Experience Count (Burn,
    K., Hagger, H. and Mutton, T.) 33

reflectiveteaching.co.uk

behaviour 52, 487
  expectations 202
behaviour intervention toolkit 220–1, 227–8
behaviour interventions 227–8
behaviour management 196–7, 223
  authority, establishing 201–8
  behaviour cycles 184*f*–6, 218–23
  classroom behaviour 197–201
  classroom episodes, managing 212–18
  engagement skills 208–12, 218–20
behaviour progression 200–1
behavioural direction 204
behaviourism 39–41*f*, 48*f*
Behaviour2Learn YouTube channel 224
Beishuizen, J. 359
beliefs 11
Benavides, F. 133
Benn, M. 160
Bennett, T. 199, 201, 225
BERA (British Educational Research Association) 84, 96, 126,
  144, 461
BERA/SAGE Handbook of Educational Research, The (Wyse, D.,
  Selwyn, N., Smith E. and Suter, L.) 103
Bereiter, C. 391–2
Berger, P. L. 560
Berlak, A. 81–2, 102, 560
Berlak, H. 81–2, 102, 560
Berlin Olympics, The (Cross, V.) 386
Berliner, D. 258, 514, 515
Bernstein, B. 484–5, 489
Berry, J. 565
Best Practice Syntheses 128
Beverage, M. 399
BICS (basic interpersonal communicative skills) 395
bilingualism 395–6
biology 51
Black, P. 76, 412, 432
Black-Hawkins, K. 103
black history 276
Blake, A. 5–6, 12
Blakemore, C. 52
Blanchard, J. 433
Blatchford, P. 254–5, 259
blocking 207
Bloom, B.S. 323*f*–4, 375
Blundell, D. 161
Blyth, A. 278
Bolster, A. 95
Bonell, C. 192
Bourdieu, P. 148, 160
Bowe, R. 566
Bowles, S. 560
Bradbury, A. 448, 474–5
brain, the 51–2 *see also* neuroscience
brain-based learning 52
brain-compatible classrooms 52
Bransford, J.D. 51–2, 75, 133, 257

Braun, A. 552, 574
Breaking the Link between Disadvantage and Low Attainment
  (DCSF) 160
Brindley, S. 103
Bringing Knowledge Back In (Young, M.) 301
British Academy, The and Royal Society, The (RS & BA) 84,
  126, 144
British Early Childhood Education Research Association
  (BECERA) 572
British Educational Research Association (BERA) 84, 96, 126,
  144, 461
Britton, J. 372
Britzman, D. 352–3
Broadfoot, P. 431, 478
Bronfenbrenner, U. 231–2*f*, 258
Brophy, J. 133
Brown, A.L. 75
Brown-Jeffy, S. 352
Bruner, J.S. 74, 75, 114, 289, 302, 352, 359–60, 365
'Building Learning Power' 66
Building Learning Power: Helping Young People Become Better
  Learners (Claxton, G.) 75
built environment of schools toolkit 260
Bullock, A. 373, 395, 398
bullying 20
Burn, K. 33
Burns, M. 341
Burton, D. 161
Butt, G. 478

CACE (Central Advisory Council for Education) 43, 302
Calhoun, E. 365
CALP (cognitive and academic language proficiency) 395
Cambridge Handbook of Expertise and Expert Performance, The
  (Ericsson, K.A., Charness, N., Feltovich, P. and Hoffman,
  R.R.) 535
Cambridge Handbook of the Learning Sciences, The (Sawyer,
  R.K.) 134
Cambridge Primary Review (CPR) 134, 566–7
Campaign for Evidence-Based Education (CEBE) 144
Campaign for the Advancement of State Education (CASE) 566
Can We Teach Children to be Good? Basic Issues in Moral,
  Personal and Social Education (Straughan, R.) 226
capitalism 276
carers 153–5
Carmichael, P. 76, 432
Carr, M. 433
Carroll, C. 192
Carter, C. 33
Cartmell, D.M. 74
CASE (Campaign for the Advancement of State Education) 566
Cassen, R. 133
CCEA (Council for the Curriculum Examinations and
  Assessment) 275
CCT (Chartered College of Teaching) 84, 131, 152, 541, 562,
  571, 572
CEBE (Campaign for Evidence-Based Education) 144

624   Index

Central Advisory Council for Education (CACE) 43, 302
CfE (*Curriculum for Excellence*)144, 275, 281*f,* 288–9, 408, 413, 559
Chambers, M. 302
Chan, M. 133
Changing Life Chances (Richardson, R.) 5
Changing Schools: Alternative Ways to Make a World of Difference (Wrigley, J., Thompson, P. and Lingard, R.) 573
Chaplain, R. 192, 200–1, 225
character education 25
Charness, N. 535
Chartered College of Teaching (CCT) 84, 131, 152, 541, 562, 571, 572
Child Poverty Action Group (CPAG) 505
childhood 26
children 26, 498–9 *see also* pupils
     body and brain, mind and behaviour 51–2
     boundaries 175
     categories 171
     conceptions of 409
     development 49–51
     health 49–51, 307, 499, 501, 509
     influences 162
     literature 385–9
     mental development 42
     mental health 49–50, 307, 501, 509, 563
     opportunity 148, 162
     peer relationships 61–2, 173, 200, 233, 489–92
     rights 120, 525
     social justice 5
     wellbeing 49–51
Children and their Primary Schools (CACE) 43, 302
Children, Power and Schooling. The Social Structuring of Childhood in the Primary School (Devine, D.) 33
Children Reading Pictures (Styles, M. and Arizpe, E.) 399
Children, Their World, Their Education. Final Report and Recommendations of the Cambridge Primary Review (Alexander, R.) 134, 160, 301
Children's Experiences of Classrooms: Talking about Being Pupils in the Classroom (Hargreaves, E.) 505
Children's Reading Choices survey 385
Christie, P. 133
civic responsibility 554
Clarke, A. 192
Clarke, S. 415, 433
class sizes 149
class/subject details 314
Classroom Behaviour: A Practical Guide to Effective Teaching, Behaviour Management and Colleague Support (Rogers, B.) 225
Classroom Dilemmas: Solutions for Everyday Problems (Kimbrough, K.) 102
'Classroom organization and management' (Doyle, W.) 225
classroom processes 518*f*–19*f,* 526–8
classroom relationships 164–5, 172–7
     classroom climate, enhancing 165–72

     fairness 177
     positive 172–3
     relationship skills 174
     rules and routines 175–6
     social and emotional learning 174
classroom sessions
     beginnings 213–14
     development 214
     endings 215–16
     transitions 214–15
     unexpected, the 216–18
classrooms *see also* spaces
     acoustics 235
     activities 335
     assessment 200
     assessment for learning in 412–28
     authority 189–90, 201–8
     behaviour. *See* behaviour management
     class sizes 149
     climate 165–72
     communication 373–4
     crises 217
     curriculum 199
     dilemmas/challenges 81–3, 85, 220–3
     displays 234, 235
     engagement 208–12, 218–20
     environment 199–200, 234–5
     group work 171, 183, 248–52, 325, 357–9, 368, 370, 380, 405, 487–8, 489–90, 508
     inclusivity 170–2
     individual work 25
     interaction categorisations 356–7
     layouts 237–9
     learning, organising for 234–42
     light 235
     My Classroom Inventory 167–8
     organisation 23–4, 43
     parental involvement 253–4
     pedagogy 200
     positive behaviour, environment for 199–200
     practices 32, 48*f*
     processes 518*f*–19*f,* 526–8
     relationships 164–77, 200
     resources 235–7, 326
     sessions 213–18
     social differentiation 484–9
     society 563–6
     survival 154, 156
     ventilation 235
     whole class teaching 247–8
Classrooms as Learning Communities (Watkins, C.) 192
Claxton, G. 75, 282–3*f,* 302
Clever Classrooms. Summary Report of the HEAD Project (Barrett, P., Zhang, Y., Davies, F. and Barrett, L.) 258
Cliff Hodges, G. 400
Close to Practice Research Project (BERA) 96, 126
closed questions 418

reflectiveteaching.co.uk

Cocking, R.R. 75, 257
Code of Values and Professional Practice (GTC NI) 554
Coe, R. 133
cognition 28
    stages of 42
Cognition and Curriculum Reconsidered (Eisner, E.) 342
cognitive and academic language proficiency (CALP) 395
cognitive challenge 317
cognitive development 39
Cognitive Development: The Learning Brain (Goswami, U.) 75
cognitive load 59
    strategies for 58
cognitive neuroscience 58
cognitive psychology 58
cognitive science 58–60
cognitive styles 64
Coleman, J.S. 560
Coles, A. 5
collaboration 88, 96, 97–99, 369
collaborative groups 248–9
collaborative learning toolkit 369
collaborative mediation 100
colleagues 13
    learning with 97–99
collection curriculum 290–1
Collins, F. 399
commands 207–8
Commentary on Assessment (TLRP) 524
Common Knowledge: The Development of Understanding in Classrooms (Edwards, D. and Mercer, N.) 399
Common Transfer File 471
communication 371–402 *see also* talk
    characteristics of classroom 373–4
    knowledge about language for 393–6
    reading 382–9
    rules 379–80
    speaking and listening 374–82
    writing 389–92
communities 61, 125, 233–4, 312, 524, 559
    culture 145
communities of practice 97, 146
Communities of Practice: Learning. Meaning and Identity (Wenger, E.) 103
Compassionate Classroom: Relationship Based Teaching and Learning, The (Hart, S. and Hodson, V.K.) 191
Complete Guide to Lesson Planning and Preparation, The (Haynes, A.) 341
comprehension 317*f*
comprehensive school system 143
concepts 275, 278–9, 293–4
concrete operations development stage 42
confidence 169–70
Confident Teacher. Developing Successful Habits of Mind, Body and Pedagogy, The (Quigley, A.) 32
conformity 182
Conner, C. 76, 432
Connolly, P. 506

consistency 212
conspirational mediation 100
Constitution of the United Kingdom: A Contextual Analysis (Leyland, P.) 552, 574
constraints 230–1
construct validity 456
constructionism 42
constructivism 42–4*f*, 48*f*
Consulting Pupils about Teaching and Learning (TLRP) 36, 119–20
Conteh, J. 400
content knowledge 292–3, 334
contexts 139–62
    people and agency 153–8
    social contexts 141–53
contextual value-added data 46
continuing professional development (CPD) 544–5 *see also* professional learning
continuous provision 11
Convention on the Rights of the Child (CRC) (UN) 120, 525, 557
Cooper, H. 352
Core Knowledge Curriculum 276–7, 317
core subjects 288, 310
Cork, V. 390
corporal punishment 221
Corsaro, W.A. 258
Coser, L.A. 560
Council for the Curriculum Examinations and Assessment (CCEA) 275
COVID-19 global pandemic 122, 147, 243, 285, 317, 486, 545–6
Cox, B. 393
CPAG (Child Poverty Action Group) 505
CPD (continuing professional development) 544–5 *see also* professional learning
CPR (Cambridge Primary Review) 134, 566–7
Craft, A. 504
CRC (Convention on the Rights of the Child) (UN) 120, 525, 557
Creating a Culture: How School Leaders Can Optimise Behaviour (DfE) 226
Creating the Conditions for Teaching and Learning (Hopkins, D., Harris, A., Singleton, C. and Watts, R.) 258
Creating the Curriculum (Wyse, D., Baumfield, V., Egan, D., Hayward, D., Mulme, M., Menter, I., Gallagher, C., Leitch, R., Livingston, K. and Lingard, R.) 301
Creative Learning Without Limits (Swann, M., Peacock, A., Hart, S. and Drummond, M-J.) 465, 506
creative mediation 89, 100
creative talk 381–2
credit approach 38
Cremin, T. 399, 400
criterion referencing 453, 454, 455
Critical Essays on Major Curriculum Theorists (Scott, D.) 301
critical pedagogy 351
Critical Pedagogy Primer (Kincheloe, J.L.) 366
Critical Practice in teacher Education: A Study of Professional Learning (Heilbronn, R. and Yandell, J.) 103

reflectiveteaching.co.uk

Crozier, G. 161, 258
Crystal, D. 400
cultural capital 16, 146, 148, 495–6, 559
cultural influences 60–3
    cultural resources and experiences 60
    family and community 61
    language, mediation of 60–1
    learning disposition 61
    media and new technology 62
    peers at school 61–2, 233
    schools 62
Cultural Literacy: What Every American Needs to Know (Hirsch, E.D.) 317
cultural psychology 146
cultural reproduction 558–9
culturally relevant pedagogy 352
culture 45, 51, 52, 145–6
    pupil 19–20, 145, 156
Culture and Pedagogy: International Comparisons in Primary Education (Alexander, R.) 128, 365
Culture of Education, The (Bruner, J.) 365
Cummins, J. 395
Cunningham, B. 573
Cunningham, P. 574
curricula 90, 111–12, 125, 150, 267–303 *see also* curriculum planning *and* national curricula
    aims and values 271–4
    balanced 284–5, 286–7, 291, 518*f*
    Bernstein, B. 484, 489
    breadth 291, 292, 518*f*, 522
    capitalism 276
    coherence 518*f*
    collection 290–1
    concepts 518*f*, 522, 524, 526–7, 529
    connection 518*f*, 524
    core knowledge 276–7
    Core Knowledge Curriculum 276–7, 317
    core subjects 288, 310
    COVID-19 global pandemic 285, 317
    decolonising 276
    differentiation 518*f*
    effectiveness 518*f*, 529
    England 65, 89, 112, 151, 271–2, 273*f*, 274, 275, 276–7, 281, 289, 291
    experienced 269
    foundation subjects 288, 310
    geography 278
    hidden 269, 282
    history 276
    implementation. *See* planning
    integrated 291
    knowledge, development and 270–1
    learning, elements of 274–85
    legislation 271
    Northern Ireland 275, 282, 288
    official 268–9
    Ofsted 526–7

PACE project 357, 451, 452*f*, 564
    personalisation 518*f*
    politics 276
    principles for curriculum provision 270–4
    progression 518*f*
    reading across 386–7
    relationships 178–81
    relevance 518*f*, 526–7
    Republic of Ireland 144
    school 151, 288
    Scotland 275, 281, 288–9, 316, 317
    social differentiation 485–6, 489
    spiral 289
    subject knowledge for teachers 292–8
    subject-based 290–1
    subjects 277, 278, 279
    UK structures 287–8
    Wales 144, 288, 307, 312
    washback 444, 445
curricular knowledge 292, 294–5
curriculum activity, time available for 239–41
Curriculum from 5 to 16, The (HMI) 274, 301, 340
Curriculum for Excellence (CfE)144, 275, 281*f*, 288–9, 408, 413, 559
Curriculum for Wales 144, 288, 307, 312, 445
curriculum planning 305–44
    breadth and balance 311
    children's needs, meeting 331–3
    coherence 312–13
    connection 311–12
    Core Knowledge Curriculum 317
    COVID-19 global pandemic 317
    differentiation 327–31
    early years – primary transition 310
    evaluation 333–9
    lesson plans 320–7
    lesson studies 336–9
    long-term 308–13
    medium-term 313–20
    personalised learning 327, 331–3, 344
    progress for all 328–31
    progression 316–18
    relevance 319–20
    schemes of work 313–15
    school curriculum 307–8
    short-term 320–333
    social differentiation 485
    statutory requirements 310
    study programmes 308–10
Cuthbert, A.S. 301

D-Day (Perrett, B.) 386
Dale, R. 121–2
Damasio, A. 39, 166
Damon, W. 173
Daring to Be a Teacher (Richardson, R.) 6, 32
Darling-Hammond, L. 127, 133

data 93, 445–8
  objective 93
  performance 83–4, 93
  subjective 93
Davies, F. 258
Day, C. 12, 13, 29–30, 33, 161
De Nisi, A. 419
Deakin Creak, R. 451
Dean, J. 259
declarative knowledge 280
Deconstructing Special Education and Constructing Inclusion (Thomas, G. and Loxley, A.) 507
Deighton, J. 192
democracy 569–71
Democracy and Education: An Introduction to the Philosophy of Education (Dewey, J.) 552, 574
democratic professionalism 540
Department for Education (DfE) 7–8
  bullying guidance 20
  COVID-19 global pandemic 285
  Creating a Culture: How School Leaders Can Optimise Behaviour 226
  Early Career Framework 14, 112, 127, 155, 329, 548
Department for Education and Science (DfES) 226
Designing and Teaching Learning Goals and Objectives (Marzano, R.J.) 134
Developing Professional Knowledge and Competence (Eraut, M.) 535
Developing Teacher Assessment (Gardner, J., Harlen, W., Hayward, L. and Stobart G. with Montgomery, M.) 478
Developing Teacher Expertise: Exploring Key Issues in Primary Practice (Sangster, M.) 535
Developing the Expertise of Primary and Elementary Classroom Teachers. Professional Learning for a Changing World (Eaude, T.) 33
development 270–1
Development of Writing Abilities (11–18), The (Britton, J. et al.) 372
Devine, D. 33
devolution 144
Devolution in the United Kingdom (Mitchell, J.) 160
Dewey, J. 87–8, 91, 94, 102–3, 552, 574
DfE (Department for Education), England. *See* Department for Education, England
DfES (Department for Education and Science) 226
diagnostic questions 377
Dialogic Education. Mastering Core Concepts through Thinking Together (Phillipson, N. and Wegerif, R.) 365, 399
dialogic learning 378–9
dialogic talk. *See* talk
dialogic teaching 115, 119, 356–7, 378–9, 398, 417
dialogue 416–19
Dialogue and the Development of Children's Thinking (Mercer, N. and Littleton, K.) 365, 399
diet 50
differentiation 19, 327–31
digital technology toolkit 261
Dilemmas of Schooling (Berlak, A. and Berlak, H.) 102

Dillow, C. 259
Dimensions of Expertise: A Conceptual Exploration of Vocational Knowledge (Winch, C.) 535
direct questions 208
directed 'choices' 208
disability 499–500
disadvantage 188
discipline 169, 170
Discipline and Group Management in Classrooms (Kounin, J.S.) 225
Discipline in Schools, Report of the Committee of Enquiry chaired by Lord Elton (Department for Education and Science) 226
disengagement 312
Displays for Learning (Andrew-Power, K. and Gormley, C.) 258
distraction 207
district authorities 472–3
diversity 144–5, 146, 276
  linguistic 395–6, 400
  social differentiation 494–501
Dixon, A. 33, 365, 506
Dombey, H. 399
Donaldson, M. 43
Don't Change the Light Bulbs: A Compendium of Expertise from the UK's Most Switched-on Educators (Jones, R.) 535
Downs, J. 160
Doyle, W. 225
drama 381–2
Drawing the Future project 29
Drummond, M-J. 33, 76, 365, 409, 428, 432, 456, 506
Drury, R. 399
dual coding 58
Duckworth, K. 505
Dudley, P. 76, 342, 432, 478
Dumont, H. 133
Duran, D. 365
Dweck, C.S. 55, 74, 75, 118
Dyer, R. 424

EAL Teaching Boo. Promoting Success for Multilingual Learners (Conteh, J.) 400
Early Career Framework 14, 112, 127, 155, 329, 548
Early Childhood Matters. Evidence from the Effective Pre-school and Primary Education Project (Sylva, K., Melhuish, E., Sammons, P., Siraj-Blatchford, I. and Taggart, B.) 134
Eaude, T. 33, 535
Ecological Psychology: Concepts and Methods of Studying the Environment of Human Behaviour (Baker, R.G.) 258
ecological systems theory 231–2f
Ecology of Human Development: Experiments by Nature and Design (Bronfenbrenner, U.) 258
Economic and Social Research Council 144
economic capital 148
economy, the 140–1, 147, 473, 558
Educating the Whole Child: Cross-curricular Skills, Themes and Dimensions (Siraj-Blatchford, I. and Siraj-Blatchford, J.) 341

education 270
  society and 555–61
Education Act (1944) 555
Education Act (1977) 221
Education Act (2022) 271
Education and Constructions of Childhood (Blundell, D.) 161
Education and the Family: Passing Success Across the Generations (Feinstein, L. Duckworth, K. and Sabates, R.) 505
'Education at a Glance' (OECD) 547
Education by Numbers: The Tyranny of Testing (Mansell, W.) 478
Education Endowment Foundation (EEF) 144, 196 *see also* EEF toolkit
  cognitive science review 58
  social and emotional learning 174
  website 134
Education Endowment Foundation (EEF) toolkit. *See* EEF toolkit
Education, Equality and Social Cohesion: A Comparative Analysis (Green, A., Preston, J. and Janmaat, J.G.) 160
education for life 108*f*, 109–11
Education Forward: Moving Schools into the Future (Price, D.) 302
Education International 85
Education on the Web: A Tool-kit to Help You Search Effectively for Information on Education (Houghton, E.) 535
education policy 89–90, 125–7, 141, 142–4, 150, 473–5, 546–50, 564, 565–71, 572 *see also* policy frameworks
Education Policy and Social Class (Ball, S.) 160
Education Reform: A Critical and Post-Structural Approach (Ball, S.J.) 552, 574
Education Reform Act (1988) 522
Education, Schooling and Learning for Life: How Meaning and Opportunity Build from Everyday Relationships (Pollard, A and Filer, A.) 191
Education Scotland 151, 541
education systems 555–60
Education Workforce Council (EWC) 8–9, 84, 152, 541, 571
educational aims 271–4, 518*f*–19*f*, 520–3
Educational Failure and Working Class White Children in Britain (Evans, G.) 505
Educational Institute of Scotland (EIS) 541, 570
educational principles. *See* principles *and* TLRP principles
Edwards, A. 259
Edwards, D. 399
EEF (Education Endowment Foundation). *See* Education Endowment Foundation
EEF toolkit 84, 106, 517, 561, 562
  behaviour intervention toolkit 220–1, 227–8
  built environment of schools toolkit 260
  collaborative learning toolkit 369
  digital technology toolkit 261
  feedback toolkit 434
  mastery learning toolkit 343
  metacognition toolkit 66, 77, 118
  parental engagement toolkit 135
  peer tutoring toolkit 435

phonics toolkit 367
reading comprehension strategies toolkit 402
setting and streaming toolkit 508
small group teaching and learning toolkit 368
social and emotional learning toolkit 193
speaking and listening activities toolkit 401
Teaching and Learning Toolkit 106, 107
teaching assistants, effective deployment of toolkit 262
Effective Teaching: Evidence and Practice (Muijs, D. and Reynolds, D.) 133, 259, 365
Effective Teaching in Schools: Theory and Practice (Kyriacou, C.) 365
Egan, D. 301
Egan, K. 342
EIS (Educational Institute of Scotland) 541, 570
Eisner, E. 342
Elliot, D. 103
Elliot, G. 278
Elton Report 224, 226
Embedded Formative Assessment (Wiliam, D.) 433
emotion 13, 28, 65–6, 115, 526 *see also* SEL
emotional capital 148, 157
emotional intelligence 526
emotional learning 193
emotional security 166–9
empathy 168
engagement 195–228, 519*f*, 527 *see also* behaviour management
  reading 384–6
  skills for 208–12
  time, use of 239–42
England 144, 149, 151, 152, 559
  assessment 468
  Chartered College of Teaching 84, 131, 152, 541, 562, 571, 572
  Common Transfer File 471
  curriculum 65, 89, 112, 151, 271–2, 273*f*, 274, 275, 276–7, 281, 286, 289, 291, 349
  Department for Education 7–8, 20, 14, 155, 226, 285
  Early Career Framework (DfE) 14, 112, 155, 548
  General Teaching Council 152, 541, 571
  learning outcomes 443
  National Education Union 571
  pedagogy 350–1
  professional learning 548
  teachers 154, 155
  Teachers Standards 548
English Language: A Guided Tour of the Language, The (Crystal, D.) 400
Enhancing Relationships Between Children and Teachers (Pianta, R.C.) 192
Enhancing Self-esteem in the Classroom (Lawrence, D.) 192
enrichment task demands 324
'Ensuring a Settled and Focused Class' (Rogers, B.) 224
entity theory (of intelligence) 55
Entwistle, N. 279
environmental sustainability 141, 557, 559
Equality Act (2010) 495

reflectiveteaching.co.uk

Equality Trust 505
equilibration 42
equity 327–33
Eraut, M. 112, 535
Ercikan, K. 133
Ericsson, K.A. 535
Ernest, P. 290
Essays on Pedagogy (Alexander, R.) 365
Essential Guide to Understanding Special Educational Needs, The (Thompson, J.) 507
established knowledge 270
ethnicity 146, 276, 496–7, 561–2
Ethnicity, Race and Education (Walters, S.) 506
EuroHealthNet 484
evaluation 317*f*, 333–9
evaluative skills 93
Evans, G. 505
Evans, W. 225
evaporated time 239
Every Child Matters agenda 120, 127
evidence gathering and evaluating 88, 92–4
evidence-informed policy 143–4
evidence-informed practice 83–6, 516*f*
evidence-informed principles 28, 106–8
Evidence-Policy and Practice in Education 84
EWC (Education Workforce Council) 8–9, 84, 152, 541, 571
Ewing, R. 12 and Manuel, J. 12
examinations 404
exercise 50
experienced curriculum 269
explicit learning 407
exploratory talk 380
Exploring Professionalism (Cunningham, B.) 573
Exploring Talk in School (Mercer, N. and Hodgkinson, S.) 259
extended professionalism 540, 541
extraneous cognitive load 59
extrinsic motivation 5

Facer, K. 259
fairness 177, 184, 221–2
faith 563–4
families 61, 148, 162
Farrar, M. 166, 192
feedback 84, 115, 392, 419–21, 487, 488–9
feedback toolkit 434
Feinstein, L. 28, 34, 134, 501–2, 505
Feltovich, P. 535
Feminism and 'The Schooling Scandal' (Skelton, C. and Francis, B.) 506
Filer, A. 49, 65, 433, 462, 479, 492–4
Finland 128
Finnish Lessons: What Can the World Learn from Educational Change in Finland? (Sahlberg, P.) 133
Fisher, D.L. 167
Fisher, R. 76
fixed mindset 55, 410, 411*f*
Fletcher-Wood, H. 534

Flook, J. 535
Florian, L. 33
flow 212–18
folk pedagogy 352
formal learning environments 232
formal operations development stage 42
formative assessment 430, 462 *see also* assessment for learning
Formative Assessment in Action: Weaving the Elements Together (Clarke, S.) 433
Formative Assessment in the Secondary Classroom (Clarke, S.) 433
Formative Assessment project (King's Medway Oxfordshire) 412, 425
foundation subjects 288, 310
Fox, A. 76, 432
Framework for Innovative Thinking (Hart, S.) 24
framework of meaningfulness 65
framing 209–10
Frances, J. 499
Francis, B. 506
Fraser, B.J. 167
Fray, L. 5
Frederikson, J.R. 415
free schools 125
free-writing books 361, 362
Freedom to Learn (Rogers, C.) 192
freeze-frame 382
Freire, P. 351, 556, 573
friendship groups 251
Frost, D. 76, 432
Furlong, J. 12

Gallagher, C. 301
Gallard, D. 74
Gallimore, R. 66
Galton, M. 196, 357, 358, 377, 472
Gardner, J. 432, 478
gender 171, 491, 497, 561
General Teaching Council England (GTC E) 152, 541, 571
General Teaching Council Northern Ireland (GTC NI) 9, 84, 541, 554, 571
General Teaching Council Scotland (GTC S) 8, 84–5, 151, 54, 571, 572
General Teaching Council Wales (GTC W) 152, 541, 571
genes 51
genuineness 169
geography 278
germane cognitive load 59
Gibson, E.J. 230
Gilbert, I. 225
Gilchrist, G. 103
Gilmore, C. 302
Gill, S. 191
Gillborn, D. 506
Gintis, H. 560
Girls, Boys and Junior Sexualities. Exploring Children's Gender and Sexual Relations in the Primary School (Renold, E.) 506

reflectiveteaching.co.uk

Index

Glaser, R. 514–15
goals 425–6, 555
    sharing 414–16
Gold, A. 566
Goldstein, H. 446–7
Good, T. 133
Goodman Turkanis, C. 258
Gore, J. 5
Gormley, C. 258
Gove, M. 109–10, 143
Goswami, U. 75
governing bodies 125, 307, 472–3
governments 96
    control 566, 567
    education policy 89–90, 125–7, 141, 142–4, 150, 473–5, 546–50, 564, 565–71, 572
    health schemes 50
    measuring educational outcomes 444, 448, 475
grammar 274, 393–4
grammar schools 142, 144
Gray, J. 472
Green, A. 160
Griffiths, A. 341
Gross, J. 192, 399
group work 171, 183, 248–52, 325, 357–9, 368, 370, 380, 405, 487–8, 489–90, 508
growth mindset 55, 408, 410–11*f*
GTC E (General Teaching Council England) 152, 541, 571
GTC NI (General Teaching Council Northern Ireland) 9, 84, 541, 554, 571
GTC S (General Teaching Council Scotland) 8, 84–5, 151, 54, 571, 572
GTC W (General Teaching Council Wales) 152, 541, 571
Gu, Q. 12, 29–30, 33, 161
Guide to Early Years and Primary Teaching, A (Wyse, D. and Rogers, S.) 5
Guide to Practitioner Research in Education, A (Menter, I., Elliot, D., Hall, J., Hulme, M., Lewin, J. and Lowden, K.) 103

Hacking School Discipline: 9 Ways to Create a Culture of Empathy and Responsibility Using Restorative Justice (Maynard, N. and Weinstein, B.) 225
Hagger, H. 33
Hall, J. 103
Hallam, S. 259, 506
Halpin, D. 95
Hargreaves, A. 13
Hargreaves, E. 505
Harlen, W. 451, 478
Harnessing Educational Research (RS & BA) 126, 144
Harris, A. 258
Harrison, C. 399, 432
Hart, S. 24, 33, 55, 191, 365, 506
Hatcher, R. 506
Hattie, J. 106, 112, 115, 118, 128–9, 134, 341, 365
Hawkins, L. 535
Haydn, T. 226

Hayes, D. 133
Haynes, A. 341
Hayward, L. 414, 467, 478
Hayward, D. 301
health 49–51, 307, 499, 501, 509
Heilbronn, R. 103
helplessness 55, 56*f*
Helsby, G. 551, 573
Her Majesty's Inspectorate (HMI) 274. 282, 301, 340
Heritage, M. 414
hidden curriculum 269, 282
Hidden Lives of Learners (Nuthall G.) 76
hierarchy of needs 21–2*f*
Higgins, S. 133
higher-order questions 375
Hightown Grammar: The School as a Social System (Lacey, C.) 505
Hirsch, E.D. 276–7, 289, 317
history 276, 386
HMI (Her Majesty's Inspectorate) 274. 282, 301, 340
Hodgkinson, S. 259
Hodson, V.K. 191
Hoffman, R.R. 535
Hogan, D. 112, 116–17, 128, 133
Hogden, J. 418
Holding Together: Equalities, Difference and Cohesion (Richardson, R.) 504
Holleran, G. 225
Hollindale, P. 385
Holmes, E. 140
Holt, J. 196, 526
home influences 233 *see also* parents and carers
Home–School Knowledge Exchange project 20–1, 120–1, 136
Hong Kong 128
Honour, L. 76, 432
Hopkins, D. 258
hot-seating 382
Houghton, E. 535
How Children Fail (Holt, J.) 526
How Children Learn at Home (Thomas, A. and Pattison, H.) 76
How Children Think and Learn: The Social Contexts of Cognitive Development (Wood, D.) 74
How Do Expert Primary Classteachers Really Work? A Critical Guide for Teachers, Headteachers and Teacher Educators (Eaude, T.) 535
How People Learn: Brain, Mind, Experience and School (Bransford, J.D., Brown, A.L. and Cocking, R.R.) 75, 127, 133, 257
'How research findings can be used to inform educational practice and what can go wrong: The Ofsted Mathematics Research Review 202' (Gilmore, C., Trundley, R., Bahnmueller, J. and Xenidou-Dervou, I.) 303
How Schools Do Policy: Policy Enactments in Secondary School (Ball, S.J., Maguire, M. and Braun, A.) 552, 574
How to Change 5000 Schools (Levin, B.) 133
How We Think: A Restatement of the Relation of Reflective Thinking to the Educative Process (Dewey, J.) 103

reflectiveteaching.co.uk

Hoyle, E. 540, 551, 573
Huberman, M. 12, 29, 33
Hudson-Sharp, N. 506
Hughes, M. 43, 72, 136
Hulme, M. 103
human capital theory 558
Human-Centred Education. A Practical Handbook and Guide (Gill, S. and Thomson, G.) 191
Human Development in Context : The Study of Risk and Resilience (Schoon, I.) 34
human rights 556–7
Hunter, R. 341
Hurry, J. 192
Hutton, P. 224

ICAPE (Independent Commission on Assessment in Primary Education) 479
Ice Trap! Shackleton's Incredible Expedition (Hooper, M. and Robertson, M.P.) 387
ICT. *See* technology
ICT in the Primary School: From Pedagogy to Practice (Beauchamp, G.) 259
idealism 5
Identifying Troublesome Classroom Behaviour (Merrett, F. and Wheldall, K.) 225
Identities and Practices of High Achieving Pupils: Negotiating Achievement and Peer Cultures (Francis, B., Skelton, C. and Read, B.) 506
identity 3–36
  language 395
  learning and identity model 492–4
  minority groups 559
  national 558–9
  personality 64
  pupils 15–25, 65, 146, 156, 234
  pupils, development and career 26–9
  social differentiation 492–4
  teachers 11–15
  teachers, becoming 5–6
  teachers, development and career 29–30
  values informing practice 6–7
ideology 142–5
'IDSR (School Inspection Data Summary) Report Guide' 84
IEAN (International Education Assessment Network) 409–10, 442, 463–5
'imaginative professional, The' (Power, S.) 34, 563
Immordino-Yang, M.H. 39, 166
Improving Behaviour in Schools, A Guidance Report (EEF) 196
Improving Children's Life Chances (Tucker, J.) 507
Improving Learning How to Learn: Classrooms, Schools and Networks (James, M., McCormick, R., Black, P., Carmichael, P., Drummond, M-J., Fox, A., MacBeath, J., Marshall, B., Pedder, D., Procter, R., Swaffield, S., Swann, J. and Wiliam, D.) 76, 432
Improving Learning through Consulting Pupils (Rudduck, J. and McIntyre, D.) 161, 191

Improving Social and Emotional Learning in Primary Schools (van Poortvliet, M., Clarke, A. and Gross, J.) 174, 192
'Improving Teaching' (Fletcher-Wood, H.) 534
Improving Teaching and Learning in Schools (James, M. and Pollard, A.) 132
incidental language 206
inclusion 170–2
incremental task demands 324
incremental theory (of intelligence) 55, 56*f*
Independent Commission on Assessment in Primary Education (ICAPE) 479
individual rights 556–7
individual work 252
individuals 153–8
  society, relationship with 140, 560
inequality 114, 147, 327–33, 483–4, 501, 509, 556
  addressing 561–2
Inequality among Lesbian, Gay, Bisexual and Transgender Groups in the UK: A Review of Evidence (Hudson-Sharp, N. and Metcalf, H.) 506
informal learning 108*f*, 112, 113–14, 120–2
informal learning environments 232–3
Information and Book Learning (Meek, M.) 386
Ingram, J. 192
initiation-response-evaluation (IRE) 376
initiation-response-feedback (IRF) 349, 376
innovative mediation 100
innovative thinking 24
Inquiring in the Classroom. Asking the Questions that Matter about Teaching and Leaning (Mitchell, N. and Pearson, J.) 103
Inside the Black Box: Raising Standards through Classroom Assessment (Black, P. and Wiliam, D.) 432
instructional tasks 112
instructional time 239
integrated curriculum 291
intelligence 53–7
interactive/authoritative talk 357
interactive/dialogic talk 357
Interactive Education project (TLRP) 121
interactive whiteboards (IWBs) 238–9, 243–5, 326
interest groups 250
interleaving 58, 59
international comparisons 84, 128, 448, 473–5, 477, 558
International Education Assessment Network (IEAN) 409–10, 442, 463–5
international knowledge accumulation 127–30*f*
Intersection of International Achievement Testing and Educational Policy, The (Volante, L.) 473–4
interthinking 380
Into the Unknown: How Great Explorers Found Their Way by Land, Sea and Air (Ross, S. and Biesty, S.) 385
intrinsic cognitive load 59
intrinsic motivation 5
Introduction to Assessment, An (Broadfoot, P.) 431, 478
Introduction to Curriculum Research and Development, An (Stenhouse, L.) 102

632   Index

Introduction to Education Studies (Bartlett, S. and Burton, D.)
        161
intuition 95, 96
*Invisible Classroom: Relationships, Neuroscience and
        Mindfulness in School, The* (Olson, K.) 191
ipsative referencing 453, 454–5
IRE (initiation-response-evaluation) 376
Ireson, J. 259, 506
IRF (initiation-response-feedback) 349, 376
Istance, D. 133
IWBs (interactive whiteboards) 238–9, 243–5, 326

Jackson, B. 246, 489–90, 506
Jackson, C. 506
Jackson, P.W. 192
Jacobson, L. 187
James, M. 76, 123, 132, 291, 300, 410, 432, 478
Janmaat, J.G. 160
Japan 336
Jenks, C. 560
Jerrim, J. 385
Jones, R. 535
Joseph Rowntree Foundation 505
journels 302
Joyce, B. 365

Kallick, B. 75, 76
Kane, M. 456, 457
Kavanagh, A.M. 302
Kehily, M.J. 506
Kennedy, A. 543*f*–4
key-person approach 172–3
Kim, M. 379
Kimbrough, K. 102
Kincheloe, J.L. 366
Kluger, A.N. 419
Knight, P. 551, 573
knowing-in-action 88, 95
knowledge 112, 270–1, 274–8
        content 292–3, 334
        core 276–7
        curricular 292, 294–5
        declarative 280
        international knowledge accumulation 127–30*f*
        about language 393–6
        nature of 270
        pedagogic content 292, 293–4, 295, 334
        procedural 280
        subject 270, 279, 292–8, 347
        teacher 95–7*f*, 334
        valued 108*f*, 111–13
knowledge exchange 20
knowledge quartet 296–8
knowledge-telling 392
knowledge-transforming 392
Kounin, J.S. 210, 225
Kress, G. 259, 394

Kutnick, P. 259
Kwek, D. 133
Kyriacou, C. 365

Lacey, C. 505
Lads and Ladettes in School: Gender and a Fear of Failure
        (Jackson, C.) 506
language 60, 346 *see also* communication
        development 373
        discipline, supporting 204–5
        English as an additional 395–6
        grammar 393–4
        knowledge about (for communication) 393–6
        mediation of 60–1
        oral 346, 349
        spoken and written, differences between 393–5
*Language for Life. Report of the Committee of Enquiry into
        Reading and the Use of English, A* (Bullock, A) 373, 395,
        398
Lantz-Andersson, A. 546
Lareau, A. 148
law of effect 39–40
law of exercise 40
Lawrence, D. 192
lay perspective of personality 63–4
Leach, J. 366
LEAF (Learning Explicit Autonomy Focus) 408
league tables 446, 480
learned helplessness 55, 56*f*, 118
learners 110, 427 *see also* pupils
        development 353–5
        learning outcomes 466, 468
        needs of 270, 528
        readiness to learn 27
learning 37–78, 123 *see also* assessment for learning *and*
        learning outcomes
        as 'acquisition' 70–1*f*, 72
        active 241–2
        activities/tasks 320, 323–5
        adjusting 425–8
        affordances for 230–1
        application beyond school 72–3
        assistance in 45–6
        autonomous 407–8
        capacity 500
        challenges 64–5*f*
        classroom organisation for 234–42
        collaborative 369
        concepts 275, 278–9, 293–4
        contexts 518*f*–19*f*, 524–5
        cultural influences 60–3
        curriculum and relationships 178–81
        curriculum for 274–85
        dialogic 378–9
        differences 55–6, 57
        disposition 16, 61
        environments 231–4

reflectiveteaching.co.uk

explicit 407
focusing on 408
helplessness 55, 56*f*
how to learn 66–8
informal 108*f*, 112, 113–14, 120–2
intentions 321, 322–3
key factors 69–70
Lesson Study 67–8
lifelong 26, 28
linear 289–9
malleable 544*f*, 545
mastery 55, 56*f*, 118, 323, 343, 421, 423–4
metacognition 77
metaphors of 70–2
national curricula 289–90
nature, nurture and agency 49–68
objectives 314, 415
over time 463–75
parental engagement 121, 135, 157
as 'participation' 71*f*, 72
personalised 65, 327, 331–3, 344
positive and negative cycles 184*f*–6, 218–23
processes 39–48*f*
progression 316–18, 414, 463–75
pupil perspectives of teachers 181–2
relationships for 178–86
risk, boredom and challenge 64–5*f*
self-regulated 77, 427
social and emotional learning toolkit 193
social differentiation 492–4
spaces. *See* spaces
styles 64
supple learning mind 272, 273*f*
teacher 108*f*, 123–4, 542–6
teacher and pupil actions, 182–3
technology 242–6
transformative 544*f*, 545
transmissive 544*f*, 545
visible 115, 119
wider benefits of 28*f*
Learning Behaviour: Lessons Learned, A Review of Behaviour Standards and Practices in Our Schools (Steer, A.) 226
Learning by Teaching. Evidence-based Strategies to Enhance Learning in the Classroom (Duran, D. and Topping, K.) 365
learning contexts 518*f*–19*f*, 524–5
Learning Curve, The 474
Learning Futures (Facer, K.) 259
learning how to learn 66–8
Learning How to Learn project (TLRP) 116, 125, 407, 408, 412, 432, 436, 450
Learning How to Learn: Tools for Schools (James, M., Black, P., Carmichael, P., Conner, C., Dudley, P., Fox, A., Frost, D., Honour, L., MacBeath, J., McCormick, R., Marshall, B., Pedder, D., Procter, R., Swaffield, S. and Wiliam, D.) 76, 432
Learning Lives project (TLRP) 110–11, 520

learning outcomes 441–80, 518*f*–19*f*, 529–30
assessment for improvement and accountability 444–8
national surveys of system performance 449–53
performance comparison 453–5
summative assessment 463–75
trusting assessments 455–62
Learning Powered School: Pioneering 21st Century Education, The (Claxton, G., Chambers, M., Powell, G. and Lucas, B.) 302
learning processes 39
behaviourism 39–41*f*, 48*f*
constructivism 42–4*f*, 48*f*
social cognition 44–7, 48*f*
'Learning Stories' approach to assessment 409
Learning Stories: Constructing Learner Identities in Early Education (Carr, M. and Lee, W.) 433
Learning Teaching from Teachers – Realizing the Potential of School-Based Teacher Education (Hagger, H. and McIntyre, D.) 33
Learning Through Life: Future Challenges (Feinstein, L., Vorhaus, J. and Sabates, R.) 34, 134
Learning to Write (Kress, G.) 394
Learning Together: Children and Adults in a School Community (Rogoff, B., Goodman Turkanis, C. and Bartlett, L.) 258
Learning Without Limits (Hart, S., Dixon, A., Drummond, M-J. and McIntyre, D.) 33, 365, 465, 506
'Learning without Limits' (Peacock, A.) 32
Leckie, G. 446–7
Lee, C. 432
Lee, W. 433
Leitch, R. 301
lesson phases/structure 320, 322
lesson plans 320–7
adult support 320, 326–7
context and previous assessment information 320, 321
differentiation 327–31
learning activities/tasks 320, 323–5
learning intentions 320, 321–2
lesson phases/structure 320, 322
personalisation 327, 331–3
research lessons 336–9
resources, ICT and safety 320, 326
success criteria 320, 325–6
lesson studies 92, 99, 336–9, 545
creative pedagogy for girls learning mathematics in Reception 180–1
cycle 338*f*
developing mathematical reasoning and verbalisation in Year 3 297–8
differentiated teaching for attainment-based groups in Year 5 330–1
groups 336, 337–9
helping children to develop skills for collaborative learning 250–1
helping children who are 'stuck' to re-engage with their learning 219–20
Japan 336

634 Index

progression with disadvantaged 8-year-olds to 'Talk for Learning' 317–18
research lessons 336–9
shared, critical thinking for learning 67–8
Lesson Study: A Handbook (Dudley, P.) 342
Levin, B. 133
Lewin, J. 103
Lewis, S. 161
Leyland, P. 552, 574
LGBTQ experiences 562
liberal values 142
life chances 32, 501–2
Life Chances, Education and Social Movements (Munro, L.) 507
Life in Classrooms (Jackson, P.W.) 192
lifelong learning 26, 28
lifelong teaching 26
Lightning Mary (Simmons, A.) 389
Lingard, B. 128
Lingard, R. 133, 301, 573
linguistic diversity 395–6, 400
Linklater, H. 33
listening 375–82
skills 189, 204
literacy 259–62, 530
Literacy and Social Inclusion: Closing the Gap (Bearne, E. and Marsh, J.) 400
Literacy in the New Media Age (Kress, K.) 259
literature, children's 385–9
Littleton, K. 365, 380, 399
Lives of Teachers, The (Huberman, M.) 12, 33
Livingstone, K. 301
local authorities 125, 472–3
Loo, S. C. 133
Looking in Classrooms (Good, T. and Brophy, J.) 133
Loughran, J. 535
Lowden, K. 103
lower-order questions 375
Loxley, A. 507
Lucas, B. 302
Luckin, R. 257
Luckman, T. 560
Lundin, M. 546
Luo, W. 133

MacBeath, J. 76, 432
McCormick, R. 76, 432
McCullough, G. 551, 573
MacGilchrist, B. 447
McGill, R.M. 433
McGoun, C. 259
McGrath, J. 5
McIntyre, D. 33, 103, 161, 191, 365, 506
McLaughlin, C. 103
McNally, J. 5–6, 12
McNally, S. 133
Maguire, M. 552, 574
Major, L.E. 133

Making a Difference in Education (Cassen, R., McNally, S. and Vignoles, A.) 133
Making Assessment Matter (Butt, G.) 478
Making Best Use of Teaching Assistants (Sharples, J., Webster, R. and Blatchford, P.) 259
Making the Grade (Becker, H.S.) 462
Male, B. 301, 341
malleable learning 544*f*, 545
Mallett, M. 386
Mallon, B. 302
managerial professionalism 540
Managing Classroom Behaviour (Watkins, C.) 225
Managing Difficult Behaviour in Schools: A Practical Guide (Bennett, T.) 225
Managing Pupil Behaviour (Haydn, T.) 226
Managing the Literacy Curriculum (Webster, A., Beverage, M. and Reid, M.) 399
Mansell, W. 478
Manuel, J. 12
Mapping of Seminal Reports on Good Teaching (Rowe, N., Wilkin, A. and Wilson, R.) 133
Mark. Plan. Teach (McGill, R.M.) 433
Marks, R. 33
Marsh, J. 400
Marshall, B. 76, 432
Marzano, R.J. 134
Maslow, A. 21
mastery learning 55, 56*f*, 118, 323, 343, 421, 423–4
mastery learning toolkit 343
mathematics 274, 295–8
Maun, I. 392
Maynard, N. 225
Maynard, T. 12
media and new technology 62
Megarry, J. 551, 573
Melhuish, E. 134
memory 52
mental health 49–50, 307, 501, 509, 563
Menter, I. 103, 301
mentoring 545
Mercer, N. 259, 349, 365, 380, 399
Merrett, F. 225
metacognition 66–8, 77
metacognition toolkit 66, 77, 118
Metcalf, H. 506
Millennium Cohort Study 501
Mills, C.W. 159
Mills, M. 133
mind, the 52
Mindset: The New Psychology of Science (Dweck, C.S.) 75
minimal intrusion strategies 206
misconceptions 113
Mitchell, J. 160
Mitchell, N. 103
modelling 359–60
Models of Teaching (Joyce, B., Weil, M. and Calhoun, E.) 365
Montgomery, M. 478

reflectiveteaching.co.uk

Moon, B. 366
Mortimer, E.F. 356–7
Moss, P. 385
motivation 5, 64–5, 118
Mottram, M. 399
'Moving beyond country rankings in international assessments: The case of PISA' (Perry, N. and Ercikan, K.) 133
Muijs, D. 133, 259, 365
Mulme, M. 301
multi-tasking 210
multilingualism 395–6
multimedia learning theory 59
multimodal texts, reading 387, 392
Munro, L. 507
Mutton, T. 33
My Classroom Inventory 167–8
My Story series 386
Myhill, D. 392, 400

NAHT (National Association of Head teachers) 566
NAPE (National Association for Primary Education) 566, 572
NAPTEC (National Primary Teacher Education Council) 541, 566
NASUWT (National Association of Schoolmasters Union of Women Teachers) 566
National Academies of Sciences, Engineering, and Medicine review 61
National Association for Primary Education (NAPE) 566, 572
National Association of Head teachers (NAHT) 566
National Association of Schoolmasters Union of Women Teachers (NASUWT) 566
National Child Development Study (NCDS) 28, 501
national curricula 90, 111–12, 150, 268–82, 285–99 *see also* curricula
    England 65, 89, 112, 151, 271–2, 273*f*, 274, 275, 276–7, 281, 286, 289, 349
    language 393
    Northern Ireland 275, 282, 288
    planning 307, 310
    Republic of Ireland 144
    Scotland 275, 281, 288–9, 316, 317
    Wales 144, 288, 307, 312
National Curriculum Council (NCC) 281
National Curriculum Review (England) 112, 289
National Education Union 571, 572
National Foundation for Educational Research (NFER) 84, 128, 130*f*
National Improvement Framework for Scottish Education 413, 445
National Primary Headteachers' Association (NPH) 566
National Primary Teacher Education Council (NaPTEC) 541, 566
National Primary Trust (NPT) 566
National Professional Qualifications 155
National Strategy for Educational Research and Enquiry 85
national systems 124–7
National Union of Teachers (NUT) 566

Nature of Learning, The (Dumont, H., Istance, D. and Benavides, F.) 128, 133
'nature' versus 'nurture' debate 49, 57, 78
NCC (National Curriculum Council) 281
NCDS (National Child Development Study) 28, 501
needs hierarchy 21–2*f*
negative cycles 185*f*–6, 220–3
neuro-linguistic programming 52
neuro-myths 78
neurobiology 166
neuroscience 27, 39, 51, 52, 78
New Lives of Teachers, The (Day, C. and Gu, Q.) 29–30, 33, 161
New Technology and Education (Edwards, A.) 259
New Zealand 128
Newell, P. 573
Newton, P. 457
Newton, P.E. 457
NFER (National Foundation for Educational Research) 84, 128, 130*f*
Nias, J. 5
non-interactive/authoritative talk 357
non-interactive/dialogic talk 357
non-legitimate censure 182–3
non-legitimate disorder 182
non-verbal communication 373
non-verbal skills 189, 204
norm referencing 453–4, 455
Norman, K. 399
North America 127
Northern Ireland 144, 152, 559
    Council for the Curriculum Examinations and Assessment 275
    curriculum 275, 282, 288
    General Teaching Council 9, 84, 541, 554, 571
    learning outcomes 443
    professional learning 548–9
    Teacher Competences 548–9
NPH (National Primary Headteachers' Association) 566
NPT (National Primary Trust) 566
NQT (Newly Qualified Teaching) years 14
NUT (National Union of Teachers) 566
Nutbrown, C. 33
Nuthall, G. 76
Nutton, G. 424
Nystrand, M. 376–7, 378

obesity 499, 501
Observational Research and Classroom Learning Evaluation (ORACLE) research 357, 377
OECD 477, 547
Office for Science
    Foresight Programme 134
official curriculum 268–9
Ofsted 287, 479, 563
    curriculum 526–7
    inspection system 151, 311
    research reviews 302–3

reflectiveteaching.co.uk

636   Index

Olson, K. 191
'On the two metaphors for learning and the dangers of choosing just one' (Sfard, A.) 70
open-mindedness 94, 95, 168, 563
open questions 216–17, 418
Opening Minds project 280
opportunity 147–50, 162
ORACLE (Observational Research and Classroom Learning Evaluation) research 357, 377 Oracle study 239
oral language 346, 349
orchestration 211–12
Organic Classroom: Organizing for Learning 7 to 12, The (Hunter, R. and Scheirer, E.A.) 341
Organising Learning in the Primary School Classroom (Dean, J.) 259
Osler, A. 574
Otero, G. 166, 192
Outstanding Differentiation for Learning in the Classroom (Bartlett, J.) 342
overlapping 210

PACE (Primary Assessment Curriculum and Experience) project 357, 451, 452*f*, 564
pacing 211
Papert, S. 42–3
parental engagement toolkit 135
parents and carers 153–5, 253–4
    as consumers 253, 466
    learning outcomes 466–8
    parental engagement 121, 135, 157
    as partners 253, 466
    reporting to 466–7
    as resources 253, 326
Passeron, J.C. 160
Pattison, H. 76
Peacock, A. 32, 465, 506
Pearson, J. 103
pedagogic content knowledge 292, 293–4, 295, 334
pedagogical discourse 352–3
pedagogy 200, 345–70
    agency and 353
    analysing 350–1, 354–5, 362
    Bernstein, B. 484, 489
    concepts 519*f*, 522, 524, 527, 529
    critical 351
    culturally relevant 352
    culture 519*f*
    dialogue 519*f*
    empowerment 519*f*, 527
    enacting 347–50
    enacting a series of lessons 360–2
    enacting learner development 353–5
    engagement 519*f*, 527
    knowledge and learning 350–3
    pedagogic principles 350
    pedagogical discourse 352–3
    principle 519*f*, 522

reflection 519*f*
relationships 519*f*
repertoire 355–60, 519*f*, 523
scaffolding 359–60
social differentiation 486–8, 489
talk 356–9
theories of mind 352
warrant 519*f*, 524
Pedagogy: A Primer (Anderson, P.M.) 365
'pedagogy of friendship: young children's friendships and how schools can support them, A' (Carter, C. and Nutbrown, C.) 33
Pedagogy of the Oppressed (Freire, P.) 351, 573
Pedder, D. 76, 432
PEER (Prove, Explain, Explore and Reapply) 421, 423*f*–4
peer-assessment 422
peer culture 61–2, 173, 200, 233
    polarisation through 489–92
peer tutoring 252
peer tutoring toolkit 435
performance 83–4, 444–7, 529
    comparison 453–5
    national surveys of system performance 449–53
    social processes 462
performance data 446–8
    international 84, 448
Perry, N. 13
personal knowledge 112
personal skills 280
personal, social, health and economic education (PHSE) 563
personalised learning 65, 327, 331–3, 344
personality analysis 63–4
Peters, S.J. 500
Petty, G. 365
Phelps, E. 173
Phillipson, N. 365, 399
'Philosophy for Children' 25
Philosophy of Education Society of Great Britain 109
Philosophy of Educational Research (Pring, R.) 103
Phonics Screening Check (PSC) 117, 461
phonics toolkit 367
PHSE (personal, social, health and economic education) 563
physical appearance 499
physical skills 280
Piaget, J. 42–3, 45, 173
Pianta, R.C. 192
Pickett, K. 151
PIRLS (Progress in International Reading Literacy Study) 448, 473
PISA (Programme for International Student Assessment) 84, 128, 448, 473, 474, 477
plasticity 52, 53
Plowden Committee report 43, 302
Pol, J. van de 359
polarisation 490–1
policy frameworks 108*f*, 124–7
    in the locality of the school 125

reflectiveteaching.co.uk

national 126–7
at school level 125
politics 89–90, 473–5, 546–7, 564
accountability 150–1
curriculum, the 276
ideology 142–3
politicians' knowledge 96, 97*f*
pressure group activity 566–71
teachers 90, 564–71
Politics and the Primary Teacher (Cunningham, P.) 574
Politics of Professionalism: Teachers and the Curriculum, The (McCullough, G., Helsby, G. and Knight, P.) 551, 573
Pollard, A. 49, 65, 132, 183, 191, 192, 291, 300, 364, 433, 462, 490, 492–4, 505
Position Paper – Re-thinking Learner Progression in a Post-Covid World (IEAN) 442
positive cycles 184*f*
positivity 169
poverty 49, 147, 495, 561
Powell, G. 302
Powell, S. 399
Powell, W.W. 560
power
between children 173
teachers' use of 169–70
Power, S. 34
'Power of Believing That You Can Improve, The' (Dweck, C.S.) 74
Power of Pedagogy, The (Leach, J. and Moon, B.) 366
'Power of Poetry, The' training day 361
Practice Makes Practice: A Critical Study of Learning to Teach (Britzman, D.) 352–3
practice task demands 324
Practitioner Enquiry: Professional Development with Impact for Teachers, Schools and Systems (Gilchrist, G.) 103
Pratt, L. 504
predictability 181–2
prefacing 206
preoperational development stage 42
'Preparing teachers for inclusive education: using inclusive pedagogy to enhance teaching and learning for all' (Florian, L. and Linklater, H.) 33
pressure group activity 566–8
Preston, J. 160
Price, D. 302
Primary Assessment Curriculum and Experience (PACE) project 357. 451, 452*f*, 564
Primary Curriculum Design Handbook, The (Male, B. and Waters, M.) 301, 341
primary resources 386
primary teachers. *See* teachers
Primary Teachers Talking (Nias, J.) 5
principles *see also* TLRP principles
international 127–30
Principles and Big Ideas of Science Education (Harlen, W. and Bell, D.) 279

Principles for Effective Pedagogy: International Responses to Evidence from the UK Teaching and Learning Research programme (James, M. and Pollard, A.) 132
Principles of Assessment in Curriculum for Excellence Building the Curriculum 5. A Framework for Assessment (Scottish Government) 479
Pring, R. 103
prior experience 108*f*, 113–14
private schools 148
procedural knowledge 280
Procter, R. 76, 432
professional artistry 88
professional development 538–9
Professional Expertise: Practice, Theory and Education for Working in Uncertainty (Flook, J., Ryan, M. and Hawkins, L.) 535
professional groups 566, 570
professional learning 537–52
CPD model 544*f*–5
mentoring 545
national policies 547–50
online 545–6
policies 546–50
political 546–7
professional organisations 541–2
professionalism 540–1
teacher learning 542–6
teacher-initiated 545
Professional Standards for Teaching and Leadership 549
professional values 7–10, 30
professionalism 540–1, 553–74
classroom teaching 563–6
education and society 555–61
inequalities 561–2
reflective teaching and the democratic process 566–71
Professionalism and Pedagogy: A Contemporary Opportunity (Pollard, A.) 350, 364
Programme for International Student Assessment (PISA) 84, 128, 448, 473, 474, 477
Progress in International Reading Literacy Study (PIRLS) 448, 473
progression 316–18, 414, 463–75
Promoting Effective Group Work in the Classroom (Baines, E., Blatchford, P. and Kutnick, P.) 259
protective mediation 100
Proust and the Squid: The Story and Science of the Reading Brain (Wolf, M.) 383
PSC (Phonics Screening Check) 117, 461
Psychology and Education (Gallard, D. and Cartmell, D.M.) 74
Psychology of Written Composition, The (Bereiter, C. and Scardamalia, M.) 391–2
puberty 27
punishment 221–2
Pupil Consultation project (TLRP) 125
Pupil Premium Grant 561
pupil teachers 87*f*
pupils 15–25, 155–8 *see also* children *and* learners

638 Index

actions, 182–3
assessment, reaction to 450–2*f*
behaviour 220–3
behaviour parameters 183*f*
boundaries 175
boy/girl performance 19
categories 171
challenging 169–70
classroom behaviour 198–9
classroom relationships 164–5
confidence and self-esteem 169–70, 492–4
culture 19–20, 145, 156
development and career 26–9
engagement 218–20
friendship groups 183
independence 219–20
learning involvement 414–16, 426
needs, understanding 20–2
opportunity 148, 162
organising 246–52
peer relationships 61–2, 173, 200, 233, 489–92
perceptions of, examining 22–5
physiology 26–8
playground culture 145
progression 316–18, 414, 463–75
qualities 16
questions 377
school, perspectives of 17–18
social influences 26, 27*f*
teacher-pupil interaction 347–9
teachers, perspectives of 17–18, 181–2
teaching and learning, consulting with 36
transfer and transition, supporting 471–2
underachievement 556
understanding 425
views of themselves in school 16–17
voice 178–81
wait time 377
Pupils at the Center: Personalized Learning with Habits of Mind (Kallick, B. and Zmuda, A.) 75, 76
Putting Assessment for Learning in to Practice (Spendlove, S.) 433

QTS (qualified teacher status) 548
qualifications 151
qualified teacher status (QTS) 548
quality, identifying 414–16
questioning 216–17, 416–19
questioning, responding, instructing and explaining 375–8
Quigley, A. 32

race 561. *See* ethnicity
racism 496–7
Racism and Education: Coincidence or Conspiracy? (Gillborn, D.) 506
Racism, Gender and Identities of Young Children: Social Relations in a Multi-ethnic, Inner-city Primary School (Connolly, P.) 506

Racism in Children's Lives: A Study of Mainly White Primary Schools (Troyna, B. and Hatcher, R.) 506
Rahim, R. 133
Raising Boys' Achievements in Writing (UKLA) 359
rationalism 275
Re-Designing Learning Contexts. Technology-Rich Learner-Centred Ecologies (Luckin, R.) 257
Read, B. 506
reader-response theory 384
readiness to learn 27
reading 382–9
   writing, relationship with 390
reading comprehension strategies toolkit 402
reading development 354
Reading Images: The Grammar of Visual Design (Kress, G. and van Leeuwen, T.) 387
Realising the Power of Professional Learning (Timperley, H.) 103
Reay, D. 161, 258, 450, 491
recall 317*f*
reciprocal groups 249
reciprocity 272, 273*f*
'Reconstructing the primary curriculum' (Turner-Bissett, R.) 341
Reese, L. 396
reflection 79–103
   classroom dilemmas/challenges 81–3, 85
   evidence-informed practice 83–6
   reflective teaching 87–100
   standards for effectiveness and career development 86–7
reflection-in-action 88
reflection-on-action 88
reflective action 87, 88
reflective agent 46
Reflective Practitioner: How Professionals Think in Action, The (Schön, D.A.) 103
reflective teaching 87–9, 100–1, 154
   aims and consequences 88, 89–90
   colleagues, learning with 88, 97–99
   as creative mediation 89, 100
   cyclical process 88, 91*f*–2
   democratic process 566–71
   evidence gathering and evaluating 88, 92–4
   teacher judgement 88, 95–7*f*
   teaching, attitudes towards 88, 94–5, 168
reflectiveness 272, 273*f*
reflexivity 11
Reid, M. 399
Reiss, M. 301
relationships 163–93
   assessment 411
   classroom 172–7
   classroom climate 165–72
   for learning 178–86
   peer 61–2, 173, 200, 233, 489–92
   special efforts 190
   teacher thinking and professional skills 186–90
Renold, E. 491, 506

reflectiveteaching.co.uk

representational repertoire 294

Reproduction in Education, Society and Culture (Bourdieu, P. and Passeron, J.C.) 160

Republic of Ireland 144, 152
    learning outcomes 443

research 84, 93, 96
    assessment 405
    assessment for learning 437–8
    classroom talk 357
    Convention on the Rights of the Child 525
    curriculum 286–7
    feedback 419
    group work 357–9, 370, 380, 405
    health 509
    home-school knowledge exchange 136
    inequality 501–2, 509
    learning how to learn 436
    literacy 530
    neuroscience 78
    NQT years 5–6
    PEER model 423–4
    personalised learning 344
    physical appearance 499
    professional learning 546
    pupils, consulting 36
    reading development 354, 388–9
    researchers' knowledge 96, 97*f*
    school league tables 480
    social environments 162
    talk 528
    teacher careers and effectiveness 35
    teacher expertise 514–15
    teacher-pupil interaction 348–9
    technology 263, 523
    underachievement 556
    writing 361–2, 391–2

research lessons (RL) 336–9

Researching and Teaching Reading: Developing Pedagogy Through Critical Enquiry (Cliff Hodges, G.) 400

Researching Literacy Lives: Building Communities Between Home and School (Cremin, T., Mottram, M., Collins, F., Powell, S. and Drury, R.) 399

Researching Schools: Stories from a Schools-University Partnership (McLaughlin, C., Black-Hawkins, K., Brindley, S., McIntyre, D. and Taber, K.) 103

resilience 272, 273*f*

resourcefulness 272, 273*f*

responsibility 94, 95, 168, 563

restricted professionalism 540

restructuring task demands 324

Rethinking Learner Progression for the Future (IEAN) 463–5

retrieval practice 58, 59

revision task demands 324

Reynolds, D. 133, 259, 365

Richardson, R. 5, 6, 32, 504

Right to Learn; A Blueprint for Creating Schools that Work, The (Darling-Hammond, L.) 133

risk, boredom and challenge 64–5*f*

Rix, J. 504

RL (research lessons) 336–9

Roberts-Holmes, G. 448, 474–5

Robertson, S. 121–2

Rogers, B. 204–6, 224, 225

Rogers, C. 168, 191

Rogers, S. 5

Rogoff, B. 258

Role of Schools in the Mental health of Children & Young People, The (Hurry, J., Bonell, C., Carroll, C. and Deighton, J.) 192

Role of Teachers in Assessment of Learning, The (ARG) 478

Rosenblatt, L. 384

Rosenthal, R. 187

Ross, G. 114, 359

Rostow, W.W. 558

routine action 87–8

routine censure 182

routine deviance 182

routine strategies 206–7

Rowe, N. 133

Rowland, S. 46

Rowland, T. 296

Royal Society 52

Royal Society, The and British Academy, The (RS & BA) 84, 126, 144

Royal Society of Arts (RSA) 125, 280, 312, 524

RS & BA (Royal Society, The and British Academy, The) 84, 126, 144

RSA (Royal Society of Arts) 125, 280, 312, 524

RSA Area Based Curriculum: Engaging the Local, The (Thomas, L.) 341

Rudduck, J. 36, 161, 191, 472

rule reminders 206

rules and routines of the classroom 175–6

Russell, A. 254–5

Ruthven, K. 30

Ryan, M. 535

Ryle, G. 280

Sabates, R. 28, 34, 134, 505

Sachs, J. 103, 540, 551, 573

Sage Handbook of Curriculum, Pedagogy and Assessment, The (Wyse, D. et al.) 414

Sahlberg, P. 133

Sammons, P. 134

Sangster, M. 535

satiation 241

Savage, J. 225, 259

Sawyer, R.K. 134

scaffolding 46, 108*f,* 114–15, 118–19, 359–60

Scardamalia, M. 391–2

Scheirer, E.A. 341

schemes of work 313–15

Scholes, R. 390

Schön, D.A. 88, 91, 95, 103

reflectiveteaching.co.uk

640   Index

School-based Research. A Guide for Education Students (Wilson, E.) 103
'School Inspection Data Summary (IDSR) Report Guide' 84
school resources 149–50, 235–7, 326
     buildings 149
     equipment and materials 149
     people 149
schools *see also* school resources
     academies 110, 125, 143, 148, 151
     aims 307
     budgets 149–50
     choice 148
     culture 62
     curriculum 151, 288
     curriculum evaluation 333–9
     curriculum planning 307–333, 339–42
     environment for positive behaviour 199–200
     free schools 125
     governing bodies 125, 307
     league tables 446, 480
     learners' experiences 110
     outside influences 89
     peers 61–2
     performance 83–4, 444–53
     policies 308
     policy frameworks 125–7
     private 148
     self-evaluation 469–70
     social differentiation 484–9
     systems 143, 148
     values 387–9
Schools and Communities: Working Together to Transform Children's Lives (West-Burnham, J., Farrar, M. and Otero, G.) 192
Schoon, I. 34
Schwab, J. 292
science 279
Scope 500
Scotland 144, 149, 151, 316, 317, 559
     Assessment is for Learning 412*f*
     curriculum 275, 281, 288–9, 316, 317
     Curriculum for Excellence 144, 275, 281*f*, 288–9, 408, 413, 559
     Education Scotland 151, 541
     Educational Institute of Scotland 541, 570
     Framework for Assessment 413
     General Teaching Council 8, 84–5, 151, 54, 571, 572
     learning outcomes 443
     National Improvement Framework for Scottish Education 413, 445
     national monitoring programme 449
     professional learning 549
     Scottish Government 479
     Scottish Survey of Literacy and Numeracy 449
     SPRinG (Social Pedagogic Research into Group-work) project 119, 358, 370
     Standard for Full Registration 549
     transfer and transition 472

Scott, D. 301
Scott, P.H. 356–7
Scottish Government 479
Scottish Survey of Literacy and Numeracy 449
seating groups 248
Secondary Curriculum Design Handbook, The (Male, B. and Waters, M.) 301, 341
SEL (social and emotional learning) 174
self-assessment 421, 422
self-esteem 169–70
self-fulfilling prophecy 23
self-perspective of personality 64
self-regulated learning 77, 427
Selwyn, N. 103, 546
SEND (Special Educational Needs and Disabilities) 40, 171, 561
sensorimotor development stage 42
setting 246
setting and streaming toolkit 508
sex 497
Sex and Relationships Education (SRE) 27, 563
sex role stereotypes 188 *see also* gender
sexism 497
sexuality 497–8, 562
Sexuality, Gender and Schooling. Shifting Agendas in Social Learning (Kehily, M.J.) 506
Sfard, A. 70–2
SFRE (Strategic Forum for Research in Education) 84, 126, 144
Shackleton, E. 387
Sharples, J. 259
Shaw, S. 457
Sheng, Y. 133
Shulman, L.S. 292, 293–4, 295, 302, 535
Simmons, K. 504
Simon, B. 350–1
Singapore 112, 116–17, 128
Singleton, C. 258
Siraj-Blatchford, I. 134, 341
Siraj-Blatchford, J. 341
Skelton, C. 506
skills 112, 275, 280–1, 286–7
Skinner, B.F. 40
small group teaching 368
small group teaching and learning toolkit 368
Smith, E. 103
SMSE (social, moral, spiritual and cultural) education 563
social and emotional learning (SEL) 174
social and emotional learning toolkit 193
social capital 148, 496
social class/status 143, 148, 171, 489, 495–6, 561
social cognition 44–7, 48*f*
social conditions 49, 114, 157
social constructionist/constructivist model 44, 46*f*
social context 140–1, 158–9
     accountability 150–3
     culture 145–6
     ideology 142–5
     opportunity 147–50, 162

reflectiveteaching.co.uk

pupils 155–7
teachers 153–5
social democratic values 142
social differentiation 485–9
social factors 115, 116, 120
social justice 5, 481–509, 555–6
diversity and differentiation 494–501
identity formation, perception and self-belief 492–4
inequality 114, 147, 327–33, 483–4
life chances 501–2
polarisation through peer culture 489–92
social differentiation 484–9
Social Justice Re-Examined. Dilemmas and Solutions for the Classroom Teacher (Arshad, R., Wrigley, T. and Pratt, L.) 504
social learning 193
social market values 142
social, moral, spiritual and cultural (SMSE) education 563
Social Origins of Educational Systems, The (Archer, M.) 573
Social Pedagogic Research into Group-work (SPRinG) project 119, 358, 370
social relationships 108*f*, 119–20
social reproduction 496 (
Social World of Pupil Assessment: Processes and Contexts of Primary Schooling, The (Filer, A. and Pollard, A.) 433
Social World of Pupil Career: Strategic Biographies through Primary School, The (Pollard, A. and Filer, A.) 33
Social World of the Primary School, The (Pollard, A.) 192, 505
society 147–8, 198 *see also* inequality
civic responsibility 554
classroom teaching and 563–6
democratic process 566–71
education and 555–60
goals of 522
individual, relationship with 140, 560
teachers' role in 554, 562–71
socio-cultural model 44–5
Sociological Imagination, The (Mills, C.A.) 159
Sociology of Childhood, The (Corsaro, W.A.) 258
Solar, J. 504
Sotto, E. 365
spaced learning 58, 60
spaced practice 59
spaces 229–63
classroom organisation for learning 234–42
environments for learning 231–4
managing pupils and adults 246–55
technology 242–6
use of 237–9
speaking 393–4
and listening 374–82
speaking and listening activities toolkit 401
Special Educational Needs and Disabilities (SEND) 40, 171, 561
Special Educational Needs: The Basics (Wearmouth, J.) 507
Spencer, E. 467
Spendlove, S. 433
Spielman, A. 286–7

spiral curriculum 289
Spirit Level: Why Equality is Better for Everyone, The (Wilkinson, R. and Pickett, K.) 161
SPRinG (Social Pedagogic Research into Group-work) project 119, 358, 370
SRE (Sex and Relationships Education) 27, 563
Stages of Economic Growth (Rostow, W.W.) 558
Standard for Full Registration 549
standards 86–7
Standish, A. 301
Starkey, H. 574
State of the Discipline project (BERA) 126
Steer, A. 226
Stenhouse, L. 91, 102, 551, 573
steps to success 16
stereotypes 146, 188, 198–9
Stobart, G. 411, 478
Stoll, L. 542–3
Stories of Self: Tracking Children's Identity and Well-being through the School Years (Warin, J.) 490
storytelling 381
Strategic Forum for Research in Education (SFRE) 84, 126, 144
strategic repertoire 205–8, 221–2, 516
strategies 205–8,
assertive 207–8
challenging behaviour 221–2
minimal intrusion 206
routine 206–7
Straughan, R. 226
streaming 246, 508
Streaming: An Education System in Miniature (Jackson, B.) 246, 489–90, 506
strictness 181
Student's Guide to Education Studies, A (Ward, S.) 161
Study of Education: An Introduction, The (Bates, J. and Lewis, S.) 161
study skills 280
Styles, M. 399
subject-based curriculum 290–1
subject knowledge 270, 279, 292–8, 347
applying 295–8
connection 296, 297
contingency 296, 297
foundation 296, 297
transformation 296, 297
subject skills 280
subjects 288
success criteria 16, 416
summative assessment 453–75 *see also* learning outcomes
accountability 444–8, 473–5
authorities 472–3
evidence over time, using to support pupil progress 470–1
governors 472–3
guiding principles 463–5
improvement 444–8
learners 466–8
non-statutory tests and tasks 469

reflectiveteaching.co.uk

642 Index

parents/carers 466–8
performance comparison 453–5
politicians 473–5
progress, understanding at national and government level 475
teacher assessment 469–50
teachers/headteachers 468–9
transfer and transition, supporting 471–2
trust 455–62
supple learning mind 272, 273*f*
support staff 254–5
Supporting Stories: Being a Teaching Assistant (Dillow, C.) 259
sustainability 141, 557, 559
Suter, L. 103
Sutton Trust 505
Swaffield, S. 76, 430, 432, 478
Swann, J. 76, 432
Swann, M. 506
Sylva, K. 134
synapses 51–2
synthesis 317*f*
synthetic phonics 274

Tabachnick, R. 94
Taber, K. 103
tactical ignoring 206
TACTYC (Association for the Professional Development of Early Years Educators) 572
Taggart, B. 134
take-up time 206
TALIS (Teacher and Learning International Survey) 547
talk 356–9, 417, 528 *see also* communication
    creative 381–2
    exploratory 380
talk partners 417–18
Tanner, J.M. 49
targets 445
TAs (teaching assistants) 254–5, 326–7
task demands 324
task groups 248
Taxonomy of Educational Objectives (Bloom, B.S.) 323*f*–4, 375
Teacher and Learning International Survey (TALIS) 547
Teacher–Child Partnership: The Negotiating Classroom (Ingram, J. and Worrall, N.) 192
Teacher Competences 548–9
'Teacher education around the world: What can we learn from international practice?' (Darling-Hammond, L.) 127
teacher expertise 513–35
    classroom processes 518*f*–19*f,* 526–8
    conceptual framework 517–30
    conceptual framework, using 531–2
    educational aims 518*f*–19*f,* 520–3
    learning contexts 518*f*–19*f,* 524–5
    learning outcomes 518*f*–19*f,* 529–30
teacher-pupil interaction 347–9
teachers 4, 123, 149, 153–5 *see also* teaching
    accountability 150–3
    actions, 182–3

activist role 90
assessment, judging 458, 464, 468, 470–1
assessment, thoughts on 450, 453
authority 189–90, 201–8
becoming 5–6
bias 188
career/professional development 12, 29–30, 80*f,* 86–7, 99, 101, 155
careers 12, 35
challenges 5, 12, 220–3
classroom relationships 164–5
content knowledge 292–3, 334
contributions of 29
curricular knowledge 292, 294–5
diaries 186–7, 222
differentiation of attention 171
effectiveness 35, 86–7
emotion 13
engagement skills 208–12, 218–20
evaluation 334
expectations 55–6, 187–8, 202–3
expertise 513–35
fairness 177
government policies 90
group work 380
idealism 5
identities 11–15
judgement 85, 88, 95–7*f,* 107
knowledge 95–7*f,* 334
language 204–5
learning 108*f,* 123–4, 542–6
lesson plans 320–7
metaphors 14
mind frames 128–9
motivations 5
NQT years 5–6, 14
pedagogic content knowledge 292, 293–4, 295, 334
perspectives 186–7
policy, influence on 566–71
politics 90, 564–71
power, use of 169–70
pressure group activity 566–71
professional capacities 470
professional development 515, 537–52
professional skills 188–9, 204
professionalism 540–1
pupil perspectives of 17–18, 181–2
pupil progression 470–1
pupil teachers 87*f*
qualities 6
representational repertoire 294
research and development 84
resilience 515
rights 566–71
self-evaluation 469–70
self-preservation 203–4, 564–5
social influences 30

reflectiveteaching.co.uk

social work role 154
society, role in 554, 562–71
staff culture 146
standards 86–7
strategic repertoire 205–8, 221–2, 516
subject knowledge 292–8
talk 356–9
teacher-pupil interaction 347–9
values informing practice 6–11
warranted practice 30
work 13–15, 81, 155
Teachers and Human Rights Education (Osler, A. and Starkey, H.) 574
Teachers and Schooling Making a Difference (Hayes, D., Mills, M., Christie, P. and Lingard, R.) 133
Teacher's Companion to Essential Motivation in the Classroom, A (Holleran, G. and Gilbert, I.) 225
Teachers Standards 548
Teachers Undefeated: How Global Education Reform Has Failed to Crush the Spirit of Educators (Berry, J.) 565
teaching 80 *see also* reflective teaching
adjusting 425–8
art of 14
behaviourism 40, 41
classroom dilemmas/challenges 81–3, 85, 220–3
cognitive science 58–60
craft of 14
dialogic 115, 119, 356–7, 378–9, 398
discourse of 346
evaluation 334
key features for effective 130*f*
lifelong 26
modelling 359–60
national curricula 289–90
NFER review 128, 130*f*
professional competence spiral 80*f*
professional learning 537–52
reading 383
reflection and evidence-informed practice 83–6
reflective 87–9
scaffolding 46, 108*f*, 114–15, 118–19, 359–60
science of 14
small group 368
society 563–6
standards for effectiveness and career development 86–7
talk for 356–9
technology 242–6
to the test 117, 473
visible 115, 119
writing 259–62, 391
Teaching and Learning in 2020 Review Group 160, 284, 331–2, 341
Teaching and Learning Toolkit 106, 107
teaching assistants (TAs) 254–5, 326–7
teaching assistants, effective deployment of toolkit 262
Teaching Backwards (Griffiths, A. and Burns, M.) 341
Teaching Council Ireland 9–10, 84
Teaching for Social Justice and Sustainable Development Across

the Primary Curriculum (Kavanagh, A.M., Waldron, F. and Mullen, B.) 302
teaching groups. *See* group work
Teaching in a Networked Classroom (Savage, J. and McGoun, C.) 259
Teaching, Learning and Assessment (Blanchard, J.) 433
Teaching Reading (Dombey, H. et al.) 399
Teaching Scotland's Future (Donaldson, G.) 155
'Teaching: The reflective profession, incorporating the Northern Ireland Teacher Competences' 548–9
Teaching Thinking: Philosophical Enquiry in the Classroom (Fisher, R.) 76
teaching to the test 117, 473
Teaching Today: A Practical Guide (Petty, G.) 365
Teaching Without Disruption in the Primary School (Chaplain, R.) 192, 200–1, 225
technology 62, 121–2, 233, 242–6, 263, 326
classroom 237, 238–9, 523
Tennant, W. 399
test questions 376
Testing, Motivation and Learning (ARG) 478
Testing Times: The Uses and Abuses of Assessment (Stobart, G.) 478
tests 404, 444, 456–7, 460–1*f*
international 473–5
non-statutory tests and tasks 469
Phonics Screening Check 117, 461
Reception baseline 461
teaching to the test 117, 473
Tharp, R. 66
theories of mind 352
theories of reading 383–4
think time 418
thinking capability 66–8
'Thinking Together' project 380
Thinking Voices: The Work of the National Oracy Project (Norman, K.) 399
Thomas, A. 76
Thomas, G. 507
Thomas, L. 341
Thompson, J. 507
Thompson, P. 573
Thomson, G. 191
Thorndike, E.L. 39–40
'Those who understand: knowledge and growth in teaching' (Shulman, L.S.) 302
thought processes, 317
time, use of 239–42
Time, Place and Society 8–13 (Blyth, A.) 278–9
Time to Talk. Implementing Outstanding Practice in Speech, Language and Communication (Gross, J.) 399
Timperley, H. 103, 542
TIMSS (Trends in International Mathematics and Science Study) 84, 448, 473, 474
Tizard, B. 43
TLRP (Teaching & Learning Research Programme) 106, 524 *see also* TLRP principles

644 Index

Commentary on Assessment 524
Consulting Pupils about Teaching and Learning 36, 119–20
Home–School Knowledge Exchange project 136
Interactive Education project 121
Learning How to Learn project 116, 125, 407, 408, 412, 432, 436, 450
Learning Lives project 110–11, 520
Pupil Consultation project 125
pupils, consulting with 36
teacher careers and effectiveness 35
Variations in Teachers' Work, Lives, and their Effects on Pupils (VITAE) project 124
TLRP principles xi, 106, 107–127, 130–1, 132, 351, 517, 522
active engagement 108*f,* 118–19
assessment for learning 108*f,* 115–17, 406, 408, 443
classroom relationships 165
curricula 268, 286, 289, 306
education for life 108*f,* 109–11
identity 4
informal learning 108*f,* 120–2
language 372
learning 38
learning contexts 141
learning environments 230
learning outcomes 443
pedagogy 347
personalised learning 344
prior experience 108*f,* 113–14
professional learning 538
professionalism 538, 554
pupil engagement 197
reflective teaching 80
scaffolding understanding 108*f,* 114–15, 118–19
social justice 482
social relationships 108*f,* 119–20
society, teachers' role in 554
teacher expertise 514
teacher learning 108*f,* 123–4
teacher strategy 347
teaching contexts 141
valued knowledge 108*f,* 111–13
values 4
topic work 388
Topping, K. 365
Towards a Theory of Instruction (Bruner, J.S.) 302
Towards Dialogic Teaching: Rethinking Classroom Talk (Alexander, R.) 399
trade unions 566, 570–1
trait theories of personality 64
transfer and transition, supporting 471–2
transformations 293–4
transformative learning 544*f,* 545
Transforming Learning Cultures (James, D. and Biesta, G.) 110
Transforming Practice: Critical Issues in Equity, Diversion and Education (Solar, J., Walsh, C.S., Craft, A., Rix, J. and Simmons, K.) 504

transmissive learning 544*f,* 545
Trends in International Mathematics and Science Study (TIMSS) 84, 448, 473, 474
tripartite school system 143
Trojan Horse Scandal 563–4
Troyna, B. 506
Trundley, R. 303
Truth About Our Schools: Exposing the Myths, Exploring the Evidence, The (Benn, M. and Downs, J.) 160
Tucker, J. 507
Turner-Bissett, R. 341

UK. *See* United Kingdom
UKLA (United Kingdom Literacy Association) 359, 542
UN. *See* United Nations
Convention on the Rights of the Child 120, 525, 557
Universal Declaration of Children's Rights 498
Universal Declaration of Human Rights 556–7
UN Convention and Children's Rights in the UK, The (Newell, P.) 573
unconscious bias 188
underachievement 556
Understanding Reading Comprehension (Tennant, W.) 399
Understanding Reading Development (Harrison, C.) 399
United Kingdom
curricular structures 287–8
education systems 124–7, 144–5, 148
wealth distribution 147
United Kingdom Literacy Association (UKLA) 359, 542
United Nations
Convention on the Rights of the Child 120, 525, 557
Universal Declaration of Children's Rights 498
Universal Declaration of Human Rights 556–7
United States, 127, 142
Universal Declaration of Children's Rights (UN) 498
Universal Declaration of Human Rights (UN) 556–7
Unlocking Assessment: Understanding for Reflection and Application (Swaffield, S.) 432
Using Assessment for School Improvement (James, M.) 478
Using Data, Improving Schools (Ofsted) 479
Using Your Voice Effectively in the Classroom (Evans, W. and Savage, J.) 225
USSR 142

value-added data 446
valued knowledge 108*f,* 111–13
values 109–10, 409
government 7–10
professional 7–10
informing practice 6–11
van Poortvliet, M. 174, 192
Variations in Teachers' Work, Lives, and their Effects on Pupils (VITAE) project (TLRP) 124
verbal skills 189, 204
Vignoles, A. 133
Visible Learning: A Synthesis of Meta-Analyses Relating to Achievement (Hattie, J.) 134

reflectiveteaching.co.uk

Visible Learning for Teachers: Maximising Impact on Learning (Hattie, J.) 128–9, 341, 365
visions 110
Visual Approaches to Teaching Writing: Multimodal Literacy 5–11 (Bearne, E. and Wolstencroft, H.) 400
VITAE (*Variations in Teachers' Work, Lives, and their Effects on Pupils*) project (TLRP) 124
voice 189, 204
Volan, M. 359
Volante, L. 474
Vorhaus, J. 28, 34, 134
Vygotsky, L.S. 45, 66, 114, 173

wait time 377, 418
Waldron, F. 302
Wales 144, 307, 312, 559
    assessment 445
    Curriculum for Wales 144, 288, 307, 312, 445
    Education Workforce Council 8–9, 84, 152, 541, 571
    General Teaching Council 152, 541, 571
    learning outcomes 443
    professional learning 549
    Professional Standards for Teaching and Leadership 549
    standards 549
Walkerdine, V. 43
Walsh, C.S. 504
Walters, S. 506
Ward, S. 161
Warin, J. 490, 505
warranted practice 30
washback 444, 445
Wassermann, S. 365
Waters, M. 301, 341
Watkins, C. 192, 225
Watts, R. 258
'We feel, therefore we learn' (Immordino-Yang, M.H. and Damasio, A.) 39, 166
wealth creation 558
wealth distribution 147, 495
Wearmouth, J. 507
Webb, M. 418
Webster, A. 399
Webster, R. 254–5, 259
Wegerif, R. 365, 399
Weil, M. 365
Weinstein, B. 225
Wenger, E. 103
Wertsch, J.V. 146
West-Burnham, J. 166, 192
What Expert Teachers Do: Enhancing Professional Knowledge for Classroom Practice (Loughran, J.)535
'What If Students Controlled Their Own Learning?' (Hutton, P.) 224
What Is, and What Might Be? (Holmes, E.) 140
What Makes Great Teaching? Review of the Underpinning Research (Coe, R., Aloisi, C., Higgins, S. and Major, L.E.) 133

What Should Schools Teach? New Disciplines, Subjects, and the Pursuit of Truth (Standish, A. and Cuthbert, A.S.) 301
'What's all the fuss about instructional time?' (Berliner, D.) 258
Wheldall, K. 225
When Teaching Becomes Learning (Sotto, E.) 365
White, B.J. 415
White, J. 301
White, M.A. 414
whole class teaching 247–8
Whole Curriculum, The (NCC) 281
wholeheartedness 94, 95, 168
Why Don't Pupils Like School (Willingham, D.) 75
'Why no pedagogy in England?' (Simon, B.) 350–1
Wiliam, D. 76, 412, 432, 433, 450, 514
Wilkin, A. 133
Wilkinson, I.A.G. 379
Wilkinson, R. 161
Williamson, J. 358
Willingham, D. 52, 75
Wilson, E. 103
Wilson, R. 133
Winch, C. 535
Wisdom of Practice – Essays on Teaching, Learning and Learning to Teach, The (Shulman, L.S.) 535
with-it-ness 210
Wolf, M. 382–3
Wolstencroft, H. 400
Wood, D. 74, 114, 359
World Yearbook of Education 1980: The Professional Development of Teachers (Hoyle, E. and Megarry, J.) 551, 573
Worrall, N. 192
Wrigley, J. 573
Wrigley, T. 504
writing 259–62, 389–92, 393–5
    reading, relationship with 390
Writing Voices: Creating Communities of Writers (Cremin, T. and Myhill, D.) 400
Wyse, D. 5, 103, 301, 414

Xenidou-Dervou, I. 303

Yandell, J. 103
Young, M. 112, 276, 301
Young Children's Rights (Alderson, P.) 574
Your Teaching Training Companion (McGrath, J. and Coles, A.) 5

Zeichner, K. 94
Zhang, Y. 258
Zmuda, A. 75, 76
Zones of Proximal Development (ZPD) 45–6, 66, 114
ZPD (Zones of Proximal Development) 45–6, 66, 114